The Record Shelf
Guide to Classical CDs
and Audiocassettes

Revised and Expanded Fourth Edition

How to Order:

Single copies may be ordered from Prima Publishing, P.O. Box 1260BK, Rocklin, CA 95677; telephone (916) 632-4400. Quantity discounts are also available. On your letterhead, include information concerning the intended use of the books and the number of books you wish to purchase.

The Record Shelf
Guide to Classical
CDs and Audiocassettes

Revised and Expanded Fourth Edition

Jim Svejda

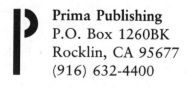

Prima Publishing
P.O. Box 1260BK
Rocklin, CA 95677
(916) 632-4400

Production by Melanie Field
Copyediting by Jane Gilligan
Typography by A-R Editions, Inc.
Interior design by Judith Levinson and Hal Lockwood
Cover design by The Dunlavey Studio, Inc.

The radio version of *The Record Shelf* is produced by Public Radio Station KUSC, Los Angeles, a broadcast service of the University of Southern California and is distributed nationally via Public Radio International.

Library of Congress Cataloging-in-Publication Data

Svejda, Jim.
    [Record shelf guide to the classical repertoire]
    The record shelf guide to classical CDs and audiocassettes / Jim Svejda. — Rev. and expanded 4th ed.
      p. cm.
    Previous ed. published under title: Record shelf guide to the classical repertoire.
    Includes index.
    ISBN 1-55958-573-0
    1. Sound recordings—Reviews. 2. Audiocassettes—Reviews. 3. Compact discs—Reviews. 4. Music—Discography. I. Title.
ML156.9.S86 1994
780.26′6—dc20   94-21510
                                            CIP

95 96 97 98 99 RRD 10 9 8 7 6 5 4 3 2 1
Printed in the United States of America

*For Ben, who made me do it,
Kevin, who should have done it,
And Diane and Michael, for everything.*

Foreword

I admit that I am not impartial when it comes to Jim Svejda. Long before I met him, I was an ardent fan of his radio program, *The Record Shelf*. His musical taste, his sardonic wit, his urbanity, and his unique connection with his listeners I find unequaled. And I am not alone. I have since learned—not from him—that of some three thousand letters received each month by KUSC, fifteen hundred are for Jim.

Some years ago, after conducting the Minnesota Orchestra, I had made dinner reservations with some musician friends. I couldn't budge them. They refused to go until they finished listening to that week's *Record Shelf*. To my surprise and ensuing delight, Jim began the program with a lusty Teutonic male choir, developed a comparison with my Sing A Longs, and concluded by featuring my oboe and English horn recordings from 1947 to 1951. Over the air, Jim anointed me his favorite oboe-English horn player of all time. The compliment was better than dessert.

When we finally did meet, my impressions were more than confirmed and we became instant friends. He truly loves music, being a former oboe player himself. The breadth of his knowledge is extraordinary. He thoroughly understands every kind of music, every conductor, composition, and nuance of performance, from early jazz through the entire classical repertoire. His taste is consummate; his integrity, unswayed by today's musical hype.

Sure, I am prejudiced, but so will you be after referring to this book for your recording needs. You may not always agree, but believe me, you'll *never be wrong* listening to Jim Svejda and *The Record Shelf Guide to Classical CDs and Audiocassettes*.

MITCH MILLER

Acknowledgments

This book grew out of the comparative survey programs that are a regular feature of my weekly radio program, *The Record Shelf*, a production of KUSC, the radio station of the University of Southern California. I would like to thank Wally Smith and the staff of KUSC for their many kindnesses and indulgences over the years. To my closest musical friends, Kevin Mostyn, Robert Goldfarb, and Henry Fogel, no amount of thanks can adequately repay what I owe them. I also owe a special debt of gratitude to Dr. Christian Rutland, without whose encouragement this book might never have been begun, and to Dr. Karl-Heinrich Vogelbach, without whose timely intervention it might never have been completed. I am singularly lucky in having such a tolerant, music-loving publisher as Ben Dominitz, whose enthusiasm seems to know no bounds. I'm grateful to my tennis partners Ed and Pat Self, Cathy Crockett, and Bill Kraft for keeping me in such excellent shape, to my friends at the Pacific Jewish Center (especially the Altschulers, the Genuths, the Magilnicks, the Medveds, the Schechters, and Harry Medved) for their warmth and hospitality, and to Kate Zeng for prodigious feats of Duck-sitting.

Introduction

Along with those of Dr. Samuel Johnson ("Were it not for imagination, sir, a man would be as happy in the arms of a chambermaid as a duchess"), Georg Christoph Lichtenberg ("Reading means borrowing"), and François, Duc la Rochefoucauld ("Love diminishes the lesser passions and augments the great, as the wind snuffs out the candle and ignites the flame"), the aphorisms that did the most to shape my youthful character were those of my paternal grandmother. She was a God-fearing woman—and the feeling was undoubtedly mutual. Of all the many maxims I imbibed at her flinty knee—including the great Czech beatitude, "Blessed are they who expect nothing, for they shall not be disappointed"—the one that made the most lasting impression was this rueful suggestion: "There's no such thing as a bargain and *everything* costs more than it's worth." A quick browse through the bins of any well-stocked CD store suggests she may have had a point. Although they are actually cheaper to produce than the late (and in some quarters, still greatly lamented) LP, CDs, for all their convenience and durability, are becoming a frightfully expensive investment. Though some stores have a no-questions-asked return policy, young or inexperienced listeners can have their views permanently distorted by a feeble or senselessly perverse interpretation. Moreover, there are so many choices (in a recent edition of *Opus*, more than eighty available versions of the Beethoven Fifth alone), how do you know that you've gotten the best possible return on that hard-earned investment, unless you've sampled a fair number of the alternatives beforehand?

That is what this book is intended to help you do.

Unlike the invaluable *Penguin Guide*, the *Record Shelf Guide* does not pretend to be all-inclusive or objective. (Not that *they're* all that objective either. For instance, in their one to three (*) rating system, you can safely deduct from one-half to a full (*) for any recording featuring a British composer, conductor, performer, or recording company, or any recording featuring liner notes by anyone associated with that admittedly finest of all music magazines, *Gramophone*). Although the *Record Shelf Guide* has grown an average of 30 percent with each edition, many things continue to slip through the cracks, while as many others have been shoved through them. Except for its indisputable giants, the Baroque still remains sparsely represented, as does the music of our time. The former because of the author's unshakable conviction that life is too short for the virtually interchangeable sewing-machine music of the Torelli-Corelli-Nardini-Spumoni-Linguini school, the latter because what in all the baffling variety of music being written today is actually worth hearing remains anybody's guess. In others words, the bulk of the book is devoted to music that people actually tend to listen to, which is to say music produced from the middle of the eighteenth century to roughly the midway point of our own.

Following the pattern of the comparative surveys that have been a regular feature of my radio program, *The Record Shelf*, from the beginning, the *Guide* attempts to say something cogent, enlightening, or amusing about the works themselves, and then blithely tells you which of the many available recordings you should actually go out and buy. Needless to say, this involves a measure of arrogance on my part—for which I make no apology—and an element of risk on the part of the reader. Actually, since the book itself isn't *all* that much more expensive than one full-priced CD, you'd still be well ahead of the game if it did nothing more than warn you off a single Nikolaus Harnoncourt recording or any of the several versions of the Górecki Third Symphony. Besides, it can always be put to other uses. (As the German composer Max Reger wrote in a famous blast to a critic: "I am seated in the smallest room in my house. Your review is in front of me. Shortly, it will be behind me.")

As to the criteria that were used in arriving at the final choices, they were surprisingly simple. In the first place, what *didn't* count was the reputation of the performer. Young, unknown musicians have made some astonishing recordings over the years; famous—yea, verily, *legendary*—musicians can on occasion perform like pigs. Nor was recorded sound much of a consideration. Never having been an audiophile, I will automatically opt for a bad-sounding recording of a great performance over a brilliant recording of a very good one. (Anyone listening to the sound of their playback system instead of what's being *played* should seriously begin thinking about finding another hobby.)

What *was* taken into consideration and what would seem to bind most of these recommendations together was the presence, in one way or another, of something that is becoming all too rare in the musical world: an instantly recognizable musical personality. Increasingly, as the late twentieth-century obsession with mechanical perfection continues—aided and abetted by the wonders of editable recording tape—commercial recordings have had less and less to say in musical and human terms. With a few notable exceptions, the world's major orchestras are losing their individuality (jet-set maestros have turned them into something with all the character of airport terminals), while the conductors themselves—again with a few notable exceptions—are becoming ever more bland and faceless, like Swiss characters in a spy novel.

For better or worse then, this *Guide* has become a celebration of musical individuality. Fortunately, the reissue of many recordings from the 1950s and '60s when such wonderfully individual musicians as Beecham, Björling, Furtwängler, Klemperer, Reiner, Rubinstein, and Walter were still active is a bittersweet reminder —as Mrs. Fisher put it in *Enchanted April*—"of better times, and better men," while the emergence of younger musicians with real personalities offers some reason for hope. The *Guide* constantly strives to sift the personal, the unique, and the truly memorable from the dull, the routine, and the mundane, selecting, wherever possible, the *one* recording of a given work currently available that seems the most exciting and individual. On occasion, this has meant giving two possible choices for a given work, not because I have any trouble making up my mind, but because there may be more than one equally exciting and individual interpretation that belongs in everyone's library.

More than any other edition of the *Guide*, this one reflects those two inevitable by-products of the coming of age of the compact disc: the disheartening, increasingly profligate, use of the deletions ax, and the heartening emergence of the bargain-basement label. Although every effort has been made to keep the *Guide* as current as possible, favorite recordings continue to vanish without warning—often to turn up in some other form. That other form, more often than not, are second exploitation labels—EMI Encore,

RCA Silver Seal, Philips Concert Classics, DG Galleria—which frequently offer superb performances in perfectly adequate sound at something less than half the cost of a full-priced CD. Even more encouraging is the arrival of labels like Naxos, which presents new digital recordings by lesser-known orchestras and artists—primarily from what used to be the Eastern Bloc—at an equally reasonable price. Wherever warranted, these recordings have been enthusiastically recommended, needless to say, for their *musical* as opposed to their economic virtues, since there are—*pace* Grandma —some bargains that no one can afford.

I continue to hope that you will find what follows useful in putting your recording library together, that it will help save you some money and make some for me (Dr. Johnson did say that "No man but a blockhead ever wrote except for money"), and that you will pardon its errors and excesses, which are wholly my own.

Adam, Adolphe-Charles

(1803–1856)

Giselle (complete ballet)

Orchestra of the Royal Opera House, Covent Garden,
Bonynge. London 433007-2 [CD].

The fame of the French composer Adolphe Adam continues
to hang on a dangerously slender thread. Apparently, though, the
thread is made of something with the tensile strength of piano wire,
since *Giselle*, the oldest Romantic ballet to retain a place in the
standard repertoire, shows no sign of losing any of its gooey appeal.
(I once saw a performance of this tenacious warhorse at the Bolshoi
in Moscow. The dancing, costumes, and scenery were beautiful, but
the auditorium was badly overheated, the audience fetid, and somewhere in the middle of the first act I managed to fall asleep.)

If this innocent, slightly oversweetened bonbon is to your
taste—although at well over two hours, "bonbon" is hardly the
appropriate metaphor—you can't possibly do better than Richard
Bonynge's sumptuous London recording. Over the years, Bonynge
has taken a good deal of undeserved heat from critics who have
suggested that he has gotten where he is *solely* because of his wife.
(Many still refer to him, churlishly, as "Mr. Joan Sutherland.") A
recording like this one should wring the neck of that honking
canard. The performance is both warm and richly detailed, with
superb playing from the Covent Garden Orchestra. But even more
to the point, this is an engagingly *theatrical* interpretation: so much
so, that for the first time ever, listening to old *Giselle*, I didn't nod
off once.

Adams, John (1947–)

The Chairman Dances; Two Fanfares, etc.

San Francisco Symphony, de Waart. Nonesuch 79144-2
[CD], 79144-4 [T].

For anyone who considers minimalism to be the dim-witted musical rip-off that it probably is, the music of John Adams presents a problem. Unlike Philip Glass, Steve Reich, Terry Riley, and the rest, Adams is a composer of demonstrable abilities and considerable charm, and this attractive Nonesuch recording will provide an excellent introduction to his humane and refreshingly *human* minimalist idiom.

While his most celebrated work to date, the controversial opera *Nixon in China* (Nonesuch 79193-2 [CD], 79193-4 [T]) may be too much of a not-so-good thing, the Chairman Dances from that work are pert, lively, and never wear out their welcome, and the five-minute "Short Ride in a Fast Machine" may be the most amusing and immediately appealing minimalist composition to date.

Edo de Waart and the San Franciscans are consistently alert and committed, and the recorded sound is close to ideal.

Albéniz, Isaac (1860–1909)

Iberia (Suite for Piano, 4 books)

De Larrocha, piano. London 417887-2 [CD].

Every so often a work becomes so completely identified with a specific performer that the interpreter and the thing being interpreted become all but indissoluble. A half century ago, Fritz Kreisler's version of the Brahms Violin Concerto, Wanda Landowska's

Goldberg Variations and the Furtwängler *Eroica* all existed on that remote, Olympian summit; so too, for more than three decades now, has Alicia de Larrocha's constantly growing version of that lexicon of modern Spanish music, Isaac Albéniz's *Iberia.*

In her latest and finest recording of the suite, de Larrocha probes more deeply, finds more color and drama, and somehow infuses *Iberia* with a rhythmic subtlety and life that even her earlier versions lacked. London's warmly detailed recorded sound is a worthy frame for a performance that will probably never lose its bloom and spontaneity.

The best available recording of the skillful orchestral suite arranged by the composer's friend Enrique Arbós—Ravel was contemplating an arrangement of his own; when he learned of Arbós's project, he abandoned the idea and wrote *Bolero* instead—is the pleasantly erotic version by the London Symphony led by Enrique Bátiz on Angel (CDC-49405 [CD]).

Albinoni, Tomaso (1671–1750)

Adagio in G minor for Strings and Organ

I Musici. Philips 420718-2 [CD], 410606-4 [T].

It is one of the minor tragedies of musical history that Tomaso Albinoni had more money than he knew what to do with. The son of a wealthy Venetian paper merchant, Albinoni described himself proudly as a "dilettante Veneto." He was never forced to earn his living as a musician, and more's the pity. Had he been made to work a bit harder at the craft for which he was so perfectly suited, he may well have become one of the giants of the Italian Baroque, instead of the tantalizing "what if?" curiosity he remains today.

Although he composed numerous instrumental concertos and nearly fifty operas, Albinoni is known primarily through the arrangements of his music made by his German admirer Johann

Sebastian Bach, and through the well-known Adagio for Strings and Organ, skillfully concocted by the modern Italian musicologist, Remo Giazotto.

As Baroque confections go, the Albinoni Adagio is very nearly as popular as Pachelbel's equally high-cholesterol *Kanon* and has been recorded almost as frequently. I Musici gives the piece one of those typically aristocratic yet meltingly lyrical performances that neither cheapen the music nor rob it of emotional impact. The twenty-year-old recorded sound remains impressive on both the CD and the tape, and the Bach and Handel concertos (to say nothing of the Pachelbel *Kanon*) that fill out the collection make this one of the more attractive Baroque albums on the market.

Albrechtsberger, Johann Georg (1736–1809)

Concertos (2) for Jew's Harp, Mandora, and Orchestra

> Mayr, Jew's Harp; Munich Chamber Orchestra, Stadlmair.
> Orfeo C-035821.

Walk into any bar in the world at any time of the day or night and suggest that *anyone* is the world's greatest conductor, pianist, violinist, or cellist and you're bound to get an argument. On the other hand, among devotees of the oft-misunderstood and much-maligned Jew's harp, only one name need do: the redoubtable Fritz Mayr—the Heifetz, Casals, Horowitz (take your pick)—of his chosen instrument. I have never had the pleasure of hearing Herr Mayr in person or even seeing a photograph of the man; I would dearly love to see what his dedication to his art has done to his bicuspids. Listening to Mayr perform, one is painfully reminded of David Niven's description of the dental malformations of the producer

Darryl Zanuck, who the actor alleged "could eat an apple through a tennis racket."

These two Jew's harp concertos by Beethoven's principal teacher are all the loonier because they were written as more or less serious works. Mayr twangs and doinks magnificently through both, and one can only hope that he and the admirable Munich Chamber Orchestra will soon get around to the five or six other such works that Albrechtsberger is alleged to have composed.

Alfvén, Hugo (1872–1960)

Midsommarvaka; Symphony No. 2

Stockholm Philharmonic, Järvi. BIS CD-385 [CD].

Any investigation of the unaccountably unexplored riches of modern Swedish music should begin with the major works of Hugo Alfvén, whose *Midsommarvaka*—an utterly delectable Swedish meatball variously known as the "Midsummer Vigil" and the "Swedish Rhapsody No. 1"—made its composer an international celebrity in the years immediately after the First World War. Though Alfvén never managed to duplicate the popular success of this enchanting trifle, his five symphonies, written between 1896 and 1952, are all important and appealing works, especially the Second Symphony of 1899.

Predictably, Neeme Järvi proves to be an ideal advocate of this warm and instantly approachable music. The version of *Midsommarvaka* is easily the finest currently available, and the performance of the Symphony is more impressive still, sounding for much of the time like early Sibelius without the static basses or rough edges.

Superb performances and strikingly lifelike recorded sound.

Allegri, Gregorio (1582–1652)

Miserere
(see Palestrina)

Alwyn, William (1905–1985)

Autumn Legend for English Horn and String Orchestra;
Lyra Angelica (concerto) for Harp and String Orchestra;
Pastoral Fantasia for Viola and String Orchestra; Tragic
Interlude for Two Horns, Timpani, and String
Orchestra

Soloists, City of London Sinfonia, Hickox. Chandos
CHAN-9065 [CD].

Symphony No. 4; Elizabethan Dances; Festival March.
London Symphony, Hickox. Chandos CHAN-8902
[CD].

For anyone with even a passing interest in twentieth-century
English music, Chandos's brilliant and courageous series devoted
to the major works of William Alwyn must be counted among
the most exciting recording projects of the last decade. A near
contemporary of Benjamin Britten, Sir William Walton, and Sir
Michael Tippett, Alwyn never achieved anything like their celebrity, for reasons that aren't difficult to explain. On the surface,
his music seems to have less in the way of a readily recognizable
personality (to say nothing of instantly memorable tunes) and his

preference for established forms—the symphony, the concerto, the string quartet—and traditional harmonic language might create the impression of a composer with nothing new or original to say. On closer examination—and Alwyn is a composer whose music absolutely *requires* repeated hearings to make its points—he emerges as one of the most rewarding of modern English composers. The music is passionate, dramatic, and uncompromising, with a craggy power and awesome sense of scale. It is also among the most intensely virile music produced in this century: forthright, unaffected, and unabashedly romantic.

Perhaps the best place to begin dipping into this epic project is the compact disc of concerted pieces, which includes the darkly beautiful *Lyra Angelica*, the composer's own favorite of all his works and possibly the finest harp concerto ever written. The other works are no less memorable—*Autumn Legend* is a kind of English *Swan of Tuonela*—and all are thrillingly played.

The symphonies are probably Alwyn's finest achievement, and none is more powerfully argued or richly orchestrated than the Fourth. Each of its three movements is brimming with mystery and character, especially the wonderful finale, a ravishing passacaglia concluding in a blaze of glorious brass. The colorful *Elizabethan Dances* and the stirring *Festival March* make for extremely attractive filler.

Although the playing of the London Symphony—like that of the City of London Sinfonia—is exemplary (as is the work of the Chandos engineers), the real secret of the series' success is the consistently inspired work of Richard Hickox. Alwyn has never had a more probing or persuasive interpreter, including Alwyn himself. While the composer's own recordings from the 1970s are currently available on a series of extremely expensive Lyrita reissues, the Hickox versions are preferable in almost every way.

Fours stars and three cheers to all concerned.

Anderson, Leroy (1908–1975)

Music of Leroy Anderson

> Orchestra, Anderson. MCA Classics MCAD2-98156 [CD],
> MCAC-531 [T].
>
> Boston Pops, Fiedler. RCA 09026-61237-2 [CD], 09026-
> 61237-4 [T].

Leroy Anderson once described the kind of music he wrote as "concert music with a pop quality," and let it go at that. It has also been described as "light" or "semi-classical" music, as well as a number of other less flattering terms by those who simply fail to get the point. The point is that he was a hugely gifted, highly original composer whose music came to epitomize the 1950s as unmistakably as Eisenhower, fallout shelters, and the Hula Hoop. By the time of Anderson's death, many of his best-known works had long since become a part of the national consciousness: as indelibly ingrained in the American ear as the paintings of his near-contemporary Norman Rockwell had been imprinted on the American eye. Although Anderson's music never plumbed the depths, stormed the heights, inflamed the passions, or stirred the soul, he had a knack for making people feel a little better, and given what life can be, that might well be the greater gift.

The most numerous and most popular of Anderson's works were those witty novelty items that became favorite Boston Pops encores and have remained pops concert staples ever since. Yet whatever the central gimmick—from the sounds of some actual office equipment, to those of a musical cat, an old time vaudeville soft shoe dancer, or a horse-drawn sleigh—it was never the sound effects or the high-concept central idea that animated the piece. It was Anderson's melodic genius and impeccable craftsmanship, coupled with an unwillingness to wear out his welcome and a genuine eagerness to please, that made him one of the most popular of American composers.

As this indispensable MCA collection of virtually his entire output proves, Anderson was a splendid interpreter of his own music. Recorded between 1950 and 1962, the forty-seven items are all invested with an irresistible freshness and sense of life, especially the more familiar pieces, which here sound newly-minted.

Arthur Fiedler hired Anderson as the Boston Pops's chief arranger and introduced most of his music to the world. Fiedler's interpretations are equally incomparable, though they tend to be a bit more literal and roughshod. Still, their energy and feeling of fun make them irresistible, and the recorded sound is marginally more up-to-date.

Arnold, Sir Malcolm (1921–)

Four Cornish Dances; Four English Dances; Four Irish Dances; Four Scottish Dances

London Philharmonic, Arnold. Lyrita SRCD-201 [CD].

With seven numbered symphonies to date, memorable scores for films such as *The Bridge on the River Kwai*, and even a zany contribution or two to the Hoffnung Festivals, Sir Malcolm Arnold has been one of the most prolific and versatile of all British composers. This Lyrita compilation of his four sets of British dances provides an ideal introduction to Arnold's eclectic, colorful, instantly digestible idiom: from the sassy Scottish Dances, with their vivid evocation of the skrill of highland pipes and the jaunty rhythms of the strathspey and reel, to the somber, often surprisingly substantial Irish Dances, written as recently as 1986. The interpretations, needless to say, are definitive, as is the swaggering playing of the London Philharmonic.

In the wake of Sir Malcolm's richly deserved and long-overdue knighthood, a relative flood of new Arnold recordings has deluged the market. Easily the most entertaining of all is a Chandos recording (CHAN-9100 [CD]) of suites from some of the finest of the composer's film scores, including *The Bridge on the River Kwai*, *The Inn of the Sixth Happiness*, and *Hobson's Choice*. Although copyright restrictions prevented using Arnold's inspired arrangement of Kenneth Alford's "Colonel Bogey March" — for the sake of continuity, the piece is played in its original version—the *Inn of the Sixth Happiness* excerpts include as much of "This Old Man" as anyone could wish. The performances by the London Symphony led by Richard Hickox are even more vivid than those heard in the actual films.

Two Hyperion albums (CDA-66172 [CD], KA-66172 [T]; CDA-66173 [CD], KA-66173 [T]) offer some of the best of Arnold's consistently imaginative, superbly crafted chamber music, but the composer himself leads a delightful program of his overtures for Reference (RR-48 [CD]), including the irrepressible *Beckus the Dandipratt* and the shockingly unknown *A Sussex Overture*.

Bach, Carl Philipp Emanuel (1714–1788)

Symphonies (6) "Hamburg Sinfonias"

C. P. E. Bach Chamber Orchestra, Haenchen. Capriccio 10106 [CD].

The most prolific and long-suffering of Johann Sebastian's sons—you'd suffer, too, if you had to spend twenty-seven years in the employ of Frederick the Great—C. P. E. Bach is finally beginning to be regarded with some of the awe with which his near-contemporaries always viewed him. For Haydn, his influence was decisive—"For what I know I have to thank Philipp Emanuel Bach"—and for Mozart, a pupil of his brother Johann Christian, the "Berlin Bach" was an even more important figure. "He is the father," Mozart said, "and we the children."

While he is still best known for his keyboard music and the innumerable works he was forced to compose for his flute-loving employer—Frederick *was* a fair musician, but a complete musical reactionary—the so-called "Hamburg Symphonies", composed for the Baron von Swieten in 1773, are a superb showcase for his robust talent. Hartmut Haenchen and the C. P. E. Bach Chamber Orchestra, playing on modern instruments, offer alert and loving interpretations of these exhilarating works, and Capriccio's recorded sound is flawless.

Another unusually attractive Capriccio release (10101 [CD]) brings together a flock of the composer's flute sonatas in performances that are equally stirring.

Bach, Johann Sebastian
(1685–1750)

The Art of Fugue, S. 1080

Juilliard String Quartet. Sony S2K-45937 [CD].

Prior to my first experience with the composer's final monumental essay in the art of counterpoint, I had been blissfully unaware that Bach had never intended *Die Kunst der Fuge* actually to be *performed*. Someone forgot to tell the music director of the small station where I broke in as an announcer. One night, early in my first week on the air, I had to introduce and then sit through the whole of *The Art of Fugue*. I've never been the same.

Although its variations on the same dreary subject seem interminable, *Die Kunst der Fuge* can make for a life-altering experience. Those with a taste for it will find the recording by the Juilliard String Quartet both valuable and revealing, provided it's ingested in the proper doses and *not* experienced while operating heavy machinery. The playing is clear and direct, admirably disentangling the most hopelessly tangled lines.

The wackiest—and by far the most entertaining—version is the arrangement made by William Malloch called *The Art of Fuguing* (Sheffield Lab SLS-502 [CD]), in which brisk tempos and an orchestral palate that owes much to Schoenberg produce an alternately amusing and hypnotic effect.

*B*randenburg Concertos (6), S. 1046–51

Academy of St. Martin-in-the-Fields, Marriner. Philips
426088/9-2 [CD]; 426088/9-4 [T].

English Concert, Pinnock. Deutsche Grammophon 410500-
2; 410501-2 [CD]; 423317-4 [T].

Just as Johann Sebastian Bach was the final summation of all
the Baroque era gave to music, the *Brandenburg* Concertos are the
apotheosis of the concerto grosso, the most diverse and important
of all Baroque instrumental forms.

For years, the standard recordings of the *Brandenburg* Concertos were those wonderfully musical performances from the
1930s by the Adolf Busch Chamber Orchestra, an interpretation
that can now be found along with Busch's equally memorable
versions of the Orchestral Suites on a brilliantly remastered set
from EMI (64047-2 [CD]). While not for Baroque purists (the
continuo is realized on a piano by a very young Rudolf Serkin), the
playing is marvelously virile and delightfully old-fashioned: a memorable souvenir of the days when Bach was generally considered a
stylistic contemporary of Robert Schumann.

Another persuasively romantic interpretation—and my favorite modern recording of the *Brandenburgs*—is that lush and stylish
account turned in by the English Chamber Orchestra conducted by
Benjamin Britten. Although the recordings surfaced for a time on
a pair of mid-priced London Jubilee compact discs, they are not
presently available—unless you're willing to import them directly
from England. (If you decide to invest that kind of time, trouble,
and money, you might as well also import Britten's incomparable
recordings of the Mozart symphonies, including his observes-all-
the-repeats version of the Symphony No. 40 that lasts longer than
most performances of Beethoven's *Eroica*. Nos. 25, 29, and the
Serenata notturna are to be found on Decca 430495-2 [CD] or
430495-4 [T], while No. 40, coupled with the *Prague*, comes on
Decca 430494-2 [CD] or 430494-4 [T].) Until the Britten *Brandenburgs* resurface, Sir Neville Marriner's engaging Philips recording will ably fill the gap. Using modern instruments, judicious
tempos, and a group of soloists who all play with individuality and
feeling, Marriner—like Britten before him—has no theoretical or
stylistic axe to grind and simply allows these marvelous works to
speak eloquently for themselves.

If Baroque "authenticity" is an absolute necessity, the best choice is the version by the English Concert and Trevor Pinnock on Deutsche Grammophon. Although the recording has drawn extravagant praise from both the English and American press, I find much of it rather prissy and effete. Nevertheless, the English Concert version is an enterprise that deserves to be taken seriously, unlike the inept and embarrassing scandal perpetrated by Nikolaus Harnoncourt and his abysmal Concentus Musicus of Vienna.

Cantatas (212)

The 200-plus cantatas that he ground out like so many sacred sausages contain much of what is most ethereal and inspired, and a great deal of what is most gloomy and depressing, in Bach's music. Some seem literally to have been produced with the aid of divine intervention, while others find one of the giants of music dutifully and ponderously marking time. A generation ago, perhaps twenty or thirty of the most enduring of them were available to the record-buying public; today, all of them have been recorded, some more than once.

Although it is impossible to make specific recommendations for all of these works—I won't pretend I've heard each and every recording: life, as we know, is *much* too short for that— I can offer a few words of warning and encouragement to the prospective Bach cantata collector, beginning with the heartfelt injunction to avoid any of the Teldec recordings as though they were (to quote Baudelaire) "the breeches of a man with the itch."

The Teldec series is divided up between Nikolaus Harnoncourt and Gustav Leonhardt, who gleefully take turns mauling the luckless pieces beyond recognition. The Harnoncourts are packed with the usual bellylaughs, and the Leonhardts aren't much better. It is almost as if these two clowns were engaged in some sort of bizarre contest as to who could conjure up the most screechy and etiolated instrumental sound and the most feeble choral outbursts. (I hate to sound like some sort of reverse sexist, but why give us a gaggle of struggling boys when a group of accomplished female singers would do even better?)

On the other hand, virtually all of the recordings made by John Eliot Gardiner, Helmuth Rilling, or Joshua Rifkin have lovely and important things to say, as do the performances in a new series from the bargain-basement label Naxos. While the names of the performers won't ring any bells, the interpretations are pointed, large-scaled, and endearingly dramatic. Besides, at six bucks a pop, how can you possibly go wrong?

*C*hristmas Oratorio, S. 248

Argenta, von Otter, Blochwitz, Bär, Monteverdi Choir, English Baroque Soloists, Gardiner. Deutsche Grammophon 423232-2 [CD], 423332-4 [T].

The reason the *Christmas Oratorio* doesn't hang together as well in actual performance as that other seasonal staple, Handel's *Messiah*, is that its composer never intended it to be downed in one gulp. The six separate and discreet cantatas were meant to be heard over a half dozen days of the Christmas period, and taken in that dosage it constitutes one of the most rewarding and affecting of all Bach's works.

As in his festive recording of the Bach *Magnificat* (Philips 411458-2 [CD]), which is also wholeheartedly recommended, John Eliot Gardiner here reaffirms his position as the foremost antiquarian of our time. From the exciting, brilliantly articulated opening with trumpets and timpani through the witty, briskly paced choruses, Gardiner infuses the music with an incomparable zest and vigor, without overlooking its gentle warmth and tenderness.

The soloists, the choir, and the always impeccable English Baroque Soloists are all at the top of their form, and if you're in the market for something to wash down the inevitable *Messiahs* and *Nutcrackers* during the holidays, search no further than this.

*C*hromatic Fantasy and Fugue in D minor, S. 903; Italian Concerto in F, S. 971

Brendel, piano. Philips 412252-2 [CD].

Rousset, harpsichord. L'Oiseau-Lyre 433054-2 [CD].

The Chromatic Fantasy and Fugue and Italian Concerto are among the most understandably popular and frequently recorded of all Baroque keyboard works. The Fantasy's often dizzying chromatic modulations can still sound strikingly modern, while the

Concerto's extroverted exuberance makes it one of the most heroic and exciting of Bach's creations.

Alfred Brendel's Bach—like his Mozart and Beethoven—owes much to the example of his teacher Edwin Fischer, who made a famous recording of *The Well-Tempered Clavier* in the early 1930s. The playing is both dramatic and meticulous, with suitably grand gestures and beautifully shaped lines.

The brilliant harpsichordist Christophe Rousset makes a very different but equally valid case on his superb L'Oiseau Lyre recital. Nothing remotely stuffy or pedantic is exhibited in these refreshing interpretations, which seem to flow out of the instrument with the utmost naturalness and ease.

Clavier Concertos (7), S. 1052–1058

Kipnis, harpsichord; London Strings, Marriner. CBS Odyssey MB2K-45616 [CD], MGT-39801/2 [T].

Most of Bach's seven surviving keyboard concertos—the first such works written by a major composer—are transcriptions of other concertos, primarily for the violin. As in all of the music that he so transformed, Bach exhibits the uncanny knack of making the music seem as though it couldn't possibly have been written for any other instrument: each of these glowing entertainments cries out "keyboard" as clearly as their original versions say "violin."

Igor Kipnis is one of those rare early-music specialists who are able to combine the often mutually exclusive qualities of scholarship and showmanship without compromising either: the interpretations are as thoughtful as they are impetuous, and he receives the usual imaginative help from Sir Neville and the gang.

Concerto in A minor for Violin, S. 1041; Concerto in E for Violin, S. 1042; Concerto in D minor for 2 Violins, S. 1043

Mutter, Accardo, violins; English Chamber Orchestra, Accardo. Angel CDC-47005 [CD].

It's hardly surprising that of all his innumerable instrumental concertos, these three works for the violin should remain among

Bach's most popular works in the form. Lyrical, dramatic, and overflowing with rich and memorable melody, these concertos were often taken up as vehicles by Fritz Kreisler, Eugène Ysaÿe, and other important turn-of-the-century violinists whose performances of any Baroque music tended to be as scarce as hockey players' teeth. Another sure sign of their enduring popular appeal was the enlistment of one of them for a key dramatic role in the hit film, *Children of a Lesser God*.

For years, the most completely satisfying recording of all three concertos was that unabashedly Romantic account by David and Igor Oistrakh, which is still available on Deutsche Grammophon. Those achingly beautiful performances would have remained my first choice in a very crowded field had it not been for the release of an even more lush and lovely interpretation by the German violinist Anne-Sophie Mutter.

When Mutter first arrived on the scene, I must admit I took little if any notice. I simply assumed that as the latest of Herbert von Karajan's many protégés, she would inevitably develop along the same cold, impersonal lines. Fortunately—if this marvelous Angel recording is any indication—she has shed all vestiges of Karajan's reptilian influence to become one of the most magnetic young musicians before the public today.

Stylistically, her performances of the Bach concertos are throwbacks. Cast on a large scale and full of late-Romantic gestures—has anyone since Kreisler made the slow movement of the E Major concerto sound as languorously sexy as this?—the interpretations are a perfect complement to her immense tone and seamless technique. As usual, Salvatore Accardo, as conductor and second violinist in the Double Concerto, brings a wealth of warmth and experience to what I suspect may become *the* indispensable Bach concerto recording.

Of the many fine recordings of the Concerto for Violin, Oboe, and Strings, the most impressive in terms of the oboist's contribution is Harold Gomberg's recording with Isaac Stern, the New York Philharmonic, and Leonard Bernstein, now available on CBS (MK-42258 [CD]; MGT-39798[T]). As always, this great artist's command of tone color, phrasing, dynamics, and breath control is little short of amazing: indeed, his physical sound is so rich and large it frequently threatens to overwhelm the violinist's. A more evenly matched contest can be found on a fine Angel recording with Itzhak Perlman and Ray Still (CDC-47073 [CD]).

English Suites (6), S. 806–811

Schiff, piano. London 421640-2 [CD].

Even for those who, like Sir Thomas Beecham, are not especially enthralled by Bach's music—"Too much counterpoint," he breezily insisted, "and what is worse, *Protestant* counterpoint"—the English Suites are very hard to resist. With their catchy tunes, engaging rhythms, and transparent textures, they represent Bach at his most joyously unbuttoned: the light-footed secular flip side of the often turgid sacred composer.

The formidably accomplished András Schiff is a nearly perfect advocate of these alluring works. While admittedly not as individual as Glenn Gould in his revelatory CBS recording (M2K-42268 [CD]), he is neither as controversial nor as perverse. Like Gould, Schiff proves that the resources of the modern piano will do no serious injury to the composer's intentions, with playing that is as luxuriant as it is natural and unforced.

Kenneth Gilbert's excellent version for Harmonia Mundi (HMC-90.1074/75 [CD]) is the best alternative for those who automatically begin to hyperventilate whenever Bach's keyboard music isn't played on the harpsichord.

Schiff is equally compelling in his version of the composer's French Suites (London 433313-2 [CD]). In addition to clear textures and lightly-sprung rhythms, nothing is remotely forced or calculated in the pianist's playing, only the obvious joy in bringing these engaging works to life.

Goldberg Variations, S. 988

Gould, piano. CBS MYK-38479 [CD], MYT-38479 [T] (1955 version). CBS MK-37779 [CD], IMT-37779 [T] (1981 version).

Pinnock, harpsichord. Deutsche Grammophon 415130-2 [CD].

The most cogent observation anyone has ever made about that mystery wrapped in an enigma, Glenn Gould, was an offhand wisecrack dropped by the conductor George Szell shortly after he had performed with the Canadian pianist for the first time. "That nut is a genius," Szell was heard to mumble, and history should probably let it go at that. Willful, unpredictable, eccentric, reclusive, and maddeningly brilliant, Glenn Gould was easily the most provocative pianist of his generation and one of the great musical originals of modern times.

It was the 1955 recording of the *Goldberg Variations* that introduced Gould to an unsuspecting world and began an entirely new chapter in the history of Bach interpretation. Legend has it that the *Goldberg Variations* were originally written as a soporific for a music-loving nobleman who was a chronic insomniac. Most recordings of the work support the legend. Gould changed all that with driving tempos, a bracing rhythmic vitality, and an ability to clarify and untangle the dense contrapuntal lines that was, and remains, amazing.

After twenty-five years of further study, Gould rerecorded the work in 1981, and the result was every bit as controversial as his original recording. While sacrificing none of the razor clarity of the earlier performance, the interpretation became more profound and reflective, with tempos that not only were dramatically slower but had been chosen—according to the pianist—to help each of the variations fit into a more homogeneous, integrated whole.

Since the release of the second version, I've been trying to choose between the two recordings, without very much success. But then, too, the choice boils down to either the youthful brashness of the original or the mature, studied brashness of the Revised Standard Version.

For those who insist on a harpsichord—though *I* am forced to agree with Sir Thomas Beecham, who said its sound reminded him of "two skeletons copulating on a corrugated tin roof"—try the alert, intelligent performance by Trevor Pinnock.

Mass in B minor, S. 232

Monteverdi Choir, English Baroque Soloists, Gardiner. Deutsche Grammophon 415514-2 [CD].

Nelson, Baird, Dooley, Hoffmeister, Opalach, Schultze, Bach Ensemble, Rifkin. Nonesuch 79036-2 [CD], 79036-4 [T].

The Baroque revival of the 1960s was a very shrewd marketing ploy of the recording industry. Compared to operas or Mahler symphonies, Baroque music was far easier and, more important (at least from *their* point of view), far cheaper to record. Thus we were inundated by not only torrents of music by composers who for centuries had been little more than names in a book, but also well-intentioned and generally lamentable recordings by organizations like the Telemann Society, and such stellar European ensembles as the Pforzheim Chamber Orchestra of Heilbron.

Next, the Baroque Boom was further complicated by the emergence of the Baroque Authenticity Movement, whose exponents argued—at times persuasively—that for Baroque music to make the points the composer intended, it had to be presented on instruments of the period. Like all such upheavals, the period-instrument revolution spawned its fair share of frauds and fanatics: untalented, uninspired charlatans who forgot that making music *does not* consist entirely of making physically repellant noises and arcane musicological points.

The work of three English musicians, Christopher Hogwood, Trevor Pinnock, and preeminently, John Eliot Gardiner, finally offers convincing evidence that the Authenticity Movement has at last grown up: Each of the three finest antiquarians before the public today is a musician first, a musicologist second. Gardiner's recording of the Bach Mass in B minor is as stirring and compassionate as his exhilarating recordings of the Handel Oratorios. He mixes grace, finesse, and dramatic grandeur into an immensely satisfying amalgam, while managing to coax more physical beauty from those old instruments than any other conductor ever has before or since.

For an interesting companion piece to Gardiner, try Joshua Rifkin—a versatile and vastly gifted musician who did as much as anyone to make the musical establishment take the music of Scott Joplin seriously—and his controversial Nonesuch recording with the Bach Ensemble. Rifkin's recording of the Mass is a radical experiment that audaciously assigns only a single voice to each of the choral parts. From a musician of lesser stature, the project easily might have degenerated into yet another Baroque Authenticity gimmick. But Rifkin, in a brilliantly argued essay, and an even more convincingly argued performance, proves that "authenticity" has to do far less with editions and instrumentation than with the authentic gifts of the performers.

A Musical Offering, S. 1079

Academy of St. Martin-in-the-Fields, Marriner. Philips
412800-2 [CD].

In addition to forging Prussia into a modern military state—
with all the pleasant consequences for the world that that would
have over the next two centuries—Frederick the Great was an
accomplished amateur flutist and composer who early in his reign
maintained one of the most musical courts in northern Europe. In
1747, he invited the aging father of his Kapellmeister, Carl Philipp
Emanuel Bach, to Potsdam and was amazed when "old Bach"
improvised a six-part fugue on a melody of the king's devising.
Back in Leipzig, Bach expanded the idea into a work consisting of
two ricercari, several canons, and a concluding trio, and dispatched
A Musical Offering to Frederick as a bread-and-butter note.

With Karl Münchinger's fine recording with the Stuttgart
Chamber Orchestra temporarily out of print, Sir Neville Marriner's
adroit, enormously musical Philips recording is the best alternative.
Unlike Münchinger, Marriner occasionally sounds a little gloomy,
particularly in the canons—which may be less a flaw in the interpretation than in the piece itself.

Organ Music

Hurford, organ. London 421337-2; 421341-2; 421617-2;
421621-2; 425631-2; 425635-2 [CDs].

It is in his organ music that Bach is at his most personal and
reactionary. This windy, glorious monstrosity was his favorite
instrument, and the music he composed for it, largely during the
Weimar period, all looked back into the past. In the forms he
inherited from Buxtehude and Frescobaldi—from the brilliant,
finger-twisting toccatas to those fantasias in which the finest keyboard composer of the Baroque era allowed his imagination free
rein—Bach wove some of the most intricate and imposing of his
inspirations. For many, the organ works represented not just his
first great creative phase, but the summit of his art.

If you're one of those Bach lovers who can't seem to get
enough of this stuff, Peter Hurford's six-volume, seventeen-CD set
on London's medium-priced Jubilee label should very nearly satisfy

you. The performances are invariably fresh, imaginative, and hugely accomplished, and the fact that the project was spread out over several years and numerous venues goes a long way to preventing any serious listener fatigue. Wisely, London has gathered together some of the best-known works on a "greatest hits" sampler (417711-2 [CD]), which is not only a revealing introduction to the series, but also one of the best single-CD collections on the market.

For the barbarians among us, London has also reissued Leopold Stokowski's Czech Philharmonic recordings of some of his gooey orchestral transcriptions (421639-2 [CD]). This breathtaking exercise in shameless self-indulgence easily ranks with the most enjoyable Bach recordings ever made.

Saint Matthew Passion, S. 244

Schreier, Adam, Popp, Lipovsek, Dresden Children's Chorus, Leipzig Radio Chorus, Dresden State Orchestra, Schreier. Philips 422088-2 [CD].

There are several ways of viewing this towering masterpiece, the most common of which is to regard it as the greatest single sacred work—and quite possibly the greatest single *musical* work— yet devised by the human mind.

As a naive yet ridiculously hypercritical youth, I once took part in a performance of the *Saint Matthew Passion* and the experience nearly killed me. Later, as a somewhat less demanding adult, I attended a production that Sir Georg Solti led early in his tenure as music director of the Chicago Symphony. Sir Georg presented his Eastertide version of the *Passion* Bayreuth-style, which is to say, it began early in the afternoon and—after a break for dinner—continued later that night. To my shame, I must admit that I and my wife (as she then was) availed ourselves of the opportunity to make a hasty getaway and take in a movie—which I still remember was the splashy, gory, well-intentioned *Waterloo*, with Rod Steiger and Christopher Plummer.

With its numberless arias, countless chorales, and interminable recitatives with the Savior speaking over an aureole of shimmering strings, the *Saint Matthew Passion* has always been a severe test of concentration and patience that I have never been fully able to pass. And if that makes me a clod and a philistine, so be it.

For those who disagree—and they are certainly in the vast majority—Peter Schreier's Philips recording will demonstrate just how dead wrong I am. Not only is this most inappropriately named of all singers (*schreier*, in German, means "screamer" or "howler") a dazzling Evangelist, he also proves to be a vastly talented conductor who moves the music along with an uncommon lightness of touch without glossing over any of its obvious profundity. The soloists, who clearly respect Schreier the tenor, sing their hearts out for Schreier the conductor; the choruses and orchestra respond just as zealously, as do Philips's engineers.

For those who require a tape—though it's impossible to imagine *anyone* listening to the *Saint Matthew* on a Walkman or while tooling down the freeway—the Harmonia Mundi recording (40.1264/65 [T]) led by Philippe Herreweghe is professional and intermittently inspired, but is no match for the triumphant Schreier set.

Sonatas (3) and Partitas (3) for Solo Violin, S. 1001–1006

Grumiaux, violin. Philips 438726-2 [CD]. Heifetz, violin. RCA 7708-4 RC6 [T].

More than any other important violinist since Fritz Kreisler, Arthur Grumiaux created the impression of a very great musician who only happened to play the violin. Although far more technically reliable than Kreisler—who never really cared for practicing and after a certain point in his career all but gave it up—Grumiaux was completely indifferent to virtuosity for its own sake. His mission in life was to illuminate great music rather than dazzle an audience.

Recorded in the early 1960s, Grumiaux's versions of the solo Partitas and Sonatas are *very* dazzling from both a musical and technical point of view. No other recordings reveal the music's structual bones quite so clearly or with such an easy, natural grace.

On tape, the Heifetz offers plenty of whiz-bang technical fireworks, although the recorded sound—like the playing itself—tends to be uncomfortably chilly and harsh.

Suites (4) for Lute, S. 995–7 and 1006a

Williams, guitar. Sony MK-42204 [CD].

Given the fact that Bob Dylan and the Beatles were the guitar's principal exponents in my youth, it's not surprising I never took the instrument all that seriously as a medium for "serious music." In the 1960s it was something that any idiot could (and frequently did) play, especially in my college dorm, which was so riddled with scruffy, smelly Dylan clones that anyone who didn't have a guitar was immediately suspected of being a secret supporter of Lyndon Johnson, napalm, and apartheid.

John Williams is such a fabulously accomplished musician that it scarcely matters what he plays. His versions of the Lute Suites are among the most musical and enjoyable of all Bach recordings, with playing that is lively, witty, and phenonemally precise. In the Sony transfer, the recorded sound is a bit bright and forward—the only minor drawback to an otherwise flawless release.

Suites (4) for Orchestra, S. 1066–1069

Academy of St. Martin-in-the-Fields, Marriner. London 430378-2 [CD].

It was Nikolaus Harnoncourt's pioneering period-instrument recording in the late 1960s that established his reputation as an interpreter of Bach's music. I remember buying it and being moderately enthusiastic at the time. Listening to it again, after nearly two decades, demonstrates what a woefully uncritical listener I was twenty years ago. It still seems to me the best of Harnoncourt's recordings, but that's a bit like trying to determine which of one's root-canal procedures bothered one the least. By no means should you waste your money buying this recording, but the next time you hear it on the radio, notice how crude and lifeless the playing is. In fact, in his driven, humorless approach to everything, Harnoncourt suggests nothing so much as a kind of technically inept Toscanini of the Baroque.

The first of Sir Neville Marriner's three separate recordings to date, the London version is a reissue of that dazzling Argo edition prepared with the help of the late English musicologist Thurston

Dart. As in Marriner's interpretation of the *Brandenburg* Concertos, the playing is brisk and ingratiating, with memorable contributions by every solo voice.

Unaccountably, John Elliot Gardiner's wonderful period-instrument recording for Erato has been withdrawn, demonstrating once again that an alarming number of children who tear the wings off butterflies and push little old ladies into manure spreaders eventually grow up to become recording executives. Until those silly people come to their senses, the best of the "authentic" versions is the warm and bracing Trevor Pinnock recording for Deutsche Grammophon (423492-2 [CD]), which comes with equally satisfying period accounts of the *Brandenburg* Concertos.

Suites (6) for Solo Cello, S. 1007–12

Starker, cello. Mercury 432756-2 [CD].

Ma, cello. CBS M2K-37867 [CD], IMT-39508/9 [T].

In the right hands, Bach's six Suites for Solo Cello can be an ennobling, thoroughly rewarding experience; in the wrong hands, they can be a crashing, unmitigated bore. There is certainly nothing boring about Pablo Casals's legendary recordings from the 1930s, still available on Angel. Professional musicians tend to admire them without reservation (Mitch Miller once told me that he developed his wonderful singing style on the oboe by trying to emulate the long lines that the cellist achieved on those famous old discs). My reaction to Casals's playing however, has always been similar to Igor Stravinsky's: "Of course, he is a very great man. He is in favor of Peace, against General Franco, and plays Bach in the manner of Brahms."

My own introduction to the Cello Suites was that superb and now recently resuscitated Mercury recording by the always provocative János Starker. Like his great Galician predecessor Emanuel Feuermann, Starker has always been a welcome foil to Casals's rough-and-tumble school of modern cello playing. His interpretations of the Bach Suites capture the essence of his unmannered, but always virile and distinctive, art with playing that mixes polish and control with fire and daring. As with all of the Mercury Living Presence recordings of the late '50s and early '60s, the sound on this one is astonishingly fresh and alive.

The eagerly anticipated account by Yo-Yo Ma, the most accomplished cellist of his generation, was a considerable disappointment. The playing itself is thrillingly beautiful, but there is a certain sameness in the performances that leaves one flat, as though we'd overheard a youthful run-through of what undoubtedly will be a great interpretation a few years down the road. Nevertheless, Ma's is still the preferred version in the tape format.

The Well-Tempered Clavier, S. 846–893

Gould, piano. CBS M3K-42266 [CD], M4T-42042 [T].

Gilbert, harpsichord. Deutsche Grammophon 413439-2 [CD].

In a charming little one-page essay called "Masters of Tone," the great American newspaperman, iconoclast, and linguistics scholar, H. L. Mencken, summed up the music of Johann Sebastian Bach as "Genesis I:1." Nowhere is Bach's seminal importance to the development of Western music more obvious than in that most significant of all Baroque keyboard collections, The Well-Tempered Clavier. Beginning with a disarmingly simple C Major prelude that makes Beethoven's Für Elise seem like the Third Rachmaninoff Concerto, The Well-Tempered Clavier moves triumphantly through all the major and minor keys with forty-eight masterworks that not only encapsulate the entire scope of Baroque contrapuntal thinking, but also epitomize the essential greatness of Bach's mature keyboard style.

Like The Art of Fugue, The Well-Tempered Clavier was probably never intended for public performance and is in fact dedicated to the "musical youth, desirous of learning." Be that as it may, some of the major keyboard artists of the twentieth century, beginning with Wanda Landowska and Edwin Fischer, have left immensely personal visions of this towering monument that continue to exert an irresistible fascination for performers today.

As a performance, the most staggering modern interpretation could be heard on a Melodiya/Angel recording by Sviatoslav Richter, now long out of print. Like Serge Koussevitzky's Beethoven, Richter's conception of The Well-Tempered Clavier may have had very little to do with the music of the composer, but as a lesson in the art of piano playing given by the most fabulously complete pianist of the last forty years, it has never been approached.

As in his recording of the *Goldberg Variations*, Glenn Gould's performance remains a model of imaginative musical brinkmanship. In spite of all the eccentricities—which include some of the fastest and slowest performances the individual preludes have ever received—the playing is a triumph of Gouldian textural clarity and pizzazz: the way he manages to make the most complicated fugues sound so trivially easy will leave the jaws of the ten-fingered dragging on the floor.

For a less personal, though by no means anonymous, vision supplied by one of today's preeminent harpsichordists, the Deutsche Grammophon recording by Kenneth Gilbert offers many quiet and unexpected revelations. With playing that is alternately relaxed and pointed, Gilbert—without ever letting us forget that we are in the presence of a major artist—allows us to focus our entire attention where it properly belongs: on the music itself.

Balakirev, Mily (1837–1910)

Symphony No. 1 in C; *Rus* (Second Overture on Russian Themes)

> Philharmonia, Svetlanov. Hyperion CDA-66493 [CD]; KA-66493 [T].

After César Cui, whose music has slipped into an oblivion from which it seems unlikely ever to emerge, Mily Balakirev (accent on the second syllable) remains the most obscure member of that group of Russian composers that critic Vladimir Stasov dubbed "The Mighty Five." As a conductor, composer, teacher, and propagandist, Balakirev probably did more for the cause of a Russian national music than anyone, including his more celebrated colleagues Borodin, Mussorgsky, and Rimsky-Korsakov.

With the glistening Oriental Fantasy *Islamey*—now best represented in a blistering account by the Hungarian pianist Jenö Jandó on a Naxos recording (8.550044 [CD]), which also includes a first-rate account of Mussorgsky's *Pictures at an Exhibition*— the Symphony in C is the most enjoyable and representative of Balakirev's works. Until Sir Thomas Beecham's classic 1955 interpretation returns to circulation, Yevgeny Svetlanov's Hyperion recording makes for a sumptuous alternative. If the performance lacks the bite and character of Beecham's, the playing of the Philharmonia is as richly overripe as Hyperion's recorded sound is richly resonant. A companion recording (CDA-66586 [CD]) makes a similar case for the composer's Second Symphony, the symphonic poem *Tamara*, and the delightful *Overture on Three Russian Themes*.

Barber, Samuel (1910–1981)

Adagio for Strings (from String Quartet, Op. 11)

Los Angeles Philharmonic, Bernstein. Deutsche Grammophon 427806-2 [CD], 423169-4 [T].

Even before achieving celebrity as "The Love Theme from *Platoon*," Barber's moltenly beautiful Adagio for Strings had acquired many powerful nonmusical associations. In fact, the case can be made that it was the moving use to which the work was put during Franklin Delano Roosevelt's funeral that established Samuel Barber's popular reputation.

Of all the many recordings that the Adagio has been given so far, none can come within hailing distance of the live performance —preserved superbly by Deutsche Grammophon—that Leonard Bernstein gave a few years ago with the Los Angeles Philharmonic. Adopting a tempo so measured that the music is almost guaranteed to fall apart, Bernstein, with vast dignity and deliberation, wrenches the last ounce of pain and pathos from the Adagio, while building one of the most devastating climaxes any piece has received in recent memory. While the Barber is clearly the principal selling point, there are also equally thrilling interpretations of Bernstein's *Candide* Overture, William Schuman's *American Festival* Overture, and Aaron Copland's *Appalachian Spring* (see page 143), thus making this one of the most exciting recordings of American music released in a decade.

For those interested in the ravishing string quartet from which the Adagio was taken, the finest recorded performance the work has yet received can be heard on a Deutsche Grammophon recording (435864-2 [CD]) by the Emerson String Quartet.

Overture to *The School for Scandal*; Essays Nos. 1–3 for Orchestra; *Medea's Meditation and Dance of Vengeance*

> New York Philharmonic, Schippers. CBS Odyssey 33230 [T].
>
> St. Louis Symphony, Slatkin. Angel CDC-49463 [CD], 4DS-49463 [T].

Except for the powerful and powerfully original Symphony No. 1, these two treasurable releases contain most of the works on which Samuel Barber's reputation as a composer of orchestral music will probably rest.

Thomas Schippers's credentials as a Barber conductor were unassailable. An intimate friend of the composer, Schippers was responsible for perhaps the finest of all Barber recordings: an ineffably tender account of the composer's masterpiece, *Knoxville: Summer of 1915*. That luminescent RCA recording with Leontyne Price has finally appeared on CD (09026-61983-2) with its original companion piece, two scenes from Barber's unjustly maligned opera *Anthony and Cleopatra*, together with material from a 1953 Library of Congress recital that includes the composer accompanying Price in the *Hermit Songs*. No singer, not even the wonderful Eleanor Steber for whom it was written, can approach Price in *Knoxville* (or, indeed, in any of these lovely works) for sheer vocal beauty or musical acuity; it is one of the principal glories in a career strewn with glory, one of the classic interpretations upon which her enormous reputation will rest.

On the Odyssey tape (and *where* the hell is the CD?), the New York Philharmonic is on its best behavior, and Schippers has never been better in the recording studio. The Adagio for Strings is also included; Schippers's is the only one that compares favorably with Bernstein's. The Overture crackles with gaiety and wit—Harold Gomberg's oboe solo is dumbfoundingly beautiful—and *Medea's Meditation and Dance of Vengeance* is unleashed with such horrifying fury that it almost persuades you that Mother's Day ought to be canceled. The gem of the collection, however, is the Second Essay for Orchestra in which lyricism, passion, and architectural integrity are kept in nearly perfect equilibrium by one of the most strangely underrated conductors of his time.

Like his electrifying version of the Barber Violin Concerto with Elmar Oliveira (Angel CDC-47850 [CD]), Leonard Slatkin's Angel recording of the same repertoire confirms *his* position as the foremost Barber conductor in the world today. The St. Louis Symphony—which is now second to no orchestra in the country—romps through the music as though it were part of the standard repertoire, and Slatkin's interpretations are both refreshing and insightful. Especially valuable are the performances of the two "unknown" Essays: the First, for a change, sounds neither as monotonous nor as grim as it frequently can, and the Third—Barber's last major work—is imbued with all the richness and dignity of a genuine valedictory. The recorded sound, like the playing, is state-of-the-art.

Songs (complete)

Studer, soprano; Hampson, baritone; Browning, piano;
Emerson String Quartet. Deutsche Grammophon
435867-2 [CD].

This is the most beautiful and important album of American music released in a decade: the first integral recording of a key facet of Barber's output, featuring two of America's finest singers accompanied by a pianist with a profound and special insight into the composer's work. John Browning, who also supplied the illuminating notes for this two-CD set of Barber's entire output of songs, was a friend of the composer and thus a uniquely qualified guide to this material, which shows an astonishing consistency of melodic and dramatic inspiration. It is impossible to imagine a better choice of singers for the project than Cheryl Studer and Thomas

Hampson. Although Studer's delivery is not ideally effortless throughout, she sings with perception and taste; if her version of the *Hermit Songs* doesn't completely efface the memory of Price and Steber, it can still be mentioned in the same breath with theirs. The singing is lush and feminine, the word-painting both subtle and shrewd. Hampson's contributions, on the other hand, add further fuel to the argument that he is currently America's finest singer. Nothing seems beyond his vocal, musical, or expressive grasp, with the *Mélodies passagères* and the haunting *Dover Beach* receiving their most haunting recorded performances ever.

All in all, a milestone in the recording history of American music.

Symphony No. 1 in One Movement; Piano Concerto; *Souvenirs*

Browning, piano; St. Louis Symphony, Slatkin. RCA 60732-2-RC [CD]; 60732-4-RC [T].

Given the fact that with the Third Symphony of Roy Harris it may well be the finest work in the form ever written by an American, Samuel Barber's Symphony No. 1 has not been all that well served by the recording industry. Apart from Bruno Walter's blazing account from the 78 era, there has never been a completely satisfying commercial recording of this taut and turbulent masterpiece. At least until now.

Besides the excellent Argo recording by the Baltimore Symphony under David Zinman and a fine version from Neemi Järvi and the Detroit Symphony that served as a makeweight for their performance of Amy Beach's *Gaelic* Symphony, the recording by the St. Louis Symphony under Leonard Slatkin is the one that finally does something like complete justice to the piece. On balance, the Slatkin is not only the most dramatically searching and impressively played of the three, it also comes with a superb performance of the Barber Piano Concerto, featuring the pianist Barber personally chose to give the world premiere. If not quite as electric as John Browning's earlier, long out-of-print recording with the Cleveland Orchestra and George Szell, the later one still towers above all the current competition. With Slatkin joining Browning for a charming two-piano version of *Souvenirs* as an encore, this is another indispensable Barber album from St. Louis.

Vanessa

Steber, Elias, Resnik, Gedda, Tozzi, Metropolitan Opera
Orchestra and Chorus, Mitropoulos. RCA 7899-2-RG
[CD].

If ever there was a contemporary opera for people who think
they hate contemporary operas, it is Samuel Barber's *Vanessa*.
The reason, of course, is obvious: *Vanessa* is a full-fledged nineteenth-century grand opera, even though it may have had its world
premiere in 1958.

From the mid-1930s until his death, Barber was something of
an anomaly among the major twentieth-century American composers. Recognition came early, his first musical champions included figures as diverse and powerful as Arturo Toscanini, Serge
Koussevitzky, and Bruno Walter, and for the next half century he
enjoyed the kind of popular and critical acclaim that might have
ruined the career of a lesser man.

To the very end, his expressive idiom remained stubbornly
and unashamedly Romantic, though it was a Romanticism guided
by a commanding modern intellect, coupled with extraordinary
elegance and finesse. After George Gershwin, he was also the most
gifted melodist of his generation, the American composer whose art
was most firmly grounded in the natural grace of song.

While *Vanessa* may not be universally regarded as a *great*
opera—though I, for one, am inclined to think that it is—there has
been little argument that it is a haunted and haunting work, with
moments of rare and voluptuous beauty. For instance, Erika's tiny
throwaway "aria," "Why must the winter come so soon?" is in
itself nearly worth the price of admission.

It was extremely decent of RCA to reissue this historic recording, made with the original cast in 1958. Eleanor Steber, for
whom the *Hermit Songs* and *Knoxville: Summer of 1915* were
written, more than lives up to the legend in the title role. The
supporting cast is uniformly excellent (Rosalind Elias and Nicolai
Gedda especially so) and that largely unsung hero of modern
music, Dimitri Mitropoulos, leads a performance in which the
unearthly lyricism and dramatic tension of the piece are given free
and equal rein.

For lovers of Barber, opera (modern or otherwise), glorious
melody, and lovely singing, this one cannot be passed up.

Bartók, Béla (1881–1945)

Bluebeard's Castle

Martón, Ramey, Hungarian State Orchestra and Chorus, Fischer. CBS MK-44523 [CD].

Bartók's greatest stage work is certainly not something for children or sissies. And this has nothing to do with the gruesome violence of the piece, since there is none. What makes *Bluebeard's Castle* so taxing for most people is that it has only two extremely talkative characters and practically no action. But because it is a work about a man who values his privacy, the pathologically private composer threw his entire being into the project, producing a score of unsurpassed richness, subtlety, and depth. Besides being prime early Bartók, it's also—since so little actually takes place on stage—an ideal opera for home listening.

While the brilliant London recording (414167-2 [CD]) has much to recommend it, especially the conducting of István Kertész, who turns in the most powerful realization of the orchestral part, it is the singing on the more recent CBS version that sets it apart and will probably keep it ahead of the competition for decades. With its inky, resonant lower register and brilliant baritonal top end, the voice of Samuel Ramey is perfect for the hero. Eva Martón, vocally phenomenal as always, here seems capable of shattering flower pots, much less wine glasses. Adam Fischer is an able accomplice, keeping the tension at an almost uncomfortably high level from beginning to end.

Concerto for Orchestra

Chicago Symphony, Reiner. RCA 09026-61504-2 [CD]; 09026-61504-4 [T].

New York Philharmonic, Boulez. CBS MK-37259 [CD], MYT-37259 [T].

Like his near contemporary George Szell, Fritz Reiner was one of the consummate orchestral technicians of the twentieth century. There was nothing that his minuscule, but infinitely various, beat could not express, and even less that escaped his hooded, hawklike eye. He was also a humorless despot who terrorized orchestras for more than fifty years. Once a jovial bass player whipped out a huge brass telescope at a Reiner rehearsal and shouted "I'm looking for the beat." The man was fired on the spot.

Like Szell—of whom one frequently hears the same nonsense —Reiner was often accused of being rather chilly and aloof in his performances, a kind of radioactive ice cube who sacrificed depth and emotion in favor of brilliantly polished surface details. Dozens of Reiner recordings ably refute that preposterous contention, none more convincingly than his stupendous version of Bartók's *Concerto for Orchestra*.

Reiner's association with the *Concerto* in fact began *before* the piece was written. Without Bartók's consent or knowledge, it was Reiner and his friend the Hungarian violinist Joseph Szigeti who persuaded Serge Koussevitzky to commission the work from the destitute, dying composer in 1942. Reiner made the first commercial recording of the *Concerto* with the Pittsburgh Symphony, and the very first stereo recording with the Chicago Symphony in 1955.

In its new compact disc format, this ageless performance sounds as though it might have been recorded a few years ago, instead of at the very dawn of the stereo era. Reiner's characteristic combination of complete flexibility and cast-iron control can be heard in every bar of the interpretation, from the dark melancholy of the opening movement to the giddy reaffirmation of life in the finale.

If Sir Georg Solti's more recent Chicago Symphony performance on a London compact disc offers clearer sound and slightly better orchestral execution, the brusque and intermittently vulgar reading is no match for Reiner's. In fact, the only serious competition comes from Pierre Boulez, who, in one of his finest New York Philharmonic recordings, offers a brilliantly analytical yet glowing performance, marred only by the occasionally slipshod playing of the Philharmonic brass. But since the Reiner compact disc offers, as a bonus, the most hair-raising of all recordings of the Music for Strings, Percussion, and Celesta and a splendidly atmospheric *Hungarian Sketches*, it constitutes—at something over sixty-five minutes—one of the few authentic bargains on the market today.

Concertos for Piano and Orchestra (3)

> Ashkenazy, piano; Chicago Symphony, Solti. London
> 425573-2 [CD].
>
> Bishop-Kovacevich, piano; London Symphony, BBC
> Symphony, Davis. Philips 426660-2 [CD].
>
> Sándor, Hungarian State Orchestra, Fischer. Sony SK-45835
> [CD].

The three Concertos, which Bartók composed primarily for his own use, are so central to the language of twentieth-century piano music that one wonders why they aren't performed and recorded more frequently. While the percussive First Concerto is still a fairly difficult pill for most people to swallow, and the fiendish Second is all but unplayable, the lyrical, sweet-spirited Third should have entered the standard repertoire years ago. A deceptively simple, often childish piece, it should pose no problem for anyone who enjoys Rachmaninoff or Tchaikovsky and, further, becomes an ideal invitation to explore the more complex pleasures of the two masterworks that precede it.

On a generously packed pair of CDs—which also feature a distinguished performance of the Sonata for Two Pianos and Percussion—Vladimir Ashkenazy, Georg Solti, and the Chicago Symphony dance their way through this demanding music with just the right blend of ardor, sarcasm, poetry, and rhythmic bite. Solti, always an imaginative and sympathetic accompanist, is especially telling in the First and Third Concertos, where the vivid backdrop he supplies is almost operatic in its theatricality. Ashkenazy, too, has some of his finest moments on records, especially in the meditative slow movements to which he brings an uncommon eloquence and restraint.

The medium-priced Philips recording of all three Concertos on a single CD is obviously a major bargain. The performances by Stephen Bishop-Kovacevich and Colin Davis, recorded between 1968 and 1975, while considerably less pointed and dramatic than Ashkenazy's, are nonetheless exceptionally fine. Lyrical, thoughtful, though peppered with moments of reckless abandon, they are a perfect foil to the more intense versions on London, especially for listeners who want to acquire them for substantially less than half the price.

Finally, for the last word in absolute authenticity, the recordings by the composer's friend György Sándor remain in a class by themselves. He not only studied the music under Bartók, but also he was chosen by the Bartók family to give the Third Concerto's world premiere after the composer's death. As in his earlier cycle for Vox (now available on CDX2-5506), Sándor brings a fire and authority to the music that no other living pianist can match.

Concerto No. 2 in B minor for Violin and Orchestra

Chung, violin; Chicago Symphony, Solti. London 425015-2 [CD].

Zukerman, violin; St. Louis Symphony, Slatkin. RCA 60749-2-RC [CD]; 60749-4-RC [T].

Like the life-affirming *Concerto for Orchestra*, which was written while the composer was dying of leukemia, the exuberant B minor Violin Concerto was produced during an unusually harrowing period of Bartók's life. Begun during the dark months of 1938, when the composer was fearing the spread of Nazism throughout Central Europe and worrying, correctly, about "the imminent danger that Hungary, too, will surrender to this system of robbers and murderers," the Second Violin Concerto is one of his most optimistic and proudly nationalistic statements. Folklike melodies permeate the entire fabric of the score, as does a giddy virtuosity that makes it one of the more challenging and rewarding works in the violinist's repertoire.

Kyung-Wha Chung brings a towering technique to the music and a sharp objectivity that many might find distant or cold. The approach works exceptionally well in the often uncompromising outer movements of the Concerto, and Georg Solti's equally cool yet idiomatic accompaniment clearly places the piece in the mainstream of twentieth-century violin concertos.

For those who prefer a more romantic view, Pinchas Zukerman with Leonard Slatkin and the St. Louis Symphony move the Concerto backwards in time by several decades without doing serious violence to the spirit or letter of the score. In addition, they serve up what is easily the best available version of the late and problematical Viola Concerto, which, like the pioneering recording by its dedicatee William Primrose, makes it seem as though there were no problems at all.

Mikrokosmos (selections); Contrasts

Bartók, piano. Sony MPK-47676 [CD].

Consisting of 153 tiny pieces in six volumes, Bartók's *Mikrokosmos* was written to teach children the logic and meaning of contemporary music. From simple studies in dotted notes, syncopation, and parallel motion to more elaborate examinations of polytonality and polyrhythms, *Mikrokosmos* represents precisely that: a series of "little worlds" in which the composer's inventive genius was at its purest and most disarming.

As these famous recordings made in 1940 clearly prove, Bartók himself was an ideal guide to these enchanting microcosms: the playing is simple and unaffected, a paradigm of that art which conceals art. With the equally famous recording of *Contrasts* made with Benny Goodman and Joseph Szigeti, this is a thrillingly immediate reminder of a great musician and great soul.

The Miraculous Mandarin (complete ballet)

New York Philharmonic, Boulez. Sony SMK-45837 [CD].

A close friend of mine had an extremely effective method of getting rid of visitors who overstayed their welcome. Rather than yawn ostentatiously, or consult his watch every five minutes, he would put on a recording of *The Miraculous Mandarin* and within minutes would find himself alone.

Although written as long ago as 1919, Bartók's savage, sensational, frequently sickening ballet remains a startlingly modern work. Emotionally, if not necessarily musically, it often seems more advanced than Stravinsky's *Rite of Spring*; at the very least, it is one of the first important musical works that seem to have completely digested the horrific implications of the recently concluded First World War.

Early in his unhappy stay in Chicago, Jean Martinon made a recording of the *Miraculous Mandarin* Suite for RCA that may always be the last word in orchestral ferocity; coupled with an equally memorable version of Hindemith's ballet on the life of St. Francis of Assisi, *Nobilissima visione*, it was one of the best of RCA's Chicago Symphony recordings and certainly deserves a CD reissue.

Pierre Boulez's stunning New York Philharmonic recording not only underscores the *Miraculous Mandarin*'s link to Stravinsky, but invests it with a lyric grace that will surprise many admirers of the ballet. Not to say that the performance soft-pedals the more savage elements: when the finale begins grunting and snarling in earnest, sissies will make for the nearest door.

Bartók's vastly different fairy-tale ballet, the warm and cuddly *The Wooden Prince* is now best represented by a sumptuous Chandos recording (CHAN-8895 [CD], ABTD-1506 [T]) by the Philharmonia Orchestra led by the ubiquitous Neeme Järvi. In addition to being the only note-complete version currently available, it is one of the most vividly graphic recordings of *any* ballet. Järvi's gifts as a musical storyteller are such that one can easily follow dramatic argument without the slightest hint of what's going on. The performance of the *Hungarian Sketches* that comes as a filler is no less splendid.

String Quartets (6)

> **Emerson String Quartet. Deutsche Grammophon 423657-2 [CD].**
>
> **Chilingirian String Quartet. Chandos ABTD-1280; 1323; 1346 [T].**

With the possible exceptions of the quartets of Dmitri Shostakovich, Arnold Schoenberg, and Leoš Janáček, those of Béla Bartók are the most significant contribution a twentieth-century composer has yet made to the form. Each of these adventurous masterworks is an important signpost in the evolution of Bartók's stylistic development: from the folklike elements that pervade the early works, to the astringent flirtation with atonality in the middle two, to a more direct and simple mode of communication in the last two works of the series.

For more than three decades, the cycle has very nearly been the private property of the Juilliard String Quartet. When their most recent recording was withdrawn (possibly to be reissued as a

CBS compact disc), many of us despaired of ever hearing its like again—at least until the arrival of the new Deutsche Grammophon recording by the Emerson String Quartet.

There are many who insist that the Emerson is the finest young American string quartet now before the public. I would agree with that assessment, if one were to drop the modifiers "young" and "American." Judging from the series of "Great Romantic Quartets" they recorded for the Book-of-the-Month Club and this hair-raising version of the Bartók Quartets, there seems to be nothing that the Emersons cannot do. They play with all the fire and polish of the old Juilliard, yet still produce a sinuous beauty of tone reminiscent of the Guarneri Quartet in their prime. It is also the only quartet in living memory that literally has no second fiddle: the two violinists change roles from concert to concert and often from piece to piece.

This is easily one of the finest Bartók cycles yet recorded, with interpretations that are large, audacious, brooding, risky, colorful, and richly "histrionic" in the best possible sense of the word. The hell-bent performance of the Second Quartet may be the most frighteningly exciting ever, and the Fifth has never seemed more amusing or profound. While no currently available tape can begin to equal the Emerson's achievement, the Chandos cassettes by the fine Chilingirian Quartet are as presentable as any.

Among other recordings of Bartók's chamber music, Gidon Kremer's versions of the two Violin Sonatas for Hungaroton (HCD 11655-2 [CD]) represent some of his finest work in the recording studio to date: The performances have a scale and intensity unlike any other, including the pioneering interpretations of the composer's friend, Joseph Szigeti.

The astonishing Sonata for Solo Violin has never been better served than in the Mark Kaplan's recent Arabesque recording which combines musical insight, breathtaking virtuosity, and flawless recorded sound (Z6649 [CD]). A program of Bartók's shorter works for violin and piano rounds out a most desirable disc.

Bax, Sir Arnold (1883–1953)

The Garden of Fand; The Happy Forest; November Woods; Summer Music

Ulster Orchestra, Thomson. Chandos CHAN-8307 [CD], ABTD-1066 [T].

After Ralph Vaughan Williams, Sir Arnold Bax, late the Master of the King's Musick and composer of the score for David Lean's immortal movie version of *Oliver Twist*, was the major English symphonist of the twentieth century. While his gentlemanly yet deeply Romantic music contains occasional echoes of Vaughan Williams and Sibelius, there is a strong, highly individual personality that informs the best of it, especially the four masterful tone poems with which the late Bryden Thomson and the Ulster Orchestra began their complete cycle of Bax's music for Chandos. In all of them, the composer's obsession with Celtic legend and his fascination with French impressionism are clearly evident: these are darkly chromatic, vividly evocative scores, which become all the more fascinating on repeated hearings.

For those who find themselves drawn to Bax—and I treasure him almost as much as Walton and Tippett—the next logical step is to explore the seven symphonies, all of which have now been recorded by Thomson and the London Philharmonic. The quality tends to vary, but at least four of them rank with the finest symphonies ever written by an Englishman. The Second, composed for Serge Koussevitzky, is a sweeping, deeply spiritual work, with an almost Baroque opulence of ornamental detail (CHAN-8493 [CD]). The mystical Third—first recorded in 1943 by Sir John Barbirolli—is perhaps the most accomplished and original of the cycle (CHAN-8454 [CD]), while the Fifth (CHAN-8669 [CD], ABTD-1356 [T]) and Sixth (CHAN-8586 [CD]) are clearly the works of an independent master who owes nothing to anyone or to any school.

Thomson and his orchestra cannot be praised too vigorously for either their meticulous execution or their ability to immerse themselves completely in the composer's unique idiom. As with that other great nature poet, Frederick Delius, Bax is decidedly an acquired taste; yet like many acquired tastes, he can quickly turn into an acquired passion.

Beach, Mrs. H.H.A. (Amy Marcy Cheney)

(1867–1944)

Symphony in E minor, *Gaelic*

> Detroit Symphony, Järvi. Chandos CHAN-8958 [CD], ABTD-1550 [T].

Mrs. H. H. A. Beach, to use the designation that this hugely proper and very gifted Bostonian preferred, wrote what has the distinction of being only the second symphony ever published by an American composer, the *Gaelic* Symphony of 1896. As with virtually all serious American music written at the time, the spirit of Dvořák hangs heavily over Mrs. Beach's major orchestral score, as do the shades of Schubert, Brahms, and Liszt. Still, the *Gaelic* is a skillful manipulation of a series of familiar Irish folk tunes and a work of considerable power and charm.

The new Chandos recording—the first since the game but not especially inspired outing released by the long-defunct Society for the Preservation of the American Musical Heritage—features the resurgent Detroit Symphony sounding better than it has in years, with Neeme Järvi providing his predictable blend of insight and enthusiasm. The versions of Barber's First Symphony and Overture to *The School for Scandal*, if not the first choice for either piece, make for an attractive and generous filler.

Mrs. Beach's attractive piano music can be heard on a pair of CDs from Northeastern (NR-223; NR-9004). Although the music is largely of the *fin de siècle* potted-palm variety, it has considerable freshness and period charm, particularly in the definitive-sounding interpretations of the wonderful Virgina Eskin. Two of the composer's more important larger works—the Piano Concerto in C-sharp minor and the Piano Quintet in F-sharp minor, which many Beacheans long have argued is her masterpiece—are available in very respectable performances on a budget Vox/Turnabout compact disc (PTV-7196).

Beethoven, Ludwig van

(1770–1826)

Bagatelles (24)

Jandó, piano. Naxos 8.550474 [CD].

There are few works that make this crusty, often forbidding giant seem more endearingly human than his three sparkling sets of Bagatelles: rarely is Beethoven this consistently charming, humorous, and relaxed.

As in the wondrous and inexplicably discontinued Philips recording by Stephen Kovacevich (née Bishop, subsequently Bishop-Kovacevich), Jenö Jandó is an ideal exponent of these attractive miniatures. The playing is both imaginative and wholly unaffected, with the natural charm of the pieces allowed to emerge.

Unfortunately, the Jandó recording does not include that most famous bagatelle of all, *Für Elise*, best represented currently on a Philips recital by Alfred Brendel (412227–2 [CD]). Along with a suitably winsome account of that frequently hackneyed work, the compact disc also includes thoroughly adult performances of the six *Écossaises* and the *Eroica Variations*.

Choral Fantasy (Fantasia in C minor for Piano, Chorus, and Orchestra)

R. Serkin, piano; Westminster Choir, New York Philharmonic, Bernstein. CBS MYK-38526 [CD], MYT-38526 [T].

This odd, hybrid piece (no one would again write for this combination of forces until Ferruccio Busoni unveiled his mammoth Piano Concerto, albeit for Piano, Orchestra, and *Male* Chorus, more than a century later) owes much of its popularity to the fact that it is usually viewed as a kind of dry run for the finale of the Ninth Symphony. It isn't, really, but its choral theme *is* a close cousin of the *Ode to Joy*, and in the right hands, it can be intriguing and uplifting.

In my experience, only one recording has ever made this peculiar hodgepodge come off, and that is the version taped in the early 1960s by Rudolf Serkin and Leonard Bernstein. As usual, Serkin's seriousness of purpose imbues the music with a dignity and significance that no other interpretation does, while Bernstein's enthusiasm proves a perfect foil to the high-mindedness (though never high-handedness) of his partner. A vintage Serkin interpretation of the Third Piano Concerto fills out both the compact disc and tape.

Concertos (5) for Piano and Orchestra

Fleisher, piano; Cleveland Orchestra, Szell. CBS M3K-42445 [CD].

Schnabel, piano; London Symphony, Sargent. Arabesque Z-6549/50/51 [CD], 9103-4 [T].

Since the extravagantly gifted William Kapell died in a plane crash near San Francisco in 1953, the careers of America's finest pianists have been the cause of great sadness, consternation, and alarm. The mercurial, highly-strung Byron Janis began canceling appearances on such a regular basis that his brilliant career was over almost before it began; similarly, the unjustly maligned Van Cliburn, after years of abuse from the critics, lapsed into a stony silence from which he has yet to emerge. Gary Graffman has been plagued in the last decade by a crippling neurological disorder, as has the most accomplished American pianist since William Kapell, Leon Fleisher.

The CBS compact disc reissue of Fleisher's classic account of the Beethoven Concertos with George Szell and the Cleveland Orchestra is a major cause for rejoicing. Rarely, if ever, have a pianist and conductor shown more unanimity of purpose and execution in this music. The rhythms are consistently crisp and vibrant. The phrasing is meticulous almost to a fault, and the hair-trigger reflexes of the Cleveland Orchestra are a perfect complement to Fleisher's then fabulous technique. Although some listeners might find the approach uncomfortably patrician, Fleisher and Szell manage to scrape off so many layers of accumulated interpretive treacle that we are able, in effect, to hear these familiar and frequently hackneyed works as if for the first time.

If state-of-the-art recorded sound and mechanical perfection are not absolute necessities, the recordings made in the 1930s by Fleisher's great teacher, Arthur Schnabel, are still the standard by which all other recordings must be judged. Never a pianist's pianist, Schnabel exhibited technical imperfections that were the butt of countless jokes among his colleagues. When told that Schnabel had been exempted from military service for physical reasons during the First World War, that mordant turn-of-the-century virtuoso Moriz Rosenthal quipped, "Naturally, the man has no fingers." Nevertheless, it was the force of Schnabel's personality that virtually rediscovered Beethoven's piano music in the 1920s and '30s, and in Arabesque's immaculate transfers, these impetuous, headstrong, and always deeply personal interpretations emerge as touchstones of twentieth-century keyboard art.

Concerto for Violin and Orchestra in D

Menuhin, violin; Philharmonia Orchestra, Furtwängler. Angel CDH-69799 [CD].

Perlman, violin; Philharmonia Orchestra, Giulini. Angel CDC-47002 [CD].

It has been argued—and argued persuasively—that Yehudi Menuhin has yet to make a finer recording than the 1932 version of the Elgar Violin Concerto, made when that extraordinary child prodigy was only sixteen years old. But in the last couple decades, Menuhin's Olympian technique has eroded alarmingly. Although the warmth and musicianship are still there in ample supply, the digital dexterity is now a mere shadow of its former self.

With the Elgar, this famous recording of the Beethoven Concerto ranks with the violinist's greatest achievements. In it, the high-minded nobility and melting tenderness of this unique musician are conspicuously on display. Add to that the surging yet impeccably disciplined accompaniment Wilhelm Furtwängler provided in one of his final commercial recordings, and we are left with something very close to a Beethoven Violin Concerto for the ages.

For those who require more up-to-date sound—although in Angel's compact disc transfer of the Menuhin recording the 1954 acoustics sound remarkably detailed and warm—the best modern version comes from Itzhak Perlman and Carlo Maria Giulini. The violinist offers his usual blend of exuberance and arching lyricism, while the conductor's elegant yet probing support confirms his reputation as one of the great modern accompanists.

Concerto for Violin, Cello, Piano, and Orchestra in C (Triple Concerto)

Beaux Arts Trio, London Philharmonic, Haitink. Philips 420231-2 [CD].

Although it doesn't exactly bear the same relationship to Beethoven's other concertos that *Wellington's Victory* does to the symphonies, the Triple Concerto can be a lame, long-winded thing, even when given the most committed kind of performance. For the already converted—I myself will remain a nay-saying heretic to the end—the Beaux Arts Trio, Bernard Haitink, and the London Philharmonic give the thing every opportunity to sound important and interesting. Everyone—including Philips's engineers—work together beautifully. Only the Concerto itself refuses to cooperate.

Creatures of Prometheus (complete ballet)

Orpheus Chamber Orchestra. Deutsche Grammophon 419608-2 [CD].

Once again, the Orpheus Chamber Orchestra seems to prove that the cheapest of all instruments is the conductor's baton. This is easily the most alert and vivid recording ever made of Beethoven's youthful ballet, which, apart from the overture and the famous tune that would turn up in the finale of the *Eroica* Symphony, is very little known. Although clearly not top-drawer Beethoven, the *creatures of Prometheus* makes for some extremely agreeable listening, especially in so fine a performance as this.

Along with those classic recordings of two other Beethoven theatrical works that absolutely *must* be returned to circulation— Sir Thomas Beecham's crackling account of *The Ruins of Athens* and George Szell's breathtaking Vienna recording of *Egmont* (part of which resurfaced briefly as filler for his London Symphony Tchaikovsky Fourth)—Michael Tilson Thomas's spirited recording of the *King Stephen* incidental music (CBS MK-33509 [CD]) really is mandatory for the Beethoven freak who has to have everything. In addition to that splendid performance—which includes the best version of the Overture since the RCA recording by Pierre Monteux —the compact disc offers first-rate versions of *Calm Sea and Prosperous Voyage* and those *genuine* choral rarities, the *Opferlied*, *Bundeslied*, and *Eligischer Gesang*.

Fidelio

Norman, Goldberg, Moll, Wlaschiha, Coburn, Blochwitz, Dresden State Opera Chorus and Orchestra, Haitink. Philips 426308-2 [CD].

Nearly two hundred years after *Fidelio*'s first successful production—and none of the composer's works would ever cost him as much time, pain, and backbreaking labor—Beethoven's one and only opera still provokes heated debates. Is the rickety rescue melodrama worthy of the magnificent music that fleshes it out? Is *Fidelio* a successful *opera* at all, or simply a breathtaking collection of musical essays in the composer's mature middle-period style?

No one ever made a stronger case for *Fidelio* both as music and as musical theatre than Otto Klemperer, whose legendary recording from the early 1960s features some of the noblest conducting ever captured on records. With a monumentality and scope that literally dwarfs the competition, the Klemperer *Fidelio* is also a gripping dramatic experience. Leonore's "Abscheulicher!" Florestan's second act aria, the dungeon scene, and the exultant finale, all crackle and pop with an immediate and vivid realism, beside which almost all other recorded performances seem flaccid and pale.

Until EMI returns that epic recording to the catalog, the Philips version with Jessye Norman and Bernard Haitink will almost fill the void. Even those of us who are not Norman fans cannot fail to be impressed by the woman's singing in this, her finest opera recording to date. Along with the usual mannerisms and fussy diction, tremendous power and conviction are exhibited in her performance: the "Abscheulicher!" for instance, is probably the most vocally imposing rendition since Kirsten Flagstad's. Although Reiner Goldberg hardly effaces the memory of Jon Vicker's legendary performance for Klemperer, the rest of the cast is excellent, and Haitink as always is superb.

Lieder

Fischer-Dieskau, baritone; Moore, piano. Orfeo C-140501 [CD].

Wunderlich, tenor; Giesen, piano. Deutsche Grammophon 429933-2 [CD].

As anyone who has ever sung in the chorus of the Ninth Symphony has probably come to suspect, Beethoven's writing for the human voice is neither comfortable nor idiomatic. Which is not to say that he didn't write some of the most inspired pages ever conceived for that instrument: the simple fact is that his vocal writing is often awkward, ungrateful, or both, and singers have been paying the price for years. While Beethoven's output of seventy-odd songs pales in comparison with that of his younger contemporary Schubert's, they still form an important link in the evolution of the Mozartean aria into the Schubert *lied*.

The Dietrich Fischer-Dieskau recital was recorded live at the 1965 Salzburg Festival when his instrument was at its freshest and most supple. Partnered by the incomparable Gerald Moore, Fischer-Dieskau is consistently sensitive and insightful, particularly in the brief cycle *An die ferne Geliebte* (To the Distant Beloved), here given its finest available performance.

The recordings that Fritz Wunderlich made in the year before his untimely death are all special, especially the soaring reading of "Adelaide," the best known Beethoven song. His voice is almost heartbreakingly beautiful throughout, and one cannot listen to "Ich liebe Dich" or "Resignation" without an involuntary shudder at the thought of what might have been.

Mass in C

Ameling, Baker, Altmeyer, Rintzler, New Philharmonia Orchestra and Chorus, Giulini. Angel CDZB-62693 [CD].

The standard reaction among people hearing this stirring work for the first time is to wonder why they had never heard it before. The Mass in C is prime middle-period Beethoven: grand, heroic, and sublime, and Carlo Maria Giulini's recording is the one that makes its comparative neglect seem most perplexing. In both its sweep and meticulous attention to detail, this is one of the conductor's finest recordings. All the participants are inspired to give their absolute best—Dame Janet Baker's performance is predictably moving—and the original sound has been freshened considerably. The only problem is that EMI has coupled the Mass with Giulini's far less memorable performance of the *Missa solemnis*, which aside from some genuinely perverse tempos (especially in the *Gloria*) has little to recommend it. Thus, what should have been a major bargain turns out to be more expense than a single full-price CD. Fie!

Missa solemnis in D

Moser, Schwarz, Kollo, Moll, Hilversum Radio Choir, Concertgebouw Orchestra of Amsterdam, Bernstein. Deutsche Grammophon 413780-2 [CD].

During his tenure with the New York Philharmonic, Leonard Bernstein made a splendidly dramatic recording of this greatest of Beethoven's choral works, a performance superseded—as is every other recording in the catalog—by this sublime interpretation, pieced together from two live performances he led in the Netherlands.

There are still people for whom Bernstein's name instantly conjures up images of glitz and glitter. For three decades, his public persona certainly encouraged many to take him less than seriously, and the publication of a shallow and vulgar biography a few years ago certainly didn't help. Yet beneath it all, Bernstein was always a profoundly serious musician, and a recording like this one only confirms what I have suspected for many years: Leonard Bernstein is, at the very least, the most consistently interesting, and in all probability, the greatest conductor the world has seen since Wilhelm Furtwängler.

Like Furtwängler, Bernstein frequently turned the act of music-making into a deeply spiritual, often mystical experience, an experience we feel from first note to last in this transcendent *Missa solemnis*. The performance itself is by no means perfect: The soprano soloist is barely adequate to her brutally demanding part, and even the normally flawless Concertgebouw Orchestra has the occasional—if barely noticeable—slip. Of course, such minor quibbles hardly matter: No recorded version of the work has ever come close to the depth and ethereal beauty of this one, and it's extremely unlikely that one ever will.

Overtures

> Bavarian Radio Symphony, Davis. CBS MDK-44790 [CD], MDT-44790 [T].
>
> Hanover Band, Goodman, Huggett. Nimbus NI-5205 [CD].
>
> Vienna Philharmonic, Abbado. Deutsche Grammophon 429762-2 [CD].

Sir Colin Davis's superbly played and flawlessly recorded collection of Beethoven's most popular overtures very nearly takes the sting out of CBS's senseless decision to withdraw its brilliant set with the Cleveland Orchestra and George Szell. (A few of the Szell recordings have returned as filler for his Beethoven cycle on Sony.) The Davis interpretations are taut and dramatic when the music demands (*Coriolan, Egmont, Leonore* Nos. 1 and 3), yet are easygoing and flexible in the more lightweight fare (*Ruins of Athens, Creatures of Prometheus*).

The performances by the plucky Hanover Band are so dramatic and spirited that even those of us with little patience for the period-instrument movement can't help but be impressed. In fact, the tangy winds and cantankerous lower strings materially add to the tension of the music, especially at the beginning of *King Stephen* and in the codas of *Egmont* and *Consecration of the House*.

Although Claudio Abbado's recording of the complete overtures offers spirited playing from Vienna Philharmonic and up-to-date recorded sound, the interpretations lack the character of some of the best from Abbado's rivals—most notably, those other DG Vienna Philharmonic recordings by Leonard Bernstein which, alas, have yet to be gathered onto one convenient disc.

Piano Sonatas (32)

> Schnabel, piano. EMI CDHH-63765 [CD].
>
> Kempff, piano. Deutsche Grammophon 429306-2 [CD].
>
> Jandó, piano. Naxos 8.550045, 8.550054, 8.550150, 8.550151, 8.550161, 8.550162, 8.550166, 8.550167, 8.550234 [CD].

Even more than in his pioneering recordings of the five Beethoven piano concertos, it was Arthur Schnabel's great recorded cycle of the Piano Sonatas that sparked the modern revival of interest in Beethoven's keyboard music and ensured (as much as mere recordings ever can) this extraordinary pianist's immortality. Originally recorded by the Beethoven Piano Sonata Society on a subscription basis between 1932 and 1935 (the idea of recording so many completely unknown works commercially was unthinkable), the Schnabel interpretations have lost none of their originality or wisdom over the years. Even the technical flaws, with time, have acquired an aura of quaintness, like the dings on a beloved jalopy or the chips in your grandmother's china. This is one of the supreme accomplishments in the history of recording and is still the place where any journey into the heart of this music must begin.

The modern cycle that most closely rivals Schnabel's in terms of depth of insight is Wilhelm Kempff's second complete recording from the mid-1960s. Although markedly less individual than Schnabel, Kempff is also less willful. The interpretations have a distinct, intellectually probing personality all their own and a stature that consistently dwarfs all the cycles by Kempff's younger contemporaries. Moreover, the bargain price makes the set all but irresistible. Although temporarily withdrawn from American circulation, the set can be readily imported from England through any of the record stores listed in *Gramophone.*

Jenö Jandó's cycle for the super-budget Naxos label is one of the most exciting in years. Virtually every performance is filled with life and a sense of discovery, and the fine digital recording captures an unusually realistic piano sound. If state-of-the-art recording is a necessity, then the Jandó is to be preferred to any other modern cycle, including those by far more famous names.

Piano Sonatas: No. 8 in C minor, Op. 13 *Pathetique*; No. 14 in C-sharp minor, Op. 27 no. 2 *Moonlight*; No. 23 in F minor, Op. 57 *Appassionata*

R. Serkin, piano. CBS MYK-37219 [CD], MYT-37219 [T].

Rudolf Serkin often told an amusing story about his Berlin debut in the 1920s, when he performed Bach's fifth *Brandenburg* Concerto with the man who would eventually become his father-in-law, Adolf Busch. Following the audience's warm reception, Busch invited the young pianist to favor them with an encore.

Serkin responded with the whole of Bach's *Goldberg Variations*. As Serkin later recalled the scene, "At the end of the evening there were only four people left in the hall: Adolf Busch, Arthur Schnabel, [the musicologist] Alfred Einstein, and me." Throughout his career, there was an endearing, almost boyish earnestness in Serkin's playing, and to the music of Beethoven, Mozart, Schubert, and Brahms he always brought a special authority and integrity none of his contemporaries could match.

In this attractive collection of three of the most popular Beethoven piano sonatas, Serkin's lofty, thoroughly committed approach serves this familiar music extremely well. The performances are vastly intelligent without ever becoming pedantic, selfless though never self-effacing, impassioned yet never overblown. Until some recording company is canny enough to reissue Ivan Moravec's impossibly beautiful, though now deleted Connoisseur Society recording of the *Moonlight* Sonata, Serkin's will remain the standard performances of all three.

Piano Sonatas: No. 21 in C, Op. 53 *Waldstein*; No. 23 in F minor, Op. 57 *Appassionata*; No. 26 in E-flat, Op. 81a *Les Adieux*

Gilels, piano. Deutsche Grammophon 419162-2 [CD].

The popular *Waldstein* and *Les Adieux* sonatas have never been given more distinguished performances than in these recordings made in the mid-1970s by Emil Gilels. Toward the end of his life, Gilels—always a searching and dynamic Beethoven interpreter—began to find a subtlety and depth in the composer's music that were unique even for him. The *Waldstein* has a mechanical perfection that few recordings can begin to match, while the wistful poignancy of *Les Adieux* recalls the historic version made by Arthur Schnabel in the 1930s. With a two-fisted, heaven-storming *Appassionata* to fill it out, this is one of the most desirable Beethoven sonata recordings now in the catalog.

Piano Sonatas: No. 28 in A, Op. 101; No. 29 in B-flat, Op. 106 *Hammerklavier*; No. 30 in E, Op. 109; No. 31 in A-flat, Op. 110; No. 32 in C minor, Op. 111

Pollini, piano. Deutsche Grammophon 419199-2 [CD].
Solomon, piano. EMI ZDBH-64708 [CD].

There are many—and for years, I had to include myself
among them—who never fully recovered from the Beethoven Bicentennial of 1970. Virtually everything was so overplayed, over-
broadcast, overrecorded, and overpackaged that more than one
sensitive sensibility snapped. It's only been in the last five years that
I have again been able to sit through the Fifth Symphony or the
Egmont Overture without feeling an uncontrollable urge to run
amok with a meat cleaver, and my best friend—who knows every
note of the man's music—has flatly refused to listen to Beethoven
for the rest of his natural life, except as penance or on salary.

Fortunately, a handful of works remained unsullied in that
shameless marketing orgy, primarily the last handful of piano sonatas which will *never* be transformed into popular commodities.
Except for the *Hammerklavier*, to which only the bravest musicians
sometimes turn during their most masochistic moments, these sublimely imponderable creations remain as mysterious and unfath-
omable to us as they must have been to audiences of the early
nineteenth century. They represent Beethoven at his most private,
withdrawn, and mystical: a voice that hardly seems to be speaking
to anyone at all, except, perhaps, to himself or to God.

While more impressive individual performances of some of
these pieces can certainly be found—Emil Gilels, for instance, turns
in a *Hammerklavier* of titanic strength and unmeasurable scale
(Deutsche Grammophon 410527-2 [CD]) and Rudolf Serkin, in the
slow movements of the last three sonatas, finds a shattering stillness
that no other pianist can seem to hear (CBS MPK-44838 [CD])—
Maurizio Pollini's integral set from the late 1970s is one of the great
modern Beethoven recordings and probably this gifted pianist's
finest outing to date. Like Gilels, Pollini brings ample amounts of
power and poetry to the music: each of the interpretations is full
of character and individuality, yet each seems utterly natural, de-
void of any pointless originality or excess. The restored recorded
sound is for the most part warm and spacious, if a touch muddy
when the going gets rough.

If recorded sound is not a consideration, then that series of
astonishing recordings made by the English pianist Solomon remain in a category by themselves. Recorded between 1951 and
1956, the year he suffered the crippling stroke that ended his career,

the performances delve as deeply into the mysteries of the music as Schnabel's did, but with far finer technique. Indeed, as examples of transcendent piano playing and profoundly moving human communication, Solomon's are among the greatest Beethoven recordings ever made. As EMI tends to withdraw its historical reissues without warning, snap this one up at once.

Quintet in E-flat for Piano and Winds

Perahia, piano; English Chamber Orchestra Winds. CBS MK-42099 [CD].

In an otherwise chatty letter written to his father in the spring of 1784 about a recent subscription concert, Mozart made the following rather startling statement: "I composed two grand concertos and then a quintet which called forth the very greatest applause. I myself consider it the best work I have ever composed." Along with Mozart himself, one of the most passionate admirers of the E-flat Major Quintet for Piano and Winds was the young Beethoven, who in 1795 composed his own work for the same combination of instruments in the same key. The quintet also *happens* to begin with a slow introduction (*Grave* as opposed to Mozart's *Largo*) and conclude with a moderately paced rondo finale (Beethoven's tempo indication is *Allegro ma non troppo*; Mozart's is *Allegro moderato.*) Although clearly not the equal of Mozart's greatest chamber works, the Beethoven Quintet was nonetheless the finest work *he* had written up to that time.

Of all the many recordings that offer the Mozart and Beethoven quintets in tandem, none is more satisfying than the version by Murray Perahia and the English Chamber Orchestra Winds. Unlike so many other couplings in which the Beethoven quintet comes off sounding like the decidedly lesser work, Perahia and company almost suggest that the exact opposite is true. Their interpretation has a scale and power unlike any other, with many tantalizing hints of the composer Beethoven would soon become.

Two other attractive early works, the Septet for Strings and Winds and the Octet for Winds in E-flat are available together on a fine Amon Ra recording (CDSAR-26 [CD]; CSAR-26 [T]), featuring period-instrument performances by the Classical Winds. If the playing is not quite as adroit as the Chamber Orchestra of

Europe's on a deleted ASV CD, it still gives considerable pleasure in these unusually appealing works.

Sonatas (5) for Cello and Piano

Harrell, cello; Ashkenazy, piano. London 417628-2 [CD].

These five alluring works have never achieved the popularity of the composer's violin or piano sonatas for reasons that are not so easy to explain. While the first two are ingratiating early pieces that contain echoes of both Haydn and Mozart, the Op. 69 is from the heart of Beethoven's heaven-storming middle period, and the pair of Op. 102 sonatas are among the most forward-looking of his final works.

With the classic Philips recording by Mstislav Rostropovich and Sviatoslav Richter currently out of circulation—though look for it to show up on one of the company's bargain "Duo" series—the choice falls between the versions of Lynn Harrell and Vladimir Ashkenazy on London or Yo-Yo Ma and Emanuel Ax for CBS. (Why, oh why, can't Ma and Ax get together with the German violinist Anne-Sophie Mutter to form the Lizzie Borden, or Ax-Ma-Mutter, Trio?) On balance, the London recording is preferable: not only is Harrell's incomparably warm and luxuriant tone ideally suited to this music, but the two men manage to play with a shade more unanimity of style and purpose as well.

Sonatas (10) for Violin and Piano

Oistrakh, violin; Oborin, piano. Philips 412570-2 [CD].

During the iciest years of the Cold War, David Oistrakh was a warm reminder that the Soviet Union was a nation not only of dour commissars and sinister KGB hoods but also of magnificent artists who had much to say to their not-so-very-different neighbors in the West. In many ways, this rumpled, pugnacious-looking fiddler was the best loved of Russia's cultural ambassadors: a violinist of inestimable accomplishment, and a human being whose rare powers of communication probably touched more hearts more deeply than any other Soviet musician of his time.

With his famous Dresden recordings of the Brahms and Tchaikovsky concertos reissued by Deutsche Grammophon (423399-2
[CD]), these superlative versions of the Beethoven Violin Sonatas
may prove to be Oistrakh's most enduring memorial. Recorded in
the early 1960s with the always polished, sensitive Lev Oborin,
Oistrakh's interpretations are textbook examples of that high art
which conceals high art. Beneath the unmannered and apparently
straightforward surfaces of the performances lies a wealth of character and finesse. While not as technically dazzling as the London
recordings by Itzhak Perlman and Vladimir Ashkenazy, this version
exhibits a knowing sense of give-and-take between the performers
that creates the feeling of a real and fascinating conversation, and
the warmth of the playing practically makes the speakers glow. The
recorded sound, though perfectly adequate, is a little mushy around
the upper edges; aside from that, this is a moving souvenir of a great
musician and an even greater man.

Sonata No. 9 in A for Violin and Piano, Op. 47 *Kreutzer*

Huberman, violin; Friedman, piano. Angel CDH-62194
[CD].

Perlman, violin; Ashkenazy, piano. London 410554-2 [CD].

I have had countless heated arguments with violinist friends
over the years whenever I made so bold as to suggest that Jascha
Heifetz was not the great violinist of the twentieth century.
Granted, his was probably the most phenomenal technique since
Paganini's, but with a couple of recorded exceptions—the Second
Prokofiev Concerto and the D Major Concerto of Erich Wolfgang
Korngold—I have always found his playing heartless, distant, and
cold. When challenged to name a finer violinist, I typically supply
a list of at least a half dozen possibilities—a list that invariably
begins with the name of Bronislaw Huberman.

Like Fritz Kreisler, Jacques Thibaud, Joseph Szigeti, and the
other giants of the era, Huberman was never a note-perfect player.
Nor was he a paragon of consistency: more often than not, his
performances were flawed by the most elementary kind of mistakes,
even though his technical finish could be nearly as impressive as
Heifetz's whenever the occasion arose. For Huberman was of that
generation of violinists for whom technique was never an end in

itself: always a great musician who only *happened* to play the violin, he was far more deeply concerned with what lay between and beneath the notes.

Compare this justly celebrated 1930 recording of the *Kreutzer* Sonata with any of the several versions that Heifetz left, and you'll begin to understand the difference between flesh-and-blood music-making and mere superhuman facility. In spite of some minor slips and the errant sour note, Huberman invests every bar of the piece with passion, profundity, and an instantly recognizable musical personality. It is an interpretation riddled with rubato, portamenti, and other Romantic liberties, yet a performance of such conviction, that everything sounds utterly natural, inevitable, and right. The playing of pianist Ignaz Friedman more than lives up to its almost mythic proportions. In addition, this priceless collection preserves virtually all the commercial recordings that the legendary Polish pianist ever made.

The most completely satisfying modern version of the *Kreutzer* is the London compact disc by Itzhak Perlman and Vladimir Ashkenazy, who also turn in a delectably verdant account of the composer's *Spring* Sonata.

String Quartets (16)

> **Alban Berg Quartet. Angel CDC-47126 (Op. 18); CDC-47130 (Opp. 59, 74, 95); DC-3973 or CDC-47134 (Opp. 127, 130, 131, 132, 135, *Grosse Fuge*).**
>
> **Talich Quartet. Calliope 4631/40 [T].**

If it is in the nine symphonies that Beethoven became the composer who had the most seismic impact on the development of nineteenth-century music, then it is with that astonishing series of sixteen string quartets that we are introduced—more revealingly than anywhere else—to the man inside the public figure. Beethoven reserved the most personal and intimate of his musical thoughts for his chamber music, and in them, the most restlessly original composer in the history of music became his most consistently adventurous.

Since the days of those pioneering, and still magically effective, recordings made by the Lener Quartet during the 78 era, virtually every important ensemble has come to terms with the cycle, and none more successfully in recent years than Vienna's Alban Berg Quartet, named after the great Viennese composer and probably without equal in the world today. They play with a finesse and finish that only the Guarneri Quartet, at the height of their fame, could begin to match. The Berg Quartet's technical prowess is reminiscent of the young Juilliard's, and the engaging warmth and mellowness of its physical sound have probably not been heard since the disbandment of the great—and greatly lamented— Quartetto Italiano.

For the audiophile or the novice listener, the Berg Quartet's complete recording of the Beethoven quartets is a nearly perfect introduction to the cycle, and even the most jaded collector will find much here that seems startlingly fresh, original, and new. The Op. 18 collection sparkles with a suitably Haydnesque wit and charm; the middle-period quartets are appropriately tempestuous and heroic. If in those final mysterious masterworks the Berg Quartet is unable to probe quite as deeply as the Busch Quartet did a half century ago, their performance is still more than adequate to leave most of the current competition far behind.

For the tape collector, the performances by the brilliant Talich Quartet, while not quite as polished as the Berg Quartet's, are full of character, bite, and youthful enthusiasm. Their recording also has the distinction of being one of the few not available solely on compact discs.

String Trios (complete)

Perlman, violin; Zuckerman, viola; Harrell, cello. EMI ZDCB-54198 [CD].

Not even the most passionate Beethoven admirer would ever suggest that the string trios are great or even very significant works. Composed between 1796 and 1798, when the brash young Rhinelander was still trying to ingratiate himself with Vienna's upper crust, the trios are far closer in spirit and execution to the late eighteenth-century serenades and divertimenti, then enjoying the final flush of their European vogue.

Except for a lovely recording of the Op. 8 Serenade from the 78 era that featured the extraordinary team of Szymon Goldberg (then concertmaster of the Berlin Philharmonic), violist Paul Hindemith, and the great Galician cellist Emanuel Feuermann, this recorded performance of Beethoven's charming early works has never been quite so fine. Indeed, they seem less performances than convenient excuses for three close friends to kick back and have a good time. Which is not to say that the playing is in any way slack or slaggard; the whirlwind finale of the G Major Trio, for instance, rushes by with a precise ferociousness that takes the breath away. The recorded sound of these concert performances is more than adequate, and most of the time the audience forgets to breathe.

Symphony No. 1 in C

English Chamber Orchestra, Thomas. CBS MDK-44905 [CD], MDT-44905 [T].

Philharmonia Orchestra, Klemperer. Arkadia CDMAD-755 [CD].

Here is a pair of superlative recordings that will go a long way to demolishing the preconceptions many listeners have about the two conductors involved: the adroit but essentially lightweight Michael Tilson Thomas, and the stodgy, ponderous Otto Klemperer, who near the end of his life made recordings that bore an uncanny resemblance to Easter Island monoliths.

Using an ensemble whose reduced forces are those of the standard Mozart orchestra, Thomas turns in a beautifully proportioned, refreshingly vigorous interpretation of the work, and Klemperer, far from being lethargic—which he most assuredly *never* was—responds with the same light and delicate touch that characterized all of his admirable Haydn recordings. Until Philips sees fit to reissue that spontaneous wonder Sir Neville Marriner and the Academy of St. Martin-in-the-Fields unleashed a decade and a half ago, these are the recordings that will probably dominate the catalogs for years.

Symphonies: No. 2 in D; No. 8 in F

London Classical Players, Norrington. Angel A26-49852 [CD].

The thought of a group of musicians actually going out of their way to wrestle with those treacherous and invariably vile-sounding antiques known as period instruments has always reminded me of my quasi-hippie, back-to-the-basics friends of the 1960s, who took such inexplicable pride in outdoor plumbing, home-ground grain, and miserably inefficient (to say nothing of vastly malodorous) wood-burning stoves. Thank goodness, times have changed. It's now possible to dismiss such nonsense for what it was without people suspecting you of having been a secret supporter of the Vietnam War.

Imagine, then, my dumbfounded amazement at being so thoroughly swept away by this electrifying period-instrument recording, further heartening proof that the Authenticity Movement has finally moved out of the finger-painting stage. The London Classical Players are obviously crackerjack musicians one and all, as opposed to the hacks and second-raters that the phrase "period-instrument" always seemed to imply. They play with genuine polish and fire and, urged on by Roger Norrington, deliver two of the most ferociously exciting Beethoven symphony recordings released in years. Had such recordings been available when the period-instrument revival began, I might have given up eating Wonder Bread years ago.

The hitch is that the performances are currently available *only* as part of a six-CD set that includes all nine symphonies. Although not quite as riveting as the Second and Eighth, the other recordings are all of a piece, and anyone interested in a period-instrument cycle can call off the search.

Symphony No. 3 in E-flat, *Eroica*

Vienna Philharmonic, Furtwängler. Arkadia CDWFE-363 [CD].

Cleveland Orchestra, Szell. CBS MYK-37222 [CD], MYT-37222 [T].

From 1922, the year he succeeded Arthur Nikisch as music director of both the Berlin Philharmonic and Leipzig Gewandhaus Orchestra, to his death in 1954, Wilhelm Furtwängler was the most potent and eloquent spokesman for a style of interpretation that could trace its roots to the work of Richard Wagner, the major conducting force of nineteenth-century music. In Furtwängler, Wagner's radical theories about phrasing, tempo modification, and the idealized image of the interpreter as an artist on equal footing with the composer were given—depending on one's point of view—their final grotesque or glorious expression.

For those who grew up under the spell of Arturo Toscanini's new objectivism, Furtwängler was an anachronism: an unpleasant reminder of a time when Romantic excesses practically made a composer's intentions unintelligible. For those who were unpersuaded by the Italian conductor's manic, though essentially simpleminded approach, Furtwängler was one of the last of the heroically subjective individualists, a man whose mystic, almost messianic faith in his own ideas transfigured all he touched with the sheer force of his personality alone.

If any other interpretation of Beethoven's *Eroica* does more to justify the symphony's subtitle, I have yet to hear it. Only Otto Klemperer found a comparable grandeur in this music; however, along with the titanic scale of Furtwängler's performance come a dramatic power and animal magnetism that remain unique. No one has ever transformed the funeral march into the stuff of such inconsolable tragedy, nor has any conductor perceived such individuality in each of the final movement's variations, or galvanized that movement into such a unified, indissoluble whole. In short, one of the great interpretations of the century.

For a more brilliant modern version of this popular work, George Szell's recording with the Cleveland Orchestra—like all the performances from his memorable Beethoven cycle has stood the test of time magnificently. The sound in both formats, especially the compact disc, simply refuses to show its age.

Symphony No. 4 in B-flat

Bavarian State Orchestra, Kleiber. Orfeo C100841A [CD].

Columbia Symphony, Walter. MYK-37773 [CD], MYT-37773 [T].

It was Robert Schumann who inadvertently invited posterity to think of the Fourth as something of a weak sister among the Beethoven symphonies when, in one of his poetic moments, he described it as a Greek maiden standing between two Norse gods. If so, this volcanic souvenir of a live performance given in Munich suggests that the maiden is one hell of an interesting girl.

With his customary flair, Carlos Kleiber virtually rethinks this essentially light and graceful symphony. The outer movements —especially the finale—rush by at a breakneck clip, while the slow movement and Scherzo are invested with an uncommon significance and weight. Given the extraordinary demands he makes upon them, the courageous Bavarian Radio Symphony's playing is exemplary. Listen especially to the principal clarinet and bassoon, who, in their cruelly difficult solos in the finale, sound like men who were born with the tongues of snakes.

For the cost-conscious collectors who can't quite bring themselves to spend their hard-earned money on any recording, however spectacular, that offers barely a half hour of music, the best alternative is Bruno Walter's gentle yet potent 1959 interpretation with the Columbia Symphony, in which the Eighth Symphony is also included.

Symphony No. 5 in C minor

Vienna Philharmonic, Kleiber. Deutsche Grammophon 415861-2 [CD], 415861-4 [T].

Dozens of recorded versions of this popular symphony have come and gone since the mid-1970s, when this withering recording introduced many of us to one of the most electric musical personalities of our time. For nearly twenty years, only one other version, that majestic and tremendously adult interpretation by Carlo Maria Giulini and the Los Angeles Philharmonic, also on Deutsche Grammophon (410028-2 [CD]), has seriously challenged what may well be the single most exciting Beethoven recording of the stereo era.

The first movement is a triumph of cataclysmic energy and hushed mystery, while the ensuing Andante con moto has never seemed more poetic and refined. Yet in the Symphony's final movements, Kleiber leaves the competition panting in the dust. The scherzo is transformed into a diabolically grotesque witches' sabbath, and the finale, with the incomparable Vienna Philharmonic in full cry, sweeps all before it in a flood of C Major sunshine.

As in his recording of the Fourth Symphony, Kleiber's Fifth offers fewer than thirty-four minutes of actual playing time. Still, considering the quality of this historic issue, either the tape or the compact disc (to coin a cliché) would be a bargain at twice the price.

Symphony No. 6 in F *Pastorale*

**Columbia Symphony, Walter. CBS MYK-36720 [CD];
MYT-36720 [T].**

Symphony No. 7 in A

Columbia Symphony, Walter. Sony SX6K-48099 [CD].

Like dog catchers, truant officers, old-time sideshow geeks, and syndicate hit men, recording company executives have always had a rather unsavory reputation: cost-conscious bureaucrats whose artistic standards—such as they are—have always taken a distant back seat to the pursuit of the almighty bottom line. In fact, with a slight change of gender, their behavior has reminded many musicians and music lovers of Dr. Samuel Johnson's pronouncement on Lady Diana Beauclerk: "The woman's a whore, and there's an end on't."

And yet the recording executive at Columbia Records—now CBS/Sony—who in the late 1950s turned the octogenarian Bruno Walter loose on the heart of his repertoire deserves some sort of medal, or at very least, our undying gratitude and admiration. For like the Homeric series of recordings that Otto Klemperer made in London during the final years of his career, Walter's protracted recording swan song is an enduring monument to one of the greatest twentieth-century conductors.

For more than six decades—and Walter had been conducting professionally for three years *before* the death of Johannes Brahms —the *Pastorale* was one of his most famous house specialties, and this beautiful recording, so full of freshness, wide-eyed innocence, and vivid nature painting, has never been approached.

Similarly, a finer recording of the A-Major Symphony does not exist. If the tempos in the first three movements tend to be on the leisurely side—and on records, only George Szell conducted the second movement as a true allegretto—the rhythms are so firm and infectious that we scarcely notice, much less mind. The finale, on the other hand, dashes off in such a good-natured jumble of barely controllable exuberance that we are reminded why Wagner called this swirling masterpiece "The Apotheosis of the Dance." Alas, the Seventh is available only as part of Walter's complete cycle, which for the price turns out to be a very good buy. In addition to an incomparable Sixth and Seventh, the First, Second, Fourth, and Eighth are unusually good too.

Among recordings with more up-to-date sound, the beautifully serene recording of the *Pastoral* with Richard Hickox and the Northern Sinfonia is a fine yet inexpensive supplement to Walter (ASV Quicksilva QS-6053 [CD]), while Carlos Kleiber's Vienna Philharmonic performance (Deutsche Grammophon 415862-2 [CD]) of the Seventh is nearly as incisive as his famous recording of the Fifth. Among available tapes, a scrappy yet endearing and virile performance conducted by Pablo Casals at one of the 1960s' Marlboro Festivals is still immensely satisfying (CBS MYK-37233).

Symphony No. 9 in D minor, *Choral*

Curtin, Kopleff, McCollum, Gramm, Chicago Symphony Orchestra and Chorus, Reiner. RCA 6532-2-RG [CD]; 6532–4-RG [T].

Shortly after the beginning of his final season as music director of the Chicago Symphony, Fritz Reiner became so seriously ill that many feared he would never lead the orchestra again. (My father and I actually had tickets for the concert where Erich Leinsdorf stepped in at the last moment to officiate at Sviatoslav Richter's American debut.) Reiner recovered sufficiently to return for the final subscription concerts of the season, programs that were devoted to Beethoven's First and Ninth Symphonies, both of which he recorded in the following week.

Perhaps it is simply my vivid memory of those concerts (and for the first five years of my career as a concertgoer, Fritz Reiner's Chicago Symphony was the only professional orchestra I ever heard), but this recording has always seemed to me something breathlessly close to the ideal realization of Beethoven's Ninth. Brilliantly played and beautifully sung, it is a suave, rugged, polished, explosive, and inspiring performance that captures Reiner's special gifts at, or very near, their peak. In its original 1963 incarnation, the sound—like that of most of the recordings made in pre-renovation Orchestra Hall—was a wonder of clarity, warmth, and detail. In RCA's elegant compact disc transfer, it still rivals all but the very best on the market today.

Trio No. 4 in D for Piano, Violin, and Cello, Op. 70 no. 1 *Ghost*; Trio No. 6 in B-flat, Op. 97 *Archduke*

Beaux Arts Trio. Philips 412891-2 [CD].

More than any other ensemble of the last quarter century, the Beaux Arts Trio have been almost as much fun to *watch* as to hear. Much of the fun came from the contrast between the group's rather stoic-looking former cellist, Bernard Greenhouse, and the trio's nervous, restless, hyperkinetic Ewok of a pianist. On stage, Menahem Pressler is alert to the point of distraction. Hunched over the keyboard like a watchmaker over a priceless heirloom, fingers flashing, eyes darting everywhere at once, he *is* quite a sight. Watching him, one is reminded of what the Pittsburgh Pirate great Willie Stargell once said of the twitchy mannerisms of the pitcher Luis Tiant: "That guy would make a cup of coffee nervous."

The recordings of Beethoven's two most popular trios are vintage Beaux Arts performances, full of energy, wit, pith, and vinegar. While the Suk Trio on Supraphon (11 0707-2 [CD]) give them a run for their money in the *Archduke*, the diaphanous playing in the *Ghost* is unapproachable, and the two trios offered together on a single CD represents a major bargain.

Variations (33) on a Waltz by Anton Diabelli, Op. 120

Serkin, piano. Sony MPK-44837 [CD].

In 1821 the Viennese music publisher Anton Diabelli asked a number of his composer friends to write a variation on a banal little waltz of his own devising. Dozens of the leading figures of the period responded, including Franz Schubert, Johann Nepomuk Hummel, Ignaz Moscheles, Mozart's son, and the eleven-year-old Franz Liszt. Beethoven, whose passion for banal tunes was obvious from all the mileage he got out of the *Eroica* theme, produced a set of thirty-three variations that rank with the *Hammerklavier* Sonata as his most important work for the instrument. With Bach's *Goldberg Variations*, it is the greatest single series of variations ever written, a masterpiece that Hans von Bülow characterized as "the microcosmos of Beethoven's genius."

Among the many versions of the *Diabelli Variations*, none has a firmer grasp of the music's architecture or its expressive possibilities than the classic performance Rudolf Serkin recorded in 1957. In his unflagging honesty and seriousness of purpose, his tensile energy, humor, power, and humility, Serkin has been the ideal guide up this pianistic Everest for two generations and will continue to be so for many generations to come.

Wellington's Victory

Cincinnati Symphony, Kunzel. Telarc CD-80079 [CD].

As if it weren't bad enough losing most of his army to the Russian winter and then getting mauled at Waterloo, poor Napoleon—and what else could actually make one feel *sorry* for that miserable little cretin?—also had to have his nose rubbed in it by two of history's supreme masterpieces of musical schlock: Tchaikovsky's refined and tasteful *1812 Overture* and this embarrassing garbage by Beethoven. Until the historic recording led by Antal Dorati is reissued (remember the miniature French and English flags you could put on your speakers so as to tell who was shooting at whom?), this generally impressive effort from Telarc should keep most people happy. The performance itself is excellent, though the musketry sounds a trifle anemic, almost as though no one was really all that angry.

Bellini, Vincenzo (1801–1835)

Norma

Callas, Stignani, Filippeschi, Rossi-Lemeni, La Scala
Orchestra Chorus, Serafin. Angel CDC-47303 [CD].

There are few words that get the true opera lover's juices flowing more effusively than the title of Vincenzo Bellini's masterpiece, *Norma*. In one of his rare bouts of genuine humility, an opera lover named Richard Wagner said that he hoped *Tristan und Isolde* would some day be seen as the German equivalent of the opera he loved more than any other. The celebrated Wagnerian soprano Lilli Lehmann insisted that a half dozen Isoldes were far less physically and emotionally exhausting than one encounter with Bellini's Druid priestess.

In this century, the great exponents of what is widely regarded as the most brutally demanding of all soprano roles can be counted easily on the fingers of one hand. In the 1920s, the matchless American soprano Rosa Ponselle began the modern *Norma* revival with an interpretation whose sheer vocal splendor has never been equaled. In more recent times, the Norma of Dame Joan Sutherland was a technical wonder, if something of a dramatic joke. And then of course, for a few brief seasons in the 1950s, there was the Norma of Maria Callas, which both as a vocal and theatrical experience ranks with Lotte Lehmann's Marschallin and the Boris Gudunov of Feodor Chaliapin as one of the supreme operatic experiences of the twentieth century.

Angel was extremely wise to choose this 1954 recording for reissue as a compact disc. Unlike her much less successful, but still overwhelming, stereo remake, in the 1954 *Norma* Callas's voice had yet to acquire many of the hooty, wobbling eccentricities for which her admirers are always needlessly apologizing and to which her detractors fasten like barnacles to a once-majestic ship. Here the voice is heard at its youthful best, from the velvety grace of the "Casta Diva," to the spine-tingling fireworks of "Mira, o Norma." The Pollione and Oroveso might just as well have phoned their performances in, but the choice of the indestructible Ebe Stignani as Adalgisa was an inspired one. Although well past her prime at the time the recording was made, this greatest Italian mezzo of the

1930s and '40s was still a worthy foil for perhaps the finest Norma history has so far known.

Run, don't walk, to buy this one.

I Puritani

Sutherland, Pavarotti, Ghiaurov, Cappuccilli, Luccardi,
Orchestra and Chorus of the Royal Opera House,
Covent Garden, Bonynge. London 417588-2 [CD].

There are at least two overwhelming pieces of evidence that unlike Ponchielli, Leoncavallo, and Mascagni, Vincenzo Bellini was more than a one-opera composer. The first is the delightfully co-quettish *La Sonnambula*—best represented by the 1957 Angel recording featuring Maria Callas and the usual suspects (CDCB-47377 [CD]); the second is his final stage work, *I Puritani*.

While the wooden, intermittently goofy story about English Roundheads and Cavaliers lacks the weight and dramatic thrust of *Norma* (although the same might be said of virtually any bel canto opera), there are some glorious things in this hugely underrated score. The aria "Qui la voce" is cut from the same radiant cloth as *Norma*'s great hit tune, "Casta Diva"; for once in a Bellini opera, the tenor has as much important music to sing as the half-mad heroine, and the hectoring duet "Suoni la tromba," which closes Act II is as fine a bit of martial drum-thumping as exists in Italian opera.

The London recording achieved something close to legendary stature on the day it was first released and has only improved with age. Whatever one might think of Joan Sutherland, she can't really be touched in a role like this one, perhaps because all—all!—Elvira really needs to do is sing magnificently without paying any special attention to the words or the dramatic context in which they appear. Dame Joan has not fluttered and warbled more thrillingly since her first recording of *Lucia di Lammermoor*, made in the late 1950s.

Yet the real stars of the show are Richard Bonynge, who tightens the often flaccid action into something as lean and mean as middle-period Verdi, and Luciano Pavarotti, who here gives the performance of his life. The singing has a suppleness and taste that recall the feats of Fernando de Lucia, Allesandro Bonci, and other late nineteenth-century giants, and the high F-sharp above high C that he uncorks in the final scene will curl the hair on a steel brush. The supporting cast is uniformly excellent—in fact, the Cappuccilli-Ghiaurov delivery of "Suoni la tromba" very nearly hijacks the show.

Berg, Alban (1885–1935)

Concerto for Violin and Orchestra

Krasner, violin; Stockholm Philharmonic, F. Busch. GM Recordings 2006 [CD].

Szeryng, violin; Bavarian Radio Symphony, Kubelik. Deutsche Grammophon 431740-2 [CD].

If there is a single work that establishes Alban Berg's credentials as one of the giants of twentieth-century music, it is his moving and powerful Violin Concerto, finished only a few weeks before his death. Written to "the memory of an Angel"—the young Manon Gropius, daughter of Alma Mahler—the Concerto was obviously Berg's own requiem as well. According to Louis Krasner, the American violinist who commissioned the work (and for whom Berg's teacher, Arnold Schoenberg, would also write *his* Violin Concerto), Berg was fully aware that the Concerto would be his final work. "It was not written with ink," Krasner would later insist, "but with his own blood."

The small Massachusetts-based company GM Recordings—a labor of love from the American composer Gunther Schuller—has released two live Krasner performances of those two extraordinary works he helped create. Although the performances are less than perfect, and the recorded sound is of the early '30s and late '50s aircheck variety, the living history it represents makes this recording an absolute necessity for anyone interested in the music of the twentieth century.

With the splendid recordings by Kyung-Wha Chung, Itzhak Perlman, and Arthur Grumiaux currently out of print—expect to see all of them reissued on medium-priced CDs in the not-too-distant future—the suave and richly romantic version by Henrik Szeryng and Rafael Kubelik is the best modern alternative.

Lyric Suite for String Quartet

LaSalle Quartet. Deutsche Grammophon 419994-2 [CD].

This great work was already clearly established as one of the cornerstones of modern chamber music when a series of sensational discoveries proved what many listeners had long suspected: There was a bit more to the *Lyric Suite* than met the eye. The composer himself offered a key to the *Lyric Suite*'s mystery, with that cryptic and, until recently, inexplicable quotation of the "Love Potion" motif from Wagner's *Tristan und Isolde* embedded in the work's final movement.

It was the brilliant American composer and Berg authority George Perle who finally discovered what the piece was really *about.* A score, annotated by Berg himself, came into Perle's possession, which contained the startling revelation that the *Lyric Suite* had in fact been written to a secret program. Called by the composer "A small monument to a Great Love," the work traces the events of a lengthy and passionate love affair the composer conducted with a lady who was not his wife. The final movement is in fact a wordless setting of "De Profundis Clamavi," a tortured poem about doomed, impossible love from Charles Baudelaire's *Fleurs du mal.*

Needless to say, while the fact that the cat, after a half century, is finally out of the bag does much to add to our understanding of Berg's motives and emotional state when he composed the *Lyric Suite*, nothing could seriously add or detract to what has been, in all that time, one of the most profound and profoundly moving of all twentieth-century chamber works.

The famous recording by the LaSalle Quartet is available only as part of a larger release that includes most of the major chamber works of Berg, Webern, and their teacher, Arnold Schoenberg. Although a considerable investment, the set is more than worth the expense. The performance of the *Lyric Suite* is especially warm and, appropriately, lyrical. And unlike so many performances, which make the music seem far more complex and forbidding than it needs to be, their fluent, natural grasp of its language and vocabulary make it as lucid and approachable as one of the middle-period Beethoven quartets.

Another Berg masterpiece, the richly intricate *Chamber Concerto* is well served by the Chamber Orchestra of Europe on Teldec (2292-46019-2). Although considerably thornier than the *Lyric Suite*, the concerto has an abundance of life and invention; it will repay handsomely any investment of time the listener is willing to make.

Wozzeck

Silja, Wächter, Jahn, Laubenthal, Zednik, Vienna Philharmonic, Dohnányi. London 417348-2 [CD].

With Puccini's *Turandot*, which had its world premiere only four months later, *Wozzeck* was the last great opera to enter the standard repertoire. From the perspective of three quarters of a century, it is now obvious that these two wildly disparate works have far more in common than was once supposed. In spite of its once radical, atonal musical language—to say nothing of its lurid subject matter—*Wozzeck*, like *Turandot*, is an old-fashioned, intensely Romantic opera that creates a darkly lyrical universe all its own. Should anyone tell you that the opera has no singable arias or memorable tunes, invite that person over to hear this lovely London recording; if it isn't *precisely* late Puccini, then it is certainly something not too far removed.

Much of the credit for the success of the recording must go to Christoph von Dohnányi, whose approach to *Wozzeck* might be loosely described as treating it as though it were a Mahler symphony with words. His eye for the larger structures is as keenly developed as his ear for the minor details: the music unfolds with all the sweep and power anyone could wish, yet in its textures and inner voices, it has the character of fine chamber music. In short, by the time Marie's orphaned child delivers his final "hop-hop" at the end of the performance, we feel as annihilated as we always should; yet it is a subtle, enthralling feeling of annihilation, as at the end of Debussy's *Pelléas et Mélisande*.

While Dohnányi and—in this music—the incomparable Vienna Philharmonic are the principal selling points of the recording, the cast is also excellent. Vocally, the title role is something of a struggle for Eberhard Wächter, although the rough-and-ready raggedness somehow suits the character very well. Anna Silja is superb as Marie, as she is in the blistering performance of Schoenberg's monodrama *Erwartung*, which comes as a generous bonus.

For those who respond to *Lulu*, Berg's repulsive, alluring, hypnotic final masterpiece, the complete opera—with the unfinished final act put into performing shape by Friedrich Cerha—is currently available in the staggering Paris Opéra production led by Pierre Boulez (Deutsche Grammophon 415489-2 [CD]).

Berkeley, Sir Lennox

(1903–1989)

Orchestral Works

London Philharmonic, Berkeley. Lyrita SRCD.226 [CD].

Sir Lennox Berkeley would have been happier as a man, no doubt—and far more respected as a composer—had he actually lived in the eighteenth century where he properly belonged. A disciple of Mozart born more than a century too late, Berkeley wrote some of the most urbane and civilized music of the twentieth century: polished, intelligent, translucent, profoundly entertaining modern music that is never pretentious, abrasive, or impossible to understand. No wonder Berkeley is currently out of fashion.

This Lyrita compact disc collects most of those delectable performances the composer recorded with the London Philharmonic in the early 1970s. From the early *Mont Juic*, a suite of Catalan dances that Berkeley arranged in collaboration with Benjamin Britten in 1937, to the enchanting Partita for Orchestra from 1965, this is serious, healthy, eminently *adult* music that might just save you several trips to the psychiatrist.

Hector (1803–1869)

...de Faust (complete oratorio)

..., Bastin, Ambrosian Singers, London
Orchestra and Chorus, Davis. Philips
[CD].

...z could never quite make up his mind about The
...st, so it's hardly surprising that posterity hasn't
...is bets by calling it "A Dramatic Legend," and
...nd has been—staged as both an opera and an
...people the piece consists of that trio of familiar
...the Will-o'-the-Wisps, Dance of the Sylphs, and
...h, based on a Hungarian tune the composer
...iend Franz Liszt.
... a good deal more to The Damnation of Faust
than that, the piece can be unbearably tedious, as any of a half
dozen previous recordings clearly prove. Sir Colin Davis's recording from the mid-1970s earns high marks for Nicolai Gedda's
singing, the crispness of the orchestral execution, and the generally
sensitive attention to detail. For those who might not need the full
catastrophe, excerpts from Sir Georg Solti's rivetingly dramatic
recording on London (410181-2 [CD]) should more than fill the
bill.

L'Enfance du Christ

Von Otter, Rolfe-Johnson, Cachemaille, Van Dam, Bastin,
Monteverdi Choir, Lyon Opera Orchestra, Gardiner.
Erato 2292-45275-2 [CD].

Like marriage, Christmas is essentially an invention of English
literature: for just as it was the poet Edmund Spenser who made
wedded love both fashionable *and* respectable, it was a great Victorian propagandist named Charles Dickens who transformed a
lovely, sacred holiday into the red-blooded, two-fisted, multibillion
dollar secular orgy we enjoy and endure today. If there *is* any
universal justice, the author of The Chimes, The Cricket on the
Hearth and A Christmas Carol is standing right now in some

cosmic Macy's or Bloomingdàles, being prodded, gouged, and jostled by large, rude people, sneered and snapped at by snotty, adolescent clerks, screamed at by whining children—in short, going through what we *all* go through at that wretched time of the year.

Whenever I feel the milk of human kindness congealing into rancid crankcase oil, a dose of Berlioz's eternally fresh and innocent *L'Enfance du Christ* is usually all it takes to get me back on track, for there is as much of the real spirit of the season in this gentlest of Christmas classics as in any work I know.

Though nothing could persuade me to give up my beloved, old Victor recording with the Boston Symphony led by Charles Munch, especially since it has been reissued on a pair of medium-priced Gold Seal CDs (RCA 09026-61234-2), the John Eliot Gardiner version has better soloists, a more idiomatic chorus, and far finer recorded sound. Next time the holiday crush leaves you feeling like a piece of chewed string, give this eternal charmer a try.

*H*arold in Italy, for Viola and Orchestra

Imai, viola; London Symphony, Davis. Philips 416431-2
[CD].

Ironically, the foremost champions of the music of France's major nineteenth-century composer have tended to be British. It was Sir Hamilton Harty—an Ulsterman by birth, and proud of it, thank you—who began the modern Berlioz revival through his revelatory performances with the Hallé Orchestra of Manchester in the 1920s, and Sir Thomas Beecham whose zany, scintillating interpretations in the middle decades of the century finally helped make the music of this strange and original composer a bona fide box office draw. From the mid-1960s onward, this long and fruitful tradition has been ably continued by Sir Colin Davis—in the opinion of many, the finest Berlioz conductor the century has so far produced.

A comparison of his two recorded versions of *Harold in Italy* provides a fascinating glimpse at Sir Colin's growth as a Berlioz conductor. In the first, made with Sir Yehudi Menuhin, Davis was much too deferential to a far more famous colleague. It was as if both the soloist and the conductor had forgotten that whatever else *Harold in Italy* may be, it is certainly *not* a viola concerto. (After all, Niccolò Paganini, who commissioned the work to show off his new Stradivarius viola, actually refused to play it in public, complaining that it gave him far too little to do.)

On the other hand, Sir Colin's second recording is clearly the conductor's show. As in all of his Berlioz performances, the image of the composer Davis tries to project is that of an arch-Romantic whose roots were firmly planted in the classical past. While the interpretation has an appealing sweep and impulsiveness, it is also meticulously controlled. The Japanese violist Nabuko Imai plays her pivotal role with great zest and distinction, offering an unusually urbane and sensitive approach to phrasing and a physical sound whose size and beauty will make you want to check the CD box to make certain she really *does* play a viola, not a cello.

Les Nuits d'été (song cycle)

Crespin, soprano; L'Orchestre de la Suisse Romande, Ansermet. London 417813-2 [CD].

Even though he never actually composed any chamber music —and what could you expect from a man whose ideal ensemble included a total of 465 musicians, playing everything from 120 violins and five saxophones to an ophicleide in C *and* an ophicleide in B?—the delicate song cycle *Les Nuits d'été* has a hushed intimacy that almost suggests what a Berlioz string quartet might have been.

Although many celebrated singers have recorded the cycle in recent years—and the dreadfully dull versions by Jessye Norman and Dame Kiri Te Kanawa are to be avoided at all costs—Régine Crespin's famous thirty-year-old recording hasn't lost a speck of its magic. With a voice more supple, luxurious, and feminine than any of her colleagues, she weaves her way around and through this fragile music with a sirenlike seductiveness. "The Spectre of the Rose" is particularly adroit and heartbreaking, proving that Crespin was one of the few singers of her generation who was equally comfortable with opera and song.

While several volumes could be written about the variety of color that Ernest Ansermet coaxes out of the orchestral accompaniment—to say nothing about the equally memorable version of Ravel's *Shéhérazade* that fills out the disc—three words will do it: Buy this *now*.

Overtures

> London Philharmonic, Hallé Orchestra, Harty. Pearl 9485 [CD].
>
> London Symphony, Davis. Philips 416430-2 [CD].

There are many who insist that the Ulster composer and conductor Sir Hamilton Harty was the finest Berlioz conductor of the twentieth century, and these electrifying recordings from the 1930s tend to bear that out. Not only are they among the most highly charged recordings ever made of this composer's music (the speeds generated in the *Roman Carnival Overture* will nearly cause you to do a double take), they are also among the most refined and sophisticated. Even through the occasionally furry sound, the subtle finish, and physical presence of the performances come through to a remarkable degree.

Among more recent Berlioz conductors, Sir Colin Davis has been as admired and influential in our time as Harty was in his. Davis's overture collection is the most consistently satisfying modern one available, combining carefully judged tempos and textures with a sophisticated feeling for detail and genuine panache.

Requiem (*Grande messe des morts*)

> Dowd, tenor; London Symphony Orchestra and Chorus, Davis. Philips 416283-2 [CD].

Of all his major compositions, including the sprawling *La Damnation de Faust*, the Requiem is probably Hector Berlioz's most problematic work. For just as that other great Requiem by Giuseppe Verdi is an opera thinly disguised as a sacred service, the *Grande messe des morts* is a dramatic symphony which, almost incidentally, takes as its point of departure one of the most moving texts of the Roman Catholic liturgy.

To date, it is Sir Colin Davis's 1970 recording that best reconciles the Requiem's not completely resolvable sacred and secular conflicts: the *Tuba mirum*, for once, sounds more like worship than the usual sonic sideshow, and throughout the performance Davis consistently maintains an appropriate sense of decorum, without ever allowing the music to become ponderous or dull.

As an eye- and ear-opening bonus, the compact disc reissue comes with an unbelievably civilized and serious reading (and how did Davis keep a straight face?) of what is surely the most embarrassing half hour of unregenerate schlock ever perpetrated by a major composer: the brazen *Symphonie funébre et triomphale*, an utterly mindless twenty-odd minutes of musical trash which, I blush to confess, I love without reservation.

R*oméo et Juliette*

> Roggero, Chabay, Sze, Harvard Glee Club and Radcliffe Choral Society, Boston Symphony, Munch. RCA 09026-60681-2 [CD]

In the last decade or so, Charles Dutoit has worked a minor miracle in Montreal, transforming a fine regional ensemble into an orchestra of international importance. On a good day—and to hear their recordings or broadcast concerts, they seem to have nothing but *very* good days—the Montreal Symphony must now be considered one of the great orchestras of the world. Beginning with their intoxicating version of Ravel's *Daphnis and Chloë*, they have had such an unbroken string of recording triumphs that their gifted music director has become the first superstar conductor of the digital age.

Dutoit's recording of Berlioz's *Roméo et Juliette*—the most far-reaching and startlingly modern of all that composer's scores—has much in common with Sir Colin Davis's famous London Symphony recording for Philips. All of the famous set pieces have tremendous character and individuality, while the connecting episodes refuse to sound (as they so often do, alas) like patchwork filler in which both the composer and the performers are merely marking time. The Dutoit performance benefits from a chorus that sings with marvelously idiomatic French inflection and feeling, to say nothing of state-of-the-art recorded sound, but the real surprise is the ease with which the orchestra outplays even the great London Symphony, which on records is an all but impossible feat.

Although temporarily out of print, look for the recording to reappear on London's mid-priced Jubilee label. Until it does, Charles Munch's impassioned—if occasionally wayward—Boston Symphony performance is a perfectly adequate stopgap.

Symphonie fantastique

Concertgebouw Orchestra of Amsterdam, Davis. Philips
411425-2 [CD].

Boston Symphony, Munch. RCA 7735-2-RV [CD], 7735-4-
RV3 [T].

In many ways, this odd and perplexing masterpiece remains
the most daringly original large-scale orchestral work produced
during the entire Romantic era. Completed barely eight years after
the premiere of Beethoven's Ninth, the *Symphonie fantastique*
helped to define an entirely new compositional aesthetic that would
have an incalculable effect on the subsequent development of nineteenth-century orchestral music. For unlike the modest nature
painting Beethoven had employed in his *Pastoral* symphony, the
Symphonie fantastique was one of the first important orchestral
works that attempted to tell a distinct and detailed story. Thus it
became one of the seminal works in the development of program
music, which would be further expanded in the tone poems of
composers from Liszt and Smetana to Richard Strauss. And in his
use of the *idée fixe*, a recurrent melody associated in the composer's
mind with the heartthrob of the symphony's hero, Berlioz anticipated the use of leitmotif technique, the structural glue that would
bind the gargantuan music dramas of Richard Wagner together.

Since the invention of electrical recording in the mid-1920s,
Berlioz's bizarre, colorful, and outrageously flamboyant score has
been handsomely served on records. Bruno Walter and Felix Weingartner made famous early recordings, though perhaps the greatest
single recording ever made—a 1929 version by Pierre Monteux and
a Parisian pickup orchestra, long treasured by 78 collectors—has
recently surfaced on CD (Pearl PEA-9012).

Sir Colin Davis has so far recorded the *Symphonie* three
times, initially with the London Symphony—a taut, dramatic performance now available on Philips's medium-priced Silver Line
series (422253-2 [CD]), and then as the first work he chose to
record with Amsterdam's great Concertgebouw Orchestra. It is
Davis's second recording that continues to offer the most balanced
and exciting view of the *Symphonie fantastique* presented in the last
half century. It goes without saying that the playing of the Concertgebouw Orchestra is a model of modern orchestral execution,
and the conception, while beautifully organized, is also wonderfully

detailed. Except for Jean Martinon, whose Angel recording is only a hair's breadth less effective, Davis is the only conductor on recordings to make use of the haunting cornet part in the Scene at the Ball. Similarly, he is the only conductor who sees fit to observe the all-important repeat in the opening section of the March to the Scaffold. The first three movements are superbly disciplined and the final two are as exciting as those of any Berlioz recording on the market today.

For a delightfully scatterbrained and thoroughly exhausting second opinion, consult Charles Munch's first Boston Symphony recording, recently reissued, with his equally madcap performance of the Requiem, on a pair of RCA compact discs. Never one of the century's great disciplinarians—at his very first session with the orchestra, Munch cut the rehearsal short and invited such members of the orchestra who were so inclined to join him for a round of golf—he, like Beecham before him, believed that *under*rehearsal was the key to excitement and spontaneity. If the menacing, insanely driven performance of the Witch's Sabbath is any indication, he certainly had a point.

Les Troyens

Lindholm, Veasey, Vickers, Glossop, Soyer, Orchestra and Chorus of the Royal Opera House, Covent Garden, Davis. Philips 416432-2 [CD].

Even though it has had its fair share of enthusiastic advocates —Sir Thomas Beecham was preparing a new production of it at the time of his death—Berlioz's elephantine opera in two parts, *The Trojans*, has always seemed to me to suffer from one of two possible flaws: it is either an hour too long or two hours too short. Part I is simply too brief to do justice to an event as fraught with possibilities as the Trojan War. The role of Cassandra, one of the most rewarding in the show, could stand to be twice again as long, as could the scenes involving Troy's royal family, who are given very short shrift. Perhaps Berlioz simply couldn't wait to get to Carthage and on with the *real* business of the opera, the romance of Dido and Aeneas, which did indeed yield some of the most inspired passages the composer would ever produce.

This quibble aside, the triumphant Philips recording ranks among the dozen or so supreme achievements in the history of the gramophone. With his uncanny, instinctive grasp of Berlioz's intentions, Sir Colin Davis tightens and clarifies the sprawling action to the point where we are almost persuaded we are listening to something as succinct and economical as *Salome* or *La Bohème*.

The cast, which could have included the incomparable Dido of Dame Janet Baker but didn't, is more than equal to the opera's formidable challenges, except, perhaps, for the Cassandra of Berit Lindholm, who sounds hard-pressed and uncomfortable much of the time. Josephine Veasey is a warm and winning Dido, and Jon Vickers's Aeneas is the stuff of legend, a worthy addition to his already storied Otello, Tristan, and Peter Grimes.

Originally released in the early 1970s, the recording was widely regarded as the outstanding entry in that flood of releases that accompanied the hundredth anniversary of the composer's death in 1969. Two decades later, it seems even more clearly the most significant Berlioz recording yet made.

Bernstein, Leonard

(1918–1990)

Candide

Anderson, Ludwig, Jones, Hadley, Gedda, Green, Ollmann, London Symphony Orchestra and Chorus, Bernstein. Deutsche Grammophon 429734-2 [CD]; 429734-4 [T].

Although *West Side Story* is the one Bernstein work that everybody knows and loves, *Candide* may well be the finer score. From a purely musical point of view it's a far more interesting show: not only for its brilliantly sophisticated parodies of everything from bel canto opera to Gilbert and Sullivan but also for its deeply affecting serious moments, from "Candide's Lament" to "Make Our Garden Grow," one of Bernstein's signature tunes.

Because of the relative failure of its initial 1956 Broadway run, *Candide* has acquired the status of a fascinating, noble flop over the years—a myth this stunning production of the score's final revised version blows to smithereens.

Based on a series of performances at the Barbican in London that Bernstein led about a year before his death, this *Candide* is—if anything—even more impressive than the composer's version of *West Side Story*. The cast is uniformly better, with June Anderson a vocally dazzling Cunegonde and Jerry Hadley a moving Candide; the decision to cast Lenny's old friend and collaborator Adolph Green as Dr. Pangloss was positively inspired, as are the cameo star turns of Christa Ludwig and Nicolai Gedda. Bernstein conducts with an effortless grace and wit, while the London Symphony Orchestra and Chorus perform with prodigious panache and precision.

In sum, this is one of the most important and enjoyable recordings in a decade.

Chichester Psalms; Songfest

> **Vienna Youth Choir, Israel Philharmonic; Soloists, National Symphony, Bernstein. Deutsche Grammophon 415965-2 [CD].**

Leonard Bernstein made no secret he was rather embittered over the reception that most of his music received. Apart from the apparently imperishable *Candide* Overture—heard to best advantage in the composer's New York Philharmonic recording for Sony (SMK-47529 [CD])—none of his pieces has established a serious foothold in the concert hall, and aside from the composer himself and a few of his friends, conductors seem reluctant to program Bernstein's music, however fine that music might be.

The *Chichester Psalms* and *Songfest*, written in 1965 and 1977 respectively, are among the most instantly affecting of Bernstein's compositions. The *Psalms*—jazzy, colorful, unpretentious, and devout—may well be the most important choral work yet written by an American; *Songfest* is a feverishly inventive orchestral song cycle, which by all rights should *not* add up to more than the sum of its wantonly eclectic parts, but somehow magically does.

The inspired, astonishingly inventive *Serenade* after Plato's *Symposium* has a fair claim to being the finest American violin concerto—in every way a match for those of Samuel Barber and William Schumann—and is given a hair-raising ride by Gidon Kremer and the composer on Deutsche Grammophon (423583-2 [CD]). In addition, Bernstein's three symphonies—the *Jeremiah* and *The Age of Anxiety* (415964-2 [CD]) and *Kaddish* (432582-2)— are among the most daring, original, and moving that any American has ever produced.

The performances, it goes without saying, are definitive.

Fancy Free; *On the Town* (ballet music); *On the Waterfront*

New York Philharmonic, Bernstein. Sony SMK-47530 [CD].

The ballet *Fancy Free* and the dances from *On the Town* contain some of the composer's most brilliantly infectious music, yet there are many—myself included—who believe there is no finer Bernstein score than the symphonic suite from *On the Waterfront*. Unfortunately, his music for Elia Kazan's classic 1954 film was Bernstein's only brush with the movies, although there was talk at one time about giving him a screen test for the starring role in a screen biography of Tchaikovsky! It's a pity that Bernstein never worked again in a medium that suited his talents so perfectly.

All the recordings are from Bernstein's vintage New York Philharmonic days, and if the sound on the later versions for Deutsche Grammophon is marginally better, the performances are not.

West Side Story

Te Kanawa, Carreras, Troyanos, Ollmann, Horne, Chorus and Orchestra, Bernstein. Deutsche Grammophon 415253-2 [CD], 415253-4 [T].

If there are any lingering doubts that *West Side Story* ranks with Gershwin's *Porgy and Bess* as one of the two greatest works of the American musical theatre, this indispensable Deutsche Grammophon recording should go a long way to dispelling them. While Bernstein may have written more important or more obviously "serious" works—the endlessly inventive Serenade for Violin, Strings, and Percussion and the deeply moving *Chichester Psalms*

—it is this inspired transformation of Shakespeare's *Romeo and Juliet* that will probably outlast anything that any American composer, except Gershwin, has ever written before or since.

The controversial choice of José Carreras as Tony—and one quickly gets used to the dramatic incongruity of a Jet singing with a heavy Spanish accent—is far less problematic than the Maria of Dame Kiri Te Kanawa. As always, listening to that gorgeous instrument is an unalloyed pleasure, and, as always, she does little with it other than make an admittedly beautiful collection of sounds. (Compare her performance to that of the brilliant Marni Nixon—Natalie Wood's voice in the Robert Wise film—and you'll begin to hear just how emotionally and theatrically deficient Te Kanawa's interpretation is.)

The rest of the performances, especially the sly, yet earthy Anita of the late Tatiana Troyanos, are uniformly excellent, yet it is the composer's conducting that is the real revelation. Each of the numbers is infused with the last degree of depth, tenderness, and animal excitement, from the inspired poetry of the love music to the jazzy bravado of "Cool" and the great Quintet.

Even if you don't normally respond to Broadway musicals, don't worry: *West Side Story* is no more a mere Broadway musical than the Grand Canyon is a mere hole in the ground.

Berwald, Franz (1796–1868)

Symphony No. 1 in G minor, *Sérieuse;* Symphony No. 2 in D, *Capricieuse;* Symphony No. 3 in C, *Singulière;* Symphony No. 4 in E-flat, *Naïve*

> Gothenberg Symphony, Järvi. Deutsche Grammophon 415502-2 [CD].

The next time you're in the mood for a Romantic symphony, but can't bear the thought of yet another dose of the Sibelius Second, Tchaikovsky's *Pathétique,* or anything else too well known or serious, the pleasant, unassuming symphonies of Franz Berwald might just do the trick. The first Scandinavian symphonist of any consequence, Berwald was a fine craftsman whose music owed much to that of his hero, Felix Mendelssohn. And though echoes of other voices—primarily those of Beethoven and Weber—can also be heard throughout his work, Berwald could often be modestly original, in a limited but altogether charming way.

Though the four Berwald symphonies have been recorded before, Neeme Järvi and the Gothenberg Symphony make the strongest case that has ever been made for them. Järvi takes a fresh, no-nonsense approach to the music, and the Gothenbergers, with their usual combination of flare and rigid discipline, waltz through these unfamiliar works as though they were cornerstones of the standard repertoire.

As a gift for the music lover who has practically everything, you can't go wrong with this—even if the gift is for yourself.

Billings, William (1746–1800)

Anthems, Hymns and Fuguing Tunes

Gregg Smith Singers, Adirondak Chamber Orchestra, Smith. Premier PRCD-1008 [CD].

Best known for the three hymns "Be Glad Then America," "When Jesus Wept," and "Chester," which the late William Schuman used as the thematic basis for his popular *New England Triptych*, the colonial composer and tanner William Billings was an authentic American original, one of those ruggedly individual genius-cranks whose later manifestations include Charles Ives and John Cage. Billings was entirely self-taught as a composer; he developed the "fuguing tune"—which in an early advertisement he claimed was "more than twenty times more powerful than the old slow tunes"—and died in abject poverty at the age of forty-five, leaving behind a wife and numerous hungry children.

In addition to the three memorable *New England Triptych* hymns in their original versions, this wonderful collection runs the entire dizzying gamut of Billingsian invention, from the wacky "Jargon," which is harmonized entirely in dissonances, to the lithely beautiful "I am the Rose of Sharon," the composer's most famous work after "Chester," which became the unofficial marching song of the Continental Army.

The performances by the Gregg Smith Singers are wonders of poise, enthusiasm, and almost superhuman accuracy; in addition, Premier's remastered sound is cleaner and sharper than the CBS originals. Gregg Smith's *The Continental Harmonist Ballet*, arranged from Billings's themes, makes for a very attractive bonus.

Bizet, Georges (1838–1875)

L'Arlésienne (incidental music); Symphony in C

**Royal Philharmonic; French National Radio Orchestra,
Beecham. Angel CDC-47794 [CD], 4AE-34476 [T].**

After *Carmen* and the sadly neglected *The Pearl Fishers* (one of the most hauntingly lovely of all French operas but, alas, hamstrung by its relentlessly vapid and dippy text), the incidental music that Georges Bizet wrote for Alphonse Daudet's play *L'Arlésienne* is the most attractive and justly popular of all his theatrical scores.

No recording has ever made the *L'Arlésienne* music seem as colorful, original, or utterly fresh as that luminous miracle that Sir Thomas Beecham taped with the Royal Philharmonic in the 1950s. As in his celebrated versions of Grieg's *Peer Gynt* and Rimsky-Korsakov's *Scheherazade*, Beecham's ability to rejuvenate and revitalize a familiar war horse remains uncanny. Each of the individual sections of the *L'Arlésienne* suites emerges like a freshly restored painting: the rhythms are consistently infectious, the phrasing is pointed and always original, and as is so often the case in a Beecham recording, the solo winds are given a degree of interpretive freedom that no other major conductor would ever dare allow.

The same qualities dominate Beecham's performance of the composer's youthful C Major Symphony. While the playing of the French National Radio Orchestra is not quite up to the standard of the Royal Philharmonic, the octogenarian conductor's obvious affection and boyish enthusiasm easily make this the preferred recording of the piece.

*C*armen

> Horne, Maliponte, McCracken, Krause, Metropolitan
> Opera Orchestra and Manhattan Opera Chorus,
> Bernstein. Deutsche Grammophon 427440-2 [CD].

Recorded in 1973 about the time of the conductor's controversial production at the Metropolitan Opera, Bernstein's *Carmen* is obviously not going to be everybody's *Carmen*. For anyone who needs the recitatives composed by Ernest Guiraud—competent bridgework by a fine journeyman composer, to be sure, but *not* the work of Georges Bizet—Bernstein's decision to return to the spoken dialogue of the original 1875 production will pose some problems, for this is *not* the standard *Carmen* most listeners know. Some will take exception to the conductor's eccentric tempos, to say nothing of Marilyn Horne's elemental characterization and occasionally butch delivery as well as James McCracken's barking and bellowing.

On the other hand, if you like to leave a performance of *Carmen* feeling like you've been hit by a freight train, then this one fits the bill. For all of its many flaws, Bernstein's *Carmen* packs a tremendous emotional wallop. The spoken dialogue intensifies the drama, and the occasional rough vocal edge seems to result from an excess of uncontrollable passion. This is old-fashioned, big-time, go-for-the-glands grand opera. Long may it grunt and groan.

*C*armen Suites

> Montreal Symphony, Dutoit. London 417839-2 [CD],
> 417839-4 [T].

For those who prefer *Carmen*'s greatest hits without the singing—and someone did define opera as "that thing fat foreigners do until you get a headache"—Dutoit's suave and slinky performances of the Suites are easily the best around, with a very honorable mention going to the overripe but completely winning CBS recording Leopold Stokowski made while in his nineties (MYK-37260 [CD], MYT-37260 [T]). Both recordings also include the *L'Arlésienne* music; Dutoit's superlative account is possibly the best since Beecham's.

Jeux d'enfants

> L'Orchestre de la Suisse Romande, Ansermet. London 433721-2 [CD].

> Katia and Marielle Labèque, pianos. Philips 420159-2 [CD].

The only time my old boss at WONO Syracuse, Henry Fogel (now the Executive Director of the Chicago Symphony) ever vetoed a piece of my programming was when I scheduled Bizet's delectable suite immediately prior to a performance of Mahler's *Kindertotenlieder*. Like all enthusiastic but inexperienced classical radio types, I went in for that kind of thematic programming in those days: morning programs devoted to music by composers who had died of syphilis (Beethoven probably, but *definitely* Schubert, Schumann, Smetana, Delius, and Wolf), and evening shows in which the first letters of the last names of the performers spelled out dirty messages to various girlfriends.

The *very* performance of *Jeux d'enfants* I scheduled at the time was Ernest Ansermet's still vivid Suisse Romande recording, now coupled with equally fine performances of the suite from *La jolie fille de Perth* and the Symphony in C. The two-piano version with the Labèque sisters is possibly even more enjoyable, with suave, coquettish playing full of wit and rhythmic bite.

Les Pêcheurs de perles

> Hendricks, Aler, Quilico, Toulouse Capitole Orchestra and Chorus, Plasson. Angel CDCB-49837 [CD].

Except for the ravishing duet "Au fond du temple saint," which many of the greatest tenor-baritone combos of the century recorded in every language except Esperanto, neither history nor the recording studio has been very kind to *The Pearl Fishers*. In 1916 the Metropolitan mounted it with a dream cast headed by Frieda Hempel, Giuseppe de Luca, and Enrico Caruso. The production was a resounding failure and, with a couple of exceptions, International Big-Time Opera has ignored it ever since.

Several years ago, the New York City Opera unveiled a new production, which proved beyond question that given half a chance, *The Pearl Fishers* will not only work but can make for a very rewarding evening. The performances featured City Opera's characteristically earnest but bargain-basement vocal talent, and some conducting from the late and greatly lamented Calvin Simmons that ranks with the finest I have ever heard in an opera house.

If this Angel recording won't convince everyone that *The Pearl Fishers* is a forgotten masterpiece, then at very least it will win it some surprised and delighted friends. The best things in the production are the Leïla of Barbara Hendricks and the conducting of Michel Plasson. The soprano makes more than almost anyone could out of what may be the dizziest role since Pamina in Mozart's *Magic Flute*, and Plasson contributes an interpretation that is full of quiet insight while maintaining the long, uninterrupted line. If John Aler and Louis Quilico don't exactly efface the memory of Caruso and De Luca, Björling and Merrill, Domingo and Milnes, and the countless others who have recorded *the* duet, both sing admirably throughout.

Carmen lovers and/or the only slightly adventurous really should give this lovely little ball of fluff a try.

Bliss, Sir Arthur (1891–1975)

A Colour Symphony; Metamorphic Variations

BBC Welsh Symphony, Wordsworth. Nimbus NI-5294 [CD].

Pastoral: Lie strewn the white flocks

Minty, Holst Orchestra and Singers, Wetton. Hyperion CDA-66175 [CD]; KA-66175 [T].

Best known for his score for Sir Alexander Korda's 1936 screen version of H. G. Wells's *Things to Come*, Sir Arthur Bliss— whose beguiling Suite, with its famous march in three-quarter time really *does* need to appear on compact disc very soon—succeeded another vastly underrated English composer, Sir Arnold Bax, as Master of the Queen's Musick in 1953. After study with Stanford, Vaughan Williams, and Holst, Bliss established himself as one of the leading figures of modern English music with some of the most ambitious British scores of the 1920s, '30s and '40s: the fascinating *A Colour Symphony*, the moving *Mourning Heros* (written to the memory of his brother and other friends killed during the First World War—Bliss himself was wounded in 1916 and gassed two years later), the ballet *Checkmate*, and the opera, *The Olympians*. A civilized tenderness in Bliss's music makes it unlike that of any other modern English composer: a tenderness heard to special advantage in the haunting pastoral, *Lie strewn the white flocks*. His music was aptly described by the critic Alec Robertson as "aristocratic," adding, "Physically, it is healthy and sane; mentally, it is distinguished without being aloof; spiritually, it is undenominational. It displays unvaryingly fine craftsmanship, a wit that has mellowed with the years, and a note of almost Mediterranean passion and liveliness."

An ideal way to meet this brilliant and urbane composer is with the superb Nimbus recording of *A Colour Symphony* and the *Metamorphic Variations*—Bliss's first important work and his last—both of which demonstrate an extraordinary facility and inventiveness that remained intact for a half century. *Lie strewn the white flocks* is one of the most serenely beautiful English choral works ever written, especially in the ravishing performance that Hilary Davan Wetton coaxes out of his small group of performers.

Bloch, Ernest (1880–1959)

Schelomo (Hebraic Rhapsody for Cello and Orchestra)

Harnoy, cello; London Philharmonic, Mackerras. RCA
60757-2-RG [CD]; 60757-4-RC [T].

Though Ernest Bloch's creative life spanned more than six decades, it is for the music the Swiss-born composer produced from about 1915 through the mid-1920s that he remains best remembered, and rightly so. For the major works of Bloch's so-called "Jewish Period"—when he made a conscious attempt to give musical expression to "the complex, glowing, agitated Jewish soul"—contain some of the most expressive and individual music written by a twentieth-century composer.

Schelomo (Solomon), the Hebraic Rhapsody for Cello and Orchestra, has long remained Bloch's most popular and frequently recorded work. Gregor Piatigorsky left an impassioned account of this brooding, exotic piece in the 1950s, a recording that was joined by equally distinguished interpretations by János Starker and Mstislav Rostropovich.

With Lynn Harrell's richly operatic London recording currently out of circulation, the version by Ofra Harnoy and Sir Charles Mackerras is clearly the one to own. The soloist is suitably impassioned and rhapsodic, while Mackerras—always a first-rate accompanist—responds in kind.

Fortunately, Arabesque has reissued the Portland String Quartet's versions of the five quartets that Bloch composed between 1916 and 1956. The recording of the somewhat Brahmsian First Quartet (Arabesque Z-6543 [CD]) is a good introduction to a group of works that not only follow the composer's development over a forty-year period, but constitute one of the undiscovered silver mines of twentieth-century chamber music. For those who become hooked, the versions of the Second and Third Quartets (6626 [CD]) and the Fourth and Fifth (6627 [CD]) are every bit as good.

Finally, the reissue of Leonard Bernstein's 1958 New York Philharmonic recording of the *Sacred Service (Avodath Hakodesh)* (Sony SMK-47533 [CD]) is a major cause for rejoicing. With deeply committed support from the various choirs and a performance from Robert Merrill that ranks with the finest of his distinguished career, Bernstein makes a virtually airtight case that this is not only Ernest Bloch's masterpiece but also one of the great choral works of the century. The remastered sound is shockingly good.

Boccherini, Luigi (1743–1805)

Quintets (3) for Guitar and Strings

P. Romero, guitar; Academy of St. Martin-in-the-Fields Chamber Ensemble. Philips 420385-2 [CD].

The Italian cellist and composer Luigi Boccherini, who spent his most productive years as court composer to the Infante Luis and later King Carlos III of Spain, was in many ways the classical era's answer to Georg Philipp Telemann: a greatly respected, fabulously prolific composer—he wrote 102 quartets alone—whose civilized, well-made music all sounds pretty much the same.

There are a few exceptions. His wildly popular "Ritirata notturna di Madrid"—a series of variations on the nightly retreat that the city's military bands would play to call the soldiers back to the barracks—was the eighteenth-century equivalent of "Stardust," and the minuet from his E Major String Quintet contains one of the most famous tunes in musical history. (This is the music Alec Guinness and his band of desperados "played" in Mrs. Wilberforce's upstairs room throughout the imperishable Ealing comedy *The Ladykillers*.) Rather unbelievably, Boccherini's one lasting contribution to Western civilization is now represented by only two recordings; the best is an excellent Vanguard CD (OVC-8006).

Among the more attractive and individual of Boccherini's works are those several quintets he wrote for guitar and strings. In them, the local color that the traditional Spanish instrument evokes is handled with enormous skill and tact—don't expect any flamenco fireworks or shouts of *Olé!*—and the three (Nos. 4, 5, and 6) that Pepe Romero and members of the Academy Chamber Ensemble present are among the composer's most appealing pieces.

The performances are flawless, as is the recorded sound.

Boito, Arrigo (1842–1918)

Mefistofele

Treigle, Caballé, Domingo, Ambrosian Opera Chorus,
London Symphony, Rudel. Angel CDCB-49522 [CD].

It is rare that a single performer, through the force of his or her personality, will provoke a drastic reevaluation of a work that had always been dismissed as unimportant or uninteresting. *Boris Godounov* never made much of an impression outside of Russia until a lunatic named Chaliapin began terrifying audiences with it shortly after the turn of the century; by the same token, most people were probably persuaded that Boito's *Mefistofele* was little more than souped-up, cut-rate Verdi until they saw and heard Norman Treigle in the title role. And it was something to hear *and* to see: the lithe, slight, almost painfully emaciated body of a consummate actor from which that unimaginably cavernous, ink-black instrument would rumble forth. On stage, the Treigle Mefistofele was one of the great operatic experiences since the end of the war; on record, this indispensable Angel recording captures much of the Treigle miracle intact.

This is also, by several light-years, the most persuasive recorded performance the opera has ever received. Another New York City Opera alumnus, Placido Domingo, is nearly perfect as Faust, and Montserrat Caballé is both alluring and dignified, keeping the scooping and drooping to a bare minimum. Julius Rudel's contribution is only slightly less distinguished than Treigle's.

The action flows more easily than it ever has, giving the lie to the nonsense that *Mefistofele* is a fatally episodic work, and in the thrilling choral passages—the celebrated "Prologue in Heaven" and in the opera's finale—Rudel musters a collection of sounds that Verdi would have been proud to have included in his Requiem.

The Hungariton recording of Boito's other opera, *Nerone* (HCD-12487/89 [CD]) is clearly worth investigating, if for no other reason than to hear what occupied the composer for virtually his entire adult life. Begun in 1877 and finished in 1915—on the last page of the final revision, the composer wrote: "The End: Arrigo Boito and Kronos"—the opera is a complex examination of good and evil in Nero's Rome. While the libretto is predictably brilliant, the music is often uncertain and forced. Nonetheless, there are moments of genuine power and beauty, as this superb recording readily reveals. The Hungarian cast is uniformly excellent—János Nagy is particularly engaging in the title role—and Eve Queler seems to do as much as humanly possible to minimize the score's weaknesses while emphasizing its strengths. *Nerone* is obviously no *Mefistofele*, but it's just as obviously worth a try.

Borodin, Alexander

(1833–1887)

Prince Igor

> Evstatieva, Mitcheva, Martinovich, Ghiaurov, Ghiuselev,
> Sofia Festival Orchestra and National Opera Chorus,
> Tchakarov. Sony S3K-44878 [CD].

Alexander Borodin was without question the greatest composer in history who was also a chemist. After his dipsomaniacal, atrabilious friend Modest Mussorgsky, he was the most original of that group of Russian composers who came to be known as "The Mighty Five," and like Mussorgsky, he left much important music unfinished at the time of his death. A true weekend composer, Borodin spent decades putzing around with his masterpiece, *Prince Igor*, which had to be wrestled into performing shape by Rimsky-Korsakov. (Borodin never bothered to write the Overture down; fortunately, Rimsky's pupil Alexander Glazunov had heard him play it so often that he was able to reconstruct it from memory.) As Borodin once ruefully confessed: "In winter I can only compose when I am too unwell to give my lectures. So my friends, reversing the usual custom, never say to me, 'I hope you are well' but 'I do hope you are ill.'"

This exceptional Sony recording is the first really adequate recorded performance Borodin's opera has ever received. The singing ranges from the very good to the truly memorable—Nikolai

Ghiaurov is tremendously imposing as the Polovtsian Khan, Kontchak—and the conductor's canny pacing tends to minimize the episodic nature of the work while revealing the peculiar color and character of every scene. Add spectacular contributions from the brilliantly drilled chorus and orchestra as well as recorded sound that is both sumptuous and realistic, and the result is an exciting, invaluable release.

Prince Igor: Overture; *Polovtsian Dances*

London Symphony, Solti. London 417689-2 [CD].

Boston Pops, Fiedler. RCA 7813-4 [T].

The most ecstatic of all recordings of the familiar *Prince Igor* Overture and *Polovtsian Dances*, an Angel recording from the early 1960s by the Philharmonia Orchestra conducted by Lovro von Matačič (available for a time on the Quintessence label), is, alas, no longer in print. Should the performance ever resurface again, or should you come across it in the LP cutout bins, buy at least a half dozen copies: three for yourself, and three to lend out to friends. (If your friends are like mine, you'll never see the records again.)

Nearly as arresting as the Matačič were those versions that Sir Georg Solti recorded with the London Symphony, out now on one of those hypercheap London Weekend Classics CDs. With a hell-for-leather dash through Glinka's *Russlan and Ludmilla* Overture and a bone-chilling reading of Mussorgsky's *Night on Bald Mountain*, this is one of the finest of all Solti recordings and a rather melancholy reminder of what a dull, housebroken musician he has since become.

Among available tapes, the performances by Arthur Fiedler and the Boston Pops, in a handsome package of Russian orchestral showpieces, are more than competitive with the best on the market today.

String Quartets: No. 1 in A; No. 2 in D

Borodin Quartet. Angel CDC-47795 [CD].

Among that pathetically small handful of works that Borodin managed to complete, the String Quartets rank very high in his canon; the lesser-known A Major Quartet is full of energy and invention, and the familiar D Major Quartet is one of the most justly popular of all Russian chamber works—made all the more so by the famous Nocturne, which has enjoyed a life of its own as a freestanding concert piece and by a couple of tunes that eventually found their way into the Broadway musical *Kismet.*

In their most recent recording, The Borodin Quartet give both works unusually thoughtful, natural-sounding interpretations, as though their eponym had actually written the music specifically for them. The playing is relaxed and efficient, with results that are deeply Romantic without ever becoming self-indulgent.

A tape of the two quartets together cannot currently be had for love or money, but an equally fine performance of the D Major by the Emerson String Quartet is available from Book-of-the-Month Club Records (21-7526 [CD], 11-7525 [T]). The good news is that the recording is every bit the equal of the Borodins'. The bad news is that it can only be had as part of a four-CD or three-tape set called "The Great Romantic Quartets." The *best* news is that their versions of the popular quartets of Ravel, Debussy, Smetana, Schumann, Tchaikovsky, Dvořák and Brahms are among the finest ever recorded. The Emerson's second recording for Deutsche Grammophon (427618-2 [CD]), however, is neither as fresh or vital as their first. Unfortunately, a note of calculation has crept into the interpretation, making it far less enjoyable than it once was.

Symphony No. 2 in B minor

National Philharmonic, Tjeknavorian. RCA 60535-2-RV [CD]; 60535-4-RV [T].

Once one of the most understandably popular of all Russian symphonies, the Borodin Second has inexplicably fallen on hard times. Incorporating many ideas that Borodin planned to include in *Prince Igor*, the Symphony is therefore—not surprisingly—an unusually tuneful and pleasantly exotic work. The powerful first movement, the composer's friend Vladimir Stasov revealed, was intended to evoke the gathering of the ancient Russian tribes, and the cheerfully orgiastic finale depicts a hero's banquet not unlike the Polovtsian blow-out that concludes *Prince Igor*'s second act. Why conductors don't program the work more frequently remains a mystery; the piece is a certified crowd-pleaser, in addition to being one of the finest of all Romantic symphonies.

With the budget reissue of Loris Tjeknavorian's vivid 1977 interpretation, the classic but rather shrill-sounding recording by Ernest Ansermet may now be honorably retired. Tjeknavorian finds nearly as much drama and poetry as his great predecessor did, but he has a finer orchestra to work with and dramatically superior recorded sound. Together with equally bracing versions of the Overture, *Polovtsian Dances*, and the *Polovtsian March* from *Prince Igor*—not *quite* as bracing as Solti's, but close—plus one of the finest versions of *In the Steppes of Central Asia* ever recorded, this is a completely irresistible bargain.

Although it lacks the last measure of the Tjeknavorian's punch and character, the Deutsche Grammophon recording by Neeme Järvi and the Gothenburg Symphony (435757-2 [CD]) has the advantage of being generously packaged with equally fine performances: the First and unfinished Third Symphonies, the *Petite Suite*, the Nocturne (Nicolai Tcherepnin's orchestration of the slow movement of the D Major Quartet), *In the Steppes of Central Asia*, and the *Prince Igor* excerpts.

Boyce, William (1711–1779)

Symphonies (8)

English Concert, Pinnock. Deutsche Grammophon 419631-2 [CD].

William Boyce found himself in the unenviable position of being a native-born English composer at a time when the English musical scene was completely dominated by a Saxon immigrant named George Frideric Handel. Like his near-contemporary Thomas Augustine Arne, the composer of a masque named *Alfred* that contained a fairly memorable ditty called "Rule, Britannia," Boyce spent his career in Handel's immense shadow, apparently without bitterness or regret. A friend said of him, "A more modest man than Dr. Boyce I have never known. I never heard him speak a vain or ill-natured word, either to exalt himself or to deprecate another."

Thanks to the '60s Baroque Boom, the eight tiny "symphonies" Boyce composed have enjoyed a considerable vogue on records. All are gems in their way, full of wit, emotion, and imagination, and—if nothing else—they prove that *something* was happening in homegrown English music between Purcell and Elgar apart from *The Beggar's Opera* and Gilbert and Sullivan.

The period-instrument recording by Trevor Pinnock and the English Concert is an undiluted joy. The Symphonies emerge not only as the work of an important talent, but of an uncommonly healthy, intensely likable man. The best are as full of life as Handel's better concerti Grossi, and if you have yet to make the acquaintance of the good Dr. Boyce, here is an ideal opportunity.

Brahms, Johannes (1833–1897)

Alto Rhapsody; *Begräbnisgesang*; *Nänie*; *Gesang der Parzen*

Hodgson, mezzo-soprano; Bavarian Radio Orchestra and Chorus, Haitink. Orfeo C-025821 [CD].

The Alto Rhapsody, the best loved of Brahms's choral works after *A German Requiem*, was easily the most peculiar wedding present ever given to anyone. The composer bestowed this fretful, stygian work on Julie Schumann, the daughter of Robert and Clara, a girl he himself had hoped to marry, but of course never would. (Brahms was never able to maintain anything approaching a normal romantic relationship. From his youth, spent playing the piano in the bordellos of Hamburg's red-light district, he developed a lifelong dependence on prostitutes that made love with "ordinary" women impossible.)

This handsome Orfeo recording combines an eloquent version of the Rhapsody with three beautifully sung performances of other Brahms choral pieces, including the rarely heard *Gesang der Parzen* (Song of the Fates) and the *Begräbnisgesang* (Funeral Ode). The late British mezzo Alfreda Hodgson had a voice whose sable resonance frequently recalls that of her great compatriot, Kathleen Ferrier. Bernard Haitink, for years a superlative Brahmsian, brings his usual virtues to all the performances: The emotions are carefully controlled but never bullied; there is passion aplenty but nothing is overstated or overdone. Now that he has been succeeded as music director of the Concertgebouw Orchestra of Amsterdam by Riccardo Chailly, who is as accomplished as the average truck driver, except that he can't drive a truck, let's hope Haitink will assume the post of Permanent Guest Conductor of the World.

Concerto No. 1 in D minor for Piano and Orchestra

R. Serkin, piano; Cleveland Orchestra, Szell. CBS MYK-37803 [CD], MYT-37803 [T].

To many, Brahms early D minor Piano Concerto has always seemed less a concerto than a large, turbulent orchestral work with a very significant piano obbligato appended almost as an afterthought. The feeling is more than understandable, for the Concerto actually grew out of discarded materials for a projected D minor symphony that the composer could not bring himself to complete. (For more than half his creative life, Brahms was constantly on the lookout for ways of making symphonic noises without actually having to produce that dreaded First Symphony. Sadly, his morbid fear of the inevitable comparison with Beethoven delayed its composition until he was well past forty.)

For more than twenty years no recording has fought more ferociously for the Concerto's identity *as* a concerto than the explosive and poetic performance of Rudolf Serkin and George Szell. Serkin's playing in this famous recording is magisterial, delicate, and shatteringly powerful—qualities that made him as effective in the music of Mozart as he was in the works of Liszt.

George Szell, in one of the best of his Cleveland recordings, provides a muscular and exciting backdrop for his old friend. The playing of the Cleveland Orchestra is above criticism, and the digitally remastered sound is superb.

Concerto No. 2 in B-flat for Piano and Orchestra

Gilels, piano; Chicago Symphony, Reiner. RCA 60536-2
[CD], 60536-4 [T].

For most of his distinguished and rewarding career, Emil
Gilels was known unfairly as "The Other Russian," a man condemned to live out his entire professional life under the enormous
shadow cast by his great contemporary, Sviatoslav Richter. While
Gilels may have lacked his friend's charisma—a short, stocky, unpretentious man, he was the very image of a third assistant secretary
in the Ministry of Textiles—he was a formidable musician whose
playing matched Richter's in its depth and intensity, even if it
lacked the last fraction of a percentage point of that unapproachable technique.

While Gilels's final recording of the Brahms B-flat Major
Concerto made with Eugen Jochum and the Berlin Philharmonic in
the 1970s is in every way exceptional, it is the Chicago recording,
made a decade before, that captures his immense talents at their
absolute best. As in all of his finest and most characteristic performances, Gilels's interpretation, while completely unmannered, is
also possessed of a unique power and panache. No recorded performance of the Scherzo communicates half of this one's driven
assurance or feverish pain, and the finale is played with such a
natural and unaffected charm that for once it is not the anticlimax
it can frequently be.

Fritz Reiner proved to be an ideal partner in this music:
generous, sensitive, and deferential, yet never afraid of showing
off a little power and panache of his own. And even if in its sonic
face-lift, the recorded sound remains a trifle thin and shrill, this is
a trivial flaw in one of the most flawless concerto recordings ever
made.

Concerto in D for Violin and Orchestra

Kreisler, violin; Berlin Philharmonic, Blech. Pearl PEA-996
[CD].

Perlman, violin; Chicago Symphony, Giulini. Angel
CDC-47166 [CD], 4XS-37286 [T].

When I am packing up the trunk of recordings to haul off to that mythic desert island—though since my mother didn't raise a fool, the island I'll probably pack myself off to is Maui—Fritz Kreisler's 1929 version of the Brahms Concerto will probably be put close to the top of the stack. While not the most perfect recording the Concerto has ever received, this is far and away the noblest and most inspiring. In the sweep of its patrician phrasing, melting lyricism, and hell-for-leather audacity, this is as close as we will ever come to a Brahms Violin Concerto from the horse's mouth. (It should be remembered that for a time in the 1880s, one of Kreisler's Viennese neighbors was the composer himself.)

Among modern recordings of the Concerto, none is more completely engaging than Itzhak Perlman's with Carlo Maria Giulini and the Chicago Symphony. Perlman is a spiritual descendant of Fritz Kreisler: a wonderful exponent of Kreisler's own music, he also plays with that indescribable, untranslatable quality that the Viennese call, in its closest, but very approximate, English equivalent, "beautiful dirt." This is a dark, luxurious Brahms Concerto cut from the same cloth as Kreisler's, but one in which the modern preoccupation with technical perfection also makes itself felt. In short, it sounds very much like the kind of performance that one would give almost anything to hear: one in which Heifetz's iron fingers were guided by Kreisler's golden heart.

Concerto in A minor for Violin, Cello, and Orchestra

> Francescatti, violin; Fournier, cello; Columbia Symphony, Walter. CBS MK-42024 [CD].

With the classic Angel recording by David Oistrakh, Mstislav Rostropovich, George Szell and the Cleveland Orchestra now inexplicably out of print, the pickings among available recordings of the Brahms Double Concerto are surprisingly slim. Until that very special performance returns to the catalogue (it was one of the final commercial recordings Szell would ever make) the Francescatti-Fournier-Walter version will have to do. Apart from some occasionally wayward contributions from the violinist, the performance is actually a very strong one: the splendid Pierre Fournier is as polished and virile as always, and Bruno Walter, whose attention seems to wander from time to time, nevertheless inspires some rich and spirited playing, especially from the Columbia Symphony strings.

A fine tape of an earlier Oistrakh recording with Pierre Fournier, the Philharmonia Orchestra, and Alceo Galliera is now available from Angel (4LZ-62854).

Ein deutsches Requiem

> Schwarzkopf, soprano; Fischer-Dieskau, baritone;
> Philharmonia Orchestra and Chorus, Klemperer. Angel
> CDC-47238 [CD].

In one of the first of his incontestable masterworks, Brahms produced what remains the most gently consoling of all the great Requiems: a work which seems to tell us, with the utmost civility and compassion, that dying is neither the most frightening nor the most terrible thing a human being can do.

Since it was first released in the 1960s, Otto Klemperer's otherworldly recording has cast all others in the shade. Along with the characteristic breadth and depth he brings to the interpretation, the frail but indomitable conductor also projects such a moving degree of fragile tenderness that the performance will quietly, but firmly, tear your heart out by the roots. Neither of the soloists ever made a more beautiful recording, and the singing of the Wilhelm Pitz–trained Philharmonia Chorus remains an enduring monument to the greatest choral director of his time.

Hungarian Dances

> Leipzig Gewandhaus Orchestra, Masur. Philips 411426-2
> [CD].
>
> Katia and Marielle Labèque, pianos. Philips 416459-2
> [CD].

After Brahms settled permanently in Vienna in 1862, his life was completely uneventful. Aside from several concert tours and summer holidays to the Austrian lakes and to Italy, his daily routine consisted of composition and those twice-daily trips to the Red Hedgehog, a coffeehouse where he caroused with his artistic cronies and from which he would set off for his regular assignations with the city's ladies of the night. He had no hobbies, and his idea of relaxation consisted of making arrangements of German folk songs for various combinations of voices and turning out trifles like the popular Hungarian Dances.

A serious and, on occasion, somewhat stolid conductor, Kurt Masur leads the Leipzig Gewandhaus Orchestra through a sparkling tour of these magical works. Here, the Leipzig winds play with as much character as those of any orchestra in Europe, and the strings gush with an authentic gypsy flair.

For the Dances as originally written for piano four-hands, the version by the Labèque sisters is without equal. The Labèques are so glamorous and have been hyped so mercilessly that we tend to forget what absolutely thrilling musicians they are.

In his first recording as music director of the North German Radio Orchestra (Deutsche Grammophon 437506-2 [CD]) John Eliot Gardiner—perhaps best known for his consistently imaginative and exciting recordings of early music—proves that he is just as comfortable on the well-worn Romantic path. In nine of the Hungarian Dances and in the Dvořák *Symphonic Variations* and *Czech Suite*, there is a feeling of unflagging enthusiasm and a sense of constant discovery. The fine North German Radio Orchestra sounds almost unbelievably fine—in fact, like a real rival of the Berlin Philharmonic—and the recorded sound is superb. Had they recorded all of the Hungarian Dances, they would have easily swept the field.

Liebeslieder Waltzes

Los Angeles Vocal Arts Ensemble; Guzelimian, Herrera, pianos. Elektra/Nonesuch 79008-2 [CD].

One of the few musical issues upon which Brahms and Wagner were in perfect agreement was their admiration for the music of Johann Strauss. The irresistible lilt of the Waltz King's music may have actually influenced Wagner in the seductive Flower Maidens scene from *Parsifal*, and it can certainly be felt in the two sets of *Liebeslieder* Waltzes that Brahms composed under the spell of his famous Viennese neighbor.

No recording of these irresistible but formidably difficult works has ever captured more of their freshness or sheer inventiveness than this one by the Los Angeles Vocal Arts Ensemble. Musically and vocally, the performances are flawless, with the singers missing none of the music's joy or romance (and few of its nuances) and the pianists offering some exceedingly deft support.

Piano Music: Two Rhapsodies, Op. 79; Three Intermezzi, Op. 117; Six Pieces, Op. 118; Four Pieces, Op. 119

Lupu, piano. London 417599-2 [CD].

When the Romanian pianist Radu Lupu first arrived on the scene in the late 1960s, I must admit that I heaved an enormous yawn at the prospect of yet *another* oppressed victim of Communism seeking artistic freedom—to say nothing of a few bucks here and there—in the West. These were the days when overzealous press agents were hailing that ham-fisted oaf Lazar Berman as the "new Horowitz"—a process which has continued even into the age of *glasnost* with the storm of nonsense generated over the very modestly equipped Vladimir Feltsman.

Lupu, as everyone quickly discovered, was something quite different: an inquisitive, deeply "spiritual" pianist whose playing reminded many of that other incomparable Romanian, Dinu Lipatti. Although over the last two decades Lupu has made comparatively few commercial recordings, each of them has been something of a milestone: witness this extraordinary series of late Brahms piano works, originally recorded in 1971.

No living pianist—and only a handful from the past—can rival either the depth or the intensity of Lupu's performances. When he is at his best, as he clearly is here, there is also a wonderfully paradoxical quality in the playing which suggests that every detail has been worked out ahead of time *and* that he is making it all up as he goes along: a kind of "interpretation" which frequently crosses that thin dividing line into active creation, without doing any disservice to the composer or his work.

No one who loves Brahms or great piano playing will fail to be moved.

Piano Quartets: in G minor, Op. 25; in A, Op 26; in C minor, Op. 60

> Domus. Virgin Classics VC-790709-2 [CD], VC-790709-4
> [T] (Opp. 25 and 60); VC-790739-2 [CD] (Op. 26).

It was with his first two Piano Quartets that the twenty-eight-year-old Brahms introduced himself to Viennese musical society in 1861. The debut was auspicious and, for the composer, rather unnerving: On the strength of these pieces, one of the city's leading critics dubbed him "Beethoven's heir," an honor and curse that would haunt him for the rest of his life. The early Piano Quartets were Brahms's first important chamber works and, with the stormy C minor String Quartet that followed three years later, they remain pillars of Romantic chamber music.

The group calling itself Domus is one of many young ensembles adding fuel to the argument that as far as chamber music performance is concerned, we may be passing through a new Golden Age. Technically, they are completely seamless, as we have automatically come to expect; musically, they show as much poise and savvy as any of the finest chamber groups in the world today. In the tempestuous finale of Op. 25, for instance, they play with a wild, fearless abandon, yet in the more somber moments of Op. 60, they probe the rueful depths of the composer's heart in a way that would make a thoracic surgeon gasp.

Coupled with the very Brahmsian Piano Quartet Movement that the teenage Gustav Mahler composed during his Vienna Conservatory days, these two generously-packed CDs set a standard in this music that's going to be very difficult to match.

Piano Quartet in G minor, Op. 25 (orchestrated by Arnold Schoenberg)

> London Symphony, Järvi. Chandos CHAN-8825 [CD];
> ABTD-1450 [T].

Suddenly and for no apparent reason—other than the obvious explanation that conductors and recording companies are belatedly discovering what a tremendously entertaining and marketable work it is—there are now *five* excellent modern versions of Arnold

Schoenberg's inspired orchestration of Brahms's G minor Piano Quartet. Arguing that in all of the performances he had ever heard, the piano part always overbalanced the strings, Schoenberg produced what has been called with some justification "The Brahms Fifth": an imaginative and for the most part utterly faithful adaption of one Brahms's most colorful chamber works.

With the brilliant version by Sir Simon Rattle and the City of Birmingham Symphony now out of print, Neemi Järvi's fine London Symphony recording is the best currently available. Although not quite as sensitive as Rattle in the arrangement's subtler niceties, it is very nearly as exciting in the finale, where all hell breaks loose.

For the most convincing reading of the Quartet as it was actually composed, the Virgin Classics recording by Domus continues to lead the field. (I blush to confess that since I first learned the Quartet through Robert Craft's old Chicago Symphony recording of the Schoenberg orchestration, the original version has always seemed slightly pale. In fact, the finale never sounds completely right without that wildly incongruous xylophone.)

Piano Quintet in F minor, Op. 34

Jandó, piano; Kodály Quartet. Naxos 8.550406 [CD].

Before Brahms's friend Robert Schumann, no major composer had ever written a work for piano and string quartet. True, Luigi Boccherini *did* toy with the form a half century earlier, but those experiments were lost in the avalanche of quintets he produced for other combinations of instruments. Like the Schumann—with which it is frequently paired on recordings—Brahms's F minor Quintet is one of his strongest chamber works, despite a lengthy, structurally tricky finale, which can seem to ramble in many performances.

There is nothing remotely rambling, however, in the interpretation by Jenö Jandó and the Kodály Quartet; powerful, incisive, yet sensitive and playful too, it is one of the most distinguished recorded performances the Quintet has ever received. Coupled with an even more dramatic version of the Schumann and available for about the same price as lunch at McDonald's, this is quite a bargain.

Quintet in B minor for Clarinet and Strings, Op. 115

> D. Shifrin, clarinet; Chamber Music Northwest. Delos
> DE-3066 [CD].

Although the two Clarinet Sonatas, the *Four Serious Songs*, and the Chorale Preludes for Organ were Brahms's actual valedictory, no composer ever wrote a more breathtakingly beautiful farewell than the slow movement of the Clarinet Quintet. In it, Brahms's celebrated mood of "autumnal melancholy" can be heard at its most burnished and wistful.

The haunting recording by Chamber Music Northwest has a fair claim to being the best currently available. In the opinion of many, David Shifrin might well be the finest clarinetist alive. His fingers are as nimble as anyone's and he plays with a tone the size of a four-bedroom house. His musical personality is a combination of heroic swagger and melting sensitivity, both of which are heard to special advantage in this great work.

Among the available tapes, the recording by Thea King and the Gabrieli String Quartet for Hyperion (KA-66107) is very nearly as fine.

Serenades: No. 1 in D; No. 2 in A

> London Symphony, Kertész. London 412628-2 [CD].

Brahms at his most relaxed, joyous, and lyrical in performances that will wash over you like the first spring rain. Superlatives fail me. *Buy* this one.

Sonatas (2) for Cello and Piano

> Rostropovich, cello; Serkin, piano. Deutsche Grammophon
> 410510-2 [CD].

One of the highlights of Rudolf Serkin's not entirely successful series of Indian summer recordings for Deutsche Grammophon were the versions of the Brahms Cello Sonatas he made with Mstislav Rostropovich. What on paper looked like a very odd pairing proved to be an inspired and mutually beneficial one, with Serkin losing some of his characteristic reserve and Rostropovich gaining an added measure of emotional discipline and control. Still, each remained very much his own man and the occasional friction served the music very well, especially in the febrile F Major Sonata, which has rarely sounded so intense. The youthful E minor is also exceptional, and the recorded sound is superb.

Sonatas (2) for Clarinet and Piano

Stolzman, clarinet; Goode, piano. RCA 60036-2-RG [CD].

The self-taught German clarinetist Richard Mühlfeld was not only a favorite musician of Richard Wagner (he was the principal clarinetist at every Bayreuth Festival from 1884 to 1896), but he was also the one responsible for Brahms's last great love affair, the composer's completely *requited* passion for the clarinet.

Like Mozart, who was born at about the same time the instrument was invented and wrote its first great pieces, Brahms was utterly taken by its richly burnished, deeply melancholy voice. Between 1891—the year he met Mühlfeld—and 1894, Brahms wrote for Mühlfeld those four towering works that constitute the instrument's New Testament and his own farewell to chamber music: the clarinet trio and quintet, and the two late Sonatas.

Richard Stolzman is at his most natural and unaffected in this superb recording with Richard Goode. Although a gentleness pervades the interpretations, whenever the music demands it, there is plenty of power, too. Rarely, for instance, has the opening movement of the F minor seemed so portentous, or the finale of the E-flat Major so blithely unbuttoned. Although the players are rather closely miked, the recorded sound is excellent.

For those interested in the composer's own transcription for viola and piano, the often wayward but always compelling Deutsche Grammophon recording (437248-2 [CD]) by Pinchas Zukerman and Daniel Barenboim should more than fill the bill.

Sonatas (3) for Piano

Richter, piano. (Nos. 1 and 2) London 436457-2 [CD].
Perahia, piano. (No. 3) Sony SK-47181 [CD].

At the time Brahms composed his youthful piano sonatas, he was already demonstrating what an unusual Romantic he was. Few composers of his generation concerned themselves with anything as cumbersome and outmoded as the sonata: for the young Romantics, the short, lyrical "musical moment" was the favored form of communication. It was Schumann who first recognized the yearning for symphonic expression inherent in these turbulent works, calling them "veiled symphonies," and it was the composer's performance of one of them that led to the famous entry in Schumann's diary, "Brahms to see me, a genius."

With Krystian Zimerman's commanding recording for Deutsche Grammophon out of print but presumably awaiting medium-price reissue, the best available versions are a pair of live performances of the First and Second from the late 1980s featuring the great Sviatoslav Richter and Murray Parahia's Sony recording of No. 3. Although Richter was in his mid-seventies and reportedly not in the best of health when the recordings were made, he still towers above almost every living pianist. If his technique is not as overwhelming as it once was, then his grasp of the music's architecture and spiritual implications remain as acute as ever. Perahia is also at his most profound and revealing in the F minor Sonata, a performance whose subtlety and scale rivals that of any recording ever made.

Sonatas (3) for Violin and Piano

> Osostowicz, violin; Tomes, piano. Hyperion CDA-66465 [CD]; KA-66465 [T].

If it was in the symphony that Brahms came closest to approximating the achievement of his hero and idol Beethoven, then it was in the apparently less demanding realm of the violin sonata that he may have actually surpassed him. Each of Brahms's three works in the form is a mature masterpiece: the earliest, the so-called *Rain* Sonata, Op. 78, is at least the expressive equal of Beethoven's *Kreutzer* Sonata, while the final two were written when the composer was in his mid-fifties and at the zenith of his powers.

Although not as well known as some who have recorded these great works, Krysia Osostowicz and Susan Tomes yield to none in terms of imagination, temperament, or technique. These carefully thought-out, beautifully executed performances also seem completely spontaneous and utterly fresh. The lovely give-and-take of the conversation is captured by one of Hyperion's warmest recordings.

Songs

Ferrier, contralto; Walter, piano. London 433476-2 [CD].

Fischer-Dieskau, baritone; Moore, piano. Orfeo C-140201 [CD].

Hotter, bass; Moore, piano. Angel CDH-63198 [CD].

Von Otter, mezzo-soprano; Forsberg, piano. Deutsche Grammophon 429727-2 [CD].

With Schubert, Schumann, and Hugo Wolf, Brahms was one of the four undisputed masters of German lieder and the only one, ironically, who did not succumb to what might be called "The Song-Writer's Disease." (Given his life-long dependence on prostitutes, it was the purest luck that he never contracted the tertiary neurosyphilis that claimed the other three.) Brahms's two hundred songs form one of the loveliest and most important parts of his output, from the eternal little *Wiegenlied* to the *Vier ernste Gesäng* (Four Serious Songs), one of the last and greatest of all his works.

Spiritually, musically, and vocally, no two singers were more perfectly suited to the Brahms lieder than were the German bass Hans Hotter and the English contralto Kathleen Ferrier. Recorded live at the 1948 Edinburgh Festival, Ferrier's performances with Bruno Walter at the piano are among the most deeply moving she ever gave. It's unlikely that any female singer—even the composer's friend Ernestine Schumann-Heink—could have gotten more pathos out of dark meditations like "Immer leiser wird mein Schlummer," and Walter's accompaniments are similarly heartbreaking. By the same token, Hotter's version of the *Four Serious Songs* is incomparable in its depth and wisdom. This is musical and human communication the like of which has not been heard in the recording studio for a generation.

The Fischer-Dieskau recital from the 1958 Salzburg Festival not only finds the singer at his most probing but also captures his voice at its freshest. Moreover, the presence of an actual audience lends an added edge of excitement to the interpretations, which also have an unforced naturalness that many of his later studio recordings do not. Anne Sofie von Otter is thoroughly natural in her fine Deutsche Grammophon recording, which mixes familiar and lesser-known items in a handsome, generous package.

String Quartets (3)

Melos Quartet. Deutsche Grammophon 423670-2 [CD].

As with the symphonies, the relative dearth of Brahms string quartets was the direct result of his festering Beethovenophobia, that debilitating fear of following his god and hero into any form the master had made his own. Brahms did not complete the C minor Quartet — cast, significantly, in the same key as his First Symphony — until sixteen years after he first sketched it. As with the Second Symphony, the A minor Quartet followed almost immediately, and the series ended abruptly a few years later with B-flat Major Quartet, Op. 67. Like the symphonies, each of the quartets is the work of a mature and confident master, and no two are even remotely alike: No. 1 somber and turbulent, No. 2 tender, graceful, elegiac, and No. 3 whimsical and good-natured.

Although finer individual interpretations of each of the three do exist — the Emerson String Quartet's tumultuous recording of the C minor (Book-of-the-Month Club Records 21-7526 [CD], 11-7525 [T]) and a glowing version of the A minor with the Gabrieli String Quartet (Chandos CHAN-8562) — the cycle by the Melos Quartet of Stuttgart is as rewarding as it is convenient. Further, it comes with the added bonus of all the Schumann quartets in performances that are equally crisp, dramatic, and sympathetic, if a bit tight-lipped and literal. While not an ideal choice, this is probably the *best* choice in repertoire that is shockingly under-recorded.

String Sextets (2)

Raphael Ensemble. Hyperion CDA-66276 [CD], KA-66276 [CD].

Given their scope, charm, and elegance, it has always been a little surprising that Brahms's two wonderful String Sextets have not been more popular. They are among the most ingratiating and symphonic of all his chamber works and inspired a largely self-taught twenty-six-year-old composer named Arnold Schoenberg to write a string sextet of his own called *Verklärte Nacht*.

The Sextets have probably never been served more handsomely than by this beautiful recording by the Raphael Ensemble. While no subtlety of surface detail or inner voicing escapes their attention, it is their response to the Romantic sweep of the music that ultimately carries the listener away.

Would that the Raphaels would now turn their attention to the ravishing String Quintets, which are ably—if not unforgettably—represented by a sturdy Elektra/Nonesuch recording (79068-2 [CD], 79068-4 [T]), featuring the Boston Symphony Chamber Players.

Symphony No. 1 in C minor

Columbia Symphony, Walter. CBS Odyssey MBK-44827 [CD].

Even though Otto Klemperer's titanic recording from the early 1960s has returned on an Angel compact disc (CDM-69651), Klemperer still faces some formidable competition from his old friend Bruno Walter, whose final recording of the Brahms First Symphony was made at about the same time.

Walter's 1936 Vienna Philharmonic recording was one of the great glories of the 78 era: lithe, sinewy, and intensely passionate, it was every bit the dramatic equal of Arturo Toscanini's famous interpretation, while investing the music with an expressive freedom of which the Italian maestro scarcely could have dreamed.

Although Walter was well past eighty when the Columbia Symphony recording was made, there is no hint of diminished concentration in the performance; if anything, the first movement unfolds with such searing intensity that we are almost forced to wonder what the elderly conductor had for breakfast that day. Although as usual, Walter is without peer in the Symphony's gentler passages, the great theme of the final movement rolls out with an unparalleled sweetness and dignity, and the performance concludes in a blaze of triumph.

Among the available tapes, the powerful and athletic recording by George Szell and the Cleveland Orchestra (CBS MYT-37775) is far and away the best.

Symphony No. 2 in D

Vienna Philharmonic, Bernstein. Deutsche Grammophon
410082-2 [CD].

Recorded live in Vienna in 1983 as part of a larger Brahms cycle, Leonard Bernstein's performance of the composer's sunniest symphony is the most invigorating since Sir Thomas Beecham's. The general mood is one of relaxed expansiveness, and while tempos tend to be on the leisurely side, the phrasing and rhythms never even threaten to become lethargic or slack. Which is not to say that the familiar Bernstein fire is not available at the flick of a baton: the finale crackles with electricity and ends with a deafening roar of the incomparable Vienna Philharmonic trombones.

As a bonus, the recording includes a performance of the *Academic Festival Overture* whose sly humor and rambunctious good spirits are all but impossible to resist. Among the current crop of tapes, George Szell's hyperkinetic CBS recording (MYT-37776) is a clear first choice.

Symphony No. 3 in F

Columbia Symphony, Walter. CBS MK-42022 [CD],
Odyssey YT-32225 [T].

Cleveland Orchestra, Szell. CBS MYK-37777 [CD],
MYT-37777 [T].

All the qualities that make Walter's recording of the First so special can be heard in even greater abundance in his version of Brahms's most concise and original symphony. If you have the chance to audition the recording before you buy it, listen to the last three minutes. For in this daring coda—which marked the first time an important symphony ended on a quiet note—Walter is so ineffably gentle that those three magical minutes should be more than sufficient to make the sale. An equally warmhearted account of the *Variations on a Theme by Haydn* fills out this unusually generous and irresistibly attractive compact disc.

George Szell's stunning Cleveland Orchestra recording runs Walter a very close second. The recorded sound and playing are both superior, and the performances shine with the typical Szell gloss. An even more impassioned Szell interpretation with the

Concertgebouw Orchestra of Amersterdam (in perfectly acceptable 1951 mono sound) is now available on London (425994-2 [CD]), coupled with their legendary recording of the Dvořák Eighth.

Symphony No. 4 in E minor

Royal Philharmonic, Reiner. Chesky CD-6 [CD].

Vienna Philharmonic, C. Kleiber. Deutsche Grammophon 400037-2 [CD].

In spite of formidable competition from Bernstein, Walter, Klemperer, and the always provocative Carlos Kleiber—whose stunning Deutsche Grammophon recording is perhaps the most impressive of those that are relatively easy to find—the recent release from the small Chesky Records label preserves one of the loveliest Brahms symphony recordings ever made. Available for a time on Quintessence, the performance was originally recorded for—are you ready for this?—one of those omnibus, great-music-for-just-plain-folks collections produced by the *Reader's Digest.*

At the playback that followed the recording sessions, Reiner was quoted as saying "This is the most beautiful recording I have ever made," and many have been tempted to agree. Wisely, Reiner chose to capitalize on the particular strengths of the Royal Philharmonic, without trying to turn them into a British carbon copy of his own Chicago Symphony. From a string section that produced a sound at once darker and less perfectly homogenized than what he was used to in Chicago, Reiner coaxed the aural equivalent of a carpet made of Russian sable. While their playing in the second movement is especially memorable, the contributions of the woodwinds and brass are equally outstanding. (At the time the recording was made, the orchestra was still, in essence, Sir Thomas Beecham's Royal Philharmonic, which is to say as fine a collection of individual soloists as any orchestra in Europe could boast.)

As an interpretation, this Brahms Fourth is vintage Reiner: tautly disciplined yet paradoxically Romantic. The outer movements are brisk and wonderfully detailed, and the recording of the energetic third movement is probably the most viscerally exciting yet made.

On tape, Szell and the Clevelanders (CBS MYT-37778) once again virtually have the field to themselves.

Trio in E-flat for Horn, Violin, and Piano

Tuckwell, horn; Perlman, violin; Ashkenazy, piano. London
414128-2 [CD].

Boston Symphony Chamber Players. Elektra/Nonesuch
T-79076 [T].

Like Aubrey Brain and his brilliant but tragically short-lived son, who was killed in his favorite sports car while rushing home from a concert at the 1957 Edinburgh Festival, Barry Tuckwell, for more than a quarter century, has been living proof of the unwritten law that says the world's foremost horn player must be an Englishman. As the longtime principal horn of the London Symphony, and throughout an equally distinguished solo career, Tuckwell has proved to be the only horn player of the last thirty years whose artistry has been compared favorably with that of the legendary Dennis Brain.

Tuckwell's impeccable recording of the Brahms Horn Trio dates from 1969, or from roughly that period when Tuckwell began his ascendancy as the preeminent horn player of his time. From a purely technical standpoint, the playing is as flawless as horn playing can possibly be. Add to that a rich, singing tone, a musical personality that is a winning blend of sensitivity and swagger, and the immaculate performances of his two famous colleagues, and we're left with a recording of the Brahms Horn Trio that will probably not be bettered for a generation.

The fine performance on Elektra/Nonesuch by members of the Boston Symphony Chamber Players can be considered competitive *only* if you have failed to acquire a compact disc player.

Trios (3) for Piano, Violin, and Cello

Golub, piano; Kaplan, violin; Carr, cello. Arabesque
Z-6607/8 [CD].

When Clara Schumann heard Brahms's B Major Trio for the first time, she found fault with everything, especially the opening movement. Bursting with confidence as usual, the composer withdrew the piece, revising it entirely thirty-seven years later. If Brahms —or anyone else—ever wrote a more beautifully poignant theme than the one that begins the Trio, it has yet to be heard. All three of the Trios, for that matter, are full of extravagantly lovely moments, in which a youthful enthusiasm vies with a mature resignation in that mood of ineffable sadness which was this composer's alone.

The Trios have enjoyed some superb recordings over the years, by the Beaux Arts and Borodin Trios, and by an ad hoc dream ensemble made up of the late American pianist and Brahms specialist Julius Katchen, cellist János Starker, and violinist Josef Suk, whose London recording of the First and Second Trios (421152-2 [CD]) remain singularly moving. And yet for all the wonders contained in those and other famous interpretations— Rubinstein-Szeryng-Fournier; Fischer-Schneiderhan-Mainardi; Istomin-Menuhin-Casals—the Arabesque recording by three young American kids shoots to the very top of the list.

Individually, pianist David Golub, violinist Mark Kaplan, and cellist Colin Carr are all world-class virtuosos poised on what will undoubtedly be major solo careers; as a trio, they have few—if any—equals. As in their superlative recording of the Schubert trios (see page 476), they demonstrate that they have already learned the secret of great chamber-music playing: the ability to function as a single well-oiled unit without losing any of their individual identities. The performances are fresh, warmhearted, audacious, lyrical, and dramatic, depending on the demands of the piece, but above all they are supremely musical, without so much as a single false or unnatural-sounding step.

Not to be missed.

Variations on a Theme by Haydn

Columbia Symphony, Walter. CBS MK-42022 [CD].

If I've managed to talk you into buying Bruno Walter's stellar compact disc recording of the Brahms Third Symphony, you have this richly various version of the *Haydn Variations* already. Wasn't that easy?

Bridge, Frank (1879–1941)

The Sea

Ulster Orchestra, Handley. Chandos CHAN-8473 [CD].

To the present day, this gifted English composer is principally known as the teacher of Benjamin Britten. In fact, for decades after his death his name was largely kept alive by that famous pupil's act of homage, the *Variations on a Theme of Frank Bridge*. As the world has belatedly begun to recognize, Bridge was one of the most individual English composers of his generation, a nature poet whose finest inspirations rank with those of Frederick Delius. His voice, if not always unique, is utterly distinctive: clearheaded, manly, subtle, with few obvious echoes of any music other than his own.

His most celebrated orchestral score, *The Sea*, is not only one of the most vividly colorful ever produced by an Englishman, it is one that can be favorably compared with *La Mer* by Debussy. Vernon Handley and the Ulster Orchestra give it a thrilling and sumptuous send-off, and the recording is rounded out by two other splendid British seascapes: Britten's *Four Sea Interludes* from *Peter Grimes* and *On the Sea Shore* by Sir Arnold Bax.

Among Bridge's other more readily approachable works, the enchanting children's opera *The Christmas Rose* easily deserves to become a seasonal classic, and very well might, were it given the kind of loving performance that the Chelsea Opera Group delivers on a recent Pearl CD (SHE CD-9582). The charming miniatures *Sir Roger Coverley*, *There Is a Willow Grows Aslant a Brook*, and *An Irish Melody*, with an exquisite arrangement of the Londonderry Air, are beautifully served by William Boughton's English String Orchestra on Nimbus NI-5366 [CD].

Part of the explanation for Bridge's slow absorption into the mainstream of modern music is that most of his music, like that of his near-contemporary Arnold Schoenberg, is uncompromising in the extreme. Any time spent coming to terms with his more thorny and demanding scores more than repays the investment, especially the four string quartets which, in the devoted performances by the Brindisi String Quartet on two Continuum CDs (CON-1035/6), reveal Bridge as the most breathtakingly daring English composer of his time.

Britten, Benjamin

(Lord Britten of Aldeburgh) (1913–1976)

An American Overture; *The Building of the House*; *Canadian Carnival*; *Diversions* for Piano (left hand) and Orchestra; *Occasional Overture*; *Praise We Great Men*; *Quatre Chansons française*; *Scottish Ballad* for Two Pianos and Orchestra; *Sinfonia da requiem*; *Suite on English Folk Tunes (A Time There Was. . .)*; *Young Apollo* for Piano, String Quartet, and Orchestra

> **Soloists, City of Birmingham Symphony, Rattle. Angel CDCB-54270 [CD].**

Apart from the *Sinfonia da Requiem*, here given one of its most powerful recent interpretations, and *Diversions*, the brilliant piano concerto he wrote on a commission from the one-armed Austrian pianist Paul Wittgenstein, this invaluable two-CD collection brings together largely unknown Britten works in performances that are not likely to be bettered any time soon. While there may not be any long-lost masterpieces lurking here, there is plenty of rewarding, enjoyable music, from the jaunty *Canadian Carnival* and *American* overtures—the latter was the *Occasional Overture*, but was renamed by the present conductor—to the surprisingly dark and substantial *Suite of English Folk Tunes (A Time There Was . . .)*. With polished, infectiously enthusiastic performances by Rattle's superb forces, this must be counted as one of the most significant Britten releases in a decade.

Billy Budd

> **Pears, Glossop, Shirley-Quirk, Luxon, Langdon, Brannigan, Ambrosian Opera Chorus, London Symphony, Britten. London 417428-2 [CD].**

Even counting *Death in Venice*, with its explicitly homoerotic theme, *Billy Budd* is in many ways the most daring of Benjamin Britten's operas. For one thing, Herman Melville's parable of good and evil on the high seas would seem far too top-heavy with symbolism to make for successful dramatic—to say nothing of *operatic*—treatment; for another, since it *is* set on a British man-o'-war, the cast is confined entirely to men. Asking an audience to sit through what might have been a waterlogged, black-and-white morality play is one thing; asking them to sit for more than two hours without hearing a single female voice is quite another.

In spite or perhaps because of these limitations, what Britten delivers with *Billy Budd* might just be his most important opera after *Peter Grimes*: a kind of all-male English *Otello* with the mood and scent of Wagner's *Flying Dutchman*. Among Britten's other stage works, only *A Midsummer Night's Dream* can rival Budd's musical inventiveness and imagination, and in Captain Vere, the essentially good and decent man trapped in an impossible moral dilemma, Britten may have created his single most memorable character.

As Vere, Sir Peter Pears gives one of the great performances of his career in this not-to-be-missed recording. But then again, under the composer's sharply disciplined yet sympathetic leadership, virtually everyone in the cast is ideal, from Peter Glossop's naive, heroic Billy to the Iago-like darkness of Michael Langdon's Claggart. The last opera project the legendary English producer John Culshaw was to undertake, the recording is a model of clarity, vividness, and realism. The CD transfer could not have been more effective, especially in the barely audible closing lines of Captain Vere's final monologue.

And as if all this—a major modern opera, brilliantly performed and produced—weren't enough, there's more. The first CD begins with two of Britten's finest song cycles featuring the composer accompanying the singers for whom they were written: Pears's last and most moving recording of *The Holy Sonnets of John Donne* and Dietrich Fischer-Dieskau's version, in almost impeccable English, of the witty, hard-edged, frequently bitter *Songs and Proverbs of William Blake.*

A Ceremony of Carols; *Hymn to St. Cecilia*; *Jubilate Deo*; *Missa brevis*; *Rejoice in the Lamb*; *Te Deum*

Choir of King's College, Cambridge, Willcocks, Ledger.
Angel CDC-47709 [CD].

For some, it wouldn't be Christmas without *Miracle on 34th Street* and Nat King Cole singing "The Christmas Song"; for others, it wouldn't be Christmas without throbbing headaches, swollen credit card balances, and those obnoxious relatives they've spent the entire year successfully managing to avoid. If Britten's *A Ceremony of Carols* hasn't yet taken its place beside plum pudding, Alastair Sim's Scrooge, *The Nutcracker*, and the other seasonal favorites, it certainly should.

The sweet-voiced King's College Choir are nearly ideal in this most appealing confection, as well as giving first-rate performances of a generous selection of Britten's other soft-sell sacred works.

God bless them, every one.

A *Midsummer Night's Dream*

Harwood, Veasey, Watts, Pears, Deller, Shirley-Quirk,
London Symphony Orchestra and Chorus, Britten.
London 425663-2 [CD].

After Verdi's *Otello* and *Falstaff*, Britten's *A Midsummer Night's Dream* may very well be the most completely successful Shakespeare setting in all of opera. Using a skillful digest of the play which loses little of its essence, Britten responded to the challenge with one of his most brilliantly imagined scores. The scenes with the four befuddled lovers have genuine romance and urgency, the fairy music is on a par with Mendelssohn's, and the play within the play, wherein the rustics put on their botched version of *Pyramus and Thisbe*, is a wickedly funny parody of the conventions of bel canto opera. While not overloaded with memorable tunes—pregnant lines like "The course of true love never did run smooth" are frequently tossed off like afterthoughts—*A Midsummer Night's Dream* can be an authentic crowd-pleaser, as recent productions by Glyndebourne and the Los Angeles Music Center Opera clearly prove.

The composer's own recording is a wondrous one, with the ethereal Oberon of countertenor Alfred Deller and the coarsely amusing Bottom of Owen Brannigan among the standouts of the large and accomplished cast. The London Symphony is in spectacular form, and the recording, which features many examples of John Culshaw's sonic wizardry, is one of London's very best.

*P*eter Grimes

Pears, Watson, Brannigan, Evans, Orchestra and Chorus of
the Royal Opera House, Convent Garden, Britten.
London 414577-2 [CD].

Along with *Classics Illustrated*—a vivid collection of comic
book versions of *Robinson Crusoe, Frankenstein*, and *Moby Dick*
that got me through many a high school book report—and the
not-to-be-missed and invariably memorized latest issue of *Mad
Magazine*, one of my most cherished bits of boyhood reading matter was a book called *A Pictorial History of Music*. I still own the
book and leaf through it from time to time.

The pictures are as entertaining as ever and the text, which I
never bothered to read as a boy, becomes increasingly fascinating.
In all seriousness, the author—Paul Henry Lang —blithely informs
us that not one of Gustav Mahler's works achieves "true symphonic greatness." (I wonder whether Solti, Haitink, Tennstedt,
and others realize they've been wasting their time all these years.)
Lang further explains that the symphonies of Anton Bruckner are
not really symphonies at all. Instead, they are massive "organ fan-
tasies" (liver? pancreas?), all of which are indistinguishable from
one another. (At least that puts Bruckner in fairly good company:
except for that "organ" business, Igor Stravinsky said almost the
same thing about every concerto Antonio Vivaldi ever wrote.)
About Benjamin Britten, Dr. Lang was even less flattering. While
duly noting his native facility, he eventually dismissed him as a
pleasant but shallow and irretrievably minor composer, a kind of
late twentieth-century English version of Camille Saint-Saëns.

These days, of course, we tend to take a decidedly different
view of Lord Britten of Aldeburgh, not only as the foremost English
composer of his generation but as the man who virtually single-
handedly roused English opera from a three-century sleep. The
most significant English opera since Purcell's *Dido and Aeneas*,
Peter Grimes—which the man who commissioned it, that inveterate mauler of the English language, Serge Koussevitzky, called "Peter und Grimes" until the end of his life—is one of the handful of
twentieth-century operas that has found a substantial audience.
And with good reason. For *Peter Grimes* is not only gripping
theatre, it is a powerful and consistently rewarding musical work.

In terms of authority and understanding, the composer's own
recording from the late 1950s cannot, almost by definition, be

approached. It features many of the singers who had created these parts, chief among them Sir Peter Pears, for whom the demanding and complex title role was written. In its compact disc reissue, this famous recording becomes more vivid and atmospheric than ever. The well-known *Sea Interludes* have an especially wonderful color and mystery, and the stature of the individual performances only grows with the passage of time.

Serenade for Tenor, Horn, and Strings

> Pears, tenor; Tuckwell, horn; London Symphony, Britten. London 417153-2 [CD].

With the possible exception of the marriage of Robert and Clara Schumann, the longtime relationship of Benjamin Britten and Peter Pears was the most productive love affair in the history of music. It was for Pears's plaintive and eccentric voice, which Britten heard in his mind whenever he composed, and for the great artist who possessed it that some of the most important vocal music of the twentieth century was written.

Nowhere is Pears's intimate understanding and complete mastery of the idiom heard to greater effect than in this last of his three recordings of the Serenade for Tenor, Horn, and Strings, a work that in the fullness of time may very well prove to be Britten's masterpiece. There is no subtle inflection, no nuance, no hidden meaning in either the words or the music that escapes Pears's attention. The composer's conducting is as warm and witty as can possibly be imagined, and the almost insolent grace with which Barry Tuckwell negotiates the formidable horn part must be heard to be believed. With equally impressive performances of two other magnificent Britten song cycles, *Les Illuminations* and the *Nocturne*, this generously packed compact disc is not to be missed.

Spring Symphony

> Armstrong, Baker, Tear, St. Clement Danes School Boys Choir, London Symphony Orchestra and Chorus, Previn. EMI CDM-64736 [CD].

What a completely enchanting, endlessly inventive work the *Spring Symphony* is! And like the incidental music that Sir Edward

Elgar composed for the 1915 play *Starlight Express*—an orchestral song cycle that concludes with a richly Edwardian peroration on the familiar Christmas carol "The First Noël"—the *Spring Symphony* ends with one of the most cleverly sprung and completely appropriate surprises in English music. For as the tenor soloist is busy trying to conclude a magnificent setting of Rafe's address to London from Beaumont and Fletcher's play *The Knight of the Burning Pestle*, the chorus and orchestra come crashing in with a lusty quotation of the bawdy medieval lyric, "Sumer is icumin in."

Like most who love this great work, I was introduced to the *Spring Symphony* by the superb London recording made by the composer in the mid-1960s. Yet as fine as that performance certainly is, André Previn's, I think, is finer still.

The key to Previn's greatness as a Britten conductor lies in his stubborn refusal to present the music as Britten the *conductor* did, and in his constant discovery of ways to shed new light on this marvelous music. Thus, as with all great interpreters, he makes the music wholly and unmistakably his own.

His approach to the *Spring Symphony* is altogether more relaxed and expansive than the composer's. In the great moments—most noticeably in the mezzo-soprano's languorous delivery of Auden's "Out on the lawn I lie in bed"—Previn tends to shy away from the faster tempos the composer favored, thus allowing more time for the mood and special character of each section to unfold. Of course, he is materially aided, in "Out on the lawn" and elsewhere, by the ravishing work of Dame Janet Baker, to whom even the admirable Norma Proctor, Britten's soloist, cannot begin to compare. The London Symphony, as always, outdoes itself for Previn (have they ever played as well for anyone since Pierre Monteux?), and the singing of both the adult and children's choirs only serves to remind us why London is, far and away, the Choral Capital of the World.

War Requiem

Vishnevskaya, Pears, Fischer-Dieskau, Melos Ensemble, Bach Choir, Highgate School Choir, London Symphony Orchestra and Chorus, Britten. London 414283-2 [CD].

Harper, Langridge, Shirley-Quirk, Choristers of St. Paul's Cathedral, London Symphony Orchestra and Chorus, Hickox. Chandos CHAN-8983/4 [CD], DBTD-2032 [T].

With Elgar's *The Dream of Gerontius* and Sir Michael Tippett's *A Child of Our Time*, Britten's *War Requiem* is one of the three most important large-scale choral works written by an English composer since the time of Handel. A poignant, dramatic, and ultimately shattering experience, the *War Requiem* is an inspired fusion of the traditional Latin Mass for the dead and the poems of Wilfred Owen, those starkly horrifying visions from the trenches of the Western Front, which are now universally regarded as the greatest poems on the subject of war yet produced in the English language.

In retrospect, it's hardly surprising that the *War Requiem*, like *The Dream of Gerontius*, was a failure at its world premiere. Its interpretive problems are so daunting, the performing forces so enormous and complex, that it was only with the release of this path-breaking London recording that the *War Requiem*'s deeply universal appeal properly can be said to have begun.

As a performance, it remains one of Benjamin Britten's greatest achievements. The playing and singing are consistently urgent, vivid, and immediate, and the composer controls the work's quickly shifting textures, from the chamber episodes to the most aggressive mass eruptions, like the undeniably great conductor he eventually trained himself to be.

The only serious flaw remains the contribution of soprano Galina Vishnevskaya. Though she is undeniably impressive in the more declamatory moments, with repeated hearings the straining and bellowing become increasingly grating—like trying to sit still in the presence of a wobbly air raid siren.

On the other hand, the interpretations of the composer's other close friends, Sir Peter Pears and Dietrich Fischer-Dieskau, will probably never be bettered. Their performance of "Strange Meeting" is all the more moving when we remember not only who, but also *what* the singers were: a lifelong British pacifist, and a former foot soldier of the Wermacht who actually spent time in an Allied prisoner-of-war camp.

Musically, emotionally, and historically, this is a milestone in the history of recording.

So, too, is the recent recording from Chandos. Never has a version of the *War Requiem* come so close to matching the communicative power of the composer's own, while in terms of execution and recorded sound, actually surpassing it. The soloists are superb, and the London Symphony Orchestra and Chorus perform prodigious feats for Richard Hickox, who now joins Simon Rattle, Jeffrey Tate, and John Eliot Gardiner as one of the outstanding English conductors of his generation. Similarly, the Chandos engineers respond with one of the most thrilling digital recordings yet made, a wonder of clarity, depth, immediacy, and physical presence.

No one who loves this great work can afford to be without either recording.

The Young Person's Guide to the Orchestra (Variations and Fugue on a Theme of Purcell)

Royal Philharmonic, Previn. Telarc CD-80126 [CD].

From almost the moment it was first heard in the British documentary film *The Instruments of the Orchestra*, Britten's *Young Person's Guide* has remained his most popular and frequently recorded work. Over the last forty years, there has been no dearth of first-rate recordings of the *Guide*, including the one I grew up with: a long-vanished but thoroughly electrifying performance made for one of those small music appreciation-type labels featuring an anonymous pickup orchestra conducted by George Szell. (As with my youth, I have been searching for a copy of that recording for years. To anyone who can locate it for me, I'm willing to trade any ten Herbert von Karajan recordings and what's left of my once-complete collection of 1957 Topps baseball cards.)

A narrated recording is probably redundant at this late date, unless of course you have an impressionable kid you'd like to hook as I once was. Among the recordings in which the *Guide* is allowed to speak for itself, which it does with great eloquence, André Previn's recent Royal Philharmonic performance is to be preferred above all others, including, rather incredibly, the composer's own. While Benjamin Britten brought a keen wit and insight to his famous London recording (417509-2 [CD]), Previn brings even more. The personalities of the various instruments are painted in broad yet wonderfully subtle strokes. Rarely, for instance, have the bassoons sounded quite as buffoonish, nor has anyone ever made the percussion cadenza seem so ingenious or so musical. The Royal Philharmonic, especially in the Fugue, plays with a hair-trigger virtuosity, and the recorded sound could not have been bettered.

Bruch, Max (1838–1920)

Concerto No. 1 in G minor for Violin and Orchestra

Chung, Royal Philharmonic, Kempe. London 417707-2 [CD].

In 1906, toward the end of his long career, the Hungarian violinist Joseph Joachim, for whom Brahms and Dvořák had written their violin concertos, left what still remains a fair assessment of the central European history of the form:

> The Germans have four violin concertos. The greatest, the one that makes the least concessions, is Beethoven's. The one by Brahms comes closest to Beethoven's in its seriousness. Max Bruch wrote the richest and most enchanting of the four. But the dearest of them all, the heart's jewel, is Mendelssohn's.

To date, the richest and most enchanting recording of Bruch's G minor Violin Concerto is the first of the two Itzhak Perlman has made for Angel Records. Unlike Perlman's digital remake with Bernard Haitink and the Concertgebouw Orchestra of Amsterdam —a strangely inert and calculated performance from two such warm-hearted musicians—the recording made with André Previn and the London Symphony (now out of print) finds Perlman at his most irresistibly boyish and romantic. There is an appealing improvisatory feeling in the playing, and the rhapsodic support that Previn supplies could not have enhanced the interpretation more. One can only hope this recording will be reissued soon.

Kyung-Wha Chung is also very fresh and spontaneous-sounding in this music. And since Perlman's earlier version is unlikely to be remastered any time soon, the brilliant young Korean's London recording should be considered the first choice among currently available compact discs. Anne-Sophie Mutter plays astonishingly well in her Deutsche Grammophon recording (400031-2), but Herbert von Karajan's cloying, manipulative, utterly sterile accompaniment drowns an otherwise lovely performance in a vat of rancid strawberry jam.

Although not quite on a par with his masterpiece, Bruch's Second Violin Concerto is more than worth investigating, especially when paired with the popular *Scottish Fantasy* and given swaggering, lyrical performances by Itzhak Perlman at the top of his form (Angel CDC-49071).

Bruckner, Anton (1824–1896)

Symphony No. 5 in B-flat

Vienna Philharmonic, Furtwängler. Arkadia CDWFE-360 [CD].

Symphony No. 7 in E

Berlin Philharmonic, Furtwängler. Arkadia CDWFE-362 [CD].

Symphony No. 8 in C minor

Berlin Philharmonic, Furtwängler. Arkadia CDWFE-356 [CD].

Symphony No. 9 in D minor

Berlin Philharmonic, Furtwängler. Music and Arts Programs of America CD-730-1 [CD].

More than those of any other great composer—and be assured, that this squat, homely, diffident man ranks with the greatest composers of the Romantic era—the symphonies of Anton Bruckner need all the help they can get. Unlike the virtually foolproof music of Beethoven, Tchaikovsky, or Brahms, which can resist all but the most rankly incompetent mauling, for the Bruckner symphonies to emerge as the great works they so obviously are, nothing less than *great* performances will do. While they contain much that is immediately appealing, including some of the most heroic brass writing in all of music, their finest moments tend to be private and internal: the deeply spiritual utterances of an essentially medieval spirit who was completely out of step with his time.

For the interpreter, the single most pressing problem in performing Bruckner is trying to maintain the level of concentration that these often mammoth outbursts require. If the intensity relaxes for a moment, the vast but terribly fragile structures will almost inevitably fall apart. In short, it's altogether possible that many who are persuaded they dislike Bruckner are confusing the composer with the *performances* of his music they've heard. Indifferent, good, or even *very* good interpretations, which in recent years is about the best the composer can expect, simply will not do.

Wilhelm Furtwängler was unquestionably the greatest Bruckner interpreter of whom we have an accurate record. All that is best and most characteristic in the composer's music—its drama, grandeur, mysticism—is revealed more powerfully and clearly in Furtwängler's recordings than in those of any other conductor. Although the recorded sound in these performances from the late 1940s and early '50s ranges only between barely adequate and good, several books could easily be written on each of the individual interpretations: from the apocalyptic holocaust that Furtwängler conjures up in the last movement of the Eighth Symphony to his unutterably beautiful performance of the Adagio from the Fifth, in which we become a party to one of the most moving spiritual journeys ever undertaken by a nineteenth-century composer. While the point could be belabored indefinitely, suffice it to say that if you have yet to experience these astounding recordings, it's unlikely that you've ever really *heard* the Bruckner symphonies at all.

For collectors who are unable (or unwilling) to come to terms with Furtwängler's intensely personal conceptions, or for those who grow impatient with less than state-of-the-art recorded sound, a handful of recent recordings can be recommended as reasonable, if not completely satisfying, alternatives. In the Symphony No. 4 (*Romantic*), Eliahu Inbal's recording of the original 1874 version with the Frankfurt Radio Symphony (Teldec 9031-77597-2 [CD]) is as persuasive as it is fascinating, including, as it does, a Scherzo entirely different from the one that is usually heard. The most completely satisfying account of the more familiar edition is by Eugen Jochum and the Berlin Philharmonic on Deutsche Grammophon (427200-2 [CD]).

Of all modern recordings of the Fifth, none has yet to surpass either the warmth or virtuosity of Bernard Haitink's Philips recording with the Vienna Philharmonic (422342-2 [CD]). For the closest thing we have to a Furtwängler Seventh and Ninth in stereo sound, Bruno Walter's handsomely remastered recordings from the early 1960s with the Columbia Symphony fills the bill (CBS MB2K-45669 [CD], MBK-44825 [CD], YT-44825 [T]). An excellent performance of the Ninth can be found on a pair of budget-priced Angel (Laser) CDs (CDZB-67279), coupled with the Vienna Philharmonic's imposing version of the Eighth, led by Carl Schuricht, that is both very Furtwänglerian and has a good deal of character of its own.

Anyone looking for recordings of all the symphonies who also wants the convenience of a boxed set will find Eugen Jochum's admirable cycle for Deutsche Grammophon (429079-2) an authentic bargain. The performances, by either the Berlin Philharmonic (1, 4, 7, 8, and 9) or the Bavarian Radio Symphony (2, 3, 5, and 6), are for the most part admirably direct and intensely noble, while the recorded sound rivals all but today's best. Similarly, another medium-priced Deutsche Grammophon collection of virtually all of the composer's choral music (423127-2 [CD]) finds Jochum in equally persuasive form. No finer versions of the three Masses are currently available; the Motets emerge with far more individuality than most interpreters find. The team of vocal soloists is excellent, the choruses sing with devotion and finesse, and the recorded sound, although no longer of demonstration quality, is still exceptionally fine.

Busoni, Ferruccio (1866–1924)

Concerto in C for Piano and Orchestra (with Male Chorus)

Ohlsson, piano; Cleveland Orchestra and Chorus,
Dohnányi. Telarc CD-80207 [CD].

Unlike his friend Gustav Mahler, Ferruccio Busoni is a composer whose time has not yet come. Best remembered for his arrangements of the music of Bach, as an inspired and influential teacher, and as one of history's consummate keyboard virtuosos (those who heard them both insisted that his playing was superior even to Liszt's), Busoni was an odd combination of Italian Romantic composer and North German philosopher-mystic who was one of the major musical heros of his age and *could* be one of ours. Perhaps the best introduction to this absorbing and endlessly complex personality is the titanic Piano Concerto he composed between 1902 and 1904, one of the most involved and entertaining concertos ever written for the instrument and—at seventy minutes—the longest.

John Ogdon's historic first recording of the work, which will undoubtedly be the English pianist's most enduring memorial, has been unaccountably withdrawn, as has the newer and exceedingly impressive recording by Peter Donohoe. Telarc's Cleveland Orchestra recording, while not quite as overwhelming as either of its predecessors, is still a good suggestion of the riches contained within the piece. Garrick Ohlsson is both thoughtful and exciting in his playing of the demanding solo part, and though the orchestra is predictably brilliant, the chorus sounds a trifle anemic.

Busoni admirers—or anyone who would like to know this captivating musician a good deal better—should waste no time acquiring Deutsche Grammophon's CD reissue (427413–2) of the composer's final opera, *Doktor Faust*. This 1969 recording, with a cast headed by Dietrich Fischer-Dieskau, confirmed what many Busoni fanciers had been claiming for years: that his last, unfinished work was not only his ultimate masterpiece but one of the most disturbingly original operas of modern times.

Butterworth, George

(1885–1916)

The Banks of Green Willow; Two English Idylls; A Shropshire Lad

English String Orchestra, Boughton. Nimbus NI-5068 [CD].

Like the poets Edward Thomas, Isaac Rosenberg, and Wilfred Owen, George Butterworth was of that tragic English generation decimated in the trenches of the Western Front. He enlisted during the week the First World War began and was killed at the battle of Somme two years later. During his brief career he was an inveterate collector of English folk songs, helped Vaughan Williams arrange material for *A London Symphony*, and composed a handful of inspired miniatures that suggest he might have become one of the most significant English composers of his time.

The four bewitching works found on this gorgeous Nimbus CD represent Butterworth at his most beguiling. If you are touched by the folk-inspired music of Delius, Holst, and Vaughan Williams, you will probably find Butterworth irresistible. And once you find yourself in his gentle, vice-like grip, don't fail to investigate a Unicorn-Kanchana recording of his Housman song cycle *Six Songs from "A Shropshire Lad"* in the winning performance by baritone Brian Rayner Cook and pianist Clifford Benson (DKPCD-9113 [CD]).

Byrd, William (1543–1623)

The Great Service

> The Tallis Scholars, Phillips. Gimmell CDGIM-011 [CD].

One of the giants of Renaissance sacred music, William Byrd was probably the first incontestably great English composer. Unlike his probable teacher, Thomas Tallis—only hearsay evidence suggests a link between the two men—Byrd wrote distinguished music in virtually every form, from keyboard works and madrigals to music for High Anglican worship.

Peter Phillips and The Tallis Scholars give an inspired performance of Byrd's stirring masterpiece *The Great Service*, a work that might have been designed for people who think they don't like older sacred music. Almost as moving is an Argo recording (430164-2 [CD]) of the Masses for three, four and five voices, elegantly sung by the Choir of Winchester Cathedral led by David Hill.

Canteloube, Joseph (1879–1957)

Songs of the Auvergne

> Te Kanawa, soprano; English Chamber Orchestra, Tate. London 410004-2 [CD] (volume 1); London 411730-2 [CD], 411730-4 (T) (volume 2).

> Von Stade, mezzo-soprano; Royal Philharmonic, Almeida. CBS MK-37299 [CD], IMT-37299 [T] (volume 1); CBS MK-37837 [CD], IMT-37837 [T] (volume 2).

For much of his life, the indefatigable French composer Joseph Canteloube devoted himself to collecting and arranging the charming, haunting, and frequently scintillating folk songs of the Auvergne region of central France. Although none of his original works ever succeeded in making much of an impression, the four-volume *Songs of the Auvergne* are well on their way to becoming modern classics. Beginning with the pioneering recordings of Natania Davrath (Vanguard VBD-2090 [CD]) and Victoria de los Angeles (Angel CDC-47970 [CD]) in the late 1950s and early '60s, famous singers have been drawn almost irresistibly to these minor masterworks, not only because they are so vocally and musically rewarding, but also because any album with *"Songs of the Auvergne"* on its cover is almost guaranteed to sell.

Dame Kiri Te Kanawa, in some of her finest work in the recording studio to date, has so far recorded two excellent collections, and her ravishing, peaches-and-cream instrument serves the music very well.

Frederica von Stade, if not as completely in tune with this music as she is with Mozart and Massenet, turns in a pair of recordings that will disappoint no one; vocally, they are delectable; musically, they are beyond reproach.

Carter, Elliott (1908–   )

Piano Sonata

Lawson, piano. Virgin Classics VC-7-91163-2 [CD].

During the last four decades, Elliott Carter has become the most uncompromising and, for many, one of the most forbidding of modern American composers. Igor Stravinsky was quoted as saying that Carter's Double Concerto of 1961 was the first true American masterpiece, and in the increasingly complex music he has written since then—from the astonishing *Concerto for Orchestra* to the mysterious *Enchanted Preludes* for flute and cello—he has proven to be, with Milton Babbitt, the most consistently challenging composer of his generation.

The Piano Sonata, finished in 1946 and revised substantially in 1982, is probably the greatest piano sonata yet written by an

American. Composed toward the middle of Carter's neoclassical phase, it is a rich, serious, elegantly made work which includes, among its many wonders, one of the finest fugues since Beethoven. Peter Lawson's electrifying Virgin Classics disc will allow you to judge whether it really *is* the Great American Piano Sonata, since, with the exception of the magnificent Piano Sonata of Charles Tomlinson Griffes, it includes the only other possible contenders: those of Samuel Barber and Aaron Copland, in equally authoritative performances.

This is easily one of the most important recordings of American piano music yet released.

An equally exciting recording of three of Carter's most important orchestral scores features Oliver Knussen leading the London Sinfonietta in revelatory performances of the *Concerto for Orchestra*, the Violin Concerto, and *Three Occasions* (Virgin Classics CDC-59271 [CD]). In Knussen's capable hands, even the thorniest of Carter's inspirations emerges with a new lucidity and emotional depth. Although nothing will ever transform this aristocratic composer into a man of the masses, this is easily—to use a particularly vile mass-marketing phrase—the most "user-friendly" Carter album yet.

Finally, to hear the starting point from which Carter's extraordinary journey began, CRI has reissued the Symphony No. 1 from 1942 (CD-552 [CD], ASC-6003 [T]). One of the most exuberant and handsomely turned-out American orchestral scores of the 1940s, the Symphony is a far cry indeed from the endlessly fascinating minefield of late Carter. The language is no more threatening than the symphonies of Hanson, Harris, and Diamond, and the musical rewards are just as immediate and considerable.

Catalani, Alfredo (1854–1893)

La Wally

Tebaldi, Marimpietri, del Monaco, Cappuccilli, Turin Lyric
Chorus, Monte Carlo National Opera Orchestra, Cleva.
London 425417-2 [CD].

Even before interest in its hit tune was reawakened by the
1981 French film *Diva*—and one wonders what became of the
movie's alluring star, Wilhelmena Wiggins Fernandez—Catalani's
sappy melodramatic potboiler had the reputation of being a one-
aria opera. This sells the work considerably short. For in addition
to "Ebben? Ne andro lontana"—admittedly, one of the loveliest
arias ever written—*La Wally* can also boast what may well be the
stupidest story in Italian opera. After the heroine arranges to have
the hero murdered because she believes he insulted her (now *that's*
touchy, even by soprano standards), she changes her mind and
rescues him. On the mountaintop they confess their love and are
promptly swept away by an avalanche.

The great Renata Tebaldi was never more irresistibly feminine
than here, in one of her last complete opera recordings. Her voice
is at its most melting—the big aria is a wonder of passionate
abandon and effortless control—and the characterization is so enthralling that you nearly forget what utter nonsense *La Wally* is.
Although Mario del Monaco reminds us, gloriously, of what the
now nearly extinct *tenore da forza* could be, and Fausto Cleva's
old-fashioned blood-and-thunder conducting defines *verismo* at
its best, this is very much Tebaldi's show, and she steals it magnificently.

Chabrier, Emmanuel

(1841–1894)

Bourrée fantastique; *España*; *Danse slave*; *Gwendoline*: Overture; *Joyeuse Marche*; *Suite Pastorale*

Detroit Symphony, Paray. Mercury 434303-2 [CD].

Gustav Mahler once shocked the members of the New York Philharmonic by calling Emmanuel Chabrier's *España* "the foundation of modern music." Precisely what Mahler meant by that we'll probably never know, but he certainly put his baton where his mouth was: During his two-year stay in America he programmed it a half dozen times, always in performances in which he took the liberty of quadrupling all the wind parts.

Although we now tend to think of *España* as not much more than the foundation of many a pops concert, there was a time when the reputation of its abrupt, lively, immensely likable composer was far more imposing than it is today. As the American musicologist Gilbert Chase once wrote, "He was the direct precursor of Debussy and Ravel, whose most daring effects he anticipated." For their part, Debussy and Ravel always admitted their fondness for the music of this late-blooming composer and celebrated salon wit. (Chabrier's caustic sense of humor was legendary. He once said, "There are three kinds of music: the good, the bad, and that of Ambroise Thomas.")

Paul Paray's wonderful Chabrier recordings from the late 1950s cannot be welcomed back into the catalog too warmly. In this repertoire—and in French music in general—Paray had few rivals among the major conductors of his generation, and he invests each of the pieces with an abundance of life and a character uniquely its own. The Detroit Symphony has rarely sounded as sensuous or alert, and the original Mercury Living Presence recording has been revived with astonishing vividness.

Charpentier, Gustave

(1860–1956)

Louise

Cotrubas, Barbié, Domingo, Sénéchal, Bacqier, Ambrosian
Opera Chorus, New Philharmonia Orchestra, Prêtre.
Sony S3K-46429 [CD].

Gustave Charpentier was nearly forty when after a decade-long gestation, *Louise* was first mounted at the Opéra-Comique on February 2, 1900. At its fiftieth anniversary performance, the composer, nearing ninety, conducted the final scene of the opera, after which he was made a Grand Officer of the Legion of Honor by the President of France. In between those two historic events, Charpentier did precious little, other than compose a dismal sequel called *Julien* in 1913 and ponder the mysteries of *Louise*'s phenomenal success. Part of that success had to do with the novelty of the opera's working-class setting and socialist leanings, and part with the fact that an unknown singer named Mary Garden took over the title role two months into the production and created a sensation. But *Louise* has other, more durable charms, including a touching and turbulent love story and a vivid evocation of turn-of-the-century Paris, which almost becomes another character in the drama.

The Sony recording makes the strongest possible case for this frequently compelling work. If Ileana Cotrubas isn't perfectly suited, vocally, to the title role—"Depuis le jour," for instance, is not ideally soaring and effortless—her dramatic reading of the little seamstress is very affecting, as is the singing of Placido Domingo as Julien. The rest of the cast is uniformly excellent, and George Prêtre delivers some of the most sensitive conducting of his career. All in all, a recording that proves that *Louise* is something considerably more than a French *La Bohème*.

Chausson, Ernest (1855–1899)

*Po*ème for Violin and Orchestra

Chung, violin; Royal Philharmonic, Dutoit. London
417118-2 [CD].

One of the most provocative of all "what if?" musical speculations concerns the effect on the subsequent development of
French music had Ernest Chausson been as accomplished a bicyclist
as he was a composer. His premature death, from injuries sustained
when he drove his bicycle into a brick wall in 1899, robbed French
music of the most distinct and original voice it had produced between those of Hector Berlioz and Claude Debussy.

With the Symphony in B-flat, the best German symphony ever
written by a Frenchman—Charles Munch's glorious Boston Symphony recording has recently returned on a Victor CD (09026-
60683-2)—and the sumptuous orchestral song cycle *Poème de
l'amour et de la mer*—best represented these days by Linda Finnie's
haunting Chandos recording (CHAN-8952 [CD], ABTD-1546
[T])—the *Poème* for Violin and Orchestra is one of the finest and
most justly popular of all Chausson's works: a finished masterpiece
by an already established master, and a tantalizing, heartbreaking
suggestion of what might have been.

The greatest performance the *Poème* has ever received on, or
probably off, records was that rich and passionate recording the
tragically short-lived French violinist Ginette Neveu made in the
late 1940s. Kyung-Wha Chung's London recording resembles
Neveu's in its emotional depth and technical facility. Only Itzhak
Perlman, in his superb Angel recording (CDC-47725 [CD]), can
create the similar illusion that this extremely thorny work is so
childishly simple to play. As usual, the support that Charles Dutoit
gives Ms. Chung is as imaginative as it is sensitive, not only in the
Poème but also in Saint-Saëns's *Havanaise* and *Introduction and
Rondo capriccioso*, and Ravel's *Tzigane*, the other popular violin
showpieces that round out this extremely appealing release.

Cherubini, Luigi (1760–1842)

Medea

Callas, Scotto, Pirazzini, Picchi, La Scala Orchestra and
Chorus, Serafin. Angel CDMB-63625 [CD].

Callas, Simionato, Vickers, Ghiaurov, La Scala Opera
Chorus and Orchestra, Schippers. Arkadia
CDLSMH-34028 [CD].

Although *Medea* has always had its admirers—Beethoven, for
one, Leonard Bernstein for another—and though its place in the
history books as "the first modern opera" is more or less assured,
the opera's fortunes as a piece of living theater have always relied
on its ability to attract extraordinary sopranos to its formidable
title role. (The first Medea, Madame Scio, was said to have died of
consumption brought on by singing the role once too often. But
that's hardly credible, since if sopranos were to die simply from
singing the wrong piece once too often, then there'd be no sopranos
left.)

No singer in living memory made more of the part than Maria
Callas, in either her very fine studio recording from Angel or in any
of the several live performances that have been preserved. Her
chilling portrait of mythology's most famous mom is imposing and
overwhelming, a musical characterization cut from the same sublime cloth as her unforgettable Norma. If *Medea* is not a great
opera, you certainly couldn't prove it from this.

Chopin, Frédéric (1810–1849)

Concertos for Piano and Orchestra: No. 1 in E minor; No. 2 in F minor

Zimerman, piano; Los Angeles Philharmonic, Giulini. Deutsche Grammophon 415970-2 [CD].

In addition to being central works in the concerto literature for the instrument, the Chopin piano concertos go a long way to dispelling several myths that continue to cling to one of history's most popular composers. There are those who still insist that Chopin was essentially an incomparable miniaturist who was un-comfortable with—and, indeed, incapable of sustaining—larger-scale forms. These are the same people, no doubt, who are con-vinced that this first important composer of piano music con-structed entirely in *pianistic* terms was thoroughly incapable of writing gracefully and idiomatically for other instruments—which is to say, for the nineteenth-century orchestra. Hogwash. Both as larger forms, and as concerted works for piano and orchestra, these two Concertos are as masterly as those any composer of the Ro-mantic era produced.

It was one or the other of these two exceptional Deutsche Grammophon recordings that probably introduced most of the world to the great young Polish pianist, Krystian Zimerman. As a general rule, I am extremely suspicious of the phrase "great young" when applied to anyone, but in Zimerman's case, it most assuredly *does* apply. He has instinct, technique, and temperament to burn, together with a maturity and insight that many pianists twice his age would be hard-pressed to match.

Zimerman's performances of the Chopin concertos are as nearly perfect as any that have been heard in a generation. In them, poetry and youthful impetuosity are combined with a highly dis-ciplined musical intelligence, and the results are an unalloyed de-light for both the heart and the mind. The backdrops provided by Giulini and the Los Angeles Philharmonic could not have been more suave or sympathetic, and the recorded sound has a warm and natural bloom.

Vigorously recommended.

Solo Piano Works

Ballades (4); Scherzos (4). Rubinstein, piano. RCA
RCD1-7156 [CD], CRK2-5460 [T].

Mazurkas (35). Rubinstein, piano. RCA 5614-2-RC [CD],
CRK2-5171 [T].

Nocturnes (21). Rubinstein, piano. RCA 5613-2-RC [CD],
CRK2-5018 [T].

Polonaises (7). Rubinstein, piano. RCA 5615-2-RC [CD],
CRK2-7036 [T].

Waltzes (19). Rubinstein, piano. RCA RCD1-5492 [CD],
CRK2-5018 [T].

Although this phenomenally popular body of music has attracted almost every important pianist of the last 150 years, it's
unlikely that Frédéric Chopin ever found, or will ever find, a more
ideal interpreter than Artur Rubinstein. To be sure, pianists like
Josef Hoffman, Leopold Godowsky, and Vladimir Horowitz gave
infinitely more brilliant performances of the music. Even some of
the brighter lights of the younger generation, Dinu Lipatti in the
1950s and Maurizio Pollini in our time, managed to find an intellectual and spiritual depth in Chopin that Rubinstein, for much
of his career, never did. Yet on balance, these remain the definitive
recordings of Chopin's piano music, as authoritative and unapproachable in their way as Furtwängler's recordings of the Bruckner symphonies, or the music of Frederick Delius led by Sir Thomas
Beecham.

The key to Rubinstein's greatness as a Chopin interpreter was
the combination of his utter naturalness as a performer and his
enormously sophisticated musical mind. Nothing ever seems forced
or premeditated; there are no sharp edges or sudden flashes of
insight. In fact, the illusion that the performances create is one
of the music flowing, without benefit of a human intermediary,
directly from Chopin's heart to the listener's. Of course, only the
most accomplished artists are able to create such illusions, and
then only after a lifetime of study, experience, self-examination
and back-breaking work.

At almost every moment in these classic recordings, Rubinstein discovers some wonder of color or phrasing, brings out a
beautiful inner voice it seems we've never heard before, and in
general creates the impression of a man for whom playing this often
fiendishly difficult music is no more difficult than making love. In

short, Rubinstein's great and completely unaffected humanity breathes such life into these performances that they will continue to move, enlighten, and inspire for as long as people require such things from recorded music.

With the Rubinsteins as the backbone of any Chopin collection, there are some superb second opinions that really should be consulted too. Most important of all are the recordings of the Czech pianist Ivan Moravec, who is probably to the present generation of Chopin interpreters what Rubinstein was to his. With playing of an almost otherworldly refinement and purity, Moravec's Elektra/Nonesuch recording of the Nocturnes (79233-2 [CD]) may well be the loveliest Chopin recording ever made. His 1976 Supraphon recording of the Preludes (11-0630-2 [CD]) is both more technically impressive than Rubinstein's and probes even deeper beneath the surface; his recent Dorian recording of the Scherzos (DOR-90140 [CD]) offers insight and excitement in virtually equal amounts.

Krystian Zimerman's Deutsche Grammophon recording of the Ballades (423090-2 [CD], 423090-4 [T]) features playing as fresh as it is powerfully dramatic, and Maurizio Pollini on another DG recording (431221-2 [CD]) demonstrates that he is still the undisputed master at solving the formidable technical and musical problems of the Études. (The set of three bargain CDs also includes his impeccable versions of the Preludes and Polonaises.)

Dinu Lipatti's unutterably moving recording of the Waltzes, made in the last year of his tragically abbreviated life, can be found on an Odyssey tape (YT-60058E). At almost no time since they were first issued in the early 1950s have these miraculous performances been out of print, and with good reason. In their unfailing eloquence and deceptive simplicity, they are not only touchstones in the history of recording, they stand among the enduring triumphs of human communication.

Finally, Testament has reissued the complete Chopin recordings made between 1932 and 1946 by the English pianist Solomon. These are clearly among the greatest Chopin recordings ever: as pure and poised as Lipatti's and delivered with an even more breathtaking technique. The 1942 version of the *Berceuse*, for instance, is one of the most nearly perfect piano recordings ever made. With splendid transfers from the original 78s and a revealing appreciation of Solomon's art from Bryce Morrison, this is one of the most important Chopin CDs yet released.

Piano Sonatas: No. 2 in B-flat minor, Op. 35; No. 3 in B minor, Op. 58

> Kapell, piano. RCA 5998-2 [CD].

Here is some very persuasive evidence that William Kapell was the finest pianist America has ever produced. Only thirty-one at the time of his death in a plane crash in 1953, he was already a performer of epic abilities. His technique was the most formidable of any pianist of his generation, and his powers of communication were broadening and deepening to the very end. With the Romantics he was dashing and fearless, and with Bach he was dignified and self-effacing. And with Mozart he impressed the dreaded Claudia Cassidy, the virtually unimpressible critic of the Chicago *Tribune*, as the purest, most effortless music-maker she had ever heard.

Kapell's versions of the two popular Chopin sonatas—one recorded in the studio, one taken from a concert given in the last months of his life—make for an exhilarating, exhausting, ennobling experience. The playing is that of one of the century's towering instrumentalists: powerful, confident, poetic, and introspective, with just the right combination of an immediately recognizable personality and absolute fidelity to the spirit of the text. One of the acid tests of any performance of this music is the ability to listen to the well-known Funeral March from the B-flat minor Sonata with a perfectly straight face. Kapell invests it with such heartrending pathos that we are left in pieces on the floor.

Rounded off with Kapell's brilliant recordings of ten of the Mazurkas, this may be the single most valuable Chopin album on the market.

Les Sylphides (ballet)

> Philadelphia Orchestra, Ormandy. Sony SBK-46551 [CD], SBT-46551 [T].

If Igor Stravinsky meant it as no compliment when he called Eugene Ormandy "the ideal conductor of Strauss waltzes," then that much-maligned musician was a nearly perfect interpreter of the Chopin-inspired ballet, *Les Sylphides*. Recorded at a time when the

Philadelphia Orchestra boasted some of the finest first-desk players of their time, the performance not only capitalizes on the wonders of the famous Philadelphia strings but also features some fabulous solo displays. In addition to this inspired Chopin travesty, the budget CD comes with equally memorable versions of the suites from Delibes's *Coppélia* and *Sylvia* and a rather disappointing *Nutcracker Suite* in which the conductor makes some exceedingly vulgar "improvements" in Tchaikovsky's orchestration.

Cilea, Francesco (1886–1950)

Adriana Lecouvreur

> Sutherland, Bergonzi, Nucci, Welsh National Orchestra and Chorus, Bonynge. London 425815-2 [CD].

Like Umberto Giordano, Alfredo Catalani, and Riccardo Zandonai, Francesco Cilea was one of those second-rung figures of the *verismo* movement who had about one really good opera in him. *Adriana Lecouvreur* is an extremely good opera, and not simply because of its unforgettable money tune, the ravishing "Io son l'umile ancella." Adriana herself—an actress at the Comédie Française in early eighteenth-century Paris—is almost as fine a character as Puccini's Tosca and in the hands of a great singer-actress will hold the stage nearly as well.

As in her surprising recording of Puccini's *Turandot* (see page 406), Joan Sutherland scores another major hit in what is hardly a "Sutherland role." With few opportunities for the dizzying bel canto display that made her famous, the Great Dame sings with enormous power and expressiveness throughout. The rest of the cast—especially the indestructible Carlo Bergonzi—is excellent, and Richard Bonynge turns in some of the most richly imaginative conducting of his career.

Coates, Eric (1886–1957)

Orchestral Music

Czecho-Slovak Radio Symphony of Bratislava, Leaper.
Marco Polo 8.223445 [CD]

London Symphony, Mackerras; Royal Liverpool
Philharmonic, Groves; City of Birmingham Symphony,
Kilbey. Classics for Pleasure CFPD-4456 [CD].

Admittedly, there are people who cannot abide the music of the English composer Eric Coates. But then, too, there are people who enjoy pulling the wings off butterflies and pushing little old ladies into manure spreaders.

With his near-contemporary, the longtime Boston Pops arranger Leroy Anderson, Coates was one of the indisputable masters of "light music." In his familiar suites and bracing marches, Coates was a man who not only knew the value of a good tune but was also singularly successful in producing them over the years, from the unforgettable "Knightsbridge March" from the *London Suite* to that equally memorable inspiration from *The Three Elizabeths*, which served as the signature tune of Public Television's *Forsyth Saga*. It is music that never tries the patience, overstays its welcome, or fails to amuse, entertain, and delight.

On the two generously packed, reasonably priced, and very aptly named Classics for Pleasure CDs, two of the all-time great Coatesians, Sir Charles Mackerras and Sir Charles Groves, bring the music so vividly to life that you suspect it will last an eternity; the contributions of the City of Birmingham Symphony under Reginald Kilbey—what a perfect name for a Coates conductor!— are hardly less enjoyable.

The Coates album from Marco Polo's British Light Music series is, if anything, even *more* enjoyable. The playing of the Slovakian musicians is so thoroughly idiomatic it's difficult to believe they haven't known and loved this music since birth, and Adrian Leaper's consistently fresh and spontaneous interpretations make even the most familiar items seems as though they were dashed off yesterday. The recorded sound and notes are also exemplary.

Rather incredibly, the Coates is not necessarily the most valuable installment in the already memorable Light Music series. The recording of Sir Edward German's music, including the irresistible *Gipsy Suite*, restores a shamefully neglected composer to the catalog (8.223419 [CD]). The CDs devoted to Frederic Curzon (8.223425), Robert Farnon (8.223401), Ernest Tomlinson (8.223413), and Haydn Wood (8.223402) are no less thoroughly delightful.

If you have the willpower, or simply the cussedness, to resist these collections, you have my admiration and sympathy.

Copland, Aaron (1900–1990)

Appalachian Spring

> Los Angeles Philharmonic, Bernstein. (Suite only) Deutsche Grammophon 431048-2 [CD].
>
> St. Paul Chamber Orchestra, Davies. Pro Arte CDD 140 [CD], PCD-140 [T].

Aaron Copland was, in many ways, the most dramatic musical manifestation of the "melting pot" genesis of American culture. For the composer who, in his most popular works, seemed to capture the very essence of Middle America and the Western frontier was in fact born in a working-class Jewish neighborhood of Brooklyn, and received his principal musical training with Nadia Boulanger in Paris.

Appalachian Spring, a ballet composed for the celebrated American dancer Martha Graham, is probably Copland's masterpiece. All the hallmarks of his "Enlightened Populist" style are heard to their best advantage. Bracing, wide-open harmonies and folksy, unforgettable melodies are bound together with Copland's expressive idiom, which mixes tenderness, exuberance, sentimentality, and sophistication, in roughly equal amounts.

Like the exhilarating recording Leonard Bernstein made with the New York Philharmonic in the 1960s, this version with the Los Angeles Philharmonic is an unqualified triumph. The orchestra plays with great delicacy and conviction, and the special excitement all Bernstein's live performances generate can be felt throughout.

For a somewhat less compelling but thoroughly satisfying look at the ballet in its original version for chamber orchestra, the performance led by Dennis Russell Davies handily defeats all other contenders, including the recording by the composer himself.

Billy the Kid; Rodeo

St. Louis Symphony, Slatkin. Angel CDC-47382 [CD], 4DS-37357 [T].

For more years than anyone can remember, Leonard Bernstein, one of Copland's oldest and closest friends, virtually owned this music. His CBS recordings of these immensely appealing cowboy ballets (both of which quote more actual frontier tunes than a typical Zane Grey novel) have been all but unapproachable in their dramatic flair and authority. That is, at least, until now.

Leonard Slatkin, who in the last decade has galvanized the St. Louis Symphony into one of America's finest orchestras, leads a pair of performances that are even more successful than Bernstein's. The rhythms are tighter and more infectious, the phrasing is consistently more alert and imaginative, and the playing of this great young ensemble sounds every bit the equal of that of any orchestra in the world. Along with demonstration-quality sound, the recording has the further advantage of presenting both ballets note-complete. While this represents only a few extra minutes of actual music, it makes what is already an immensely attractive recording virtually irresistible.

Fanfare for the Common Man; Danzón Cubano; El salón México; Appalachian Spring

New York Philharmonic, Bernstein. CBS MYK-37257 [CD], MYT-37527 [T].

The advantage of this particular lineup—and CBS is repackaging Bernstein's hugely marketable Copland recordings in a variety of combinations—is that it brings together all but definitive performances of three of the composer's shorter works and a version of *Appalachian Spring* that is second only to the conductor's Los Angeles Philharmonic recording for Deutsche Grammophon.

If the *Fanfare* is slightly compromised by the wobble of the Philharmonic's principal trumpet, the performance as a whole is gloriously gutsy. (Be warned, though: This is not the original version of the score, but instead an extract from its memorable appearance in Copland's Third Symphony.) On the other hand, the two Latin items are unapproachable, especially *El salón México*, which here becomes a triumph of salsa and swank.

Lincoln Portrait

Hepburn, speaker; Cincinnati Pops Orchestra, Kunzel.
Telarc CD-80117 [CD].

Among the many interesting choices to deliver the president's lines in Copland's *Lincoln Portrait*—former British Prime Minister Margaret Thatcher and Desert Storm hero Norman Schwarzkopf notwithstanding—Telarc's decision to hire Katharine Hepburn is perhaps the most interesting of all. Not since Adlai Stevenson read the lines in his recording with Eugene Ormandy and the Philadelphia Orchestra, have the words meant quite so much as they do here. Kunzel and the Cincinnati Pops orchestra rise memorably to the occasion, as they do in the other items in this Copland anthology, including rarities like the *Ceremonial Fanfare*, *John Henry*, and the *Jubilee Variations*. While Sherrill Milnes's performance of the first set of *Old American Songs* is full of zest and fun, William Warfield's classic recording of both sets remains unapproachable (CBS MK-42430 [CD]).

Symphony No. 3; Quiet City

New York Philharmonic, Bernstein. Deutsche Grammophon
419170-2 [CD].

Among the candidates for the musical equivalent of the Great American Novel, the Copland Third has always ranked very high on most people's lists. I have never been persuaded that this is, in fact, the Great American Symphony—my own nominee is the Roy Harris Third—nor am I usually inclined to think of it as a great American *anything*. The gritty, affably belligerent Scherzo is prime Copland, the incorporation of the *Fanfare for the Common Man* is clever, exciting, and all of that, but for the most part the Symphony has always seemed to me a melancholy victory of manner over matter: one of the major *shallow* masterpieces of American music. Except when conducted by Leonard Bernstein.

His final version, taken from a live New York Philharmonic performance, proves once again that this composer never had a more eloquent advocate. No other recording of the work, including the two the composer made himself, can begin to match this one in nervous tension and sustained energy. Moreover, what can seem merely rhetorical in other hands is miraculously transformed in Bernstein's into deeply felt emotion; no one, for instance, has ever made the *Fanfare*'s final apotheosis seem more inevitable or just.

With one of the loveliest of all versions of *Quiet City* as the welcome filler, this would seem to be a recording that no Copland lover could afford to pass up.

*T*he Tender Land

The Plymouth Music Series Soloists, Orchestra, and Chorus, Brunelle. Virgin VCD-791113-2 [CD].

Copland never wrote a more gently affecting piece than his only full-length opera, *The Tender Land*. Although the touching little story of a farm girl and a drifter has no big arias and no big scenes, it is suffused with the same folksy richness that animates *Appalachian Spring*. In fact, the opera's most memorable moment, the Act I finale called "The Promise of Living" is based on "Zion's Walls," the same tune Copland used in one of the *Old American Songs*.

The performance by the Plymouth Music Series is as accomplished as it is affectionate. The soloists—especially Elizabeth Comeaux and Dan Dressen as the young lovers—all seem perfectly cast, while conductor Philip Brunelle allows the undeniable charm of the opera to quietly unfold. An equally moving performance of the orchestral suite features the composer in one of his earliest recordings as a conductor leading the Boston Symphony on RCA (6802-2-RG [CD], 6802-4-RG [T]).

Corelli, Arcangelo (1653–1713)

Concerti grossi (12), Op. 6

English Concert, Pinnock. Deutsche Grammophon 423626-2 [CD].

Along with being one of the finest violinists of the Baroque era and a man who did as much as anyone to codify the form and substance of the sonata and concerto grosso, the penurious Arcangelo Corelli was far and away the most tight-fisted cheapskate in the history of music. He refused to buy new clothes until the old ones literally disintegrated on his back, and although he was an avid collector of paintings and sculpture, he never went to public galleries on days when admission was charged.

Yet for all his personal idiosyncracies, Corelli was as admired by his contemporaries as he is largely unappreciated today. The richly inventive collection of Op. 6 Concerti grossi were among the most influential works of the High Baroque. In addition to the well-known *Christmas* Concerto—which is about as Christmasy as a Fourth of July Parade—the eleven other works in the set contain one felicitous idea after another. In addition to the innovative melodic and harmonic thinking, the craftsmanship is of an order that would not be surpassed until Handel's own Op. 6 collection, which owes Corelli's an incalculable debt.

Trevor Pinnock's enthusiastic period-instrument performances make an exceptionally strong case for these works. The interpretations are as bracing and articulate as the music itself, and the recorded sound is wonderfully lifelike and clear.

Corigliano, John (1938–)

Symphony No. 1

Chicago Symphony, Barenboim. Erato 2292-45601-2 [CD].

Unlike Henryk Górecki's vapid Symphony No. 3 (see page 219), John Corigliano's Symphony No. 1 might have been a similarly opportunistic exercise in political correctness were it not for the fact that it is as genuinely moving as it is sincerely felt. Written in memory of friends of the composer who have died of AIDS, the Symphony is a gruff, angry, impassioned, lyrical, deeply personal outburst, and it is the composer's seething indignation that makes it such an intensely wrenching experience. Whether it will prove to be a '90s equivalent of Luciano Berio's *Sinfonia* or something more enduring, only time will tell.

Barenboim and the Chicago Symphony give a suitably shattering performance, which is captured to perfection by Erato's engineers.

Couperin, François
(1668–1733)

L'apothéose de Lully; *Dans le goût théatral*; *Le Parnasse* *(L'apothéose de Corelli)*

English Baroque Soloists, Gardiner. Erato 2292-45011-2 [CD].

As a sage English philosopher once insisted, "Murder, like talent, seems occasionally to run in families," especially if talent (or murder, for that matter), *also* happens to be the family business. His title "le Grand" (the Great) was as much a means of identification as an accolade, for François Couperin was merely the most illustrious member of a family that for two centuries produced illustrious professional musicians. Beginning with Charles Couperin, a merchant and organist of Chaumes in the province of Brie, the line continued with his eldest son Louis, who became organist of St. Gervais in Paris in 1653. Louis was succeeded in that post, without interruption, by other members of the family and its descendants until the line became extinct in 1826 with the death of Gervais-François, grandson of François "le Grand's" cousin Nicolas.

These three engaging works by the first great French composer of instrumental music are given nearly ideal performances by John Eliot Gardiner and his superb ensemble. Even those not usually drawn to the stately pronouncements of the French Baroque should readily respond to both the magnificent music itself and the equally magnificent performances.

By the same token, Kenneth Gilbert's monumental recording of Couperin's complete *Pièces de clavecin* on four densely packed boxed sets of CDs from Harmonia Mundi (HMA-190351/53, HMA-190354/56, HMA-190357/58, HMA-190359/60) establishes a standard for scholarship and enthusiasm that will probably not be approached for the remainder of the century.

In a far less comprehensive release from Deutsche Harmonia Mundi (77219-2-RC), Skip Sempé demonstrates why he is one of the most talked-about harpsichordists in the world today; his imaginative, impassioned playing is rare among pianists.

Debussy, Claude (1862–1918)

Children's Corner Suite; Images for Piano, Books I and II

> Michelangeli, piano. Deutsche Grammophon 415372-2
> [CD].

Without much question, Arturo Benedetti Michelangeli is the most exasperating musician of his generation. A monstrously gifted pianist and a wholly unique musical personality, Michelangeli could have become a household word long ago had he only been a little more interested in playing the piano. The public appearances of this cult figure, who has a small but fanatical following, have been likened to the sightings of a rare and exotic bird. Michelangeli plays whenever he feels like it (which isn't often), and records even less.

This Debussy collection, taped in the early 1970s, reveals just what kind of spellbinder this fabulous oddball was in his prime. The playing itself is largely unbelievable, and the interpretations have an almost Promethean originality. Only Ivan Moravec could find such wondrous charm in the familiar *Children's Corner Suite*, and even the great Walter Gieseking would have been hard-pressed to wring more color or individuality from the bewitching *Images*.

What a pity that one of the accomplished musicians of modern times should have been such a thoroughgoing spook.

La Demoiselle élue; L'Enfant prodigue

> Cotrubas, Norman, Carreras, Fischer-Dieskau, Stuttgart
> Radio Symphony and Chorus, Bertini. Orfeo 012821
> [CD].

It was on his third attempt to win the prestigious Prix de Rome that Debussy finally succeeded with the cantata *L'Enfant prodigue* in 1884. Debussy consciously tailored the music to the tastes of the conservative members of the jury; the strategy paid off handsomely: One of the judges, Charles Gounod, pronounced it a work of genius.

Debussy left for Rome—and a three-year residence at the Villa Medici—in January of 1885. He despised the city, the food, the people, and resented having to regularly send back musical envois to the Prix de Rome's judges. His final envoi, the cantata *La Demoiselle élue* so disturbed the Prix de Rome judges, they refused to allow it to be performed.

While neither of these early works offers many clues as to the composer Debussy would become, both are richly romantic, beautifully scored, and handsomely served on this Orfeo recording. The soloists are all first-rate, especially Jessye Norman, who sings the best-known moment in either score, the "Air de Lia" from *L'Enfant prodigue* with exceptional refinement, and Gary Bertini coaxes some meltingly Gallic playing from his fine Teutonic forces. The recorded sound is excellent.

The orchestral fragments from another intriguing Debussy choral work, *Le Martyre de Saint Sébastien* can be heard to memorable advantage in the classic Boston Symphony performance conducted by Charles Munch, available now on a medium-priced RCA CD (09026-60684-2).

Images for Orchestra

Montreal Symphony, Dutoit. London 425502-2 [CD].

Chicago Symphony, Reiner. RCA 60179-2-RG [CD] (*Ibéria* only).

Claude Debussy both despised and distrusted the term *impressionism* whenever it was applied to his own music, largely because he did not want anyone to think that he had merely created a slavish aural imitation of the paintings of Monet and the poetry of Stéphane Mallarmé. Of course, the composer was absolutely right. For his music represents one of the great turning points in the history of music: a rethinking of musical color and texture so complete that its influence would rival that of Wagner's harmonic upheaval, or the rhythmic revolution begun in Stravinsky's *Rite of Spring*.

As in their near-historic series of Ravel recordings, Dutoit and his fabulous orchestra turn in performances of the *Images* that are all but unapproachable in their sensitivity to the almost infinite variety of Debussy's orchestral sound. Not only are the performances brilliantly lit and colored, they are also remarkable for their rhythmic acuity and dramatic flare. With one exception, *Ibéria* has never sounded so richly various in a commercial recording.

The exception is the legendary Reiner version, which has a fair claim to being the finest recording that often sadistic perfectionist ever made. As in his version of *La Mer* (see below), no detail of Debussy's complex orchestration escapes his hooded, hawklike glare. Yet along with the wondrous details come a grasp of form and a projection of life that, after four decades, continue to make the performance unique. By adding equally compelling versions of Ravel's *Alborada del gracioso, Pavane pour une Infante défunte, Rhapsodie espagnole,* and *Valses nobles et sentimentales,* the Reiner CD makes for one of the great French orchestral collections.

La Mer

Chicago Symphony, Reiner. RCA 60875-2 [CD].

New Philharmonia Orchestra, Boulez. CBS MYK-37261 [CD], MYT-37261 [T].

When Pierre Boulez's recording of Debussy's most evocative work was first released two decades ago, it was widely hailed as a major revelation, and, to be fair, no other recording has ever succeeded in presenting this stunning, magically atmospheric work with greater precision and clarity. Still, the final test of any performance of *La Mer* is the extent to which it makes you see, taste, and smell the sea.

The wonderful recording Fritz Reiner made with the Chicago Symphony in the late 1950s still does that more effectively than any other. In the compact disc reissue, the range of color in this virtuoso performance is as incredibly rich and varied as ever, and the drama that Boulez's otherwise fine interpretation lacks, Reiner finds in abundance. Listen, for instance, to the electrifying playing in the final bars, where the conductor whips up such visceral excitement that you might almost suspect you're listening to the finale of a Tchaikovsky symphony.

Originally, and rather incongruously, coupled with Reiner's final and finest recording of Strauss's *Don Juan,* the digitally remastered tape now offers gleaming performances of Ravel's *Alborada del gracioso* and *Rhapsodie espagnole*; the compact disc brings you the sexiest of all commercial recordings of Rimsky-Korsakov's *Scheherazade* (see page 431).

Nocturnes for Orchestra; *Jeux*

Concertgebouw Orchestra of Amsterdam, Haitink. Philips
400023-2 [2CD].

Boston Symphony, Munch. RCA 6719-4 [T].

I blush to confess that it took me far too long to see the light on the subject of Bernard Haitink. As an ardent admirer of his great predecessor in Amsterdam, Eduard van Beinum, and an absolute fanatic on the subject of van Beinum's predecessor, Willem Mengelberg, for years I regarded Haitink as merely a competent journeyman, a talented but rather anonymous figure who could be relied on for polite and handsomely organized performances, little more. For the last decade, with the release of every new Haitink recording I have eaten what amounts to Brobdingnagian helpings of crow. In almost every recording he has made, recordings that cover an unusually broad range of repertoire, he combines intelligence, passion, craftsmanship, and utter professionalism more thoroughly than any other conductor before the public today. If Haitink, like Felix Weingartner and Pierre Monteux before him, may not be the most glamorous conductor of his generation, he is probably the most consistently satisfying.

Naturally, he faces formidable competition in one of the most popular of Debussy's major works, yet no other modern recording of the Nocturnes can begin to match the effortless perfection of this one. The interpretation of "Nuages" is a masterpiece of mood and texture, "Fêtes" crackles with electric excitement, and "Sirènes" is so seductively alluring that you begin to understand why countless ancient mariners were more than willing to crack up on these dangerous ladies' reefs.

And Haitink's interpretation of *Jeux* is nothing less than a revelation. Whereas other conductors have made this strange tennis-court ballet seem an interesting work at best, Haitink dares to suggest that it may actually be an unjustly neglected masterpiece.

Charles Munch's Boston Symphony recording is one of his very best, an engaging mixture of color, brilliance, and panache that makes it the first choice among currently available tapes.

Pelléas et Mélisande

Alliot-Lugaz, Golfier, Henry, Carlson, Cachemaille, Thau,
Montreal Symphony and Chorus, Dutoit. London
430502-2 [CD].

From its disastrous premiere in 1902 to the present day, *Pelléas et Mélisande* has never been a popular opera. Although the first-night disturbances were organized by friends of the playwright Maurice Maeterlinck, who disowned the project when he was told that his mistress Georgette Leblanc would not be cast as the heroine, there is more than enough in *Pelléas* to irritate the more conservative opera-lover, beginning with a virtual absence of memorable arias. Moreover, it has no big scenes, no dramatic outbursts —in the entire score there are only four *fortissimos*—and the work can seem to move in a hazy, ill-defined half light.

It is also an opera that overflows with the most subtle musical invention, offers ample dramatic challenges (it was *Pelléas* that made Mary Garden a star), and creates an expressive universe wholly and unmistakably its own. Its adherents insist it is the one indisputably great French opera after *Carmen*, a claim its finest recording to date would seem to substantiate.

With this triumphant new recording, Charles Dutoit proves yet again that he is the most resourceful and sensitive conductor of French music before the public today. Although almost without exception the cast of superb singers do everything that is asked of them and more—Colette Alliot-Lugaz and Didier Henry are both radiant and utterly believable as the lovers, while Gilles Cachemaille is probably the most three-dimensional villain since the legendary Martial Singher—it is ultimately Dutoit's wondrous conducting that will make this a *Pelléas* to dominate the catalog for years.

Prélude à l'après-midi d'un faune; *La boîte à joujoux*; *Jeux*

London Symphony, Thomas. Sony SK-48231 [CD].

Becoming a father for the first time late in life changed Debussy dramatically both as a man and as a musician. In writing the *Children's Corner Suite* for his three-year-old daughter (the dedication reads "with her father's apologies for what follows"), Debussy finally allowed a measure of humor to creep into his work. The tender feelings an increasingly doting father felt for his only child would also manifest themselves in the charming ballet for children, *La boîte à joujoux*, composed in 1913.

So fine a performance as the one led by Michael Tilson Thomas makes the neglect of the work all the more inexplicable. Thomas finds precisely the right combination of sophistication and wide-eyed innocence in Debussy's toy-box ballet, to say nothing of a properly athletic grace in *Jeux*, making it a performance worthy of comparison with Haitink's classic interpretation. With one of the best played, best recorded versions of the *Prelude to the Afternoon of a Faun* now available, this is one of the most impressive Debussy discs in years.

Preludes for Piano, Books I and II

Jacobs, piano. Elektra/Nonesuch 73031-2 [CD], 73031 [T].

The American pianist Paul Jacobs has the tragic distinction of being the first well-known musician to die of AIDS. A versatile performer who brought a special fire and poetry to the music of the twentieth century, he was one of the most persuasive advocates of modern American piano music, and his recordings of the music of Arnold Schoenberg (Elektra/Nonesuch 71309-2 [CD], 71309-4 [T]) were among the few that can be mentioned in the same breath with those of the composer's friend and pupil, Eduard Steuermann.

Even though he faces formidable competition in this popular repertoire, Jacobs's recordings of the Debussy Preludes are second to none. His humanely analytical approach and meticulous attention to detail serve all of the music—especially the better-known pieces—extremely well. Like the restorers of the Sistine Chapel, he scrapes the decades of accumulated interpretive treacle off favorites like "The Girl with the Flaxen Hair," yet manages to do so without robbing them of any of their essential tenderness and charm. There are also healthy helpings of passion and fireworks whenever they are required, together with a sly and knowing wit.

In all, this is one of the most satisfying of all Debussy recordings and a suitable memorial to a fine and talented man.

Mitsuko Uchida's recording of the twelve Etudes for Philips (422412-2 [CD]) gives the lie to the notion that she is solely a Mozart specialist. Her command of color and suggestion is as phenomenal as her manual dexterity, and the recorded sound is almost unbelievably real. Although the sound of Ivan Moravec's incomparable interpretations of the three *Estampes* has clearly begun to fade, the performances never will. Not even Walter Gieseking managed such control of dynamic shading in these sublimely subtle works; with the most pianistically sophisticated recording of the *Images* for Piano now available, this bargain Vox Unique CD (VU- 9005) is some bargain indeed.

Sonatas (3) for various instruments

Athena Ensemble. Chandos CHAN-8385 [CD].

Debussy was already in the final agonizing stages of cancer when he began writing the curiously anachronistic series of works that would conclude his career: three instrumental sonatas modeled on eighteenth-century forms. Though occasionally they might suggest a diminished concentration (especially in the Violin Sonata, his final piece), the Sonatas contain an abundance of intriguing ideas and ripe invention. The Cello Sonata seems, for the most part, to be deliberately written *against* the instrument's principal strengths; the Sonata for Flute, Viola, and Harp is so ethereal it seems the work of the inhabitant of another world.

All the performances by the Athena Ensemble are highly distinguished, and as a bonus the compact disc includes the *Petite pièce* and *Première Rapsodie* for Clarinet and Piano, together with the haunting *Syrinx* for solo flute. If the absolute last word on the Violin Sonata is absolutely necessary, then the listener can hear it spoken by violinist Kyung-Wha Chung and Radu Lupu in their suave and electrifying London recording (421154–2).

Songs

Ameling, Command, Mesplé, Souzay, von Stade; Baldwin, piano. Angel CDMC-64095.

This elegant collection on three medium-priced CDs gathers fifty-five of Debussy's eighty-plus songs in performances that represent some of the best Debussy singing ever captured in a recording studio. With the always sensitive and resourceful Dalton Baldwin as the common denominator, the series traces Debussy's growth as a composer of *chansons* from the beginning to the end of his career. Elly Ameling, Frederica von Stade, and Gerard Souzay are all but incomparable in this repertoire, with readings that teem with insight and surge with life. The recorded sound from the early- to mid-1970s is warm and natural, and although English translations of the texts would have been a helpful touch, this is a minor drawback to an absolutely indispensable release.

String Quartet in G minor

Guarneri Quartet. RCA 60609-2 [CD], 60909-4 [T].

A relatively early work (even though it was the last piece Debussy would compose in an identified key and to which he assigned an opus number), the String Quartet is nonetheless the finest of the composer's chamber works and a cornerstone of the modern quartet literature.

For years, the most meltingly beautiful of all its many recordings was a version by the Guarneri Quartet for RCA, now reissued on a dirt-cheap, no-frills (such as program notes) CD. Though the Guarneri have been perhaps the most maddeningly inconsistent of the world's great quartets, they are at their absolute best in both the Debussy and its inevitable companion piece, the String Quartet of Maurice Ravel. The playing has such a natural ease, sensitivity, and unanimity of frankly Romantic purpose that the recording easily sweeps a very crowded field.

Suite bergamasque; Estampes; Images oubliées; Pour le piano

Kocsis, piano. Philips 412118-2 [CD].

Given the fact that Debussy was responsible for some of the most original and popular piano music produced after Chopin, there is a surprising (one is tempted to say *scandalous*) dearth of first-rate recordings now in print. Perhaps we are simply going through one of those predictable droughts, during which the major recording companies are gearing up to reissue the Debussy piano treasures in their vaults as compact discs. Whatever the explanation, virtually none of the definitive recordings made by that arch-poet Walter Gieseking are readily available, apart from his shimmering recording of the Preludes (Angel CDH-61004 [CD]), and Debussy's greatest living interpreter, the Czech pianist Ivan Moravec, is currently represented by only a few tantalizing bits and pieces (see page 155).

This generous and brilliantly played collection by the young Hungarian pianist Zoltán Kocsis is one of the few genuine treasures in a shockingly barren field. Kocsis, who obviously possesses an important technique, plays with great subtlety and refinement. The *Suite bergamasque* is particularly successful, offering considerable wit, admirable control, and an attractively understated account of the famous *Clair de lune* (which the incomparable Victor Borge, before all of his inimitable performances, invariably introduced by saying, "English translation: Clear the saloon"). The recorded sound offers one of the most realistic recreations of piano timbre that has yet been heard.

Delibes, Léo (1836–1891)

Lakmé

Sutherland, Vanzo, Bacquier, Monte Carlo Opera
Orchestra, Bonynge. London 425485-2 [CD].

In the days when the glamorous Lily Pons was its most famous exponent, Delibes's tuneful and exotic *Lakmé* was known primarily for the tinkling "Bell Song," which the famous soprano typically sang with great abandon and a quarter step flat. (Her pitch was always a problem: Once, while working on a film with Max Steiner, she tearfully confessed on the sound stage that she could not sing properly "without *l'amour*." When Steiner picked up her then-husband Andre Kostelanetz at the airport the next day, he said, "Andre, do you think you could pump her up a half step or two?") Recently, thanks to its use in certain TV airline ads and in a peculiar film called *The Hunger*, the melting Act I duet "Dôme épais, le jasmin" has gone on to enjoy a similar life of its own.

For anyone interested in getting to know the rest of *Lakmé* —and what a lovely and fascinating opera it is—the London recording provides a near ideal introduction. Although Joan Sutherland's reading of the title role is something of a wash dramatically, her work in the "Bell Song" and "Dôme épais" is breathtaking. The rest of the cast is excellent, as is the recorded sound and Richard Bonynge's conducting.

Those not content with the fine Ormandy/Philadelphia Orchestra recording of the suites from *Coppélia* and *Sylvia* (Sony SBK-46551 [CD], SBT-46551 [T]), will find Bonynge's versions of the complete ballets equally delightful. The electrifying performance of the familiar "Procession of Bacchus" from *Sylvia*—listen especially to the swagger of the National Philharmonic brass—is almost in itself worth the price of the compact disc (London 425475. His version of *Coppélia* (414502-2 [CD], 414502-4 [T]) presents the ballet's finest recording ever and some of Bonynge's most pointed and imaginative work to date.

Delius, Frederick (1862–1934)

*Over the Hills and Far Away; Sleigh Ride; Marche
caprice; Brigg Fair (An English Rhapsody); Florida
Suite; Dance Rhapsody No. 2; Summer Evening; On
Hearing the First Cuckoo in Spring; Summer Night on
the River; A Song Before Sunrise; Intermezzo from
Fennimore and Gerda; Prelude to Irmelin; Songs of
Sunset*

> Forrester, contralto; Cameron, baritone; Beecham Choral
> Society, Royal Philharmonic Orchestra, Beecham. Angel
> CDCB-47509 [CD].

With the possible exception of the amoral, egomaniacal, virulently anti-Semitic, and treacherous Richard Wagner, who repaid
the unswerving loyalty of at least two of his most ardent supporters
by sleeping with their wives, Frederick Delius, of all the great
composers, was probably the most thoroughly unpleasant human
being. Cruel, ruthless, pathologically selfish, and a self-styled incarnation of Nietzsche's idealized Nordic superman, Delius fought
his long, lonely struggle for recognition while making the lives of
everyone around him (especially that of his devoted, long-suffering
wife Jelka) miserable. As much as his apologists, his amanuensis
Eric Fenby and the Australian composer Percy Grainger have tried
to pardon his unpardonable behavior, Delius, to the day he died (a
blind and paralyzed victim of tertiary neurosyphilis) was a complete and thoroughgoing beast.

And yet contained within this difficult, often despicable man
was one of the most original and rarified talents in musical history.
At its best, Delius's music is among the most delicate and ineffably
gentle ever produced by an English composer, and as one of the last
of the late-Romantic nature poets, he remains unique.

For those of us who are hopelessly addicted to his admittedly
limited but irresistibly appealing art, or for those perfectly sensible,
though sadly misguided souls who gag at the very mention of his
name, this comprehensive Angel recording is the most valuable
single release since the introduction of the compact disc. For contained on these two tightly packed and handsomely remastered

CDs are all the stereo recordings of Delius's music that his greatest champion, Sir Thomas Beecham, ever made.

In Beecham's hands (though, alas, in few others' since the conductor's death) the music of Delius clearly emerges as that of a major composer. Almost every bar of these famous performances is shot through with Beecham's special interpretive wizardry. *On Hearing the First Cuckoo in Spring* very nearly says as much as the whole of Beethoven's *Pastorale* Symphony, and the legendary version of *Brigg Fair* sounds not only like the finest Delius recording ever made, but also preciously close to the most magical fifteen minutes in recording history.

For dyed-in-the-wool Delians, this is an invaluable release; for the unconverted, an ideal invitation to join us.

Sea Drift; *Songs of Farewell*; *Songs of Sunset*

Soloists, Bournemouth Symphony Orchestra and Chorus, Hickox. Chandos CHAN-9214.

As a partial setting for Walt Whitman's moving poem "Out of the Cradle Endlessly Rocking" (which is said also to have inspired the cradle scenes in D. W. Griffith's screen classic *Intolerance*), *Sea Drift* not only has a fair claim to being Delius's masterpiece but is also one of the few indisputably great choral works of the twentieth century. Whitman's tale of a child's coming to terms with the terror and beauty of death struck a resonant chord in Delius. He captures to perfection the poignant little drama of the seabird losing and mourning its mate, and evokes the scents and sounds of the sea as magically as any composer ever has.

At the beginning of his career, Richard Hickox made a thrilling recording of this great work for English Decca, available until recently on a London compact disc. Happily, the new version for Chandos is in every way more sumptuous and refined. Hickox coaxes committed and rapturous performances from his alert forces and Chandos's engineers, as usual, respond with their very best sound. Together with versions of the *Songs of Farewell* and *Songs of Sunset* that rival those of Fenby and Beecham, this is the finest recording of Delius choral music now available.

*A*quarelles (2); *Caprice and Elegy*; *Fantastic Dance*;
Prelude to *Irmelin*; "La Calinda" from *Koanga*;
Cynara; *Idyll*; *A Late Lark*; *A Song of Summer*; *Songs of Farewell*

> Soloists, Ambrosian Opera Chorus, Royal Philharmonic,
> Fenby. Unicorn DKPC-9008/09 [CD].

These recordings by Eric Fenby, who took dictation and abuse from Delius during the composer's final years, would be remarkable for their historic value alone. To hear the molten *Song of Summer* led by the man who actually wrote it down, note by note, makes for a slightly eerie experience. For that matter, Delius's ghost hangs almost palpably over all these proceedings, as well it should, since they are overseen by someone who knew him—both as man and musician—as intimately as anyone.

Beyond their documentary interest, these are absolutely marvelous performances, as loving and individual as Beecham's, which they complement, but in no way supplant. While the versions of *A Song of Summer*, the *Irmelin* Prelude (which Fenby arranged), and the little-known *Fantastic Dance* (a piece Delius dedicated to Fenby) are understandably authoritative, it is the conductor's handling of the larger works that makes the recording so priceless. The extended love scene called *Idyll* (for soprano, baritone, and orchestra) has a Puccini-like redolence, and the *Songs of Farewell*, in Fenby's hands, emerges as one of the composer's most singular and unforgettable works.

The sensitive, devoted contributions of the soloists, the Ambrosian Singers, and the great Royal Philharmonic only help to prove that for this composer, there *is* life after Beecham.

A Village Romeo and Juliet

> Field, Davies, Hampson, Mora, Dean, Schoenberg Chorus,
> Austrian Radio Symphony, Mackerras. Argo 430275-2
> [CD].

A Village Romeo and Juliet, the fifth of Delius's six operas, is easily his most successful work for the stage. The familiar, matzo-thin plot, centered on a feud between a pair of Swiss families and the two children tragically caught in between, drew from the composer some of his most ravishing music, including the unspeakably touching "Walk to the Paradise Garden."

The gap left by the withdrawal of Sir Charles Groves's sumptuous recording from the 1970s has been brilliantly filled by Sir Charles Mackerras's new version, which is far and away the finest recording of a Delius opera yet made. All of the singers—especially Helen Field and Arthur Davies as the kids and the heartthrob baritone Thomas Hampson as the Dark Fiddler—are excellent, and Mackerras's conducting has a warmth and felicity that recalls Beecham at his best.

One only hopes this is the first in a series.

Violin Concerto; *Légende* for Violin and Orchestra; Suite for Violin and Orchestra

Holmes, violin; Royal Philharmonic, Handley. Unicorn DKPCD-9040 [CD], DPKC-9040 [T].

The Delius Violin Concerto is one of several works that give the lie to the notion the composer was essentially a miniaturist uncomfortable with the larger musical forms. True, the architecture and underlying organization of Delius's most ambitious instrumental work may not be as obvious as in the more traditional concertos of Elgar and Walton, but with some help from an inspired soloist and an insightful conductor, the Delius seems to emerge as the equal of either.

Ralph Holmes is a meticulous and passionate advocate of the Concerto, a musician who spares no effort to illuminate the music without a hint of self-serving display. In addition to the warmth and beauty of the playing, the natural flow of the musical argument has never been captured more convincingly. In this the soloist is aided and abetted by one of the great Delians of modern times. Like Beecham, Vernon Handley has an instinctive grasp of the composer's highly individual idiom, all the more obvious in the far weaker but thoroughly agreeable *Légende* and Suite, which round out the disc.

Perhaps even more impressive is Handley's recording with the Ulster Orchestra for Chandos of two major Delius scores, the *North Country Sketches* and the *Florida Suite* (CHAN-8413 [CD]). Again like Beecham, Handley makes the youthful suite by the twenty-five-year old composer seem far more forward-looking and original than it probably is, while the much later *North Country Sketches* is revealed again as one of the composer's supreme achievements.

Diamond, David (1915–)

Symphony No. 2; Symphony No. 4; *Concerto for Small Orchestra*

Seattle Symphony, New York Chamber Symphony, Schwarz. Delos DE-3093 [CD].

It is in the work of David Diamond that a particular species of American symphony may have reached its most polished and exuberant form of expression. During the late 1940s and early '50s, Diamond became one of the principal purveyors for the neoclassical American symphony, a composer whose finest works in the form rival the best brought forth upon this continent.

The three works presented in the first volume in Delos's Diamond series show the composer at his most characteristic and attractive. If Gerard Schwarz's performance of the wonderful Symphony No. 4 doesn't completely efface the memory of Leonard Bernstein's pioneering recording from 1958, it is still a superb reading, with warmth, energy, and individuality to burn. Here, as in the other pieces, Schwarz continues to reveal himself as the most sympathetic and significant champion American music has had since the death of Howard Hanson.

The subsequent installments in the Diamond series have proven no less valuable. The powerful Symphony No. 3, together with the elegant *Romeo and Juliet*, the moving *Psalm*, and the eloquent *Kaddish* for Cello and Orchestra fill the second volume (DE-3093 [CD]). The Symphony No. 1, Second Violin Concerto, and the fascinating tone poem based on e.e. cumming's *The Enormous Room* make up volume 3.

Anyone responding to Diamond's fresh and bracing idiom will certainly want to investigate the music of two of his near-contemporaries. The sparkling *Symphony for Classical Orchestra* by Harold Shapero, together with the snappy *Nine-Minute Overture*, are brilliantly served by André Previn and the Los Angeles Philharmonic (New World NW-373-2 [CD]).

The extent of what American music lost when the gifted Irving Fine died in 1962 at the age of forty-seven may be guessed from his stunningly effective Symphony, written in the last year of his life. Captured in a live performance by the Boston Symphony under the composer's direction, it is now available from Phoenix (PHCD-106 [CD]). Fine's *Partita* of 1948, which has a fair claim to being the finest woodwind quintet yet written by an American, can be found on a superlative album of Fine's chamber music from Elektra/Nonesuch (79175-2 [CD], 79175-4 [T].)

Dohnányi, Ernst von

(1877–1960)

Variations on a Nursery Song

Wild, piano; New Philharmonia Orchestra, C. von Dohnányi. Chesky CD-13 [CD].

Until relatively recent times, the smart money insisted that Ernst von Dohnányi was the greatest Hungarian composer of the twentieth century. A late Romantic whose painstaking craftsmanship earned him the sobriquet "the Hungarian Brahms," Dohnányi would eventually be overtaken and almost completely overshadowed by his younger, more radical contemporaries Béla Bartók and Zoltán Kodály. In fact, the extent to which Dohnányi's reputation is now in eclipse may be gathered from the fact that only a handful of recordings of his most popular piece, the witty and ingratiating *Variations on a Nursery Song*, are available.

Why the American pianist Earl Wild is not better known has always been something of a mystery. Technically, he is one of the most formidably equipped pianists of his generation. And although a musician of considerable taste and refinement, he is also among the more viscerally exciting musicians of our time. As in his superb set of the Rachmaninoff concertos (see page 411), this recording from 1967 finds him at the peak of his form. The interpretation is as fiery as it is playful, featuring a combination of a thunderous pianism that recalls the legends of the old barnstorming days and an ability to spin out the music's delicate filigree that is almost unheard of today.

Christoph von Dohnányi is a predictably sympathetic advocate of his grandfather's music, in both his best-known piece and the virtually unknown *Capriccio* in F minor that accompanies it. Another Wild performance—in both senses of the phrase—rounds out this bargain release: the old *Reader's Digest* recording of the Tchaikovsky First Concerto that could stand a cue ball's hair on end.

Donizetti, Gaetano

(1797–1848)

L'elisir d'amore

> Sutherland, Pavarotti, Malas, Cossa, Ambrosian Opera Chorus, English Chamber Orchestra, Bonynge. London 414461-2 [CD].

Even as one who has never been carried away by Dame Joan "The Woman Without a Tongue" Sutherland, and who cordially (well actually, *virulently*) despises what the self-indulgent, self-congratulatory Luciano Pavarotti has become—even *I* can recognize one of the great Donizetti recordings when I hear it. As a comedienne, Sutherland is deliciously effective: coy, girlish, warmly and irresistibly human—in short, all of those things that she so rarely is elsewhere. Pavarotti, too, is tremendous fun as the lovesick Nemorino, and his singing of the show's hit tune, "Una furtiva lagrima," contains some of the best work of his career. Spiro Malas's Dr. Dulcamara is a wonder of transparent, W. C. Fields–like hokum, and Richard Bonynge's touch is as light-fingered as a pickpocket's.

The same team is responsible for an equally engaging recording of Donizetti's *Daughter of the Regiment* (London 414520-2 [CD])—indeed, the *very* recording in which Pavarotti pops all those ringing high Cs. Sutherland is at her most imposing in the 1987 recording of *Anna Bolena* (London 421096-2 [CD]), with Samuel Ramey leading the excellent supporting cast. London has also reissued its effervescent 1964 Vienna recording of *Don Pasquale* (433036-2 [CD]), with the droll Fernando Corena in the title role and István Kértesz conducting as though to the bel canto manner born.

Lucia di Lammermoor

> Callas, Tagliavini, Cappuccilli, Ladysz, Philharmonia Orchestra and Chorus, Serafin. Angel CDCB-47440 [CD], 4AV-34000 [T].

More than any other of Gaetano Donizetti's sixty-odd operas, which were often produced at the mind-boggling rate of eight to ten per year (a contemporary caricature shows the composer seated at a desk, his famous mop of hair askew, writing with two hands simultaneously), *Lucia di Lammermoor* is the archetypal representative of all that is best *and* most ridiculous in bel canto opera. As theater, it is both grippingly effective and utterly absurd. The famous Sextet is one of the high-water marks of nineteenth-century ensemble writing, the long and demanding mad scene a silly and thinly veiled excuse for a twenty-minute coloratura concert. (Of course, it could be argued that Lucia's lengthy conversation with an equally energetic flute is no more preposterous than that goofy scene the recently stabbed Gilda, fresh from her gunnysack, is asked to deliver at the end of Verdi's *Rigoletto*, or the similarly exhausting vocal and dramatic tour de force the consumptive Violetta uses to conclude that same composer's *La Traviata*.) But then again, loving opera has always been dependent on a healthy disregard for common sense. And *Lucia di Lammermoor*, with the proper attitude, and more important, the proper cast, can be as rewarding an experience as the opera house has to offer.

Vocally, the most impressive Lucia of modern times was the young Joan Sutherland, whose 1959 London recording recalled the exploits of the almost mythic Luisa Tetrazzini, the great turn-of-the-century diva who today is best remembered for the recipe for the chicken and spaghetti dish that bears her name. (Tetrazzini's astonishing artistry is now conveniently preserved on a set of five handsomely produced Pearl CDs [GEMM CDS-9220], which contain all the singer's known recordings from 1903 through 1922. As examples of vocal legerdemain, these recordings may never be surpassed, and the set is required listening for anyone interested in opera, singing, or the possibilities of the human voice.) Dramatically and emotionally, the Sutherland Lucia was a rather different matter, and in her far less impressive remake with her husband Richard Bonynge, what were once merely Sutherland eccentricities had already become annoying clichés. The diction made almost every word incomprehensible, and that droopy, sad-little-girl delivery made you want to throw her down the nearest open manhole.

What the opera *should* be, as both a dramatic and vocal experience, is still best suggested by the classic recording made by Maria Callas. Like the Callas *Norma*, it is an exceedingly rich and beautiful characterization. It contains some of the finest singing that Callas would ever deliver in a recording studio. The famous mad scene, for once, is not the unintentionally uproarious joke it usually is, but a riveting piece of theater cut from the same cloth as Shakespeare's scene on the blasted heath in *King Lear*. The rest of the cast, even the aging tenor, Ferrucio Tagliavini, is more than adequate. And the veteran Tullio Serafin gives us countless thrilling moments that confirm his reputation as one of the last of the great blood-and-thunder opera conductors. For Callas fans, or for anyone interested in making the rare acquaintance of *Lucia di Lammermoor* as convincing musical drama, this one is an absolute must.

Dukas, Paul (1865–1935)

The Sorcerer's Apprentice

New York Philharmonic, Bernstein. CBS MYK-37769 [CD], MTY-37769 [T].

Don't let any of those slightly smug and self-important music lovers who are going through that inevitable, pseudosophisticated "Trashing the Warhorses" phase of their development sway you. In spite of the fact this piece *did* serve as the backdrop for one of Mickey Mouse's greatest performances, in that otherwise turgid and self-conscious classic *Fantasia*, it is still one of the most dazzlingly inventive tone poems in musical history.

Of the twenty of so versions of *L'apprenti sorcier* that are currently available, the winner and still champ is Leonard Bernstein's early CBS recording. The conductor earns high marks for both wit and drama, and the performance also has a visual acuity that makes the playing extremely cinematic in the best possible sense of the word.

For those who might find the thirty-year-old recorded sound a trifle muddy—and it was not, even in its day, one of Columbia's more impressive sonic efforts—Mariss Janson's EMI recording with the Oslo Philharmonic (CDD 64291 [CD]) is one of the most spectacular sounding in years.

The best available recording of Dukas's "other" work, the ballet *La Péri*, remains the 1958 Ernest Ansermet recording, now recycled as part of the Ansermet Edition from London (433714-2 [CD]). If the sound has become slightly tubby and brittle, the performance is still pretty sensational, especially in the thrilling fanfare. Ideally, either David Zinman's recording for Philips or Pierre Boulez's on CBS should be reissued; until they are, Ansermet will do just fine.

Duruflé, Maurice (1902–1986)

Requiem

Murray, Allen, Corydon Singers, English Chamber
Orchestra, Best. Hyperion CDA-66191 [CD].

Like his teacher Paul Dukas, the talented French organist and
composer Maurice Duruflé seems destined to be remembered for
a single work, the sweetly beautiful Requiem composed in 1947.
Consciously modeled on the Requiem of Gabriel Fauré, Duruflé's
masterpiece is similar in its structure, thematic content, and gently
consoling message, although the similarities on repeated hearings
prove increasingly superficial. The Duruflé stands on its own as a
sincerely felt, quietly moving work with more real religious feeling
than many Requiems three times its age and twice its size.

Matthew Best leads his fine Corydon singers through an eloquent performance of the piece, with singing that seems the last
word in refinement and devotion. Ann Murray and Thomas Allen
are wonderfully expressive soloists and the chamber orchestra accompaniment is both pointed and discreet. With the composer's
starkly haunting *Four Motets on Gregorian Chants*, this is the ideal
introduction to an unassuming masterpiece.

Dutilleux, Henri (1916–)

Symphony No. 1; *Timbres, espace, mouvement*

Lyon Orchestre National, Baudo. Harmonia Mundi 905159 [CD].

Over the years the French composer Henri Dutilleux has maintained a consistently lower profile than his far more celebrated near-contemporary Olivier Messiaen. For one thing, Dutilleux has tended to work in more traditional forms, thus earning him the undeserved reputation of being an "academic" composer; for another, he tends to produce music utterly free of the sort of gimmickry—from catchy, politically correct subjects and titles to tiresome Left Bank mysticism—that helped Messiaen to catch on. Although posterity will of course be the judge, I tend to suspect that when the smoke clears in the middle of the next century, Dutilleux will emerge the far more significant voice.

One of the best ways to make the acquaintance of this highly individual composer is through the fascinating First Symphony, written in 1951 to portray the birth and death of a dream. In the composer's words, "The music emerges from the shadow in the first movement only to return whence it came in the very last ones. Thus there is established a transition between the real and imaginary world. It is a little like the inception and unfolding of a dream." The music is suitably fanciful and mysterious, with an astonishing range of orchestral color and texture and no mean emotional clout. Serge Baudo and the Lyon Orchestra play it as though it were a standard repertoire item, which it certainly deserves to be.

Those who repond to the Symphony and its later, equally gripping companion piece should waste no time investigating the stunning *L'Arbre des songes*, one of the most beautiful of contemporary violin concertos, written in 1985 for Isaac Stern (Sony MK-42449 [CD]), or the darkly poetic string quartet, *Ainsi la nuit* available on IMP Masters (MCD-17 [CD]).

Dvořák, Antonín (1841–1904)

Concerto in B minor for Cello and Orchestra

Feuermann, cello; Berlin State Opera Orchestra, Taube.
Pearl GEMM CDS-9077 [CD].

Fournier, cello; Berlin Philharmonic, Szell. Deutsche
Grammophon 429155-2 [CD], 429155-4 [T].

Du Pré, cello; Chicago Symphony, Barenboim. Angel CDC-
47614.

The events that led to the composition of this greatest of all
cello concertos are movingly documented in Josef Škvorecký's magnificent 1987 novel *Dvořák in Love* (Knopf), probably the finest
fictional treatment of the life of any composer. The Concerto's
second movement was written as an elegy for the composer's sister-
in-law, the only woman with whom Dvořák was ever in love. In
fact, embedded in this poignant outpouring of grief is a quotation
from an early song Dvořák wrote for Josefina Čermáková, a few
years before he married her sister, Anna.

The Dvořák Cello Concerto has been brilliantly served in the
recording studio, beginning in 1929 with what remains the most
spellbinding realization of the solo part. In that classic recording by
cellist Emanuel Feuermann, the recorded sound is fairly dismal even
by the standards of the time, and the Berlin State Opera Orchestra
under Michael Taube was barely equal to the task. Still, it is this
recording, more than any other, that demonstrates so conclusively
why Feuermann, and not Pablo Casals, was the great cellist of the
twentieth century. The combination of bravado, patrician phrasing,
and flawless technique that Feuermann brought to the Concerto has
never been duplicated. Hearing this fine Pearl restoration, together
with versions of the Haydn D Major Cello Concerto, Bruch's *Kol
Nidrei*, and a half dozen charming encore pieces, makes us realize
anew what the world lost when Emanuel Feuermann died during
a routine operation in 1942, a few months short of his fortieth
birthday.

The modern recording that comes closest to approaching the
brilliance and passion of Feuermann's, is that pointedly dramatic
interpretation by Pierre Fournier and George Szell, recorded in
Berlin in the 1960s and now available on Deutsche Grammophon.

Fournier plays the solo part with fire, subtlety, and conviction, and Szell, who led the Czech Philharmonic in Casals's famous recording of 1937, gives what is arguably his most intense and involving recorded performance. (For a Feuermann-Szell recording in up-to-date sound, I would willingly trade my priceless baseball autographed by Mickey Mantle, 10 percent of my annual income, and my first-born male child.)

Jacqueline Du Pré's Angel recording with Daniel Barenboim and the Chicago Symphony is also very special. It is a red-blooded, slightly (but always persuasively) wayward interpretation in which the playing may owe something to that of her teacher, Mstislav Rostropovich, but which fortunately lacks his tendency to vulgarity and self-indulgence. Barenboim, the cellist's husband, offers a sweepingly romantic yet sensitive accompaniment, and both the orchestra and recorded sound are absolutely first-rate.

Concerto in A minor for Violin and Orchestra

Perlman, violin; London Philharmonic, Barenboim. Angel CDC-47168 [CD].

Somewhere between that Mount Everest of cello concertos and the foothills of his likable but hopelessly minor Piano Concerto lies the concerto that Dvořák wrote for violin, a work that has never quite managed to challenge the popularity of the Bruch or Tchaikovsky concertos, though in terms of quality it is easily the equal of either.

Written for Brahms's great friend, the Hungarian-born virtuoso Joseph Joachim, the piece cost Dvořák an unusual amount of time and anguish. The maniacally fastidious Joachim kept the score for nearly two years, finally returning it with so many suggestions for "improvements" that Dvořák all but rewrote the solo part. The result—which Joachim never got around to actually playing—is one of the most broadly rhapsodic of nineteenth-century violin concertos, a lush, yearning, quintessentially Romantic work rounded off by a spirited rondo-finale whose principal theme, once heard, is all but impossible to forget.

Despite some fine recent releases—the teenage Japanese violinist Midori's stylish outing for CBS (MT-44923 [T]), and a swashbuckling Deutsche Grammophon recording by Schlomo Mintz—

Itzhak Perlman's Angel recording from the 1970s still comfortably dominates the field. The most striking thing in the Perlman interpretation is the ease with which he evokes the "Bohemian" elements in the score. The playing, in fact, is so idiomatic that one wonders if he might not have more than a few drops of Czech blood in his veins. Daniel Barenboim is an alert and able partner, and the remastered recorded sound more than holds its own with the best today.

In spite of its weaknesses, the Dvořák Piano Concerto has never gone begging for first-rate recordings; the most memorable features the great Rudolf Firkusny on RCA (09026-60781-2 [CD]). Recorded recently in Prague at the concert that marked his return to his homeland after an exile of nearly a half century, Firkusny's performance is not only full of warmth and character, it is also remarkably vibrant and technically secure for a pianist approaching eighty. As an historic document it is undeniably moving, as touching in its way as the recordings of concerts that another prodigal son, the conductor Rafael Kubelík, gave at about the same time.

Overtures

Ulster Orchestra, Handley. Chandos CHAN-8453 [CD].

Czech Philharmonic, Ančerl. Supraphon 11-0605-2 [CD].

Although they usually turn up as filler on recordings of the symphonies, the three overtures Dvořák composed in 1891 were conceived—and should be presented—as a single, indissoluble work with the general title *Nature, Life, and Love*. The "Life" section—the *Carnival* Overture—became an instant sensation, and still overshadows the evocative *In Nature's Realm*, and what is, by far, the greatest panel of the tryptych, the searing Shakespearean fantasy, *Othello*.

Though *Carnival* has had more brilliant and daring performances—those by Rafael Kubelík, István Kertész, George Szell, and especially Fritz Reiner are not easily forgotten—the excellent Ulster Orchestra under Vernon Handley bring more than enough moxie to that pops-concert favorite, and offer the strongest versions of *Othello* and *In Nature's Realm* currently in print. *In Nature's Realm* is the verdant tone poem the composer intended, and *Othello* seems the stuff of genuine tragedy, without once flirting with melodrama or hysterics. The interpretation of the *Scherzo capriccioso* that fills out the disc is also top drawer, as are the orchestral execution and recorded sound.

Considerably less well recorded are the classic interpretations from the 1960s by the Czech Philharmonic led by Karel Ančerl. In addition to the late trilogy, the CD offers brilliantly idiomatic readings of the *Hussite* and *My Home* Overtures played as only this orchestra can. The quality of the music making and the reasonable price more than make up for the distant, slightly fuzzy recorded sound.

Piano Music

Firkusny, piano. Vox CDX-5058 [CD].

Dating from the early 1970s and available now as part of a two-CD set that also features rarely heard piano works by Smetana, Benda, Dussek, Tomásek, and Vorisek, Rudolf Firkusny's performances of some of the most important of Dvořák's solo piano music are the most distinguished yet recorded. In addition to the Mazurkas and the Humoresques—his version of the famous G-flat Humoresque is a model of disarming simplicity—the *Poetic Tone Pictures* are played with a tenderness and affection all but impossible to resist.

Among the other works featured on this treasurable recital is the most famous sonata written by the great keyboard virtuoso of the late Classical period, Jan Ladislav Dussek. As Frederick Marvin's splendid cycle on a series of Genesis LPs clearly proved, Dussek's sonatas were second only to Beethoven's in terms of quality and depth. Firkusny's poised yet fiery performance of *L'Invocation* will leave you anxious to hear more.

Quintet for Piano and Strings in A, Op. 81; Quartets (2) for Piano and Strings; Bagatelles

Firkusny, piano; Juilliard String Quartet. Odyssey MB2K-45672 [CD].

By any definition, these two dirt-cheap Odyssey CDs constitute an incredible bargain. Though not as well known, perhaps, as the *American* Quartet or the *Dumky* Trio, the A Major Piano Quintet is among the most attractive and accomplished of Dvořák's chamber works, which places it with the greatest chamber music of the Romantic era. The Piano Quartets are hardly less appealing, and the delectable Bagatelles, scored for the unusual combination of strings and harmonium, make a haunting physical sound unique in nineteenth-century music.

That dean of Czech pianists, Rudolf Firkusny, is obviously an ideal exponent of an idiom that has flowed through his veins since childhood. (As a very young boy, he played some of Janáček's music for the aging composer, who was mightily impressed.) The Juilliard String Quartet prove to be perfect accomplices in an enterprise that will steal your heart without leaving you broke.

Requiem

Soloists, Ambrosian Opera Chorus, London Symphony Orchestra, Kertész. London 421810-2 [CD].

At the height of his European fame in 1884, Dvořák made his first trip to England, where, like Mendelssohn a generation earlier, he was treated as a conquering hero. From his first appearance in London in March 1884, leading a performance of the Stabat Mater at the Albert Hall, the English took Dvořák to their hearts, just as he took them to his. It was for the oratorio-mad English that Dvořák would write some of his most ambitious scores: the cantata *The Spectre's Bride*, the epic Oratorio *St. Ludmilla* and the devout and haunting Requiem.

If not quite the equal of those by Verdi and Brahms, then the Dvořák Requiem is one of the most moving such works of the late-Romantic era, especially in a performance as intensely involved and involving as this one. István Kertész again reveals his natural affinity for Dvořák's music with an interpretation that disguises the Requiem's weaker moments while emphasizing the stronger ones. The powerfully dramatic ebb and flow of Kertész's interpretation is captured in vintage London late-'60s sound; with magnificent versions of Kodály's *Hymn of Zrinyi* and *Psalmus hungaricus* as the generous filler, this medium-priced two-CD set is a not-to-be-missed bargain.

Rusalka

Beňačková, Soukupová, Ochman, Novák, Prague
Philharmonic Chorus, Czech Philharmonic Orchestra,
Neumann. Supraphon 10-3641 [CD].

On his return home after his protracted stay in America, where he was both deeply homesick and phenomenally productive, Dvořák entered what would prove to be the most nationalistic phase of his career. In the last years of his life, he devoted himself entirely to symphonic poems and operas based on Czech folk stories: from the series of orchestral ballads based on stories by Karel Jaromir Erben (see page 181), to the fairy-tale opera in which a water sprite confesses to the moon that she has fallen in love with a prince and now wishes to become human.

The last but one and by far the most successful of Dvořák's thirteen operas, *Rusalka* received its first performance in March 1901, five months before the composer celebrated his sixtieth birthday. Like all of Dvořák's operas, *Rusalka* has had some difficulty holding the stage over the years (I once saw a wonderful performance at the National Theater in Prague which in spite of the brilliant production and glorious singing seemed about a half hour too long), yet its dramatic shortcomings are barely noticeable in this spellbinding recording, featuring the reigning Czech diva of our time and the incomparable Czech Philharmonic in the pit. Gabriela Beňačková's performance of the molten "Mesicku na nebi hlubokem"—the love theme from *Driving Miss Daisy*—is ravishing, as is the work of the orchestra throughout. All in all, this is a performance that finally begins to suggest the greatness of one of Dvořák's most beautiful scores.

Serenade for Strings in E, Op. 22; Serenade for Winds in D minor, Op. 44

Academy of St. Martin-in-the-Fields, Marriner. Philips
400020-2 [CD].

There has never been a day so wretched, a problem so insoluble, a night so long, a winter so bleak, a toothache so painful that one or the other of these enchanting works couldn't cure it. On those days when I walk in the door drained, disgruntled, disillusioned, full of contempt for all things human, and beating down an insane desire to kick the cat, I put on one of the Dvořák Serenades, make for the nearest chair, and within a few minutes a dippy grin—the external manifestation of a mood of avuncular forgiveness and beatific peace—invariably steals over my face. If only this inexhaustibly charming music were a little better known, many of the nation's psychiatrists would have to start looking for honest work.

Sir Neville Marriner's glowing Philips recording contains the most radiant performances of both Serenades on the market today. The string tone in the Op. 22 is the aural equivalent of a morning in early June; the wind playing in the Op. 44 is a marvel of individuality and character. (The thin, nasal twang of English oboes has never been one of my favorite sounds; here, I hardly notice.)

In a word, yummy.

Slavonic Dances, Opp. 46 and 72

Cleveland Orchestra, Szell. CBS/Sony 44802 [CD], Odyssey 34626/7 [T].

Royal Philharmonic, Dorati. London 411735-2.

Once, during the interval of a Cleveland Orchestra rehearsal at Severance Hall, a member of the orchestra greeted a visiting friend by saying, after carefully looking over his shoulder to see who might be listening, "Welcome to the American home of Bohemian Culture." And throughout his tenure with the orchestra, George Szell was an enthusiastic champion of the music of Dvořák, Smetana, and that Moravian giant, Leoš Janáček. Although born in Budapest, Szell had considerable Czech blood in his veins; he studied in Prague, and early in his conducting career was a familiar fixture in the Bohemian capital.

Szell's recordings of these most popular works are the only ones that bear favorable comparison with Václav Talich's unsurpassable versions from the late 1940s, available now on Supraphon SUP-111897 [CD]. (Talich's pioneering recording from 1935, whose sound probably makes it a "collectors only" item, has surfaced on Music and Arts CD-658-1 [CD]). The playing of the Cleveland Orchestra is a wonder of brilliance and flexibility, and the conductor, while demanding the last word in virtuoso execution, never overlooks the music's wealth of subtle color and irrepressible charm.

From a somewhat less dizzying height, Antal Dorati's London recording is also very satisfying, especially if nearly flawless recorded sound is an absolute must.

Songs

Beňačková, soprano; Firkusny, piano. RCA 09025-60823-2 [CD].

For a composer with such an effortless gift of melody, it's rather surprising that song should have accounted for such a relatively unimportant part of Dvořák's total output. Although written at virtually every stage of his career—from a small 1865 collection of four items published as his Op. 2 through the *Biblical Songs* of 1895—the songs tend to be charming rather than significant: poetic, delightful, and decidedly minor works.

In their generous and well-chosen collection, interspersed with songs by Janáček and Martinu, Gabriela Beňačková and Rudolf Firkusny offer one of the finest recitals of Dvořák songs ever recorded. Whether expressing the aching sorrow of the darker *Biblical Songs* or the robust joys of the *Gypsy Songs*, these two great artists seem ideally suited to both the material and each other.

String Quartet No. 12 in F, Op. 96 *American*

Talich Quartet. Calliope CAL-9617 [CD], 4617 [T].

Written during a few days of the summer vacation the composer spent in the amiable, hard-drinking Czech colony of Spillville, Iowa, where he also completed the *New World* Symphony, Dvořák's *American* Quartet is only the most famous and colorful of those fourteen works which, taken together, constitute the most important contribution a nineteenth-century composer would make to the form after the death of Franz Schubert. Like the *New World* Symphony, the *American* Quartet was inspired by Dvořák's passionate love affair with the sights and sounds of the United States, although like the Symphony it does not contain, as has been so frequently suggested, a single American folk tune. (The subtitle, incidentally, was not the composer's, but instead the idea of a discreet publisher who sought to correct the brazen stupidity of an unforgivably insensitive time. Shamefully, on the original title page, the F Major Quartet was called "The Nigger.")

With the warmly appealing Deutsche Grammophon recording by the Prague Quartet available only in the sumptuous nine-CD box from Deutsche Grammophon (429193-2) that contains all of the composer's string quartets, this handsome Calliope recording by the Talich Quartet can be recommended without hesitation. The group, founded by a nephew of the great Czech conductor Václav Talich, plays with an engaging mixture of polish and youthful enthusiasm. Like the Prague and Smetana Quartets, they have this music in their bones, and unlike non-Czech groups, which tend to overemphasize the music's "New World" color, they never forget that this great work is first and foremost an intensely Bohemian score. Also, their performance of the Op. 61 Quartet (No. 11) is so engaging that if you haven't begun to explore Dvořák's lesser-known chamber works, the urge to do so will probably be overwhelming.

String Quartets: No. 10 in E-flat, Op. 51; No. 12 in F, Op. 96 *American*; No. 13 in G, Op. 106; No. 14 in A-flat, Op. 105

> Panocha Quartet. Supraphon C37-7910 [CD] (Nos. 10 and 13); C37-7565 [CD] (Nos. 12 and 14).

If they stay together and stay healthy (to use an indispensable sportscaster's cliché), the young Panocha Quartet should become one of the dominant chamber ensembles of the next quarter century. On the basis of the recordings they have made so far, and some firsthand experience hearing them on their last American tour, I am convinced they are already one of the finest quartets around.

Paradoxically for a quartet, their principal strength—aside from a highly evolved musicality and very sophisticated technique—is their unwillingness to forget their own individual identities for the sake of that mushy, pasteurized uniformity so many groups seem obsessed with these days. If they have a counterpart among the older outfits, it is the Borodin Quartet, another collection of rugged individualists who are not only instantly recognizable *as* individuals but who also add up to an even more appealing whole.

There are no better versions of these late Dvořák quartets currently available. The performances are understandably fresh and youthful, but are also (to coin a phrase) mature beyond their years. Only the Talich Quartet digs into this music with such abandon, authority, and finesse.

If this is the beginning of a cycle of *all* the Dvořák quartets, be prepared to drop some serious cash. You won't regret it.

Symphonic Poems (complete)

Scottish National Orchestra, Järvi. Chandos CHAN-8798/
99 [CD], DBTD-2019 [T].

Although they are not as consistently inspired as his symphonies and overtures, Dvořák's symphonic poems are mature, colorful settings of some of the wonderfully gruesome folk stories collected by K. J. Erben: stories rife with murder, betrayal, dismemberment, and assorted mayhem—something for the whole family.

While not quite as magical as the recently withdrawn Kubelik set or the legendary recordings that Václav Talich made in the early 1950s, the performances by the Scottish National Orchestra under Neeme Järvi are nonetheless very fine. Like Kubelik, Järvi is a natural and arresting storyteller who leads the listener through the gory plots so graphically that one need not necessarily know what's going on to enjoy them. (People with sensitive stomachs would probably *not* want to know.) As always, the Scottish National Orchestra under Järvi sound like one of the best in Europe, and as always, the Chandos recording is ideal.

Symphonies (9)

Berlin Philharmonic, Kubelik. Deutsche Grammophon
423120-2 [CD].

Fifty or even twenty-five years ago it would have been nearly impossible to convince the average music lover that there were really nine, as opposed to only three Dvořák symphonies. Ironically enough, it was the composer himself who became the principal culprit in the misunderstanding, since he considered the F Major Symphony (No. 5) of 1875 his first mature work in the form and preferred to forget the rest. (He quite literally forgot a couple of the early works, neither of which would be performed during his lifetime.)

These days, there are perhaps as many as five Dvořák symphonies that have wormed their way into general awareness: in addition to the final three, the D Major (No. 6) has begun showing up on concerts with increasing frequency, as has the exuberant, rowdy No. 5, which finally seems to be shaking off the dust of more than a century of neglect.

The unique value of Kubelik's classic cycle of all the Dvořák symphonies is the extent to which they demonstrate that the early pieces were not merely apprentice works or dry runs for what was to follow, but important, attractive, often inspired stages in the evolution of a great Romantic symphonist. While Kubelik's performances of the last four symphonies are among the very best available today, it is the special excitement the conductor generates in the lesser-known works that makes the cycle the modern classics they are.

The Second, Third and Fourth Symphonies contain a wealth —sometimes, an almost *embarrassing* wealth—of ingenious melodic ideas, and even the gabby, frequently clumsy *Bells of Zlonice* (No. 1) is made to seem the creation of a sleeping giant who is just on the verge of waking up. (Strangely enough, Kubelik had little affection for the First Symphony and only recorded it as a favor to Deutsche Grammophon to make the cycle complete. It was—and remains—one of the glories of his recording career.) The Berlin Philharmonic plays with its usual phenomenal precision, but also a warmth and freedom it rarely displayed during the Karajan era, and if you weren't told, you couldn't begin to guess that the recording is more than twenty years old.

Symphony No. 7 in D minor

Concertgebouw Orchestra of Amsterdam, Davis. Philips 420890-2 [CD].

Given the fact that it *is* the man's greatest symphony—and many would argue, his greatest work—you would think there would be a huge selection of first-rate recordings of the Seventh Symphony from which to choose. Think again. Compared to more than fifty recordings of the *New World* Symphony, the Seventh's total remains approximately a dozen and a half—and some of those (by Järvi, Levine, and Maazel) run the scintillating gamut from ho to hum.

With the dramatic and darkly shaded interpretation that comes as part of Kubelik's superlative set, the best single-disc version now on the market is this Sir Colin Davis recording for Philips. While Davis doesn't plumb the tragic depths as deeply as Kubelik —or Szell or Giulini in their badly missed recordings—his is a keen, powerful, elegantly organized performance that is superbly played and recorded.

An even finer version of the Eighth Symphony fills out this unusually desirable disc.

Symphony No. 8 in G ; Symphony No. 9 in E minor, *From the New World*

Cleveland Orchestra, C. von Dohnányi. London 421082-2 [CD].

Czech Philharmonic, Talich. Supraphon Collection 11-0627 2 [CD] (No. 8), 11-0290-2 [CD] (No. 9).

Unlike their recording of the Dvořák Seventh—which, admittedly, has been enthusiastically, even ecstatically, praised elsewhere —it was this recording of the Eighth, more than any other, that confirmed the Cleveland's reemergence as one of the world's great orchestras. Although standards were never allowed to slip during Lorin Maazel's unsettled and unsettling tenure as the orchestra's music director, the orchestra nevertheless played as though their hearts weren't quite in it. At very least, the old Szell electricity was clearly gone.

Their splendid recording of the most amiable and open-hearted of Dvořák's mature symphonies proved, triumphantly, that the Cleveland Orchestra's spirit, under Christoph von Dohnányi, has been thoroughly revived. Not since Szell has the orchestra given another conductor such awesome precision. But the healthiest indication that Dohnányi's was not to be a caretaker regime can be heard in the work of the middle and lower strings, who play with an even darker, more burnished quality than they did under Szell. The interpretation itself reminds me more than anything of Bruno Walter's immensely rewarding CBS recording (MK-42038 [CD]), though one in which the Walter charm is matched by a Szell-like bite. For instance, in the rousing coda of the final movement Dohnányi makes a point that many conductors seem to miss: namely, that this three minutes of unbridled enthusiasm is nothing more than a thinly-veiled Slavonic Dance.

On the other hand, if the quality of the recorded sound is not an issue, then the 1954 Talich recording will probably remain without equal in both this world and the next. Listen to only two minutes of the third movement and the ineffably sorrowful yet impish thing that he makes of it, and you'll understand why Talich has always been regarded as the greatest Dvořák conductor of all time.

The same qualities that characterize both conductors' recordings of the Eighth Symphony can be heard in their very different versions of the *New World*. Dohnányi, in the best modern tradition, is completely unforced and natural, with rhythms that nonetheless have plenty of snap, and execution that is hair-raising in its perfection. Talich allows himself far more rhythmic liberties, and the result is an approach to phrasing which at times seems to mirror the inflections of speech. It is one of the most deeply communicative versions of the *New World* ever recorded and something perilously close to representing Talich at the zenith of his art.

Te Deum; *Psalm 149*; *Heirs of the White Mountain*

Soloists, Prague Philharmonic Choir, Czech Philharmonic Orchestra, Neumann. Supraphon C37-7230 [CD].

For the first ten years of his career as a composer, only his closest friends knew that Dvořák was writing music. He supported himself during these years by teaching and playing the viola in the orchestra of Prague's Provisional Theater. It was a time he would later describe as being full of "hard study, occasional composing, much revision, a great deal of thinking, and very little eating." In 1873 he gave up his orchestra post to become organist at St. Adalbert's Church in Prague. The year before, he had written a cantata for mixed chorus and orchestra on a patriotic poem by

Vitezslav Halek that expressed the undying love of the Czechs for their country. The work drew from the thirty-two-year-old Czech composer a musical expression of a love he had never ventured musically before. First performed by the three-hundred-voice Prague Choral Society on March 9, 1873, *Heirs of the White Mountain* was an enormous critical and popular success, the first of Dvořák's career. Similarly, his setting of the *Te Deum* proved to be a work of considerable historic significance: it was the piece that Antonín Dvořák used to introduce himself to America on October 21, 1892, at a concert in New York's Carnegie Hall.

Both of these exciting and memorable works, together with the composer's setting of *Psalm 149*, are given bracing and authoritative performances on this invaluable Supraphon CD. Although Neumann can occasionally be a lethargic Dvořák conductor, no lack of commitment or exuberance is exhibited here. All the pieces, particularly the *Te Deum*, are given what sound like definitive performances, and Supraphon's lush but detailed sound is excellent.

Trio No. 4 in E minor for Piano, Violin, and Cello, Op. 90, *Dumky*

Borodin Trio. Chandos CHAN-1157 [CD], ABDT-1157 [T].

The liner notes that tell you that a *dumka*—of which *dumky* is the plural—is a kind of Czech dance (and I've never read a liner note that didn't) haven't got it quite right. A *dumka* isn't a dance at all, and the word isn't Czech, but Russian. Its literal meaning is a "passing through," as in ". . . this vale of tears," which Dvořák understood as meaning something essentially *sad*. (He may have associated it in his mind with an ancient form of song or poem that brooded, as lugubriously as possible, on the heroic deeds of a long-vanished past. This particular kind of brooding has always been a key element in the Czech national character: witness the ruminations of that Moravian neurologist, Sigmund Freud, or the jovial fictions of Prague's foremost novelist, Franz Kafka.) As a matter of fact, Dvořák was never really certain *what* the word meant, but that's beside the point. What is important is that he was in the mood to write something *excessively* melancholy, and the *Dumky* Trio became just that.

Coupled with Smetana's equally disturbing piano trio, a work written in response to the death of his eldest daughter, this Borodin Trio recording is probably not the sort of thing you'd want to give to someone with even the mildest suicidal tendencies. Yet for deeply felt forays into two of the darker corners of Romantic chamber music, it exhibits a rare and sinister beauty that no other recording of either piece ever has. In the *Dumky*, the musicians come to terms with the frequent mood swings of the piece with the sensitivity of three adept psychiatrists; their performance of the Smetana unfolds as a long, unbroken cry of grief.

Though the playing may be "too intense for younger audiences," for the more experienced, it should prove uncommonly rewarding.

Dyson, Sir George

(1883–1964)

Concerto da Camera for String Orchestra; *Concerto da Chiesa* for String Orchestra; *Concerto Leggiero* for Piano and String Orchestra

Parkin, piano; City of London Sinfonia, Hickox. Chandos CHAN-9076 [CD].

Sir George Dyson was always something of an outsider, one of the few composers of his generation whose work remained virtually untouched by the English folk-song movement. Best known for his sacred music and *The Canterbury Pilgrims*, a cantata based on a modern translation of extracts from Chaucer's classic work, Dyson was also the composer of some powerfully individual instrumental music, as this revelatory Chandos recording proves. In addition to the engaging *Concerto Leggierio* for Piano and Orchestra, in which Erik Parkin performs with his usual effortless panache, the *Concerto da Camera* and *Concerto da Chiesa* are clearly works to be mentioned in the same breath with Elgar's *Introduction and Allegro* and Vaughan Williams's *Tallis Fantasia*. Lovers of modern English music owe Richard Hickox their gratitude for unearthing yet another series of neglected masterworks. The performances by the City of London Sinfonia could not have been more alert or sympathetic, and the recorded sound is impeccable.

Elgar, Sir Edward (1857–1934)

Concerto in E minor for Cello and Orchestra

Ma, cello; London Symphony, Previn. CBS MK-39541 [CD], IMT-39541 [T].

Anyone who has ever been sprung from an institution of higher learning has understandable feelings of affection and gratitude to Elgar for his best-known work. It is usually to the stirring strains of the *Pomp and Circumstance* March No. 1 in D Major, also known in England as "Land of Hope and Glory," that most high school and college inmates make their final, glorious escape. Though the average music lover still persists in thinking of him as little more than the stuffy, official musical voice of Edwardian England, Sir Edward Elgar was one of the last of the incontestably great Romantic composers. Finding one's way into Elgar's rich and occasionally overripe world certainly isn't easy. I should know. For it was only after years of mulish resistance that I finally embraced Elgar as one of my greatest musical passions.

There is no more rewarding way of jumping into the real Elgar than with his last major composition. The Cello Concerto, the only work in the literature that can be compared favorably with Dvořák's, was never better served than by the young Jacqueline Du Pré, who made her ardent, rhapsodic recording at the beginning of her fame in 1965, a recording that has been unaccountably withdrawn. (A live Albert Hall performance by Du Pré from 1963 is currently available from Intaglio [INCD-7351] which gives a far less accurate indication of what her interpretation was all about.) Until it returns to circulation—as it most certainly must—Yo-Yo Ma's tautly expressive and phenomenally well-played version with André Previn will fill the gap more effectively than any other. In addition to an Elgar Concerto of genuine stature, the recording offers what is probably the finest available account of another English masterpiece, the Cello Concerto of Sir William Walton.

Concerto in B minor for Violin and Orchestra

Takezawa, violin; Bavarian Radio Symphony, Davis. RCA 09026-61612-2 [CD].

Like the symphonies of Anton Bruckner, this longest and, many would say, noblest of all violin concertos has one minor flaw. For in spite of its incomparably majestic length, it is still *much* too short. The Concerto dates from one of the most fertile periods of Elgar's creative life. Originally composed for the Viennese violinist Fritz Kreisler, during the waning years of the Edwardian era—a period that also saw the composition of Elgar's two symphonies—it was one of several key works in which Elgar tried to confine his flood of melodic invention and naturally expansive temperament within the limits of more rigid musical forms.

Apart from its sheer size (in most performances, the Concerto requires nearly fifty minutes to play), the work presents other challenging interpretive problems, chief among them an immense (and immensely original) accompanied cadenza in the final movement. In his 1932 recording with the sixteen-year-old Yehudi Menuhin, the composer demonstrated that the Concerto's difficulties are trivial when compared to its enormous rewards, and fortunately, after years of neglect, a new generation of violinists is beginning to agree.

With the superb recordings by Nigel Kennedy, Itzhak Perlman, and Kyung-Wha Chung currently out of print and the recent version from Pinchas Zuckerman on RCA a major disappointment, the recording by the young Japanese virtuoso Kyoko Takezawa now assumes pride of place. It's a vivid, sweepingly romantic interpretation that is as meticulous in its attention to detail as it is thrillingly played, while Davis and his German orchestra offer some beautifully turned-out support. Not a great performance, perhaps, but the best in a shockingly uncrowded field.

The Dream of Gerontius

Palmer, Davies, Howell, London Symphony Orchestra and
Chorus, Hickox. Chandos CHAN-8641/42 [CD],
DBTD-2014 [T].

When Elgar wrote "This is the best of me" in the score of his
setting of Cardinal Newman's mystical poem, he might also have
written, "This is not only the best work written by an English
composer in three centuries, but also the greatest oratorio written
since the days of Handel."

To date, *The Dream of Gerontius* has had three unassailably
great recordings: an impassioned account led by Sir John Barbirolli,
which was available briefly on CD and then maddeningly withdrawn; the heroic version by Sir Adrian Boult now available in
England on a pair of EMI CDs (47208-8); and a fascinating interpretation by Benjamin Britten in which one great English composer pays homage to another, which in the last couple years has
flitted in and out of the catalog on a pair of London CDs.

The modern interpretation which comes closest to approaching them in stature is the recent Hickox recording for Chandos.
Although his trio of soloists is not quite as memorable as some from
the past—Sir Peter Pears's vulnerable and deeply human Gerontius
in the Britten recording was unforgettable, while Dame Janet Baker's performance as the Angel in the Barbirolli set is as close as we'll
ever come to hearing it done by the real thing—Hickox has the
undeniable advantage of a spectacular modern recording that
makes the big moments like "Go in the name of Angels and Arch-
angels" irresistibly thrilling. The performance also has enormous
warmth and depth, with perhaps the finest choral contribution of
any *Gerontius* yet.

The other panels of Elgar's sacred triptych, *The Apostles* and
The Kingdom are currently available in the best recorded performances they have ever received, also led by Hickox. In marked
contrast to the Boult recordings, which took their own sweet (albeit
noble) time in allowing these magnificent works to make their
points, the Chandos versions invest the music with passion, urgency, and above all, dramatic life. *The Apostles* (CHAN-8875/76
[CD], DBTD-2024 [T]) smolders with a sacred fervor that recalls
the Verdi Requiem, and *The Kingdom* (CHAN-8788/89 [CD],
DBTD-2017 [T]) perfectly captures the mood of rapt piety mixed
with opulent turn-of-the-century decadence.

In the most recent recording in his Elgar series, Hickox leads a stirring account of the closest thing we have to an Elgar opera, the dramatic cantata *Caractacus* (CHAN-8428 [CD]). Although nearly hamstrung by its impossible libretto, Elgar rose to the occasion with wonderful set pieces like the "Sword Song" and Triumphal March (in truth a triumphal chorus), as well as some of his most inspired orchestration. Hickox and his forces respond triumphantly, as do the Chandos engineers. The marvelous *Severn Suite* for full orchestra is the extremely attractive bonus.

Enigma Variations

Royal Philharmonic, Previn. Philips 416813-2 [CD].

With the passing of Sir John Barbirolli and Sir Adrian Boult, many admirers of Elgar's music feared it would suffer the same fate that Frederick Delius's did following the death of Sir Thomas Beecham. Of course, there was never any serious danger of that: unlike the rarified, specialized genius of his younger contemporary, Elgar's was always the far more important and universal gift. Although no major Delius conductor has emerged to take the place of the inimitable Baronet, the Elgar tradition continues to grow and flourish in the hands of a brilliant new guard of sympathetic advocates, whose brightest light is clearly André Previn.

As in his superlative recordings of the symphonies of Ralph Vaughan Williams (see page 564), Previn not only speaks the traditional Elgarian language as though it were his native tongue but also—and wisely—has never resisted the temptation to throw in a few new accents of his own. While his early Angel recording of the *Enigma* Variations was characterized by a refreshing openness and spontaneity, this new version with the Royal Philharmonic is clearly the work of a mature master. The vibrancy and sense of discovery have certainly not vanished, but along with the still-youthful enthusiasm we can hear a far more confident grasp of the larger ebb and flow of the piece. Each of these inspired and inventive variations has great individual character and identity, yet that episodic quality which sabotages so many performances is nowhere to be found. In short, this is the one *Enigma* on the market today in which the whole adds up to considerably more than the sum of the admittedly striking parts.

Introduction and Allegro for Strings; Serenade for Strings

London Chamber Orchestra, Warren-Green. Virgin Classics 59546 [CD].

The debut recording of the resurrected London Chamber Orchestra presents virtually ideal recordings of two of Elgar's most appealing shorter works. Completed in 1892, the *Serenade for Strings in E minor* was the most substantial piece the late-blooming Elgar had written up to that time. Prior to his marriage in 1889, the largely self-taught composer had busied himself mostly with popular and functional music; it was his intelligent, supportive wife who urged him to become more serious and ambitious and the *Serenade* was one of the happy results.

In 1904 the recently knighted Sir Edward Elgar was approached to write a new work to help celebrate the founding of the London Symphony Orchestra. The composer's closest friend, the music editor A. J. Jaeger—"Nimrod" in the *Enigma* Variations—suggested "a real bring-down-the-house torrent of a thing such as Bach would write." What Elgar delivered was a sophisticated up-dating of the eighteenth-century concerto grosso, the *Introduction and Allegro for Strings*.

The small (seventeen-member) London Chamber Orchestra perform both works with phenomenal precision under Christopher Warren-Green. Yet in addition to the near-perfect execution, the performances bustle with Elgarian energy: the "devil of a fugue" in the *Allegro* is tossed off with a supremely insolent swagger, and the opening theme of the *Serenade* is amiability itself. With equally inspired accounts of Vaughan Williams's *Lark Ascending*, *Greensleeves*, and *Tallis Fantasia*, this is a recording that no lover of English string music can afford to be without.

Pomp and Circumstance Marches (5); *Cockaigne Overture; The Crown of India Suite*

Scottish National Orchestra, Gibson. Chandos CHAN-8429 [CD], CBT-1012 [T].

This is the confident, public, tub-thumping Elgar, a man far removed from the thoughtful, melancholy Romantic who produced the Cello Concerto or the visionary mystic of *The Dream of Gerontius*. The supremely stirring *Pomp and Circumstance* Marches and the jingoistic *Crown of India* are the musical high noon of the British Empire, the perfect reflection of a self-satisfied society celebrating the fact that it had stolen half the world fair and square.

Sir Alexander Gibson rouses his Scottish musicians to great heights of eloquence and enthusiasm in the Marches and the Suite, while *Cockaigne* (a cognate of "Cockney"), crackles with working-class London life.

In another and possibly even finer Chandos recording (CHAN-8430 [CD]), the same forces (together with excellent soloists and a top-notch chorus) are equally persuasive in Elgar's *Coronation Ode*, in which the great striding tune of the D Major March first became "Land of Hope and Glory." Another masterwork of Elgarian occasional music, the wartime cantata *The Spirit of England*, is offered as a generous bonus.

Symphonies: No. 1 in A-flat; No. 2 in E-flat

Philharmonia Orchestra, Hallé Orchestra, Barbirolli. EMI CDM-64511 [CD] (No. 1); EMI CDM-64724 [CD] (No. 2).

With the dark and dramatic Symphony No. 1 in A-flat, whose brooding principal theme was used to such memorable effect in *Greystoke: The Legend of Tarzan*, Elgar's Symphony No. 2 in E-flat is one of the absolute summits of late-Romantic symphonic thought. The Second Symphony (as with *The Dream of Gerontius*), represents much of what is best in Elgar: From the striding confidence of the opening movement through the ineffably poignant closing bars of the finale, it is a sort of gentlemanly and gently refined Götterdämmerung of the entire Edwardian era. As a matter of fact, the composer was already at work on the Symphony's emotional heart, the devastating Largo, when word reached him that the man who gave the age its name had died. This long, beautifully painful, inexpressibly moving elegy for Edward VII is one of the great farewells in all of music.

The recordings that Sir John Barbirolli made in the early 1960s are among his greatest achievements, and no recorded versions before or since have captured quite so much of the passionate, red-blooded side of these magnificent scores. For instance, the finale of the First Symphony seethes with a barely containable power, and the *Largo* of the Second is all but insupportable in its outpouring of grief. Listen, too, to the mood of feverish delirium the conductor conjures up toward the end of the Second Symphony's Scherzo or the triumphant grandeur with which he invests its final march. For all the special insights of the composer's own recordings (EMI CDCC-54560 [CD]), to say nothing of those by Boult, Solti, or Slatkin, it is this pair of performances that continue to persuade us that these *are* the great English symphonies to date.

Given EMI's shameful record of allowing Barbirolli's classic Elgar recordings to slip out of print, snatch these up without delay.

The Wand of Youth Suites; *Nursery Suite*

Ulster Orchestra, Thomson. Chandos CHAN-8318 [CD], ABTD-1079 [T].

All of the basic musical material for these enchanting works came from the composer's boyhood sketchbooks. As Elgar wrote of the second *Wand of Youth* Suite in 1908, "The music is now presented for the first time as imagined by the author: & in adapting to a modern orchestra these juvenile ideas the suggested instrumentation has been carried out as nearly as possible. Occasionally an obviously commonplace phrase has been polished out but on the whole the little pieces remain as originally planned." In truth, Elgar was having some fun at his readers' expense. Only the tunes remained from boyhood; the harmonic and contrapuntal treatment was clearly that of a mature composer in his prime.

The late Bryden Thomson's recordings of these endearing miniatures rank with his very best, capturing the vigor and abiding innocence of the music as no recordings ever have. One of the conductor's final Elgar recordings (Chandos CHAN-9022 [CD]) features the exquisite *Sea Pictures* and the rarely heard *The Music Makers* in sumptuous readings by the London Philharmonic. With the classic Baker/Barbirolli version of *Sea Pictures* presently unavailable, this lovely performance with contralto Linda Finnie is now the one to own. Similarly, Thomson and company make the strongest possible case for *The Music Makers*, a work in which Elgar liberally quotes Elgar, including a rapt choral setting of *Nimrod* from the *Enigma* Variations.

Music from another engaging reworking of Elgarian juvenilia, *The Starlight Express* (which is not to be confused with Andrew

Lloyd Webber's witless abomination of that same name), together with a suite from the incidental music for the play *Arthur*, a modern adaptation of Malory's famous romance, *Morte d'Arthur*, can be found on another delightful Chandos recording (CHAN-8428 [CD]) in glowing performances by the Bournemouth Sinfonietta conducted by George Guest.

Enescu, Georges (1881–1955)

Romanian Rhapsody No. 1

RCA Victor Symphony, Stokowski. RCA 09026-61503 [CD].

Although the most important of all Romanian composers produced symphonies, an opera, and numerous elegantly crafted chamber works, Georges Enescu remains best known for a single score, the indestructible *Romanian Rhapsody No. 1*, which offers folksy melodies and gypsy passions decked out in spectacular orchestral garb.

Rarely has the old warhorse seemed as spry as in the mercurial performance from Leopold Stokowski's *Rhapsodies* album, now reissued in RCA's Living Stereo series. Even though Stoky couldn't resist the temptation of tinkering with Enescu's inspired orchestration (nothing personal—he routinely meddled with the work of master orchestrators like Rimsky-Korsakov, Stravinsky, and Ravel), the performance surges with life. From the coy opening to the wild gypsy finish, this is vintage Stokowski, as are the versions of Liszt's *Hungarian Rhapsody No. 2*, Smetana's *Vltava*, and excerpts from Wagner's *Tristan und Isolde* and *Tannhäuser*, which includes perhaps the most unabashedly pornographic version of the *Venusberg Music* ever recorded.

For those wishing to meet the other Enescu, a Hyperion recording (CDA-66484 [CD]) offers two of the composer's violin sonatas—he was also a brilliant violinist—in fiercely committed performances by the Romanian virtuoso Adelina Oprean accompanied by her brother Justin. While the Second Sonata is an appealing early piece, the Third is one of the finest such works produced in this century.

Although his setting of the Sophocles story has been completely overshadowed by Stravinsky's *Oedipus Rex*, Enescu's lyric tragedy *Oedipe* may actually be the finer work. It is a vivid and powerfully compelling score, as the startling new EMI recording (CDCB-54011 [CD]) makes blindingly clear. With a nearly perfect cast headed by José van Dam in the title role and inspired conducting from Lawrence Foster, *Oedipe* is finally revealed as one of the major stage works of modern times.

Falla, Manuel de (1876–1946)

Nights in the Gardens of Spain

De Larrocha, piano; London Philharmonic, Frühbeck de Burgos. London 410289-2 [CD].

When she first walks out on stage, Alicia de Larrocha looks like nothing so much as a slightly plump, demurely elegant Barcelona housewife—which, when she is not off on one of her concert tours, is precisely what she happens to be. Yet the moment she begins to play we are instantly ushered into the presence of one of the great pianists 'of modern times. Her Mozart shimmers with crystalline purity and inner strength, and her Liszt is an exhilarating amalgam of volcanic intensity and urbane sophistication, but it is with the colorful, evocative music of her fellow countrymen that de Larrocha is unique. It's unlikely that Isaac Albéniz, Enrique Granados, or Manuel de Falla ever had a more sympathetic or persuasive interpreter of his piano music, and barring some unforseen miracle, they will probably never have one of this quality again.

In her most recent recording of Falla's exquisitely dreamy *Nights in the Gardens of Spain*, de Larrocha plays with all the sensitivity and profound understanding that make her new London version of Albéniz's *Iberia* one of the classics of recent recording history. Unlike the many pianists who are unable to resist the temptation of flooding the *Nights* with too much local color, de Larrocha is able to approach it with the ease and assurance of one who speaks its musical language fluently. Never has the music seemed more natural, or more naturally indebted to the piano music of Ravel and Debussy, nor has there ever been a performance so utterly spontaneous that it creates the illusion the soloist is simply making all this up as she goes along. Rafael Frühbeck de Burgos provides her with some richly idiomatic support, and the recorded sound is breathtaking in its dynamic range and presence. Clearly, this is the recording of the *Nights* that will dominate the catalogs for years to come.

The Three-Cornered Hat; *El amor brujo*

L'Orchestre de la Suisse Romande, Ansermet. London 433908-2 [CD].

In its intoxicating rhythms and harmonic language, its color, wit, and distinctive, highly original use of the resources of the modern orchestra, *The Three-Cornered Hat*—originally composed for Sergei Diaghilev's Ballets Russes—is the most important large-scale orchestral work ever written by a Spanish composer. All of its freshness and overt, provocative sensuality have remained intact for more than seventy years, and, with that masterpiece by a great French tourist, Bizet's *Carmen*, the ballet remains one of the most vivid of all musical distillations of the sights and sounds of Spain.

While *The Three-Cornered Hat* has never gone begging for first-rate recorded performances—Ernest Ansermet, who gave the work its world premiere in 1919, left a commandingly vivid interpretation in 1961, superseded by an even finer Angel recording by André Previn and the Pittsburgh Symphony two decades later—Charles Dutoit's effort for London captured more of the ballet's drama and atmosphere than any other. Alas, that recording has been temporarily withdrawn, presumably to reappear as a London Jubilee mid-price reissue.

Until the Dutoit returns to circulation, the Ansermet will hold the fort quite nicely, especially since it is generously packaged on a pair of medium-priced CDs with de Larrocha's brilliant first recording of *Nights in the Gardens of Spain*, Ansermet's fiery *El amor brujo*, one of the finest available versions of the intriguing *Harpsichord Concerto*, and the best recording *ever* of Falla's most enchanting score, *El retablo de maese Pedro* (Master Peter's Puppet Show), the last two in gleaming, wholly idiomatic performances led by Simon Rattle.

La vida breve

De los Angeles, Rivadeneyra, Cossutta, Higueras, Orfeon Donostiarra Chorus, National Orchestra of Spain, Frühbeck de Burgos. Angel CDM-69590 [CD].

It is often suggested that the reason Falla's colorful two-act opera has never really caught on is weakness in the story. One suspects that there's more to it than that, since if weaknesses in the story *are* a serious consideration, then half of the most popular operas ever written would never have caught on. It's probably because *La vida breve* (The Short Life) is such an intensely Spanish opera that non-Spanish companies are reluctant to give it a try. Which is a pity, since in terms of its musical inspiration it ranks not far behind the early Puccini operas or with the very best Massenet.

Victoria de los Angeles is an ideal exponent of Salud, the gypsy girl who collapses and dies of a broken heart at the wedding of her treacherous lover (okay, so it's not Ibsen). She breathes an irresistible life and color into the role and has rarely been more impressive vocally, while Frühbeck de Burgos's conducting could not have been more sympathetic or resourceful. On a single medium-priced CD, this neglected masterpiece has never been easier to investigate.

De los Angeles is also very compelling in her classic 1951 recording with pianist Gerald Moore of the *Siete canciones populares espagñolas* (usually translated as *Seven Popular Spanish Songs*, but more properly *Seven Songs of the Spanish People*). It is the one recording of the cycle that comes closest to the electrifying version from the 78 era made by the composer's friend Maria Barrientos. As in her great predecessor's interpretation, de los Angeles's singing is alternately pure, suave, insinuating, and *very* unladylike.

Fauré, Gabriel (1845–1924)

Dolly Suite; Pavane

> Boston Symphony, Ozawa. Deutsche Grammophon
> 423089-2 [CD].

Originally a work for piano, four-hands—and heard to seductive advantage in that form on a Philips CD by the Labèques (420159-2)—the *Dolly Suite*, in the orchestration by Henri Rabaud, is one of the most enchanting of Fauré's inspirations. Though clearly no match for Sir Thomas Beecham's magical, recently withdrawn recording (but then again, there has never been one that is), Seiji Ozawa's professional, frequently charming realization of the score offers typically suave and aristocratic playing from the Boston Symphony. The versions of the *Pavane*, *Après un rêve*, and Fauré's suite from the *Pelléas et Mélisande* incidental music are equally efficient.

Bargain hunters should take note that Ernest Ansermet's lovely, if somewhat harshly recorded, versions of the *Pelléas et Mélisande* incidental music and *Masques et bergamasques* have now turned up on a London Weekend Classics CD (421026-2).

Piano Music

> Barcarolles (13). Crossley, piano. CRD 3422.
>
> Impromptus (5). Crossley, piano. CRD 3423.
>
> Nocturnes (13). Crossley, piano. CRD 3406/7.

As with his *mélodies*, Fauré produced piano music throughout his entire creative life, from the *Trois Romances sans paroles* written when he was eighteen, to the B minor Nocturne composed nearly sixty years later. Like his songs, many of these miniatures are among Fauré's most characteristic and nearly perfect creations. In fact, given all the wonders they contain, these are "miniatures" only in terms of duration, for they are also microcosms of the man's emotional life and expressive art.

As in his superb Poulenc and Ravel series (see page 389), Paul Crossley maintains a consistently high level of inspiration throughout his admirable Fauré project, as evidenced in the complete recordings of the Barcarolles, Impromptus, and Nocturnes. For anyone not wishing to make quite so substantial an investment, the French pianist Pascal Rogé is polished and insightful on an attractive London recital (425606-2 [CD]), which offers some of the best of the above together with the *Valse caprice* and the *Trois Romances sans paroles*. Of historic interest, the recordings of the composer's friend Marguerite Long are finally available on a Pearl CD (PEA-9927).

Quartets (2) for Piano and Strings

Domus. Hyperion CDA-66166 [CD].

The two Fauré piano quartets are among the most completely civilized chamber works ever written. For many, the conversation can become *too* civilized and introspective, often degenerating into elegant small talk; for others, they are the most cultivated and musically rewarding works in the form since those of Mozart.

The members of Domus obviously share the second opinion, and their immensely accomplished performances are among the most rewarding Fauré compositions ever recorded. The playing is not only extraordinarily refined, it also captures the music's warmth and subtle passions as no modern recordings have. With their versions of the Brahms Quartets (see page 102), these are Domus's most distinguished recordings to date.

Another superb Hyperion recording (CDA-66277 [CD], KA-66277 [T]) features Domus's pianist Susan Tomes and violinist Krysia Osostowicz in lovely performances of the glorious Violin Sonatas, with the two gifted young musicians handily outperforming many far more famous teams.

Requiem

Ashton, Varcoe, Cambridge Singers, City of London Sinfonia, Rutter (1893 version). Collegium COLCD-109 [CD], COLC-109 [T].

Battle, Schmidt, Philharmonia Orchestra and Chorus, Giulini (1900 fully orchestrated version). Deutsche Grammophon 419243-2 [CD].

The French consider Gabriel Fauré the consummate musical embodiment of their culture—and certainly, no French composer ever produced a more cultivated body of chamber music, piano works, and songs—but for most non-French ears, Fauré, to use the tired metaphor, is the classic example of a rare, virtually priceless wine that simply refuses to travel. Outside his native country, his discretion, restraint, and natural reticence are still insufficiently appreciated. Then again, to expect anything but an educated Gallic audience to respond to the subtle delicacies of a song cycle like *La Bonne Chanson*, is a little like expecting a non-German listener to fully grasp the more thorny lieder of Hugo Wolf.

Along with the melancholy and sinuously beautiful pops-concert staple, the *Pavane*, one of the rare Fauré works that has enjoyed considerable popularity in the rest of the world, is the gentlest and most reserved of the great nineteenth-century requiems. As in all of his important music, the Fauré *Requiem* makes its subdued points without so much as wrinkling an inch of its immaculately polished surface. From first note to last, the music flows in an inevitable, unhurried way, offering not only quiet spiritual consolation but an extraordinary and original sonic beauty.

The Collegium recording, the first to present the work in the composer's original chamber music instrumentation, makes the strongest case for the Requiem that has yet been made. In fact, the reduced scale of the performing forces is such a perfect complement to the intimate nature of the music that one wonders why no one ever thought of recording it before. Both the singing and playing are engagingly fresh and youthful, and Collegium's spacious but detailed recording captures every nuance of an extremely subtle interpretation.

For those who prefer a Fauré Requiem with a little more meat on its bones, Carlo Maria Giulini's iridescent Angel recording of the 1900 orchestration, while maintaining the restrained poise of a fine chamber music performance, still overflows with old-fashioned romanticism and warmth.

Songs

Ameling, soprano; Souzay, baritone; Baldwin, piano. Angel CDMD-64079 [CD].

Nowhere is the exquisite refinement of Gabriel Fauré's art more evident than in his *chansons*, which taken as a whole represent the greatest contribution to the art of song made by any French composer. From the age of twenty when he wrote his first song, "Le Papillon et la fleur," based on a text by Victor Hugo, through the cycle *L'Horizon chimérique*, composed only two years before his death, Fauré's lifelong devotion to the form produced some of the most nearly perfect fusions of words and music in musical history. The brilliance extends from early miracles such as "Après un rêve," through mature masterpieces like "Au cimetière," "Chanson d'amour," "Clair de lune," and the greatest of his song cycles, *La Bonne Chanson*.

This historic set from Angel gathers all the songs together on four CDs in performances by two incomparable Fauré interpreters, Elly Ameling and Gérard Souzay. If Souzay's voice is not quite as fresh as it was in his earlier Philips recordings, his sheer musicality and depth of understanding more than makes up for any minor vocal imperfections. On the other hand, the indestructible Elly Ameling is girlish and radiant throughout, with an instinctive grasp of Fauré's rarified idiom to match Souzay's own. Dalton Baldwin, as always, is an ideal partner for both, and the recorded sound remains very fine.

Feldman, Morton (1926–1987)

Rothko Chapel; *Why Patterns?*

Abel, viola; Rosenak, celeste; Winant, percussion; UC Berkeley Chamber Chorus, Brett. New Albion NA-039CD [CD].

In 1971 the American composer Morton Feldman was in Houston for the opening of a chapel for which Mark Rothko had painted fourteen enormous canvases. While there, he was asked to write a musical tribute to Rothko to be performed in the chapel the following year. The result is one of the most original and starkly hypnotic works ever written by an American. Scored for chorus, viola, celesta, and percussion, *Rothko Chapel* has an astonishing effect on listeners whenever we put it on the air, especially among those who are convinced they can't stand contemporary music. In addition to being a thoroughly spellbinding piece, it is a very moving and spiritual one, with a number of personal references in the score including a haunting soprano melody written on the day of Stravinsky's funeral and, in the composer's words, "Certain intervals (which) have the ring of the synagogue."

The UC Berkeley Chamber Chorus and company give *Rothko Chapel* a suitably rapt and ethereal performance in its second commerical recording, with flawless digital sound adding immeasurably to its sense of purity and limitless space. If *Why Patterns?* from 1978 seems less convincing and original, it's probably because *Rothko Chapel* was such a once-in-a-lifetime inspiration.

Finzi, Gerald (1901–1956)

Clarinet Concerto; Five Bagatelles for Clarinet and Piano

Johnson, clarinet; Royal Philharmonic, Groves. ASV DCA-787 [CD].

Gerald Finzi is not one of the better-known twentieth-century British composers. His output was relatively modest (he died of leukemia at the age of 55), and he tends to be at his best in the music he wrote for the human voice, which is hardly the way to guarantee *any* composer's popularity. A recent ripple of interest in his music —he was never popular enough to enjoy a "revival"—has led to no fewer than five recordings of the 1948 Clarinet Concerto, one of Finzi's loveliest and most characteristic works.

Those—especially clarinetists themselves—who complain that too few important works have been written for the instrument really do need to hear the Finzi Concerto, which easily ranks with those of Carl Nielsen and Aaron Copland as one of the finest produced in this century. In fact, repeated exposure to its lush, almost Brahmsian opening movement, its deeply expressive Adagio, and the unbuttoned but unhurried finale has persuaded me that it may well be *the* clarinet concerto of modern times.

In her brilliant ASV recording, Emma Johnson assumes the mantle of the great Reginald Kell, taking her rightful place among the world's great clarinetists. Her breath control and command of dynamic shading are both little short of astonishing, revealing possibilities of expression and color that no recording of the Finzi Concerto ever has. She also offers a similarly inspiring account of the gorgeous Five Bagatelles, the second of which movie buffs will immediately recognize as John Barry's inspiration for the big tune from *Dances with Wolves*.

Those who respond to either of these unique works should waste no time investigating the composer's Cello Concerto in the Chandos recording (CHAN-8471 [CD]) by Rafael Wallfisch and the Royal Liverpool Philharmonic conducted by Vernon Handley. If anything, it is an even more ambitious and important work than the Clarinet Concerto: an alternately dark and exhilarating piece, performed here with intelligence and passion.

Songs

> Hill, tenor; Varcoe, baritone; Benson, piano. Hyperion CDA-66161/62 [CD].
>
> Varcoe, baritone; City of London Sinfonia, Hickox. Chandos CHAN-8743 [CD], ABTD-1382 [T].

Here is compelling evidence for the argument that Gerald Finzi was among the most important song composers of the twentieth century. The Hyperion set offers five of Finzi's cycles based on the poetry of Thomas Hardy, a total of forty-three songs that present an astonishing range of musical and emotional expression: from the roistering charm of "Rollicum-Rorum" through the heart-tugging wistfulness of "Childhood Among the Ferns" to the *Winterreise*-like desolation of "At Middle-Field Gate in February," completed only a few months before the composer's death. With richly imaginative support from pianist Clifford Benson, tenor Martyn Hill and baritone Stephen Varcoe are ideal guides to this hugely rewarding repertoire. Although the piano sounds a bit distant, the balance is otherwise very natural.

Perhaps an even more attractive introduction to Finzi's vocal music is the Chandos recording of *Let Us Garlands Bring*, five of the most inspired of all modern Shakespeare settings. While Finzi's versions of "O Mistress Mine" and "It Was a Lover and His Lass" are every bit the equal of the far more familiar settings of Peter Warlock, the beautiful centerpiece of the cycle, "Fear no more the heat o' the Sun" from *Cymbeline* ranks with the very greatest of English songs. Varcoe is again the perfect exponent of this material, with Hickox lending his typically impeccable support. With equally inspired performances of other items by Butterworth, Elgar, Ireland, Quilter, and Vaughan Williams, this is one of the loveliest albums of English vocal music now available.

Flotow, Friedrich von

(1812–1883)

Martha

Popp, Jerusalem, Ridderbusch, Nimsgern, Bavarian Radio Chorus and Orchestra, Wallberg. Eurodisc 7789-2-RG [CD].

Given the disturbing frequency with which the world's opera companies are mounting revivals of dead-from-the-neck up bel canto howlers, dark, unsingable downers by dour Finns, to say nothing of the operas [*sic*] of Philip Glass, it's astonishing that Flotow's *Martha* should be so scandalously ignored. Not only is it delightful theater, it abounds in memorable arias, from the several unforgettable appearances of the English folk song "The Last Rose of Summer," to the radiant and justly famous tenor aria "Ach so fromm," which Caruso—to say nothing of every other significant Italian tenor of the century—recorded as "M'appari."

As in his splendid recording of another neglected masterpiece, Weinberger's *Schwanda the Bagpiper* (see page 602), Heinz Wallberg leads a lush and lively performance of the old charmer, with excellent contributions from most of the cast. The exceptions are Siegfried Jerusalem, well *beyond* excellent in his dashing portayal of Lionel, and the late Lucia Popp, whose intelligence, musicianship, dramatic flair, and gleaming voice make her one of the great Lady Harriets history has known.

To be investigated at once.

Françaix, Jean (1912–   )

L'horloge de Flore for Oboe and Orchestra

De Lancie, oboe; London Symphony, Previn. RCA 7989-2-RG [CD].

As they do to most right-thinking people, the perky, tuneful, mercilessly cheerful excretions of Jean Françaix—the A. A. Milne of French music—usually fill me with an irresistible urge to rip out daisies by the roots and hurl bricks at the nearest chirping bird. Except for *The Flower Clock*.

Written for John de Lancie, the former principal oboist of the Philadelphia Orchestra, *L'horloge de Flore* is one of the most ingratiating and gratefully written of all modern oboe concertos and forms the centerpiece of a recording that no lover of the instrument—or of elegant French music—can afford to be without. With suave and stylish accompaniments by André Previn and the London Symphony, de Lancie turns in equally definitive performances of the Ibert *Symphonie concertante* and the ethereal *Gymnopedies* by Erik Satie.

As a bonus, the CD reissue includes a 1987 recording of the Richard Strauss Oboe Concerto, a work the elderly composer was prompted to write thanks to a chance conversation with an American GI named John de Lancie. Although one could wish the oboist had recorded it in his prime, this version is easily the finest now available and an historic document of considerable significance.

Franck, César (1822–1900)

Le Chasseur maudit

Czech Philharmonic, Fournet. Supraphon 11-0613-2 [CD].

A fondness for Franck's splendidly gruesome *Chasseur maudit* (The Accursed Huntsman) usually accompanies similar passions for B horror-pictures of the 1940s (usually the ones with Rondo Hatton, Martin Kosleck, or both). The tone poem is one of the key works in an honorable line of black-schlock masterpieces that stretches back to Bach's "Mein Herze schwimmt im Blut" and looks forward to the Shostakovich eighth.

With Charles Munch's wonderfully gruesome Boston Symphony recording unavailable, the version with Jean Fournet and the Czech Philharmonic is the best stop-gap. The interpretation is forceful and direct and comes with a very fine performance of the youthful curiosity *Les djinns* and a more than serviceable version of the Symphony in D minor.

Piano Quintet in F minor

Bingham, piano; Medici String Quartet. Nimbus NI-5114 [CD].

Like the Janáček string quartet called "Intimate Pages," Franck's F minor Piano Quintet was inspired by his passion for a much younger woman, in this case one of his students. In addition to the boiling emotions—and in no other work by this master of form and gesture are the emotions in more imminent danger of boiling over—there is more than a touch of mysticism in this otherworldly piece, Franck's first unqualified masterpiece.

Even compared to the classic London recording by Sir Clifford Curzon and the Vienna Philharmonic Quartet, the newer Nimbus recording by John Bingham and the Medicis is very impressive. Emotionally, it burns on a consistently higher flame, yet does not ignore the music's spiritual dimension or carefully balanced textures. It's a pity that Fauré's String Quartet is included on this Nimbus CD instead of Franck's, especially since none of the available recordings of the composer's final masterpiece can be recommended with enthusiasm.

Sonata in A for Violin and Piano

Perlman, violin; Ashkenazy, piano. London 414128-2 [CD].

Like Leoš Janáček, who did not begin to produce his greatest music until he entered his seventh decade of life, Franck was a classic late bloomer among the major composers. He produced some shockingly dreadful music early in his career (*Hulda*, for instance, has a better than average claim to being the worst French opera of the nineteenth century, and *that's* saying something), and yet, toward the end, he found his own distinct voice in a tiny handful of masterworks that will probably endure forever.

Franck's Violin Sonata (known in some irreverent corners of the classical music radio trade as the Frank Sinatra) stands with those of Brahms and Schumann as one of the finest violin sonatas after those of Beethoven. As in all of Franck's most powerful and characteristic music, the work represents a conscious attempt to contain Romantic sentiment within formal classical structures, a tendency his French critics lambasted mercilessly, charging the composer with an unseemly and almost treasonous fondness for German formalism. (As preposterous as it might seem, many of those same critics took George Bizet's *Carmen* to task for being so obviously and slavishly "Wagnerian.")

While I still have the fondest memories of a long-vanished Decca interpretation by the fabulously musical Viennese violinist Erica Morini, Itzhak Perlman's London recording from the mid-1970s easily surpasses all currently available recordings of the work. Poised and elegant throughout, the playing of both the violinist and Vladimir Ashkenazy is also shot through with a wonderful sense of dramatic urgency and immediacy. In their hands, for instance, the turbulent second movement emerges as one of the composer's greatest creations.

Symphony in D minor

Chicago Symphony, Monteux. RCA 6805-2-RG [CD].

There are people whose friendship I value and whose musical opinions I respect who absolutely cannot abide Franck's Symphony. (Curiously enough, they tend to be the same people who have an inexplicable revulsion for the music of Frederick Delius. Consequently, I never argue either subject with them, but instead tend to look their way with a mixture of benign sorrow and genuine confusion.) For if truth be told, what's *not* to like in this tuneful, brilliant, melancholy, triumphant work? It has something for everyone: despair, adventure, exuberance, romance, and an English horn solo in the second movement for which anyone who ever played the instrument, myself included, would cheerfully sell his grandmother to the gypsies.

For students of English horn playing, the legendary Laurence Thorstenberg gives one of the greatest performances of his incomparable career in this 1961 RCA recording. For those whose interests are a bit less parochial, Larry's luscious playing can be heard in what also happens to be the greatest recorded performance that the Franck Symphony has ever been given.

If further proof were needed that Pierre Monteux was one of the most consistently satisfying conductors of the twentieth century, this stunning performance goes a long way to underscoring the point. With the youthful impetuosity that only this ageless octogenarian could muster, he levitates Franck's often problematical symphony almost to the level of those of Johannes Brahms. The first movement seethes with a barely containable intensity, the slow movement is a seamless, diaphanous love song, while the finale becomes a Tchaikovskian explosion of exuberance and romance. With his London Symphony *Daphnis and Chloë* and Boston Symphony version of Stravinsky's *Rite of Spring*—two works that Pierre Monteux introduced to the world—this is one of the principal monuments of a unique and irreplaceable talent. To make the reissue all the more attractive, RCA has packaged the performance with two Boston Symphony recordings led by Charles Munch: a scintillating account of Berlioz's Overture to *Béatrice et Bénédict* and what remains the most distinguished available recording of d'Indy's *Symphony on a French Mountain Air.*

With the classic recording by Sir Clifford Curzon of Franck's other great orchestral score, the *Symphonic Variations*, no longer available, most of the better alternatives—Bolet, Entremont, Firkusny—mean getting stuck with yet *another* recording of the Symphony in D minor. Which therefore leaves the field to Artur Rubinstein (RCA 09026-61496-2 [CD], 09026-61496-4 [T]), who in addition to a pleasantly brooding interpretation of the Franck, offers a beautifully atmospheric version of Falla's *Nights in the Gardens of Spain* and possibly the finest-ever recording of the Second Piano Concerto of Camille Saint-Saëns.

Fucík, Julius (1872–1916)

Marches and Waltzes

Czech Philharmonic, Neumann. Orfeo C-147861 [CD].

In many of the more benighted corners of the planet, the Czech composer Julius Fucík is known as "The John Philip Sousa of Bohemia." Those of us who know better refer to the March King as the American Julius Fucík. Best known as the composer of the immortal circus march *Entrance of the Gladiators*, Fucík also wrote many tunefully appealing waltzes which, if they don't exactly eclipse those of Johann Strauss II, are at very least cut from the same entrancing cloth.

Václav Neumann proves to be an enthusiastic advocate of his countryman's music, and with the great Czech Philharmonic at its most precise and congenial, Fucík emerges as a composer of genuine character, originality, and charm. Besides, without a first-rate recording of his imperishable masterwork, what will you do if you suddenly acquire an elephant?

Gabrieli, Giovanni

(ca. 1557–1612)

Canzoni for Brass Choirs; Intonazioni d'organo; Seven Motets; Three Mass Movements; Sonata in the Ninth Tone for Eight Parts

Biggs, organ; Gregg Smith Singers, Texas Boys' Choir, Edward Tarr Brass Ensemble. CBS MK-42645 [CD].

This handsome collection called "The Glory of Venice—Gabrieli in San Marco" made quite some noise when it was first released in 1967 and still sounds pretty spectacular today. Recorded in the incomparable acoustics of St. Mark's Cathedral, the original venue in which most of these pieces were first heard, Gabrieli's antiphonal writing has never seemed more inspired, nor were many of the participants ever moved to more joyously inspired work. Hearing these thrilling performances, you almost believe they had just read the Biblical injunction to "make a *joyful* noise unto the Lord."

If brassy Gabrieli is your cup of sacramental wine, then by all means try another exciting CBS album (MK-44931 [CD], MT-44931 [T]), featuring thirteen canzoni played by the Canadian Brass, aided by the first-desk men of the Boston Symphony and New York Philharmonic.

Gershwin, George (1898–1937)

An American in Paris; Concerto in F; *Rhapsody in Blue*

Golub, piano; London Symphony, Miller. Arabesque Z-6587 [CD].

At the very *least*, this is the greatest single Gershwin recording ever made. Where it ranks among the great classical recordings of the last twenty-five years only time will tell, though I suspect it will rank very high. Among so many other things (peerless oboist, television star, and recording executive whose list of discoveries reads like a *Who's Who* of American popular music), Mitch Miller is also one of the most revealing and exciting conductors in the world today. This Arabesque recording of music by his friend George Gershwin may well be the crowning achievement to date in a long and colorful career.

What Miller brings to Gershwin's music is an unusual combination of freshness and authority. But paradoxically, the freshness comes from simply playing the music as the composer intended, intentions Miller discovered firsthand while playing in the orchestra for the composer's 1934 American tour, and in the original production of *Porgy and Bess*. Working from scores that Miller carefully marked from Gershwin's own interpretations and instructions, the performances emerge from this astonishing recording sounding like no others you've ever heard before. While infinitely more lyrical, expansive, and direct in their emotional expression, they are also more intricate and subtle than those of any other Gershwin recording on the market today. The important but rarely heard inner voices are coaxed out of the background with a startling clarity, and the jazz inflections, for once, are not simply tossed in as cheap effects but can clearly be heard for what they were all along: part of the music's natural organic structure.

The playing of the London Symphony ranges from the merely sensational to the absolutely terrifying—at times, the brass section wails with the electrifying unanimity of purpose of the old Count Basie band—and the technically spellbinding but intelligent and poetic playing of David Golub suggests that he is clearly one of the finest pianists before the public today. For Gershwin lovers, the recording is an obvious necessity; for those who have never been able to warm to the composer's more obviously "serious" music, this is an excellent opportunity to hear it—quite literally—for the very first time.

Piano Music

Bolcom, piano. Nonesuch 79151-2 [CD].

The major qualitative difference between the songs of Franz Schubert and those of George Gershwin is that, by and large, Gershwin worked with better texts. The best of the songs that he wrote to lyrics by his brother Ira *are* the enduring lieder of the twentieth century. Often, all that differentiates works like "An die Musik" and "The Man I Love" are their harmonic language and emotional content; as to their ultimate merit, five hundred years from now the connoisseur of art songs will probably be hard-pressed to choose between them.

In addition to the "Gershwin Song Book"—arrangements made by the composer himself of eighteen songs—this inviting Nonesuch recording gathers together most of Gershwin's music for solo piano in performances as stylish as they are unaffected.

An eclectic and frequently arresting composer in his own right, William Bolcom speaks Gershwin's musical language without any discernable accent: the frequently recorded Three Preludes sound more mysterious and rhythmically intriguing than they ever have before, and the *Rialto Ripples* are tossed off with a typically Gershwinesque wise-guy smile.

*P*orgy and Bess

Haymon, Blackwell, Clarey, White, Baker, Evans,
Glyndebourne Festival Chorus, London Philharmonic,
Rattle. Angel CDCC-49568 [CD].

Although many of its arias have long since become popular standards (is there anyone who can forget their first encounter with "Summertime"?) Gershwin's last great achievement, *Porgy and Bess*, remains a neglected classic. Its initial run, while more than respectable for an opera, was disastrous by Broadway-musical standards, and ever since its ill-fated first production, *Porgy and Bess* has had the undeserved reputation of being a hard-luck show.

The handsome RCA recording by the Houston Grand Opera (the same adventurous company that recently brought us John Adams's *Nixon in China*, whether we wanted it or not) proved conclusively that Gershwin knew precisely what he was about. For with the proper care and dedication—which does not necessarily mean the services of world-class voices or an internationally famous conductor—*Porgy and Bess* can clearly be heard as the closest thing we have to the Great American Opera. Not since the path-breaking Columbia recording Goddard Lieberson produced in 1950 has any recorded version of the opera made such a convincing case for *Porgy and Bess*'s greatness. What a pity that RCA had the short-sightedness to withdraw it from circulation.

Having spent considerable time relistening to the Angel recording led by Sir Simon Rattle, I must confess that I've warmed to it considerably. The singers are every bit as good as the Houston group—Harolyn Blackwell's version of "Summertime" seems to get sexier every time I hear it—and Rattle's sense of pacing and attention to detail become increasingly impressive. I'll still miss the Houston *Porgy*, but perhaps just a little less.

Gilbert, Sir William S.

(1836–1911) and

Sullivan, Sir Arthur

(1842–1900)

H.M. S. Pinafore

D'Oyly Carte Opera Company, Sargent (recorded 1930). Arabesque Z-8052-2 [CD].

Iolanthe

D'Oyly Carte Opera Company, Godfrey. London 414145-2 [CD].

The Mikado

D'Oyly Carte Opera Company, Nash. London 425190-2 [CD].

Patience

D'Oyly Carte Opera Company, Godfrey. London 425193-2 [CD].

The Pirates of Penzance

D'Oyly Carte Opera Company, Godfrey. London 414286-2 [CD].

Along with their inedible cuisine (who but they would even consider *looking* at such emetics as "Steak and Kidney Pie" and "Beans on Toast"?) and their public monuments (are there any structures in the civilized world quite so ugly as the Albert Memorial or the facade of Euston Station?), another of the great and presumably imperishable English traditions are the fourteen operas written by two of the strangest and most unlikely bedfellows in theatrical history, W. S. Gilbert and Arthur Sullivan. The myth that the two were close, inseparable friends is precisely that. From beginning to end, the relationship was characterized by mild mutual respect tempered by constant suspicion, distrust, and frequently open, albeit gentlemanly, contempt. In fact, all the two men had in common was an unshakable belief that each was prostituting his sacred talent for the sake of making money.

Those of us who are hopelessly drawn to the Gilbert and Sullivan operas tend to treat the affliction as any other incurable disease. For except among ourselves, to admit a passion for Gilbert and Sullivan is a bit like admitting to something slightly embarrassing, like being, to quote Sheridan Whiteside in *The Man Who Came to Dinner*, "the sole support of a two-headed brother."

For anyone similarly smitten, or for those who are thinking of taking the ghastly plunge for the first time, the recordings listed above represent a fair cross-section of the D'Oyly Carte Opera Company's finest achievements. While the *Iolanthe, Mikado, Patience, Pirates*, and Godfrey-led *Pinafore* recordings are among the very best that the late and greatly lamented company founded by Gilbert and Sullivan themselves would ever make (John Reed, the last in the unbroken line of Savoy patter comics, is especially delightful, and Donald Adams is an incomparable Dick Deadeye and Pirate King), the 1930 *Pinafore* remains in a class by itself. The principal attraction here, aside from the buoyant conducting of the young Malcolm Sargent, is one of the few complete recorded performances left by the greatest Savoyard of all. After a career spanning more than fifty years, Sir Henry Lytton was the only Gilbert and Sullivan performer ever knighted for his services. Even the great Martyn Green could not approach the horrible perfection of Lytton's Sir Joseph Porter, K.C.B. Dramatically, it is a triumph of bumbling incompetence and unbridled lechery. Musically, it is absolutely glorious, thanks in no small part to an inimitable "voice" that can best be described as a cross between a soggy Yorkshire pudding and a badly opened beer can.

Glazunov, Alexander

(1865–1936)

Concerto in A minor for Violin and Orchestra; *The Seasons*

Shumsky, violin; Scottish National Orchestra, Järvi.
Chandos CHAN-8596 [CD], ABTD-1285 [T].

Of all the well-known composers, Nikolai Rimsky-Korsakov had, by far, the most hideous wife. And considering the dispositions of women like Frau Haydn and the dread Pauline Strauss, that's saying something.

At her husband's funeral in 1908, Madame Rimsky-Korsakov, with an atypical rush of human feeling (to say nothing of a completely unprecedented flash of perception), noticed that the deceased's prize pupil, a young man named Igor Stravinsky, was utterly disconsolate. In an effort to comfort him, the woman put her hand on Stravinsky's shoulder and said, "Don't despair. We still have *Glazunov*."

Such was the extent of Alexander Glazunov's reputation at the turn of the century, although we now tend to think of him primarily as Rimsky's acolyte and as the teacher of Dmitri Shostakovich. That he did not quite become what everyone thought he would—the towering giant of Russian music—came as a shock to everyone, except, perhaps, to the composer himself.

But then, too, neither was he the cut-rate Tchaikovsky he was widely considered a generation ago. In the last few years, the musical world, especially the recording companies, has begun to reassess this minor but immensely attractive musical personality, with some extremely gratifying results.

Not surprisingly, that indefatigable Estonian recording machine, Neeme Järvi, is in the vanguard of the current Glazunov revival. While neither recording of the composer's two most enduring achievements, the Violin Concerto and the ballet *The Seasons*, is the last word in delicacy or excitement, both are the best available versions of these once-popular works and might help steer the listener in the even more interesting direction of the Glazunov symphonies.

With the Bamberg Symphony and Bavarian Radio Orchestra, Järvi has recorded all eight of the completed symphonies for Orfeo (a ninth exists as a fragmentary single movement), and almost without exception, both the pieces themselves and the performances are sources of undiluted pleasure. For those who'd prefer to begin slowly rather than investing in the entire set, the best place to begin is at the beginning, with the youthful, invigorating Symphony No. 1. Coupled with the brashly heroic Symphony No. 5 (Orfeo C-093101 [CD], M-093101 [T]), this is an excellent introduction to a body of work that deserves to be far better known.

Glière, Reinhold (1875–1956)

Symphony No. 3 in B minor, *Ilya Murometz*

BBC Philharmonic, Downes. Chandos CHAN-9041 [CD].

Best known for the ballet *The Red Poppy* and its (try as you will) unforgettable "Russian Sailor's Dance," Reinhold Glière was the Norman Rockwell of Soviet Socialist Realism, a man whose native musical conservatism (he was in fact irretrievably reactionary) fitted in perfectly with what the tone-deaf Joseph Stalin thought a "revolutionary" society ought to hear.

Glière's most important work, a mammoth programmatic symphony celebrating the life of a legendary Russian hero, is also his most controversial. The debate centers on just *how* bad the *Ilya Murometz* Symphony is.

Heavily edited, as it was in a famous recording by Leopold Stokowski, it was merely awful; given an uncut and committed performance—as it is here—it is *obscene*. Vulgar, vapid, stupid beyond description, it is a pathetic melange of bathos, bombast, and empty, knuckleheaded gestures. It is also terribly loud and terribly long.

If you love *Ilya* as helplessly as I do, you will acquire this splendid, virtually note-complete recording without delay. On the other hand, you might want to hold up on acquiring the other installments in the series. Coupled with the tone poem *The Za-porozhy Cossacks* (whose frightful title says it all), Glière's Second Symphony is rather like a bad steak in that the more you chew it, the bigger it gets (CHAN-9071 [CD]). The youthful First Symphony is even worse, with, to push the unfortunate metaphor even further, the unsavory texture of either very old meat or very new cheese. To make matters worse, the album forces you to endure the *whole* of *The Red Poppy* (CHAN-9160 [CD]).

For Glière in a substantially smaller and infinitely more palatable dose, his attractive Harp Concerto from 1938 (going on 1880) sounds sweeter than ever in another recent Chandos recording (CHAN-9094) from the City of London Sinfonia and Richard Hickox.

Gluck, Christoph Willibald

(1717–1787)

Orfeo ed Euridice

> Horne, Lorengar, Donath, Orchestra and Chorus of the
> Royal Opera House, Covent Garden, Solti. London
> 417410-2 [CD].

Listening to this best known of Gluck's "reform" operas today, it is all but impossible to understand the violent passions it unleashed more than two centuries ago. In Paris, where Gluck had set up shop in 1773, the composer's insistence that drama, instead of florid singing, should be the true focus of the operatic stage generated heated public debates. As a matter of fact, it even provoked a number of private duels, in which many of his partisans and those of his principal rival, Nicola Piccinni, were killed. Today, of course, Gluck's revolutionary operas seem rather tame and timid stuff, largely because the reforms he inaugurated have long been accepted as elementary tenets of how opera should behave.

After Purcell's *Dido and Aeneas*, *Orfeo ed Euridice* is the earliest extant opera performed with any frequency today. Though the action is generally static, and the characters are little more than cardboard cutouts, *Orfeo* has some beautiful moments that still have the power to move us deeply, including the celebrated "Dance of the Blessed Spirits" and the haunting aria, "Che, farò senza Euridice".

With Dame Janet Baker's Glyndebourne Festival recording currently unavailable, the Solti recording is an acceptable, if not wholly satisfying, alternative. Vocally, Marilyn Horne makes an impressive hero: her deep, throaty sound and virile delivery are both positive assets in the role of Orfeo. If Pilar Lorengar, as Euridice, has seen better days—the characterization is surprisingly tentative and the sound is insecure and unfocused—then Sir Georg Solti, who would seem to be rather out of his element in this staid and stately music, gives one of the better recorded performances of his career. The conducting is as tasteful as it is pointed, and rarely—as in "The Dance of the Blessed Spirits"—has this music conveyed more genuine feeling or quiet charm.

Goldmark, Karl (1830–1915)

Rustic Wedding Symphony

Royal Philharmonic, Butt. ASV CD DCA-791 [CD].

The son of an impoverished synagogue cantor born in the small Hungarian town of Keszthely, Karl Goldmark would eventually become one of the most popular and respected composers of his generation, thanks largely to a group of three works dashed out in short order between 1875 and 1878, beginning with the exotic and tuneful opera *The Queen of Sheba*. Among its many lovely moments is the ethereally beautiful tenor aria, "Magische Töne," superbly sung by Siegfried Jerusalem in the fine recording of the complete opera from Hungaroton (HCD-12179/82). Three years after writing *Queen of Sheba*, Goldmark produced one of the most instantly appealing of all late-Romantic violin concertos, which has never sounded more like the standard repertoire item it clearly deserves to be than in Itzhak Perlman's sumptuous Angel recording (CDC-47848 [CD]) with André Previn and the Pittsburgh Symphony.

Goldmark's masterpiece, though, is the delightful *Rustic Wedding Symphony* of 1876, which Brahms described as "clear-cut and faultless," and the young Mahler obviously admired it, too. The ASV recording by the Royal Philharmonic led by Yondani Butt is the most impressive since Leonard Bernstein's New York Philharmonic version from the late 1960s. Like Bernstein, Butt resists the temptation of making the bucolic and purposefully naive music sound more sophisticated than it was intended to be; the result is a wholly natural, spontaneous-sounding performance, which contains not the slightest hint of strain or condescension. In place of the more familiar Overture *Im Frühling*, the slightly windy (eighteen-minute) but generally charming *Sakuntala* Overture is the generous filler.

Górecki, Henryk

(1933–)

Symphony No. 3, *Symphony of Sorrowful Songs*

Upshaw, London Sinfonietta, Zinman. Elektra/Nonesuch 79282-2 [CD], 79282-4 [T].

There are some bits of bitter, pessimistic wisdom that you desperately hope aren't true—from Voltaire's glib assertion that "Marriage is a dull meal at which dessert is served at the beginning," to Dostoyevsky's rueful suggestion that "I believe the best definition of man is the ungrateful biped."

The Third Symphony of the Polish composer Henryk Górecki is almost enough to make you believe that history's most cynical curmudgeons may actually have had a point. In a recent *Record Shelf* called "Flim-flams, Frauds, and Floozies"—an angry look at some of the more blatant of recent musical frauds—the Górecki Third was the featured work after due consideration was given to the following: Zamfir, undisputed master (since who else in their right mind would want to bother?) of the ridiculous pan flute; the smarmy cocktail piano Puccini of John Bayless; the *Three Tenors Concert*, which offers a lot of shouting, bellowing, and generally second-rate singing; Paul McCartney's kitschy and excruciating *Liverpool Oratorio*; the sophomoric, amateurish, misbegotten swill called *The Juliet Letters* by Elvis Costello; the aptly named *Low* Symphony (adapted from the music of David Bowie) by Philip Glass; and Górecki's most serious competitor, the sleazy and oafish Lesley Garrett, a soprano of transcendentally modest accomplish- ment whose willingness to display herself on album covers in various degrees of sexual arousal has earned her a fortune.

In a two-page ad taken out in *Gramophone*, that most important and influential of English classical music magazines, Elektra/Nonesuch, the publishers of Górecki's Third Symphony, reproduced a sampling of the witheringly negative reviews the piece had received, from *The Evening Standard*'s abrupt, "A load of gloomy piffle," to Michael Kennedy's admonition, "Why this really rather dreary symphony has sent all those people to the record shops baffles me." On another page, they offered statistics in place of opinions, including the most important one of all from their point of view: Over 300,000 copies sold.

The implication is obvious: How can that many satisfied customers be wrong? To answer the purely rhetorical question, they can be wrong as easily as all those people who bought another surprising classical best seller of a generation ago. Merely a dull exercise in tone clusters, had the work been called Etude No. 2 it would have gone completely unnoticed; called "Threnody for the Victims of Hiroshima," it created a sensation.

Based on various sacred and secular laments, including one inscribed on a wall at Gestapo headquarters in Warsaw, the politically correct Third Symphony is equally dull, but dull in a slightly different way. For the concentrated dullness of Penderecki's *Threnody* is merely diluted in Górecki's Symphony. As Dr. Johnson said of Thomas Gray, "He was dull in a new way, and that made many people think him great." Or, even more to the point, as the good doctor said of Sheridan: "He is dull, naturally dull; but it must have taken him a great deal of pains to become what we now see him. Such an excess of stupidity, Sir, is not in nature."

Over 300,000 copies sold. The mind reels.

Gounod, Charles (1818–1893)

Roméo et Juliette

> Malfitano, Kraus, Quilico, Van Dam, Bacquier, Capitole de Toulouse Orchestra and Chorus, Plasson. Angel CDCC-47365 [CD].

Poor Charles Gounod has fallen on decidedly hard times. Then again, it's rather difficult to work up any real sympathy for one of the luckiest musicians who ever lived. It was a major miracle that the man who was perhaps the tenth best French composer of his generation parlayed a gift for sugary melody into one of the greatest successes in the history of the operatic stage. His opera *Faust* was at one time performed with such monotonous frequency that a turn-of-the-century wag recommended that the Metropolitan in New York be renamed the "Faustspielhaus."

That *Faust* may finally be losing its viselike grip on the world's affections is suggested by the fact that there are currently only about a dozen available recordings of it, and only one of them really works: the recent (and magnificently sung) Angel recording with Cheryl Studer, Richard Leech, Thomas Hampson, José van Dam, and the Capitole de Toulouse Orchestra led by Michel Plasson (CDCC 54228 [CD]).

In marked contrast to the composer's immensely lucrative Goethe travesty, his setting of Shakespeare's *Romeo and Juliet* is a far less presumptuous and probably far finer work. With the proper cast, this genuinely touching but sadly neglected opera can make a very moving impression, as this superb Angel recording easily proves. While the two principals don't exactly efface the memory of the legendary performances Jussi Björling and the Brazilian soprano Bidú Sayão gave at the Metropolitan Opera shortly after the end of the war, both are exceptionally fine: Catherine Malfitano is a melting, delectably innocent Juliette, and the Romeo of the aging but always canny Alfredo Kraus is a triumph of interpretive savvy and consummate musicianship over a voice that has clearly lost its bloom. As in his *Faust* recording, Michel Plasson's conducting is consistently sensitive, supportive, and richly romantic. The orchestra plays wonderfully, and the recorded sound is first-rate.

Grainger, Percy (1882–1961)

Composer, conductor, pianist, enthnomusicologist, linguistic theorist, the Australian-born Percy Grainger was one of the certifiable madmen of twentieth-century music. He thought his true mission in life was to purge the English language of its corrupting Latin influences; hence, in his scores he eschewed words such as *crescendo* in favor of toothsome phrases such as "louden lots." He experimented in polyphony plus electronic and "chance" music well in advance of almost everyone. And true to his iconoclastic nature, Grainer was married before a cheering crowd of fifteen thousand during an intermission at a Hollywood Bowl concert in 1928, at which he conducted the premiere of *To a Nordic Princess*, written for his bride.

As for his musical philosophy, Grainger maintained that the three greatest composers in history were Bach, Frederick Delius, and Duke Ellington, and following the example of the English philosopher Jeremy Bentham, who left his entire fortune to the University of London on condition that his corpse be present at all subsequent meetings of the Board, stipulated in his will that his remains be stuffed and placed on display at the Grainger Museum at the University of Melbourne. (Alas, cooler heads prevailed.)

In addition to being an irrepressible zany, Grainger was one of the most distinctive musical talents of his generation: a great pianist in an era of great pianists, a fearlessly quirky and individual composer, and perhaps the most inspired arranger of folk music who has ever lived.

His evergreen *Lincolnshire Posy* is available again in the classic recording by the Eastman Wind Ensemble led by Frederick Fennell (Mercury 432754-2 [CD]), whose equally memorable versions of Grainger standards like "Country Gardens," "Mock Morris," and "Handel on the Strand" can be found on another Mercury CD (434330-2). Kenneth Montgomery leads the Bournemouth Sinfonietta in a Chandos anthology (CHAN-6542 [CD]), which is every bit as enjoyable (the version of "Blithe Bells," a "free ramble" on Bach's "Sheep May Safely Graze" is alone worth the price of the CD), and the Michigan State University Symphonic Band step off very smartly on a Delos CD (DE-3101) called "To the Fore!"

The music Grainger "dished up for piano" is brilliantly realized by Martin Jones on a series of five Nimbus recordings (volume 1: NI-5220-2 [CD], NC-5220 [T]; volume 2: NI-5232-2 [CD], NC-5232 [T]; volume 3: NI-5244-2 [CD], NC-5244 [T]; volume 4: NI-5255 [CD]; volume 5: NI-5286 [CD]). Jones's playing is as fresh and imaginative as the music itself, and there isn't a single less-than-intriguing performance (or piece for that matter) in the entire collection. The arrangements for piano four-hands are also delectably served by the duo piano team of Thwaites and Lavender on a pair of Pearl CDs (SHE CD-9611/23), and Richard and John Contiguglia have recorded Grainger's inspired Gershwin transcriptions on a beautiful recording for MCA (MCAD-6626 [CD], MCAC-6626 [T]).

Finally, Grainger's own extraordinary gifts as a pianist are on abundant display in a Pearl recital (GEMM CD-9957 [CD]) that features the music of Bach, Chopin, Schumann, Grieg, Debussy, and Grainger in recordings made between 1923 and 1948. The playing is among the most individual and incandescent ever captured in a recording studio, and the transfers are superb.

Granados, Enrique

(1867–1916)

Goyescas Piano Suite

De Larrocha, piano. EMI CDMB 65424 [CD].

When the S.S. *Sussex* went down in the English Channel, torpedoed by a German U-boat in the second year of the Great War, she took with her one of the most original talents that Spain had ever produced.

With his friend Isaac Albéniz, it was Enrique Granados who reawakened serious music in Spain, with a group of colorful, electric, rhythmically vibrant reactions to the etchings and paintings of Francisco Goya. The suite for piano, *Goyescas*, helped to establish the vocabulary and parameters of modern Spanish music, and has remained a pianistic tour de force to be undertaken only by the most fearless virtuosos. (Granados would later adapt the music into an opera by the same name, adding an orchestral Intermezzo that would eventually become his most familiar work).

As in her most recent recording of Albéniz's *Iberia*, Alicia de Larrocha is literally incomparable in this music. Other pianists have certainly tried to invest *Goyescas* with this kind of wit, passion, and insouciance, but none has ever come close. She makes it all sound so natural and preposterously easy, that we need only sit back, relax, and enjoy the spells cast by one of the most beguiling sorceresses in living memory.

Grieg, Edvard (1843–1907)

Concerto in A minor for Piano and Orchestra

Perahia, piano; Bavarian Radio Orchestra, Davis. CBS
MK-44899 [CD].

One of the most apt but not completely flattering descriptions
of the music of Edvard Grieg came from Claude Debussy, who
called the diminutive Norwegian composer "a bonbon filled with
snow." The implication, of course, is that along with the bracing
Nordic freshness of his music, Grieg was essentially a miniaturist,
a composer of delicious little trifles and nothing more. For more
than a century, one of the most popular of all Romantic piano
concertos has given the lie to the suggestion that Grieg was only at
his best when he was thinking small. True, his finest work *does* tend
to come in smaller packages, but this enduring classic demonstrates
that he was perfectly comfortable in large-scale forms as well.

From a recording made at an actual concert, Murray Perahia
and Sir Colin Davis turn in a performance of uncommon dramatic power and interpretive finesse, one of those rare recordings in
which everyone concerned seems to walk the tightrope between
Romantic anarchy and modern control. The disciplined and completely unobtrusive German audience almost forgets to breathe,
and the recorded sound is supremely transparent and warm.

If sound is not a major consideration, no recording has ever
duplicated the poetry and insight of Dinu Lipatti's eternal 1947
performance, now available on a lovingly remastered Angel CD
(CDH-63497) or on an Odyssey tape (YT-60141).

Holberg Suite

Orpheus Chamber Orchestra. Deutsche Grammophon
423060-2 [CD].

Written in 1884 for the bicentenary of the birth of Ludvig
Holberg, the patriarch of Danish literature, the *Suite from Holberg's Time* is, after *Peer Gynt* and the Piano Concerto, the most
popular and most frequently recorded of Grieg's larger works.

The recording by the Orpheus Chamber Orchestra finds that brilliant conductorless ensemble at the top of its form, in both the *Holberg Suite* and the *Two Elegaic Melodies*. It's a pity that in place of the very fine version of the Tchaikovsky *Serenade for Strings*, they couldn't have recorded another major Grieg work. Better yet, perhaps Deutsche Grammophon could graft Orpheus's performances onto an exceptional Grieg recording by Neeme Järvi and the Gothenberg Symphony. That strenuously recommended release (419431-2 [CD]) brings you the finest available versions of the *Lyric Suite*, the *Norwegian Dances*, and the *Symphonic Dances*. Not only a great Grieg bash, but also a great buy.

Lyric Pieces for Piano

Gilels, piano. Deutsche Grammophon 419749-2 [CD].

Here are some of the most bewitching piano miniatures ever, in performances that are not likely to be equalled, much less surpassed. Emil Gilels might seem to be well outside his regular territory in this music, but his recording remains a standard against which all others will be judged. The playing reaches stratospheric heights, and the mixture of the familiar with the scarcely known works makes this one of the most desirable Grieg recordings ever made.

Anyone seriously devoted to this composer's piano music will find all of it—yes, *all* of it—on a monumental set of ten Bis compact discs (BCD-104/113) that features the gifted and apparently indefatigable Eva Knardahl. If her playing cannot really compare with Gilels's, it is not to be taken lightly, either. The interpretations are for the most part balanced, idiomatic, and unobtrusive, yet are not lacking in fire and individuality whenever the spirit moves her or the music demands. Not the least of the innumerable attractions of this gallant undertaking is the recorded sound. As we might expect from Bis, Robert von Bahr's small but maniacally perfectionist Swedish label, this is as close to being in a room with an actual piano as modern technology has come.

The Hungarian pianist Balázs Szokolay is recording a new series for the super-budget label Naxos, and on the evidence of the first two volumes (8.550450, 8.550477 [CDs]), it will be a very distinguished series indeed. There is an unforced natural charm in

Szokolay's playing, together with a feeling of utter spontaneity that places the best of his performances on the same rarified heights as Gilels's. These are two of the most enjoyable Grieg recordings currently available, and at a mere six bucks a pop represent a rather incredible bargain.

*P*eer Gynt (incidental music)

Hollweg, soprano; Beecham Choral Society, Royal Philharmonic, Beecham. Angel CDM-69039 [CD].

Carlsen, Hanssen, Bjørkøy, Hansli, Oslo Philharmonic Chorus, London Symphony, Drier. Unicorn-Kanchana UKCD-2003/04 [CD].

Like Tchaikovsky, who thoroughly despised his *Nutcracker* Suite, and Rachmaninoff, who often became violently nauseated at the prospect of having to give yet another performance of his C-sharp minor Prelude, Grieg was not especially fond of his most frequently performed work. In a famous letter written to the playwright Henrik Ibsen, he had this to say of the soon-to-be world-famous *In the Hall of the Mountain King*: "I have written something for the hall of the Troll king which smacks of so much cow dung, ultra-Norwegianism and self-satisfaction that I literally cannot bear to listen to it." In that, of course, Grieg has always been a minority of one. For the score he composed for a production of Ibsen's poetic drama *Peer Gynt* contains some of the best-loved moments in all of music.

For anyone who cut his or her musical teeth on the chestnuts from the two *Peer Gynt* Suites, the world premiere recording, from Unicorn, of the complete incidental music will come as a major and unfailingly delightful surprise. (By the way, all the other recordings that claim to contain the "complete" incidental music are stretching the laws of truth in advertising. With Neemi Järvi's recent, and slightly less successful, Deutsche Grammophon recording, and the virtually complete EMI recording with Jeffrey Tate, there are now precisely *three*.) Containing nearly an hour of unknown *Peer Gynt* music, the performance led by the fine Norwegian conductor Per Drier makes for an enlightening experience, to say the very least. The "heavy hits" are all done to near-perfection, but it is the cumulative impact of the other, completely unfamiliar episodes that creates the more indelible impression. Far from being the lightweight collection of saccharine lollipops it can often become, the *Peer Gynt* music for once emerges as vivid and powerful drama. Drier leads his forces with great individuality, charm, and authority; the Norwegian cast and chorus are consistently brilliant and idiomatic, and the playing of the London Symphony is above reproach.

The only serious flaw in this otherwise flawless recording is one that none of these dedicated performers could possibly control. For all its professionalism and devotion, it is simply *not* in the same stratospheric league with that vocally klutzy, harshly recorded source of wonder and despair Sir Thomas Beecham perpetrated a generation ago. In its new compact disc incarnation, this ageless performance seems even more magnetic and unsurpassable than ever. *Anitra's Dance* contains some of the most graceful playing ever captured in a recording studio, *The Death of Aase* becomes a muffled outcry of insupportable grief, and *Morning* dawns with a sylvan freshness that suggests the very first morning of the world. Yet it is in the *Hall of the Mountain King* that Beecham really makes us wonder what the composer's whining "cow dung" letter was all about. Unless, of course, Beecham read it too, and took that as his cue to do his best, in this macabre and terrifying performance, to scare a similar substance out of his listeners.

Grofé, Ferde (1892–1972)

Grand Canyon Suite

> Cincinnati Pops, Kunzel. Telarc CD-80086 [CD], CS-30086 [T].

There is a special category of quasi-classical pieces (one resists the term *semi-classical* since it immediately conjures up images of the 101 Strings and Mantovani) of which the *Grand Canyon Suite* seems to be the most stubborn survivor of all. Other examples include *Victory at Sea*, the *Warsaw Concerto*, the *Red Shoes* ballet (conducted in the movie by Sir Thomas Beecham), and one that never received anything like the attention it deserved: the suite from the music that Norman Dello Joio composed for the CBS News series *Airpower*, which was recorded (and how!), by Eugene Ormandy and the Philadelphia Orchestra. For want of a term both more succinct and more descriptive than *semi-* and/or *quasi-classical*, let's call this stuff Music Serious Music Lovers Wouldn't Be Caught Dead Admitting They Liked, Even If They Did.

Apart from its intrinsic merits—which are considerable—Ferde Grofé's celebration of the world's most inspiring ditch was given enormous credibility by the advocacy of Arturo Toscanini, who loved this brilliantly effective tour of his favorite spot on earth. (Since it was also the vehicle of one of the Maestro's few palatable NBC Symphony recordings, one wonders why RCA didn't issue it, instead of those dreadful Beethoven, Brahms, and Verdi catastrophes, as part of the first installment of the Complete Toscanini on CD.)

Among modern recordings of the *Grand Canyon Suite*, none is more spectacular than Erich Kunzel's Cincinnati Pops outing for Telarc. Part of the gimmick (and who doesn't love a good gimmick when it works?) is a second version of the *Cloudburst* movement, which includes a frighteningly realistic recording of an actual desert thunderstorm captured by Telarc's engineers. The performance itself is an exceptionally fine one: the orgasmic climax of *Sunrise* is beautifully built, and *On the Trail* lopes along with just the right touch of innocent humor.

I wonder if Kunzel ever watched *Airpower*? (Apparently, the American conductor Davis Amos did. His version of Dello Joio's score, in an earnest though something less than soaring performance by the Krakow Philharmonic, is now available on Koch 3-7020-2 [CD], 3-7020-4 [T].)

Halévy, Jacques

(1799–1862)

La Juive

> Varady, Anderson, Carreras, Gonzales, Furlanetto,
> Ambrosian Opera Chorus, Philharmonia Orchestra,
> Almeida. Philips 420190-2 [CD].

On February 23, 1835, the French-born son of a celebrated
Hebrew poet introduced an opera whose central character, a devout Jewish goldsmith, proved to be the last role the twentieth
century's greatest singer undertook. Enrico Caruso was scrupulous
in his preparation for Eléazar, the hero of Jacques Halévy's *La Juive*
(The Jewess); for months, he haunted New York's Orthodox syn-
agogues, consulting with various rabbis on virtually every gesture
and costume detail. It was in *La Juive* that Caruso gave his final
performance on Christmas Eve, 1920.

Halévy's most popular opera also has the distinction of being
the first important work by a Jewish composer on a Jewish theme
to achieve international popularity. With a sympathetic conductor
and a good cast—and it has both in this virtually complete Philips
recording—*La Juive* is every bit the equal of the best of Meyerbeer's
operas: a skillful mixture of intimate pathos and public spectacle
that helped defined the limits of French grand opera.

This recording began in 1986 without José Carreras, who had
recently been diagnosed with leukemia. By 1989, however, he
had recovered sufficiently to dub in his part. The results, predictably, are mixed. Carreras sings with control and conviction, yet the
ensemble pieces inevitably suffer—not as obviously as in the famous recording of *Aida* from the early '70s in which Aida and
Rhadames never actually appeared together, but some of the dramatic give-and-take is clearly missing. Otherwise, it is a marvelous
performance, with Julia Varady an emotionally rich Rachel and
June Anderson a fiery Princess Eudoxia. Antonio de Almeida keeps
things moving without compromising the stately progress of the
piece, while the Philips engineers capture it all, including the
dubbed-in Carreras bits, in spectacularly vivid recorded sound.

Handel, George Frideric

(1685–1759)

Concerti Grossi (12), Op. 6

**Academy of St. Martin-in-the-Fields, Brown. Philips
410048-2 [CD].**

**English Concert, Pinnock. Deutsche Grammophon 410897/
9-1 [CD].**

I somehow manage to shock people when I tell them I have always preferred the music of George Frideric Handel to that of Johann Sebastian Bach. I find Handel not only the far more appealing composer, but also the far more interesting man. Assiduously devoting his extramusical energies to prayer and the production of twenty-odd children, Bach seems to have been a classic seventeenth-century Lutheran homebody, whose life story makes for singularly boring reading. Handel, who was an internationally famous figure while Bach was still a provincial kapellmeister, was a mass of fascinating contradictions. In spite of his many physical and psychological afflictions—he was nearly felled by several major strokes, went blind at the end of his career, and for more than sixty years exhibited many of the classic symptoms of manic depression—Handel was nevertheless one of the healthiest composers in the history of music, a man whose many enthusiasms and vigorous love of life can be heard in virtually every bar of music he ever wrote.

Nowhere is the essence of Handelian exuberance and inventiveness more clearly in evidence than in these dozen concerti grossi he composed, largely for money, in 1739. (Dr. Johnson may have actually had Handel in mind when he framed one of the most irrefutable of all his aphorisms: "No man but a blockhead ever wrote, except for money.") Though much of the thematic material was purloined from the works of other composers, the collection is full of an utterly original and irresistible beauty. The dance movements are as infectious as any written by a Baroque composer, the slow movements are often poignant and invariably memorable, and the slap-dash, good-natured fugues remain as impressive as any Bach ever wrote.

Of all the fine recordings that are currently available, pride of place clearly goes to the elegant Philips set by the Academy of St. Martin-in-the-Fields. While detailed and scholarly, these non-period-instrument performances have none of the musty, stuffy, academic quality that has marred so many recent Handel recordings. Under Iona Brown, as they had for years under Sir Neville Marriner, the St. Martin's Academy plays with an appealing combination of bravado and finesse, and the Philips engineers have provided a warm but lively acoustic that is the perfect mirror of the performances themselves.

For the Baroque Authenticity Purists, Trevor Pinnock's only slightly less desirable Deutsche Grammophon recording offers a fine period-instrument alternative.

Concertos (16) for Organ and Orchestra

Hurford, organ; Concertgebouw Chamber Orchestra, Rifkin. London 430569-2 [CD].

As a boy, my idea of ultimate torture—besides watching the deeply detested Chicago Cubs win the occasional game—was being made to sit still while someone was playing the organ. It undoubtedly had something to do with spending Sunday mornings languishing in a hot, stuffy Premethepiscobapterian church that smelled of dust and peppermint, while a sweet but hopelessly inept matron fumbled her way through hymn after ghastly hymn. To this day, it takes a lot to make me listen to the organ; Peter Hurford almost makes it a pleasure. Of course, he has a bit of help here from George Frederic Handel.

Handel's organ music could not be further removed from either the horrifying experiences of my youth or the leaden, insufferably self-righteous outpourings of many of the other Baroque masters. (Legend has it that Bach walked two hundred miles to hear Dietrich Buxtehude play; I would have *run* several miles in the opposite direction to have avoided it.) Even in the least of these works—and the general level of quality is phenomenally high—imagination and exuberance are to be found on every page, and Hurford's stylish, manly enthusiasm is difficult to resist. On a pair of medium-priced CDs, this is a tremendous amount of enjoyment for twenty bucks. If you can resist, your willpower is far more highly developed than mine.

Coronation Anthems (4)

Academy and Chorus of St. Martin-in-the-Fields, Marriner. Philips 412733-2 [CD].

If until very recently the House of Windsor has seemed one of the least interesting and most dim-witted of Britain's royal families, the Windsors have been rocket scientists compared to the ill-starred and unlamented Hanoverian kings. George I, the founder of the line, not only refused to learn English during his reign but also succeeded in enraging his British subjects even more by refusing to trade in his German mistresses for English ones. His unstable grandson, George III, who suffered from recurrent bouts of madness throughout his life, was responsible for the loss of the nation's American colonies. In fact, the only significant accomplishment the entire dynasty can point to with pride was its employment of the Saxon composer George Frideric Handel, who produced for them some of the greatest ceremonial and occasional music ever written.

The magnificent *Coronation Anthems* are all that survive from the thoroughly bungled coronation of George II in 1727. At their first performance, the sequence of the hymns, together with most of the actual ceremony, was somehow thrown completely out of whack, thereby making it a typically Georgian event. Still, the anthems that Handel provided are so stirring in their grandeur, so rich in their invention and execution, that upon hearing them even the most tenaciously republican of her former colonists might almost be tempted to ask Her Majesty to take us back.

Neville Marriner's Philips recording offers suitably grand, though never grandiose, performances of these imposingly noble works. The interpretation of the seven-minute *Zadok the Priest*, with its mysteriously hushed opening and thundering final fugue on the word *Alleluia*, is in itself worth more than the price of the recording. For anyone addicted to eighteenth-century pomp and circumstance, or who simply wants to be convinced that there *will* always be an England, this is a recording that cannot be passed up.

The Faithful Shepherd; *The Gods Go a'Begging* (suites arranged by Beecham); *Handel at Bath* (suite arranged by Allan Bennett)

> Royal Philharmonic, Menuhin. RPO Records 9004 [CD].

Rather than step out into the alley and try to settle *this* one again, suffice it to say that anyone who admires the works and pomps of that marvelous hybrid composer, Handel-Beecham (a very close relative of Handel-Harty) will love these confections in the extremely tasty performances served up here by Sir Yehudi Menuhin. Handel-Bennett, while less distinguished, is still very endearing, as are the performances of the only *echt* Handel pieces on the program, the Overture and familiar "Arrival of the Queen of Sheba" from *Solomon*.

All that's needed now to propel us Baroque lowbrows into ersatz-Handel heaven is a CD reissue from Angel of Beecham's own recording of his masterpiece in the form, *Love in Bath*, which includes among its numerous wonders a trombone quotation of "Rule, Britannia" and an *allegro* setting of the famous Largo.

Messiah

> Marshall, Robbin, Rolfe-Johnson, Hale, Brett, Quirke,
> Monteverdi Choir, English Baroque Soloists, Gardiner.
> Philips 411041-2 [CD].

While his dramatic oratorios *Jeptha* and *Theodora* are probably finer works (Handel considered the chorus "He Saw the Lovely Youth" from *Theodora* his absolute masterpiece), *Messiah* has more than earned its status as the best-loved sacred work of all time. Its level of inspiration is astronomically high, and its musical values are phenomenally impressive, given the fact that the whole of the oratorio was dashed off in something under three weeks.

Although there are nearly two dozen *Messiah* recordings currently available, Sir Thomas Beecham's famous recording of the stunning arrangement by Sir Eugene Goossens remains unique. And until you've heard *Messiah* with Jon Vickers's singing, Beecham's racy tempos, and an orchestra that includes trombones, tubas, tam-tams, cymbals, snare drums, and gong, you haven't really lived (RCA 09026-61266-2 [CD]).

A wonderful version of that greatest *Messiah* arrangement of all has also turned up on RCA (7786-2-RC [CD], 7786-4-RC [T]): Sir Charles Mackerras's loving interpretation of Mozart's German edition, in which the ingenious wind parts that were grafted on to Handel's string torso make for such an intoxicating amalgam of Christ and *Don Giovanni*. Perhaps the most beautifully played and sung of all *Messiahs* is Sir Colin Davis's Philips recording with the London Symphony, now reissued (420865-2) on the company's medium-priced Silver Line series and *not* to be confused with his disappointing digital remake with the Bavarian Radio Orchestra.

John Eliot Gardiner's triumphant period-instrument version can be confidently mentioned in the same breath with any of the great *Messiah* recordings of the past. In fact, in many ways, it is the most completely satisfying *Messiah* ever released. Using the reduced performing forces and older instruments that are common to almost every *Messiah* recording of the last decade, Gardiner nevertheless succeeds in projecting almost all of the oratorio's size and significance in a performance that is still very intimate in its physical dimension and sound. The soloists are all intelligent and musical, the chorus—in which Gardiner has wisely opted for sopranos instead of the more "authentic" boys—sings with joy and devotion, and the English Baroque Soloists, while they play with great precision and high-minded intensity, still give the unmistakable impression that they're all having an enormous amount of fun. Though nothing will ever make me part with my well-worn copies of the Davis, Beecham, and Mackerras recordings, the exultant new Gardiner version now joins that select circle of *Messiahs* I cannot do without.

*M*usic for the Royal Fireworks

> London Symphony, Szell. London 417694-2 [CD], 417694-4 [T].

> Cleveland Symphony Winds, Fennell. Telarc CD-80038 [CD].

It was through the arrangements for modern orchestra by the gifted Ulster composer and conductor Sir Hamilton Harty that Handel's *Music for the Royal Fireworks* and *Water Music* first became accessible to twentieth-century audiences. And although that curious hybrid composer Handel-Harty is now persona non grata in most musical circles, George Szell's gorgeous London recording from the mid-1960s proves just how ridiculous such snobbery is. The arrangements, while admittedly anachronistic, are as tasteful as they are exciting, and if you can bear the scorn of the Baroque-purist crowd, this recording will offer you countless hours of undiluted pleasure and delight.

Thanks to the classic series of recordings he made with the Eastman Wind Ensemble for Mercury, the name of Frederick Fennell is far more closely associated with Sousa marches than with Baroque Authenticity. Nevertheless, on this brilliant Telarc recording he leads the finest "authentic" performance of the *Royal Fireworks Music* currently available. Because, as its title implies, the work was originally intended for performance in the open and soon to be sulfur-clogged air, Handel's original scoring called for instruments that had a fighting chance of making themselves heard above the ruckus: a huge wind band dominated by oboes and bassoons. Fennell's forces make a spectacular noise on this high-tech Telarc recording. You can almost hear every buzzing vibration in that forest of double reeds, and the brass are so emphatic and lively you can nearly smell the valve oil. For audiophiles, Handel lovers, and anyone who has ever spent time in a high school band, this is an absolutely essential recording.

*O*de for St. Cecilia's Day

> Lott, Rolfe-Johnson, English Concert and Chorus, Pinnock.
> Deutsche Grammophon 419220-2 [CD].

Like his oratorio *Israel in Egypt*, which can be heard on a superb Erato recording led by John Eliot Gardiner (ECD-88182 [CD]), Handel's setting of Dryden's "A Song for St. Cecilia's Day" is at once one of his most brilliant and shameful works: brilliant because it finds Handel the composer of choral music at the summit of his powers; shameful because all of the *Ode for St. Cecilia's Day*, as with most of *Israel in Egypt*, was cribbed from other sources. The oratorio drew its "inspiration" from several directions, whereas the thematic material of the *Ode* was stolen in its entirety from a collection of harpsichord pieces published by Handel's older contemporary Georg Muffat.

Of course, it is what Handel *made* of Muffat's melodies that matters, and with the *Ode for St. Cecilia's Day* he fashioned the finest of his smaller-scale vocal works. Though several of the arias that celebrate the patron saint of music are among the most exceptional Handel would ever produce—the gently insinuating "What passion cannot Music raise and quell?" and the hectoring "The trumpet's loud clangor" are only two—it is in its choruses that the *Ode* rises to its full greatness. For instance, the final fugue on Dryden's couplet, "The dead shall live, the living die,/ And Music shall untune the sky!" is among the principal treasures of Baroque music.

What Trevor Pinnock's period-instrument performance may lack in sumptuousness of sound it makes up for in stylishness and vigor. The reflective passages are brought off with the utmost sensitivity; the more boisterous items have an admirable snap and bustle.

Devotees of Handel's later Dryden ode, *Alexander's Feast*, will find it elegantly realized on a Philips recording (422053-2 [CD]) in a performance led—surprise! surprise!—by John Eliot Gardiner. *And* as long as you're browsing through the Handel section of your favorite store, you might just as well pick up Gardiner's exciting, illuminating, incorruptible versions of *L'Allegro, il Penseroso ed il Moderato* (Erato 2292-45377-2 [CD]), *Dixit Dominus* (Erato 2292-45136-2 [CD], 2292-45136-4 [T]), *Saul* (Philips 426265-2), *Semele* (Erato 2292-45982-2 [CD], and *Solomon* (Philips 412612-2 [CD], 412612-4 [T]) and save yourself some extra trips.

Judas Maccabaeus is currently best served by the 1979 Vanguard recording (OVC-4071/72 [CD]) featuring a sterling quartet of soloists (Harper, Watts, Young, and Shirley-Quirk) with the English Chamber Orchestra and Amor Artis Chorale conducted by Johannes Somary. Somary and company are even more impressive in the late masterpiece, *Theodora* (OVC-4074/5 [CD], which contains the composer's own favorite of all his works, the magnificent chorus "He Saw the Lovely Youth."

Water Music

Los Angeles Chamber Orchestra, Schwarz. Delos DCD-3010 [CD].

My unremitting enthusiasm for the recording by the Los Angeles Chamber Orchestra has absolutely nothing to do with civic pride. The only Southern California cultural institutions for which

I have a blind and uncontrollable passion are the Dodgers and Disneyland. This is, quite simply, the most thrillingly played of all recorded performances of Handel's popular score, and, by a comfortable margin, the craziest. The insanity here consists largely of what might best be described as virtuosity gone berserk. In a performance that features nearly as many added ornaments as notes in the score, Gerard Schwarz leads his brilliant ensemble through one of the great recorded bravura exercises of the last decade. The playing is dumfounding in its swaggering effortlessness: listen especially to the LACO oboes and horns for some of the most breathtaking technical legerdemain to be heard on recordings today.

Among available tapes of the complete *Water Music*, Trevor Pinnock's affable period-instrument recording for Deutsche Grammophon (410525-4) is easily the preferred version.

Hanson, Howard (1896–1981)

Symphony No. 2, *Romantic*

Seattle Symphony, Schwarz. Delos DCD-3073 [CD].

One of the most embarrassing of the numerous embarrassing moments I have suffered during my radio career occurred at a small station in upstate New York in the mid-1970s, shortly after I introduced this moltenly beautiful symphony as being a work by "the late Howard Hanson." Midway through the first movement, the "late" Dr. Hanson phoned the station and proceeded to point out, in the most charming way imaginable, that my information was not entirely accurate.

For anyone who attended the National Music Camp at Interlochen, Michigan, the principal theme of the *Romantic* Symphony has many powerful associations. Since the late 1930s it has served to conclude every concert as the "Interlochen Theme" and was for years the signature theme of the camp's weekly NBC broadcasts. (More recently, Jerry Goldsmith used it to memorable effect at the end of his score for Ridley Scott's sci-fi thriller *Alien*.)

This Delos recording by Gerard Schwarz and his superbly trained Seattle Symphony is not only the finest recording of the *Romantic* we are likely to hear for the rest of the century, it is an interpretation whose sweep and energy rival those of the several recordings the composer made himself. The playing is as full of genuine sentiment as it is totally lacking in mawkish sentimentality, and the rhythmic tingle Schwarz wires into the jazzy sections of the final movement is a delight to hear. Offering equally convincing performances of the gorgeous *Nordic* Symphony and the rarely heard but deeply touching *Elegy in Memory of My Friend Serge Koussevitzky*, this is an important, exciting recording.

If anything, the subsequent releases in Delos's Hanson series have proven even more valuable. The greatest of the symphonies — the Third — together with the *Fantasy Variations on a Theme of Youth* and the Symphony No. 6 are all given gripping performances on Delos DE-3092 [CD]; the most personal work in the canon, the Fourth — called the *Requiem* since it was written in memory of his father — is grouped on Delos DE-3105 [CD] with the outrageously beautiful *Lament for Beowulf*, one of the finest and most deeply moving choral works ever written by an American, and the exciting suite from the composer's opera, *Merry Mount*. The Fifth and Seventh, the two symphonies with texts by Walt Whitman, are coupled with the colorful *Mosaics* for Orchestra on Delos DE-3130 [CD].

The only possible way to improve this brilliant series would be a complete version of *Merry Mount*, together with a Schwarz-led survey of early Hanson works such as the *Symphonic Legend*, the tone poems *Before the Dawn* and *Exaltation*, and the Organ and Piano Concertos.

Harris, Roy (1898–1979)

Symphony No. 3

New York Philharmonic, Bernstein. Deutsche Grammophon 419780-2 [CD].

If Roy Harris was not the most original and important symphonist America has so far produced, then the only other possible candidate for that distinction is William Schuman, whose Third Symphony is paired with Harris's here. This superb recording of two live New York Philharmonic performances of what are probably the finest symphonies both men composed affords us an excellent opportunity to make up our minds.

On balance, the Harris Third, which had a tremendous vogue during the 1940s, still seems the fresher and more startling work. And in its day, this concise, dramatic, and often soaringly lyrical piece attracted more than the usual New Music Crowd audience. Harris received fan mail on a regular basis from all sorts of people, including cab drivers, politicians, and baseball managers. The Schuman Third, while it may lack the Harris Symphony's apparent ease of inspiration, is nonetheless a starkly proud and powerful statement by a keen and frequently astringent musical mind. It may also be the better made of the two works, which, given Harris's fanatical approach to craftsmanship, is saying a very great deal.

Leonard Bernstein's invigorating interpretations of both symphonies will provide an ideal introduction to anyone who has yet to become familiar with these seminal works in the development of American symphonic thought. Though the conductor made some very fine studio recordings of both symphonies during his years with Columbia, the excitement of these concert performances easily outstrips the earlier versions'.

Serge Koussevitzky commissioned Harris's masterpiece, and his uniquely powerful interpretation—together with a live 1934 recording of the *Symphony 1933* (Symphony No. 1)—is now available on a Pearl anthology of classic Koussey recordings of American music, which include works by Copland and Arthur Foote. Although it's good to have Vladimir Golschmann's vigorous performance of the *Folksong Symphony* (No. 4) back in circulation (Vanguard OVC-4076 [CD]), it would be better still to have Maurice Abravanel's even more stirring account reissued by EMI. If the reissue on Albany (AR 012-2 [CD]) of Robert Whitney's business-like Louisville Orchestra recording of the Fifth Symphony is little more than a stop-gap until something better comes along (perhaps, beat still my heart, a Harris cycle from Schwarz and the Seattle Symphony?) then Keith Clark's brilliant realization with the Pacific Symphony of the *Gettysburg* (No. 6) is one of the most exhilarating Harris recordings in years (Albany TROY-064 [CD]).

Harty, Sir Hamilton

(1879–1941)

Irish Symphony; *A Comedy Overture*

Ulster Orchestra, Thomson. Chandos CHAN-8314 [CD], ABTD-1027 [T].

The Ulsterman Sir Hamilton Harty is best known for being half of one of history's most celebrated hyphenated composers. It was Harty's joyous and accomplished arrangements for modern orchestra of Handel's *Royal Fireworks* and *Water Music* that introduced the composer to several generations of music lovers before the snobbish and pedantic period-instrument movement made such "tampering" unfashionable. In addition to elevating the Hallé Orchestra of Manchester to the very front rank of European ensembles, Harty was a charming and resourceful composer whose best works evidence a profound understanding of the possibilities of the modern orchestra and an abiding passion for his native Ireland.

An examination of Bryden Thomson's admirable cycle of Harty recordings should begin with *An Irish Symphony*, a beautifully made potpourri of traditional Irish airs, and the sparkling *Comedy Overture*. The performances by the Ulster Orchestra are so bracing and affectionate that most people will want to investigate other recordings in the Chandos series, beginning with the sturdy and tuneful Violin Concerto and thoroughly charming *Variations on a Dublin Air* (CHAN-8386 [CD]), followed by those two haunting vocal works that may well be Harty's finest achievements, *The Children of Lir* and the *Ode to a Nightingale* (ABR-1051 [T]), which also find the wonderful soprano Heather Harper at her most fetching.

Haydn, Franz Joseph
(1732–1809)

Concertos (2) for Cello and Orchestra

Schiff, cello; Academy of St. Martin-in-the-Fields, Marriner. Philips 420923-2 [CD].

For reasons that are not so easy to explain, Haydn's D Major Cello Concerto has never been the basic staple of the cellist's rather limited solo repertoire it certainly deserves to be. Witness the fact that the C Major Concerto, which was not discovered until the 1960s in Prague, is nowadays heard almost as frequently. Perhaps it has something to do with the fact that neither concerto is a crowd-pleasing whiz-bang display piece, and that if orchestras are going to hire big-name players they generally want more drawing power than these modestly elegant eighteenth-century works are likely to supply.

Heinrich Schiff, partnered by a conductor with impeccable Haydn credentials, gives each of the concertos a vibrant, immaculately shaped performance: the C Major is especially graceful and lighthearted, but the D Major isn't far behind. Philips provides an unusually warm and natural acoustic for an unusually heartwarming release.

Concerto in E-flat for Trumpet and Orchestra

Marsalis, trumpet; National Philharmonic, Leppard. CBS MK-37846 [CD], IMT-37846 [T].

Though he was the literal father of the classical symphony and string quartet (the nineteenth century didn't call him "Papa" for nothing), few of the numerous operas, keyboard sonatas, or instrumental concertos Haydn composed throughout his life have ever been very popular, with the exception of the delightful and justly famous Trumpet Concerto. Along with its abundance of memorable melody and virtuoso fireworks, the Concerto is also a work of considerable historical significance. It was the first work by a major composer written for a newfangled contraption that was several generations ahead of its time: the initial, but not completely practical, incarnation of the *valved* trumpet.

When Wynton Marsalis's now famous recording was first released a few years ago, it was accompanied by an enormous amount of ballyhoo and hype. As the first classical recording by one of the finest jazz musicians of the younger generation, it promised little more than Barbra Streisand's ill-starred venture into art song, or the wonderful Cleo Laine's horrendous Frankenstein-Meets-the-Wolfman encounter with Schoenberg's *Pierrot Lunaire*. What it delivered, on the other hand, was one of the most stylish and spellbindingly brilliant recordings this beloved work has ever received.

Formidable competition comes from Gerard Schwarz on Delos and a majestic (and alas, now deleted) Deutsche Grammophon recording by the recently retired principal trumpet of the Chicago Symphony, Adolf Herseth, but Marsalis continues to set the standard for both lyric expressiveness and bravura display. The cadenzas he supplies are so electrifying that the playing would make the hair on a bald man's head stand on end.

Concertos (2) for Violin and Orchestra; *Sinfonia concertante* in B-flat for Oboe, Bassoon, Violin, Cello, and Orchestra

Wallfisch, violin; Orchestra of the Age of Enlightenment. Virgin CDC-59266 [CD].

Even more than his cello concertos, Haydn's violin concertos are among the most strenuously ignored of all his works. Admittedly, neither of these youthful scores is a masterpiece, but each contains a lovely slow movement and a typically bubbly Haydn finale, and both are bound to give considerable pleasure, especially in performances as enthusiastic as these. The Orchestra of the Age of Enlightenment is equally persuasive in the graceful, much-harder-than-it-sounds *Sinfonia concertante*, and the recorded sound is both warm and refined.

Although of doubtful authenticity, the C Major Oboe Concerto is an unfailingly delightful work (*whoever* wrote it), particularly in the Deutsche Grammophon recording (431678-2 [CD]) by Paul Goodwin and the English Concert led by Trevor Pinnock. In addition to a very stylish version of the D Major *Clavier Concerto*, the recording also comes with a version of Haydn's greatest concerto for the keyed trumpet. Sounding like a cross between a maladjusted steam valve and a saxophone with very bad adenoids, the trumpet produces noises that are a sheer delight.

The Creation

Augér, Langridge, D. Thomas, City of Birmingham Chorus and Symphony, Rattle. Angel CDCB-54159 [CD].

One of the high water marks in the sacred music of the Age of Enlightenment, *The Creation* is an innocent, dramatic, unaffected, and beautifully made celebration of the God of whom Haydn said so frequently, "When I think of Him, my heart leaps with joy." Even those who do not typically respond to lengthy religious works will find that *The Creation* overflows with such a wealth of inspired melodic and theatrical invention, only the most adamant of pagans are able to resist its glories. For instance, the choral outburst on the words "Let there be light" must certainly rank with the most exultant moments in all of music.

For the last thirty years, *The Creation* has led a charmed life on records. With the exception of Herbert von Karajan's last effort, a performance recorded at the 1982 Salzburg Festival that is so sinister in its calculation it would warm the cockles of an atheist's heart, there has really never been a *bad* recording of *The Creation*. Even Karajan's 1969 Deutsche Grammophon version has much to recommend it, especially the unbelievably moving singing of tragically short-lived Fritz Wunderlich, captured in one of the final commercial recordings that incomparable tenor would make.

The most consistently rewarding version of the oratorio was Sir Neville Marriner's masterful interpretation for Philips, now withdrawn but presumably awaiting resurrection on one of the company's popular "Duo" sets. Sir Simon Rattle's English-language version is also an exceptionally fine one, notably in its highlighting of the naive programmatic effects that so delighted Beethoven. In its bluff, Handelian confidence and humor, together with its recourse to the English text of which the composer readily approved, it is the kind of performance that proves Haydn, if not the Lord Himself, *must* have been an Englishman.

Mass No. 11 in D minor, *Nelson Mass*

Lott, Watkinson, Davies, Wilson-Johnson, English Concert and Chorus, Pinnock. Deutsche Grammophon 423097-2 [CD].

Blegen, Killebrew, Riegel, Estes, Westminster Choir, New York Philharmonic, Bernstein. Sony SM2K-47563 [CD].

Most of the dozen great Masses Haydn composed date from the final years of his extraordinarily productive career. The fact that they contain some of the most wonderful music Haydn (or anyone else, for that matter) ever wrote bears eloquent testimony to his willingness to learn and grow.

The period-instrument performance of the *Nelson* Mass led by Trevor Pinnock is among this accomplished musician's most successful yet. It is one of high drama, soaring lyricism, and unflagging energy, all captured in state-of-the-art recorded sound.

Leonard Bernstein's powerful CBS recording from the 1970s has been reissued with an equally successful version of the Mass No. 10, *Mass in Time of War*, as part of Sony's "Royal Edition," the series with all those painfully ordinary watercolors by H.R.H. The Prince of Wales on the covers. The interpretations are both sensitive and highly charged, with brilliant singing and playing from everyone involved. If anything, Bernstein's recording of the Mass No. 14, *Harmoniemesse*, is even more inspired. Listening to his infectiously bouncy opening of the *Benedictus*, one realizes why

Haydn, when asked why his sacred music was so strangely light-hearted, said: "Why, because when I think of God, my heart leaps with joy." The performance is only available on a pair of Sony CDs (SM2K-47560) coupled with the conductor's very fine recording of *The Creation*, providing an excellent German complement to Simon Rattle's outstanding English version.

*T*he Seasons (Die Jahreszeiten)

> **Bonney, Rolfe-Johnson, Schmidt, Monteverdi Choir, English Baroque Soloists, Gardiner. Deutsche Grammophon 431818-2 [CD].**

Compared to *The Creation*, Haydn's final oratorio has always remained far less popular for reasons that are hardly a well-kept secret. The subject matter is the heart of the problem, for how can the mere turning of the year compare with the relatively dramatic acts recounted in *Genesis*? For many since Haydn's time, the bucolic joys of *Die Jahreszeiten* have offered about as much excitement as watching the grass grow.

Like Sir Thomas Beecham, who made a gripping recording of the oratorio in the early days of stereo, John Eliot Gardiner couldn't disagree more. He finds drama and excitement aplenty throughout the score—*Die Jahreszeiten*'s storms were Beethoven's model for his *Pastorale* Symphony—together with abundant lyrical grace and an earthy, Breugel-like humor. The soloists are exceptionally eloquent and Gardiner's chorus and orchestra respond with their usual sensitivity, enthusiasm, and prodigious skill.

*S*onatas for Keyboard

> **Brendel, piano. Philips 416643-2 [CD].**
> **Bilson, fortepiano. Elektra/Nonesuch 78018-2 [CD].**
> **Gould, piano. CBS M2K-36947 [CD].**

They turn up, occasionally, as opening works on recitals—not being terribly demanding, they give the performer a chance to warm up—and they are heard on the radio from time to time, usually as a palate-cleanser after a Mahler symphony. Haydn's keyboard sonatas (and he composed more than sixty) have never had the popular appeal of Beethoven's or even Mozart's, although the best of them are a constant source of astonishment.

Alfred Brendel has done more than anyone in recent years to bring this music some of the attention it has been denied during the last couple centuries. His performances are enthusiastic, compelling, and quirky but always convincing and thoroughly personal; in fact, they represent some of the finest work that this intelligent, versatile artist has yet done in the recording studio.

Malcolm Bilson is one of those rare period-instrument specialists who gives the impression that he is following the lonely road of the fortepianist out of choice, rather than of necessity. He is a personable, magnetic performer who persuades us—as long as he is playing—that those tinny, tinkly sounds really *are* the only appropriate ones for the keyboard music of the period. His Haydn recordings are lively and entertaining, and only make us wish that more were generally available. (At this writing, two of his Titanic LPs are still in the catalog, though one can only assume that their days are numbered.)

If not quite as perverse as his infamous Mozart recordings, the Gould interpretations of the late sonatas are completely insane. A stylistic amalgam of Bach and Prokofiev, Gould's Haydn is a strange and strangely appealing invention, proving that these underrated works—like all important music—are open to an almost limitless variety of points of view.

String Quartets (6), Op. 76

Kodály Quartet. Naxos 8.550314; 8.550315; 8.550129 [CDs].

It was with the historic collection published as his Op. 20 that Haydn, in effect, invented the single most important vehicle of Western chamber music, the modern string quartet. In all the quartets he had written previously, the function of the viola, second violin, and cello was to support and embellish the first violin's solo line; with Op. 20, all four instruments began to become the equal partners they have remained ever since.

Of the eighty-two string quartets—from many of his earliest published compositions to the unfinished D minor fragment he was working on at the time of his death—none have proven to be more popular than the Op. 76 collection, which contains the *Quinten*, the *Sunrise*, and the *Emperor*, three of the most familiar of all string quartets.

At any price, the recordings by the Kodály Quartet on the superbudget Naxos label would be the ones to own. The performances are shot through with a sense of wonder and discovery, without a single routine or ill-considered phrase. Few recordings (few live performances, for that matter) seem as fresh, spontaneous, and openhearted as these, except, perhaps, for their equally memorable versions of the Op. 54 (8.550395 [CD]) and Op. 55 (8.550397 [CD]) collections, their first installment of the early quartets from Op. 1 and 2 (8.550399 [CD]), or the moving versions of the unfinished Op. 103 fragment coupled intelligently with *The Seven Last Words of Christ on the Cross* (8.550346 [CD]). When complete, the Kodály's cycle of all the Haydn string quartets should prove as valuable and important as Antal Dorati's historic recording of the symphonies. Thus far, it has been an undiluted joy.

The Tátrai Quartet play with a warm, idiomatic grasp of the material in their cycle for Hungaroton, with interpretations that manage to remain straightforward without ever sounding impersonal or dull. Their recording of the pivotal Op. 20 collection is highly recommended (Hungaroton HCD-11332/3 [CD]), as are their versions of the colorful Op. 33 set, which includes the *Joke* and the *Bird* (Hungaroton HCD-11887/8 [CD]).

Symphonies (104) (complete)

> Philharmonia Hungarica, Dorati. London 425900-2 (1–16);
> 425905-2 (17–33); 425910-2 (34–47); 425915-2 (48–
> 59); 425920-2 (60–71); 425925-2 (72–83); 425930-2
> (84–95); 425935-2 (96–104) [CDs].

In both its scope and level of accomplishment, Antal Dorati's justly famous cycle of the complete Haydn symphonies is one of the supreme achievements in the history of recorded music. Under the watchful eye of that greatest of Haydn scholars, H. C. Robbins Landon, Dorati and his musicians turned in a series of performances that were remarkable for their vigor, imagination, and consistency. The familiar symphonies reveal themselves with a wonderful sense of discovery and life, while the more obscure ones all tend to sound like preposterously neglected masterworks. The recorded sound from the 1970s is still exceptionally clear and warm, and Robbins Landon's program notes are among the most literate and enjoyable ever written. For offering so much enjoyment and enlightenment in such an attractive and economical package, London deserves everyone's heartfelt thanks.

Symphonies: No. 6 in D, *Le Matin*; No. 7 in C, *Le Midi*; No. 8 in G, *Le Soir*

> **English Concert, Pinnock. Deutsche Grammophon 423098-2 [CD].**

In these appealing early works in which we hear the embryonic form of the classical symphony beginning to coalesce in the hands of its first great master, Trevor Pinnock and the English Concert give alert and lively performances, although the lack of string vibrato may get on the nerves of some listeners. Still, this is world-class Haydn and the best single CD of these charmers for anyone who wants a period-instrument alternative or doesn't care to invest in the Dorati box.

Symphonies: No. 22 in E-flat, *The Philosopher*; No. 63 in C, *La Roxelane*; No. 80 in D minor

> **Orpheus Chamber Orchestra. Deutsche Grammophon 427337-2 [CD].**

The French academics who chastised César Franck for the revolutionary idea of including an English horn in his D minor Symphony had obviously forgotten about (or had never heard) Haydn's *Philosopher* Symphony, which uses not one English horn but *two*. The studied ruminations at the beginning of the E-flat Major Symphony are some of the cleverest of Haydn's early inspirations and the Orpheus players respond with a wonderful tongue-in-cheek *gravidas*. The rest of the Symphony is performed with their typical enthusiasm and fanatical attention to detail, as are the *Roxelane* and the dramatic Symphony in D minor. With performances of three symphonies instead of the usual two, this is the most desirable issue in the Orpheus's admirable Haydn series to date.

Symphonies: No. 45 in F-sharp, *Farewell*; No. 48 in C, *Maria Theresia*; No. 102 in B-flat

Capella Istropolitana, Wordsworth. Naxos 8.550382 [CD].

As in their cycle of recordings of the Haydn string quartets by the Kodály Quartet, the ongoing Naxos series of the symphonies with Barry Wordsworth and the Capella Istropolitana represent another heartening refutation of my grandmother's staunchly held maxim: "There's no such thing as a bargain and *everything* costs more than it's worth." For a little less than six dollars, or about two bucks per symphony, we're offered warm, witty, and well-executed performances in very fine modern sound. Though there are versions of the B-flat Major Symphony with unquestionably more punch and flavor, Wordsworth's interpretations of the *Farewell* and the *Maria Theresia* yield to none in terms of geniality and warmth. Similarly, even if buying his equally satisfying versions of the *Trauer*, *London*, and Symphony No. 88 (8.550287 [CD]) or *La Reine*, *Oxford*, and the *Drum Roll* (8.550387 [CD]) involves some duplication, then at these prices, who should care?

Symphonies 82–87, the *Paris* Symphonies

New York Philharmonic, Bernstein. Sony SM2K-47550 [CD].

One of Leonard Bernstein's first recordings after being appointed music director of the New York Philharmonic in 1958 was a version of Haydn's *London* Symphony, originally paired with Mendelssohn's *Italian* on a Columbia LP. I vividly remember everything about the album because it was the very first premium I got as a member of the Columbia Record Club, which I joined in the seventh grade. The Club's fliers would follow me through graduate school and beyond, with something approaching the tenacity of *The Watchtower* and *Awake*. (These days, when door-to-door evangelists try to interest me in whatever it is they're selling, I simply tell them: "No thank you, I'm a Druid and I've been washed in the blood of a tree.")

From that excellent *London* Symphony, Bernstein went from strength to strength as a Haydn conductor, reaching his early peak in these versions of the *Paris* Symphonies, recorded between 1962 and 1967. In addition to their grace and virility, the level of humor in these colorful interpretations is extraordinarily high, from oboist Harold Gomberg's inspired clucking in *The Hen* to the droll grumbling of the basses in the finale of *The Bear*. The remastered sound is excellent.

Symphonies: No. 88 in G; No. 92 in G, *Oxford*

Vienna Philharmonic, Bernstein. Deutsche Grammophon 413777-2 [CD].

Listening to any of his 107 works in the form (in addition to the 104 numbered pieces, there are 3 others we now know with some certainty were his), one is invariably tempted to paraphrase Will Rogers: "I never heard a Haydn symphony I didn't like." In no other body of work can one hear such a consistently high level of invention and craftsmanship, or a greater delight in the sheer act of creativity, as in that marvelous series of symphonies that history's finest professional composer produced throughout his career.

Leonard Bernstein's Vienna recording of these two popular G Major symphonies is one of the most desirable Haydn recordings of the last decade. The interpretations are warm, witty, and, in the slow movements, unabashedly and unashamedly romantic. The *Oxford* Symphony has never sounded more lively or luxuriant on records, and this unbuttoned, brilliantly executed, yet meltingly tender performance of No. 88 is the only one that can be mentioned in the same breath with Wilhelm Furtwängler's famous, wonderfully screwball 1951 recording for Deutsche Grammophon, now inexplicably withdrawn. (An even crazier Furtwängler live performance with the RAI Turin Orchestra recorded in the following year is available on AS Disc 371 together with a sublimely demented reading of Tchaikovsky's Symphony No. 5.)

Symphonies 93–104, the *Salomon* (or *London*) Symphonies

Cleveland Orchestra, Szell. Odyssey MB2K-45673 [CD] (Nos. 93–98).

Royal Concertgebouw Orchestra, Davis. Philips 432286-2 [CD] (Symphonies Nos. 93–104).

London Philharmonic, Jochum. Deutsche Grammophon
437201-2 [CD] (Nos. 93–104).

Here, in three reasonably priced box sets, are the most popular of the Haydn symphonies in performances that represent the
very highest standards of modern Haydn conducting. The Szell
interpretations are phenomenally precise, with hair-trigger attacks
and releases and crisply immaculate phrasing, but they also bubble
over with an infectious good humor: the bassoon belch in the slow
movement of No. 93 must rank with the funniest musical effects
ever recorded; the famous slow movement of the *Surprise* Symphony has rarely sounded so mischievous. A minor hitch is the
remastered recorded sound, in which all the original tape hiss continues to fizz away and the upper strings are made to seem uncharacteristically brittle and dry.

On the other hand, the Philips engineers lavished some of
their most richly detailed sound on Sir Colin Davis's performances,
which remain some of the most successful Haydn recordings ever
made. Although generally straightforward, all of the interpretations
have this conductor's stamp of intelligence and gentlemanly passion, and the Concertgebouw Orchestra ensures that they are
among the best-played versions on the market today.

Finally, there are no more enjoyable Haydn symphony recordings than those Eugen Jochum made with the London Philharmonic in the early 1970s. The outer movements crackle with
energy and wit—the finales tend to be unusually fleet—and the slow
movements sing, providing that one of the supreme Bruckner conductors of his generation was enough of a Romantic after all.
Rarely has an orchestra seemed to enjoy itself as palpably as the
London Philharmonic does in these incandescent performances,
and the recorded sound doesn't seem to have aged a day.

Symphonies: No. 94 in G, *Surprise*; No. 96 in D, *Miracle*

Academy of Ancient Music, Hogwood. Oiseau-Lyre
414330-2 [CD], 414330-4 [T].

While the story of how the *Miracle* Symphony earned its
name is probably apocryphal (allegedly, the audience at the world
premiere in London were so moved by the music that they rushed
up en masse to congratulate the composer a few seconds before a

massive chandelier crashed into their recently vacated seats), and while every Haydn symphony is a "surprise" symphony in one way or another, in this delicious Oiseau-Lyre recording two of the composer's most popular works more than earn their subtitles. The playing of Christopher Hogwood's spirited Academy of Ancient Music really *is* quite miraculous in both symphonies, and the revelations in texture and balance that these period-instrument performances afford *are* a source of endless surprise. The winds play with such individuality and character that you begin to suspect the conductor must have swallowed an entire bottle of Sir Thomas Beecham pills, and Hogwood himself provides innumerable subtle comments from his chair at the fortepiano. The familiar slow movement of No. 94 has rarely seemed so sly or tensely dramatic, and the finale of the *Miracle* Symphony rushes off with such a flurry of unbridled high spirits and good humor that we can easily believe the old chandelier story might, after all, have been true.

Symphonies: No. 95 in C minor; No. 101 in D, *Clock*; No. 88 in G

> "Fritz Reiner Orchestra," Chicago Symphony, Reiner. RCA 09026-60729-2 [CD], 09026-60729-4 [T].

The recordings of the C Minor and *Clock* Symphonies were the very last Fritz Reiner made. As a great conductor's swan song, it is of course tempting to read a little something more into these performances, which are wonderful enough on their own. Still, there is a warmth and charm, a genial wisdom in the playing unique among Reiner recordings. For instance, the version of Symphony No. 88, which originally appeared as side four of the conductor's LP recording of Mahler's *Das Lied von der Erde*, is vintage Reiner: precise, witty, beautifully controlled. The others, recorded with a New York pickup orchestra, are simply among the most gracious and ethereal Haydn recordings ever. Don't pass them up.

Symphonies: No. 100 in G, *Military*; No. 103 in E-flat, *Drum Roll*

> Orchestra of St. Luke's, Mackerras. Telarc CD-80282 [CD].

For a single disc pairing of these two popular symphonies in splendid performances with up-to-date sound, you can't do much better than this. As in his wonderful Mozart recordings with the Prague Chamber Orchestra, Sir Charles Mackerras proves he also has the full measure of the other master of the classical symphony; these performances overflow with charm and good humor, not unlike the readings that another musical knight, Sir Thomas Beecham, used to give. Mackerras's versions of the *Clock* and *London* Symphonies are no less desirable (CD-80311 [CD]).

Trios for Piano, Violin, and Cello, Nos. 24–31

Beaux Arts Trio. Philips 422831-2 (24–27); 420790-2 (28–31) [CDs].

Along with Antal Dorati's magnificent cycle of the complete Haydn symphonies for London, one of the major accomplishments of recent recording history was the Beaux Arts Trio's go-round of all forty-three of the Haydn piano trios. As valuable as the Dorati recordings certainly are (fully half of them remain the finest individual performances that the symphonies have yet received), the Beaux Arts' may have been even more so, for how many of us are familiar with even the best known of these inexplicably neglected works? Why history has treated the Haydn trios so shabbily is a perplexing mystery, since the best of them seem every bit as inventive and beautifully made as the finest of the composer's quartets.

Although still difficult to track down in this country, the complete recording of all the trios has recently been issued in Europe on nine jam-packed CDs. Listening to this incredible wealth of treasure over a period of a few weeks will only strengthen the conviction that Haydn was the finest professional composer who ever lived.

Herrmann, Bernard

(1911–1975)

Symphony No. 1

Phoenix Symphony, Sedares. Koch 3-7135-2 [CD].

Best known for his classic film scores from *Citizen Kane* and the *Ghost and Mrs. Muir* as well as from Hitchcock's *Psycho*, *Vertigo*, and *North by Northwest*, the mordant and explosive Bernard Herrmann—called "a virtuoso of unspecified anger" by his friend David Raksin—was also the composer of more obviously serious music, such as this fine symphony written in 1941. Although somewhat longwinded and occasionally derivative, the Herrmann Symphony reflects its composer's superb sense of mood and atmosphere: This is evocative and dramatic music which is also "cinematic" in the best possible sense.

Though it may not be quite as authoritative as the composer's own recording made not long before his death, James Sedares and his superbly trained Phoenix Symphony give a handsome, utterly convincing account of the work. Those who respond to the Symphony will want to investigate what may well be an even finer piece, the cantata *Moby Dick*, given a stunningly effective performance under the composer's direction (Unicorn-Kanchana UKCD-2061 [CD]).

Hildegard of Bingen

(1098–1179)

Hymns and Sequences

Gothic Voices, Page. Hyperion CDA-66039 [CD],
KA-66039 [T].

Cleric, mystic, poet, playwright, naturalist, musician, and composer, Hildegard—later St. Hildegard—of Bingen was one of the most fascinating characters of the Middle Ages. In addition to writing extensively on theology and natural history, she maintained a voluminous correspondence with several popes and Holy Roman Emperors; she published a collection of her mystical visions in 1151, and wrote the morality play, *Ordo virtutum*, which was accompanied by some eighty-seven plainsong melodies of her own devising.

As one of the first composers of either sex of whom we have an accurate record, Hildegard's historical significance goes without saying. Yet she was also a creative musician of genuine abilities, as this astonishing Hyperion recording of some of her hymns and sequences clearly shows.

For those who place listening to plainsong close to the bottom of their list of things to do (and how aptly named this numbingly dull stuff has always seemed), Hildegard's rare and hypnotic talent will come like a splash of cold water in the face. In the exquisite, innocent singing of the Gothic Voices, the simple melodies with their static drone accompaniments seem infinitely more varied, subtle and resourceful than they have any right to be. They also possess an emotional and spiritual tranquility whose calming spells are almost impossible to resist. (This from someone who respectfully gags on almost any form of early sacred music.)

An unqualified, and—for a pagan like me—completely surprising winner.

Hindemith, Paul

(1895 –1963)

Kammermusik (complete)

Members of the Royal Concertgebouw Orchestra of Amsterdam, Chailly. London 433816-2 [CD].

In the generation since his death, Paul Hindemith's reputation has declined alarmingly. Once a leading voice of the twentieth-century avant-garde, a composer whose thorny, elegantly crafted experiments in dissonant counterpoint caused many to liken him to a modern Bach, Hindemith has now been unfairly dismissed as a stuffy "academic" composer who has little to say to a generation brought up on the mindless delights of minimalism.

Though much of his music *can* seem rather dry and forbidding, musicians love Hindemith, since he never wrote a piece of music that wasn't at least as much fun to play as it was to hear. Witness the *Kammermusik* (Chamber Music), a series of concertos composed in the 1920s as a deliberate twentieth-century equivalent of the *Brandenburg* Concertos of Bach. In addition to the delightful *Kammermusik* No. 1 with its irrepressible "Finale: 1922," the other concertos in the collection (one each for piano, cello, violin, viola, viola d'amore, and organ) find Hindemith at his most inventive and appealing. The performances by members of the Royal Concertgebouw Orchestra of Amsterdam are both precise and flamboyant, representing Riccardo Chailly's most impressive work with the orchestra so far.

Among other recordings of the composer's chamber music, none is more valuable than the two-CD set from Sony (SM2K-52671), containing Hindemith's sonatas for brass instruments (alto horn, horn, trumpet, trombone, and tuba) with the principal brass players of the Philadelphia Orchestra and pianist Glenn Gould. The Canadian pianist's well-known passion for Hindemith's music is evident in every bar, and the brass playing is close to perfection.

Symphonic Metamorphosis on Themes by Carl Maria von Weber; *Mathis der Maler* (symphony); *Trauermusik* for Viola and String Orchestra

San Francisco Symphony, Blomstedt. London 421523-2 [CD].

The bulk of Paul Hindemith's reputation now rests on a scant handful of works, including the two Herbert Blomstedt and the San Francisco Symphony have recorded so successfully for London. Among available versions of the symphony drawn from that most famous of all unknown twentieth-century operas, *Mathis der Maler* (the first production was canceled by the Nazis in 1934, causing Wilhelm Furtwängler to resign from the Berlin State Opera in protest), only the last commercial recording Jascha Horenstein ever made (Chandos CHAN-6549 [CD], ABT-1243 [T]) is clearly superior. But Blomstedt has no serious competition in the gravely eloquent *Trauermusik* written for the funeral of King George V.

George Szell's incomparable version of the *Symphonic Metamorphosis* has resurfaced on a budget Sony CD (SBT-53258), along with the wonderful *Variations on a Theme by Hindemith* by Sir William Walton and a rather lackluster *Mathis der Maler* Symphony from Eugene Ormandy and the Philadelphia Orchestra. Szell's performances of both the *Symphonic Metamorphosis* and the Walton are quite sensational, giving the impression of a cross between a perfectly tuned Ferrari and an elegant Swiss watch.

Since we are still in the midst of a major Hindemith drought as far as recordings are concerned, three others deserve mention: James DePriest's spotless versions of *The Four Temperaments* and *Nobilissima visione*, the haunting ballet based on the life of St. Francis of Assisi (Delos DCD-1006 [CD]); the deeply felt requiem on a text by Walt Whitman, *When Lilacs Last in the Dooryard Bloom'd*, in a moving performance led by Robert Shaw, who commissioned the work (Telarc CD-80132 [CD]); and the composer's own superlative versions of the Symphony in B-flat, the Concert Music for Strings and Brass, and *Nobilissima visione*, coupled with Dennis Brain's definitive recording of the Horn Concerto on Angel (CDH-63373 [CD]).

Although it means duplicating *Mathis* and *Metamorphosis* (in excellent performances led by Paul Kletzki and Claudio Abbado, respectively), David Oistrakh's 1962 recording of the Violin Concerto with the composer conducting the London Symphony (London 433081-2 [CD]) is very possibly the greatest Hindemith recording yet made. The late Russian violinist makes it seem one of the most passionately beautiful of all violin concertos, and the recorded sound remains astoundingly fresh and alive.

Hoffnung Music Festivals

Various artists, Hoffnung Festival Orchestra, various conductors. Angel 63303-2 [CD].

It's all here, on a pair of shiny new compact discs: Chopin on tubas, "Let's Fake an Opera," Dennis Brain playing Mozart (albeit Leopold) on a garden hose, the *Leonore* Overture No. 4, the "perfectly straight" excerpt from Walton's *Belshazzar's Feast* conducted by the composer, as well as those two *magnum opera* the *Concerto Populaire*, brilliantly pieced together from dozens of well-known piano concertos, and the *Horrortorio*, in which Dracula's daughter is wed to "that freak, that zombie, that unnatural growth," Frankenstein.

With all due respect to P.D.Q. Bach, it was the series of three musical festivals inspired by the incomparable and tragically short-lived English cartoonist, Gerard Hoffnung, which set a standard for murdering the classics that only Spike Jones, at his most inspired, could begin to approach. With a typically English combination of parchment-dry wit coupled with unbridled lunacy, the Hoffnung concerts made loving fun of virtually everything musical that could be made fun of, and did it with a touch that could be both extremely sophisticated and phenomenally crude.

Hoffnungians—those of us who have long since committed every note and nuance of this transcendental nonsense to memory—will be delighted by the quality of the CD transfers, which capture the sense of occasion far better than the old recordings did. For those who have never experienced this divine madness, I envy you your virgin run. Cherish it, for like your first romance, it is an experience that will never come again.

Holst, Gustav (1894–1934)

Brook Green Suite; *A Fugal Concerto*; *Lyric Movement* for Viola and Small Orchestra; *Morris Dances*; *St. Paul's Suite*

> New Zealand Chamber Orchestra, Braithwaite. Koch 3-7058-2 [CD].

Along with the rarely heard *A Fugal Concerto* and *Lyric Movement*, two impeccably crafted and instantly rewarding concerted works, this extremely appealing Koch recording is devoted to music that reflects the composer's abiding love for English folk song, including the lovely *Brook Green Suite* and the jaunty *St. Paul's Suite*, both written for the orchestra of the St. Paul's Girls' School in London where Holst was music master for nearly thirty years.

Founded as recently as 1987, the brilliant New Zealand Chamber Orchestra play with a sense of style and unanimity of purpose that completely belie their youth. Much of the credit for these exhilarating performances must go to Nicholas Braithwaite, who, as a Holstian, seems as deeply steeped in the idiom as Sir Adrian Boult or the composer's daughter Imogen, whose recordings do not seem any more authoritative than these. The recorded sound is quite exceptional.

The Cloud Messenger; *The Hymn of Jesus*

> London Symphony Orchestra and Chorus, Hickox. Chandos CHAN-8901 [CD], ABTD-1510 [C].

These gorgeous choral works define the two radically disparate poles of Gustav Holst's spiritual life: the Anglican humanism of his youth, which reached its culmination in his sacred masterpiece *The Hymn of Jesus*, and the preoccupation with Eastern mysticism in the years immediately before the First World War, which led to works like the opera *Savitri* (beautifully realized in another Hickox-led performance on Hyperion CDA-66099 [CD]), the ethereal *Choral Hymns from the Rig Veda* (performed magically by the Holst Singers on Hyperion CDA-66175 [CD], KA-66175 [T]), and on this CD, the ravishing *The Cloud Messenger*, based on ancient Sanskrit texts.

Richard Hickox leads the London Symphony Orchestra and Chorus in performances that make both pieces, particularly *The Cloud Messenger*, seem like two of the forgotten masterworks of modern choral music. The level of inspiration in both the singing and playing is unusually high, and the Chandos recording captures the complex textures perfectly. Even for devoted Holst fans, this should prove an important discovery.

The Planets

London Philharmonic, Boult. Angel CDM-69045 [CD].

Every conductor who has ever tried to come to terms with this phenomenally popular score has had to do so under an enormous shadow. Even the composer himself, who made his own recordings during the 78 era, was no match for the man who led the world premiere of *The Planets* in 1918, and during the next six decades, Sir Adrian Boult would record the work no fewer than seven times.

Over the years, the legendary Boult interpretation changed very little. In fact, the tempos remained so consistent that the variance in timings from one recording to another amounted to no more than a few seconds — except, that is, in his final version, which the conductor recorded in his ninetieth year.

The conductor's last look at *The Planets* is one of the great modern orchestral recordings. Beginning with a *Mars* of such weight and menace that all other performances seem positively pacifist in comparison, Boult somehow manages to find new expressive possibilities that even he had previously overlooked. *Venus* is more subtle and dreamy, *Jupiter* roars with a Falstaffian good humor, and *Uranus* lumbers along with a wit and rhythmic point that no other recording can really begin to match.

Suites (2) for Military Band

Cleveland Symphonic Winds, Fennell. Telarc CD-80038 [CD].

Among old bandsmen (and even if they give it the more snooty name of "wind ensemble," a band is still a band), the name of Frederick Fennell has been the stuff of legend for more than thirty years. An old bandsman himself—whose principal instrument, believe it or not, was the bass drum—Fennell made a classic series of Mercury records with the Eastman Wind Ensemble that were probably the finest band recordings ever made. They not only forced the classical music establishment to take the "wind ensemble" more seriously, but also, along with their celebrated, spit-and-polish Sousa albums, gave many of the first recorded performances of some absolutely wonderful music.

While Fennell's Eastman versions of these first great classics of the modern band repertoire were indispensable in their day, his latest recording of Holst's magnificent Suites for Military Band is finer still. The Cleveland Symphonic Winds play with the same gusto and precision as the old Eastman crowd, and Fennell's interpretations, if anything, have become even more suave and energetic with the passage of time. If these marvelous performances fail to raise the hair on the back of your arms (or possibly even a lump in your throat), all that proves is that you've never experienced the indescribable thrill of sidestepping horse droppings at a brutal 120-beat-per-minute cadence during a Memorial Day parade.

Honegger, Arthur (1892–1955)

Symphonies (5)

Czech Philharmonic, Baudo. Supraphon 11 1566-2 [CD].

Of that group of a half dozen rebellious young composers who in the 1920s banded together into a loose but like-minded confederation called *Les Six* with the mercurial Jean Cocteau as their spokesman, only three went on to achieve lasting recognition as major composers. If Darius Milhaud possessed the most robust and prolific talent and Francis Poulenc the most rarefied and individual gifts, the most powerful and versatile voice in the group belonged to Arthur Honegger.

His best music is characterized by a neoclassical formal economy in which driving rhythms, astringent harmonies, and a facile, often moving, Gallic lyricism are thrown together to form a very heady and original brew. His oratorio *Le Roi David* is one of the most significant sacred works of the twentieth century, and his five symphonies constitute one of the last largely undiscovered treasure troves of modern orchestral thought.

Given Erato's inexplicable decision to withdraw the superb Honegger symphony series led by Charles Dutoit, Serge Baudo's excellent cycle from the 1960s is clearly the one to have. The performances have plenty of subtlety as well as punch (No. 5 is unusually fine), and the recorded sound has been dramatically improved. As a bonus, the set comes with equally memorable performances of the *Mouvement symphonique No. 3*, *La Tempête* (a prelude to Shakespeare's *The Tempest*) and Honegger's most famous work, *Pacific 231*.

Erato has partially redeemed itself by reissuing Dutoit's powerfully dramatic 1970 recording of *Le Roi David* on its mid-priced Hommage series (2292-45800-2 [CD]) in a performance that uses the composer's original chamber-like scoring.

Hovhaness, Alan (1911–)

Symphony No. 2, *Mysterious Mountain*

Chicago Symphony, Reiner. RCA 5733-2-RC [CD].

One of history's most prolific composers (it has been suggested that *profligate* might be a better description of his output), Alan Hovhaness is generally known for only two of his hundreds of mature works: *And God Created Whales*, which incorporated taped recordings of actual whale song, and *Mysterious Mountain*, which became famous through Fritz Reiner's Chicago Symphony recording. I have had an enormous affection for the piece from the first moment I heard it, and for reasons that are not entirely musical.

I was playing the record one day when my paternal grandmother wandered in and asked what I was listening to. I had barely said "Hovhaness" when she fled screaming from the room, appalled at my rudeness. The composer's name bears a resemblance to an exceedingly vulgar Czech word for the by-product of a basic bodily function.

Contrary to the associations his name has for Czech speakers, Hovhaness's Symphony reaches misty heights that exert a powerful allure, especially in the sublimely peaceful opening movement. The performance is even more perfect than it seemed to me as a boy, and packaged with Reiner's glistening accounts of Stravinsky's *Song of the Nightingale* and Divertimento from *The Fairy's Kiss*—the recordings that may have led the composer to pronounce the Chicago Symphony, under Reiner, "the most precise and flexible orchestra in the world"—the CD represents an outstanding bargain.

In the first recording of their new Hovhaness series for Delos (DE-3137), Gerard Schwarz and the Seattle Symphony make elegant work of the composer's *City of Light* (No. 22) and *Mount St. Helens* (No. 50) Symphonies. If both pieces are somewhat structurally amorphous and repetitive, you can scarcely tell so from the brilliantly focused, superbly atmospheric performances.

Howells, Herbert (1892–1983)

Hymnus Paradisi; *An English Mass*

Soloists, Royal Liverpool Philharmonic Orchestra and Choir, Handley. Hyperion CDA-66488 [CD].

A younger contemporary of Ralph Vaughan Williams and Gustav Holst, whom he succeeded as music master at St. Paul's Girls' School in 1936, Herbert Howells has remained far less well known for two obvious reasons: his musical personality is not as instantly recognizable or immediately appealing as theirs, and the bulk of his creative energies were devoted to church music. Composed after the death of his nine-year-old son, Howells's gravely beautiful *Hymnus Paradisi* ranks with the great sacred works of the twentieth century, an impassioned but dignified outpouring of grief that becomes increasingly moving and powerful on repeated hearings.

Vernon Handley leads a performance so committed and compassionate, you soon begin to wonder why this great work has not yet entered the standard repertoire. With an equally compelling performance of another Howells masterpiece, the quieter, less ambitious *An English Mass*, the recording makes an ideal introduction to a preposterously neglected talent.

On an equally impressive Argo CD (430205-2), Stephen Cleobury leads the Choir of King's College, Cambridge in some of the magnificent Anglican church music Howells composed for that choir over the years. On Hyperion (CDA-66139 [CD]) the group called Divertimenti give a glowing performance of the evocative String Quartet No. 3, *In Gloucestershire*, coupled with the gripping *Three Rhapsodies* for String Quartet by Howells's friend, Sir George Dyson.

Humperdinck, Engelbert (1854–1921)

Hänsel und Gretel

Schwarzkopf, Grümmer, Felbermeyer, Ilosvay, Philharmonia Orchestra, Karajan. Angel CDMB-69293 [CD].

Now that this best loved of all children's operas has finally made its debut on compact disc, how appropriate that it should be this magical recording from 1953 that captures more of the wonder and wide-eyed innocence of *Hänsel und Gretel* than any other performance ever has or ever will. Elisabeth Schwarzkopf and Elisabeth Grümmer are unsurpassable as Humperdinck's immortal tykes, and Herbert von Karajan's warm and glowing conducting provides a depressing reminder of what a superlative musician that chilling, arrogant wretch once was. The supporting cast sings with immense character and devotion, and the original recorded sound has been made to seem extraordinarily fresh and alive in the CD transfer.

Jeffrey Tate leads an outstanding modern *Hänsel und Gretel* on Angel (CDBC-54022 [CD]), which frequently approaches the Karajan in terms of mystery and wonder. Although Barbara Bonney and Anne Sofie von Otter are not quite as magical as their famous rivals, they sing with exceptional beauty, and the recorded sound is thrilling.

Husa, Karel (1921–)

Music for Prague 1968

Eastman Wind Ensemble, Hunsberger. CBS MK-44916 [CD], MT-44916 [T].

If you've become convinced that Contemporary Music now means either minimalist drivel or incomprehensible noise, you have yet to hear the music of Karel Husa, the major musical voice to have emerged from Czechoslovakia since Bohuslav Martinů, and one of the most powerful and original composers of our time. While his idiom is thoroughly, and often aggressively, modern, Husa is essentially a conservative: a composer who believes that music must carry enormous emotional and expressive burdens above and beyond the notes on the printed page. With his String Quartet No. 3, which won the 1969 Pulitzer Prize and is now available on a Phoenix CD (PHCD-113) in the spellbinding performance by the Fine Arts Quartet, Husa's most celebrated work to date has been *Music for Prague 1968*, which has so far amassed the astonishing total of more than seven thousand performances.

Written in reaction to the tragic events that engulfed the Czech capital in the fall of that year, *Music for Prague 1968* is a furious, brutally dramatic, and hauntingly beautiful evocation of a city and a people which, in the last ten centuries prior to 1990, have known precisely twenty years of political freedom. With its vivid colors, brilliant craftsmanship, and searing intensity, this piece is one of the handful of authentic large-scale masterworks of modern times.

The Eastman Wind Ensemble performance, while a fine one, lacks the sweep and passion of the composer's own on a now-deleted Golden Crest recording. The recording to wait for is of a performance given on February 13, 1990, when Husa, at the invitation of President Václav Havel, introduced it to the city for which it was written.

I once devoted a program to Husa's music, which bore the purposefully provocative title "The Greatest Living Composer?" I should now confess what I *really* think. Lose the question mark.

Ibert, Jacques (1890–1962)

Escales

French National Orchestra, Martinon. EMI CDM-64276 [CD].

Several decades after his best-known work had become firmly entrenched in the standard repertoire, the dapper French composer Jacques Ibert ruefully told a reporter: "I have written twenty important works since *Escales*, but always when they speak of Ibert, they talk about *Escales*." Based on his impressions collected on a Mediterranean cruise made while serving in the French Navy during the First World War, *Escales* (Ports of Call), with its unforgettable evocation of Palermo, Tunis, Valencia, and Nefta is like a technicolor version of Debussy's *La Mer*: an obvious but highly skillful swatch of local color that deserves all the popularity it has enjoyed.

Paul Paray's classic 1962 interpretation on Mercury (432003-2 [CD]) and Jean Martinon's 1974 recording are the finest ever made: vivid, atmospheric, and in the languorous second movement, supremely erotic. Martinon's has the advantage of being packaged with two rarely performed Ibert works (Paray's comes with a Ravel collection): the shallow but engaging *Ouverture de fête*, and the uneven but fascinating *Tropisms pour des amours imaginaires*, his last completed score.

The obstreperous *Divertissement*, the only other Ibert score to begin to match *Escales* in popularity, is given a suitably boisterous performance by the Ulster Orchestra under Yan Pascal Tortelier (Chandos CHAN-9023 [CD]). The delightful *Trois pièces brèves* is given a scintillating performance by the Berlin Philharmonic Wind Quintet in a superb Bis anthology (CD-536 [CD]) of French wind music.

Ives, Charles (1874–1954)

Songs

DeGaetani, soprano; Kalish, piano. Elektra/Nonesuch 71325-2 [CD], 71325-4 [T].

Alexander, soprano; Crone, piano. Etcetera KTC-1020 [CD], XTC-1020 [T] (vol. 1); KTC-1068 [CD] (vol. 2).

Hampson, baritone; Guzelimian, piano. Teldec 9031-72168-2 [CD].

Ramey, bass; Jones, piano. Argo 433027-2 [CD].

Like virtually everything he wrote, the 114 songs Charles Ives produced between 1884 and 1921 could not have been written by anyone else. Alternately serious, nostalgic, cranky, spontaneous, ridiculous, patriotic, cynical, featherheaded, and sentimental, they cover an astonishing range of musical and emotional expression and represent, with those of Ned Rorem, the most significant body of art songs yet produced by an American.

With her flawless intonation and uncanny rhythmic sense, Jan DeGaetani was an ideal interpreter of this highly individual repertoire, capturing the quirky charm of "Ann Street" and the tender beauty of "A Christmas Carol" to perfection. Roberta Alexander is almost as perceptive in her two generous Etcetera recordings, offering a total of fifty-four songs in warmly sympathetic readings. As part of a fascinating recital of American songs on German texts, Thomas Hampson's performances are as intelligent as they are deeply musical, while Samuel Ramey's lush and virile singing is ideally suited to both the Ives material and Copland's *Old American Songs*, which also appear on his splendid Argo recording.

String Quartets (2)

Emerson String Quartet. Deutsche Grammophon 435864-2 [CD].

The Ives String Quartets are the great Jekyll and Hyde act of American chamber music. The First, a work that wouldn't offend your grandmother, was written when the composer was a twenty-one-year-old Yale undergraduate, still very much under the influence of Horatio Parker; the Second dates from the years 1907–1913, the very heart of his most forbidding, dad-blamed cussedest manner. As the title page describes the work: "SQ for four men—who converse, discuss, argue (in re 'politics'), fight, shake hands, shut up—then walk up the mountainside to view the firmament." That just about says it.

Although it would be delightful to have the old Columbia recording by the Juilliard String Quartet returned to circulation, the newer version by the Emersons is also very impressive. If things are kept a little too sedate and homogenized in the First Quartet, they really let the Second rip: this is Ives at his most original and explosive, with most of the bark left on. A lovely performance of the Barber Quartet comes as the aptly chosen filler.

Symphony No. 2; Symphony No. 3, *The Camp Meeting*; *The Unanswered Question*

New York Philharmonic, Bernstein. CBS MK-42407 [CD].

Concertgebouw Orchestra of Amsterdam, Thomas. Sony
Classical SK-46440 [CD] (Symphonies No. 2 and 3
only).

It was Leonard Bernstein's famous Columbia recording of the
Second Symphony that almost single-handedly sparked the Ives
revival of the 1960s. Prior to the release of that classic recording by
the man who had led the work's world premiere more than a half
century after it had been composed, Ives had been an obscure figure
with a small but knowledgeable following. Within a few years, he
was to become an American Original, a cult phenomenon, a composer who, in Bernstein's words, was "the Washington, Jefferson,
and Lincoln of our music."

Now that the hoopla which surrounded the Ives centennial in
1974 has begun to fade into the distance like one of those crack-
brained parades that haunt his music, a more balanced guess at the
stature of his achievement can finally begin to be made. Like another insurance executive who was also a diligent weekend artist,
the Hartford poet Wallace Stevens, Ives possessed an important,
original, and peculiarly American talent. And if, as his admirers
claim, he was one of the most forward-looking composers of his
generation—and he *did* anticipate many of the most important
trends in twentieth-century music, years and often decades before
anyone else—there was also in Ives a good deal of the archetypal
American Crank, a kind of musical Rube Goldberg raised to the nth
degree.

The Second Symphony remains his most approachable and
instantly likable work. In fact, it's difficult *not* to like a work whose
principal themes include "Bringing in the Sheaves" and "Where, O
Where, Are the Pea Green Freshmen?"—a Yale student song that
sounds like an impossibly civilized version of "Dixie"—and which
concludes with a fabulous peroration on "Columbia, the Gem of
the Ocean," flanked by reveille and the most spectacular orchestral
raspberry (an eleven-note chord cluster) anyone ever wrote.

In its compact disc reissue, Bernstein's performance sounds
more joyous, committed, and spirited than ever, and his versions of
the *Camp Meeting* Symphony and the intriguing *Unanswered
Question* should still be considered the definitive performances of
both works. Though very fine, the conductor's more recent Deutsche Grammophon recording lacks some of the bite of the old
Columbia outing.

Michael Tilson Thomas's more recent digital recording is also a tremendous amount of fun. While the performance may lack the last measure of Bernstein's savvy and gusto, this is the first commercial recording of the critical edition of the Symphony No. 2, and the playing of the Concertgebouw Orchestra, as playing per se, can't really be approached.

Washington's Birthday, Decoration Day, Fourth of July, Thanksgiving and/or Forefather's Day (Holidays Symphony); Central Park in the Dark; The Unanswered Question

Chicago Symphony Orchestra and Chorus, Thomas. CBS MK-42381 [CD].

From the off-kilter barn dance in *Washington's Birthday* to the spendthrift use of an entire chorus to intone a single verse of "God! Beneath Thy Guiding Hand" in *Thanksgiving and/or Forefather's Day*, the *Holidays* Symphony contains some of Ives's most characteristic and supremely eccentric inspirations.

Some of the pieces have had superb individual performances, most notably those of Leonard Bernstein, but it is this eye-opening recording by Michael Tilson Thomas and the Chicago Symphony that finally persuades us the *Holidays* are not only arresting parts but also an even more satisfying whole. (Ives himself indicated that he didn't care if they were performed separately or as a unit; then, too, the only thing that George Bernard Shaw would ever tell his actors was, "Speak the lines clearly and have a good time.") Never have the tempos and textures of the four pieces seemed so interconnected and interdependent, nor has any performance, at least in my experience, created the feeling of such an inevitable musical *and* dramatic flow.

The playing of the orchestra—from the barely audible opening of *Washington's Birthday* to the raucous march in *Decoration Day*, where the Chicago brass sound like the old Sousa band—is quite phenomenal, as is the recorded sound. With equally atmospheric performances of *Central Park in the Dark* and *The Unanswered Question*, this may be the single most important Ives recording yet made.

The finest recording of Ives's masterpiece, *Three Places in New England*—one of Michael Tilson Thomas's first—is now out on a Deutsche Grammophon compact disc (423243-2.) To get it, you have to put up with Seiji Ozawa's rather lackluster walk-through of the Fourth Symphony, but the *Three Places* are done so magically that they're more than worth the price.

Janáček, Leoš (1854–1928)

Capriccio for Piano (left hand) and winds; Concertino for Piano and Chamber Orchestra

> Firkusny, piano; Czech Philharmonic, Neumann. RCA 09026-60781-2 [CD].

As in his recording of the composer's solo piano music (see page 275), Rudolf Firkusny is all but unapproachable in this repertoire. Completed in 1925, the Capriccio for Piano (left hand) and wind instruments was written for Ottokar Hollman, who, like the Austrian pianist Paul Wittgenstein, lost his right arm during the First World War. Originally called *Defiance*, undoubtedly as a tribute to Hollman's stubborn courage, the Capriccio contrasts wind writing of unusual richness and complexity with piano writing of a deceptive and elegant simplicity. The Concertino, written the year before, is a less obviously demanding but no less original work.

Made in Prague after an exile of nearly fifty years, Firkusny's recordings have an insight and authority that no others will ever match. His old teacher Leoš Janáček, with whom he studied composition, not piano, would have been proud.

The Cunning Little Vixen

> Popp, Jedlička, Randová, Vienna Philharmonic, Mackerras. London 417129-2 [CD].

Had Leoš Janáček died at the same age as Beethoven, he would be remembered today—if at all—as a very minor late-Romantic composer, conductor, and organist, whose name would occasionally turn up in the more complete biographies of his friend Antonín Dvořák. It was not until 1904, at the age of fifty, that he began to produce, apparently from out of nowhere, that startling series of works on which his reputation as one of the most powerfully original twentieth-century composers now rests. Janáček's sudden transformation from a provincial nobody into a modern giant is without precedent in the history of music. In the other arts, only William Butler Yeats's relatively late emergence as the great English-language poet of the twentieth century offers a similar example of such mysterious and wonderful growth.

The cornerstone of Janáček's achievement is his series of eleven operas, which are slowly being recognized as some of the most important works of the modern operatic stage. Their general acceptance was understandably delayed by the difficulty of the Czech language itself, and the fact that they are by definition untranslatable, since Janáček's musical language was intimately connected with the rhythms and inflections of Czech speech. Then, too, their subject matter is often so peculiar that theaters outside of Czechoslovakia once thought them to be all but impossible to produce. For instance, the heroine of *Věc Makropulos* (The Makropulos Case—though a more correct translation would be The Makropulos Thing), is a three-hundred-year-old opera singer; *Z mrtvého domu* (From the House of the Dead) is set in a Czarist prison camp; and the cast of characters in *Příhody lišky Bystroušky* includes a dog, a badger, a cricket, a grasshopper, and a group described simply as "the various vermin." In spite of its profound and delightful eccentricity, *The Cunning Little Vixen* is neither nonsense nor simply another children's story, but one of the most bewitching and enchantingly beautiful operas ever composed.

Sir Charles Mackerras's grasp of the special power, charm, and expressive potential of Janáček's music is without equal in the world today. As a student, he studied the scores with the man who gave many of them their world premieres, the composer's friend, Václav Talich. At this late date it is absurd to ask whether Mackerras, an American-born Englishman of Australian parentage, can possibly speak Janáček's language as idiomatically as a native; it is doubtful that any Czech conductor, except for Talich, has ever begun to speak it half as well.

Sir Charles's version of *The Cunning Little Vixen* is one of the greatest in an already triumphant series of Janáček recordings. He leads the Vienna Philharmonic through the difficult, delicate score as though it were no more challenging than an early Haydn symphony. The predominantly Czech cast is largely wonderful, especially since most of them drop the wobbly, intrusive vibrato that so many Eastern European singers are apparently taught from birth. Most wonderful of all, however, is the exquisite Vixen of Lucia Popp, one of the most hugely gifted sopranos of the last half century. Her passion, precision, and the extraterrestrial beauty of her physical sound make this one of the great characterizations of the last twenty years, and further makes an already invaluable recording a completely indispensable one.

The orchestral suite Janáček's friend Václav Talich arranged this opera is available again in the conductor's inspired recording with the Czech Philharmonic (Supraphon SUP-111810 [CD]).

Jenůfa

**Söderström, Popp, Randová, Dvořsky, Ochman, Vienna
Philharmonic, Mackerras. London 414483-2 [CD].**

Jenůfa was the first of Janáček's great operas, and it remains the most popular and instantly approachable. It is also, by a comfortable margin, the most conventional of all his works for the stage. Set in a sleepy Czech village, the direct but not-so-simple story of jealousy, vengeance, violence, and redemption is a dramatic amalgam of Smetana's *Bartered Bride* and Mascagni's *Cavelleria rusticana*. Musically, however, *Jenůfa* is an entirely different matter: a fresh, tuneful, and powerfully dramatic score in which one of history's major operatic composers first found his distinct and utterly original voice.

Like all the recordings in Sir Charles Mackerras's historic cycle of the Janáček operas, this is the *Jenůfa* that will probably dominate the catalogs until well into the next century. It is also one of those rare studio recordings that have all the immediacy and excitement of a live performance. Elisabeth Söderström—is there a finer Janáček heroine in the world today?—is both ineffably tender and witheringly powerful in the title role, and the rest of the cast, together with the orchestra and conductor, are all captured at the very top of their form.

If you are one of those people who are convinced, perhaps with good reason, that opera came to a screeching halt with the death of Giacomo Puccini, give *Jenůfa*—especially this *Jenůfa*—a try.

Kát'a Kabanová

Söderström, Kniplová, Dvorsky, Jedlíča, Krejčik, Svehla, Vienna Philharmonic, Mackerras. London 421852-2 [CD].

Kát'a Kabanová is the most powerful of the Janácek operas, a work which, when done properly, can leave an audience as shattered as Berg's *Wozzeck* or Strauss's *Elektra*. As anyone who saw Rafael Kubelik's now legendary San Francisco Opera production in the late 1970s knows, the combination of a potent dramatic soprano and a conductor who knows his business can make *Kat'a* an overwhelming experience. Elizabeth Söderström sings as memorably for Mackerras as she did for Kubelik, and although this is a studio recording, the dramatic power and subtlety of the characterization fairly bursts from the speakers. It, too, is destined to become the stuff of legend: a piece of operatic history to be mentioned in the same breath with the Lehmann Marschallin or the Callas Tosca.

In this first installment of his Janáček cycle, Sir Charles Mackerras inspires the Vienna Philharmonic to capture both the strength and intricacy of the often difficult writing and to respond with a wonderful sense of atmosphere and mood. With excellent to inspired contributions from the all-Czech supporting cast, this recording argues most persuasively that *Kát'a Kabanová* is indeed the composer's masterpiece.

Piano Music

Firkusny, piano. Deutsche Grammophon 429857-2 [CD].

Like his operas and orchestral scores, Janáček's piano works are the product of a wholly original musical mind. In all the pieces in this recital from the early 1970s, Rudolf Firkusny demonstrates why he is the foremost Janáček pianist history has so far known.

The playing has a seamless perfection and an evocative magic that make this entrancing music spring to life in virtually every bar: *In the Mists* will probably never have a more refined and poetic performance; the Piano Sonata emerges with an uncommon sense of unity and depth. It's a pity that Book 1 of *On an Overgrown Path* couldn't be included, but the reissue returns fair value for the dollar, and the recorded sound holds up extremely well. In the pianist's second, more recent version for RCA (60147-2-RC), the interpretations are remarkably similar, but the digital sound is not significantly better than Deutsche Grammophe's analogue recording made twenty years before.

Sextet for Winds, *Mládi (Youth)*; *Idyll* for String Orchestra

> Los Angeles Chamber Orchestra, Schwarz. Elektra/
> Nonesuch 79033-2 [CD].

No work more dramatically illustrates Janáček's phenomenal growth as a composer than the youthful *Idyll* for String Orchestra, written when he was twenty-four. It is a charming, wholly derivative late-Romantic piece with echoes of Dvořák, Smetana, Brahms, and Wagner—the young Janáček was at least admirably catholic in his tastes—and one which gives not the slightest indication of the twentieth-century dynamo its composer would later become. The brilliantly inventive wind sextet *Mládi* (Youth), a youthful product of the composer's fertile old age, is a perfect compliment to the earlier score. Ironically, the Sextet seems like the work of an impetuous twenty-year-old, the *Idyll* that of a tired old man.

Gerard Schwarz and the Los Angeles Chamber Orchestra give rousing performances of both, especially *Mládi*, which feature some of the most adroit wind playing in years.

Sinfonietta; Taras Bulba

> Vienna Philharmonic, Mackerras. London 410138-2 [CD].

Beginning with George Szell's stunning Cleveland Orchestra recording from the 1960s, Janáček's most popular orchestral work, the blazingly heroic *Sinfonietta*, has had some wonderful recordings. As both an interpretation and a recording of demonstration quality, Sir Charles Mackerras's Vienna Philharmonic performance will be difficult to better for the foreseeable future. As usual, not even the most subtle detail of Janáček's complex language escapes this conductor's attention. The occasionally intricate rhythms and always complicated inner voicing are invested with a drive and clarity they have never been given before. The last time the Vienna Philharmonic brass (augmented for the occasion by a dozen extra players) were heard to play with such ferocious bite and mind-boggling unanimity was in Sir Georg Solti's famous recording of Wagner's *Ring*, made two decades ago.

The *Sinfonietta*'s inevitable companion work, the orchestral rhapsody *Taras Bulba*, is given an equally memorable performance. In fact, Mackerras invests it with such surging life and drama that some will be persuaded—as I must admit I always *have* been—that *Taras* may in fact be the more important and rewarding piece.

Athough not quite on the same level, the performances by the Slovak Radio Symphony under Ondrej Lenárd on Naxos (8.550411 [CD]) are very fine indeed and come with the best available version of the enchanting *Lachian Dances*, all for less than it costs to take yourself to a bad movie.

Slavonic Mass (Mša glagolskaja)

> Söderström, Drobková, Livora, Novák, Czech Philharmonic Orchestra and Chorus, Mackerras. Supraphon 10-3575 [CD].

> Lear, Rössel-Majdan, Haeflinger, Crass, Bavarian Radio Symphony Orchestra and Chorus, Kubelik. Deutsche Grammophon 429182-2 [CD].

To call Janáček's *Slavonic Mass* one of the great sacred works of twentieth-century music is as accurate as it is slightly misleading. Written in the composer's seventy-second year, the *Slavonic Mass* was originally thought to be a final act of contrition by a life-long agonistic. When a Prague music critic described it as being the work of a "pious old man," the composer immediately shot back a postcard with the single line, "Neither old nor pious, *young* man."

The unshakable faith the *Slavonic Mass* expresses with such moving tenderness and medieval grandeur has to do less with the composer's religious convictions, which were all but nonexistent, than with his almost messianic belief in the survival of the Czechoslovak Republic, whose tenth anniversary in 1928 the *Slavonic Mass* was written to celebrate.

The Mackerras recording is one of the most successful in his brilliant Janáček series: the playing of the Czech Philharmonic is as vivid and emphatic as it has ever been on records; the soloists are exceptional, the chorus alert and powerful, and the recorded sound is shattering in its realism and impact. Rafael Kubelik's older Deutsche Grammophon recording still holds up remarkably well. Less driven and more gently lyrical than the Mackerras version, it nevertheless has more than its share of electrifying moments. Bedřich Janáček (whom I believe is no relation) is spellbinding in the titanic organ interlude; in the Mass's brazen postlude, the Bavarian Radio Symphony trumpets play with such wild abandon that you can almost see the musicians' tongues popping out of their instruments' bells.

String Quartets: No. 1, *The Kreutzer Sonata*; No. 2, *Intimate Pages*

Smetana Quartet. Denon C37-7545 [CD].

Leoš Janáček was a man whose vigor and appetites remained exorbitantly intact to the end of his long and unusual life. Taking its cue from Smetana's famous E minor Quartet, *From My Life*, the quartet subtitled *Intimate Pages* is one of music's most extraordinary autobiographical works. In it, the aging composer confessed the pangs and torments of a hopeless love he had conceived for a much younger woman. (In truth, with his honeyed tongue and twinkling eye, Janáček ran into little or no trouble during what scandalized quarters of Bohemia and Moravia continue to regard as a legendary erotic career.) With the equally individual *Kreutzer Sonata*, based on the Tolstoy novella inspired by the Beethoven work, *Intimate Pages* is one of the most highly charged and original of twentieth-century chamber pieces. In the proper hands, both can easily seem to rank with the finest quartets of Bartók and Schoenberg.

With the Smetana Quartet, they are in just such hands. No more committed or impassioned performance of either work has yet been recorded: The Smetanas' intensity is such that at any moment you feel any one of the players may be on the verge of breaking a bow or snapping a string. Even in their live performances recorded a few years later for Supraphon, they would never match this level of beautifully controlled violence again. This is thoroughly adult music, meant for a thoroughly adult audience; if you qualify, enjoy.

Joplin, Scott (1868–1917)

Rags

Rifkin, piano. Angel CDM 64668-2 [CD], EG 64668-4 [T].

Well before Scott Joplin's music was belatedly made into a national institution in the hit movie *The Sting*, I had already become hopelessly addicted to his piano rags, thanks entirely to Joshua Rifkin. It was Rifkin's path-breaking series of Nonesuch recordings that all but introduced the world to the subtle, infectious, endlessly inventive music of a man who, in essence, transformed the musical wallpaper of turn-of-the-century bordellos into a high, and distinctively American, art. In his Angel recording— those on Nonesuch have been foolishly withdrawn—Rifkin's self-effacing, yet enormously colorful and individual interpretations are still the definitive solo piano versions of these works.

For the serious Joplin lover, the Houston Opera production of the composer's rather quaint but utterly engaging ragtime opera *Treemonisha*, in a warm and thoroughly captivating performance led by Gunther Schuller (Deutsche Grammophon 435709-2 [CD]), is vigorously recommended.

Josquin des Prés (c. 1450–1521)

Missa Pange lingua; Missa La sol fa re mi

Tallis Scholars, Phillips. Gimell CDGIM-009 [CD], 1585T-09 [T].

Though not normally an enthusiastic consumer of "monk music"—perhaps I saw the movie *Beckett* once too often, or read too many cheerful books about the Spanish Inquisition as a boy—I must confess (so to speak) to an abiding admiration for the music of the greatest of the Flemish contrapuntists, Josquin des Prés. I feel a deep personal connection with him, not because he was one of the most venerated and influential composers of his era, but because he had a name that was as frequently mangled as mine.

In the *Baker's Biographical Dictionary of Musicians*, Nicolas Slonimsky lists Després, Desprez, Deprés, Depret, Deprez, Desprets, Dupré, Del Prato, a Prato, a Pratis, and Pratensis as a few of the ways it was most commonly spelled, while Josquin—from the Flemish Jossekin, the diminutive of Joseph—was apparently mauled just as often.

The fabulous Tallis Scholars give loving performances of two of Josquin's finest masses for Gimell, a small but exceptionally fussy English label that consistently produces some of the best-sounding recordings anywhere. The *Missa Pange lingua* is the more familiar of the two, but the *Missa La sol fa re mi* (which was *not* the basis for that wretched song in *The Sound of Music*) is equally captivating.

Kabalevsky, Dmitri

(1904–1987)

The Comedians (symphonic suite)

London Philharmonic, Slatkin. RCA 09026-60968-2 [CD], 09026-60968-4 [T].

Unlike most of the Stalinist hacks who disgorged reams of musical slop in support of the political and social programs of the then Soviet Union (an early and inspiring example of political correctness in action), Dmitri Kabalevsky was a Bolshevik with talent. Although he wrote his fair share of crap with titles such as *Requiem for Lenin, My Great Fatherland, People's Avengers, Leninists,* and *Before Moscow,* an opera celebrating the defense of the city in 1942, followed in 1951 by *The Family of Taras,* another opera describing the heroic struggle against the fascist invaders, Kabalevsky also produced pages of genuine charm and substance, especially as exhibited in the Second Cello Concerto, the opera *Colas Breugnon,* and the incidental music he wrote in 1938 for the children's play, *The Inventor and the Comedians.*

The ten brief movements that Kabalevsky gathered into an orchestral suite called *The Comedians* has remained the composer's most popular work, especially the infectious little *Galop* that was used as the signature tune—and wouldn't Stalin have been proud!—for *Masquerade Party,* a popular program on Capitalist-Imperialist television during the McCarthy era. Leonard Slatkin and the St. Louis Symphony give a scintillating performance of the Suite on their attractive "The Russian Album," which also features first-rate readings of popular works by Khachaturian, Mussorgsky, Prokofiev, and Stravinsky. Kabalevsky's only other standard repertory item, the sparkling *Colas Breugnon Overture* is available in an incomparable performance by Fritz Reiner and the Chicago Symphony on RCA 09026-61958-2 [CD].

Kalinnikov, Vasily (1866–1901)

Symphonies (2)

> State Academic Symphony of the USSR, Svetlanov.
>   Melodiya SUCD 10-00171 [CD] (No. 1); SUCD-
>   10-00170 [CD] (No. 2).

The life of the Russian composer Vasily Kalinnikov reads like one of the more poignant short stories of Anton Chekhov. As a matter of fact, the two men were neighbors for a time at one of those Black Sea spas in the Crimea where both had gone to die of tuberculosis. Chekhov would be remembered as one of the giants of Russian literature, whereas Kalinnikov became one of the great "what ifs" of Russian music, a composer of tremendous talent and promise whose name is almost completely forgotten today.

After studying bassoon at the Music School of the Moscow Philharmonic Society (he was forced to leave the more prestigious Moscow Conservatory because he was unable to pay the tuition), Kalinnikov managed to eke out a meager living playing in the city's theater orchestras. As a result of living most of his life in the squalor of the proverbial garrets and composing assiduously, a combination of overwork and undernourishment undermined his health; he died at Yalta two days before his thirty-fifth birthday.

While the Second Symphony of 1898 is a lovely work, the earlier G minor Symphony, written when he was twenty-nine, remains his masterpiece. Lyrical, exuberant, and utterly haunting—once heard, its principal themes will not be forgotten quickly—the symphony is one of the jewels of Russian late Romanticism, a work that ranks with any of the early symphonies of Glazunov, Tchaikovsky, or Rachmaninoff.

The performances by Evgeny Svetlanov and the State Academic Symphony of the USSR (in Russian, their name is even longer) are among the most startling ever to have come out of what used to be the Soviet Union. Note especially the playing in the finale of the G minor Symphony, an ecstatic, exultant whirlwind of color and energy that will leave most listeners shouting for more.

Though cleaned up considerably, the sound of the original Melodiya recordings from 1967 and 1975 is still pretty fierce and brittle. Of course, that problem does not affect the Chandos CDs

(CHAN-8861 [No. 1], CHAN-8805 [No. 2]) in which Neeme Järvi and the Scottish National Orchestra are given full-bodied, whisper-clean sound. Although first-rate performances in every way, they can't begin to match the electricity of Svetlanov's.

Khachaturian, Aram

(1903–1978)

Gayane Suite; Spartacus Suite

Royal Philharmonic, Temirkanov. Angel CDC-47348 [CD].

One can only hope that wherever that happy-go-lucky music lover Joseph Stalin is roasting these days, he is exposed to a continuous dose of the ballet *Gayane*, Aram Khachaturian's subtle celebration of the joys of collective farming. Of course, it's easy to chortle at *Gayane* and its pile-driving "Sabre Dance," or to point out with a chill—that this is what the Soviet government once hailed as ideal proletarian music, when Shostakovich and Prokofiev were catching hell. (Actually, Khachaturian himself also came under fire at the infamous Zhdanov Conference in 1948.)

For the most part, *Gayane* is good, clean Socialist Realist fun, with hummable tunes, plenty of local color, and a kind of childlike innocence that retains its freshness and seems immune to all manner of cynical trashing after nearly half a century of wear and tear. If Yuri Temirkanov's interpretations of the ballet's heavy hits—to say nothing of a blissfully truncated suite from the truly macabre *Spartacus*—are neither the most theatrical nor the most imaginative ever recorded, they are easily the best on the market today. The recording Kyrill Kondrashin made of *Gayane* and Kabalevsky's *The Comedians* is all but screaming for a CD reissue from RCA.

David Oistrakh's definitive interpretation of the Violin Concerto can now be found on Praga 250017 [CD], in a thrilling live performance from 1947 with Rafael Kubelik and the Prague Radio Symphony. A live performance of the Piano Concerto with William Kapell and the NBC Symphony from a 1945 broadcast (VAI Audio VAIA/IPA 1027 [CD]) is one of the most electrifying Khachaturian recordings ever made, making the piece seem infinitely more musical and important than it can possibly be.

Knussen, Oliver (1952–)

Where the Wild Things Are

Hardy, King, Harrington, Rhys-Williams, London Sinfonietta, Knussen. Arabesque Z-6535 [CD].

Needless to say, it is a bit too soon to tell what history, the Great Aesthetic Trash Compactor, will make of *Where the Wild Things Are*. My own suspicion is that the work will prosper as one of the enduring children's operas—if not precisely the late twentieth-century equivalent of *Hänsel und Gretel*, then at least something very close to it.

Oliver Knussen's setting of Maurice Sendak's tale of the archetypal Bad Kid and the Horrible (i.e., thoroughly lovable) Monsters is not only magnetic theater, but also highly inspired music-making. Knussen packs more mystery, enchantment, and pure fun into his forty minutes than many another operatic composer has been able to draw out of an entire evening; the soloists— especially Rosemary Hardy as the incorrigible Max—all seem ideal in their parts, and the composer-conducted performance is undoubtedly definitive.

If you have any little wild things running around under foot, sit them down in front of the speakers and see what they think. This aging Bad Kid loved it.

Kodály, Zoltán (1882–1967)

Dances of Galanta; Dances of Marósszek; Variations on a Hungarian Folk Song (Peacock Variations)

Philharmonia Hungarica, Dorati. London 425034-2 [CD].

After his friend and near-contemporary, Béla Bartók, Zoltán Kodály was the most significant composer Hungary had produced since the death of Franz Liszt. Kodály began his career writing serious, and politely ignored, chamber works, but it was his discovery of Hungarian folk music in the early 1920s that transformed him into an internationally famous composer. Beginning with the folk opera *Háry János*, Kodály combined the unmistakable flavors of Hungarian folk song with a technique that owed much to Debussy and Ravel, and created some of the most refreshingly distinctive and original music of the twentieth-century.

Dorati's London recording of these popular works, together with a very fine *Háry János* Suite, is one of the most accomplished and generous Kodály recordings now available, offering seventy-six minutes of world-class music-making on a single medium-priced CD. If the performances of *Galánta*, *Marosszék*, and *Háry János* might lack the final ounce of magic the conductor squeezed out of his famous Minneapolis Symphony recordings for Mercury (now reissued on 432005-2 [CD]), they are still full of charm, panache, and gypsy fire and are certainly *not* to be missed.

Háry János

Takács, Sólyom-Nagy, Gregor, Hungarian State Opera Orchestra and Chorus, Ferencsik. Hungaroton HVD-12837/38 [CD].

Háry János Suite

Cleveland Orchestra, Szell. CBS MYK-38527 [CD], MYT-38527 [T].

Though the Suite that Zoltán Kodály extracted from his 1926 folk opera *Háry János* remains his most universally loved and frequently recorded work, the opera itself is one of the treasures of the modern lyric theater. Its fantastic plot is a series of tall tales told by a retired hussar from the village of Abony Magna—the irrepressible Háry János—who after single-handedly defeating Napoleon and his legions has nearly as much trouble fending off the attentions of Napoleon's ardent wife.

Fortunately, the lone recorded performance of the complete opera is an extremely attractive one. Beautifully played, and, for the most part, beautifully sung, the performance projects much of the opera's unique and unmistakable color. Since much of the humor is lost on non-Hungarian listeners, one can only hope that London will some day reissue István Kertész's dazzling recording from the early 1970s, which not only included all of the opera's musical numbers but also featured the inspired Peter Ustinov in all the speaking roles.

For those who feel they don't really need to go beyond the popular *Háry János* Suite, George Szell's tender, flamboyant, meticulous, and uproarious CBS recording has never been equaled.

Sonata for Unaccompanied Cello

Starker, cello. Delos DCD 1015-[CD].

On greeting visitors to his impressive European estate, Janos Starker has often been heard to say, "Welcome to the house that Kodály built!" Thus far, the great Hungarian-born cellist has recorded the Sonata four times, most recently in Japan in 1970. Many, the present writer included, would rank the Sonata alongside the *Peacock* Variations and *Psalmus hungaricus* as one of Kodály's supreme achievements, thanks in no small part to Starker's classic interpretation. He not only makes the work's frightening difficulties seem inconsequential, he also invests it with an incredibly broad emotional range, from quiet despair to reckless excitement and everything in between. A splendid version of the Duo for Violin and Cello with Joseph Gingold is the handsome and appropriate filler.

Korngold, Erich Wolfgang

(1897–1957)

Concerto in D for Violin and Orchestra

Heifetz, violin; Los Angeles Philharmonic, Wallenstein. RCA 7963-2-RG [CD].

Perlman, violin; Pittsburgh Symphony, Previn. Angel CDC-47846 [CD].

A child prodigy whose accomplishments were compared to those of Mozart by no less an authority than Gustav Mahler, and the man who first brought genuine symphonic music to Hollywood films, Erich Wolfgang Korngold was one of the most fascinating musical figures of the twentieth century. His opera *Die tote Stadt* (The Dead City), begun when he was only nineteen, made him world famous, and his frightening abilities even convinced Richard Strauss that Korngold would inevitably supplant him as the century's foremost composer of German opera. Erich Leinsdorf's generally gorgeous recording, save for the wobbly singing of the hero, has once again been withdrawn by RCA, demonstrating why the late conductor always referred to that organization as his *bête noire*. Personally, I'm tempted to call them something a bit less polite, since they've also withdrawn their several invaluable recordings of Korngold's film music.

Forced to flee Europe after Hitler's annexation of Austria, Korngold eventually settled in Hollywood. There, with the scores for *Anthony Adverse*, *King's Row*, *The Adventures of Robin Hood*, *The Sea Hawk*, and other classic Warner Brothers films of the 1930s and '40s, he established the grammar and syntax of an entirely new musical language, whose influence can still be clearly and distinctly heard in the scores of John Williams and countless other film composers.

The Korngold Violin Concerto, whose thematic material was derived from several of his movie themes, is one of the most startlingly beautiful works in the instrument's repertoire. Sentimental, exciting, and unabashedly Romantic, it is as instantly approachable as it is impossible to forget. Although written for the Polish violinist Bronislaw Huberman, it was Jascha Heifetz who gave the work its world premiere and made the first commercial recording. Technically, of course, the playing is flawless; yet here Heifetz invests the music with a warmth and humanity that almost none of his other recordings possess. Itzhak Perlman's Angel recording is also exceptionally lovely. If in the quicksilver finale Perlman lacks the last measure of Heifetz's dizzying abandon, he milks the molten slow movement like the wonderfully shameless Romantic he has always been.

Orchestral Works

> Northwest German Philharmonic, Albert. CPO 999-037-2
> (*The Snowman*: Incidental Music; *Dramatic Overture*;
> *Sinfonietta*); 999 046-2 (*Symphonic Overture*; *Much
> Ado About Nothing*: Incidental Music; Piano Concerto);
> 999 077-2 (*Baby-Serenade*; Cello Concerto; *Symphonic
> Serenade* for String Orchestra); 999 146-2 (*Straussiana*;
> Symphony in F-sharp; *Theme and Variations*) [CDs].

The first comprehensive recorded examination of Korngold's orchestral music from the small European label CPO provides the ideal means of better understanding this unique composer's achievement, and judging from the evidence these four handsome CDs present, the achievement is considerable. Even in the earliest works, produced when Korngold was not yet out of kneepants, one immediately detects the presence of a distinct, confident, and fully formed musical personality; in mature works like the Symphony in F-sharp, which Dimitri Mitropolous called "the perfect modern score," one hears the heir of Mahler and Richard Strauss at the peak of his late-Romantic powers.

While there have been finer performances of individual works —the Violin Concerto is very well served by two classic recordings (see above), and the compelling debut recording of the Symphony, with the Munich Philharmonic led by Rudolf Kempe, has just resurfaced on Varèse Sarabande (VSD-5346 [CD])—the series, as a whole, is a major triumph, offering carefully thought out, wholly sympathetic performances in beautifully rich recorded sound.

Kraft William (1923–)

Piano Concerto; Timpani Concerto; *Veils and Variations* for Horn and Orchestra; *Evening Voluntaries*

Golabek, piano; Akins, timpani; van der Schmidt, horn; Alabama Symphony, Polivnick; Berkeley Symphony, Nagano. Harmonia Mundi HMU-907106 [CD].

In his entry on William Kraft in *Baker's Biographical Dictionary of Music and Musicians*, Nicolas Slonimsky offers a typically apt summation: "As a composer, he explores without prejudice all genres of techniques, including serial procedures; he develops the rhythmic element to the full."

That Kraft's music should be among the most rhythmically vital and imaginative ever written by an American is hardly surprising: after study with the New York Philharmonic's storied Saul Goodman, he became a percussionist with the Los Angeles Philharmonic in 1955 and its timpanist in 1962, later becoming its assistant conductor and composer-in-residence. In addition to its rhythmic life, Kraft's music is also remarkable for its mixture of experimental techniques with a musical personality that is both challenging *and* surprisingly accessible, making it some of the most enjoyable modern music now being written. In short, Kraft is that great rarity: an avant-garde humanist.

Written between 1972 and 1988, the four works featured on this Harmonia Mundi CD are among Kraft's most resourceful and intriguing compositions, especially the Timpani Concerto, the most significant solo work yet written for the instrument. The performances, supervised by the composer, are definitive, and the recorded sound is wonderfully rich and transparent. In short, a recording of modern music that proves there really *is* hope.

Kramář, František (Krommer, Franz) (1759–1831)

Octet-Partitas for Winds (4)

Sabine Meyer Wind Ensemble. Angel CDC-54383 [CD].

The Moravian composer František Kramář was one of innumerable musicians of the eighteenth century whose sheer numbers led the rest of the continent to call Bohemia-Moravia "The Conservatory of Europe." Like most of the talented musicians from that part of the world, Kramář teutonized his name to find employment in the German-speaking world, and as Franz Krommer he held a number of important court posts, including imperial kapellmeister in Vienna.

Kramář wrote symphonies, concertos, and a fair amount of sacred music, but he is best remembered for some of the most accomplished and engaging wind music of the entire classical period, including the four irresistible Octet-Partitas heard on this delightful EMI recording. The performances by the Sabine Meyer Wind Ensemble are flawless, as is the playing of clarinetist Sabine Meyer herself: if you can listen to her dizzying noodling on the final track of the disc and *not* have to suppress a giggle (or a least a smile), then you have my admiration and deepest sympathy. Warm, remarkably lifelike recorded sound.

Kreisler, Fritz (1875–1962)

Violin Pieces and Arrangements

Perlman, violin; Sanders, piano. Angel CDC-47467 [CD].

In addition to being one of the great violinists of history whose recordings of the Beethoven, Brahms, and Mendelssohn concertos remain unsurpassed in their Romantic daring and philosophical depth—all of which can now be found on an indispensable two-CD set from Pearl (PEAS-9362)—Fritz Kreisler was also the composer of some of the most enchanting music ever written for the instrument. Evergreen classics like *Caprice viennois*, *Liebesfreud*, and *Schön Rosmarin* were the apotheosis of turn-of-the-century Viennese charm and helped make their creator an immensely rich and famous man.

Nowhere does Itzhak Perlman reveal himself more clearly as Kreisler's natural heir than in this delectable recording of Kreisler miniatures and arrangements. While less free and arbitrary than the master (whose celebrated recordings from the 1930s and '40s keep slipping in and out of print), Perlman brings huge reserves of sensitivity and schmaltz to the proceedings, always drawing the fine but inviolable line between sentiment and sentimentality. Samuel Sanders is a wholly sympathetic partner, and the mid-'70s recorded sound remains ideal.

Kurka, Robert (1921–1957)

The Good Soldier Schweik Suite

Atlantic Sinfonietta, Schenck. Koch 3-7091-2H1 [CD].

With Ernst Krenek's *Jonny spielt auf* and Jaromir Weinberger's *Schwanda the Bagpiper*, Robert Kurka's *The Good Soldier Schweik* has for years been at the top of my list of Neglected Operas I Would Most Like to See. Completed shortly before Kurka's death from leukemia at the age of thirty-six, *Schweik* is a setting of Jaroslav Hašek's celebrated four-volume antiwar novel, which introduced one of the classic characters of modern literature, a seemingly "feebleminded" Everyman who endures the lunacies of modern warfare with indestructible optimism and triumphant good humor.

Judging from the brilliant six-movement Suite that the composer extracted from the opera, Kurka—himself of Czech descent—captured the very essence of Hašek's darkly hilarious vision. In this sparkling performance by the Atlantic Sinfonietta under the late Andrew Schenck, it emerges as one of the unique works of modern American music: a memorable, tuneful, colorfully dramatic score—this in spite of the fact that the instrumentation calls for winds and percussion only.

Don't miss it.

Lalo, Édouard (1823–1892)

Symphonie espagnole for Violin and Orchestra

Perlman, violin; Orchestre de Paris, Barenboim. Deutsche Grammophon 400032-2 [CD].

One of the most individual and restlessly inventive of all nineteenth-century French composers, Édouard Lalo is now known for only two apparently indestructible works: the D minor Cello Concerto and the *Symphonie espagnole*, which is not, in fact, a "symphony" at all, but rather a form of the composer's own devising that incorporates the structural elements of the concerto and the suite. As one of the most inspired of all French musical tourist works, *Symphonie espagnole* is to the brighter elements of Spanish musical culture what Bizet's *Carmen* is to the darker side: a virtuoso evocation of a specific time and place that few other works can match.

With some vivid, expressive support from Daniel Barenboim and the Orchestre de Paris, Itzhak Perlman here gives one of his most buoyant and colorful recorded performances. Along with its fabulous dexterity, the playing combines a bracing rhythmic vitality with tasteful schmaltziness in a way that only Perlman, these days, seems able to do.

Lalo's only other well-known piece, the Cello Concerto, is now admirably served by a half dozen first-rate recordings, the best of which features the impressive young Matt Heimovitz in his debut recording (at age nineteen) for Deutsche Grammophon (427323-2 [CD]). His playing is both gutsy and sophisticated, and amazingly assured for a performer his age. The recording comes with an equally memorable performance of the inevitable companion piece, the Cello Concerto No. 1 by Saint-Saëns, as well as something we have needed for some time: an unimpeachable version of Bruch's *Kol Nidrei*.

Lambert, Constant

(1905–1951)

Concerto for Piano and Nine Instruments; *Horoscope* (ballet suite); *The Rio Grande* for Contralto, Piano, Orchestra, and Chorus

Soloists, BBC Singers, BBC Concert Orchestra, Wordsworth. Argo 436118-2 [CD].

As a droll and perceptive English friend put it recently, "In mid-twentieth-century British music, there were two major schools of composition: drunken and homosexual." Constant Lambert was one of the most brilliant and tragic representatives of the former. Having achieved early fame with *The Rio Grande*, a formally indescribable jazz-inflected piano concerto cum cantata on a near-nonsense text by Sacheverell Sitwell, Lambert was never quite able to repeat its success. He turned increasingly to drink and music criticism, becoming the most engaging British music critic since George Bernard Shaw and the author of the classic *Music Ho!: A Study of Music in Decline*, which should become required reading for anyone having anything to do with the profession. He died in 1951 at the age of forty-six.

In addition to a spirited performance of *The Rio Grande*, this indispensable Argo recording offers excellent versions of two other important Lambert works: *Horoscope*, not only one of the great English ballets but one of the great modern English scores, and the Concerto for Piano and Nine Instruments, an angry, often acerbic elegy written to the memory of the equally hard-drinking Peter Warlock. Another score inspired by Warlock's death, the ambitious *Summer's Last Will and Testament*, a setting of some disturbing plague lyrics by the Elizabethan poet Thomas Nashe that may very well be Lambert's masterpiece, is available in a shattering performance on Hyperion (CDA-66565 [CD]) with another superb performance of *The Rio Grande* and the touching *Aubade Héroïque*, inspired by memories of Holland prior to the Nazi invasion.

Lehár, Franz (1870–1948)

The Merry Widow

Schwarzkopf, Steffek, Gedda, Wächter, Philharmonia
Orchestra and Chorus, Matačič. Angel CDCB-47177
[CD], 4AV-34044 [T] (excerpts only).

He never quite scaled the golden heights of Johann Strauss's
Fledermaus, Gypsy Baron, or Night in Venice—the primary reason
his music has since been designated the summit of the Viennese
operetta's "Silver Age"—but Franz Lehár was a charming and
entirely individual composer whose stage works represented the
final, bittersweet sunset of one of the most endearing of all musical
forms. Though *Giuditta* and *The Land of Smiles* are probably finer
works, it was the effervescent and eternally glamorous *Lustige
Witwe* that became the only operetta in history (short of the Savoy
Operas of Gilbert and Sullivan), to mount a serious popular challenge to the absolute supremacy of *Die Fledermaus*.

Even if Viennese operettas in general, or Lehár operettas in
particular, are not exactly your cup of *kaffee mit schlag*, I guarantee
you will find this ageless recording one of the most thrilling musical experiences of your life. Elisabeth Schwarzkopf, the greatest
Marschallin and Mozart singer of her time, gives what may well be
the performance of her career as Hanna: regal, witty, sentimental,
and unbelievably sexy, the characterization all but leaps into your
living room. As a matter of fact, there have been only two or three
other opera recordings in history that begin to match the uncanny
sense of presence this one generates from its very first notes. The
admirable Nicolai Gedda and Eberhard Wächter also turn in something close to the performances of *their* careers, and under the
inspired leadership of Lovro von Matačič, who casts what amounts
to a magical spell over the proceedings, this *Merry Widow* effortlessly swirls its way into the ranks of the greatest recordings of
all time.

Lovers of Lehár's highly addictive melodies should take note
that many of the best of them, in recordings led by the composer
himself from 1934–1942, are available on a compact disc called
"Lehár conducts Lehár" from Preiser (90150). In addition to the

voices of Lehár specialists Esther Rethy, Maria Reining, and the exquisite Jarmilla Novotna, the disc features the incomparable recordings of the composer's friend Richard Tauber, the great Austrian tenor for whom many of these roles were written.

On a very attractive Angel compact disc (47020), Willi Boskovsky leads the Vienna Johann Strauss Orchestra in a program of Lehár waltzes.

Leoncavallo, Ruggiero

(1858–1919)

I Pagliacci

> **Callas, di Stefano, Gobbi, Panerai, La Scala Orchestra and Chorus, Serafin. Angel CDCC-47981 [CD].**

Since the days when Enrico Caruso virtually adopted Canio's histrionic Act I aria "Vesti la giubba" as his signature tune, Leoncavallo's *Pagliacci*, with its inseparable companion piece, Mascagni's *Cavalleria rusticana*, has remained a staple of the operatic repertoire. Based on an actual case that the composer's father, a local magistrate, tried when Leoncavallo was a boy, *I Pagliacci* is one of the two quintessential works of the slice-of-life verismo school of Italian opera: a work in which the uncontrollable passions of ordinary people result in a delightful mosaic of jealousy, betrayal, and violent death.

The famous La Scala recording from the early 1950s is more earthy and bloodcurdling than ever in its recent compact disc reincarnation. Tito Gobbi is a wonderfully sly and malevolent Tonio, and the Nedda of Maria Callas is unapproachable in its vulgar animal magnetism and dramatic intensity. Still, *I Pagliacci* has always been the tenor's show, and it is this recording, perhaps more than any other, that demonstrates what Giuseppe di Stefano *might* have been. As it stood, he had probably the most brilliant career of the postwar Italian tenors; had it been managed with greater intelligence and care, it might have been *the* career since Caruso's. His Canio is painted in very primary colors, and for the most part, is very beautifully sung; still, for all its power, we can hear the unmistakable signs that his incredible instrument had already seen its best days.

Of the more recent *Pagliaccis*, RCA has wisely reissued the 1971 recording with Monserrat Caballé, Placido Domingo, and Sherrill Milnes, all in peak condition, supported by some stylish, blood-and-thunder conducting from Nello Santi. The recording also benefits from vintage early '70s recorded sound and the inclusion of the frequently cut Nedda-Silvio duet.

For the *really* adventurous opera lover, the Orfeo recording of Leoncavallo's *La Bohème* (023822 [CD]) is an intriguing oddity. It was over lunch one day that Leoncavallo told his friend Giacomo Puccini that he was at work on an opera based on Henri Murger's *Scènes de la vie de Bohème*; Puccini thought it was a splendid idea and immediately set to work on the same text. Leoncavallo never forgave him. Listening to Leoncavallo's *La Bohème* in light of Puccini's makes for a fascinating experience, rather like meeting your father's long-lost (and far less interesting) brother. Nothing sounds quite right or good enough, although on its own terms and in such a devoted performance, it emerges as a most attractive score.

Liadov, Anatol (1855–1914)

Orchestral Music

USSR Symphony, Svetlanov. Melodiya SUCD-10-00140
[CD].

Slovak Philharmonic, Gunzenhauser. Marco Polo 8.550328
[CD].

The history of modern music might have been entirely different had Anatol Liadov not been the most pathologically lazy composer since Gioacchino Rossini. In 1910 Liadov so dithered and dawdled over an important ballet commission that a frantic Sergei Diaghilev was forced to take a chance on a young and completely unproven composer named Igor Stravinsky. In retrospect, Liadov probably would not have been able to write *The Firebird* even if he had been able to muster the requisite gumption. He was by nature a miniaturist, as his modest output of enchanting little masterworks clearly shows. The best of them, like the *Eight Russian Folksongs* or the tone poem *Kikimora*, with its unforgettable English horn melody and concluding piccolo tweak, are among the most perfectly crafted gems of late-Romantic Russian music, an aural equivalent of the Fabergé Easter eggs.

The Melodiya album from 1970 collects most of the best of Liadov in generally superlative performances captured in more than adequate late-Bolshevik recorded sound. While the performances on Marco Polo are only slightly less magical, the sound is markedly better.

Both are guaranteed to delight, and perhaps enthrall.

Liszt, Franz (1811–1886)

Concertos for Piano and Orchestra: No. 1 in E-flat;
No. 2 in A

> Richter, piano; London Symphony, Kondrashin. Philips
> 434163-2 [CD].

Composer, conductor, philosopher, ascetic, charlatan, religious mystic, prodigious sexual athlete, and, in all probability, the greatest pianist who has ever lived, Franz Liszt was the epitome of the Romantic musician: a restless bundle of ambition, nervous energy, and insatiable appetites. His influence on the development of nineteenth-century music was so enormous that it still remains difficult to assess. As a composer, he all but invented the tone poem, one of musical Romanticism's most enduringly popular forms. His experiments in thematic transformation were decisive in the leit-motif technique perfected by his son-in-law, Richard Wagner. And in churning out endless reams of fiendishly difficult piano music for use on his innumerable concert tours, he helped provide gainful employment for virtuoso pianists from his day to our own.

Liszt's Piano Concertos have long been staples of the concert repertoire, and each is a revealing glimpse at the two complimentary, and often contradictory, sides of the composer's essential makeup: the brash, outgoing, self-indulgent E-flat Major Concerto, and the moody, poetic, introspective Concerto No. 2 in A Major.

No modern interpretations have ever captured more of the Concertos' poetry and barnstorming excitement than this sensational Philips recording by Sviatoslav Richter. On a purely technical level, they are among the most hair-raising piano recordings ever made. Yet along with the phenomenal virtuosity, Richter brings such a measure of grandeur and profundity to the music that those who were tempted to dismiss it as empty-headed bombast will never be tempted to do so again.

Among recordings with more up-to-date recorded sound, the Deutsche Grammophon version (423571-2 [CD]) with the Polish pianist Krystian Zimerman is extremely impressive. Though Zimerman's playing, per se, can't quite match the depth or brilliance of Richter's, the interpretations are poised and adult, and Seiji Ozawa and the Boston Symphony are admirable accomplices. The recording also includes a suitably spooky performance of the always tasteful *Totentanz*, a work that should never be listened to in a dark room or after having just consumed a pizza.

A Faust Symphony

Riegel, tenor; Tanglewood Chorus, Boston Symphony Orchestra, Bernstein. Deutsche Grammophon 431470-2 [CD].

Except for the final movement of Gustav Mahler's "Symphony of a Thousand," *A Faust Symphony* is probably the most inspired of all musical treatments of Goethe's great philosophical play. It may also be Franz Liszt's masterpiece. Each of its three movements is an elaborate character sketch of the play's three central figures: a brooding, heroic, poetic movement devoted to the title character, a lyrical second movement called "Gretchen," and a finale devoted to Mephistopheles, in which Liszt, like Milton before him, could not resist giving the Devil all the best lines. One of the lengthiest and most challenging symphonies written up to that time, *A Faust Symphony* still makes tremendous demands on its interpreters, and the recording that is most successful in solving the work's innumerable problems was the one recorded in the mid 1950s by Sir Thomas Beecham. Lyrical, pensive, impetuous, and shot through with a demoniacal wit, its only serious drawback was the rather shrill and harsh recorded sound, which the compact disc remastering brilliantly managed to correct.

With the Beecham recording now withdrawn from circulation it is an even greater pleasure to welcome Leonard Bernstein's back. Both the recorded sound and the orchestral execution are marginally better than Beecham's, and the interpretation is vintage Bernstein; among its many glories, the disc features the most shamelessly licentious version recorded so far of the lovely "Gretchen" movement and a "Mephistopheles" in which the playing will curl your tail. While not the most pornographic of Bernstein's recordings, it will certainly do, and I, for one, welcome it back with open arms.

Hungarian Rhapsodies (19)

Szidon, piano. Deutsche Grammophon 423925-2 [CD].

Close to the top of my "Whatever became of . . ." list, just behind the Italian conductor-wunderkind of the 1950s, Piero Gamba, is the Brazilian pianist Roberto Szidon, who made a couple of recordings in the early 1970s and then seemed to vanish without a trace.

It took a certain amount of bravado to choose as one of his first recordings these popular works that everyone and his mother have been recording since time began. The results came as quite a jolt to HR collectors: not only were they among the most exciting performances heard in a generation, they brought a refined musicality to these frequently flogged warhorses that is almost never heard. A few individual performers (Cziffra, Kapell, Horowitz in his maniacal transcription of No. 2) have outscored Szidon at various points, but no more satisfying interpretation of the entire cycle has ever appeared. The playing has authentic poetry and finesse, plus electrifying moments of out-on-the-limb derring-do. This was clearly a major career in the making, and we can only wonder again what happened.

None of the recordings of the orchestral versions of the Rhapsodies are anything to write home about, so do yourself a favor and save the stamp.

Piano Sonata in B minor

Brendel, piano. Philips 410040-2 [CD].

Wild, piano. Etcetera KTC-2010 [CD].

Richard Wagner was especially fond of his father-in-law's only piano sonata. Shortly after Liszt sent him the manuscript, Wagner wrote back, saying, "It is sublime, even as yourself." Though Johannes Brahms was also particularly keen to hear it performed, at the private concert that Liszt arranged in his honor Brahms showed his gratitude by falling asleep. Much of Liszt's piano music is little more than gaudy ephemera, his B minor Sonata, with those of Schubert and Chopin, remains the Romantic era's most enduring contribution to the form, and one of that tiny handful of nineteenth-century piano sonatas that are every bit the equal of any that Beethoven ever wrote.

Until London Records returns Sir Clifford Curzon's Homeric and inspired interpretation on a compact disc, the choice among available recordings of the work lies between the studied intro-spection of Alfred Brendel and the flamboyant virtuosity of Earl Wild. Brendel, whose link to the composer is a direct one (his teacher, Edwin Fischer, was a pupil of the Liszt pupil Eugen D'Al-bert), gives an immensely intelligent performance on his Philips compact disc. If Brendel's playing is not the last word in individ-uality or animal excitement, he nevertheless reveals the Sonata's complex structure with a disarming lucidity and ease. Earl Wild, though a bit less thoughtful than Brendel, makes the music flash and thunder like one of the hell-for-leather virtuosos of the past. Now, the ideal recording of the Liszt Sonata would be a combi-nation of Wild's fire with Brendel's brains—which is *precisely* what Sir Clifford Curzon gave us two decades ago. (Got the message, London?)

Les Préludes (Symphonic Poem No. 3)

London Philharmonic, Solti. London 417513-2 [CD].

Of the thirteen works with which Franz Liszt all but invented the tone poem, only *Les Préludes* is heard with any frequency today. Listening to Bernard Haitink's heroically ambitious cycle for Philips (now available on a pair of Philips "Duo" compact discs (438751-2, 438754-2), will quickly show you why. For in spite of the best of intentions and some of the best recorded performances any of these works are ever likely to receive, most of the Liszt tone poems are unmitigated junk. (It *is* difficult to think of another great composer whose ratio of trash to masterworks was quite as high as his.) Often as schlocky and bombastic as the rest, *Les Préludes* is saved in the end by its grandiose gestures, flood of memorable melody, and utter sincerity. Schlock it most certainly is, but of a wonderfully urgent and lovable variety.

Sir Georg Solti's recording with the London Philharmonic is one of his most completely successful recordings. While the playing is undeniably exciting, rarely has *Les Préludes* been invested with such power and genuine nobility. Packaged with equally riveting and dignified performances of the rarely heard *Tasso* and *Prometheus*, this is probably the strongest case for the Liszt tone poems any single recording has ever made.

MacDowell, Edward

(1860–1908)

Piano Concertos (2)

> Amato, piano; London Philharmonic, Freeman. Olympia OLY-353 [CD].

Edward MacDowell, the foremost American composer of the nineteenth century (unless one counts the gifted Stephen Foster), wrote musical compositions equivalent to the poetry of Longfellow, Holmes, and Whittier; for MacDowell's work is "American" only in the sense that he was born in this country. After studying in Germany with Joachim Raff and Franz Liszt, MacDowell began turning out a series of pleasant works on European models, including the two Piano Concertos with their echos of Mendelssohn, Schumann, and, not surprisingly, Liszt.

While Van Cliburn's eternally fresh and glittering interpretation of the D minor Concerto remains something very special (RCA 60420-2-RG [CD], 60420-4-RG [T]), this newer recording makes an even stronger case for the musical merits of these pieces. Donna Amato, the London Philharmonic, and Paul Freeman are eloquent advocates of both works. Without minimizing the influences on MacDowell's music, they emphasize its peculiar strengths: its open-hearted melodic thinking, its manliness and warmth. Amato's playing offers abundant lyricism and dash, while Freeman's accompaniments are both sensitive and brilliant.

Mahler, Gustav (1860–1911)

Das Lied von der Erde

King, tenor; Fischer-Dieskau, baritone; Vienna
Philharmonic, Bernstein. London 417783-2 [CD].

The popularity Gustav Mahler's music now enjoys would
have been all but unthinkable a generation ago. Most of the symphonies remained unrecorded, and of those that were, many featured mediocre to wretched performances that could only begin to
hint at the greatness contained in these noble, neurotic, enervating,
and uplifting works. Today, recordings of the Mahler symphonies
are nearly as common as those of Beethoven's, which is as it should
be. For just as the Romantic symphony was born in that series of
nine works Beethoven produced at the beginning of the nineteenth
century, its convulsive, extravagantly beautiful death can be heard
in the works Mahler wrote at the beginning of our own.

For most of his eighty-five years, Bruno Walter—Mahler's
disciple and protégé—was the composer's most impassioned and
indefatigable champion. Walter led the world premieres of the
Ninth Symphony and Das Lied von der Erde, and he left recordings
that remain some of the most telling and authoritative.

This famous 1952 version of the great symphonic song cycle
Das Lied von der Erde is not only one of Walter's greatest recorded
performances but one of the most intensely moving Mahler recordings ever made. The credit for this must be shared with the incomparable Kathleen Ferrier, whose haunting, richly sabled singing of
the concluding "Abschied" has never been matched, and the superb
Viennese tenor Julius Patzak, whose thin, leathery voice and consummate musicianship recall the art of another leather-voiced Viennese magician, Richard Tauber. But it is the conductor's gentle
intensity that makes this one of the major triumphs in the history
of the gramophone. All the passion and subtlety of this brilliantly
executed interpretation can be heard with remarkable clarity in
London's remastered recording. The compact disc was especially
miraculous in the way it makes the original 1952 recording seem
as though it had been completed the day before yesterday. Shamefully, it has now been withdrawn.

In its absence, Leonard Bernstein's Vienna Philharmonic recording, one of his very first with the orchestra, remains a noble and engrossing, if not entirely convincing experiment. Tenor James King sings well enough and the orchestra goes out of its mind; the problem may lie in hearing a baritone sing the contralto's songs. Fortunately, the baritone is Dietrich Fischer-Dieskau at his most reserved, penetrating, and dignified. The principal selling point is Bernstein's rather unbelievable conducting, which he would certainly equal on records, but never surpass.

Songs of a Wayfarer; *Kindertotenlieder*; *Rückert Lieder*

Baker, mezzo-soprano; Hallé Orchestra, New Philharmonia Orchestra, Barbirolli. Angel CDC-47793 [CD].

Even in a career as long and memorable as Dame Janet Baker's, the performances captured on these recordings stand out as pinnacles of her vocal art. Never have the *Songs of a Wayfarer* sounded as Schubertian in their refinement, and *Kindertotenlieder*, while devastating in their sorrow, are both tenderly consoling and totally lacking in self-pity.

Sir John Barbirolli was not only a great Mahler conductor but also a perfect partner for the mezzo-soprano; they seem to sense each other's needs and desires not simply bars but literally *pages* ahead of time, and yet move together so naturally that it sounds as though it were all being made up on the spur of the moment.

Dame Janet's Hyperion recording of the piano version (with Geoffrey Parsons) of the *Songs of a Wayfarer* plus some early Mahler rarities is recommended just as highly (CDA-66100 [CD]).

Symphony No. 1 in D

Concertgebouw Orchestra of Amsterdam, Bernstein. Deutsche Grammophon 427303-2 [CD].

Completed when Mahler was only twenty-eight, the D Major Symphony—still known, in spite of the composer's violent objections, as the *Titan*—contains many of the key compositional ingredients of the mature Mahler style. Its Olympian length, the sheer size of the performing forces, the gentle Viennese charm, the obsession with death in the gallows humor of the funeral march, and the ecstatic, almost hysterical triumph of its closing bars are all significant portents of what was to come.

More than three dozen versions of the work are currently in print, but none can come within shouting distance of that overwhelming and endlessly inventive recording Jascha Horenstein made with the London Symphony in the late 1960s, now shamefully withdrawn. Available for a time on the Elektra/Nonesuch label, and then on a Unicorn CD, it was one of the few studio recordings that managed to convey the on-the-spot sense of creation we encounter in only the most gripping live performances. A triumph of excess, exaggeration, and personality (and certainly no conductor ever made the final ten minutes seem more exultant or monumental), it was the Mahler First of a lifetime, and one we shouldn't have expected to be bettered any time soon.

Leonard Bernstein's final version *is* a recording of a gripping ("stupefying" would be far closer to the point) live performance. While the first two movements sound more serene and bucolic than usual—the Ländler is an amusing country bumpkin affair—the Funeral March is straight out of Edgar Allen Poe (or possibly Alfred Hitchcock), and the finale is one of those apocalyptic firestorms that threaten to incinerate everything in sight.

Symphony No. 2 in C minor, *Resurrection*

Armstrong, soprano; Baker, mezzo-soprano; Edinburgh Festival Chorus, London Symphony Orchestra, Bernstein. CBS M2K-42195 [CD].

When Leonard Bernstein's second stereo recording of the *Resurrection* Symphony was first released, most of the critics pounced all over it for its alleged self-indulgence and exaggerations. Of course, to say that of *any* performance of this inherently self-indulgent and exaggerated work would have been a bit like busting a Sodom and Gomorrah city councilman for indecent exposure. In fact, the recordings of the *Resurrection* that fail most decisively—those by Kubelik, Maazel, and Sinopoli, for example—are those that try to make the work more polite, coherent, and civilized than it can possibly be. To his great credit, Bernstein simply yanks out all the stops and allows this paradoxical hodgepodge of pathos, bathos, banality, and nobility to speak eloquently, and unforgettably, for itself.

Symphony No. 3 in D minor

Procter, mezzo-soprano; Wandsworth School Boys Choir, Ambrosian Singers, London Symphony, Horenstein. Unicorn-Kanchana UKCD-2006/07 [CD].

Ludwig, mezzo-soprano; Brooklyn Boys Choir, New York Choral Artists, New York Philharmonic, Bernstein. Deutsche Grammophon 423328-2 [CD].

Baker, mezzo-soprano; London Symphony Orchestra and Chorus, Thomas. CBS M2K-44553 [CD].

The longest symphony ever written by a major composer (and because of that fact, one of the few classical works that earns a place in *The Guinness Book of World Records*), the Third is obviously one of the more challenging Mahler symphonies to perform. In concert, it can make for a long and uncomfortable evening if the conductor has not done his homework; in the living room, it can offer countless excuses to turn off the receiver and see what's on TV.

And yet for all its daunting challenges, the Third has probably accounted for more important recordings than any other Mahler symphony, led by the three listed above. As extravagant as it may sound for such a work (the Mahler Third is hardly the Beethoven Fifth), I would suggest buying all three recordings, not only because I am unable to distinguish a clear-cut winner, but also because I would be unwilling—wild horses not withstanding—to be dragged away from the other two.

The oldest of the three, Jascha Horenstein's famous utterance of a generation ago, seems only to grow in stature over the years. In terms of both sweep and detail, he hardly misses a trick. The first movement marches in with a beautiful relentlessness, and the finale, taken at a dangerously slow pace, more than justifies Horenstein's courage: here it sounds like the greatest single movement in all of Mahler.

The Bernstein recording, taped at a live performance, is also overwhelming. (Mark Swed, the critic I trust more than any other, was present at the concert and came away talking to himself.) The relatively dry acoustic can't compromise either the lush romance or the cumulative power of the performance; it is—as it should be—a thoroughly exhausting experience.

If Michael Tilson Thomas does not yet have the reputation of being a great Mahler conductor, then his version of the Third should change that immediately. Huge in scale, meticulous in its ornamentation, and bursting with energy, it more than holds its own with those of his older colleagues—which is to say with the finest Mahler recordings ever made.

Again, each of these triumphant releases is an unqualified winner. If you must narrow it down to only one, I suggest you toss a three-headed coin.

Symphony No. 4 in G

Raskin, soprano; Cleveland Orchestra, Szell. Sony SBK-46535 [CD].

This most concise, charming, and popular of the Mahler symphonies is how most people find their way into the composer's music: it's the Mahlerian equivalent of Bruckner's *Romantic* Symphony. Yet like that other Fourth Symphony, the Mahler G Major is probably the composer's least characteristic work. Genial, untroubled, and, except for a few dark moments in the third movement, completely lacking in any neurotic symptoms, the Fourth is as happy as Mahler can be and still remain Mahler. Even the inevitable presentiment of death in the finale is a singularly trusting and innocent vision of heaven through the eyes of a child.

This classic 1965 interpretation remains one of the most completely successful Mahler recordings ever made. With a charm and glowing humanity that many of his enemies rarely accused him of possessing, George Szell handles the music with a deceptively relaxed but always exceedingly firm grip. Climaxes—even the shattering one at the end of the third movement—merely seem to happen, and in fact the entire performance creates the illusion of unfolding by itself, without the intervention of human will.

Judith Raskin gives one of the most engrossingly spontaneous performances of her brilliant career in the final movement; the Cleveland Orchestra has never been better, and in spite of some slightly intrusive hiss from the original analog tapes, the compact disc restoration is remarkably fine.

Symphony No. 5 in C-sharp minor

Chicago Symphony, Solti. London 414321-2 [CD].

Chicago still suffers from its age-old "Second City" complex, and is hence a place where superlatives tend to get thrown around more casually than anywhere else. The local Republican newspaper, the *Chicago Tribune*, calls itself "The World's Greatest Newspaper" on the masthead, hence the call letters of its television and radio stations, WGN. WLS, its Sears-owned competitor, is a reminder of "The World's Largest Store." Only in Chicago would things like the World's Tallest Building (the Sears Tower) or the World's Busiest Airport (O'Hare International) be pointed to as objects of civic pride, and only in Chicago would the city's orchestra, fresh from its first European tour, be cheered by a crowd who had probably not, for the most part, ever set foot in a concert hall, with banners proclaiming it (what else?) the World's Greatest Orchestra.

I was there in Orchestra Hall when Sir Georg Solti led an absolutely spellbinding performance of the Mahler Fifth during his first season as music director of the Chicago Symphony. The recording that was made several weeks later not only captured much of the overwhelming excitement of the interpretation, but also served to announce that the orchestra, after its stormy association with Solti's predecessor Jean Martinon, was at last back in form. They *do* sound very much like The World's Greatest Orchestra in one of the first recordings they made with their new music director. The woodwinds and brass negotiate this difficult music with supreme confidence and bravado, and the strings, both in the famous, gentle Adagietto and in the whirlwind finale, give Solti everything he asks for, which here amounts to the last word in excitement and finesse. Along with the playing itself (and this is, by a comfortable margin the best-played Mahler Fifth ever released), Solti's interpretation is a subtle, yet powerfully dramatic one, and the somewhat harsh sound of the original recording has been improved considerably.

Warning! Do not confuse this recording with the conductor's far less compelling 1990 remake (433329-2 [CD], 433329-4 [T]) in which all concerned seem to be doing little more than going through the motions.

Symphony No. 6 in A minor, *Tragic*

Vienna Philharmonic, Bernstein. Deutsche Grammophon 427697-2 [CD].

The Sixth Symphony occupies a unique position in Mahler's output as perhaps the most paradoxical work this endlessly paradoxical composer would ever produce. It is simultaneously the most objective and deeply personal of all his symphonies, the most rigorous in its formal organization, and the most devastating in its emotional effect. It is the only one of his ten completed works in the form (including *Das Lied von der Erde*) which, in its original version, adhered to the traditional format of the classical symphony, and the only one that ends on a note of catastrophic, inconsolable despair.

Bernstein's DG version of this dark masterpiece easily eclipses his earlier CBS recording, which in its day was the most compelling recorded performance available. Although the conductor's tempo in the first movement might seem a shade brisk to some, his shaping of the problematical finale is nothing short of masterly. The music rises heroically after each of the catastrophes signaled by one of those famous "hammer blows of fate"; the desolation he conjures in the final bars gives you the chilling feeling that someone has just walked on your grave. Thomas Hampson's beautifully sung *Kindertotenlieder* is the extremely attractive bonus.

Symphony No. 7 in E minor

City of Birmingham Symphony, Rattle. EMI CDC-54344 [CD].

The Seventh is by far the most difficult of all the Mahler symphonies to approach, and, finally, to love. In the mysterious Scherzo, flanked by two movements called *Nachtmusik*, the composer would write some of his most harmonically adventurous, forward-looking music. And if the opening movement presents more than its share of structural problems, the finale has always seemed, in comparison, utterly fragmented and frightfully banal.

In a pirated tape of a live London Symphony concert that has had a vigorous circulation in the underground market, Jascha Horenstein proved conclusively that the work's many problems are only surface deep. Not only was the conductor's grasp of the subtle, complex atmosphere of the three central movements amazing, he was also able to make the usually thin-sounding, patchwork finale seem as cogent and triumphant as the finale of the Mahler Fifth.

Sir Simon Rattle makes the point even more dramatically. Recorded in concert at the Aldeburgh Festival, the performance is one of the most thrilling of *any* Mahler symphony. In addition to an opening movement of incomparable thrust and power, the cen tral movements are so brilliantly characterized that the Scherzo and especially the second *Nachtmusik* for once don't seem too long. Yet it is in the final movement that Rattle moves from the ranks of the very good Mahler conductors to those of the great. The tempo relationships are so brilliantly judged that at no point is the movement's forward momentum allowed to flag, thereby creating a unique feeling of rightness and inevitability. The playing is not only phenomenally accurate but also burns with a fierce conviction and a sense of excitement that only a live performance can provide. If you have any lingering doubts about Mahler's problem child, then this is the performance to clear them up.

Symphony No. 8 in E-flat, *Symphony of a Thousand*

> Harper, Popp, Auger, Minton, Watts, Kollo, Shirley-Quirk, Talvela, Vienna State Opera Chorus, Vienna Singverein, Vienna Boys Choir, Chicago Symphony, Solti. London 414493-2 [CD].

Sir Georg Solti has said in print that he considers the Eighth the greatest of the Mahler symphonies, and on the basis of this stupendous Chicago Symphony recording, taped in Vienna, even the most rabid admirers of the Sixth and Ninth would be tempted to agree. On a singularly tight recording schedule (and the tension, at times, is almost palpable), Solti unleashes the greatness of the music in a way that even Leonard Bernstein, in his famous London Symphony recording, is not quite able to match.

The performance of the opening movement, a setting of the medieval hymn *Veni, creator spiritus*, is almost withering in its joyous excitement, and the lengthy setting of the closing scene from

Part I of Goethe's *Faust* is wonderfully operatic, in the best possible sense of the word. Solti loses no opportunity to exploit either the high drama or endless color of the score, from the hushed and sinister opening bars of the second movement to the vast and vastly moving chorus with which the Symphony concludes. The massed choruses sing with tremendous accuracy and enthusiasm, and the performance boasts the strongest collection of soloists of any Mahler Eighth on the market today. Yet it is the superhuman playing of the Chicago Symphony that tips the scales, perhaps forever, in Solti's favor. Rumor has it that members of the Vienna Philharmonic who attended the recording sessions were deeply shaken by what they heard. Many left the hall speechless, while others were heard mumbling incoherently to themselves.

Symphony No. 9 in D

Concertgebouw Orchestra of Amsterdam, Bernstein. Deutsche Grammophon 419208-2 [CD].

Even before that historic series of concerts in May of 1920, when Willem Mengelberg presided over the first important festival of his friend's music, the Concertgebouw Orchestra of Amsterdam has begun the longest unbroken Mahler tradition of any of the world's major orchestras. The composer himself was a frequent guest conductor in Amsterdam, and in addition to Mengelberg's famous interpretations, those of his successors, Eduard van Beinum and Bernard Haitink, have gone a long way to cementing the Concertgebouw Orchestra's reputation as the finest Mahler orchestra in the world. Furthermore, the greatest living Mahler conductor of recent times also appeared with them on a regular basis, and this live performance of the Ninth Symphony must now be counted with the three or four greatest Mahler recordings yet made.

In the two decades since his New York Philharmonic recordings became the principal impetus for the modern Mahler revival, Leonard Bernstein's approach to the composer's music both deepened and grew more extreme. The surface drama became increasingly turbulent (his detractors have called it "self-indulgent" and "overwrought"), while its deeper implications have been plumbed with an understanding that was ever more lucid and profound.

This performance of the composer's most shattering work is a triumph of extremes. Where other conductors have been intense in this music, Bernstein is almost savagely so; where others have heard the final movement as Mahler's poignant farewell to life, Bernstein transforms it into the stuff of universal tragedy, a farewell to *all* life, possibility, and hope. In essence, the conductor's final version of this great work is as much Bernstein's Ninth as it is Gustav Mahler's. Besides, during the final years of Lenny's life, the distinction really *had* begun to blur.

Martin, Frank (1890–1974)

Concerto for Seven Wind Instruments, Percussion, and Strings; *Petite Symphonie Concertante*; *Six Monologues from Jedermann*

> Soloists, L'Orchestre de la Suisse Romande, Jordan. Erato 2292-45694-2 [CD].

It's both astonishing and inexplicable that the music of Frank Martin, the greatest composer that Switzerland has ever produced and one of the most distinctive musical voices of the twentieth century isn't far better known. Like the work of any truly major composer, Martin's music creates and inhabits a unique sonic world, with a refined sense of color and texture, an emotional range and depth, and a rigorous (though by no means rigid) internal logic and order unmistakably its own. Although he was touched by most of the major twentieth century movements, from the impressionism of Debussy through the French neoclassicism of the 1920s to Schoenberg's twelve-tone techniques, Martin remained an utterly distinctive voice in modern music and one whose present neglect is a perplexing mystery.

Each of the works contained on this superb Erato recording has a fair claim to being Martin's masterpiece: the *Six Monologues from Jedermann*, a setting of excerpts from Hugo von Hoffmansthal's dark and despairing *Everyman*, ranks with the greatest twentieth-century song cycles, and the two reinterpretations of the *sinfonia concertante,* which established Martin's early reputation in the 1940s. The performances are all sympathetic and compelling—the *Petite Symphonie Concertante* particularly so—and the recording is ideally warm, detailed, and spacious.

Martinů, Bohuslav
(1890–1959)

The Epic of Gilgamesh

> Soloists, Slovak Philharmonic Orchestra and Chorus, Košler. Marco Polo 8.223316 [CD].

With the work of his Polish near-contemporary Karol Szymanowski, the music of the Czech composer Bohuslav Martinů remains one of the last largely undiscovered treasure troves of twentieth-century music. Like Szymanowski, Martinů was a restless eclectic whose music nevertheless spoke with a thoroughly original voice. In all of the more than four hundred works he eventually produced, one can hear the same quality that so impressed Igor Stravinsky in the music of Sergei Prokofiev—an elusive commodity Stravinsky called "the instant imprint of personality."

Nowhere is Martinů's personality heard to more original or powerful effect than in the vast *Epic of Gilgamesh*, based on the Babylonian poem—thought to be civilization's oldest—that he set to music in 1954. Like the music Szymanowski composed for the cathedral scene in his opera *King Roger*, Martinů's choral writing is infused with an eerie, almost medieval grandeur that serves the ancient tale exceedingly well. The performers respond to this hypnotic and mysterious score with enthusiasm and devotion, as do the Marco Polo engineers. Admirers of Honegger's *Le Roi David* or Walton's *Belshazzar's Feast* will find *Gilgamesh* no less compelling.

Frescos of Piero della Francesca; Double Concerto for Two String Orchestras, Piano, and Timpani

Soloists, Prague Radio Symphony, Mackerras. Supraphon 10-3393-2 [CD].

The Swiss conductor Paul Sacher commissioned Martinů's Double Concerto for his Basel Chamber Orchestra in 1938, two years after he introduced Bartók's Music for Strings, Percussion, and Celesta. Though considerably less well known than Bartók's masterpiece, the Double Concerto—unleashed by Martinů's anguish over the recently signed Munich Pact that allowed the Nazi occupation of the Sudentenland—is every bit its equal. Concentrated, sweepingly dramatic, and vibrantly alive, the Concerto is one of the most powerfully inventive orchestral scores of the twentieth century. By the same token, the *Frescos of Piero della Francesca*, written following a motor tour of Italy in 1955, is one of Martinů's most accessible and physically beautiful scores.

Sir Charles Mackerras here proves that he speaks Martinů's distinctive language as fluently as he speaks Leoš Janáček's. As in his brilliant (though alas, now deleted) recording of the colorful ballet *Špaliček*, there seems to be no detail of the often complex texture that he doesn't clarify or make even more beautiful. The Prague Radio Symphony has never sounded better, and the recording, while somewhat reverberant, is nonetheless well-focused and clear.

Nonet for Winds and String ; *La Revue de cuisine*; Trio in F for Flute, Cello, and Piano.

Dartington Ensemble. Hyperion CDA-66084 [CD].

In addition to bringing us some of the finest performances of Martinů's chamber music that have yet been made, the invaluable Hyperion recording by England's Dartington Ensemble also provides a representative cross-section of the three major phases of Martinů's creative life. *La Revue de cuisine* (The Kitchen Revue) is a sassy, jazzy ballet produced during the composer's seventeen-year stay in Paris; the Trio in F, composed during Martinů's American exile in 1944, is one of the most Czech and ebullient of all his works. Yet the gem of the collection is the bright, and deceptively simple-sounding Nonet, composed five months before the composer's death in 1959. In its serenity, melodic inventiveness, and structural elegance, it is easily one of the most nearly perfect and instantly enjoyable chamber works written since the end of the Second World War.

A recent recording by the Stamitz Quartet for Bayer (100152/54 [CD]) features the seven string quartets that Martinů composed between 1918 and 1947. The level of inspiration might not be quite as consistently high as it is in the composer's symphonies, yet the best of them—especially the Fifth and Sixth—rank not far behind those of Bartók and Schoenberg. The performances are excellent, as is the recorded sound.

Symphonies (6)

Bamberg Symphony, Järvi. Bis CD-362 (Nos. 1 and 2);
CD-363 (Nos. 3 and 4); CD-395 (Nos. 5 and 6) [CDs].

Neeme Järvi, the conductor of the Detroit Symphony (among other ensembles) is, to say the very least, an enigma. One of the most frequently recorded of contemporary conductors, he has plugged more holes in the catalog than a hundred little Dutchboys could. In repertoire that is either unknown or well off the beaten track, the burley Estonian tends to be vigorous, imaginative, and persuasive; on more familiar ground (witness his generally drab and uneventful cycle of the Dvořák symphonies), he sometimes disappoints.

Among his most valuable contributions to date are the recordings of the six Martinů symphonies made for the Swedish label Bis. The decision to use the Bamburg Symphony as opposed to his own Gothenberg Orchestra was a wise one, resulting in idiomatic, intensely committed playing.

Martinů did not produce a symphony until he was fifty-two, so all six are the products of a fully mature musical personality. The First, a gleaming, rhythmically ingenious work commissioned by Serge Koussevitzky, was followed by the relaxed and rustic Second, Martinů's *Pastoral* Symphony. The Third is a brooding, violent, often desperate commentary on the events of the Second World War, while the Fourth, written in the spring of 1945, mixes joy, hope, and idyllic tenderness, and features a Largo that rivals the somewhat more familiar Largo from Dvořák's *New World* Symphony in depth and complexity. The Fifth is another of the composer's obstinately life-affirming statements, and the Sixth, the *Fantaisies symphoniques*, is the most ambitious and far-reaching of all his orchestral scores.

With playing and recorded sound that are both nearly perfect, this constitutes an ideal introduction to a major symphonic talent.

Mascagni, Pietro
(1863–1945)

Cavalleria rusticana

Milanov, Björling, Smith, Merrill, Robert Shaw Chorale, RCA Victor Orchestra, Cellini. RCA 6510-2-RG [CD].

Long before he died in abject poverty and disgrace—like Giacomo Puccini, he had been one of Mussolini's most ardent supporters—Pietro Mascagni was one of the most tragic figures in operatic history. At the age of twenty-six, he achieved world fame with *Cavalleria rusticana*, and for the next fifty-six years he was condemned to live out his life haunted by an overwhelming early success he was never able to repeat. "I was crowned before I was King", was the composer's own rueful assessment of his career, and history has been forced to agree.

While this lurid tale of betrayal and revenge has very little to do with "rustic chivalry," the literal translation of its title, *Cavalleria rusticana* has remained the most justly popular one-act opera ever written. Like Leoncavallo's *Pagliacci*, with which it is usually paired, Mascagni's masterpiece is the central work of the Italian *verismo* school. Like *Pag*, *Cav* explodes with vivid drama and raw emotions, though it also boasts a musical subtlety and sensitivity to character that only the best of Puccini's mature operas can begin to match.

The recording that captures more of the opera's finesse and earthiness than any other is this classic RCA recording from the mid-1950s, recently released on compact disc. Zinka Milanov was one of the century's great Santuzzas. Passionate, vulnerable, immensely feminine, she was also equipped with a voice as physically impressive as those of Leontyne Price and Rosa Ponselle. This recording catches her at something past her prime, but with her temperament and most of her instrument still intact, the interpretation still makes for an overwhelming experience. With the insouciant and spectacularly well-sung Turridu of Jussi Björling, and the sensitive, yet richly powerful, garlic-laden conducting of Renato Cellini, this remains, for me, the only recording of the opera to own.

Since that other fine RCA recording with Placido Domingo has been withdrawn, presumably to be resurrected soon on compact disc, none of the modern versions can be recommended with any enthusiasm. As with *Pag*, the *Cav* situation is pretty bleak, the choice coming down to Pavarotti sweating bullets on London or Karajan sliming his way through the thing on Deutsche Grammophon.

Pavarotti, however, is at his most appealing in the Angel recording (CDCB-47905 [CD]) of Mascagni's "other" opera, *L'Amico Fritz*, which is as gently amusing and charming as *Cavalleria rusticana* is seething and passionate. If there are no other moments in the score to match the famous "Cherry Duet," then the opera still holds up well to repeated use, especially in this warmly affecting 1969 recording that also offers the young Mirella Freni at the beginning of her career.

Massenet, Jules

(1842–1912)

Manon

De los Angeles, Legay, Dens, Boirthayre, Berton, Chorus
and Orchestra of the Opéra-comique de Paris, Monteux.
Angel CDMC-63549 [CD].

At the time of his death in 1912, the suave and urbane Jules
Massenet was one of the wealthiest composers who ever lived. His
impeccably crafted, gently sentimental operas are among the finest
and most popular ever written by a French composer. Audiences
love them for their directness, dramatic realism, and inexhaustible
flow of lovely melody. Singers love them because they are so carefully and gracefully written that even the most demanding Massenet role will invariably make even a fair or barely adequate singer
sound exceptionally good.

With the reappearance of the classic Monteux *Manon*, one of
the great operatic recordings returns to the catalog. Even those who
normally do not respond to Victoria de los Angeles's singing (one
opera-loving friend refers to her as "an air-raid siren with feet")
cannot fail to be bowled over by the freshness and sheer dramatic
ingenuity of the performance. Pierre Monteux's conducting is a
wonder of panache and aching sensitivity, the rest of the cast is
splendid, and the only real drawback is the rather fierce recorded
sound.

Those who absolutely must have more up-to-date sound will
find Beverly Sills at her most attractive in a fine Angel recording
conducted by Julius Rudel (CDMC 69831 [CD]). And Sir Colin
Davis's utterly memorable version of *Werther* on Philips (416654-2
[CD]) remains, with the Monteux *Manon*, one of the most completely satisfying Massenet recordings yet.

Maxwell Davies, Sir Peter (1934–)

Eight Songs for a Mad King; *Miss Donnithorne's Maggot*

Eastman, speaker; Thomas, mezzo-soprano; Fires of
London, Maxwell Davies. Unicorn-Kanchana
DKPCD-9052 [CD].

On first hearing *Eight Songs for a Mad King*, most people are
flabbergasted. As well they should be, since it is the most frighteningly original musical work produced by an Englishman in this
century.

Employing some of King George III's actual demented ruminations, the piece is so grotesque, poignant, ridiculous, touching,
stupid, and powerful that it defies description. Julius Eastman, who
"interprets" the role of the king, is quite unbelievable: his repertoire
of sighs, shrieks, howls, and moans is astounding, as is his ability
to draw us into the mind of the character and make us feel genuine
compassion and concern.

Miss Donnithorne's Maggot, a similarly unhinging tribute to
the actual eccentric who provided Dickens with his model for Miss
Havisham in *Great Expectations*, has many intriguing moments,
but pales in comparison to the *Songs*.

I should admit that when I first heard this dizzy work, I was
convinced that everyone concerned with the project—composer,
performers, recording company executives—was in desperate need
of serious psychiatric care. I'm now fairly certain that *Eight Songs
for a Mad King* is a major twentieth-century masterpiece.

Mendelssohn, Felix

(1809–1847)

Concertos for Piano and Orchestra: No. 1 in G minor; No. 2 in D minor

Perahia, piano; Academy of St. Martin-in-the-Fields, Marriner. CBS MK-42401 [CD].

While far less familiar than the justly ubiquitous Violin Concerto, Mendelssohn's Piano Concertos are full of memorable ideas and exquisite surface detail. And though they are easy on the ear and psyche, they are by no means powder puffs: the stormy opening movement of the G minor is as substantial as anything in Mendelssohn, and the slow movements of both Concertos are superbly crafted and richly felt.

It's hardly surprising that such a fine Mozart pianist as Murray Perahia should be such a cunning advocate of these works, which so clearly have their roots in the eighteenth century. Their essentially classical poise and structure are not lost on him, nor does he ignore that breath of early Romanticism that makes all of Mendelssohn's music what it is. Sir Neville Marriner, as always, is a witty and generous partner, and the CD version comes with equally impeccable performances of the Prelude and Fugue No. 1, the *Rondo capriccioso* and the *Variations sérieuses*.

A must for Mendelssohn lovers or Perahia fans.

Concerto in E minor for Violin and Orchestra

Menuhin, violin; Berlin Philharmonic, Furtwängler. Angel CDC-69799 [CD].

Lin, violin; Philharmonia Orchestra, Thomas. CBS MDK-44902 [CD], MDT-44902 [T].

This fresh, buoyant, eternally sweet-spirited work is probably the best-loved violin concerto ever written. And in spite of the apparent effortlessness of its invention, the E minor Concerto had an unusually long and painful gestation: from first sketch to finished score, it occupied the usually deft and facile composer's attention for the better part of six years.

Every important violinist of the century has recorded the work, and many of them more than once, but there is still something very special in Sir Yehudi Menuhin's 1954 recording with Wilhelm Furtwängler and the Berlin Philharmonic. Unlike their monumental interpretation of the Beethoven Concerto, which fills out this unusually generous compact disc, the performance of the Mendelssohn is a marvel of quiet intimacy and elfin grace. Menuhin's playing (which in recent years has been seriously compromised by a neurological disorder) was never more poignantly innocent than it is here, and the conductor, who had only a few months left to live, turns in one of the freshest and most impetuous of all his recorded performances.

Among more recent versions, the sensational debut recording by the Chinese-American violinist Cho-Liang Lin is not only the most exciting recording the Concerto has received in years, but also our first glimpse at what should undoubtedly develop into one of the great careers of the next generation. Like his near-contemporary, cellist Yo-Yo Ma, Lin is already a dazzlingly equipped musician. His technique is formidably seamless, and his musical personality is an engaging combination of outgoing bravado and introspective warmth. With the lush, yet witty support supplied by the Philharmonia Orchestra and Michael Tilson Thomas, this is considerably more than a very impressive first recording by an important new artist. It is, with Menuhin's thirty-five-year-old wonder, *the* recording of the Mendelssohn Concerto to own.

Elijah

Plowright, Finnie, Davies, White, London Symphony Orchestra and Chorus, Hickox. Chandos CHAN-8774/ 75 [CD], DBTD-2016 [T].

From its startling opening recitative, which actually begins before the dirge-like overture, through such powerfully dramatic choruses as "Hear our cry, O Baal," the oratorio *Elijah* is one of the great de facto Romantic operas: a gripping, lyrical, wonderfully theatrical work which, with a little lighting and makeup, could hold the stage as easily as the early Wagner operas.

The glowing performance led by the ever-imaginative Richard Hickox transforms *Elijah* into something very far removed from the sanctimonious Victorian monstrosity that Shaw used to complain about. This is vivid, utterly committed music-making as well as compelling theater: Mendelssohn's inspiration shimmers in every bar, and the drama is made to seem consistently immediate and real. Hickox's team of soloists is exemplary and the exhilarating work of the London Symphony Chorus only confirms his growing reputation as the finest European choral director since the legendary Wilhelm Pitz.

For those in whom the Old Testament grandeur of *Elijah* strikes a responsive chord, Mendelssohn's New Testament oratorio, *St. Paul*, can be found on Erato 45279-2 [CD] in a devout and moving performance led by Michel Corboz.

A Midsummer Night's Dream (incidental music), Opp. 21 and 61

Watson, Wallis, London Symphony Orchestra and Chorus, Previn. Angel CDC-47163 [CD].

The famous overture Felix Mendelssohn composed for Shakespeare's festive comedy, *A Midsummer Night's Dream*, has a fair claim to being the greatest single musical work ever written by a teenager. Only Mozart and Schubert produced music of similar quality at a comparable age. The remainder of the incidental music Mendelssohn would write over the next twenty years was also of a very high caliber, including the finest example of a form he would make forever his own, the quicksilver Scherzo, and one of the most famous five minutes in all of music, the stirring, and, for many, bloodcurdling Wedding March, to whose famous strains countless freedom-loving people have trooped off to join the ranks of the Living Dead.

On records, André Previn has established a well-deserved reputation as one of the finest interpreters of the music of the major modern English composers, and of other big-name twentieth-century figures from Rachmaninoff and Prokofiev to Debussy and Ravel. That he is equally comfortable in the mainstream of the Austro-German tradition is amply documented by a recording like this one, in which he proves, quite conclusively I think, that he is the finest Mendelssohn conductor in the world today.

All of the familiar moments—the Overture, Scherzo, Inter-mezzo, Nocturne, and the Wedding March—are invested with an exhilarating freshness and immensely individual character, while the less familiar set pieces and linking passages are given a weight and significance that no other recording can begin to match. The spooky menace and rhythmic point of "You Spotted Snakes" is alone worth the price of the recording.

Octet in E-flat for Strings

Academy of St. Martin-in-the-Fields Chamber Ensemble. Philips 420400-2 [CD]. Chandos ABTD-1423 [T].

When I was sixteen I read something from the second volume of George Bernard Shaw's *Dramatic Opinions and Essays* that struck a painfully responsive chord:

> With the single exception of Homer, there is no eminent writer, not even Sir Walter Scott, whom I can despise so entirely as I despise Shakespeare when I measure my mind against his. It would positively be a relief to me to dig him up and throw stones at him.

At an age when I was wasting my life fighting acne and the oboe, yelling at girls, and trying to beat out three other guys for one of the two defensive-end spots on my high school football team, Felix Mendelssohn was composing his miraculously inspired E-flat Major Octet. After weeks of excruciating soul searching, leavened by the then major triumphs of making the team, and thereby at-tracting the attentions of an exceedingly cute cheerleader, I resolved to stop hating Mendelssohn by simply facing the irrefutable facts. I was a perfectly normal Midwest high school kid; he was a genius.

Nowhere is Mendelssohn's youthful brilliance revealed more felicitously than in the finest single work ever composed for this particular combination of instruments. The level of melodic in-spiration and richness of ornamental detail is so phenomenal, the Octet is obviously the work of a mature master, not a boy of sixteen. Both of these superlative recordings capture almost all of the Octet's melting warmth and blindingly brilliant inspiration. In fact, a choice between them will depend largely on your preference for the tape or the compact disc format.

Overtures

Bamberg Symphony, Flor. RCA 7905-2-RC [CD].

With Weber, Berlioz, and Rossini, Mendelssohn was one of the supreme early-Romantic masters of the concert overture, as this delightful RCA collection readily proves. In addition to the familiar warhorses *Midsummer Night's Dream* and *Fingal's Cave*, which has not had a more atmospheric, darkly mysterious performance since Furtwängler's in the early '30s, *Calm Sea and Prosperous Voyage* and *Ruy Blas* are marvelous works. *Athalia* and *The Marriage of Camacho*, the overture to his first opera, will come as delightful surprises.

Claus Peter Flor and the Bamburg Symphony have yet to make a finer recording than this one. A freshness and sense of discovery is exhibited in their playing, coupled with an aristocratic control that makes it difficult to imagine that any more completely satisfying recordings will show up any time soon. Like the performances, the recorded sound is immaculate.

Songs without Words

Barenboim, Piano. Deutsche Grammophon 423931-2 [CD] (complete); 415118-2 [CD] (excerpts).

Along with being able to hear the *William Tell Overture* without immediately thinking of the Lone Ranger, one of the acid tests of the true music lover is the ability to listen to Mendelssohn's "Spring Song" without breaking into fits of convulsive laughter. With the second Hungarian Rhapsody, it was pilloried in more cartoons of the 1940s and '50s than any other musical work, and its unaffected innocence *can* degenerate into saccharine ditziness if the performer fails to treat it like the delicate blossom it is.

Unlike so many performances of the *Songs without Words*, which have treated these magical, fragile miniatures like Victorian potted palms, Daniel Barenboim's reveal the wondrous little tone poems that lie buried beneath the decades of calcified interpretive treacle. While obviously affectionate, the interpretations have just enough twinkle of wit to prevent things from getting mushy. And even when the pianist does turn on the ooze, he does so with a charming fin de siècle graciousness—a pretty neat trick for a musician born in 1942.

If all eight sets seem like a bit much (though listening to them is precisely analogous to eating peanuts) a judicious selection, together with the three *Liebesträume* of Liszt and Schubert's *Moments musicaux* are available on a single unusually enjoyable Deutsche Grammophon CD.

Symphonies (12) for String Orchestra

English String Orchestra, Boughton. Nimbus NI-5141/43 [CD].

Mendelssohn's string symphonies scarcely sound like what they are: the apprentice work of a composer not yet out of knee pants. Written for concerts at the family home on the fashionable Neue Promenade in Berlin, the earliest were composed when Mendelssohn was only twelve; the latest when he was fourteen. They show such an astonishing confidence and fertility of invention that it's easy to hear why the aging Goethe, on meeting Mendelssohn during this period, accepted the frail boy on terms of absolute equality.

The performances by the English String Orchestra under William Boughton are as full of youthful enthusiasm as the works themselves. No attempt is made to inflate the music beyond its inherent limits or to make it seem more significant than it is. The result is playing of the utmost naturalness and grace, which lets these precocious little charmers speak for themselves.

Symphonies: No. 1 in C minor; No. 5 in D, *Reformation*

Bamburg Symphony, Flor. RCA 09026-60391-2 [CD].

Mendelssohn first conquered England with his youthful C minor Symphony. Following its world premiere in London on March 31, 1824, the composer endeared himself to both the orchestra and the audience by personally shaking hands with every member of the London Philharmonic. In spite of its late-sounding opus number, the *Reformation* Symphony is also an early work. In it, Felix Mendelssohn-Bartholdy enthusiastically quotes Martin Luther's *Ein feste Burg ist unser Gott*. (One can only wonder what the composer's grandfather Moses, a philosopher known as the "Jewish Plato," would have made of his grandson's homage to such a notorious anti-Semite.)

As in their recording of Mendelssohn's overtures, the performances by Claus Peter Flor and the Bamburg Symphony are fresh, inventive, and immaculately played, making this one of the most attractive Mendelssohn recordings now available.

Symphony No. 3 in A minor, *Scottish*

London Symphony, Maag. London 433023-2 [CD].

Chicago Symphony, Solti. London 414665-2 [CD].

It is no accident that in Great Britain, Felix Mendelssohn is revered as one of the most important of all composers. In addition to writing the incidental music for Shakespeare's *Midsummer Night's Dream*, he supplied the oratorio-mad English with *Elijah*, one of the greatest nineteenth-century examples of their favorite form of musical entertainment. And with the *Hebrides Overture* and *Scottish* Symphony (the latter dedicated to Queen Victoria), he wrote two of the best and most popular of all musical travelogues based on British themes.

No recording of the *Scottish* Symphony has come within hailing distance of the astonishingly vivid and spontaneous performance by the London Symphony led by the Swiss conductor Peter Maag since it was first released more than thirty years ago. Impulsive yet highly polished, beautifully detailed yet sweepingly cinematic, the interpretation remains one of the great glories of the stereo era. Offering as it does Sir Georg Solti's brilliant Israel Philharmonic recording of the *Italian* Symphony (you simply will not believe the ferocious pace of the finale), this disc is one of the major bargains now on the market. Solti's slightly driven, yet compellingly dramatic Chicago Symphony recording of the Third is the best alternative. With thrilling playing and dazzling recorded sound, this would be the first choice among all *Scottish* Symphony recordings, were it not for the once-in-a-lifetime combination of freshness and poetry that Peter Maag found in the score so long ago.

Symphony No. 4 in A, *Italian*

Cleveland Orchestra, Szell. CBS MYK-37760 [CD], MT-37760 [T].

More than any other work, it is the colorful, impeccably crafted *Italian* Symphony that best fixes Mendelssohn's place in the development of Western music. Essentially a classicist who was touched by the first winds of the Romantic movement, Mendelssohn reconciled eighteenth-century structural decorum with nineteenth-century emotionalism more comfortably than any other composer of his time. The *Italian* Symphony is one of the great transitional works of the early Romantic era, a piece whose formal organization is as tight as the symphonies of Haydn and Mozart, but whose expressiveness clearly points the way to Berlioz, Chopin, and Schumann.

The performance that most successfully projects both sides of the *Italian* Symphony's essential character is this immaculate and exciting CBS recording. Along with the highly buffed playing of the Cleveland, the finest Mozart orchestra of modern times, George Szell finds countless ways to remind us that this is also an intensely Romantic work. The Pilgrim's March, even at a rather brisk tempo, has a wonderfully melancholy grandeur, and in the concluding tarantella, taken at a break-neck clip, there are many dark and disquieting moments lurking beneath the swirling, giddy surface. With equally lucid and revealing performances of the best known moments from the *Midsummer Night's Dream* music, this is one of the classic Mendelssohn recordings of the stereo age.

Trios (2) for Piano, Violin, and Cello

Golub, piano; Kaplan, violin; Carr, cello. Arabesque Z-6599 [CD].

Besides the phenomenal Octet for Strings, the two Piano Trios represent Mendelssohn's major achievement as a composer of chamber music. With their singing slow movements, sparking Scherzos, and powerfully dramatic finales, both of these passionate, elegantly wrought works rank with the finest chamber music of the Romantic era.

Although for years the recordings by the Beaux Arts set the standard in both pieces, the newer versions by this brilliant trio of young Americans handily surpasses them. A freshness in the approach and an effortlessness in the execution make the performances seem both utterly natural and thoroughly alive.

While the composer's six String Quartets are not on the same consistently high level as the Trios, they contain much wonderful music and can be heard in a very fine Deutsche Grammophon collection (415883-2 [CD]) by Stuttgart's Melos Quartet.

Messiaen, Olivier

(1908–1992)

Turangalila Symphony; *Quartet for the End of Time*

City of Birmingham Symphony, Rattle. Angel CDCB-47463-2 [CD].

To give credit where credit is due, Olivier Messiaen is the only composer of serious music whose work has ever made me throw up. I was listening to a new recording of *Vingt regards sur l'Enfant Jésus* (which one announcer of my acquaintance always translates on the air as "Give my regards to Jesus") when I felt that unmistakable feeling and made it to the restroom just in time. True, I was running a fever of 102 degrees; true, there was a particularly virulent form of intestinal flu making the rounds; and true, I *had* consumed an inhumanly large and greasy cheeseburger not an hour before. Nevertheless, I firmly believed that it was Messiaen who was responsible, and I still believe it today.

Numerous respected musicians, and a fair-sized public, take Messiaen's mumbling mysticism and interminable bird calls seriously, so he can't be dismissed out of hand. Recently, for sins too horrible to mention, I assigned myself the penance of listening to Sir Simon Rattle's recording of the endless *Turangalila Symphony*. If you're drawn to this gibberish, you'll find the interpretation all you could possibly hope for: like André Previn's deleted Angel recording, the performance may even be far too good for the piece.

An older recording of that other Messiaen favorite, the knee-slapping *Quartet for the End of Time*, which was composed in a concentration camp and *sounds* like it, rounds out what is, for my taste, a far too generous release.

Meyerbeer, Giacomo

(1791–1864)

Les Huguenots

> Sutherland, Arroyo, Tourangeau, Vrenios, Cossa, Bacquier, Ghiuselev, Ambrosian Opera Chorus, New Philharmonia Orchestra, Bonynge. London 430549-2 [CD].

Like Felix Mendelssohn, Jakob Liebmann Beer was the son of a wealthy Berlin banker. His maternal grandfather bestowed an immense legacy on the boy with the sole stipulation that he add his grandfather's name to his own. After his early success as a composer of Italian opera, he Italianized his given name and as Giacomo Meyerbeer, in a career that spanned more than half a century, he did more than anyone to establish the grammar and syntax of what would come to be known as grand opera.

Though they have largely fallen out of favor—in part because they were tailor-made to the gaudy tastes of the mid-century Parisian public, and in part because so few singers are capable of performing them today—Meyerbeer's operas were among the most successful written during the entire nineteenth century. In fact, Richard Wagner's hysterical, life-long anti-Semitism was only flamed by his envy of Meyerbeer. In the revolting pamphlet *Jewry in Music*, begun shortly after he attended a Paris performance of

Meyerbeer's *Le Prophète*, Wagner argued that Jews had no place in German life and art—arguments that would later have a profound influence on Wagner's ardent admirer, Adolf Hitler.

Les Huguenots, Meyerbeer's epic treatment of the St. Bartholomew's Day Massacre of 1572, is one of the composer's most impressive works. Even Wagner considered its beautiful Act IV love duet one of the finest moments in all of opera, and the powerful Viennese critic Eduard Hanslick, Wagner's model for the narrow-minded town clerk Sixtus Beckmesser in *Die Meistersinger*, insisted that a failure to appreciate the dramatic power of *Les Huguenots* suggested serious deficiencies in the listener's critical faculties. In addition to its splendor and spectacle, the opera offers a love story of genuine depth and feeling, together with an almost embarrassing wealth of memorable set pieces and highly singable tunes.

Except for Dame Joan Sutherland, the level of singing on this fine London recording from 1970 is not quite what one imagines it was on those evenings at the turn of the century when *Les Huguenots* was used as the vehicle for those "nuits des sept étoiles." Although the other six stars here range from the very good to the barely adequate, much of the opera's appeal and power still manage to come through, thanks largely to the brilliant conducting of Richard Bonynge, who has never been more passionately persuasive. For anyone wondering what all the shouting was about in the middle of the last century, this recording will offer many clues.

Milhaud, Darius (1892–1974)

La Création du monde

National Orchestra of France, Bernstein. Angel CDC-47845 [CD].

One of the most prolific and entertaining composers that history has known, Darius Milhaud was also one of the largest. In fact, to find a composer of comparable girth, one has to go back to the late-eighteenth-century Bohemian composer and keyboard virtuoso, Jan Ladislav Dussek, who became so obese toward the end of his career that his hands could no longer reach the keyboard of his piano. (Fortunately, for posterity, Milhaud never learned to play the instrument, and thus was free to compose all of his music while seated at a desk.)

La Création du monde (The Creation of the World), the jazz ballet written after the composer's encounter with American jazz in 1923, is probably Milhaud's finest and most characteristic work. It is given a racy, vibrant performance in the Bernstein recording, which also includes spirited interpretations of Milhaud's *Saudades do Brasil* and *Le Boeuf sur le toit*, the equally jazzy and surrealistic ballet whose scenario, by Jean Cocteau, calls for (among other things) a Paris gendarme to be decapitated by an overhead fan. My kind of ballet.

Moeran, E.J. (1894–1950)

Symphony in G minor; *Overture to a Masque*

> Ulster Orchestra, Handley. Chandos CHAN-8577 [CD], ABTD-1271 [T].

It is frankly astonishing that a work as fine as Moeran's G minor Symphony should be so completely unknown outside of Britain. Brilliantly argued and crafted, with its roots firmly planted in British folk song, it is a work to stand alongside most of the Vaughan Williams symphonies, and it is one that would undoubtedly attract a large following were it simply to be played more often.

Given an unusually pointed and powerful performance by Vernon Handley and the fine Ulster Orchestra, the Symphony has a moiling, craggy intensity that recalls late Sibelius, although it has more than enough character and personality of its own. With an equally smashing account of the rambunctious *Overture to a Masque*, this is both an ideal introduction to an important, strangely neglected composer and an absolute must for lovers of modern British music.

Moeran's Cello Concerto is no less fine a work and is given a sumptuous performance by Raphael Wallfisch and the Bournemouth Sinfonietta led by the late Norman Del Mar, who is equally persuasive with the refreshing *Sinfonietta* (Chandos CHAN-8456 [CD], ABTD-1167 [T]). Another superb Chandos recording (CHAN-8807 [CD], ABTD-1435 [T]) features the lovely Violin Concerto with its many references to Irish folk song, handsomely played by Lydia Mordkovich and the Ulster Orchestra conducted by Vernon Handley.

Finally, two collections of Moeran part songs, *Songs of Springtime* and *Phyllida and Corydon* contain some of the composer's most moving inspirations. Exquisitely performed by the Finzi Singers (Chandos CHAN-9182 [CD]), they seem among the finest vocal works produced by an Englishman in this century.

Monteverdi, Claudio

(1567–1643)

Madrigals

Consort of Musicke, Rooley. Virgin 59621 [CD].

Though this anthology of works on frankly erotic themes is possibly not the most representative of the Consort of Musicke's irreproachable series of recordings of the Monteverdi Madrigals—more balanced collections include their versions of the complete Book 2 (Virgin 59282 [CD]), Book 3 (Virgin 59283 [CD]), or Book 6 (Virgin 59605 [CD], VC-7-91154-4[T])—none are more uplifting. As in Elizabethan poetry, the use of the phrase "to die" (and its many cognates) as a euphemism for achieving sexual climax was an honored convention among the Renaissance madrigal composers. Needless to say, there is nearly as much dying here (often accompanied by the most funky, salacious harmonies) as there was in the Papal Wars.

Anthony Rooley's singers make one feel like an honored guest at an immensely civilized orgy, and the rich but cozy recorded sound is close to ideal. Recommended only for those who are willing to practice safe listening.

*O*rfeo

> Rolfe-Johnson, Baird, Dawson, von Otter, Argenta,
> Robson, Monteverdi Choir, English Baroque Soloists,
> Gardiner. Deutsche Grammophon 419250-2 [CD].

Jacopo Peri's *Dafne* predates it by a decade, but Monteverdi's *Orfeo* is now generally regarded as the first genuine opera, as the word is commonly understood today. Even though *Orfeo* is an extended vocal work that attempts to tell a continuous, coherent story, it is not "operatic" in the same sense *Carmen* and *Aida* are. The action, as in most operas before those of Mozart, tends to be static to the point of stagnation, and the characters are often less than two-dimensional. As a matter of fact, to the untrained ear, *Orfeo* can seem little more than a sequence of one- and two-part madrigals (if that's not a contradiction in terms), thrown together with exquisite imagination and taste.

John Eliot Gardiner's interpretation is every bit as persuasive as the recently deleted Angel version led by Nigel Rogers. As always, this most spirited of antiquarians finds the perfect balance between the demands of textual authenticity and the needs of human communication. The story unfolds crisply and cleanly, yet with ample amounts of drama and color, making it seem a far more modern and digestible experience than it usually is. All of the soloists, especially the virtuoso tenor Anthony Rolfe-Johnson, are exceptional, and Gardiner's Monteverdi Choir and English Baroque Soloists turn in their usual flawless performance.

*V*espro della Beata Vergine

> Soloists, Monteverdi Choir and Orchestra, Gardiner.
> Deutsche Grammophon 429565-2 [CD].

The test of any performance of Monteverdi's *Vespers of 1610* is how many of the faithful remain awake at the end of the experience. Unlike *Messiah*, which contains many "hit tunes" to cling to and can thus be sampled, in pieces, like so many sacred chocolates, the *Vespers* must be swallowed and digested—all two hours of it—as a complete and indissoluble whole.

Unlike his earlier (1974) version for London, which used modern instruments, John Eliot Gardiner's newer and even finer Deutsche Grammophon recording uses period instruments and the incomparable acoustics of the Basilica of St. Mark's in Venice; the music here emerges with a sweep and grandeur that none of the more scholarly recordings can begin to match. For anyone unfamiliar with this glorious score, here is the perfect introduction.

Mozart, Wolfgang Amadeus (1756–1791)

Once, when filling out an application for a summer job, on that line next to "other" under the heading of Religion, I wrote *Mozart*. The personnel officer was not amused, but then, I hadn't intended it as a joke. For there was a time when I was convinced that Mozart was at least as divinely inspired as Moses, Christ, the Buddha, Lao-tse, or Mohammed, and I suppose I still am. For in no other works of the human imagination can the divine spirit be heard more distinctly than in the miraculous music this often vulgar, unpleasant, and difficult man produced during his pathetically brief thirty-five years. Were this book to do him justice, the section devoted to Mozart's music would take up more than half the total pages. What follows, therefore, is a painfully compressed selection.

The Abduction from the Seraglio

Augér, Grist, Schreier, Neukrich, Moll, Leipzig Radio Chorus, Dresden State Orchestra, Böhm. Deutsche Grammophon 423459-2 [CD].

As we learned from Milos Forman's *Amadeus*, a stylized, brazenly inaccurate account of Mozart's life, which I have seen only

128 times, it was with *The Abduction from the Seraglio* that Mozart made his initial splash in Vienna, and through which he met the soprano Katharina Cavalieri (the original Constanze), with whom he may or may not have had a brief but toasty affair. (If true, that would have placed the soprano in some not terribly select company, for the composer of *Don Giovanni* certainly knew whereof he wrote.) In *The Abduction*, Mozart transformed the decidedly lowbrow entertainment called *Singspiel* into high art, a form to which he would return a decade later in *The Magic Flute*. In the process, he produced the first great opera of the German language and the earliest opera in *any* language that still commands a place in the standard repertoire.

With the classic Beecham recording waiting in the wings for its CD reissue, it might seem foolish to recommend any other *Abduction* now. And yet Karl Böhm absconds with so much of the opera's wit and warmth that even with Sir Thomas in the picture, this may not necessarily be the second choice.

In addition to a generally stronger cast and superior recorded sound, the primary strength of the Böhm performance is the singing of the late Arleen Augér. Her Constanze is a wonder of pert, innocent sexiness, which conceals a smoldering sensuality lying just beneath the surface. Vocally, she is equally impressive; her "Martern aller Arten," sung with breathless abandon and deadly accuracy, is among the most exiting performances this popular aria has ever received.

The forces of the Dresden Opera (the scene of Karl Böhm's rather shady activities during the war) respond with disciplined affection for their old führer, and the recorded sound is superb.

La clemenza di Tito

> Baker, Minton, Burrows, Popp, von Stade, Lloyd, Chorus and Orchestra of the Royal Opera House, Covent Garden, Davis. Philips 422544-2 [CD].

Mozart's final opera was one of the final examples of opera seria, a once-popular form that was already dying while Mozart's ink was still wet on the page. And although most representatives of the species do tend to be unendurably static and stultifying (it was opera seria that Tom Hulce, as Mozart, was castigating in *Amadeus* when he complained that the characters were so remote and lofty that they "shit marble"), *La clemenza di Tito* is a sublime master-piece, though one perhaps better suited to the living room than the operatic stage.

Sir Colin Davis and his unbelievably fine cast make a very strong case for the work. Dame Janet Baker has never seemed more agile or noble, and even the smallish roles are covered by singers of the stature of Frederica von Stade. The Covent Garden forces respond as enthusiastically as they ever have on records, and the remastered sound is exceptionally vivid.

Heartily recommended.

Concerto in B-flat for Bassoon and Orchestra, K. 191;
Concerto in C for Oboe and Orchestra, K. 314;
Concerto in A for Clarinet and Orchestra, K. 622

> Turnovsky, bassoon; Gabriel, oboe; Ottensamer, clarinet;
> Vienna Mozart Academy, Wildner. Naxos 8.550345
> [CD].

Although these concertos may have had more distinguished individual performances—the bewitching and shamefully deleted EMI recording of the Bassoon Concerto with Gwydion Brooke, the Royal Philharmonic and Sir Thomas Beecham, or John de Lancie's limpid account of the Oboe Concerto, now available only as part of a three-CD set of the complete wind concertos in the rather uneven performances conducted by Eugene Ormandy (Sony SM3K-47215[CD])—this handsome Naxos CD offers performances that rank with the very best available, not to mention up-to-date sound *and* at a superbudget price. Best of all is Stepan Turnovsky's droll reading of the Bassoon Concerto, although oboist Martin Gabriel and clarinetist Ernst Ottensamer also have some pointed and very stylish things to say. As with so many Naxos releases, this is an incredible bargain.

Concerto in A for Clarinet and Orchestra, K. 622;
Sinfonia Concertante in E-flat Major for Violin, Viola, and Orchestra, K. 364

> Marcellus, clarinet; Druian, violin; Skernick, viola;
> Cleveland Orchestra, Szell. CBS MYK-37810 [CD],
> MT-37810 [T].

This is one of the most nearly perfect Mozart recordings ever made. Robert Marcellus, then the Cleveland Orchestra's principal clarinetist, gives a flawless, dramatic performance of the late and strangely uneven Clarinet Concerto, with some customarily precise and enthusiastic support provided by his colleagues under George Szell, and the gleaming version of the great Sinfonia Concertante is probably Szell's finest Mozart recording. Instead of using big-name soloists, the conductor wisely chose to place the Cleveland's immensely accomplished concertmaster and principal violist in the spotlight. The result is an interpretation of such total generosity and uncanny unanimity of purpose that even after thirty years, it must still be heard to be believed. For much of the time, the soloists seem like a single player with two sets of arms. Each of the beautifully wrought phrases is shaped with precisely the same dynamic shading and inflection, and even the tiniest details are never left to chance. For instance, the trill at the end of the second-movement cadenza is a miracle of timing and expressiveness. Szell's accompaniment is as energetic as it is patrician, and at the time the recording was made, the orchestra, as a Mozart ensemble, had no rival in the world.

Concerto in C for Flute, Harp, and Orchestra, K. 299; Concerto for Flute and Orchestra No. 1 in G, K. 313

Galway, flute; Robles, harp; London Symphony, Mata. RCA 6723-2 [CD], 6723-4 [T].

For most people, the choice of a recording of the finest work that Mozart composed for an instrument he thoroughly detested used to boil down to which of the various versions of the Flute and Harp Concerto James Galway or Jean-Pierre Rampal has so far made. Since yuppiedom's once-insatiable appetite for flute music has apparently begun to be sated (and why should this basically cold and inexpressive instrument have gotten so hot all of a sudden?), there are only two Galway versions listed in the current catalog and only a couple for Rampal.

A far more shameless ham than his French colleague, Galway has also been a consistently finer player—wide vibrato, syrupy phrasing, penny-whistle antics and all. His RCA recording, while clearly a Galway show, is not the undiluted Ego-thon that many of his recent escapades have tended to be; the brilliant Marisa Robles more than holds her own, and we are even led to suspect that the conductor, Eduardo Mata, might have had a few things to say.

In RCA's Papillon Collection packaging, the performance comes with a flamboyant yet stylish interpretation of the G Major Concerto. Beware the recently deleted RCA tape (AGK1-5442), which includes Galway's pointless, moderately offensive transcription of the Mozart Clarinet Concerto. It isn't quite so gruesome as Zamfir playing "Un bel di" on his wretched pan flute, but it will do.

Concertos (4) for Horn and Orchestra

> Brain, horn; Philharmonia Orchestra, Karajan. Angel
> CDH-61013 [CD].

> Tuckwell, horn and conductor; Philharmonia Orchestra.
> Collins Classics 11532 [CD].

Written for a man named Ignaz Leutgub (or Leutgeb), one of the most delightfully vulgar of Mozart's Salzburg cronies and the favorite butt of many of his practical jokes, the four Horn Concertos are among the most enchanting of all his works. From the evidence of the difficult solo parts, Leutgub must have been a virtuoso of considerable accomplishment. For as taxing as they are even for the modern performer, the Concertos were originally written for the waldhorn, an instrument without valves.

In their recent compact disc reissue, the classic recordings from the mid-1950s made by the legendary Dennis Brain are a moving, inspiring reminder of a man who was not only the century's greatest horn player but also one of its finest musicians. The secret of Brain's art lay in the fact that his approach to the instrument was that of a great vocalist. His phrasing, command of dynamics, and dramatic coloration rivaled those of the finest Mozart singers of his generation. In fact, the slow movements of the Concertos become, in effect, hauntingly beautiful arias without words.

The modern recording that comes closest to duplicating Brain's achievement is the most recent of four recordings made thus far by Barry Tuckwell. The great Australian-born virtuoso gives the liveliest and most technically accomplished performances yet recorded since Dennis Brain's death. If they lack the final measure of depth and tenderness of Brain's famous recordings, then Tuckwell's are still a magnificent accomplishment in their own right and are vigorously recommended.

Concertos (25) for Piano and Orchestra

**Perahia, piano and conductor; English Chamber Orchestra.
CBS SX12K-46441 [CD].**

**Brendel, piano; Academy of St. Martin-in-the-Fields,
Marriner. Philips 422507-2 [CD].**

With the possible exceptions of his operas and last half dozen symphonies, it is in the series of piano concertos he wrote throughout his career that the full scope of Mozart's achievement can best be understood. From the earliest of these pieces, some of which were merely arrangements of the music of his teacher Johann Christian Bach, through the towering masterworks of his final years, the Concertos also offer the most dramatic evidence of Mozart's evolution from the most celebrated child prodigy in the history of music to the greatest composer who has ever lived.

Each of these triumphant sets of the complete Piano Concertos is a milestone in the recent history of recording, and, as Murray Perahia and Alfred Brendel are among the most compelling Mozart performers of the last three decades, a choice between them will have to be made on personal rather than musical grounds. For those who respond to the "intellectual" approach to Mozart, Brendel's thoughtful, always self-possessed and disciplined playing serves almost all the Concertos exceptionally well. Like his teacher Edwin Fischer, Brendel is always acutely aware of the shape and architecture of the music. Everything is calculated—in the best possible sense of the word—to make subordinate the individual details to the needs of the greater whole. Which is not to say that Brendel's playing is in any way academic or lacking in emotion. Whereas other pianists, including Perahia, can never let an especially grateful episode pass them by without embellishing it with the stamp of their own personality, Brendel always does. The result is many of the most satisfying and natural-sounding Mozart recordings available today.

Sir Neville Marriner's accompaniments are invariably invigorating, refined, and stylish, and the recorded sound, primarily from the 1970s, is both as brilliantly detailed and as warmly unobtrusive as the performances themselves.

Like Daniel Barenboim and Géza Anda before him, Murray Perahia serves as his own conductor in his consistently fascinating CBS set. As it turns out, the decision was a sound one, not only because the arrangement helps to underscore Perahia's essentially chamberlike approach to the Concertos, but also because his ideas are so firm, and intensely personal, that the presence of another musical personality would have simply gotten in the way.

If in the most general and oversimplified terms the Brendel recordings represent the modern classical vision of Mozart, then Perahia's are a bold and generally successful attempt to rethink the Romantic approach taken by the great pianists of a half century ago. In virtually all the recordings, Perahia finds something fresh and personal to say, especially in the slow movements, which are drawn out almost to the point of languor. The phrasing is consistently imaginative and spontaneous, and the physical sound of both the soloist and the orchestra, while decidedly hedonistic, also has a wonderful feeling of openness and inevitability. Though many listeners will find the performances a trifle precious and fussy, an equal number will consider them an endless source of discovery and delight.

A clear-cut choice between these two superb cycles is not an easy one to make. And needless to say, either of them, given the current highway-robbery pricing of compact discs, represents a substantial investment. The wise collector should probably just bite the bullet (or perhaps persuade one of the kids to take a part-time job at McDonald's), and acquire them both.

Piano Concertos: No. 19 in F; No. 20 in D minor

R. Serkin, piano; Cleveland Orchestra, Szell. CBS
MYK-37236 [CD], MYT-37236.

Why the nineteenth century tended to take a rather dim view of Mozart remains one of music's most perplexing historical mysteries. Of course, that it chose to venerate its own, far lesser figures at his expense was nothing particularly unusual or new. The wholesale dismissal of the accomplishments of preceding ages was already a time-honored institution by the late fifteenth century: "The Dark Ages" — and for that matter "Renaissance" — were both terms that Renaissance propagandists coined.

Even so, how the Romantic era could have dismissed Mozart as that rococo lightweight with the powdered wig is all but impossible to fathom, especially given works like the D minor Piano Concerto, which, with *Don Giovanni*, Symphony No. 40, and the

G minor String Quintet, is among the darkest outpourings of tragedy in all of music.

Having known each other since their student days, George Szell and Rudolf Serkin—an especially formidable combination in the music of Mozart, Beethoven, and Brahms—always managed to communicate with each other as if by some mysterious musical telepathy. Their performance of the D minor Concerto is one of the most profound and deeply serious ever recorded. Serkin's playing seethes with a brooding, impassioned intensity, and Szell's contribution, as usual, is a model of cooperative understanding that still maintains a distinct and potent personality of its own. The interpretation of the F Major Concerto is just as impressive, lending to what is often tossed off as a far lighter work an unexpected and startlingly novel significance and weight.

Piano Concerto No. 21 in C

Kempff, piano; Bavarian Radio Symphony, Klee. Deutsche Grammophon 415920-4 [T] (with concerto No. 21).

Jandó, piano; Concentus Hungaricus, Ligeti. Naxos 8.550202 [CD] (with concertos Nos. 12 and 14).

Since its memorable appearance in Bo Widerberg's lovely 1967 film *Elvira Madigan*, the Concerto No. 21, or at very least its ravishing second movement, has become one of the most popular of all Mozart's works, with recordings for every conceivable taste in every price range. Listening to Wilhelm Kempff's relaxed and elegant interpretation from the early 1960s, one can readily believe the legend that the great German pianist was never nervous before a performance. (Kempff came from a town called Jüterbog where his father and grandfather before him had been the local kapellmeisters; the young Kempff was thus apprenticed to the family business with no more fuss or fanfare than was accorded the son of any other tradesman.) His playing, as always, is full of life and wisdom, as are Ferdinand Leitner's insightful accompaniments. It's a pity they haven't yet been transferred to CD.

When completed, Jenö Jandó's Mozart cycle may well prove to be as distinguished as Perahia's or Brendel's and, at Naxos's prices, might even be more desirable. His performance of the Concerto No. 21 is an exceptional one, with an extraordinarily beautiful slow movement and a finale that crackles with wit. Along with equally memorable versions of the No. 12 and No. 14 Concertos, this is quite a bargain even by Naxos standards.

Piano Concertos: No. 22 in E-flat; No. 23 in A

Uchida, piano; English Chamber Orchestra, Tate. Philips 420187-2 [CD].

Few musicians these days are more disquieting to watch than the brilliant Japanese pianist Mitsuko Uchida. Her array of ticks, grimaces, and other facial contortions is as impressive in its way as Glenn Gould's repertoire of grunts, sighs, and off-pitch moans. Fortunately, those antics apparently never get in the way of her playing, and on a recording, of course, they matter not at all.

Uchida's versions of these two popular concertos are not only among the most musically satisfying these works have yet received, but they are among the most rewarding of any Mozart concerto recordings now available. Rarely has the Concerto No. 22 seemed so luxuriant yet precise or its great companion piece, the Concerto No. 23, so superbly graceful and majestic. The accompaniments by the English Chamber Orchestra led by Jeffrey Tate are full of character, with the warmth and clarity of the performances matched by the recorded sound.

Piano Concertos: No. 23 in A; No. 25 in C

Moravec, piano; Czech Philharmonic, Vlach. Supraphon 11-0271-2 [CD].

It was probably no accident that when the producers of *Amadeus* were casting about for a pianist to supply the music for the picture, they should have settled on Ivan Moravec. For a quarter of a century, this unassuming Czech musician has been one of the great Mozart interpreters of the modern era. His versions of these two popular concertos are graced with a unique poetry and insight. The playing is so effortless that we are constantly reminded of the composer's advice to future pianists, "Make it flow like oil." Joseph Vlach and the Czech Philharmonic provide exceedingly civilized settings for these gemlike performances, and the recorded sound remains admirably focused and warm.

Piano Concertos: No. 24 in C minor; No. 21 in C

Casadesus, piano; Cleveland Orchestra, Szell. CBS MYK-38523 [CD], MT-38523 [T].

The ideal companion piece to the stormy Concerto No. 24 in C minor is the equally troubled No. 20 in D minor. In that pairing, a recording repackaged from Alfred Brendel's complete cycle for Philips (420867-2 [CD]) is extremely desirable, especially at medium price and with the delectable D Major Rondo thrown in as a bonus.

On the other hand, as a *performance* of the C minor Concerto, none has yet to seriously challenge this classic recording by Robert Casadesus and George Szell. On the face of it, the Casadesus-Szell partnership—and they recorded many of the Mozart concertos together—must have seemed to many a rather peculiar one. On the one hand, there was Szell the fanatical perfectionist; on the other, the frequently inspired Frenchman whose approach to technical niceties could be shockingly cavalier. Yet somehow, together, their differences always seemed to cancel each other out.

Their version of the C minor Concerto is as poised and turbulent as any Mozart concerto recording ever made. While the soloist's contribution is not the last word in mechanical perfection, the playing communicates a sense of tragic grandeur no other performance does. Szell, as he did so often, rises not only *to*, but frequently *above*, the occasion. The conducting is so quick to pick up the music's dark and shifting moods, so tightly coiled in its pent-up intensity, that we can only wonder what kind of unspeakably shattering experience a Szell recording of *Don Giovanni* might have been.

The other recordings in the Casadesus-Szell Mozart series have been repackaged on a set of three medium-priced Sony CDs (SM3K-46519) that offer incredible value for the dollar. Except for the Concerto No. 25, which Szell recorded with his protégé Leon Fleisher (and which appears as filler in their box of the Beethoven concertos), Nos. 21–27 are all here, together with a version of the Double Concerto in E-flat (No. 10) with Casadesus's talented wife Gaby and the Philadelphia Orchestra under Eugene Ormandy. The level of inspiration and execution is phenomenally high, and the slightly thinning late '50s–early '60s recorded sound remains more than adequate.

Piano Concertos: No. 25 in C; No. 26 in D, *Coronation*

**Ashkenazy, piano and conductor; Philharmonia Orchestra.
London 411810-2 [CD].**

If conclusive proof was ever required for the case that an artist's work need not necessarily reflect the circumstances of the artist's life, it is to be found in these final two piano concertos, which Mozart composed during the last three years of his life. By any standard, these thirty-six months were a nightmare for the composer. His spendthrift wife was seriously ill, and the always fickle Viennese public had clearly grown tired of his music. He was living in abject penury, and his health, frail to begin with, was slowly succumbing to at least a dozen potentially fatal diseases. Depressed, discouraged, and racked by continuous pain, he nevertheless produced two of the greatest and most buoyantly extroverted of all his piano concertos during this period: the irrepressibly optimistic Concerto No. 25 and the magisterial *Coronation* Concerto.

As both soloist and conductor, Vladimir Ashkenazy is close to the top of his form in his recordings of both works. The performance of the *Coronation* Concerto, while capitalizing fully on the work's overtly ceremonial elements, makes it seem far more personal and significant than usual. On the other hand, Ashkenazy's interpretation of No. 25 is an irresistible explosion of gaiety and sunshine, made all the more brilliant by the lustrous playing of the Philharmonia Orchestra and the equally gleaming recorded sound.

Piano Concertos: No. 27 in B-flat; No. 10 in E-flat for Two Pianos

**Gilels, piano; Vienna Philharmonic, Böhm. Deutsche
Grammophon 419059-2 [CD]**

Emil Gilels never made a more completely winning recording than this version of Mozart's last great piano concerto. There is an Olympian ease in his playing that comes only after an artist fully understands both the music and himself, and Gilels's grasp of the Concerto No. 27 in B-flat is both effortless and profound. By the same token, Karl Böhm brings the same qualities to his accompaniments that he brought to his famous recording of *Così fan tutte*: here, as there, wisdom and humor pervade every bar.

The version of the delightful Double Concerto is no less enjoyable, joining versions by Perahia-Lupu on Sony and Brendel-Klein on Prieser as some of the very best available. The communication between Gilels and his daughter Elena is predictably natural and intimate, with Böhm again lending glowing support.

Concertos (5) for Violin and Orchestra

Perlman, violin; Vienna Philharmonic, Levine. Deutsche Grammophon 415958-2 (No.1, Adagio, and Rondos); 415975-2 (Nos. 2 and 4); 410020-2 (Nos. 3 and 5) [CDs].

Of all the incredible stories that form the Mozart legend, one of the most farfetched also happens to be absolutely true. Mozart was never taught how to play the violin. One day at the age of seven, he simply picked it up and that was that.

Within a year he was performing in public on a half-size instrument—on one momentous occasion before the Empress Maria Theresa herself. (Although he once sat on her voluminous lap, Mozart never thought very highly of the controversial monarch, who was said to be the real-life model for *The Magic Flute*'s sinister Queen of the Night; for her part, Maria Theresa dismissed the entire Mozart family as "useless people, running around the world like beggars.")

Written in Salzburg in 1775 when the nineteen-year-old composer was resting between concert tours, the five Violin Concertos are not only an arresting amalgam of the Italian, French, and German traditions he had absorbed during his travels, they are also, in their proud bearing and graceful melodic invention, a perfect reflection of late-Rococo tastes.

In these brilliant recordings, Itzhak Perlman occasionally creates the impression that he is trying to disguise his own virtuosity, as if to suggest that too much technique might rob these youthful works of their freshness and charm. For the most part, he succeeds admirably, except in moments like the "Turkish" episodes from the finale of the A Major Concerto, when the sleeping volcano simply *must* blow its top. James Levine is an unassuming but never anonymous accompanist, and the Vienna Philharmonic is on its very best behavior—which is saying something in a city that consistently boasts the most dreadfully sloppy Mozart playing in the world.

Così fan tutte

Schwarzkopf, Ludwig, Steffek, Kraus, Taddei, Berry,
Philharmonia Orchestra and Chorus, Böhm. Angel
CDMC-69330 [CD].

Caballé, Baker, Cotrubas, Gedda, Ganzarolli, Van Allen,
Orchestra and Chorus of the Royal Opera House,
Covent Garden, Davis. Philips 422542-2 [CD].

While it has never attained the popularity of *Don Giovanni*, *The Marriage of Figaro*, and *The Magic Flute*, the effervescent *Così fan tutte* certainly belongs in the company of the greatest operas Mozart—which is to say, anyone—ever wrote. Its lightweight but enchanting plot about the ever-present danger of female infidelity (the best approximation of the title is "So do they all" or "They're all like that") is not as male-chauvinist as it might seem, and Lorenzo da Ponte's witty and ingenious libretto drew from Mozart some of the most inspired music he would ever write for the stage.

Since as characters, the two romantic couples are as deliberately interchangeable as the four ditzy lovers in Shakespeare's *Midsummer Night's Dream*, and since the old misogynist Don Alfonso and the scheming maid Despina merely exist to move the delightfully complicated plot along, *Così fan tutte* is of necessity an ensemble opera, and probably the finest ever composed. It has its share of memorable arias, but its greatest moments are the duets, trios, and quartets in which operatic polyphony reached heights of inventiveness it would never again approach.

Among all the recordings the work has ever received, none can equal the wit, unanimity, and astonishingly generous give-and-take that can still be heard in the historic Angel recording from the early 1960s. Though all the principals are dazzling vocally and dramatically, Elisabeth Schwarzkopf and Christa Ludwig, as the sisters Fiordiligi and Dorabella, give two of the most delectable performances ever put on record, and the elfin yet ruefully world-weary Don Alfonso of Walter Berry is one of the great comic portrayals of modern times.

The more recent and extremely entertaining Philips recording offers some particularly captivating singing from Monserrat Caballé and Dame Janet Baker and spirited conducting from Sir Colin Davis, as well as more modern recorded sound.

Divertimentos (complete)

New York Philomusica, Johnson. Vox CDX-5049/51 [CD].

Here, on three tightly packed budget-priced Vox Boxes, is the greatest aural wallpaper ever produced: the miraculous Divertimentos Mozart composed as background music for the various social gatherings of his tin-eared employer, the Prince Archbishop of Salzburg. Even in the slightest of these pieces, Mozart's genius blazes forth in every bar: the melodic invention, harmonic ingenuity, and obvious sheer delight in the act of music-making prove these endlessly enchanting works could not possibly have been written by anyone else.

Recorded in the early 1970s by some of the finest studio musicians in New York, the performances by the New York Philomusica are as full of life as the music itself. If there are still lingering doubts that American wind playing is the standard of the world, these recordings should silence them. And the freshness of the playing is matched by the recorded sound, which in its warmth, transparency, and presence remains in the demonstration class. All in all, one of the best Mozart buys on the market today.

Don Giovanni

Sutherland, Schwarzkopf, Sciutti, Alva, Wächter,
Cappuccilli, Frick, Philharmonia Orchestra and Chorus,
Giulini. Angel CDCC-47260 [CD].

Since the Giulini *Don Giovanni* was first released in 1963, there have no doubt been a few people who've waited for a finer recording of the greatest opera ever written. Good luck to them, and to those who await the Great Pumpkin, the Tooth Fairy, honest politicians, and anything worth hearing from Philip Glass.

In the title role, Eberhard Wächter may not have the animal magnetism and dramatic savvy of a Cesare Siepi or Ezio Pinza, but his performance is nevertheless exceptionally musical and intelligent, and very beautifully sung. And Wächter was the *weakest* link in the chain. All the other roles are represented by what still remain their finest recorded performances, from the suave, sweet-spirited Don Ottavio of Luigi Alva (who makes the character seem for once like something other than the mealy-mouthed chump he probably is) to the horrifying Commendatore of Gottlob Frick. Yet it is that incomparable trio of ladies, Elisabeth Schwarzkopf, Joan Sutherland, and Graziella Sciutti, together with the phenomenally inspired direction from the man in the pit, which levitates this *Don Giovanni* onto a plane shared by only a handful of opera recordings.

Exsultate, jubilate

Mathis, soprano; Bavarian Radio Orchestra, Kubelik.
Deutsche Grammophon 429820-2 [CD].

As a Freemason and lifelong free thinker, Mozart was not always at his most inspired in the church music he wrote at virtually every stage in his career; when the spirit genuinely moved him, the results could be overwhelming, as they are in the five justly famous sacred works contained on this medium-priced CD. From Edith Mathis's gleaming realization of the youthful motet *Exsultate, jubilate* (with that most famous of "Alleluias"), to the heartbreaking *Ave, verum corpus*, finished less than six months before the composer's death, all the performances here rank with the finest currently available, especially Kubelik's unusually dramatic reading of the *Coronation* Mass. For those wanting all five together, this reasonably priced anthology should be the answer to your prayers.

Idomeneo

McNair, Martinpelto, Rolfe-Johnson, Von Otter, English
Baroque Soloists, and Monteverdi Choir, Gardiner.
Deutsche Grammophon 431674-2 [CD].

Written for the Munich carnival season in 1781, *Idomeneo* was revived only once during Mozart's lifetime and was not heard in the United States until a performance at the 1947 Tanglewood Festival. Composed in part to show off the extraordinary virtuosity of the castrato del Prato, *Idomeneo* has acquired the reputation of a rather staid and static example of opera seria at its worst; this in spite of the great Mozart scholar Alfred Einstein's opinion that it is "one of those works that even a genius of the highest rank, like Mozart, could write only once in a life."

No recording makes Einstein's case more persuasively than this electrifying live performance conducted by John Eliot Gardiner. With his customary blend of impeccable scholarship and passionate music-making, he makes the opera come alive as no other conductor ever has. Inspired by his vision of *Idomeneo* as living theater, all the principals sing with both beauty and dramatic conviction, while the fabulous Monteverdi Choir and English Baroque Soloists perform with their customary fervor and finesse. The recording includes every note of *Idomeneo* that Mozart composed, making this the lengthiest version of the opera as well. It is all done with such obvious joy, one might begin to suspect that it's still too short.

In sum, a revelation.

The Magic Flute

Popp, Gruberová, Lindner, Jerusalem, Brendel, Bracht, Zednik, Bavarian Radio Orchestra and Chorus, Haitink. Angel CDCC-47951 [CD].

For Bruno Walter, *The Magic Flute*, not the Requiem, was Mozart's last will and testament. For in the characters of the questing hero Tamino, the noble priest Sarastro, and the vulgar, buffoonish, bird-catcher Papageno, Walter saw the three essential components of Mozart's complex and often contradictory personality. Like most of the great conductor's speculations, this one carries a certain gentle authority, and in fact may contain more than a grain of truth. The most divinely simple of all his great operas, *Die Zauberflöte* affords some even more tantalizing grist for the speculation mill: Had he lived, would Mozart have continued the process of simplification heard here and in other later works? And if so, what effect would this new directness have had on the infant Romantic movement?

In his recording debut as an opera conductor, Bernard Haitink leads one of the warmest and most dramatic performances *The Magic Flute* has ever received. The unusually strong cast includes many of the finest living Mozart singers. Lucia Popp is an adorably sensual Pamina, Siegfried Jerusalem, a subtle yet vocally exciting Tamino, and the Czech soprano Edita Gruberová, as the Queen of the Night, recalls the most brilliant and commanding German coloraturas of the past. In all, this is one of the great Mozart recordings of the last decade and will probably tower above the competition for years to come.

Surprisingly, there is no completely acceptable recording of the opera currently available on tape. Karl Böhm's Deutsche Grammophon recording (419566-4), while the strongest of all, is still a very mixed bag. On the one hand, it offers the magical Tamino of Fritz Wunderlich, and an imposing Sarastro in Franz Crass; on the other, it asks you to endure Roberta Peters's rather shrill Queen of the Night, and worse, the mugging and shameless hamming of Dietrich Fischer-Dieskau as Papageno.

The Marriage of Figaro

Schwarzkopf, Moffo, Cossotto, Wächter, Taddei, Vinco, Philharmonia Orchestra and Chorus, Giulini. Angel CDMB-63266

The same qualities that make the Giulini *Don Giovanni* one of the classic opera recordings of the stereo era can be heard to equally memorable advantage in his version of what is widely regarded as the greatest comic opera ever written. Though the contributions of the stunning cast cannot be praised too highly —for instance, the Countess of Elisabeth Schwarzkopf is in every way as great a creation as her Marschallin in Strauss's *Rosenkavalier*—it is Giulini's magical conducting that seems to place a stamp of immortality on the recording.

Only Erich Kleiber, in his famous, early stereo version for London managed to draw as much from both the singers and from the score itself. Yet if the Kleiber performance offers an abundance of sparkling wit, vocal beauty, and effortless grace, the Giulini offers even more. Virtually every moment of the performance yields some startling yet utterly natural insight, and the ineffable purity Giulini conjures out of the Act IV finale makes it one of the most ethereally beautiful five minutes ever heard on a commercial recording.

Mass in C minor, *The Great*

Cotrubas, Te Kanawa, Krenn, Sotin, John Alldis Choir, New Philharmonia Orchestra, Leppard. Angel CDC-47385 [CD].

Apart from the unfinished Requiem, the C minor Mass is the most important of all of Mozart's choral works, and the equal to the finest of that towering series of masses that his friend Franz Joseph Haydn completed at the end of his career. Like the Requiem, *The Great* C minor Mass is a dark and disturbing work, full of uncharacteristic doubts and unsettling tensions.

Raymond Leppard leads an extremely humane and civilized interpretation of the work in a performance that features both a choir and orchestra of chamber proportions. The soloists are all very individual and moving; Kiri Te Kanawa gives us one of her finest recorded performances. Her singing, as well as that of Ileana Cotrubas, is as physically beautiful as any to be heard on records today, and she also invests the music with a character and sense of involvement most of her recordings rarely reveal.

Overtures

Royal Philharmonic, Davis. EMI CDE-67777 [CD].

Capella Istropolitana, Wordsworth. Naxos 8.550185 [CD].

Here, for less than it costs to take a spouse and two-and-a-half children out for frozen yogurt (not counting gas and parking), are a pair of superbudget recordings offering no fewer than twenty-two Mozart overtures in spirited, well-recorded performances led by a well-established Mozartean and a younger colleague who is about to become one.

Sir Colin Davis's recordings with the Royal Philharmonic were models of grace and enthusiasm a generation ago and have lost little of their appeal over the years. The stylish playing has abundant energy and wit, in marked contrast to this conductor's increasingly sedate recent efforts.

In addition to all the familiar classics—*Così fan tutte, Don Giovanni, The Magic Flute,* and *Figaro*—Barry Wordsworth's Naxos collection offers ten other items, some of which are little more than names in a book for most people: the early opera serie *Mitridate, rè di Ponto* and *Lucio Silla* and the Intermezzo (and surely you remember it?) *Apollo et Hyacinthus seu Hyacinthi Metamorphosis*, written when Mozart was eleven. As in their recordings of the Haydn and Mozart symphonies, the performances by the Capella Istropolitana are both alert and affectionate, and the recorded sound is first-rate.

Piano Sonatas (17)

Barenboim, piano. Angel CDZE-67294 [CD].

No one has ever suggested that Mozart's piano sonatas are in any way comparable in stature or importance to the concertos he wrote for the instrument; with a couple of exceptions—the A minor Sonata, K. 310, and the eternally popular A Major Sonata, K. 331—they are relatively unimportant in Mozart's output. Of course the operative word is *relatively*. In absolute terms, they are as instructive and enjoyable as any keyboard works written between Bach and Beethoven, and for undemanding, "easy" listening (a phrase we Serious Music types are supposed to deplore), they are worth five times their weight in Vivaldi concertos.

Since the days when only Arthur Schnabel and Walter Gieseking seemed interested in playing them (Gieseking's peerless Angel set from the early 1950s really does need to be issued on compact disc without delay), there has been an explosion of Mozart sonata recordings, with superb complete cycles from András Schiff, Mitsuko Uchida, and Ingrid Haebler, among others, including a largely unheralded series from Peter Katin on the small Olympia label, which includes some of the most enjoyable performances of all. Two outstandingly fine budget cycles have only complicated the choice further: those by the late Walter Klien on Vox and Jenő Jandó on Naxos (although at rock-bottom prices, both could be added to virtually any collection without busting the budget).

On balance, though, the immensely individual and richly red-blooded interpretations by Daniel Barenboim continue to dominate the field. If he doesn't make the mistake of looking for hidden Beethoven in these generally modest pieces, he doesn't coddle them either. In other words, the playing is neither forced nor deliberately understated. There is also a sense of perfect balance between style and substance in the performances, greatly enhanced by unusually natural recorded sound.

Quartets (4) for Flute and Strings

Robison, flute; Tokyo String Quartet members. Vanguard OVC-4001 [CD].

On his old nightly radio program on WOR in New York, Jean Shepherd used to do a wonderful Music Minus One version of one of these quartets with a nose flute obbligato. Of late, America's greatest humorist has been far less visible than his fans would wish, although those who have listened to *A Prairie Home Companion* or watched *The Wonder Years* have been delighted to see how wide his influence has spread. His classic volumes of short stories, *In God We Trust, All Others Pay Cash* and *Wanda Hickey's Night of Golden Memories, And Other Disasters* not only rank with the best work of Shepherd's own hero, George Ade, but with that of Mark Twain and Anton Chekhov as among the most darkly amusing visions of what is drolly referred to as the Human Experience.

After Shepherd, it is Paula Robison who has given me the most pleasure over the years in these charming works Mozart wrote for an instrument he disliked so intensely. Her playing has an almost elfin grace, as well as an extraordinary musicality and purity of tone. The members of the Tokyo String Quartet play at the top of their early form, and the '60s recorded sound has held up incredibly well.

Quartet in F for Oboe and Strings, K. 370

Mack, oboe; Cleveland Orchestra Ensemble. Crystal C-323 [T].

Holliger, oboe; Orlando Quartet. Philips 412618-2 [CD].

One of the principal glories of twentieth-century American wind playing—which by common consent is now regarded as the most vital and distinguished in the world—is the incomparable sound of the American oboe, the final stage in the evolution of an instrument that began life as the raucous business end of the medieval bagpipe. Essentially a fusion of the flexibility of the French school with the strength and solidity of the German sound, it came to final fruition in the example and precept of Marcel Tabuteau, the longtime principal oboist of the Philadelphia Orchestra and professor of music at the Curtis Institute, and in the playing of the first great native-born virtuoso, Mitch Miller.

The greatest of Tabuteau's pupils, longtime principal of the New York Philharmonic, and in the opinion of many the finest player who ever drew an incredibly deep breath, the legendary Harold Gomberg recorded this alpha and omega of the instrument's chamber literature twice: once in the 1950s for American

Decca, and again toward the end of his career for Vanguard. Until the latter is returned to circulation (and with such a treasure at their disposal, how *could* Vanguard reissue that limp essay in the art of wobbling by André Ladrot?), lovers of the Mozart Quartet will have to make the best of a bad situation. The finest available performance of the piece, by the Cleveland Orchestra's adroit John Mack, can only be had on a Crystal cassette; first choice among CDs must therefore go, by default, to the Philips recording by Heinz Holliger.

To call Holliger the "Karajan of the Oboe" would be both unfair and misleading: there is nothing in the least bit sinister, musically or personally, about this quiet and reserved Swiss musician. In fact, he happens to be an extremely nice man. Yet aside from the nasal, slightly cloying physical sound, his playing is distinguished primarily by an obsession with mindless technique. He can play anything put before him, including some impossibly difficult things he composed for himself, but it all comes out sounding manufactured and glib. Here, the end result is a performance of the Mozart Oboe Quartet that makes it seem merely flashy and hence, insignificant.

Quartets (2) for Piano and Strings

Giuranna, viola; Beaux Arts Trio. Philips 410391-2 [CD].

As much as any of the composer's chamber works, these glorious quartets have led a charmed life in the recording studio, beginning with Arthur Schnabel's 1934 recording of the G minor Quartet with the Pro Arte, available now on Angel (CDHB-63870 [CD]). George Szell's brilliant 1946 versions with the Budapest String Quartet can be found on a Sony Masterworks Portrait CD (MPK-47685), and the transcendent 1952 performances by Sir Clifford Curson and the Amadeus, while in the London CD catalog briefly, have now been withdrawn.

The modern recordings that most clearly belong in this distinguished company are those by the Beaux Arts Trio and company. The playing has sparkle and purpose, and the recorded sound is admirably vivid and clear. The elegant performances by Gyula Kiss and the Tátrai Trio on White Label (HRC-170 [CD]) offer a fine budget-priced alternative.

Quintet in A for Clarinet and Strings, K. 581

**Shifrin, clarinet; Chamber Music Northwest. Delos
DCD-3020 [CD].**

Mozart thoroughly despised the flute and the tenor voice, but his initial reaction to the recently invented clarinet was love at first sound. He encountered it at the court of Mannheim in the late 1770s, and during the next decade he would produce the first great works written for the instrument: the E-flat Major Trio, K. 498, and the most popular of all his chamber works, the great A Major Clarinet Quintet.

From the recording made during the 78 era by the legendary English clarinetist Reginald Kell to that poignant little performance with a group of captured Chinese musicians led by Major Charles Emerson Winchester III (David Ogden Stiers) in the concluding episode of *M.A.S.H.*, the Quintet has received countless memorable performances over the years, and is currently represented by at least a half dozen superlative recordings.

Less well known than his glamorous near-contemporary Richard Stoltzman, David Shifrin is every bit his equal, as this sterling Delos recording clearly shows. Physically, Shifrin's sound is as large and as beautiful as any in the world today. Musically, he is one of the most imaginative and individual performers of his generation, mixing an attractive, instantly recognizable musical personality with an unerring sense of decorum and good taste. Though cast on a somewhat grand and Romantic scale, Shifrin's interpretation is also superbly detailed and intimate. With sensitive and enthusiastic support from four of his Chamber Music Northwest colleagues, and dazzling recorded sound, this is easily the most appealing recording the Quintet has received in at least a dozen years.

Currently, Stolzman's recording with the Tokyo String Quartet (RCA 60723-4) is the best of the available tapes.

Quintet in E-flat for Piano and Winds, K. 452

**Perahia, piano; English Chamber Orchestra members. CBS
MK-42099 [CD], IMT-42099 [T].**

In an otherwise chatty letter written to his father around the time of the E-flat Major Quintet's premiere, Mozart said he considered it the finest work he had written up to that time. Not the finest *chamber* work, mind you, but the finest work, *period.* And the music he had written up to that time included most of the string quartets, all the masses (except the Requiem), and all but the last three symphonies.

Among its many admirers was the young Beethoven, who just happened to produce a quintet for the same combination of instruments—piano, oboe, clarinet, bassoon, and horn—in the exact same key. (Recording company executives have been eternally grateful to Beethoven for his thoughtfulness: the Op. 16 Quintet invariably serves as the companion piece for the Mozart, as on this CBS release.)

Murray Perahia's bracing, eventful performance with the winds of the English Chamber Orchestra has much in common with his versions of the Mozart piano concertos. Although Perahia is clearly the leader of the band—the piano is the dominant voice, as it was certainly meant to be—the four wind players are given an unusual amount of freedom in terms of texture and phrasing, and all seem to fall in happily with Perahia's plans. Neil Black, the finest oboist the British have produced since Leon Goossens, is especially stylish and playful, but his ECO colleagues aren't far behind. With an equally spry and sensitive account of the Beethoven (which, if it can't compare with the Mozart, is still a very impressive work for a rude, uncouth kid from the Rhineland), this is one of the most enjoyable chamber music recordings in years.

Quintets (6) for Strings

Gerecz, Lesueur, Grumiaux Trio. Philips 422511-2 [CD].

Sandwiched between the C minor Quintet, which he arranged from his unsettling Serenade for Winds, K. 388, and the Quintet in E-flat Major, his last significant chamber work (completed a few months before his death), are two of Mozart's greatest compositions in any form: the sunny Quintet in C Major, K. 515, and its tormented companion piece, the Quintet in G minor, K. 516. Cast in the composer's favorite "tragic" key, the G minor Quintet is one of music's most desperate outcries, the work—in Alfred Einstein's vivid phrase—"of a lonely man surrounded on all sides by the walls of a deep chasm."

If other recordings may have plumbed that chasm more dramatically, none have done it with greater understanding or more sheer beauty than that accomplished ensemble led by the Belgian violinist Arthur Grumiaux. In fact, in all these sublime works one can hear some of the purest and most responsive chamber music playing ever recorded.

Whenever an eminent critic of my acquaintance feels himself in danger of buying a surplus Sherman tank and giving the human race what it probably deserves, he heads for a cabin in the woods armed only with mineral water and cassettes of these performances. So far, he has always returned restored and refreshed with renewed hope for the species. Considering what even used tanks must be going for these days, this recording may be one of your shrewder long-term psychiatric investments.

Requiem

> Price, Schmidt, Araiza, Adam, Leipzig Radio Chorus, Dresden State Orchestra, Schreier. Philips 411420-2 [CD].

After Fritz Wunderlich, who died in a tragically senseless household accident at the age of thirty-six, Peter Schreier was probably the most gifted tenor to have come out of Germany since the end of the war. Like Wunderlich, he possessed a voice of uncommon physical beauty during his prime, and even after it began showing signs of wear and tear his intelligence easily compensated for what time had taken away. Now, as Schreier's singing career draws inevitably to a close, he is proving to be an equally polished and sensitive conductor.

Schreier's Philips recording of the great unfinished Requiem is as perceptive and powerful as any recorded performance has ever been. Tempos are judiciously chosen; the brilliantly disciplined chorus sings with equal amounts of gusto and devotion, and the Dresden State Orchestra has been honed to a fine cutting edge. Yet as in his stunning recording of Bach's *St. Matthew Passion*, it is with his stellar quartet of soloists that Schreier gets the most electrifying results. Perhaps it is simply because he has a natural understanding of their needs and problems, or perhaps it is because *they* know they are singing for one of the greatest singers of his time, but each of these fine singers—particularly Margaret Price— gives one of the most impressive recorded performances of his or her career. Philips's recorded sound is as warm and dramatic as the performance itself, rising to shattering heights in the *Die irae*, while fading to a hushed whisper in the *Lacrimosa*.

Serenade No. 6 in D, *Serenata notturna*; Serenade No. 17 in D, *Haffner*

Prague Chamber Orchestra, Mackerras. Telarc CD-80161 [CD].

Few people begin what Voltaire called "that dull meal at which dessert is served at the beginning" as memorably as did the offspring of one of Salzburg's most prominent families, for whose marriage Mozart composed the *Haffner* Serenade. Like most of the composer's lighter occasional works, this one contains deep and unsuspected riches: within its eight diverting movements is a de facto violin concerto.

Oldřich Viček, the concertmaster of the Prague Chamber Orchestra, acquits himself admirably in the demanding solo part, and Sir Charles Mackerras never loses sight of the essentially frivolous—albeit divinely frivolous—nature of the music. From first to last, this is a spirited, good-natured romp characterized by sprightly tempos, pointed rhythms, and uncomplicated emotions. As a generous bonus, the recording comes with an equally persuasive account of the *Serenata notturna*.

Although Mackerras's companion version of the *Posthorn* Serenade (No. 9) is also outstanding, it isn't *quite* as outstanding as Sir Neville Marriner's performance on Philips (412725-2 [CD]). In the outer movements, the Academy of St. Martin-in-the-Fields has never sounded more lively and alert, nor have they ever seemed as cultivated as they are in the darkly fragile Andantino.

As superb a *Posthorn* as this certainly is, the irresistible performances of the two little Marches, K. 335, very nearly steal the show.

Serenade No. 10 in B-flat, *Gran partita*; Serenade No 11 in E-flat; Serenade No. 12 in C minor

Chamber Orchestra of Europe, Schneider. ASV CDCOE-804 (No. 10); ASV CDCOE-802 (Nos. 11 and 12) [CDs].

Even counting the *Music for the Royal Fireworks*, the Dvořák D minor Serenade, the Holst suites, and that score of deathless masterworks by John Philip Sousa, these three Mozart serenades are probably the greatest music ever written for winds. In its variety, invention, and sheer humanity, the *Gran partita* is one of the best arguments ever put forward for being alive—and at nearly an hour, it is *still* too short. The E-Flat Major Serenade is all but a dictionary definition of geniality, while its C minor companion piece is one of the most mysterious works Mozart ever wrote. (We know nothing about the occasion for which he produced this turbulent outburst, whose complexity and depth of emotion are so at odds with what is supposed to be an essentially lightweight form. Nor can we guess how it must have been received by its first audience. It would be similar to a modern audience trooping off to see a Neil Simon comedy and being treated to something on the order of *King Lear*.)

Without making too much of the May-December metaphor, the combination of the young, enthusiastic Chamber Orchestra of Europe and the sage, vastly experienced Alexander Schneider must account for some of the special chemistry of these glowing performances. The kids and the Old Man get on like a house afire, with results that are so wide-eyed *and* knowing it reminds you of one of the key lines from Edgar Lee Masters's *Spoon River Anthology*: "Genius is wisdom and youth."

Serenade No. 13 in G, K. 525, *Eine kleine Nachtmusik*

Columbia Symphony, Walter. CBS MYK-37774 [CD], MYT-37774 [T].

Recordings of this imperishable charmer come and go, but none has ever seriously challenged that miracle of freshness and amiability Bruno Walter recorded in the final years of his career. If the strings of the Columbia Symphony are not as clean and precise as they could have been, or the remastered recorded sound still retains its tubby bottom and hissy top, what does it matter? The music unfolds with such affectionate deftness and spontaneity, you'll almost suspect the ink was still wet on the page.

In addition to this most ingratiating of all recorded versions of the Serenade, the album also features vintage Walter interpretations of the *Impresario*, *Così fan tutte*, *Marriage of Figaro*, and *Magic Flute* Overtures, together with the moving, important, yet rarely heard *Masonic Funeral Music*.

Sonatas (16) for Violin and Piano

Goldberg, violin; Lupu, piano. London 430306-2 [CD].

These elegant, deeply musical recordings of the mature Violin Sonatas were the fruits of a unique collaboration. The concertmaster of Wilhelm Furtwängler's Berlin Philharmonic who, despite the conductor's impassioned defense of his Jewish musicians, was forced to flee Nazi Germany in 1934, Szymon Goldberg was also, for a time, the violinist of a famous string trio whose other members were cellist Emanuel Feuermann and *violinist* Paul Hindemith. When he recorded the Mozart sonatas in 1975 with the then young Romanian pianist Radu Lupu, Goldberg was in his mid-sixties, a player of vast experience and understanding with almost all of his technique intact.

Though other teams, such as Perlman and Barenboim, have brought more color and flash to these marvelous works, no recordings have ever presented the Sonatas more naturally or shown so much mutual respect and affection as these. For just as the youthful pianist is inspired to play with a burnished wisdom, so the playing of the aging violinist seems infused with a springlike glow. The result, in short, is a series of performances as ageless and timeless as they are undeniably beautiful.

String Quartets Nos. 14–19, *Haydn* Quartets

Quartetto Italiano. Philips 422512-2 [CD].
Chilingirian Quartet. CRD 4062/4 [T].
Juilliard String Quartet. Odyssey MB3K-45826 [CD].

Begun in 1782 after a nine-year period during which he composed no string quartets at all, the six works Mozart wrote under the influence of, and eventually dedicated to, his friend Franz

Joseph Haydn constitute one of the great summits in the history of chamber music. Haydn himself was overwhelmed by his young friend's touching act of homage. It was this music that led Haydn to tell Mozart's father, "I swear before God and as an honest man, that your son is the greatest composer known to me, either in person or by reputation."

Collectors who would like to buy the six Quartets together in a convenient package now find themselves in one of those difficult quandaries the recording companies seem to take such delight in. The most charming and completely memorable versions of the *Haydn* Quartets, those classic performances by Quartetto Italiano, are now available only as part of an eight-CD box from Philips, which also brings us superb performances of the rest of Mozart's twenty-three quartets. To be sure, this represents a substantial outlay of money, but this "medium-priced" set (and how long will it be before compact disc prices start becoming rational?) actually is a bargain in the long run. Compared to the hit-and-miss six-CD set with the Amadeus Quartet on Deutsche Grammophon, the all-important pleasure-per-dollar ratio is extremely high.

Of the recordings that feature the *Haydns* all by themselves, the lively, insightful interpretations by the Chilingirian Quartet are probably the most consistently rewarding. The Odyssey recording by the Juilliard String Quartet offers brilliant playing and a budget price, along with a slightly fierce recorded sound and absolutely no documentation.

Symphonies: Nos. 1–20

Academy of St. Martin-in-the-Fields, Marriner. Philips 422501-2 [CD].

Sir Neville Marriner's admirable set of the early symphonies, the first volume of Philips's epic Complete Mozart Edition—a 45-volume, 179-CD collection of the man's *entire* output—offers refreshingly vibrant and consistently stylish interpretations of the first twenty numbered symphonies, together with eleven other equally agreeable works. Mozart's early essays are clearly juvenilia—although being *Mozart's* juvenilia, virtually every scrap has something enchanting or revealing to say. Expect no hidden masterworks here, just a fascinating glimpse into the evolution of the most extraordinary genius the world has ever known.

Symphonies: No. 25 in G minor; No. 28 in C; No. 29 in A

Prague Chamber Orchestra, Mackerras. Telarc CD-80165 [CD].

At an age when most teenage boys are beginning to think about whom to ask to the junior prom, Mozart was busy writing music like this for his boss, the reactionary Prince Archbishop of Salzburg. On hearing the "Little G minor" Symphony for the first time, His Eminence's only comment was, "Far too modern."

This trio of youthful works—surely the greatest symphonies ever written by an adolescent—have had no finer recorded performances than these by Sir Charles Mackerras and the Prague Chamber Orchestra. Benjamin Britten's famous versions of 25 and 29 (available in the UK, though alas, not here) were exceptionally dramatic and resilient, but Mackerras yields nothing to those classic interpretations in terms of sparkle or elegance.

As in the other releases in his exceptional Mozart symphony series, Mackerras takes the middle ground between the grand opulence of a Walter or a Klemperer and the desiccated stinginess of period-instrument recordings. The orchestra, using modern instruments, is of chamber proportions, but the slightly reverberant acoustic creates the impression of space and depth without sacrificing any of the detail. Tempos tend to be brisk but judicious, and the execution is as meticulous as it is exuberant. With No. 28 tossed in for *very* good measure, this amounts to nearly eighty minutes of world-class music-making—a best buy in anybody's book.

Symphonies: No. 35 in D, *Haffner*; No. 39 in E-flat

Cleveland Orchestra, Szell. CBS MYK-38472 [CD], MYT-38472 [T].

Nowhere are George Szell's considerable skills as a Mozart conductor more conspicuously on display than in his recordings of these two amiable symphonies. From its thrilling opening flourish, the performance of the *Haffner* crackles with unfailing energy and transcendent wit; No. 39 strides serenely through its comfortable progress as in a pair of old but very fine shoes given a spanking new shine. The Cleveland Orchestra proves again that it was the finest

Haydn-Mozart ensemble of its time, and the remastered sound, while slightly shrill, is perfectly adequate.

Symphonies: No. 36 in C, *Linz*; No. 38 in D, *Prague*

Vienna Philharmonic, Bernstein. Deutsche Grammophon 415962-2 [CD].

Leonard Bernstein's vision of these two popular symphonies by Mozart has much in common with his final recordings of the music of Haydn. Shunning the chamber dimensions and drier sound favored by younger conductors in recent years, Bernstein's Mozart remains a bracing anachronism. The interpretations are ripe and richly Romantic, characterized by luscious textures, extreme but always persuasive tempos, powerfully dramatic gestures, and forward thrust. The opening of the *Prague* Symphony has never sounded more vividly operatic (after all, it *was* written at the same time as *Don Giovanni*), nor has the *Linz* ever sounded quite so exhilarating or rhapsodic. In recent years, the Vienna Philharmonic has rarely played better for anyone. In fact, it is only the sense of electric excitement that hints that the recordings were made during concert performances.

Symphonies: No. 40 in G minor; No. 41 in C, *Jupiter*

Philharmonia Orchestra, Klemperer. Angel CDMD-63272 [CD].

With their transcendentally serene and good-natured companion piece, No. 39 in E-flat, the G minor and *Jupiter* Symphonies form a trilogy that represents the high-water mark of eighteenth-century symphonic thought. In these great and mysterious works (why or for what occasion Mozart wrote them has never been known) the classical symphony reached its final stage of perfection. After Mozart, there was literally no place left for the form to go, other than through the bold and convulsive experiments of Beethoven, which signaled the beginning of the symphony's inevitable end.

Otto Klemperer's monumental performances from the early 1960s have a fair claim to being the greatest recordings each of the last two symphonies has ever received. It is not simply the breadth of the interpretations that makes them so extraordinary, for other conductors have adopted tempos in the outer movements that are nearly as slow. It is the conductor's Olympian insight, whether in probing the depths of despair in No. 40 or the heights of the *Jupiter's* exultation, that gives the performances a unique sense of scale and scope. There have been more turbulent recordings of the G minor Symphony, and more exciting readings of the *Jupiter*, but there are none that capture more of the tragedy and triumph of Mozart's farewell to the symphony than these.

If Klemperer's Mozart is to your taste—for *my* hard-earned money, his Mozart conducting ranks with Beecham's and Walter's as the greatest we are ever likely to hear—this four-CD set combines these two recordings with versions of eight of the other late symphonies into one convenient, not-to-be-missed box.

Bruno Walter's integral recording of the last six symphonies is equally indispensable, especially at Odyssey's budget price (MB2K-45676). All the performances glow with this conductor's unmistakable warmth and humanity, and the sound of the recordings, made in the early '60s at Hollywood's Old Legion Hall, has retained much of its presence and bloom.

Variations for Solo Piano (complete)

Barenboim, piano. Angel CDCC-54362 [CD].

This handsome three-CD set is obviously not to be digested over the course of one or two evenings, but, like Boswell's *Life of Johnson* is to be dipped into indiscriminately whenever the spirit needs a quick fix of civilizing charm. From famous sets like the twelve variations on "Ah, vous dirai-je, Maman" to oddities like the six variations on "Mio caro Adone" by Antonio Salieri, Daniel Barenboim is here as consistent and imaginative as he was in his magnificent cycle of the piano sonatas, bringing to each set a sense of eager discovery that makes even the least of them seem unique.

Mussorgsky, Modest

(1839–1881)

Boris Godunov

Vedernikov, Arkhipova, Koroleva, Sokolov, Shkolnikova,
USSR Radio and Television Orchestra and Chorus,
Fedoseyev. Philips 412281-2 [CD].

In any of its several versions—the two by the composer himself and the famous revision made by a well-intentioned friend—Mussorgsky's *Boris Godunov* is not only the most powerful and original Russian opera ever written but also one of the most relentlessly gripping theatrical experiences of the operatic stage. Since the days when Feodor Chaliapin's famous, overwhelming interpretation made it a major box-office attraction in the West, most listeners have come to know *Boris* through Rimsky-Korsakov's brilliant arrangement. While that wizard of the late-Romantic orchestra deserves the lion's share of credit for the opera's subsequent popularity, in Mussorgsky's 1872 revision the opera emerges as a cruder, rougher, and more starkly original piece.

For years, we have needed an absolutely convincing recorded performance of Mussorgsky's final revision, and this admirable Philips recording is probably as close as we are likely to get in the foreseeable future. The greatest strengths in the performance are precisely what they need to be: the intensely dramatic conducting of Vladimir Fedoseyev, and the broodingly powerful Boris of Alexander Vedernikov. Other basses—Chaliapin, Alexander Kipnis, Boris Christoff, George London—have brought finer voices and more refined musicality to the part, but in the big scenes, Vedernikov more than delivers the goods. The Clock Scene is especially unhinging in the way Vedernikov slowly begins losing his grip, and in Boris's Farewell and Death, he is perhaps more credible (and genuinely moving) than any performer since George London. The supporting cast is generally excellent, though the Pretender is more wobbly and inadequate than usual. In the massed choral scenes (and in *Boris*, as in Puccini's *Turandot*, the chorus is at least as important as any of the opera's other major characters) the USSR Radio and Television Chorus sings magnificently, with that characteristic Russian combination of wild exuberance and ink-black despair.

Khovanshchina

Lipovsek, Burchuladze, Atlantov, Haugland, Borowska, Kotscherga, Popov, Chorus and Orchestra of the Vienna State Opera, Abbado. Deutsche Grammophon 429758-2 [CD].

Set against the backdrop of the political turmoil that swept Russia at the time the forward-looking Peter the Great ascended to the throne in 1689, *Khovanshchina* is in many ways a more ambitious opera than *Boris Godunov* and, in most respects, far less universal. Essentially a sweeping historical panorama, it lacks the cohesiveness, to say nothing of the riveting central character, that animates Mussorgsky's masterpiece. But in its best moments—the lovely prelude "Dawn on the Moscow River," the wonderfully suggestive "Dance of the Persian Slaves," the thrilling choral passages, the deeply poignant closing scene in which the Old Believers opt for a *Götterdämmerung*-like immolation rather than renounce their faith—*Khovanshchina* clearly springs from the same source of inspiration that yielded the greatest of Russian operas.

Captured during actual performances at the Vienna State Opera, Claudio Abbado's *Khovanshchina* is one of the conductor's finest recordings. Aided by an alert and sensitive cast, he infuses the often episodic action with an uncharacteristic urgency and sense of purpose. Apart from the occasional cough or stomping entrance, the live recording only heightens the sense of drama and occasion.

For anyone even remotely interested in Russian opera, this is an indispensable recording.

Pictures at an Exhibition

New York Philharmonic, Bernstein. CBS MYK-36726 [CD], MYT-36726 [T].

Richter, piano. Odyssey YT-32223 [T].

Either in its original piano version or in the familiar orchestration that Serge Koussevitzky commissioned from Maurice Ravel in 1925, *Pictures at an Exhibition* is among the most inventive and original works ever written by a Russian composer. Beginning with the pioneering recordings by Koussevitzky (now available in a spectacularly fine-sounding transfer on RCA 09026-61392-2 [CD]) and Arturo Toscanini (RCA 60287-2-RG [CD] and 60287-4-RG [T], a performance complete with the famous un-written timpani roll toward the end of "The Great Gate of Kiev," which suggests the maestro's devotion to the inviolability of the score was not quite as fanatical as his legend would have you believe), the Ravel edition of the *Pictures* has probably received more great recordings than any other twentieth-century orchestral score.

One of Leonard Bernstein's earliest recordings after assuming the directorship of the New York Philharmonic in 1958 also remains one of his best. It was also the most impressive stereo recording CBS (then Columbia) had made up to that time. Bright and richly detailed, with a particularly solid and resonant bottom end, the physical sound remains astonishingly impressive in its compact disc transfer, and Bernstein's performance, after thirty-some years, remains the one to beat. In no recording do all the individual pictures emerge with such character and clarity, from the heavy ponderousness of the "Ox-cart" section to the delicate humor of the "Ballet of the Chicks in Their Eggs." Yet it is with the final two portraits that Bernstein leaves the competition at the museum door. The "Hut on Fowl's Legs" is a wonder of demonic fury and intensity, and the performance concludes with the most thrilling and majestic "Great Gate of Kiev" ever put on records. The explosive version of *Night on Bald Mountain* that accompanies the *Pictures* makes it seem like a very wild evening indeed.

Among recordings of the original piano suite, none—not even Vladimir Horowitz's famous Carnegie Hall recording, or the gleaming new version by the recent Tchaikovsky Competition winner Barry Douglas—can be mentioned in the same breath with Sviatoslav Richter's historic 1960 recording. In spite of the relatively drab and distracting recorded sound (it was taped at a recital in Sofia, Bulgaria, on a night when the entire city, apparently, was dying of terminal smoker's hack), there has never been a version of the *Pictures* to match it. It is not only the most electrifying performance Mussorgsky's suite is ever likely to receive, but also one of the dozen greatest recordings any modern pianist has made of *anything.*

Songs (complete)

**Christoff, bass; Labinsky, Moore, pianists; ORTF
Orchestra, Tzipine. Angel CHS-63025 [CD].**

If Mussorgsky had written nothing but the music contained
in this collection, he would still be remembered as one of history's
most powerfully original composers. Like the Dostoyevsky novels
or the Chekhov plays, Mussorgsky's songs create a reality both
unmistakably Russian and thoroughly universal. With the lieder of
Hugo Wolf, they are also the most disturbingly "modern" of nineteenth century art songs, not simply because they tend to avoid the
great traditional Romantic subjects of love and nature, but because
in their essentially ironic vision of human experience they anticipate
the defining attribute of the twentieth-century mind.

Recorded in the late 1950s, Boris Christoff's tour of this dark,
sarcastic, satiric, frequently beautiful universe is one of the major
achievements in recording history. Like Chaliapin and Alexander
Kipnis before him, the great Bulgarian bass is the kind of consummate singer-actor who is able to capture the full measure of the
composer's range, from the black humor in the famous "Song of
the Flea"—for which he produces the most menacing laugh since
Chaliapin's—to the delicate nostalgia of "Sunless" and the *Nursery
Songs.*

Lovers of lieder, Mussorgsky, and great singing will have
replaced their worn LPs the day this three-CD set hit the stores.
Everyone else should get a copy now.

Nielsen, Carl (1865–1931)

Choral Works (*Hymnus amoris*; Motets; *The Sleep*; *Springtime in Funen*)

> Soloists, Copenhagen Boys' Choir, Danish National Radio
> Choir and Orchestra, Segerstam. Chandos CHAN-8853
> [CD], ABTD-1470 [T].

Whenever you find yourself in the midst of a romantic campaign with an object who refuses to melt, introduce him/her/it to Nielsen's *Hymnus amoris* and relax. For years, a singularly ugly friend of mine (if you pushed his face in a big wad of dough you'd get gorilla cookies) has been using the ploy with astonishing success. Just put it on and prepare to be jumped.

In addition to the heart-dissolving beauties of the *Hymn of Love*, this loveliest of all Nielsen discs offers the entrancing *Springtime in Funen*, the challenging and dramatic *The Sleep*, and the gravely beautiful Motets. Both the performances and the recorded sound are ideal.

Symphonies: No. 3, *Sinfonia espansiva*; No. 5

> Royal Danish Orchestra, New York Philharmonic,
> Bernstein. Sony SMK-47598 [CD].

For a time during the mid-1960s, it seemed to many that the late-Romantic Danish composer Carl Nielsen was belatedly going to join his Finnish contemporary Jean Sibelius as one of the last and most popular practitioners of modern symphonic form. Though the Nielsen revival has obviously begun to lose momentum in recent years, Nielsen's remains a charming, provocative, and utterly original voice, especially in the *Sinfonia expansiva*, the first of the three major symphonies on which most of his future reputation will be based.

It's difficult to imagine a more inspired performance of it than the one on this Sony recording, which did so much to advance the Nielsen revival. Leonard Bernstein's enthusiasm for the work is as obvious as it is infectious. The Royal Danish Orchestra catch fire in what is probably the finest performance they have given in their collective memory, from their thunderous exuberance in the swaggering opening movement to the way they assault the normally flaccid finale as though it were an undiscovered masterwork of Johannes Brahms.

Bernstein's version of the Fifth, if not quite as overwhelming, still sets a standard for commitment and intensity that has yet to be approached. In this fabulously difficult work, the New York Philharmonic responds with one of its pluckiest performances; Bernstein inspires the snare-drummer to play with the verve and individuality of an Art Blakey, and recording engineers almost succeed admirably in disentangling the Symphony's complex web of sound.

Symphony No. 4, *Inextinguishable*

San Francisco Symphony, Blomstedt. London 421524-2 [CD].

Even the bungled acoustics of its horrid new concert hall cannot obscure the fact that the San Francisco Symphony, under Herbert Blomstedt, has entered its Golden Age. In less than a decade, this unpretentious musician has so completely rejuvenated the old band that it now must rank among the world's very best: the woodwinds play with grace and character, the brass are a model of fearless solidity, and the strings play with a burnished warmth that suggests a fine German orchestra at the top of its form.

Blomstedt's new version of the Nielsen *Inextinguishable* is one of his most impressive recordings to date: an interpretation of high tension, soaring lyricism, and withering drama, thrillingly played and recorded. In fact, it is the only recent *Inextinguishable* that can be mentioned in the same breath with Jean Martinon's classic RCA recording with the Chicago Symphony. The performance of the Fifth Symphony that fills out the CD is every bit as strong.

Blomstedt's versions of the composer's delightful First Symphony and the problematical Sixth, the not-so-simple *Sinfonia Semplice*, are equally impressive in capturing the freshness of Nielsen's youthful masterpiece and the bitter irony of his swan song (London 425607 [CD]). As in the other recordings in the series, no praise would be too extravagant for the San Francisco Symphony's playing or the work of London's engineers.

While their version of the Second Symphony, *The Four Temperaments*, is excellent, too, the performance of the *Espansiva* is really no match for Bernstein's (see page 370). Thus a more attractive pairing on Bis (CD-247 [CD]) features a thrilling interpretation of the Symphony with the enchanting *Aladdin Suite* in near-perfect performances by the Gothenberg Symphony led by Myung-Whun Chung.

Wind Chamber Music (complete)

Bergen Wind Quintet, et. al. Bis CD-428 [CD].

When he isn't busy being epic and heroic, i.e., "expansive" and "inextinguishable," Nielsen is at his absolute best doing charming little things, as in his naively disarming songs (Angel has a moral obligation to reissue the Danish tenor Aksel Schiøtz's immortal recordings) and the brief masterworks contained on this treasurable Bis CD.

The centerpiece is clearly the great Wind Quintet of 1922 (which, along with Hindemith's *Kleine Kammermusik* and the Wind Quintet of Arnold Schoenberg, are surely the twentieth century's most important examples of the form) but the other items are no less appealing, from the Allegretto for Two Recorders to that inspired study in tongue-in-cheek winsomeness, the *Seranata in vano*. The Bergen Wind Quintet and their friends play this music with unquenchable enthusiasm and grace, and the Bis recorded sound, as usual, is close to perfection.

Among recordings of the two wind concertos that Nielsen lived to complete (he had planned to compose one each for the five friends who gave the Quintet its premiere), the Bis version (CD-616 [CD]) of the unsettled and far-reaching Clarinet Concerto is easily the finest to date. Ole Schill's effortless handling of the all-but-impossible solo part is a marvel, as is the conducting of Myung-Whun Chung. If anything, his Bis recording of the Flute Concerto (CD-454 [CD]) is even more exhilarating, thanks to flutist Patrick Gallois, who gives the most imaginative recorded performance yet of the solo part. In such an inspired interpretation, the Nielsen sounds suspiciously like *the* great modern flute concerto.

To round out a collection of all three Nielsen concertos, Cho-Liang Lin's CBS recording (MK-44548[CD]) of the Violin

Concerto is easily the most startling that has so far appeared. The playing of both the soloist and the Philharmonia Orchestra under Esa-Pekka Salonen is so fiercely committed that this curiously underrated piece seems at very *least* the equal of the far more familiar work that fills out the recording, the Violin Concerto of Jean Sibelius.

Novák, Vítěslav (1870–1949)

Slovak Suite; South Bohemian Suite

Czech Philharmonic, Vajnar. Supraphon CO-1743 [CD].

There is a kind of piece with which everyone in classical music radio is familiar, and which some of us—especially the patient, gallant people who man the switchboards—have come to dread. These might be called, for want of a better phrase, the "What-was-that?-Where-can-I-buy-it?-What-the-hell-do-you-mean-it's-out-of-print!" recordings, those odd, offbeat, obscurities that seem to affect listeners like catnip. Morton Feldman's mesmerizing *Rothko Chapel* is one such work that will invariably light up the phone banks; the *Slovak Suite* by Vítěslav Novák is another.

A student of Dvořák whose early work was vigorously praised by Johannes Brahms, Novák—like his friend Josef Suk—was among the last of the Bohemian late Romantics, composers who were deeply influenced by Dvořák's example but who also managed to make highly individual statements of their own. Like Suk's youthful Serenade for Strings, the *Slovak Suite* is so warm-hearted, subtle, sophisticated, and opulent that it will have the most jaded listener sighing for more. (If you can persuade someone in the store to audition the CD for you, tell him or her to cue up the movement called "Two in Love." If they don't sell out their stock and take another half dozen orders for more, I would be greatly surprised.)

Both the *Slovak Suite* and the equally hypnotic *South Bohemian Suite* are given definitive performances by the Czech Philharmonic, who used to play Novák's music as standard repertoire items when they were led by the composer's friend and drinking buddy, the great Václav Talich. František Vajnar is no Talich, but his interpretations are loving, generous, and beautifully lit.

For the absolute last word in this music, if not in recorded sound, Talich's matchless recording from the early '50s has finally resurfaced on a Supraphon CD (SUP 11-0682-2), together with his equally incomparable versions of Janáček's *Taras Bulba* and *The Cunning Little Vixen* Suite.

Those responding to Novák's gentle, enchanting idiom will find much to admire in the most ambitious of his orchestral scores, the five-movement symphonic poem *Pan*, which has finally been given a decent modern recording by the Slovak Philharmonic led by Zdenek Bílek on Marco Polo (8.223325 [CD]). Though perhaps not as consistently inspired as either of the Suites, there are some thrilling moments in this long and fascinating work. The performance of what might be a major discovery for most people is rapt and solicitous, and the sound is very good.

Offenbach, Jacques

(1819–1880)

Gâité Parisienne

Pittsburgh Symphony, Previn. Philips 411039-2 [CD].

Like *Les Sylphides* and *La Boutique fantasque*, those ersatz ballets arranged from the piano music of Chopin and Rossini, *Gâité Parisienne*, Manuel Rosenthal's inspired adaptation of melodies from the Offenbach operettas, still tends to raise eyebrows (and many noses) among the Serious Music set. Though as a smug and jaded musical curmudgeon, I yield to no one in my arrogance or pickiness, I've never understood how it's possible *not* to like this dazzling confection, especially in a performance as lively and charming as this.

The ballet has received numerous fine recordings, including one by Rosenthal himself, but none can approach the urbane wit and Gallic grace of this superb Philips recording by André Previn. All the great set pieces—the Barcarole from *The Tales of Hoffman*, the "Can-Can" from *Orpheus in the Underworld*—are given the most lively and affectionate performances imaginable. In fact, the recording is a triumph of bracing rhythms, inventive phrasing, and tasteful sentimentality from beginning to end.

Overtures

> Philharmonia Orchestra, Marriner. Philips 411476-2 [CD].

Many of the best-loved of Offenbach's overtures—*Orpheus*, *La Périchole*, *La Belle Hélène*—are not, strictly speaking, his own work. Like Sir Arthur Sullivan, Offenbach frequently left much of the actual business of arranging and orchestrating the tunes from the operettas to others. Since the overtures were rarely more than potpourris, he would simply indicate which melodies he wanted in what order and then proceed to get on with more important things, such as writing or producing his next project or chasing after his most recent amour.

Sir Neville Marriner captures the spirit of these immortal trivialities perfectly, largely because he is able to maintain a light, flippant-sounding touch without making any of it *seem* trivial. The Philharmonia Orchestra is coaxed into that rare, wonderfully paradoxical state of relaxed alertness, and the recorded sound is superb.

The Tales of Hoffman

> Sutherland, Domingo, Tourangeau, Bacquier, Cuénod,
> Orchestra and Chorus of Radio Suisse Romande,
> Bonynge. London 417363-2 [CD].

Throughout his long and lucrative lifetime as the father of the operetta (his astonishing output of tuneful, racy, musical satires earned him the sobriquet, "The Mozart of the Boulevards"), Jacques Offenbach dreamed of writing a single, serious opera that would be the crowning achievement of his career. With *Tales of Hoffman*, finished a few months before his death (which occurred while the work was in rehearsal for the first production), the diminutive German-born cellist turned lighthearted French composer realized his goals. Though overshadowed in popularity by Gounod's once-ubiquitous *Faust*, Offenbach's immortal adaptation of stories by E. T. A. Hoffman is the only French opera which, in the quality and consistency of its inspiration, can be mentioned in the same breath with *Carmen* and Debussy's *Pelléas et Mélisande*.

The stunning London recording from the early 1970s is still the single most satisfying recorded performance *Hoffman* has ever received. Joan Sutherland, who undertakes all four of the opera's heroines, has never been more impressive. While Antonia and Giulietta are a trifle lacking in character, both are splendidly sung. As the doll Olympia, however, she turns in a virtuoso tour de force of such staggering dimensions that even those of us who do not count ourselves among her most rabid fans come away in a state of slack-jawed amazement. As the opera's several villains, Gabriel Bacquier is as suavely malevolent as any singer who has ever undertaken the roles, but the gem of the production is Placido Domingo's Hoffman. For nearly two memorable decades now, Domingo's achievements have rivaled those of the greatest tenors of the century's Golden Age. Vocally and dramatically, this Hoffman is one of his most impressive creations, a performance which —if it hasn't already—will one day become the stuff of legend.

Orff, Carl (1895–1982)

Carmina Burana

Armstrong, English, Allen, St. Clement Danes Boys' Choir, London Symphony Orchestra and Chorus, Previn. Angel CDC-47411 [CD], 4AM-34770 [T].

Like acne, and an insatiable lust for Milk Duds, Carl Orff's *Carmina Burana* is a juvenile affliction that most people eventually outgrow. As that torrent of unspeakably dull and repetitious music clearly proved, Carl Orff was not just a one-work but a one-*idea* composer. This astonishingly simple, musically primitive setting of some bawdy medieval lyrics can be a dazzlingly effective experience the first couple of times you hear it. It is only after repeated encounters that the vulgarity and yawning vapidity of *Carmina* really begin to get on a person's nerves.

For those who have an affection for this trash (and I must admit *I* always have), André Previn's Angel recording is one of the finest ever made. To his credit, Previn does nothing to cheapen the work further than its composer already has, but instead constantly seeks out its humor, limited subtlety, and frequently engaging wit. Which is not to say that the performance attempts to housebreak *Carmina Burana*. For at the end, we are thoroughly convinced that this is music that a gland would write, if only it could.

Pachelbel, Johann

(1653–1706)

Kanon in D

**Stuttgart Chamber Orchestra, Münchinger. London
411973-2 [CD].**

What violent emotions Pachelbel's sweet little Kanon continues to provoke! It is now one of the most frequently recorded of all classical works, but there are those of us who still can't quite understand what all the shouting is about. At best, Pachelbel was a third-rate Baroque nonentity who occasionally rose to the level of the second-rate in some of his organ music. And though the *Kanon* was composed more than a century before Napoleon showed the world what *really* heavy ordnance could do, it still unquestionably qualifies as *large bore*.

If you really *must*, Karl Münchinger leads the Stuttgart Chamber Orchestra in a tender, yet admirably disciplined performance on London. This compact disc version is especially useful, in that you can program the *Kanon* to repeat again and again, and thus save yourself untold thousands of dollars by putting off that frontal lobotomy you had planned.

If you're in need of a tape version, Raymond Leppard and the English Chamber Orchestra are equally attractive on a CBS recording (MYT-38482).

Paganini, Niccolò (1782–1840)

Caprices (24) for Unaccompanied Violin

Perlman, violin. Angel CDC-47171 [CD].

Unlike his rather lumpy and charmless violin concertos, the Paganini Caprices are among the most intriguing works ever written for the violin, by the man who was, by all accounts, its greatest master. Stories of Paganini's virtuosity are legion. For a week after a concert in which he played the whole of Beethoven's *Kreutzer* Sonata on a single string, he was the talk of Paris; when his driver asked for a considerable raise since his master was becoming so famous, Paganini readily agreed, provided he be driven everywhere on a single wheel.

Musically and technically, this recording made by Itzhak Perlman in the early 1970s has yet to be bettered. The playing is as sensitive as it is audacious, and for once even the most difficult of the individual pieces emerge with a color and freshness that suggest miniature tone poems, instead of mere excuses for wanton virtuoso display.

Concerto No. 1 in D for Violin and Orchestra

Kaplan, violin; London Symphony, Miller. Arabesque Z-6597 [CD].

Having written off this piece years ago as feeble, empty-headed fluff, I must now recant completely. Then again, I never understood that Paganini's popular D Major Concerto was in reality a miniature Rossini opera without words. At least that's the way Mark Kaplan and Mitch Miller make it seem in their electrifying Arabesque recording.

Though Kaplan is not yet as well known as some of his more highly publicized female colleagues, he proves conclusively here that he more than deserves to be. Technically, he is on a par with any violinist in the world today; musically, he is already a highly evolved personality, whose daring and bravado are matched only by his intelligence and wit.

Throughout the Paganini, and in the blazing performance of the Wieniawski D minor Concerto that accompanies it, he treats the dog-eared classics as music, not simply as a convenient vehicle for showing us what he can do. With a shrewd conductor who also adopts, or perhaps inspired, that refreshing attitude, both of the tired old warhorses are up and running like thoroughbreds from the opening bars.

In spite of formidable competition in both pieces, these recordings leave all others in the dust.

Paine, John Knowles

(1839–1906)

Symphonies (2)

New York Philharmonic, Mehta. New World NW-374-2
[CD] (Symphony No 1; *As You Like It* Overture);
NW-350-2 [CD] (Symphony No. 2).

John Knowles Paine was the John Greenleaf Whittier of American music. Portland-born and Berlin-trained, Paine's music looked to European models for precept and sustenance, and except for certain titles like *Columbus March and Hymn*, his is no more distinctly American music than "Maud Muller" is an especially American poem. Although formal and derivative, Paine's two Symphonies—the first ever published by an American composer— are richly imagined, elegantly crafted, moving, manly, and surprisingly memorable works. Though admittedly it has scant competition, Paine's Second Symphony—called *Im Frühling* as a nod to his beloved Schumann—is easily the strongest American symphony produced during the nineteenth century. If the earlier work in C minor is less determined and individual, it is still full of clever touches and fine tunes and more than repays repeated hearings.

It is difficult to imagine more eloquent champions than Zubin Mehta and the Philharmonic, who give both Symphonies and the snazzy *As You Like It* Overture top-drawer performances, captured in admirably lifelike recorded sound.

Palestrina, Giovanni

(c. 1525–1594)

*M*issa *Papae Marcelli*

Tallis Scholars, Phillips. Gimell CDGIM-339 [CD].

It's the gloomy winter of 1563, and the Council of Trent, concerned that the whacked-out new church music is taking everyone's mind off the meaning of the words being sung, is about to outlaw the use of polyphony—music in which several voice parts are heard simultaneously. (If the old monotonous monophonic chants were good enough for Pope Gregory and the boys, then by Jesu, they should be good enough for us!)

At which point young Giovanni Pierluigi, who's from the town of Palestrina, just outside of Rome (actually, at thirty-eight he isn't all *that* young), bursts in with the manuscript of his latest polyphonic Mass, which is not only utterly gorgeous but so skillfully written that you can understand *every* single syllable. The Council relents, decides that polyphony is not the work of the Devil, and the subsequent history of Western music—from Bach to the Beatles—is assured.

It would make a terrific movie. In fact, it *did* make an intriguing opera: Hans Pfitzner's somewhat long-winded but erratically inspired *Palestrina*. The only problem with one of music's most dramatic stories is that it almost certainly never took place. Polyphonic music was saved in 1563 because of the viselike pressure put on the Council by the music-loving Emperor Ferdinand I, not because the prelates were impressed with Palestrina's work.

Be that as it may, the most famous Mass of the Church's greatest composer has never sounded more, well, heavenly than it does in this transcendent performance by the Tallis Scholars. The starkly beautiful *Vox Patris caelestis* by the Tudor composer William Mundy and Gregorio Allegri's catchy *Miserere* (which with time may yet become the ecclesiastical Pachelbel *Kanon*) round out one of the best recordings of sacred music available today.

Parry, Sir Hubert (1848–1918)

Symphony No. 3 in C, *The English*; Symphony No 4

London Philharmonic, Bamert. Chandos CHAN-8896 [CD], ABTD-1507 [T].

It isn't *quite* true that no significant music was produced by native-born English composers between the death of Henry Purcell in 1695 and the appearance of Elgar's first undoubted masterpiece, the *Enigma* Variations, in 1899: the Savoy operas of Gilbert and Sullivan are among the most valuable theatrical commodities ever devised by the mind of man, and the symphonies and choral works of that eminent Victorian, Sir Charles Hubert H. Parry, are clearly those of an important composer, possibly even a major one.

Best known for that stirring anthem, *Jerusalem*, Parry was a musician cut from the same cloth as his younger contemporary Elgar. There is a stately, and occasionally self-satisfied, Victorian grandeur in his best pages, coupled with a natural vigor and deep-seated melancholy, that make him an appealing and completely approachable "private" composer as well.

Parry's Third Symphony, finished in 1889 and called *The English* because of its many folklike melodies, is an ideal introduction to his vaguely Elgarian, yet still utterly individual world. If anything, the Fourth Symphony is an even finer work, bursting with ideas and a dignified energy.

The London Philharmonic under Matthias Bamert play these marvelous works with an ease and confidence that almost suggests they are standard repertoire items; in fact, the performances make *such* a strong case, you almost wonder why they aren't. The other recordings released thus far in their Parry symphony cycle are just as enjoyable: the Symphony No. 2, *The Cambridge*, offered with the resourceful *Symphonic Variations* (CHAN-8961 [CD], ABTD-1553 [T]), and the agreeably Brahmsian Symphony No. 5 paired, appropriately, with the *Elegy for Brahms* (CHAN-8955 [CD], ABTD-1549 [T]).

More impressive than any of the symphonies, though, are the deeply moving "sinfonia sacra," *The Soul's Ransom*, and the politely sensuous *Lotus Eaters*, on a text by Tennyson—two of Parry's greatest choral works, which draw from Bamert his finest recorded performances to date. Packed onto another Chandos CD (CHAN-8990) lasting nearly eighty minutes, this is a release that no one interested in choral and/or English music can afford to miss.

Pärt, Arvo (1935–)

Arbos; *Pari Intervallo*; *An den Wassern zu Babel*; *De Profundis*; *Es sang vor langen Jahren*; *Stabat Mater*

> Various soloists, Hilliard Ensemble, Hillier. ECM
> 78118-21325-2 [CD], 78118-21325-4 [T].

The music of the Estonian composer Arvo Pärt resembles the bumblebee: by all the laws of aerodynamics neither should be able to fly, and yet somehow, preposterously, they do. To call Pärt a minimalist is both accurate and misleading. Although he seems to adopt many of the static, lifeless procedures of Philip Glass and that crowd, his *real* source of inspiration would appear to be the hypnotic stasis of Gregorian Chant. In Pärt's music, there is little in the way of development of musical ideas—in fact, there are few *ideas* at all. Somehow, though, he manages to wring genuine substance and feeling from his stubbornly thin materials: his gravely austere setting of the *Stabat Mater*, for instance, is absolutely bewitching, and the brief *An den Wassern zu Babel* has a stark grandeur that utterly belies its modest size.

The performances sound definitive.

Piston, Walter (1894–1976)

Symphony No. 2

Boston Symphony, Thomas. Deutsche Grammophon 429860-2 [CD].

In addition to being a great musical pedagogue whose pupils included Leonard Bernstein and whose books *Harmony* and *Orchestration* remain standard texts, Walter Piston was one of the finest of all American composers. His music combines an Italianate lyricism (the family name was Pistone) with a ruggedly virile individuality that often suggests the rocky coast of his native Maine. At his best, as he is in the powerful, exquisitely crafted Second Symphony of 1943, Piston reveals himself as one of our most important symphonists and an immediately appealing, instantly recognizable voice. In this flawless and exhilarating performance by Michael Tilson Thomas and the Boston Symphony, the Piston Second is the centerpiece of an invaluable American compact disc that also contains Paul Zukovsky's electrifying recording of William Schuman's Violin Concerto and a once-in-a-lifetime interpretation of Carl Ruggles's overwhelming *Sun-Treader*.

Gerard Schwarz's hugely successful Piston series for Delos is highlighted by a splendid recording of the Fourth Symphony, the Serenade for String Orchestra and the *Three New England Sketches* (DE-3106), and the composer's most popular work, the suite from the ballet *The Incredible Flutist*, is now represented by a colorful, high-voltage performance by Leonard Slatkin and the St. Louis Symphony, coupled with an equally fine account of the Sixth Symphony (RCA 60798-2-RC [CD]).

Pizzetti, Ildebrando

(1880–1968)

Messa di Requiem; *Tre composizioni corali*; *Due composizioni corali*

Danish National Radio Chamber Choir, Parkman. Chandos
CHAN-8964.

A contemporary of Respighi, Montemezzi and Malipiero, Ildebrando Pizzetti was perhaps the most urbane and poetic Italian composer of his generation and the one whose current neglect is the most difficult to explain. (With Rossini and Schoenberg, he was also one of the most superstitious of all composers: in addition to decorating his scores with four-leaf clovers, he refused to begin any new work on a Tuesday and would mark the seventeenth page of each of his scores a "16 + 1.") With Montemezzi's *L'amore dei tre re*, Pizzetti's *Debora e Jaele* and *Assassinio nella Cattedrale* (a setting of T.S. Eliot's *Murder in the Cathedral*) are among the most original and effective Italian operas written after Puccini's, and his elegantly wrought choral music is among the most moving produced in this century.

Pizzetti composed what may well be his masterpiece, the intensely beautiful *Messa di Requiem* in 1920 following the death of his first wife. (Deeply affected, he would continue to wear the black clothes of mourning even after his second marriage and indeed wore nothing else for the remainder of his life.) Making memorable use of the medieval *Dies irae*, Pizzetti's *Requiem* is an extraordinarily simple and eloquent work that wastes not a note nor a second of the listener's time. Along with five shorter but no less striking a capella choral works in equally gripping performances by the brilliantly drilled Danish National Radio Chamber Choir, this is the most distinguished Pizzetti recording in a generation.

Ponchielli, Amilcare

(1834–1886)

La Gioconda

Callas, Barbieri, Amadini, Poggi, Silveri, Neri, Turin Radio
Orchestra and Chorus, Votto. Fonit-Cetra CD0-8 [CD].

Caballé, Baltsa, Pavarotti, Milnes, Hodgson, London Opera
Chorus, National Philharmonic, Bartoletti. London
414349-2 [CD].

The next time you're at a party with people who really think
they know a lot about opera, challenge any one of them to relate,
in its simplest terms, the plot of *La Gioconda*. In retrospect, it's
almost impossible to fathom how the future librettist of Verdi's
Otello and *Falstaff* and the composer of *Mefistofele*, Arrigo Boito,
could have come up with such a hopelessly confusing pile of gibberish, or how Amilcare Ponchielli, a composer of limited abilities,
could have fashioned from it one of the most powerful and enduring works of the Italian operatic stage. *La Gioconda* would have a
decisive influence on almost every Italian opera that followed, including the later operas of Verdi and those of Ponchielli's most
celebrated pupil, Giacomo Puccini.

For more than three decades, the only Gioconda has been that
of Maria Callas. It is one of the most gripping of all her recorded
characterizations and one that seems to inspire everyone around
her, from the other principal singers to every member of the chorus
and orchestra, to give his or her absolute best. The recorded sound,
from a 1952 broadcast, is surprisingly lively and realistic.

The only real modern competition for this classic recording
comes from the splendid London set, which counts among its principal strengths recorded sound of astonishing clarity and presence,
and one of the finest performances Luciano Pavarotti has given in
years. The rest of the cast, other than Montserrat Caballé's rather
stiff and unimaginative heroine, is generally excellent, and Bruno
Bartoletti—like Antonino Votto on the Fonit-Cetra set—conducts
like a man possessed.

Poulenc, Francis (1899–1963)

Aubade for Piano and 18 instruments; Concerto for
Piano and Orchestra; Concerto in D minor for Two
Pianos and Orchestra

**Tacchino, Ringeissen, pianos; Monte Carlo Philharmonic,
Prêtre. EMI CDM-64714 [CD].**

If ever a composer wrote music that bore an uncanny resemblance to the way he actually looked, it was the tall, gangly, always slightly off-kilter Francis Poulenc. There is a pervasive and goofy oddness in all the work this deft, graceful, and highly original composer produced. Had he been just a little less peculiar, he might have been as important as Debussy; as it stands, he is responsible for some of the major French art songs of the twentieth century and is, perhaps, modern France's major composer of sacred music. In addition to being an important composer, Poulenc was also a gifted pianist, often accompanying the incomparable French baritone Pierre Bernac, his longtime companion.

Toward the end of Poulenc's life, Georges Prêtre was the composer's favorite conductor, as might be gathered from these saucy and authoritative recordings of three of his most delightful scores. Prêtre misses none of the tenderness or the tongue-in-cheek charm of these enchanting scores, and Gabriel Tacchino—like the composer and Jacques Février before him—is a thoroughly idiomatic exponent of the solo parts.

Dialogues des Carmélites

**Van Dam, Dubosc, Yaker, Gorr, Dupuy, Lyon Opera
Orchestra, Nagano. Virgin CDCB-59227 [CD].**

Ever since it was introduced at Milan's La Scala on January 26, 1957, Poulenc's masterpiece, *Dialogues des Carmélites* has been universally accepted as one of the half dozen finest operas written since the end of the Second World War. Set in Paris at the time of the revolution, it is the story of fourteen Carmelite nuns who prefer death on the guillotine to dissolving their order. Like the most inspired of Poulenc's sacred music, the opera is full of an exultant spirituality, along with a soaring, dignified lyricism and a quietly shattering dramatic intensity. The final scene, in which the Prioress and her followers mount the scaffold singing the *Salve Regina* as one by one their voices are silenced, is among the most powerful in modern opera.

If anything, the recording by the Lyon Opera Orchestra led by Kent Nagano is even more impressive than their electrifying version of Prokofiev's *The Love for Three Oranges*. The new version of Poulenc's opera either matches or supersedes virtually everything in the first recorded version on Angel led by Pierre Dervaux. The cast is without exception superb—the ageless Rita Gorr is particularly gripping as Madame de Croissy, as is Catherine Dubosc as the volatile Sister Blanche—and Nagano conducts as though guided by an inner light. For anyone persuaded that *Turandot* was the last great twentieth-century opera, this haunting masterpiece will come as a major surprise.

Gloria in G; Concerto in G minor for Organ, Strings, and Timpani

Carteri, soprano; Duruflé, organ; French National Radio
Orchestra and Chorus, Prêtre. Angel CDC-47723[CD].

Composed only two years before his death, Poulenc's *Gloria* is one of his most consistently inspired, touching, and exhilarating works. Not since Haydn had anyone set the *Laudamus Te* quite so joyously, and the work's closing bars easily rank with the most divinely inspired moments composed in this century.

Not only was George Prêtre's Angel recording the first to be made of this great modern sacred work, it was done with the composer himself in attendance. Only Leonard Bernstein, in a CBS recording now available on CD (MK-44710), found the same immensely appealing combination of fun and devotion in the *Gloria*, although for the most part, the Prêtre interpretation is far more charming and, hence, far more French. The recording has the further advantage of having been made with the composer on hand. It's a sensation that is impossible to explain in words, but while listening to the music, you can actually feel his presence.

Similarly, with composer Maurice Duruflé as soloist, the performance of the Organ Concerto has a full-throated authority, while Prêtre's accompaniment is equally incisive. Although slightly brittle around the edges, the 1960s recorded sound has held up remarkably well.

L'histoire de Babar (le petit éléphant)

Amis, speaker; Howard, piano. Chandos NI-5342 [CD].

Having spent my childhood devouring pictorial histories of music and the Second World War, and having no children of my own yet (of whom I'm aware), I'm a fairly recent Babar convert. A friend introduced me to Jean de Brunhoff's plucky pachyderm through a Christmas gift of *Le Roi Babar*, and I've been hooked ever since. (I can sing the *Chanson des éléphants* in my sleep—"Pata Pata, Ko Ko Ko" and so on—but enough of that.)

Although not quite a match for Peter Ustinov's scandalously deleted Angel recording, this newer version by John Amis has plenty of character and charm, too. Why this modern children's classic doesn't boast at least as many recordings as Prokofiev's *Peter and the Wolf* is anybody's guess; I suppose we should be grateful to have at least one.

Piano Music

Rogé, piano. London 417438-2 [CD].

Poulenc's piano music, like his *chansons*, has attracted far too few major interpreters. In the case of the songs, that's almost understandable: the memory of performances by the composer and Pierre Bernac (Poulenc's longtime lover and the man for whom many of the best of them were written) remains vivid and indelible (EMI CDC-54605 [CD]), and few singers are anxious to go up against such a legend. Then too, the songs have a quivering, elusive enchantment that makes them extremely difficult to perform well, as do many of the composer's finest piano works.

For the uninitiated or the unconvinced, Paul Crossley's heroic survey of the complete piano music for CBS (M3K-44921) may prove a bit intimidating, especially when it comes time to fork over the cost of three full-priced CDs. The set is more than worth the expenditure, since Crossley is a subtle, imaginative pianist whose performances are as astute as they are enjoyable.

Pascal Rogé's London recording might prove a far more manageable introduction. In addition to including some of Poulenc's most important and characteristic piano works—the three *Mouvements perpétuels*, the *Novelettes*, and a judicious sampling of the mercurial *Improvisations*—the playing is fairly sensational, full of capriciousness, sentiment, and Poulencian wisecracking, all captured in remarkably realistic sound.

Sextuor for Piano and Wind Quintet; Sonata for Clarinet and Piano; Sonata for Flute and Piano; Sonata for Oboe and Piano; Trio for Oboe, Bassoon, and Piano

> Portal, clarinet; Gallois, flute; Bourgue, oboe; Wallez, bassoon; Cazalet, horn; Rogé, piano. London 421581-2 [CD].

Poulenc's most consistently entertaining contribution to twentieth-century music could very well be the series of fourteen instrumental chamber works he produced at every stage of his long and colorful career: from the modest Sonata for Two Clarinets of 1918 (written, in Poulenc's words, "for entertainment and without pretention") through the magnificent Clarinet Sonata of 1962.

Here, conveniently gathered together on a single CD, are five of Poulenc's most ingratiating chamber works in performances that range from very good to near-definitive. If some of these marvelous pieces have had finer individual performances—both Richard Stolzman and Gervaise de Peyer have managed to project more character in the Clarinet Sonata, and Poulenc's own Columbia recording of the *Sextuor* with the Philadelphia Wind Quintet cries out for a CD reissue—the wind playing is witty, pungent, and suitably Gallic, and pianist Pascal Rogé again proves his mastery of the idiom.

Praetorius, Michael

(1571–1621)

*T*erpsichore Dances

London Early Music Consort, Munrow. Angel CDM-69024
[CD].

When the extravagantly gifted David Munrow died by his own hand in 1976, the cause of early music lost one of its most devoted and appealing advocates. As committed to the "authentic" performance of Renaissance and medieval music as any musician of his generation, Munrow was also a great entertainer and a compelling performer, as this stupendous 1973 recording of music by Praetorius clearly shows.

Rarely have the famous *Terpsichore* Dances sounded more lively, lovely, or utterly infectious, and the lesser-known, but stunningly beautiful motets from *The Muses of Zion* here emerge as one of the most important vocal collections of the period.

If, like a highly respected critic and my sometime tennis partner, you are usually tempted to dismiss Renaissance dance fare as "village idiot music", this wonderful monument to David Munrow's towering talent will make a believer out of almost anyone.

Prokofiev, Sergei (1891–1953)

*A*lexander Nevsky (cantata)

Cairns, mezzo-soprano; Los Angeles Master Chorale, Los
Angeles Philharmonic, Previn. Telarc CD-80143 [CD].

The way to come to Sergei Eisenstein's 1938 film *Alexander Nevsky* is *not* through a modern recording of the cantata that Prokofiev cannibalized from his score for it. I should know. After committing Fritz Reiner's interpretation to memory but never having seen the picture itself until I entered college, I eagerly made my way to one of Ann Arbor's little revival houses in the late 1960s, fully prepared for one of the cinematic experiences of my life. And so it proved to be.

With growing incomprehension, I sat through the sloppy editing, the hammy acting, the inexcusable "humor," and the execrable sound, until the fateful moment when I turned to my date, a beaded, willowy quasi-hippie named Heather (I still think it should be against the law for parents to name their children after anything that can be found in a field) and asked, far more loudly than I had intended, "What *is* this shit?" I was resoundingly booed by the cognoscenti, and retired from the theater in disgrace.

To this day, I fail to understand *Nevsky*'s status as one of the milestones of cinema. An OK Stalinist propaganda orgy, sure: The scene where the comic-book Teutonic Knights throw the kids in the fire is grisly and disturbing, though tame stuff indeed compared to what would actually happen three years later. But a great film? If so, I have no idea what the phrase "great film" could possibly mean. From the wretched soundtrack, which was nonetheless unable to disguise an inept, hideously out-of-tune performance, it would be hard to tell that Prokofiev did indeed produce a wonderful score; for that we can thank the recording companies, who with various versions of the *Alexander Nevsky* Cantata have given this thrilling piece a life of its own.

As splendid as Reiner's classic recording is, the fact that he used an English text all but cripples the performance. The words—in a perfectly accurate translation—are so irretrievably silly, and the diction of Margaret Hillis's Chicago Symphony Chorus is so flawless, that even the most sympathetic listener (as I have always been) is hard pressed not to crack up.

Among the Russian versions of *Nevsky*, in which gems like "Arise! Arise! Ye Russian folk,/In battle just to fight to death!" are mercifully blocked by the language barrier, André Previn's Telarc recording, if not quite so vibrant as his older outing with the London Symphony, is clearly the first choice. Previn's *Nevsky* has become much darker and richer over the years, and the Philharmonic's deeper voices—the lower strings and brass, and the orchestra's exceptional bass clarinetist, David Howard—respond with a wonderfully menacing rumble. Yet the performance also has its moments of blazing, flood-lit grandeur: "Alexander's Entry into Pskov" will push your speaker's tweeters—to say nothing of your neighbor's patience—to their absolute limit.

Christine Cairns sings her solo beautifully, and the chorus, like the orchestra, is enthusiastic, responsive, and when the score requires, very, *very* loud. As we have come to expect from Telarc, the recorded sound is miraculous.

Concerto No. 3 in C for Piano and Orchestra

Graffman, piano; Cleveland Orchestra, Szell. CBS MYK-37806 [CD], MT-37806 [T].

The most popular of Prokofiev's five piano concertos has received numerous first-rate recordings since the composer himself left his historic account of this profound, ebullient piece in the 1930s. Incidentally, that exhilarating performance with the London Symphony conducted by Piero Coppola (grandfather of the film director) can now be found on Pearl (PEA-9470 [CD]). The greatest modern performance of the Third Concerto is on this CBS recording, which also includes equally gripping run-throughs of the audacious First Concerto and the Third Piano Sonata. This generously packed reissue includes some of the finest playing Gary Graffman ever did in a recording studio, and is further cause for lament that that brilliant career was cut short by a neurological disorder. In both concertos, the accompaniment George Szell provides is spellbinding, and the late-1960s recorded sound is still more than adequate.

Concertos (2) for Violin and Orchestra

Mintz, violin; Chicago Symphony, Abbado. Deutsche Grammophon 410524-2 [CD].

No two works will better explain Prokofiev's position as one of the most popular of all twentieth-century composers than these magnificent violin concertos, written just before and immediately after his long, self-imposed exile from the recently created Soviet Union. While the youthful D Major Concerto is one of the freshest and most original works Prokofiev had produced up to that time, the G minor Concerto is among the greatest modern works for the instrument. Lyrical, dramatic, sardonic, and overflowing with that utterly distinctive melodic personality that makes all of Prokofiev's music unique, the Second Concerto ranks with the finest of all the composer's mature works, which is to say, with the finest music written since the turn of the century.

The Israeli violinist Shlomo Mintz is an ideal advocate of both of these wonderful works. His technique and temperament easily overcome all the formidable challenges the music presents. The accompaniments provided by Claudio Abbado are as poised and passionate as one could hope for, and Deutsche Grammophon's recorded sound is something close to ideal.

Lieutenant Kijé Suite; *The Love for Three Oranges* Suite; Symphony No. 1, *Classical*

Philadelphia Orchestra, Ormandy. Odyssey MBK-39783 [CD].

During the many years when he was one of the world's most frequently recorded conductors, Eugene Ormandy never made a finer recording than these versions of three of Prokofiev's most popular scores. Even if the interpretation of the *Classical* Symphony leaves out the final measure of sassy wit, and the outer movements of *The Love for Three Oranges* Suite could use a touch more maniacal energy, none of the pieces has ever been better played in a recording studio. At almost every turn, Ormandy's great orchestra manages some wonder of unanimity or solo display. At Odyssey prices, this is a phenomenal bargain that must not be missed.

For those who are interested in *Kijé* alone, the magic of two performances from the 1960s has never been surpassed. George Szell's CBS recording (MYK-38527 [CD], MT-38527 [T]) is coupled with that finest of all recorded performances of Kodály's *Háry János* Suite (see page 286), and Fritz Reiner's dazzling RCA recording (60176-2 [CD], 60176-4 [T]) accompanies that conductor's incomparable—though alas, English language—version of *Alexander Nevsky*.

Prokofiev's endlessly inventive opera has finally received an adequate recording: a sparkling French-language production of *L'Amour des trois oranges* by the Lyon Opera under Kent Nagano (Virgin Classics 59566 [CD]). Those who have long suspected from the famous suite that *The Love for Three Oranges* must be one of the great twentieth-century operas will be heartened to discover that they were absolutely right.

Peter and the Wolf

> Flanders, narrator; Philharmonia Orchestra, Kurtz. EMI
> CDM-63177 [CD], Seraphim 4XG-60172 [T].

You have to be a pretty irredeemably crusty curmudgeon not to respond to the warmth and wonder of Prokofiev's best-known work. Like *Hänsel und Gretel*, *Peter and the Wolf* transcends the traditional limits of a conventional "children's work"; its simplicity can be grasped and loved by the tenderest of musical ears, while its immense wit and sophistication can appeal to the most refined of musical tastes.

For years, the most delectable of all recordings of the work has featured a wonderfully sly narration (complete with some marvelously personal sound effects) by Michael Flanders. Anyone familiar with his *At the Drop of a Hat* "after dinner farragos" with Donald Swann—available, finally, in a three-CD boxed set from EMI (CDS-7974642), which includes *The Bestiary of Flanders and Swann*—realizes how uniquely charming a performer he was; together with his equally memorable readings of Saint-Saëns's *Carnival of the Animals* and Britten's *Young Person's Guide to the Orchestra*, this *Peter and the Wolf* is an endearing memorial to an irreplaceable talent.

Piano Sonatas Nos. 6–8

> Pogorelich, piano. Deutsche Grammophon 413363-2 [CD]
> (No. 6).
>
> Pollini, piano. Deutsche Grammophon 419202-2 [CD]
> (No. 7).
>
> Richter, piano. Pyramid 13503 [CD] (No. 8).

Written between 1942 and 1944 during the darkest days of the Great Patriotic War, Prokofiev's wartime piano sonatas are not only his most important works for the instrument but are also, conceivably, the most significant contribution to the form made by a twentieth-century composer. Formidably difficult and emotionally exhausting, they place enormous burdens on both the performer and the listener. While only the most courageous virtuosos need bother to approach them, an immense technique is not enough: they all plumb depths that require a considerable expressive maturity and an unusual degree of self-knowledge.

These three recordings are among the respective pianists' finest achievements, especially Ivo Pogorelich's spellbinding version of No. 6, the A Major Sonata, his most exciting single recorded performance to date. Maurizio Pollini, too, proves in the Seventh that in addition to a rarified poetic sensibility he also possesses a thunderous technique, whereas Sviatoslav Richter is simply being Richter in his astounding live performance of the Eighth Sonata — which is to say, the greatest pianist of his time.

Approaching that same rarified company is Barry Douglas's electric interpretation of the rarely heard Second Sonata (RCA 60779-2-RC [CD]), along with a powerfully dramatic version of the Seventh that would probably be the preferred recording were it not for Pollini's. For those who want the less familiar works in the series, Boris Berman's Chandos cycle is absolutely first-rate. Each sonata comes with an attractive anthology of shorter works, all of them performed with wit, fire, and a seemingly instinctive grasp of the idiom. Buy any with confidence.

*R*omeo and Juliet (complete ballet)

Boston Symphony, Ozawa. Deutsche Grammophon 423268-2 [CD].

At the Paris premiere of his Second Symphony in 1925, Prokofiev is alleged to have turned to a companion and asked the rueful question, "Can it be that I really *am* a second-rate composer?" Any of a dozen works will answer that, including what may well be the greatest full-length ballet ever written.

Romeo and Juliet is not only a worthy successor to *Swan Lake* and *The Sleeping Beauty*, it is superior to both in many significant respects. The level of melodic and rhythmic invention is generally more inspired than it is in either Tchaikovsky masterpiece, and as drama it is far more immediate, cogent, and profound. It is not the path-breaking work that Stravinsky's *Rite of Spring* clearly was, but as an old-fashioned epic on the grand scale, nothing like it would emerge from twentieth-century Russia.

With André Previn's superlative Angel recording temporarily out of circulation, Ozawa's excellent Boston recording will fill the gap more than adequately. Here, this frequently glib conductor resists doing his usual traffic cop routine: the playing has genuine bite and a feline grace, and climaxes rise to splendidly noisy proportions. The Boston Symphony brilliantly covers any inadequacies in the interpretation with playing the likes of which one never hears at the ballet.

Among single-disc versions (although since DG fits the entire ballet on two CDs, an excerpts disc hardly seems worth the trouble), Joel Levi's Cleveland Orchestra recording for Telarc (CD-80089 [CD]) is the most desirable since Erich Leinsdorf's stunning but now deleted Boston Symphony anthology for RCA.

At present, there is only a single complete recording of Prokofiev's other great ballet *Cinderella*; fortunately, it is a superb one. In their London recording (410162-2 [CD]), the Cleveland Orchestra plays with even greater dash and finesse for Vladimir Ashkenazy than they did for Lorin Maazel in their intoxicating (and sadly deleted) recording of *Romeo and Juliet*. In fact, the interpretation is so vivid and colorful, it makes *Cinderella* seem every bit as inspired.

String Quartets (2)

> Chilingirian String Quartet. Chandos CHAN-8929 [CD], ABTD 1531 [T].

Unlike Shostakovich, whose cycle of fifteen string quartets encompassed most of his creative life and represented, after the symphonies, his finest achievement, Prokofiev was curiously indifferent to the form, producing only two quartets during his entire career. Although they have yet to enter the standard quartet repertoire, both are strong and individual pieces, redolent with Prokofiev's unmistakable melodic quirkiness and wit.

The Chilingirians make a virtually airtight case for both works. The earlier and more difficult First Quartet of 1930 nearly comes off as the more musically incisive of the two, but the folksiness of the wartime Second Quartet casts the more appealing spell. The recorded sound is every bit as fine as we have come to expect from Chandos's adept engineers.

Symphonies (7)

> French National Radio Orchestra, Martinon. Vox Box CDX-5001 [CD] (Symphonies 1, 4, 5, 7, *Russian Overture*; *Overture on Hebrew Themes*); CDX-5054 [CD] (Symphonies 2, 3, and 6).

Of all the recordings released during the composer's centennial year of 1991 (his death went practically unnoticed, as it fell on the exact same day as Joseph Stalin's), none was more welcomed than this phenomenal bargain. For little more than what it costs to buy a single full-priced CD, one can enjoy Jean Martinon's idiomatic and understanding Prokofiev cycle on four generously packed compact discs.

By far the strongest performances are of precisely what one would want: the elusive and difficult middle symphonies. No more persuasive or understanding versions of Nos. 2, 3, 4, and 6 currently exist, and if Martinon and his game French orchestra face serious competition in the other works, these are still extremely enjoyable readings that will please all but the most fanatically discriminating tastes. Excellent notes and remastered sound.

Symphony No. 5 in B-flat

New York Philharmonic, Bernstein. Sony SKM-47602 [CD].

Since it first began to be known in the late 1940s, the Fifth has remained the most popular, and is probably the most important of the composer's seven symphonies. Like the equally celebrated Fifth Symphony of Dmitri Shostakovich, it is one large-scale symphonic work to have emerged from the Soviet Union that seems destined to occupy a permanent place in the standard repertoire, and rightly so. For the Prokofiev Fifth, like the Shostakovich, is a big, powerful, intensely dramatic, and unmistakably *Russian* composition that will probably continue to move and inspire audiences well into the next century, and beyond.

The Prokofiev Fifth has had some memorable recent recordings—Leonard Slatkin's amazing RCA version has the St. Louis Symphony (09026-61350-2 [CD], 09026-61350-4 [T]), sounding like the Berlin Philharmonic in overdrive—but Leonard Bernstein's first release is easily the most overwhelming performance of this popular work yet recorded. Tempos are all on the extreme side, as is the emotional content of what can often be heard as a rather cool and sardonic work. Bernstein builds some of the most tremendous climaxes heard these days on commercial recordings: the Scherzo whips by with a tremendous sense of urgency, and the Finale contains some of the most exhilarating moments this conductor, which is to say *any* conductor, has so far left.

Ptaszynska, Marta (1943–)

Jeu-parti for Vibraphone and Harp

Rutkowski, vibraphone; Mazurek, harp. Olympia OCD-324 [CD].

I should confess that I have not exactly memorized Marta Ptaszynska's *Jeu-parti* for Vibraphone and Harp, nor do I expect to do so any time soon. It is the composer's all-but-unspellable (and for most people, unpronounceable) name that instantly captured my attention. For obvious reasons, my heart immediately goes out to anyone with a difficult surname, and I would hate to think that Ptaszynska's worthy music might go unheard simply because a prospective buyer would be too linguistically intimidated to ask for it.

So if you're afraid you might get tongue-tied or otherwise embarrass yourself in the record store, simply open the book to this page, point to the woman's name, and say, "I want the *Jeu-parti* for Vibraphone and Harp by *her*." (Asking for it by number is no fun, and five will get you ten that the salesperson won't have a clue about how to pronounce it either.)

Better still, this CD devoted to percussion music of contemporary Polish composers also features the recording premieres of works by Krzysztof Baculewski, Zbigniew Bargielski, Pawel Buczynski, Andrzej Krzanowski, and Zbigniew Penherski, together with pieces by the older and more established Witold (not to be confused with the lesser-known Zbigniew) Rudzinski and Kazimierz Serocki.

Again, I bought the recording not only because I think all of us unpronounceables should stick together, but also because I wanted a companion album to Olympia OCD-316, which features piano music by—among others—Andrzej Dutkiewicz, Marian Borkowski, Stefan Kisielewski, the world-famous Witold Lutoslawski, Artur Malawski, Zbigniew (not to be confused with the better-known Witold) Rudzinski, Tadeusz Szeligowski, and Romuald Twardowski.

Puccini, Giacomo (1858–1924)

Arias

> Caballé, soprano; London Symphony, Mackerras. Angel
> CDC-47841 [CD].
>
> Callas, soprano; Philharmonia Orchestra, Serafin. Angel
> CDC-47966 [CD].
>
> Pavarotti, tenor; various orchestras and conductors. London
> 425099-2 [CD]; 425099-4 [T].
>
> Price, soprano; New Philharmonia Orchestra, Downes.
> RCA 5999-2-RC [CD].

Here, in a nutshell—in fact, in a series of incomparable nutshells—is why Giacomo Puccini was the most important and popular Italian operatic composer after Verdi. For like Verdi, Puccini had the great gift of expressing emotion and character through some of the most ravishing and unforgettable melodies ever conceived by the mind of man.

Each of these splendid aria collections represent the recent art of Puccini interpretation at something close to its best, from Maria Callas's dramatically incisive readings to the sheer sumptuous beauty of those by Montserrat Caballé. Luciano Pavarotti's London recording captures the tenor at the height of his thrilling early form, and Leontyne Price demonstrates that, although she is far more familiar as a Verdi heroine, her Puccini is also a model of passion, insight, and breathtaking control.

La Bohème

> De los Angeles, Björling, Amara, Merrill, RCA Victor
> Orchestra and Chorus , Beecham. Angel CDCB-47235
> [CD], 4X2G-47235 [T].

This astonishing recording—certainly one of the greatest commercial recordings ever made—was thrown together at the last possible moment and, in fact, was very nearly never made at all. For more than thirty years it has been the standard recording of

Giacomo Puccini's most popular opera, and will undoubtedly remain so for as long as recordings are made.

Apart from a superlative cast (Victoria De los Angeles and Jussi Björling are especially wonderful as the lovers), most of the real magic of this most magical of all Puccini recordings comes from the pit. Several volumes could be written about the special insights, beautifully shaped phrases, aching tenderness, and surging passion Sir Thomas Beecham finds in Puccini's score. No one has ever made the love music bloom so effortlessly, or captured more of the high spirits or bitter tragedy of the work than Beecham did on what was an impossibly tight recording schedule. Robert Merrill, the superb Marcello, once told me that Sir Thomas caused great consternation by insisting that his duet with Björling "Ah Mimi, tu più non torni," be recorded again, even though time was running out and the first try had seemed to be a virtually perfect performance. Later, when the producer, who could hear no difference in the two versions, asked the conductor why he insisted on a second take, Beecham replied with characteristic glee, "Oh, because I simply *love* to hear those boys sing it!" That this very special recording *was* a labor of love from beginning to end is as obvious now as on the day it was first released.

Crisantemi for String Quartet; Songs

**Alexander, soprano; Crone, piano; Raphael String Quartet.
Etcetera KTC-1050 [CD], XTC-1050 [T].**

Aside from the charming *Crisantemi* (Crysanthemums), which has begun to appear as an encore piece at string quartet concerts and has been recorded a half dozen times, none of these engaging early Puccini works are well known—unless one counts the little song "Sole e amore," which eventually became the main theme for the Act III quartet from *La Bohème*. The rest of the songs and fragments on this release offer fascinating, often delightful glimpses into the young Puccini's workshop, and the performances are devoted and enthusiastic. Placido Domingo and Julius Rudel are even more persuasive on a delectable CBS compact disc called "The Unknown Puccini" (MK 44981), which offers some of the same items with the benefit of world-class voices.

La fanciulla del West

> Neblett, Domingo, Milnes, Howell, Orchestra and Chorus
> of the Royal Opera House, Covent Garden, Mehta.
> Deutsche Grammophon 419640-2 [CD].

Many people continue to wonder why *The Girl of the Golden West*, Puccini's major effort between *Madama Butterfly* and *Turandot*, has never caught on. It certainly got off to a galloping start at its Metropolitan Opera premiere: Arturo Toscanini—temporarily on speaking terms with the composer—was in the pit, and the principals included the dream trio of Emmy Destinn as Minnie, Enrico Caruso as Dick Johnson, and Pasquale Amato as Jack Rance.

Although the opera has always had its passionate advocates (and I include myself among them), the problem is so obvious that it hardly seems worth mentioning: *La fanciulla del West*, in spite of its many wondrous beauties, is really, *really* dumb. And it's not that the action, based on a play by *Butterfly*'s author David Belasco, is either foolish or implausible; in many ways, it is one of the better dramatic constructs Puccini was given to work with. *Fanciulla*'s central impossibility, at least for American audiences, is the language. How are we to credit a literal horse opera in which the miners, cowboys, and Indians all sing in Italian? (The acid test is the first scene of Act II. If you can listen to Billy Jackrabbit and his squaw Wowkle grunting and ugh-ing at each other in between bouts of flawless Italian and not burst out laughing, you have my undiluted admiration.)

The Deutsche Grammophon recording makes the strongest case for the opera since the magnificent 1958 London set with Renata Tebaldi and Mario del Monaco, which is now available on a pair of compact discs (421595-2). While still a stunner—Tebaldi's Minnie is arguably the most finely crafted of all her Puccini heroines—the older recording yields to the newer one on a pair of important points: the far more sensitive and sympathetic Johnson of Placido Domingo and the more expressive, imaginative conducting of Zubin Mehta.

Madama Butterfly

> Tebaldi, Bergonzi, Cossotto, Sordello, Santa Cecilia
> Academy Orchestra and Chorus, Serafin. London
> 425531-2 [CD].

That this radiant, heart-stopping opera was a fiasco at its world premiere in 1904 still seems impossible to most opera lovers today. We forget that the audience at Milan's La Scala was not exactly eager to embrace a love story between an occidental and a fifteen-year-old Japanese girl, and that the composer (as he later admitted) had made a serious miscalculation in the structure of his new work. What we now know as the second and third Acts of the opera were once a single, uncomfortably lengthy act that would have tested the patience of even the most ardent of the composer's admirers.

As one of the best-loved operas ever written, *Madama Butterfly* has had more than its fair share of memorable recordings, but none was ever more poignant than this classic 1958 version, with the sumptuous Renata Tebaldi in the title role. Tebaldi's Cio-Cio-San is a marvel of dramatic evolution, from the innocent child of the opening scene to the towering, tragic heroine of the opera's final moments. The supporting cast, especially the beautifully sung Pinkerton of Carlo Bergonzi and the vastly resourceful Suzuki of the young Fiorenza Cossotto, could not have been improved upon. Tullio Serafin's conducting is its usual admirable amalgam of sensitivity, understanding, and dramatic bite, and the original late-1950s acoustics have held up surprisingly well.

*M*anon Lescaut

> Callas, di Stefano, Fioravanti, La Scala Orchestra and
> Chorus, Serafin. Angel CDCB-47392 [CD].

It was no accident that on stage the Callas–Di Stefano love scenes always had the fiery ring of truth, since all of them had been rehearsed many times behind closed doors. The singers' offstage love affair not only made good grist for the tabloid mills, it gave their moments together a magic no other operatic duo of the 1950s could even approximate.

Manon Lescaut, Puccini's first major success as a composer, provided the vehicle for one of the best of their recorded collaborations, with Maria Callas at her most penetrating and believable and Giuseppe di Stefano at his most musical and refined. (There are many who still remember him as a kind of bellowing, lyric-tenor version of his great contemporary, the bellowing *tenore da forza*, Mario del Monaco. Here di Stefano displays both the ardor and vocal sophistication—to say nothing of the naturally beautiful physical sound—that led many to predict a career as long and brilliant as Beniamino Gigli's.)

The always reliable Tullio Serafin catches fire and turns in the best-conducted *Manon Lescaut* yet recorded, and even the mono sound proves no serious distraction: from the opening scene we are caught up in the poignant drama and are soon swept away.

Messa di Gloria

Soloists, West German Radio Choir, Frankfurt Radio Symphony, Inbal. Philips 434170-2 [CD].

The twenty-year-old Puccini was still a student at the Milan Conservatory when he completed his *Messa di Gloria* in 1880. It is an ambitious, frequently vulgar, utterly confident work that here and there shows unmistakable signs of the Puccini to come: the *Gratias*, for instance, has the shape and feel of many later Puccini arias, and the sweet-spirited *Angus Dei* would later be cannibalized for *Manon Lescaut*. The march that dominates the *Gloria* is an obvious (and stirring) homage to Verdi's *Aïda*, and the climatic fugue is an astonishing achievement for so young and inexperienced a composer.

It's good to have Philips's medium-priced reissue of the fine performance led by Eliahu Inbal back in circulation, although the Erato recording by Claudio Scimone would have been more welcome still. Nonetheless, the playing and singing are sincere and to the point, providing an excellent introduction to a work that is something considerably more than a youthful oddity.

La Rondine

Te Kanawa, Domingo, Rendall, Nucci, Ambrosian Opera Chorus, London Symphony, Maazel. CBS M2K-37852 [CD].

During a visit to Vienna in 1912, Puccini was asked by an enterprising Austrian publisher to write a Viennese operetta. Presumably, what the publisher had in mind was a kind of *Madama Butterfly* meets *Die Fledermaus*. The result was *La Rondine*, the lightest and least performed of the composer's mature works.

While certainly no *Bohème*, *La Rondine* (The Swallow) is just as certainly not the misbegotten disaster its detractors have always claimed it to be. If the opera is not exactly riddled with unforgettable Puccinian melodies, the tunes are still ingratiating enough to be worth anyone's time. Moreover, the characters are likable, the action is swift and sure, and the orchestral fabric is full of wonders from the composer's top drawer.

The CBS recording makes by far the strongest case for the piece that any version ever has. Kiri Te Kanawa's luscious voice is ideally suited to the heroine, Magda, an appealing cross between Violetta and the Merry Widow, and Placido Domingo lavishes his usual care and intelligence on a role that is far more interesting than it might otherwise seem. Although Lorin Maazel's conducting is not ideally subtle and relaxed, he still coaxes some marvelous playing from the London Symphony as well as skilled contributions from the rest of the cast.

There are really no excuses left for not exploring this charmer.

Tosca

Callas, di Stefano, Gobbi, La Scala Orchestra and Chorus, de Sabata. Angel CDCB-47174 [CD], 4AV-34047 [T].

If there ever was such a thing as a perfect opera recording, this is it. It features, among other things, Maria Callas, the greatest Tosca of the modern era, the most elegantly sung of tenor Giuseppe di Stefano's heros, and a villain—the Baron Scarpia of Tito Gobbi—that will stand your hair on end. But what puts this *Tosca* on a level that will probably never be approached is the conducting of Victor de Sabata. Though not as well known as his near-contemporary, Arturo Toscanini, de Sabata, I think, was always the finer conductor. Like Toscanini's, his dramatic sensibilities were very highly developed, yet unlike the Maestro, de Sabata had an immensely complex musical mind that not only probed the music with greater depth but allowed it sufficient space to breathe. His conducting throughout this inspired recording is nothing less than miraculous, from the soaringly beautiful support he lends to the love music, to that chillingly violent moment in the second act when the evil Baron finally "gets the point."

In short, this is a classic recording which no opera lover can afford to be without.

Il trittico (Il tabarro; Suor Angelica; Gianni Schicchi).

> Donath, Popp, Seiffert, Panerai, Munich Radio Orchestra,
> Patané. Eurodisc 7775-2-RC (*Il tabarro*); 7806-2-RC
> (*Suor Angelica*); 7751-2-RC (*Gianni Schicchi*) [CDs].

One hit, one near-miss, and a dud: not a bad average, unless your name happens to have been Giacomo Puccini. *Il trittico*, the composer's trilogy of one-act operas that had its premiere at the Met on December 14, 1918, has rarely been presented in that form since. *Gianni Schicchi*, the comedy, was a resounding success from the beginning and is frequently heard alone. Though the melodramatic curtain raiser, *Il tabarro* (The Cloak), is enjoyably gruesome and direct, nothing, apparently, will ever save *Suor Angelica*—the literal weak sister of the set—although some very great divas have given Puccini's nun-with-a-past a try.

You might think that with all the big-name talent—Renata Scotto, Ileana Cotrubas, Marilyn Horne, Placido Domingo, and Tito Gobbi—the CBS recording would have the field to itself. Much of the reason the upstart Eurodisc version knocks the giant off so easily has to do with the conducting of Giuseppi Patané. Unlike Lorin Maazel, a competent stick-waver but little more, the Italian constantly searches out—and usually finds—precisely the right color or mood the moment demands.

In addition to the exemplary conducting, the Munich *Trittico* features some striking individual performances: the droll, sharply drawn Schicchi of Rolando Panerai is more than a match for Gobbi's legendary characterization, and if Lucia Popp can't quite save the feckless Angelica, she makes her an exceptionally lovely thing to hear.

Turandot

> Sutherland, Pavarotti, Caballé, Pears, Ghiaurov, Jon Alldis
> Choir, London Philharmonic, Mehta. London 414274-2
> [CD], 421239-4 [T] (highlights).

The emergence of *Turandot* as an opera whose popularity has begun to challenge that of Puccini's other major works is a relatively recent phenomenon. For years, all anyone ever knew about

Turandot was the beautiful third-act aria, "Nessun dorma," and the fact that the opera remained unfinished at the time of the composer's death. For all its obvious flaws and inconsistencies (the unfinished love duet would have undoubtedly been the crowning achievement of Puccini's career, and the problems with the hero's character would have unquestionably been ironed out had the composer been given time to revise the score), *Turandot* is a great opera—as daring, original, and phenomenally beautiful a work as Puccini ever wrote.

When it was first released in the early 1970s, this now legendary London recording shocked the opera world. What was Joan Sutherland, the reigning bel canto diva of her time, doing recording a role that she never had, and obviously never would, sing on stage? Whatever the reasons, the gamble paid off handsomely. As Puccini's icy princess, Sutherland gave one of her finest recorded performances. The interpretation is full of fury, dramatic intensity, and—in the final scene—a startling warmth and femininity that have never been this singer's strongest suits. Similarly, Luciano Pavarotti, who recorded the role of Calaf before he ever sang it on stage, is brilliant as the Unknown Prince. Unlike the work of the Pavarotti of recent years, who seems to shout and croon his way through almost every performance, this is not only an interpretation by a great tenor in his prime but a sad reminder of what a vulgarian this once-electrifying artist has allowed himself to become.

Though I have never been Zubin Mehta's greatest fan, here he delivers one of the finest performances of his career. No detail in Puccini's astonishing orchestration is overlooked, and the conducting is as tenderly lyrical as it is compellingly dramatic. If you have yet to make the acquaintance of what may well be the composer's masterpiece, this is the *Turandot* for you.

Also very special is RCA's Rome recording made during the summer of 1960 and now available on both CD (RCD2-5932) and cassette (AGK3-3970). The chief glories of this memorable performance are the molten Calaf of Jussi Björling (who manages to transform "Nessun dorma" into "Nessun-ah dorma") and the powerful Birgit Nilsson in the title role. Although the Rome Opera House forces are clearly no match for London's superbly disciplined group, Erich Leinsdorf brings a measure of soaring lyricism to the score that Mehta can't quite match.

Purcell, Henry (1659–1695)

The Bell Anthem; *Come Ye Sons of Art* (Ode on the Birthday of Queen Mary, 1694); *My Beloved Spake* (anthem); *Ode for St. Cecilia's Day*, "Welcome to All the Pleasures"

The Deller Consort. Vanguard OVC-8027 [CD].

Although the performance of early music in general, and Purcell in particular, has changed considerably since the late Alfred Deller and his Consort made these famous recordings in the early 1960s, time has not diminished either their warmth or infectious enthusiasm. Deller's countertenor voice was one of the most instantly recognizable of its time. Coming from this large, bearded, burly man, the ironically high, reedy, plangent instrument was used with tremendous intelligence and consummate skill. Rarely have these glorious odes and anthems seemed so fresh or expressive as they do here, and the recorded sound has kept its presence and focus to a surprising degree.

Although not quite as pungent as his early Vanguard recording, Deller's Harmonia Mundi version (HMC-90242 [CD], HMC-40242 [T]) of some of Purcell's delightfully smutty catches and glees reminds us how splendidly bawdy the Restoration was and how irresistibly naughty its greatest composer could be.

Dido and Aeneas

Norman, Allen, McLaughlin, Kern, Power, English Chamber Orchestra and Chorus, Leppard. Philips 416299-2 [CD].

More than any other recording of the last generation, this new version of *Dido and Aeneas* demonstrates why this incredible work by the thirty-year-old Henry Purcell is the oldest of all operas that can still hold a place in the standard repertoire today. Under Raymond Leppard's inspired direction, the work leaps to life in a way that it rarely has on commercial recordings. Jessye Norman's Dido rivals those of Kirsten Flagstad and Janet Baker in its depth and intensity, and Thomas Allen is the most manly and heroic Aeneas

I can remember hearing. For those who usually find this greatest of English operas too thin in its characterization, or too slight in its development, this magnificent and luxuriant new version will probably change their minds.

The Fairy Queen

Soloists, Monteverdi Choir, English Baroque Soloists, Gardiner. Deutsche Grammophon 419221-2 [CD].

Not an adaptation of the epic poem by Edmund Spenser (which of course would have made it *The Faerie Queen*, as well as something that would have been at least two days long) but of Shakespeare's *A Midsummer Night's Dream*, this ridiculously underperformed "semi-opera" contains some of the most miraculous music Purcell ever composed. Tuneful and fanciful, with a gossamer lightness and extraordinary rhythmic life, *The Fairy Queen* should be far more familiar, and undoubtedly would become so were it routinely given performances as vital and engaging as this.

With his customary blend of unassailable scholarship and boyish enthusiasm, John Eliot Gardiner misses no opportunity to underline the manifold glories of the score, yet does so with a deftly unobtrusive hand. The only other Purcell recording quite like it is Gardiner's Erato version (2292-45211-2 [CD]) of *King Arthur*, the most important of Purcell's collaborations with another seventeenth-century giant, John Dryden. In both recordings Gardiner makes an extremely convincing case that *each* work is in fact the composer's masterpiece, and with both he reminds us with a renewed sense of wonder and tragedy what music lost when Henry Purcell died at the age of thirty-six.

Music for the Theater

Kirkby, Nelson, Bowman, Hill, Covey-Crump, Keyte, Thomas, Academy of Ancient Music, Hogwood. Oiseau-Lyre 425893-2 [CD].

More than six hours of the incidental music Purcell composed for various largely forgotten plays might be too much of a good thing for most people, yet these classic recordings by the Academy of Ancient Music remain a source of unalloyed delight. Christopher Hogwood's soloists prove ideal accomplices, with vocal timbres skillfully adjusted to match the sound of the antique instruments.

Rachmaninoff, Sergei

(1873–1943)

The Bells (choral symphony)

> Troitskaya, Karczykowski, Krause, Concertgebouw Orchestra and Chorus, Ashkenazy. London 414455-2 [CD].

Outside the English-speaking world, where he has always been something of an embarrassment to the literary establishment, Edgar Allan Poe is widely regarded as a major figure in modern poetry. In France, for instance, where one sees more statues to his memory than to that of Shakespeare, his reputation is enormous, thanks largely to the passionate advocacy of Charles Baudelaire. The great Frenchman's translations are markedly superior to their models, perhaps because Poe's poetry tends to lose so much in the original.

Working from an excellent Russian translation of Poe's noisiest masterpiece, Rachmaninoff fashioned a dramatic, volatile, supremely colorful cantata that easily ranks among his greatest works. To date, *The Bells* has had no finer or more inspired recording than Ashkenazy's impulsive version for London. As with André Previn's inexplicably withdrawn Angel recording, Ashkenazy brings just the right combination of expansiveness and control to the interpretation, together with a sense of unpredictability that the Previn lacks. With superb soloists, to say nothing of the great Concertgebouw Orchestra and flawless recorded sound, this is *The Bells* that should ring yours admirably.

Capriccio bohémien (Capriccio on Gypsy Themes); *Isle of the Dead*; *Prince Rostislav* (symphonic poem, after Tolstoy); *The Rock* (symphonic fantasy); Scherzo for Orchestra; Symphonic Dances; *Vocalise*; *Youth Symphony*; *The Bells*; Russian Songs; *Spring* [Vesna] (cantata)

> **Soloists, St. Louis Symphony and Chorus, Slatkin. Vox CD3X-3002 [CD].**

Although some of these works may be represented by finer individual performances, this three-CD Vox Box, which includes all of Rachmaninoff's music for orchestra excluding the concertos and symphonies, makes for an exceptionally attractive bargain. In general, the best performances tend to be (as one might hope) of the lesser-known works: indeed, Slatkin's polished, dramatic readings of the vivid *Capriccio bohémien*, the windy but entertaining *Prince Rostislav*, the enchanting Scherzo for Orchestra, and the hugely underrated, Tchaikovskyesque *The Rock* are the finest now available. As the other performances are on a comparably high level and the late '70s recorded sound remains superb, even if this involves some duplication, at these prices, it should scarcely matter.

Concertos for Piano and Orchestra (4); *Rhapsody on a Theme of Paganini*

> **Wild, piano; Royal Philharmonic, Horenstein. Chandos 8521/22 [CD].**

In one form or another, these thrilling recordings have remained in circulation since the mid-1960s, when they were originally recorded for *Reader's Digest*. The American pianist Earl Wild and the dapper, impulsive Russian-born conductor Jascha Horenstein had never worked together before, though it would be difficult to gather that from this finest integral recording of the Rachmaninoff Concertos ever made.

The success of the project rested primarily on the almost perfect fusion of two surprisingly similar musical temperaments; for in spite of the differences in their ages and backgrounds, the youthful soloist and the aging conductor were from the same arch-Romantic mold.

Even more than the composer's own recordings with Stokowski and Ormandy and the Philadelphia Orchestra, or Ashkenazy's cycles with Haitink and Previn, the electricity that Wild and Horenstein generated together remains unique. On records, only a handful of pianists can match Wild's thunderous impetuosity in this music, and the conductor brought the same sort of measured lunacy and passionate brinkmanship to the accompaniments that can be heard in his famous Mahler recordings.

With beautifully remastered recorded sound that completely belies its age, this is an ideal choice for anyone who wants all four concertos and the *Paganini Rhapsody* in a convenient, hugely exciting, and unusually economical package.

Concerto No. 2 in C minor for Piano and Orchestra

Richter, piano; Warsaw Philharmonic, Wislocki. Deutsche Grammophon 415119-2 [CD].

Graffman, piano; New York Philharmonic, Bernstein. CBS MYK-36722 [CD], MYT-36722 [T].

Although the composer himself, who was certainly one of the great pianists history has so far known, left a series of famous, authoritative recordings of all his major works for piano and orchestra, no recording of his most popular concerto has ever generated more sheer wonder or excitement than Sviatoslav Richter's famous version from the mid-1960s. Interpretively, the performance is something of a madhouse. Tempos are invariably extreme, from the slowest of Adagios, to a breakneck clip in the final movement that will leave most listeners panting on the floor. Yet as eccentric as the interpretation certainly is, it is also utterly convincing, thanks to the technique and temperament of the foremost pianist of our time.

For those who prefer a cassette version of this high-cholesterol classic, Gary Graffman's version with Leonard Bernstein remains as polished as it is poetic, with one of the finest modern versions (in fact, my favorite) of the *Rhapsody on a Theme of Paganini* as the extremely attractive filler.

Concerto No. 3 in D minor for Piano and Orchestra

Horowitz, piano; New York Philharmonic, Ormandy. RCA RCD1-2633 [CD].

Some very reliable rumors insist that Rachmaninoff stopped playing his D minor Concerto in public shortly after he heard it performed by the young Vladimir Horowitz. And for the better part of fifty years, the Rachmaninoff D minor was a cornerstone in what was surely the tiniest concerto repertoire any major pianist has ever possessed. Though I have always felt about Horowitz much the same way I feel about his father-in-law, Arturo Toscanini, and his near-contemporary, Jascha Heifetz, give the man his due: In this particular music, no pianist of the century has ever come close. Of course, for something close to the ultimate in hair-raising piano fireworks, the 1951 studio recording Horowitz made with Fritz Reiner and the RCA Victor Orchestra (RCA 7754-2-RG [CD], 7754-4-RC [T]) surpasses this 1978 live performance. But as a souvenir of the century's most phenomenal technicians, this recording belongs in almost every collection.

The Isle of the Dead ; Symphonic Dances

Amsterdam Concertgebouw Orchestra, Ashkenazy. London 410124-2 [CD].

Best known for his once ubiquitous piano music, during his lifetime Sergei Rachmaninoff was equally celebrated as a composer of orchestral music and songs. The dark and richly atmospheric *Isle of the Dead*, one of the most accomplished of all his compositions, and the four *Symphonic Dances*, his last major work, have never been served more brilliantly than in this London recording by the Concertgebouw Orchestra, under Vladimir Ashkenazy. The *Symphonic Dances* were actually composed for and dedicated to Eugene Ormandy and the Philadelphia Orchestra—the last of their several recordings can still be found on Sony (SBK-48279 [CD], SBT-48279 [T])—but Ashkenazy's version is in every way more colorful, rhythmically vibrant, and intense. For those who are still persuaded that the heart of Rachmaninoff's output was the Prelude in C-sharp minor and the syrupy Vocalise, these wonderful performances of a pair of masterworks should come as an extremely pleasant surprise.

Piano Music

> Rachmaninoff, piano. RCA 7766-2-RG [CD],
> 7766-4-RG[T].

This collection of twenty-five shorter works and transcriptions offers convincing evidence that Sergei Rachmaninoff was one of the greatest pianists of whom we have an accurate record. For a composer of such overtly Romantic music, Rachmaninoff the pianist was strikingly modern in his outlook and technique. In these recordings, made between 1925 and 1942, the year before his death, he takes surprisingly few liberties: the approach is generally free of rubato and other rhythmic distortions, and any suggestion of nineteenth-century rhetoric is conspicuously absent. The playing itself ranges from the revelatory to the spellbinding. The famous C-sharp minor Prelude is done in the darkest possible tones, with a feeling of completely detached understatement; the technical legerdemain in encores like the *Midsummer Night's Dream* Scherzo will stand your hair on end.

An exciting and invaluable document.

Preludes (23) for Piano

> Ashkenazy, piano. London 414417-2 [CD].

Incredibly enough, given their wealth of invention, emotional and musical variety, and fabulous melodic richness (as with a Chopin melody, a Rachmaninoff tune can be maddeningly impossible to forget), only one completely successful recording of all twenty-three of these miniature miracles has been made, this London version by Vladimir Ashkenazy. The pianist is uncannily successful in drawing out the special character of each of the individual pieces, and, in general, the playing has a wonderful audacity, mixed with a lyrical tenderness and engaging wit. Though the Ashkenazy compact discs should be snapped up by anyone interested in stupendous piano playing or the music itself, Hyperion's set by Howard Shelley (CDA-66081/82 [CD]) offers a fascinating and distinctly *non*-Russian second opinion. Some of the interpretations might seem a bit odd—the famous C-sharp minor Prelude lumbers along like a brontosaurus with bad knees—but even the oddest of the pianist's ideas are strangely persuasive, as is Hyperion's ultrarealistic sound.

With Ashkenazy's formidable versions of the complete *Études-Tableaux* currently out of print, Shelley's incisive, technically fluent Hyperion interpretations (CDA-66091 [CD], KA-66091 [T]) are the most desirable now available.

Sonata in G minor for Cello and Piano

Ma, cello; Ax, piano. Sony SK-46486 [CD]; ST-46486 [CD].

After suffering his famous nervous breakdown at the turn of the century and undergoing hours of autosuggestion at the hands of an eminent Moscow physician named Dahl—"You will compose again . . . You will write a piano concerto . . . You will write with great facility . . . "—Sergei Rachmaninoff broke his creative logjam with the C minor Piano Concerto, which he gratefully dedicated to his therapist. The same resurgence of creativity that would lead to one of Rachmaninoff's best-loved works would also produce one of his finest, the Cello Sonata, which followed the Second Piano Concerto by only a few months.

There are those who suggest the Sonata may be Rachmaninoff's masterpiece, and it's easy to hear why. In this intimate yet turbulent work, the composer avoids most of the rhetorical pitfalls that can sabotage his other large-scale pieces; there is no hint of empty gesture or padding, and no suggestion that the music has been overcomposed. Instead, the Sonata's emotions—most notably its aching melancholy—are expressed with a disarming honesty and directness.

As in the brilliant, inexplicably deleted London recording by Lynn Harrell and Vladimir Ashkenazy, Yo-Yo Ma and Emanuel Ax are passionate, eloquent advocates of this great work: their interpretation has sweep, refinement, and character, while the playing has the subtle give-and-take of musicians who have been playing together for years. Prokofiev's handsome Cello Sonata is equally well served here.

Symphony No. 1 in D minor

Royal Philharmonic, Litton. Virgin CDC-59547 [CD].

Rachmaninnoff's First Symphony very nearly killed him. Its scandalously ill-prepared first performance on March 27, 1897 was such a disaster that the composer suffered a complete nervous breakdown; during his long and painful recovery, he contemplated suicide on more than one occasion. "There are serious illnesses and deadly blows from fate which change a man's character," he later wrote. "This was the effect of my own Symphony upon myself. When the indescribable torture of this performance had at last come to an end, I was a different man."

Certainly not the most cogent or well-behaved of Rachmaninoff's larger works, the First Symphony is a colorful and entertaining score—Monty Python fans will instantly recognize the fanfare that begins the final movement as one of their signature tunes—and a logical continuation of the Russian symphonic tradition established by Tchaikovsky and Borodin.

Andrew Lytton's recording with the Royal Philharmonic is one of the most impressive the talented young music director of the Dallas Symphony has made thus far. Instead of apologizing for the work's Romantic excesses, this expressive, rubato-laden interpretation revels in them at every opportunity. The playing has the old-fashioned sweep of another era, and the recorded sound ranks with Virgin's very best to date.

Symphony No. 2 in E minor

London Symphony, Previn. RCA 60791-2-RV [CD], 60791-4-RV [T].

There are two ways of viewing Rachmaninoff's E minor Symphony: as a late-Romantic dinosaur, completely out of step with its time, or as one of the lushest and loveliest symphonies ever written Both views are correct. Compared to what was going on in music at the time it was written (1907), Rachmaninoff's finest orchestral work was a complete anachronism, a throwback to an era when unabashed sentiment was not yet a cause for embarrassment. For all its old-fashioned sentimentality, however, the Symphony is also an utterly genuine expression of the essence of the Romantic spirit.

For instance, if there is a Romantic symphony with a lovelier slow movement than the famous Adagio of this one, it has yet to be discovered.

André Previn has so far recorded the Symphony three times, and although his finest version, a London Symphony recording for Angel made in the mid-1970s, has been withdrawn, his first outing for RCA has now been reissued to fill the gap. Aside from a few standard cuts, the performance has all the thrust, exuberance, and compassion of the later recording, and what it may lack by way of the final measure of confidence, it makes up for with youthful exuberance and panache. An equally fine interpretation of *The Rock*, one of the composer's most strangely underrated and underplayed scores, is the generous filler.

Symphony No. 3 in A minor

Concertgebouw Orchestra of Amsterdam, Ashkenazy. London 410231-2 [CD].

If an enthusiasm for this majestic anachronism might be inexcusable (for who, aside from the Hollywood film composers, was producing this kind of deep-pile, wall-to-wall lushness in 1936?), then I beg to be excused. The Third Symphony, like the Second, is so hopelessly likable that I've never been able to understand those who shun it. I'd even go so far as to suggest that people who aren't moved at least in some small way by the great subordinate theme of the first movement (the one that sounds so much like the folksong "Shenandoah") are probably capable of *anything*: drowning puppies, eating babies, attending Philip Glass concerts . . .

Vladimir Ashkenazy whips up the Concertgebouw Orchestra into a fine Russian frenzy from the opening bars and never apologizes or attempts to housebreak the Symphony into something it isn't. Instead, in the words of Dostoyevsky, he lets it all hang out —which it does magnificently.

Vespers for Contralto, Tenor, and Unaccompanied Mixed Chorus

Robert Shaw Festival Singers, Shaw. Telarc CD-80172 [CD].

Composed only two years before the October Revolution, Rachmaninoff's *Vespers* of 1915 was probably the last important sacred work written in Russia; soon, such impulses would be totally subsumed in a state-controlled "spirituality" that would lead to countless deathless masterworks in praise of Stalin, the Motherland, and the latest hydroelectric dam.

Although we don't usually think of Rachmaninoff as a composer of sacred music, the *Vespers* contains moments of extraordinary depth and beauty: the evocation of the spirit—and often, it seems, the letter—of the Eastern Orthodox worship is uncanny, especially of those dark, unmistakably Russian services that combine awe and terror in roughly equal doses.

Although not as idiomatic as several Soviet recordings that have appeared over the years (and where else in the world can one find those rumbling, impossibly resonant basses?) Robert Shaw's performance is the best Western recording this singular masterpiece has yet received. Predictably, Shaw's forces are technically flawless, and they also manage to inject an unusually high percentage of the ineffable "spook element" into the score. The recording is suitably rich and warm.

Raff, Joachim (1822–1882)

Symphony No. 5 in E, *Leonore*

> Berlin Radio Symphony, Bamert. Koch Schwann CD-311013 [CD].

There are few more sobering musical illustrations of the cruel vagaries of fame than the career of the German composer Joachim Raff. At the time of his death, Raff's reputation was comparable to that of Wagner and Brahms; by the turn of the century he had already begun to enter that stony oblivion from which he may never fully emerge.

Like the *Rustic Wedding Symphony* of his near-contemporary Karl Goldmark, a once hugely popular composer whose reputation suffered a similarly Carthagenian decline, Raff's *Leonore* Symphony is a splendid example of high-Romantic kitsch. Based on a penny-dreadful ballad about a doomed love affair (as if Romantic love affairs were anything *but*), the Symphony is full of good tunes and wonderfully cornball effects, such as the unconscionably long-winded march that represents the arrival and departure of the soldier-lover's regiment. Needless to say, the hero is killed, but eventually returns, only to be transformed into a skeleton during an *Erlkönig*-like night ride with his beloved. (I've been on many such dates myself.)

As fine as Bernard Herrmann's now-deleted recording with the London Philharmonic certainly was, the new version by Matthias Bamert and the Berlin Radio Symphony is finer still. For one thing, Bamert's tempos tend to be more lightly sprung; for another, his textures are far more transparent. The happy result is that *Leonore* seems a much less stodgy work. Fortunately, it still emerges as the endearingly silly schlock masterpiece that it is—all bombast, bathos, and blather.

All in all, party records don't come much better than this.

Ravel, Maurice (1875–1937)

Alborada del gracioso; *Boléro*; *Rapsodie espagnol*; *La Valse*

Montreal Symphony, Dutoit. London 410010-2 [CD].

For anyone interested in four of Ravel's most popular show pieces in state-of-the-art performances and recorded sound, it would be difficult to improve upon this, one of Charles Dutoit's most impressive recordings to date. The playing of the Montreal Symphony is quite sensational: *La Valse* and *Rapsodie espagnol*, in particular, are barn-burners; *Boléro* has rarely sounded so sensual *and* civilized, and the brief *Alborada del gracioso* is an unmitigated delight. Superlatives fail me on this one. Buy it, and enjoy.

*A*lborada del gracioso; *Pavane for a Dead Princess;* *Rapsodie espagnole; Valse nobles et sentimentales*

Chicago Symphony, Reiner. RCA 60179-2-RG [CD].

If you can listen to Reiner's recording of the *Prélude à la nuit* (the first movement of the *Rapsodie espagnole*) and *not* want to commit some indiscretion upon the person of your significant other, then it's time to make an appointment with your neighborhood endocrinologist. These are among the most erotic of all Ravel recordings, as well as some of the most nearly perfect: even the normally chaste *Pavane for a Dead Princess* seems full of the most *un*chaste suggestions, and the remainder of the *Rapsodie* and all of the *Valse nobles et sentimentales* ooze sensuality from every bar. Packaged with the most vivid and sophisticated version of Debussy's *Ibéria* ever recorded, this remains my desert island French album.

*C*oncertos (2) for Piano and Orchestra

De Larrocha, piano; St. Louis Symphony, Slatkin. RCA 09026-60985-2 [CD].

Ravel completed both of his piano concertos in 1931. They would prove to be his last major works, and the composer himself considered them his most important ones. (Ravel's pronouncements on his own music, like those of any composer, should be taken with a few pounds of salt, however. He once said, of *Boléro*, "I have written only one masterpiece. Alas, it contains no music.") The jazzy, elegant G Major Concerto, consciously written in the spirit of the Mozart concertos, and the dramatic Concerto for the Left Hand, produced for the Austrian pianist Paul Wittgenstein who had lost his right arm during the First World War, are certainly *among* Ravel's finest and most enduring efforts. Apart from being a brilliant solution to an impossible technical challenge, the Concerto for the Left Hand is an endlessly imaginative and resourceful work (who but Ravel would introduce the soaring principal theme on the contrabassoon?). In addition to its wit and gaiety, the G Major Concerto contains one of Ravel's most ethereal inspirations, a seamless love song that recalls a Bach arioso.

Beginning with Marguerite Long, who introduced the G Major Concerto in 1932, both works have enjoyed a singular run of first-rate female interpreters, including their greatest living exponent, Alicia de Larrocha. From her thunderous entrance in the Concerto for the Left Hand to those otherworldly musings in the G Major's slow movement, there is virtually nothing in either concerto that she doesn't do better than anyone else. Leonard Slatkin's accompaniments are both polished and stylish, as is RCA's recorded sound.

Daphnis et Chloé (complete ballet)

Montreal Symphony, Dutoit. London 400055-2 [CD].

Ordinarily, London's withdrawal of Pierre Monteux's classic recording of the work that is widely regarded as Ravel's masterpiece could be viewed as an act of insensitivity bordering on criminal negligence. It was Monteux who introduced this spellbinding work to the world in 1911, and it was his recording, from the early days of the stereo era, that no one ever seriously expected to be surpassed. Although for historical reasons alone, London never should have even considered withdrawing it from its catalog, Charles Dutoit's stupendous recording takes at least some of the sting out of London's unforgivable crassness.

In many ways, the initial installment in Dutoit's already fabulous Ravel series is still the most impressive. The dynamic range of both the performance and the recording is phenomenal, from the most delicate whispers in Ravel's diaphanous orchestration to the thunderous outbursts in the orgiastic final scene. Dutoit's command of the idiom is as complete and masterly as that of the greatest Ravel conductors of the past, and the playing of his impeccable orchestra cannot be praised too extravagantly. Clearly, this is already one of the milestones of the early digital era.

Introduction and Allegro for Harp, Flute, Clarinet, and String Quartet

> Allen, harp; Wilson, flute; Shifrin, clarinet; Tokyo Quartet.
> Angel CDC-47520 [CD].

Although this recording is essentially a showcase for the talented, lovely American harpist Nancy Allen, the highlight is the performance of Ravel's Introduction and Allegro, surely one of the composer's most finespun inspirations and one of the most beautiful of twentieth-century chamber works. Allen and flutist Ransom Wilson are especially effective in mining the Introduction's dreaminess and gaiety, with excellent support from the rest of the high-powered talent. The Ravel and Debussy miniatures that fill out the CD are also handsomely done.

I generally disapprove of using serious music for background noise, aural wallpaper, or any other nonmusical purpose (such as a sleeping pill or an aphrodisiac), but this is one of those recordings which, when slipped on after a particularly miserable day, will make almost anyone human again.

*P*avane *for a Dead Princess; Mother Goose; Le Tombeau de Couperin; Valses nobles et sentimentales*

> Montreal Symphony, Dutoit. London 410254-2 [CD].

With the two brilliant recordings listed above, these stunning interpretations of four more popular works by Ravel all but complete Charles Dutoit's triumphant Ravel cycle. Versions of the two piano concertos with Pascal Rogé (London 410230-2 [CD]) are the only modern performances worthy of comparison with Alicia de Larrocha's hair-raising recording with Leonard Slatkin and the St. Louis Symphony (see page 420).

As in the performances of *Daphnis et Chloé, Boléro, La Valse,* and the rest, Dutoit breathes an incredible freshness and vigor into these familiar works. For once, the famous *Pavane* does not come off as a cloying wad of sentimentality, and the other works are given performances as refined as they are exciting. Rarely have the closing bars of *Mother Goose* sounded so imposing, or the fabulously difficult music that begins *Le Tombeau de Couperin* been tossed off with such apparent ease. Again, London's engineers have provided Dutoit with demonstration-quality recorded sound, and again, the Montreal Symphony sounds like nothing less than one of the greatest orchestras in the world.

Piano Music (complete)

Crossley, piano. CRD 3383/84 [CD].

Like his witty, sensitive survey of the complete Poulenc piano music for CBS (see page 389), Paul Crossley's Ravel omnibus is one of the most engaging recordings of French piano music to have been released in years. While several individual performances might be preferred—the spellbinding *Gaspard de la nuit* from Ivo Pogorelich on Deutsche Grammophon (413363-2 [CD]) or Vlado Perlemuter's technically suspect but uniquely authoritative *Miroirs* for Nimbus (NIM-5005 [CD])—each of Crossley's polished, stylish, refreshingly self-effacing interpretations ranks with the very best available today.

As a colorist, Crossley has much in common with that master of impressionistic understatement, Walter Gieseking; as a technician, his performances recall the pure, unobtrusive beauty Alicia de Larrocha brought to her Ravel recordings. *Le Tombeau de Couperin* has an almost Mozart-like poise and elegance, and in the gnarlier moments of *Valses nobles* and *Miroirs* Crossley has plenty of ready technique at his disposal. CRD's recorded sound is as pristine and luminous as the performances themselves.

Song Cycles: *Chansons madécasses*; *Don Quichotte à Dulcinée*; *Cinq Mélodies populaires greques*; *Trois poèmes de Stéphane Mallarmé*; *Schéhérazade*

Norman, soprano; van Dam, bass; Gomez, soprano; Harper, soprano; Ensemble InterContemporain, BBC Symphony, Boulez. CBS MK-39023 [CD].

Except for *Schéhérazade*—which is still best served by Régine Crespin's meltingly sensual London recording (417813-2 [CD])— Ravel's small but distinguished output of song remains preposterously unknown. From the darkly erotic *Chansons madécasses* to the touching and fragile *Don Quichotte à Dulcinée*, his last completed work, these are among the most exquisite of Ravel's creations.

With four excellent soloists receiving consistently imaginative support from Pierre Boulez, this Sony CD provides an ideal introduction to Ravel's little-known music. Although Jessye Norman is especially persuasive in the cycle based on Madagascar folk poetry, each of the singers is in top form throughout, while the accompaniments are as meticulous as they are spontaneous.

String Quartet in F Major

See Debussy String Quartet, page 157.

Trio for Violin, Cello, and Piano

Borodin Trio. Chandos CD-8458 [CD].

Amid Ravel's scant output of chamber music, the Trio for Violin, Cello, and Piano is second in importance only to the great String Quartet. In many ways, the Trio is the more complex and interesting work, although its built-in austerity and restraint can make it far more elusive.

The Borodin Trio bring an unaccustomed passion to the music that ultimately serves it very well: this is far and away the most intensely emotional of all their recordings; even those who might find it slightly overheated won't fail to respond to the undeniable eloquence. Although versions of the Ravel sonatas might have been far more welcome as the filler, the performances of Debussy's Cello and Violin Sonatas are superb, as is the warm and focused recorded sound.

Among available recordings of the Ravel Violin Sonata, Dmitri Sitkovetsky and his mother Bella Davidovich offer a brilliant performance as part of an extremely attractive Ravel recital on Orfeo (C-108841-A [CD], M-108841-A [T]), which also offers intelligent, virtuoso accounts of the *Berceuse sur le nom de Fauré*, the *Sonate posthume* from 1897, and the popular *Tzigane*. Two members of the Borodin Trio offer a wonderfully introspective account of the late Sonata for Violin and Cello on an intriguing Chandos recording (CHAN-8358 [CD], ABTD-1121 [T]) together with other works by Honegger, Martinů, and Jean Rivier for that unusual combination of instruments.

Respighi, Ottorino (1879–1936)

Ancient Airs and Dances for Lute (3 sets); *The Birds*

Australian Chamber Orchestra, Gee. Omega OCD-1007
[CD].

Although the Sydney and Melbourne Symphonies—to name the two ensembles that are probably best known "Up Over"—have each made fine recordings, this may be the *finest* orchestral recording to have come out of Australia. If the Australian Chamber Orchestra's recordings of Schubert symphonies with Sir Charles Mackerras and an album of Strauss and Stravinsky with Christopher Lyndon Gee suggested they were a top-notch outfit, then this version of four popular Respighi works proves they are one of the great chamber orchestras of the world.

The competition in both *The Birds* and the popular *Ancient Airs and Dances* suites is ferocious. Sir Neville Marriner's recordings with the Academy of St. Martin-in-the-Fields and the Los Angeles Chamber Orchestra, to say nothing of Antal Dorati's classic version with the Philharmonia Hungarica, have set a standard in the *Ancient Airs* that many of us thought would never be approached. Similarly, wonderful recordings of *The Birds* have appeared and vanished, including a surprisingly nubile interpretation from Eugene Ormandy that CBS really can't afford *not* to reissue.

So along comes this recording by Gee and his plucky Aussies that blithely mops up the floor with all of them. Not only are the performances extremely sophisticated, especially in the subtly shifting colors of the *Ancient Airs*, they also manage to convey a sense of discovery, wonderment, and enthusiasm that few recordings by professional musicians ever do. The recorded sound, like the playing itself, is absolutely impeccable, so much so that further Omega releases by the ACO are awaited with the keenest interest.

Nearly as skillful as the *Ancient Airs and Dances* are Respighi's technicolor orchestrations of the music of the giant of the German Baroque, some of which are now available on a stunning Delos CD called "Symphonic Bach" (DE-3098). The arrangements are generally more idiomatic and tasteful than the more famous transcriptions by Leopold Stokowski, and the performances by

Gerard Schwarz and the Seattle Symphony are everything a Baroque Romantic could hope for, with some especially thrilling contributions from the SSO brass.

La Boutique fantasque

Toronto Symphony, A. Davis. Sony MDK-46508 [CD].

Like those other classic pastiche ballets, Stravinsky's *Pulcinella* and Vincenzo Tommasini's adaptation of some Scarlatti sonatas called *The Good-Humored Ladies*, Respighi's *La Boutique fantasque* is a startlingly successful fusion of two distinct styles and centuries. And nowhere is the orchestral genius of Ottorino Respighi more clearly evident than in this fizzing, luxurious concoction arranged from the melodies of Rossini.

Under Andrew Davis's inspired direction, the Toronto Symphony dance their way through this sparkling music as though they were one of the great orchestras of the world. No detail of the subtle, imaginative orchestral tissue escapes their attention, and the ballet's inner life emerges in a rush of joyous energy. The recorded sound is as sumptuous as the orchestration. The equally attractive fillers (Bizet's *Jeux d'enfants* and *L'Arlésienne* Suite No. 2) and Sony's medium price make this extremely difficult to turn down.

Three other, far less familiar, pastiche ballets by Respighi have surfaced on an attractive CD from Marco Polo (8.226646 [CD]), which seems intent on recording the man's entire output. Like the *Ancient Airs*, *Sèvres de la vielle France* draws its inspiration from seventeenth- and eighteenth-century models, and *Le astuzie di Colombina* makes use of popular Venetian melodies. Best of all, though, is *La Pentola magica*, which rifles through some fairly unfamiliar (albeit undeniably charming) Russian works by Gretchaninov, Arensky, Anton Rubinstein, and Vladimir Rebikov. The Czecho-Slovak Radio Symphony plays with skill and obvious relish, and Marco Polo's engineers respond with warm—if somewhat distant—recorded sound.

The Fountains of Rome; The Pines of Rome; Roman Festivals

Philadelphia Orchestra, Muti. Angel CDC-47316 [CD].

How unfortunate it is that this tremendously gifted composer had virtually no musical conscience or taste. (I have always thought it no accident that the word *pig* can actually be found within his name.) A wizard of the modern orchestra, and Italy's only significant nonoperatic composer of the prewar era, Ottorino Respighi is best remembered for this triptych of tone poems celebrating the sights and sounds of his beloved Rome. Respighi's command of orchestration rivaled that of any composer who has ever lived, which is largely why these three pieces of unadulterated trash rank with the most popular orchestral showpieces of the twentieth century. (And like everyone else who has ever fallen under their vulgar spell, I love all three to distraction.)

Though nothing will ever make me give up my cherished RCA recording of the *Fountains* and *Pines* by Fritz Reiner and the Chicago Symphony (RCA 09026-61401-2 [CD], 09026-610401-4[T]), the performances contained on Riccardo Muti's Angel recording are very much in that same rarefied league. In addition, Muti gives us a spine-tingling run-through of the grisly *Roman Festivals*, my own nomination as the greatest single piece of musical schlock produced by anyone in the last hundred years. (The only other possible contender, Richard Addinsell's *Warsaw Concerto*, was written for a movie and only accidentally went on to a macabre life of its own.) As in so many of their recent recordings, the playing of the Philadelphia Orchestra really must be heard to be believed. The last vestiges of Eugene Ormandy's "Philadelphia Sound" were all but eradicated by his dynamic successor. And while Muti may not be the most consistently profound or interesting conductor before the public today, he certainly deserves enormous credit for having revitalized a great American orchestra.

Metamorphosen modi XII; *Belkis, Queen of Sheba* (suite)

Philharmonia Orchestra, Simon. Chandos CHAN-8405 [CD].

One of the marks of true genius is its infinite capacity to renew, rejuvenate, and surpass itself. *Metamorphosen* is an academic, agreeably turgid series of variations on a medieval tune, but the music from *Belkis, Queen of Sheba* is something very special, even for Respighi.

Compared to *Belkis, Roman Festivals* is the *St. Matthew Passion*. The suite from this 1934 biblical ballet (and what one wouldn't give to hear the whole thing!) is so smarmy, so brazenly crude, so ineluctably vile, that *schlock* is a poor and trifling word to describe it. At this stratospheric level, trash ceases to be mere trash, and *Belkis* is a kind of final apotheosis of Respighian vulgarity. It's hardly surprising that the composer died only two years later. What was left to be done?

It goes without saying that I loved every millisecond of it, especially in Geoffrey Simon's resolutely wanton interpretation. The Philharmonia Orchestra comports itself like a band of shameless harlots, and the Chandos engineers capture every grunt and groan to perfection.

Sinfonia drammatica

BBC Philharmonic, Downes. Chandos CHAN-9213 [CD].

Whatever else might be said about Respighi's *Sinfonia drammatica*: It's definitely *not* the sort of thing you want to meet some night in a dark alley. Completed shortly before the outbreak of the First World War and only a couple of years before *Fountains of Rome* would make him famous, Respighi's only symphony is, on the surface, a long, noisy, irresponsible pastiche of Franck, Rimsky-Korsakov, and Richard Strauss, in which one overblown climax follows another until the exhausted composer finally throws in the towel with what can only be described as a lumbering, quasi-Biblical tango! Yet for all its goofiness and pomposity, the *Sinfonia drammatica* is the work of a man with something important to say and who is desperately trying to find a way of saying it. A dark, almost endearing urgency is in the best pages of the score, together with the composer's soon-to-be-legendary genius for manipulating great waves of orchestral sound.

The work's third commercial recording has indeed proven to be a charm, with the BBC Philharmonic under Sir Edward Downes playing as though their lives depended on it. Unlike its rival performance on Marco Polo, there is a passionate intelligence at work here, which not only gives the *Dramatic Symphony* more shape and substance than it has ever had before, but infuses it with a genuine seriousness of purpose and something approaching real respectability. The recording, like the performance, is in the demonstration class.

Il Tramonto (cantata, after Shelley); *Three Botticelli Pictures*; *The Birds*; *Adagio con variazioni* for Cello and Orchestra

Finnie, mezzo-soprano; Wallfisch, cello; Bounemouth Sinfonietta, Vásáry. Chandos CHAN-8913 [CD], ABTD-1517 [T].

Even the most gleeful Respighi-basher (and I blush to confess, I *have* been one in my time) cannot fail to be moved by *Il Tramonto* (The Sunset), a hauntingly beautiful setting of Shelley's poem, which ranks with the loveliest moments in Puccini. By that same token, the *Three Botticelli Pictures* find Respighi at his most sensitive and refined, especially in the melting second movement with its sinuous oboe solo.

Linda Finnie gives one of the finest of all her recorded performances in *Il Tramonto*, with her large, feminine, richly expressive instrument easily eclipsing all the current competition. Cellist Raphael Wallfisch is similarly convincing in the youthful *Adagio con variazioni*, while Tamas Vásáry proves an ideal exponent of this evocative music, missing none of its subtle color or dramatic point. More recordings like this one and we won't have Respighi to kick around any more.

Rheinberger, Joseph

(1839–1901)

The Star of Bethlehem (Christmas cantata) for Soprano, Baritone, Chorus, and Orchestra

Streich, soprano; Fischer-Dieskau, baritone; Bavarian Radio Chorus, Graunke Symphony Orchestra, Heger. Carus 83.111 [CD].

The first composer of note to have emerged from the Duchy of Liechtenstein, Joseph Rheinberger is remembered today (if he is remembered at all) as a composer of some of the most fastidious and handsomely made organ music of the nineteenth century. The two concertos and twenty sonatas keep flitting in and out of the recording catalogs, and still show up on concerts and recitals from time to time. What Rheinberger *should* be remembered for is *Der Stern von Bethlehem*, a touchingly innocent, sweet-spirited work that has somehow managed to escape becoming the Christmas classic it assuredly deserves to be.

This fetching recording, which was available for a brief time in the 1960s from Angel, is a charmer from beginning to end. Without so much as a wink of condescension, Robert Heger and his dedicated forces make their way through this guileless little masterwork as though it were entitled to the same care and devotion usually lavished on the *Christmas Oratorio*. The result is one of the most captivating sleepers in recent memory.

Rimsky-Korsakov, Nikolai (1844–1908)

Capriccio espagnol

New York Philharmonic, Bernstein. CBS MYK-36728
[CD], MYT-36728 [T].

CBS won't exactly make bargain hunters ecstatic with this skimpy release, which combines Rimsky's Spanish travelogue with Tchaikovsky's *Capriccio italien*. Even in the long-vanished LP days that kind of "radical cheap" packaging would have been ballsy; given today's CD and tape prices, it took—as my grandmother used to say—"some *real* stones."

On the other hand, the performances are vintage early Bernstein and are thus, in terms of sheer animal excitement, extremely difficult to surpass. *Capriccio espagnol*, which was the original filler for the conductor's *Pictures at an Exhibition*, is as seductive and vibrant as ever; the solo display—most notably from the orchestra's oboist, Harold Gomberg—matches anything from the rival Philadelphia Orchestra's heyday, and the closing bars flash by in a blinding swatch of local color.

Scheherazade

Chicago Symphony, Reiner. RCA 09026-60875-2 [CD], 09026-60875-4[T].

Royal Philharmonic, Beecham. Angel CDC-47717 [CD].

It's difficult to think of anyone who better deserves the title of History's Greatest Minor Composer. Camille Saint-Saëns actually predicted that that was how posterity would remember *him*, but he was forgetting about the work of this Russian near-giant. An orchestrator and teacher of genius (his brilliant edition saved his friend Mussorgsky's *Boris Godunov* from oblivion, and his best-known pupil, of course, was Igor Stravinsky), Rimsky-Korsakov never quite grasped the greatness that always seemed to be just within reach. For moments, even for entire acts of dazzling operas like *Le Coq d'or*, *Mlada*, or *The Snow Maiden*, you can hear him on the verge of actually *doing* it, and then, inevitably, the music draws back at the very last.

By that same token, *Scheherazade*, one of history's most colorful and beautifully made orchestral scores, is also, in a sense, one of its most heartbreaking. It is a work that never quite adds up to much more than the sum of its fabulous parts: an elegant, vivid, brilliant, clever, colorful piece, but never a great one.

Among the many memorable recordings *Scheherazade* has had over the years, none has ever made it seem closer to being a great piece than the performance recorded in the late 1950s by Fritz Reiner and the Chicago Symphony. In spite of formidable competition from Sir Thomas Beecham and the Royal Philharmonic, whose legendary interpretation recorded at about the same time remains the last word in individuality, charm, and staggeringly inventive solo display, Reiner's combination of near-perfect execution, finesse, and unadulterated sex makes this—by a whisker— *the* performance of *Scheherazade* to own. The original recorded sound has been dramatically improved in the compact disc, which, as a bonus, includes that most electrifying of all recordings of Debussy's *La Mer*.

Suites from the Operas (*Christmas Eve*; *Le Coq d'or*; *Legend of the Invisible City of Kitezh*; *May Night* (overture); *Mlada*; *The Snow Maiden*; *Tsar Saltan*)

Scottish National Orchestra, Järvi. Chandos CHAN-8327/ 29 [CD].

As Dmitri Shostakovich may or may not have pointed out in *Testimony* (the authorship of the controversial memoirs is still in question), for more than a decade Rimsky-Korsakov suffered from a debilitating emotional disease called Piotr Ilyich Tchaikovsky. "Tchaikovsky kept Korsakov from composing, interfered simply by existing," Shostakovich (or someone) observed. "For ten years, Rimsky-Korsakov couldn't write an opera and after Tchaikovsky's death he wrote eleven operas in fifteen years. And it's interesting to note that this flood began with *Christmas Eve*. As soon as Tchaikovsky died, Korsakov took a theme already used by Tchaikovsky and rewrote it his way."

Whoever proposed the theory, it does have a dreary and peculiarly Russian ring of truth; for with the passing of his arch-antagonist, Rimsky-Korsakov did enter the most fruitful period of his creative life, producing the bulk of the music on which his reputation, at least in Russia, continues to rest.

Why his operas have never gained a significant toehold in the West remains a baffling mystery. Some, like *Le Coq d'or*, are as masterly as any Slavic opera short of Smetana's *Bartered Bride* and Mussorgsky's *Boris Godunov*, and many of them—as this gorgeous series of recordings from Chandos will show—contain some of his most distinctive and original music, from the eerie mystery of the *Invisible City of Kitezh* to the delightful *Christmas Eve*, whose stirring Polonaise is alone worth the price of admission.

This is possibly the best, and certainly one of the most valuable, of the many recordings the rather overexposed Neeme Järvi has made. Honed to a fine edge, the Scottish National Orchestra cuts through the formidable difficulties of this music with ease, and the conductor has a genuine knack for revealing both its obvious and hidden treasures. Those with a sweet tooth for *Scheherazade* will have a fine time gorging themselves on these equally tasty goodies; the more shameless gluttons will also want Järvi's more workmanlike, yet utterly worthy, versions of *Antar* and the other two symphonies, *Capriccio espagnol*, and the *Russian Easter Overture*, all shoehorned onto a pair of Deutsche Grammophon compact discs (423604-2).

Rodrigo, Joaquin (1901–)

Concierto de Aranjuez for Guitar and Orchestra

Williams, guitar; English Chamber Orchestra, Barenboim. CBS MK-33208 [CD].

Angel Romero, guitar; London Symphony, Previn. Angel CDC-47693 [CD].

Like the dippy Pachelbel *Kanon*, Joaquin Rodrigo's *Concierto de Aranjuez* has become a big classical hit in the last dozen years, and its popularity is richly deserved. Written with the great Andrés Segovia in mind, Rodrigo's *Concierto* is easily the finest such work ever written for the instrument: a work which not only exploits virtually all of the rather limited expressive possibilities of the guitar, but also provides us with one of the most haunting of all musical evocations of the sights and sounds of Spain.

To date, John Williams has recorded the *Concierto* no fewer than four times, and it is his version with Daniel Barenboim and the English Chamber Orchestra that is still the most completely satisfying recording the piece has ever received. Technically, Williams is without equal among living guitarists, and here, as in all his recordings, he tosses off the *Concierto*'s formidable difficulties as though they didn't even exist. Yet unlike his other versions, this performance has a freshness and spontaneity that no other recording can begin to match. Thanks, no doubt, to Daniel Barenboim's rich and flexible accompaniment, Williams is allowed to phrase and emote with a freedom he has rarely shown on records before or since.

On the Angel CD, Angel Romero's playing is nearly as brilliant and refreshing as Williams's, and instead of the Villa-Lobos Guitar Concerto that comes with the Williams recording, this one offers the more conventional (and desirable) coupling of Rodrigo's equally enchanting *Fantasia para un gentilhombre*.

Concierto madrigal for Two Guitars and Orchestra; *Concierto Andaluz* for Four Guitars and Orchestra

The Romeros, guitars; Academy of St. Martin-in-the-Fields, Marriner. Philips 400024-2 [CD].

It has been suggested that with the *Concierto de Aranjuez* of 1939, Rodrigo stumbled upon a formula so successful that he was content to build a career out of rewriting the piece indefinitely. Even if this were perfectly true (which it isn't, quite), who could possibly care? Only the naive or the very young tend to prefer the idea of originality to the reality of cleverness, since the latter is a precious, hard-won skill and the former, for all practical purposes, simply doesn't exist. Besides, if an idea is a good one and the market will bear it, by all means, use it again. Bach, Handel, Rossini, Stravinsky, and numberless other lesser figures never felt any qualms about recycling their own, as well as other composer's, ideas; and the composer of *Star Wars* and other hugely successful film scores has grown wealthy and famous by scrupulously avoiding *any* musical idea that might even remotely be called his own. (The list of composers and specific works that have "inspired" John Williams is a long and eclectic one and would make a fascinating little book; at very least, it might be turned into a documented monograph that the powers that be at ASCAP might be interested to read.)

If they *are* warmed-over versions of *Concierto de Aranjuez*, then *Concierto madrigal* and *Concierto Andaluz* prove what every mother knows, to wit, that leftovers can often be every bit as delicious—if not more so—than the original meal. These gracefully melodious and instantly assimilable works are thoroughgoing delights, especially in performances such as these. The gifted, extrovert Romeros play the concertos as though they had been written specifically for them—which as a matter of fact, they were.

Sir Neville Marriner's accompaniments and Philips's recorded sound are worthy of both the soloists and the music itself.

Rorem, Ned (1923–)

Songs

Rees, soprano; Rorem, piano. Premier PRCD-1035 [CD].

Song Cycles: *Nantucket Songs*; *Some Trees*; *Women's Voices*

Curtin, soprano; Wolff, contralto; Gramm, baritone; Rorem, piano. CRI CD-657 [CD].

It is both astonishing and shameful that the most accomplished American composer of art song should be currently represented in the catalog by only two recorded collections. As these superb anthologies demonstrate, however, Ned Rorem's songs are imaginative, memorable, and uniquely sensitive to their texts, perhaps more so than those of any American composer. Until some enlightened and enterprising recording company begins a systematic examination of Rorem's amazingly rich and varied output, these collections will have to hint at what treasures lie awaiting discovery. On a more positive note, the performances with the composer, himself a skilled and seductive pianist, are definitive.

Fortunately, Vox has recently reissued Maurice Abravanel's spirited recording with his Utah Symphony (CDX-5092 [CD]) of Rorem's bracing Third Symphony, one of the most entertaining (and predictably tuneful) yet written by an American. Although packaged with works by Virgil Thomson, Howard Hanson, William Schumann, and Edward MacDowell, it is Rorem's irresistibly fresh and rambunctious score that steals the show.

Rossini, Gioacchino

(1792–1868)

Arias

> Anderson, soprano; Teatro Communale de Bologna
> Orchestra and Chorus, Gatti. London 436377-2 [CD].
>
> Horne, mezzo-soprano; L'Orchestra de la Suisse Romande,
> Lewis. London 421306-2 [CD].
>
> Bartoli, mezzo-soprano. London 436075-2 [CD]; 425430-2
> [CD].
>
> Ramey, bass; Welsh National Opera Orchestra and Chorus,
> Ferro. Teldec 9031-73242-2 [CD].

Even more than those of Bellini or Donizetti, the arias of Gioacchino Rossini define the true parameters of bel canto singing, for they include some of the most limpidly beautiful (and murderously difficult) vocal passages ever written: passages that in requiring an entirely new system of breath distribution helped lay the foundations for modern vocal technique.

June Anderson's London recital only enhances her reputation as Dame Joan Sutherland's logical successor as the reigning queen of bel canto. Her technique rivals Sutherland's, but she is a far more convincing actress. In these dazzling interpretations, both the notes *and* the characters leap off the page.

In terms of sheer vocal opulence, Marilyn Horne's famous London recital, now available on the medium-priced Gala series, remains in a class by itself. As an extended and breathtaking essay in technical virtuosity, singing of this caliber is rivaled only by Tetrazzini, McCormack, and a handful of the greatest singers of the past.

Both of Cecilia Bartoli's Rossini anthologies have gotten some fairly ecstatic press and for very good reason. In addition to an extraordinary command of the idiom, the projection of character is comparable to the sorts of things that Maria Callas used to do. This is a big, important voice used with tremendous skill and intelligence, one that will no doubt set the limits of the art for years to come.

Finally, Samuel Ramey's Teldec recital confirms his status as the foremost basso cantante of his generation, a worthy successor to Norman Treigle, Cesare Siepi, and Ezio Pinza. As with the recordings of his greatest predecessors, it's difficult not to be amazed that such an immense and thunderously powerful instrument can be used with such delicate agility. For some reason, there has always seemed to be room for only one or two star basses per generation; more than any of his recordings so far, this one demonstrates why Ramey, for this generation, is it.

The Barber of Seville

Callas, Alva, Gobbi, Philharmonia Orchestra and Chorus, Galliera. Angel CDCB-47634 [CD].

Despite some formidable competition from the beautifully sung and brilliantly recorded Philips recording led with high and obvious zest by Sir Neville Marriner (411058-2 [CD]), this imperishable Angel release, for all its flaws, remains the most enchanting and infectious recorded performance of the world's most popular opera buffa. The supporting cast is consistently excellent, especially the irreplaceable Tito Gobbi and the exceptionally suave Almaviva of Luigi Alva, and the star of the show, Maria Callas, in one of her rare comic roles proves that she was every bit as successful a comedienne as she was a tragic heroine. Listen, especially, to the way she teases the phrases in "Una voce poco fa," and you'll begin to understand why we Callas cuckoos immediately begin to salivate at the mere mention of the woman's name. Although niggling cuts have been made throughout the performance and the recorded sound is not up to today's standards, there is a sparkling, good-natured sense of fun in this famous interpretation that will probably never be captured in a recording studio again.

La Cenerentola

> Baltsa, Araiza, Alaimo, Raimondi, Ambrosian Opera
> Chorus, Academy of St. Martin-in-the-Fields, Marriner.
> Philips 420468-2 [CD].

Rossini's daffy retelling of the Cinderella story is proof positive that there was always more to the composer than a handful of overtures and *The Barber of Seville*. Until the bel canto revival of the 1950s and '60s, it certainly might have seemed that those were his only works, for the simple reason that the florid vocal writing in operas like *Cinderella* is so daunting that most singers simply opted for the better part of valor. To compound the problem, the title role, like that of Isabella in *L'Italiana in Algeri*, is written for a coloratura contralto, which is about as common these days as articulate vice presidents or two-headed sheep. (For that matter, *true* contraltos of any kind are an all but extinct species. If you don't believe it, dig out any of Ernestine Schumann-Heink's old recordings and try to find even the vaguest approximation of that sort of instrument today.)

The only solution in such a vocally benighted age as ours is a mezzo with the range and agility of an Agnes Baltsa. Though she is not entirely believable as Rossini's helpless waif—the size and power of the voice place it roughly in the dreadnought class—Baltsa's energy and accuracy more than save the day. With stylish contributions from Francisco Araiza and Ruggero Raimondi, and the bubbly conducting of Sir Neville Marriner, *La Cenerentola* emerges as the uproarious masterpiece many are only now discovering it to be.

In *L'Italiana in Algeri*, an even funnier opera (not witty, not amusing, but bust-a-gut-laughing *funny*), Baltsa and Raimondi are even more impressive, while Claudio Abbado's conducting, like Marriner's, is an essay in the art of comic timing. The sense of presence in this Deutsche Grammophon recording (427331-2 [CD]) is exceptional, as is the playing of the Vienna Philharmonic.

Side-splittingly funny, too, is Abbado's recording (Deutsche Grammophon 415498-2 [CD]) of the crackbrained *Il vaggio a Reims*, which one might assume is about a journey to Rheims but isn't, since it never takes place. Like an extended Italian version of the gala sequences that traditionally interrupt the second act of Strauss's *Die Fledermaus* at the Vienna Staatsoper's New Year's Eve productions, the opera is little more than an excuse for ten-star performers to strut their stuff. Abbado's cast does that and more, with some elegant support from the Chamber Orchestra of Europe.

Overtures

Academy of St. Martin-in-the-Fields, Marriner. Philips
434016-2 [CD] (complete).

Orpheus Chamber Orchestra. Deutsche Grammophon
415363-2 [CD].

London Symphony, Abbado. Deutsche Grammaphon
419893-2 [CD].

Philharmonia Orchestra, Giulini. Angel CDM-69042 [CD].

London Classical Players, Norrington. Angel CDC-54091
[CD], 4DS-54091 [T].

Chicago Symphony, Reiner. RCA 60387-2-RG [CD],
60387-4-RG [T].

For anyone seriously interested in many of the most famous and scintillating orchestral miniatures ever written, Sir Neville Marriner's four-CD set from Philips containing all the surviving Rossini overtures is an excellent investment. The performances of the more familiar pieces are among the best on the market today, and even the least interesting of the unfamiliar works are more than worth a hearing. Besides, you never know when you might receive a request for the overture to *Demetrio e Polibio*, and wouldn't it be nice to be prepared? In any event, each of the performances is bursting with vitality—the gallop from *William Tell* rushes by like the wind—and an unmistakably Rossinian sense of humor.

Humor and vitality also characterize the performances by the Orpheus Chamber Orchestra. In what may still be their finest recording to date (and given their list of outstanding releases, that's saying a very great deal), they demonstrate fairly conclusively that a conductor's baton is the cheapest instrument there is.

Among recordings made by Italian conductors, those by Claudio Abbado and Carlo Maria Giulini are the most appealing. Aside from being superbly idiomatic, each brings out the lovely singing quality of the music and more than a little of its whiplash excitement. For instance, the Giulini *William Tell* goes out in such a spectacular cloud of dust that a colleague of mine—after a stunned pause of several seconds—announced on the air: "And just think, he was originally going to call it *Pavane for a Dead Princess*."

Roger Norrington and his plucky London Classical Players offer a series of hair-trigger performances on period instruments that manage to sound neither pedantic nor stodgy. The conductor's tempos have an exhilarating bite and lift, the orchestral fabric a wonderfully piquant edge.

Finally, as performances or recordings, no versions of these popular works have ever superseded the scintillating recordings that Fritz Reiner and the Chicago Symphony made in 1958. The brass play with an awesome grandeur and solidity, the strings are rich yet nimble, and the woodwinds have all the personality of characters straight out of commedia dell'arte. This is a gifted conductor and the great American orchestra of its time captured at the height of their powers in phenomenally remastered recorded sound.

*S*emiramide

> Sutherland, Horne, Serge, Rouleau, Malas, Ambrosian
> Singers, London Symphony, Bonynge. London 425481-2
> [CD].

In spite of Gustave Kobbé's grim prognosis in his celebrated *Complete Opera Book* that "*Semiramide* seems to have had its day," this rather preposterous tale of love, sacrifice, murder, betrayal, and redemption—clearly another of those "something for everyone" evenings—may actually be the most musically rewarding of all Rossini's more obviously serious operas. It certainly contains some of his most rewarding and technically challenging duets, the best of which requires a soprano and mezzo of extraordinary technical accomplishment.

Recorded in 1966 when both singers were reaching the peak of their forms, the London *Semiramide* is probably the most brilliant of the many Sutherland-Horne collaborations. Dame Joan is both phenomenally agile and endearingly human as the murderous Queen of Babylon, and Marilyn Horne in the trouser role of Prince Arsace gives one of her most commanding performances in or out of the recording studio. Richard Bonynge manages to keep things moving nicely while remaining sensitive to the score's many felicitous details, and London's recorded sound remains ideally warm, focused, and brilliantly detailed.

Gustave, *says you.*

Sonatas (6) for Strings

> Orchestra of the Age of Enlightenment (members).
> Hyperion CDA-66595 [CD].

The question of how one of the laziest composers in history managed to accomplish so much in such little time—after the premiere of *William Tell*, he retired to a life of unprecedented indolence at the age of thirty-seven—is answered in part by these six miraculous little works: he got a *very* early start. Composed when Rossini was only twelve, the String Sonatas, like the equally precocious Wind Quartets, reveal a talent that was almost as highly evolved as Mozart's was at a comparable age.

If you have a youthful musical underachiever in your household, these sparkling performances on period instruments by members of the Orchestra of the Age of Enlightenment (whose performances are as refreshingly unassuming as their name is embarrassingly pretentious) might just do the trick: the *wunderkind* will either be spurred on to greater efforts by the young Rossini's example or will be discouraged completely. Either way, you can't lose.

Stabat Mater

> Field, Jones, Davies, Earle, London Symphony Chorus, City of London Sinfonia, Hickox. Chandos CHAN-8780 [CD], ABTD-1416 [T].

From the time he finished *William Tell* in 1829 until his death in 1868—like another celebrated musical triskaidekaphobe, Arnold Schoenberg, the deeply superstitious Italian also died on the thirteenth of a month—Rossini wrote little other than a pair of enchanting sacred works and those delectable miniatures he published in the thirteen volumes of *Péchés de vieillesse* (Sins of Old Age).

With the *Petite messe solenelle* of 1863, which at present, alas, has no recorded performance that can be recommended with any conviction, Rossini's setting of the *Stabat Mater* is one of the most thoroughly disarming sacred works ever written. Like the sacred music of Haydn and Poulenc, it doesn't have a sanctimonious bone in its lusty, yea-saying body: everything is high spirits and joyful noise, with one irrepressible Rossini tune after another.

Even more than the late István Kertész in his out-of-print London recording, Richard Hickox understands the sublime goofiness of the piece, allowing it to go its merry way with little or no editorial comment, while still demanding the most alert and enthusiastic singing and playing. The result will warm the hearts of believers and make most heathens think twice.

*W*illiam Tell

Pavarotti, Freni, Milnes, Ghiaurov, Ambrosian Opera Chorus, National Philharmonic, Chailly. London 417154-2 [CD].

Shortly after its triumphant first production at the Paris Opera in 1829, *William Tell* began to fall victim to the editor's blue pencil. Within the year, performances were being cut ever more drastically. There is a famous story that has one of the composer's ardent admirers telling him, "I heard Act Two of *William Tell* at the opera last night." "What?" Rossini is alleged to have replied. "The whole of it?"

The whole of this uneven work that Rossini consciously intended to be his masterpiece can last upwards of five hours in the theater. It is far more easily—and profitably—digested in the comfort of one's living room, especially in as compelling a production as this one. Opting for Italian instead of the original French, Riccardo Chailly leads a fiery, deeply committed, handsomely sung performance that makes one overlook the opera's excessive length. (When consumed an act at a time, it doesn't seem excessive at all.)

All of the principals are excellent, particularly Sherrill Milnes in the title role, and London's top-of-the-line 1978 recorded sound remains breathtaking.

Roussel, Albert (1869–1937)

Bacchus et Ariane (complete ballet); *Le Festin de l'araignée* (suite)

French National Orchestra, Prêtre. EMI CDM-64690 [CD].

Among the major composers—and a major twentieth-century composer is what this punctilious Frenchman is now, belatedly, thought to be—Albert Roussel is unique. After preparing himself for a naval career, he did not begin to study music seriously until he was in his mid-twenties, at roughly the same age a Polish seafaring man who would become the novelist Joseph Conrad set himself the task of learning English. In spite of what should have been an impossibly late start for a life in music, Roussel slowly evolved into one of the most arresting composers of his generation, a figure only slightly less potent and individual than his near-contemporaries Debussy and Ravel.

As an introduction to Roussel's stubbornly original idiom, this recording of his two most popular ballets is ideal. The sly, poetic *Festin de l'araignée* (The Spider's Feast) is the better known work, but it is *Bacchus et Ariane* that can be mentioned in the same breath with Ravel's *Daphnis et Chloé* and Debussy's *Jeux* as one of the most important of modern French ballets.

Georges Prêtre's sumptuous, immaculately recorded versions of both scores are the finest that have ever been available: The performance of *Le Festin* is the most authoritative since the composer's own recording from the early 1930s, and no one has ever generated quite so much explicit sexual tension in the febrile orgy that concludes *Bacchus et Ariane*, transforming it into a prurient grunt-and-groan-a-thon that rivals the final scene of *Daphnis*.

*P*admâvatí (opera-ballet in two acts)

Horne, Gedda, van Dam, Chorus and Orchestra of the
Capitole de Toulouse, Plasson. EMI CDCB-47891 [CD].

Begun during the First World War and finished after ill health
forced his retirement from the navy, the opera-ballet *Padmâvatí* is
the most ambitious and one of the most thoroughly original of all
Roussel's works. Inspired by a four-month cruise to India and the
Orient the composer had taken in 1909, *Padmâvatí* is an exotic,
resplendent score that contains some of Roussel's most inspired
music. Had the libretto proven more of a springboard than a
stumbling block, it might hold the stage more effectively than it
does. As it stands, the work is very nearly the finest and most unusual unknown French opera ever written.

Padmâvatí's dramatic limitations are scarely noticeable in this
stunning EMI recording. Marilyn Horne gives a sumptuous, beautifully detailed performance as the Hindu queen, and although
Nicolai Gedda is clearly past his best, he sings with his customary
intelligence and transcendent musicianship. Michel Plasson is sen-
sitively attuned to the Eastern flavors of the score, without allowing
them to become overdone or quaint, and the always stylish Capitole de Toulouse Orchestra responds with prodigious viruosity.

*S*ymphonies: No. 3 in G minor; No. 4 in A

L'Orchestre de la Suisse Romande, Ansermet. London
433719-2 [CD].

Detroit Symphony, Järvi. Chandos CHAN-8996 [CD];
ABTD-1578 [T] (No. 3); CHAN-9072 [CD] (No. 4).

If to say that the composer's final two works in the form are
among the greatest symphonies ever written by a French composer
would seem to be damning them with the faintest of faint praise,
then put it another way: Roussel's Third and Fourth Symphonies
are among the finest such works produced by any composer, French
or otherwise, in this century. In his early works, especially the
haunting *Poem of the Forest*, Roussel's distinctive brand of musical
impressionism is heard to lovely, often exquisite effect; the later
scores, particularly the lean and fiercely driven G minor Symphony
of 1930, are among the key works of modern neoclassicism, whose

finest passages place them on a nearly equal footing with Stravinsky's *Symphony in Three Movements* and *Symphony in C.*

With Charles Dutoit's superb Erato cycle now inexplicably withdrawn (and for sheer irresponsibility in wielding the deletions ax, Erato is rapidly approaching the gory standards of Angel/EMI), the early stereo versions of the Third and Fourth that Dutoit's mentor Ernest Ansermet recorded in 1956, despite the obvious limitations of the recorded sound and the occasional scrappiness of ensemble, are the best currently available. Järvi's version of the Third is a witty and powerful one, as is his version of the second suite from *Bacchus et Ariane.* What a pity Chandos chickened out and packaged them with mediocre run-throughs of Ravel's admittedly more marketable *Boléro* and *La Valse.* Similarly, Järvi's superlative accounts of the Fourth and the engaging Sinfonietta for Strings are watered down with yet another superfluous *La Mer* and a strangely inert and hamfisted reading of *Suite provençale* that manages to rob Darius Milhaud's marvelous travelogue of most of its charm.

An earlier Detroit Symphony Roussel recording, Paul Paray's incomparable version of the piquant and energetic *Suite in F,* has finally been reissued on a Mercury Living Presence CD (434303-2), coupled with a stunning Chabrier program (see page 133).

Rózsa, Miklós (1907–)

Symphony in Three Movements; *The Vintner's Daughter*

New Zealand Symphony, Sedares. Koch 37244-2 [CD].

Although best known for his work in film, including the Academy Award-winning scores for *Spellbound, A Double Life,* and *Ben Hur,* the Hungarian-born Miklós Rózsa also has been a diligent composer of more obviously serious music throughout his long career. His youthful *Theme, Variations, and Finale* from 1933 was one of the works on the famous New York Philharmonic broadcast concert in 1943 that catapulted Leonard Bernstein to national celebrity, and the Sonata for Solo Violin from 1985 suggests that the composer had lost none of his zest for life or music after entering his seventies.

Written in 1930 when the composer was only twenty-two, Rózsa's Symphony is an entertaining and energetic work, with a lovely slow movement and an exhilarating, hell-for-leather *perpetuum mobile* finale. If the language occasionally suggests his older compatriots Bartók and Kodály, it is still one of the most distinctive and substantial European symphonies from the era between the World Wars: a big, tuneful, user-friendly score, which those with an interest in twentieth-century music should snap up immediately.

As in their earlier Koch recording of Rózsa's *Hungarian Sketches*, *Notturno ungherese*, *Overture to a Symphony Concert*, and the *Theme, Variations, and Finale* (KIC-7191 [CD]), James Sedares and the New Zealand Symphony are wonderfully eloquent exponents of his music, as an enthusiastic testimonial from the composer printed on the CD cover clearly attests. The playing is both refined and vital, a perfect complement to this youthful but precocious piece.

The gorgeous Violin Concerto Rózsa composed for Jascha Heifetz has been reissued along with the violinist's equally definitive recordings of concertos by those other film composers Erich Wolfgang Korngold and Franz Waxman on RCA (7963-2 [CD]). The Viola Concerto, which may actually be the finer piece, is handsomely served by the brilliantly gifted American violinist/violist/composer Maria Newman on Varese Sarabande (VSD-5329 [CD]).

Rubbra, Edmund (1901–1986)

Symphony No. 3; Symphony No. 4; *Resurgam* (concert overture)

Philharmonia Orchestra, Del Mar. Lyrita SRCD-202 [CD].

That Edmund Rubbra has remained one of the least well-known of modern English symphonists isn't difficult to explain. The seriousness of purpose and ferocious integrity in his music has made it all but immune to fashionable modern trends. His orchestral palate tends to be serviceable to the point of austerity, with scarcely a bar or an instrument going to waste—in his Sixth Symphony, for instance, he requires a xylophone for only a single bar of the Scherzo, after which it is not heard from again—while his essentially conservative musical language has no other purpose than to serve his frequently profound, frequently mystical, richly polyphonic musical thought.

The late Norman Del Mar's superlative recordings of the Third and Fourth Symphonies provide an excellent introduction to Rubbra's uniquely intense and noble world. Written immediately before and during the Second World War, neither work betrays much of the dark turbulence of the era; each is persuasively argued and beautifully made, reflecting a personality which, in spite of some superficial resemblances to Sibelius and his teachers Vaughan Williams and Gustav Holst, is at once wholly admirable and wholly its own.

Rutter, John (1945–)

Gloria; Anthems

The Cambridge Singers, Philip Jones Brass Ensemble, City
of London Sinfonia, Rutter
Collegium COLCD-100 [CD], COLC-100 [T].

Requiem

Ashton, Dean, The Cambridge Singers, City of London
Sinfonia, Rutter. Collegium COLCD-103 [CD]; COLC-
103 [T].

Although undeniably modest, the gifts of the English composer John Rutter are also undeniably genuine: he knows how to
fashion a memorable tune, how to write for the human voice, how
to engage the listener's emotions, and how *not* to overstay his
welcome. And if his music never really scales the heights or plumbs
the depths, then it doesn't pretend to be anything other than the
quietly moving, gently comforting, refreshingly unassuming experience that it is.

It's unimaginable that warmer or more deeply committed
recordings than those made under the composer's expert direction
will ever be made. Once locked in the firm but loving coils of the
exuberant *Gloria* or the tenderly consoling Requiem, the listener is
a goner, thanks to the fact that the performances, like the music
itself, know more than a thing or two about the mysteries of human
communication.

Ryba, Jakub Jan (1765–1815)

Czech Christmas Mass

Soloists, Czech Philharmonic Chorus and Orchestra,
Smetáček. Fidelio CD-1809 [CD].

This vastly productive, thoroughly miserable composer—he
wrote more than 120 Masses alone and died by his own hand at the
age of forty-nine—was one of the first Bohemians to write serious
music to Czech texts. As such, Ryba has belatedly begun to be
recognized in Czechoslovakia as one of the most important pre-
cursors of Smetana and the other members of the national school.

An utterly enchanting Mass setting interspersed with a folksy
retelling of the nativity tale, the *Czech Christmas Mass* is probably
Ryba's masterpiece. Disarming, simple, and completely unaffected,
it is—like Rheinberger's *The Star of Bethlehem* (see page 430)—a
work that could easily become one of the best-loved Christmas
classics if only given half a chance.

Václav Smetáček and his forces make a wholly sympathetic
case for the piece: the performance glows with good will and
innocent warmth, and the recorded sound, while slightly distant, is
otherwise superb.

Those who respond to this disarming charmer will also want
to invesigate Ryba's *Bohemian Shepherd's Mass*, a work with many
of the same endearing qualities, recently recorded by the St. Nikolai
Chamber Orchestra for Signum (X-20-00 [CD]).

Saint-Saëns, Camille

(1835–1921)

Carnival of the Animals

> New York Philharmonic, Bernstein. CBS MYK-37765
> [CD], MT-37765 [T].

Ironically enough, it was for a work he refused to have performed in public during his lifetime that the vastly prolific, and once enormously popular Camille Saint-Saëns remains best known today. While much of his tuneful, ingratiating, always impeccably crafted music has apparently begun to lose its grip on the modern imagination, the ageless *Carnival of the Animals* has never gone begging for first-class recorded performances.

I have some very vivid memories of a Leonard Bernstein Young People's Concert in which it was first explained to me that the cuckoo was represented by the clarinet, the swan by the cello, and so forth. I bought the Bernstein recording soon afterward (one of the first records in my collection that did *not* have an erotic cover) and have cherished the performance ever since. Bernstein brings an obvious and unmistakable enthusiasm to both his narration and to the music. The soloists and the orchestra play with passion and devotion, and the early-1960s recorded sound is still very serviceable. In its most recent incarnation, the performance comes with an equally memorable—and when the horns get wound up, terrifically scary—interpretation of Prokofiev's *Peter and the Wolf*.

Concertos (5) for Piano and Orchestra

> Rogé, piano; London Philharmonic, Philharmonia
> Orchestra, Royal Philharmonic, Dutoit. London
> 417351-2 [CD].

To use an unusually disagreeable contemporary phrase, the five Saint-Saëns Piano Concertos are very "user-friendly" works, meaning, among other things, that they are very easy "to access." (This gradual pollution of the language through daily wear and tear is what the French poet Paul Valéry was thinking about when he was asked what poets really *did*. "That's simple," he said. "Each night you have to take a ten-franc whore and try to turn her into a virgin.")

Pleasant, shallow, unstintingly professional, and as easy on the mind as they are on the ear (for a man like Saint-Saëns, requiring his listeners to think simply wouldn't have been civilized), they rank with the Tchaikovsky suites and the Vivaldi concertos as some of the greatest elevator music ever written.

Pascal Rogé releases all their genuine charm without trying to turn them into something they're not. For instance, in the popular Second Concerto, which pianists are often tempted to inflate into something larger than it can really become, he maintains a decidedly laissez-faire interpretive touch, which compromises neither the work's essentially lighthearted character nor its moments of virtuoso display. Charles Dutoit is an equally levelheaded advocate of this music, providing accompaniments that give the composer and the listener precisely what they want.

Among recordings of Saint-Saëns's other instrumental concertos, Yo-Yo Ma is at his most elegant in his version of the A minor Cello Concerto; Cho-Liang Lin and Michael Tilson Thomas give us what is easily the most electric performance of the Third Violin Concerto ever recorded, and possibly the most exiting Saint-Saëns recording now in print. Sony has sensibly rereleased these exceptional recordings—together with Cecile Licad's fine performance of the Second Piano Concerto—on a single CD (MDK-46506) or tape (MDT-46506).

*D*anse macabre; *Le Rouet d'Omphale*; *Phaéton*; *Carnival of the Animals*

Philharmonia Orchestra, Dutoit. London 414460-2 [CD], 414460-4[T].

What would have made this an even more welcome addition to the catalog is a recording of the last of Saint-Saëns's four tone poems, *La Jeunesse d'Hercule*, instead of the surprisingly lackluster run-through of *Carnival of the Animals* that accompanies the other three. But no matter, for these are the most articulate and individual versions of *Danse macabre* and *Omphale's Spinning Wheel* in a generation, and even the slightly stuffy *Phaéton*, in Dutoit's tactful face-lift, seems fresher than it ever has before.

*H*avanaise for Violin and Orchestra; *Introduction and Rondo capriccioso* for Violin and Orchestra

Perlman, violin; New York Philharmonic, Mehta. Deutsche Grammophon 423063-2 [CD].

With Sarasate's *Carmen Fantasy* and Ravel's *Tzigane*, Saint-Saëns's pair of virtuoso spellbinders are among the most popular shorter works in the violin's literature. All four, together with Chausson's ravishing *Poème*, are given typically hair-raising accounts in Itzhak Perlman's most recent recordings, performances that mix phenomenal virtuosity with poetic insight, making them the most exciting *and* musical versions now available. As always, Mehta is an adroit and savvy accompanist, and the recorded sound is very good.

*S*amson and Dalila

Domingo, Obtraztsova, Bruson, Lloyd, Thau, Chorus and Orchestre de Paris, Barenboim. Deutsche Grammophon 413297-2 [CD].

After *Carmen* and *Faust*, *Samson and Dalila* has been the most enduringly popular of all French operas, in spite of the fact that it took a surprisingly long time to catch on. When a single act was given in Paris in 1875, two years prior to the Weimar premiere, critics chided it for its lack of memorable melody and mundane orchestration. Of course, in addition to its lavish spectacle, exotic orientalisms, and moving human drama, *Samson*'s wealth of unforgettable, luxuriantly scored melody is what has kept it alive all these years.

Of the available recorded *Samsons*, Daniel Barenboim's version is by far the best compromise. Placido Domingo makes an imposing, gloriously sung hero, and Barenboim's conducting misses none of the score's grandeur (the big choral scenes are especially thrilling) and very few of its more subtle details. The problem is Elena Obtraztsova, who is curiously sexless as the Philistine sexpot.

Rita Gorr, on a competing Angel set, makes a sensationally vivid Dalila, but that performance is seriously marred by Georges Prêtre's unimaginative conducting. The long-rumored Dutoit version may change the picture completely, but until then, this generally exciting (and moderately priced) effort will do.

Symphony No. 3 in C minor, *Organ*

Hurford, organ; Montreal Symphony, Dutoit. London 410201-2 [CD].

Zamkochian, organ; Boston Symphony, Munch. RCA 60817-2-RG [CD], 60817-4-RG[T].

The only one of Saint-Saëns's symphonies that is ever performed these days owes much of its current popularity to the recording industry. In the mid-1950s, when the record companies were casting about for "sonic spectaculars" to show off the revolutionary wonders of stereo, the *Organ* Symphony began to enjoy a new lease on life. Along with Paul Paray's wonderful Mercury recording with the Detroit Symphony, Charles Munch's classic Boston Symphony recording dominated the catalogs for decades. It had fire, a healthy measure of Munchian madness, stupendous playing from the orchestra, and recorded sound to raise the roof— which it still does in its compact disc reissue. In fact, the Munch recording would remain the obvious first choice were it not for the even more extraordinary interpretation led by Charles Dutoit.

What makes the Dutoit such a great performance is as easy to hear as it is difficult to describe. In its simplest terms, this is the one recording of the *Organ* Symphony that actually makes the piece sound like what it most assuredly is *not*: a great work. The conductor captures most of the Symphony's color and dramatic gestures, but for once the gestures seem internal and natural, as opposed to the empty, bombastic postures that they probably are. In short, along with its freshness, intelligence, and subtlety, this is the only version of the *Organ* Symphony in my experience in which we seem to be hearing music of genuine grandeur, instead of something merely grandiose.

Although none of his earlier works in the form begin to approach the achievement of the *Organ* Symphony, they all make for appealing listening in the recordings Jean Martinon and the

French National Radio Orchestra recorded in the mid-1970s, available now on a pair of Angel CDs (CDMB-62643 [CD]). The Second Symphony is the strongest of these unknown scores, with an effervescent Scherzo and a wild, tarantella finale, but even the juvenile A Major Symphony, written when Saint-Saëns was only fifteen, is not that far removed in quality from Bizet's Symphony in C. The performances are both affectionate and highly accomplished, and the recorded sound scarcely betrays its age.

Satie, Erik (1866–1925)

Piano Music

Rogé, piano. London 410220-2 [CD], 410220-4 [T].

Whether the arch-eccentric Erik Satie was an important composer or merely a fascinating crank is really beside the point. Since the 1960s he has attracted an ever-widening public, and for the time being he should be taken as seriously as the relatively brisk sales of Satie recordings would seem to demand.

Aside from the famous crackpot titles ("Desiccated Embryos," "Flabby Preludes for a Dog," and "Sketches to Make You Run Away" must be the choicest), the celebrated publicity stunts (for the premiere of his ballet *Parade*, Picasso painted a huge sign on the curtain which read, "Erik Satie is the greatest composer in the world. Anyone who disagrees with this statement is kindly asked to leave"), and the unquestioned influence he had on younger French composers, Satie was essentially a gifted, if largely unlettered, dilettante whose most inspired creation was his own bizarre public image.

Pascal Rogé's recital of some of the composer's best-known works will go a long way to making at least partial believers out of the more devout Satie skeptics, like me. The beautifully austere and justly popular *Gymnopédies* are given serenely rapt performances, and the versions of the six *Gnossiennes*, *Embryons desséchés* (which isn't quite as good as its title), and miniatures such as *Je te veux* and the *Bureaucratic Sonatine* are hardly less inspired. A second volume (421713-2 [CD]) in what presumably will be an ongoing Satie series is just as memorable, though in the case of this composer, more can quickly turn out to be much, *much* less.

For those who really *do* need more, Angel has reissued Aldo Ciccolini's pioneering Satie recordings on compact disc in five separate volumes "First and Last Works" (CDC-49702; "Mystical Works" CDC-49703; "Etudes" CDC-49713; "Whimsical Works" CDC 49714; "Music for the Dance"CDC-49760). And in a single, tightly-packed two-CD package (EMI CDZB-67282) running more than two and a half hours, Ciccolini performs many of the most familiar works, including the *Gymnopédies, Gnossiennes, Sarabandes,* and the three *Mouvements en forme de poire.* If his performances are not quite as sophisticated as Rogé's, they are nonetheless infectiously enjoyable, and the recorded sound remains immediate and well-lit.

Scarlatti, Domenico
(1685–1757)

Keyboard Sonatas

Pinnock, harpsichord. Deutsche Grammophon 419632-2 [CD].

Pinnock, harpsichord. CRD CD-3368 [CD].

Kipnis, harpsichord. Chesky CD-75 [CD].

Pogorelich, piano. Deutsche Grammophon 435855-2 [CD].

An exact contemporary of George Frideric Handel and Johann Sebastian Bach (1685 was one of the great vintage years in the history of music), Domenico Scarlatti was to the harpsichord what Chopin would later be to the piano: the first important composer to study the special characteristics of his chosen instrument, and then write music specifically designed to show off its individual character and peculiar strengths. His output of keyboard music was as prodigious as it was inspired. In 1971 a facsimile edition of the complete music for keyboard was published in eighteen densely-packed volumes. The truly devoted and/or demented can now acquire all 555 of them on a set of thirty-four (34) Erato compact discs (2292-45309-2), wheelbarrow not included.

It's a great pity that all the recordings featuring the father of modern Scarlatti scholarship, Ralph Kirkpatrick, are now out of print. His book *Scarlatti*, published in 1953, not only instantly became the standard work written about the composer, but also helped clear up the centuries-old muddling of the order of composition of Scarlatti's numerous works. Kirkpatrick's performances were predictably enthusiastic and sympathetic, as are those of Trevor Pinnock, whose several recordings for Deutsche Grammophon and CRD are also models of modern Baroque scholarship and musical sensitivity.

Reissued on the audiophile Chesky label, Igor Kipnis's scintillating interpretations from a quarter of a century ago continue to demonstrate why he has been one of the most joyously entertaining of all early music specialists. The performances have a distinctive wit and passion unlike those of any other player, and the recorded sound remains phenomenally good.

Among the most predictably personal of all recent collections, Ivo Pogorelich's Deutsche Grammophon anthology makes no attempt to place the music in any sort of historical context, but instead offers a uniquely individual, and exceedingly musical, view of the sonatas as formative building blocks of modern keyboard technique. The playing is both patrician and very moving.

Schiff, David (1945–)

Divertimento from *Gimpel the Fool*; *Scenes from Adolescence*; Suite from *Sacred Service*

Chamber Music Northwest. Delos DE-3058 [CD].

Of all the younger American composers whose music consciously tries to mix serious and popular styles, David Schiff may be the most consistently successful. In a note written for this delightful Delos recording, he explains: "To me, the interesting thing is to write a klezmer piece not using klezmer instruments, a rock/bebop piece not using rock instruments, or synagogue tradition combined with classical form."

Though the most striking piece here is the Divertimento from Schiff's opera based on Isaac Bashevis Singer's story *Gimpel the Fool*—it has real claims to being the single most entertaining American chamber work of the last quarter century—the Bop- and Motown-inspired *Scenes from Adolescence* is also very ingratiating, as is the lovely *Sacred Service* Suite. Chamber Music Northwest plays the music as though it had been written for them (the Divertimento actually *was*), and the recorded sound ranks with Delos's best.

Schoenberg, Arnold

(1874–1951)

Choral Music

> Shirley-Quirk, narrator; BBC Singers, London Sinfonietta,
> BBC Symphony Orchestra and Chorus, Boulez. Sony
> S2K-44571 [CD].

For a man who not all that long ago wrote the deliberately provocative (and ultimately assinine) diatribe *Schoenberg est mort*, Pierre Boulez has become one of the composer's most ardently committed interpreters. This two-CD collection of Schoenberg's choral music contains some of his most inspired creations, from the withering *A Survivor from Warsaw*, which in seven minutes accomplishes nearly as much as *Schindler's List* did in three and a quarter hours, to the great—and as the composer came to think of it—*accursed* motet *Frieda auf Erden*. (Because the deeply superstitious Schoenberg assigned his Op. 13 to a work called *Peace on Earth*, he later became convinced that that was the actual *cause* of the First World War. Nor was this breathtaking lack of modesty without its amusing side. Once, when some of his students took a sample of his script to a handwriting analyst and were told, "This man thinks he's at very least the Emperor of China," Schoenberg asked in all innocence, "But did she say if I was justified?")

Not only are these the most powerful and meticulous recorded performances these works have yet had, they are also the most physically beautiful. As much as anyone, Boulez fully understands the deeply Romantic underpinnings of Schoenberg's art, projecting it as gloriously as anyone ever has.

An alluring, indispensible recording.

Concerto for Cello and Orchestra (from a harpsichord concerto of Georg Matthias Monn)

> Ma, cello; Boston Symphony, Ozawa. CBS MK-39863
> [CD].

As much as I am tempted to ride this personal hobbyhorse into the ground, I will resist making any emotional (and they would be thoroughly heartfelt) appeals on behalf of the music of Arnold Schoenberg, the most significant composer of the twentieth century, and probably the *best* composer since Johannes Brahms. The Schoenberg debate will continue to rage long after all of us are gone and forgotten. (Why is it that in writing of Schoenberg, one always, and almost automatically, slips into such cheerful images and turns of phrase? Perhaps because this melancholy figure remains the most thoroughly misunderstood composer in history). In fact, the great bogeyman of the early twentieth-century avant-garde, the man whose experiments with atonality, serialism, and the twelve-tone technique "destroyed" music as we know it, was in fact the most conservative composer since Bach: an arch-Romantic who perceived—correctly—that if Western music were to go on at all, it needed an entirely new language. (The five-hundred-year-old system of triadic tonality that had made such music possible had simply worn out.)

Even if you shudder at the mere mention of Arnold Schoenberg's name, you probably won't be able to resist the Cello Concerto, a work so puppy-dog friendly that even the most musically shy five-year-old can embrace it with pleasure. Beginning with a happy little tune that bears a striking resemblance to "Rule, Brittania," Schoenberg's adaptation of a harpsichord concerto by the eighteenth-century Austrian composer Georg Matthias Monn is one of his most impressive essays in virtuoso orchestration: bells tinkle, the woodwinds jabber, and the solo instrument is all but asked to stand on its head. Although the cello part is allegedly one of the most difficult ever written for the instrument, Yo-Yo Ma glides through it with ease and obvious relish, and Seiji Ozawa's contribution could not have been more sympathetic or alert.

A more substantial but equally unthreatening work, the Concerto for String Quartet and Orchestra, presents Schoenberg the pedagogue showing Handel, in one of his occasionally slipshod Op. 6 concerti grossi, how the thing *really* ought to have been done. Listening to one great master gently wagging his finger at another— and producing a freestanding masterpiece in the process—is a delightfully amusing experience, particularly in the witty, open-hearted performance by the American String Quartet and the New York Chamber Orchestra led by Gerard Schwarz (Nonesuch 79145-2 [CD]).

Concerto for Piano and Orchestra; Concerto for Violin and Orchestra

Brendel, piano; Zeitlin, violin; Bavarian Radio Symphony, Kubelik. Deutsche Grammophon 431740-2 [CD].

The late Clara Steuermann, widow of the foremost interpreter of Schoenberg's piano music, once said the opening of the Piano Concerto should be played "as though it were a Mendelssohn *Song without Words.*" Which is precisely the tack Alfred Brendel takes in the second and finer of his two recordings of this magnificent work. His lyrical, rhapsodic approach to music places it firmly within the great Romantic tradition where it properly belongs, and Kubelik's alternately passionate and sensitive support only enhances that impression. Coupled with a fine, though considerably less inspired reading of the Violin Concerto, this medium-priced CD is now the best avenue to enter these challenging yet highly rewarding works.

Five Pieces for Orchestra

Berlin Philharmonic, Levine. Deutsche Grammophon 419781-2 [CD].

After leading the American premiere of the *Five Pieces for Orchestra* in Boston, the misanthropic German conductor Karl Muck announced with his customary tact, "I can't tell you whether we've played *music*, but I assure you we've played every one of Schoenberg's notes, just as they were written." Curiously, there are still those who entertain similar doubts about this modern masterpiece, more than eighty years after it was composed. With *Pierrot Lunaire*, the monodrama *Erwartung*, and the closing moments of the Second String Quartet, the Five Pieces represent the summit of Schoenberg's experiments with nontonal (he detested the word *atonal*) music: a work of stupefying originality and beauty that should be heard as frequently as the "Eroica" Symphony or *The Rite of Spring.*

In one of his best recordings in years, James Levine leads the Berlin Philharmonic in a subtle, powerful, superbly colored performance of this early Schoenberg masterpiece, in which the musical argument becomes very nearly as lucid as anything in the music of Schoenberg's favorite composers, Mozart and Brahms. With equally loving and perceptive versions of Berg's Three Pieces for Orchestra and Webern's Six Pieces, Op. 6, this is now the best single-disc collection of orchestral music by the three giants of the Second Viennese School.

Now then, if the same forces would only move on to one or two other Schoenberg items, such as the Op. 31 *Variations for Orchestra* (which the Berlin Philharmonic introduced under Furt-wängler in 1928), the orchestral versions of the Chamber Symphonies, the Violin Concerto (with Perlman), the Piano Concerto (with Pollini), *A Survivor from Warsaw* (which might take some guts), the brief but delectable *Begleitungsmusik zu einer Lichtspielszene*, and the rarely heard Suite in G for Strings, I could die a happy man.

Gurrelieder

> Norman, Troyanos, McCracken, Klemperer, Tanglewood Festival Chorus, Boston Symphony Orchestra, Ozawa. Philips 412511-2 [CD].
>
> Jerusalem, Dunn, Fassbaender, Hotter, St. Hedwig's Cathedral Choir, Düsseldorf Municipal Choral Society, Berlin Radio Symphony, Chailly. London 430321-2 [CD].

Gurrelieder, Schoenberg's magnificent orchestral song cycle/ oratorio, is both the perfect introduction to the composer's early style and one of the last great masterpieces of Romantic music. If you are one of those people who turn up your nose at the mere mention of Schoenberg's name, *Gurrelieder* might just be the medicine to cure you of a most unfortunate ailment.

While this Philips recording is not the ideal *Gurrelieder*, it is, for the most part, a very good one. The strongest things about it are the Tove of Jessye Norman, the speaker of Werner Klemperer, the playing of the Boston Symphony, and the excitement a live performance always generates. James McCracken struggles heroically with one of the most difficult tenor parts ever written, but this is not an especially comfortable or attractive performance, and the usually reliable Tatiana Troyanos is unexpectedly wobbly as the Wood Dove. Seiji Ozawa, as usual, leads an interpretation that scores very high marks for the beauties of its physical sound and the attention to detail, but that nonetheless tends to gloss over the more profound elements in the music. Still, in spite of its flaws, this recording belongs in every collection, especially since a *Gurrelieder* from Carlos Kleiber or Klaus Tennstedt is *not* on the horizon and probably shouldn't be expected any time soon.

Although the London performance has much to recommend it, too—preeminently, the singing of the most impressive of recorded Waldemars, Siegfried Jerusalem, as well as demonstration quality recorded sound—Riccardo Chailly's conducting seems efficient but superficial, as it usually does. Still, of all recorded *Gurrelieders* it makes the most impressive noise.

*M*oses und Aron

Mazura, Langridge, Bonney, Haugland, Chicago Symphony Orchestra and Chorus, Solti. London 414264-2 [CD].

There will always be a special place in hell for the well-known foundation (name withheld to prevent all right-thinking people from sending them several letter bombs per day) that turned down Arnold Schoenberg's modest request for sufficient funds to complete his oratorio *Jacobsleiter*, and one of the great unfinished works in musical history, *Moses und Aron*. (This same foundation, by the way, regularly doles out hefty grants to feckless boobs who, to quote my grandfather, if they had to take a trip on brains wouldn't have to pack a lunch.) Be that as it may, even without the music of its third act (the composer did complete the moving text), *Moses und Aron* easily ranks with the most intriguing and important of all twentieth-century operas. Were it given performances like this one on a regular basis, it might become, if not another *Bohème*, then at least a work that would be performed with something approaching the frequency it deserves.

Sir Georg Solti, in one of the finest recordings he has made since the completion of London's Vienna *Ring*, places both the opera and Schoenberg where they properly belong. It has often been suggested that Schoenberg only wanted to rewrite the music of Johannes Brahms for the twentieth century. The suggestion is ludicrous, of course, but it contains at least a grain of truth. For Schoenberg, even in the most advanced of his twelve-tone works, remained an unrepentant Romantic to the very end. Unlike the other fine recordings of *Moses und Aron* (by Pierre Boulez and Michael Gielen, both out of print), it is the Solti version that most clearly recognizes the romantic elements in this rich and moving opera and makes them work. Rarely, for instance, has the most famous moment in the score, "The Dance Around the Gold Calf," sounded more lurid (in fact the entire scene is a triumph of prurient interest, as the composer intended), and never have the difficult principal roles been more effortlessly or beautifully sung.

The Chicago Symphony, as always, is miraculous in its poise and execution, and the recorded sound is stunning in its warmth and detail. Be warned, *Moses und Aron* is no *Aida*; still, it is a very great work that will repay in abundance any investment of time and energy the listener is willing to make.

Piano Music (complete)

Pollini, piano. Deutsche Grammophon 423249-2 [CD].

I suspect that the reason Schoenberg's piano music turns up so rarely on recitals has less to do with the resistance of the audience than it does with the perfectly understandable unwillingness of pianists to play it. There is nothing about this important, serious music that could possibly attract a shallow or self-serving performer, and pianists—bless them—are no more profound or altruistic as a group than are any of the rest of us.

Like the composer's friend and longtime champion Eduard Steuermann, whose old Columbia recordings were among the great documents of modern music-making, Maurizio Pollini is one of those rare performers who are able to grapple with the music on its own uncompromising terms and yet make it seem as though they were doing it out of love and not some misplaced sense of duty. The performances are as sensitive and dramatic as his interpretations of Beethoven, Schubert, and Chopin, and should win these passionate, rarefied, uniquely lyrical works many friends.

Pierrot Lunaire

DeGaetani, speaker; Contemporary Chamber Ensemble, Weisberg. Nonesuch 79237-2 [CD], 71251-4 [T].

Stravinsky's *Rite of Spring* and Schoenberg's *Pierrot Lunaire* are the two great watersheds of modern music. The latter is a piece of such staggering originality and inventiveness that it still seems as though it might have been written yesterday, instead of the year 1912.

This classic recording with Jan DeGaetani and Arthur Weisberg's Contemporary Chamber Ensemble on Nonesuch is the closest thing we have yet had to an ideal realization of *Pierrot Lunaire*. DeGaetani, who made her formidable reputation by singing the most impossibly difficult contemporary music as though it had been written by Stephen Foster, weaves her way through Schoenberg's eerie, mysteriously beautiful *Sprechstimme* as though she were telling us stories from Mother Goose (which, after all, is not that far removed from what the *Pierrot* speaker is supposed to do.) The highest praise that can be lavished on the accompaniment she receives from Weisberg and company is that it is altogether worthy of this legendary modern performance.

String Quartets (5)

LaSalle Quartet. Deutsche Grammophon 419994-2 [CD].

Like so many of his major works, Schoenberg's Quartets have been shrouded in misunderstanding and neglect for so many decades that coming to them for the first time can make for both a bewildering and exhilarating experience. The early D Major Quartet of 1897, with its echoes of Dvořák and Schubert, is among the most buoyant and approachable of all Schoenberg's works; the first and fourth of the numbered Quartets have much to recommend them, the middle two rank with the masterworks of modern chamber music. The Second Quartet, in whose final movements Schoenberg first abandoned traditional harmony, is among his most boldly original works—in addition to the nontonal experiments, there is a haunting part for soprano voice—and the Third Quartet, one of his finest twelve-tone scores, erupts with a passionate intensity not far removed from the smoldering mood of *Erwartung*.

It is good to have the sensitive, impassioned recordings by the LaSalle Quartet back in circulation, for as performances they have even more to communicate on a human level than the more technically dazzling versions by the Juilliard String Quartet, no doubt slated for CD reissue by CBS/Sony. In addition to the Schoenbergs, this four-CD box offers the major works for string quartet by Berg and Webern, including what is probably the finest *Lyric Suite* since the old Dial recording by the Kolisch Quartet.

For lovers of contemporary chamber music, this is a major cause for rejoicing.

Verklärte Nacht

Ensemble InterContemporain, Boulez. Sony SMK-48465 [CD].

Santa Fe Chamber Music Ensemble. Nonesuch D4-79028 [T].

The early *Verklärte Nacht* (Transfigured Night), written by a largely self-taught twenty-six-year-old composer, is one of the most amazing works in the history of nineteenth-century music. (And as with Brahms, the composer he admired most of all, the ratio of masterworks to lesser pieces in Schoenberg's output is extraordinarily high.) The lush sonorities, the wealth of ornamental detail, the advanced harmonic thinking, and the expressive confidence of the work completely belie the composer's youth and relative lack of experience. Had Schoenberg never written another note of music, he would still be remembered, for this piece alone, as one of the most fascinating voices of the entire late-Romantic era.

Among recordings of the orchestral version of *Verklärte Nacht*, Pierre Boulez's is an almost ideal fusion of Romantic ardor and modern clarity in which both the passions and the architecture of Schoenberg's early masterpiece emerge in the sharpest possible relief. Packaged with equally impressive versions of the pivotal *Variations for Orchestra* and the fascinating one-act opera *Die glückliche Hand*, this clearly is the *Verklärte Nacht* to own.

Among recordings of the original version of the piece, the Nonesuch release recorded at one of the Santa Fe Chamber Music Festivals remains unapproached. In fact, the only significant drawback in this otherwise virtually perfect recording (which is coupled with a blazing account of a late Schoenberg masterpiece, the great String Trio) is that it has yet to be issued on compact disc.

Schubert, Franz (1797–1828)

Impromptus (8) for Piano

Perahia, piano. CBS MK-37291 [CD], IMT-37921 [T].

Like Mozart and Mendelssohn, Franz Schubert was one of the authentic miracles of Western art. At sixteen, he composed the first great German *lied*, "Gretchen am Spinnrade," and in the remaining fifteen years of his tragically brief life became not only the undisputed master of German art song (he wrote more than seven hundred), but also the most important composer of symphonies, chamber music, and piano sonatas after his hero and idol, Beethoven. Though the two men lived in Vienna for years, the almost pathologically modest and self-effacing Schubert never screwed up the courage to meet the older man. He did serve as a pallbearer at Beethoven's funeral in 1827, which took place a scant twenty months before his own. No other composer, including Mozart, had a greater or more facile gift for melody, and none—even the indefatigable giants of the Baroque era—was more prolific.

The two sets of Impromptus are among the most charming and characteristic of Schubert's piano works, and all have been served handsomely on records since the 78 era. On the basis of his CBS recording, Murray Perahia must be considered one of the great Schubert interpreters in the world today. The playing has a light, direct openness that is genuinely refreshing, but also plenty of *Schwung* and sinew whenever the music demands. In fact, these popular works have probably not been in better hands since the days of Arthur Schnabel and Edwin Fischer.

Masses No. 4 in C; No. 5 in A-flat; No 6 in E-flat

Soloists, Bavarian Radio Orchestra and Chorus, Sawallisch. Angel CDM-69222 [CD] (Nos. 4 and 5); CDM-69233 [CD] (No. 6).

If Schubert's six Mass settings don't typically contain his most inspired music, then they still serve to remind us that the mediocre music of a master is preferable to the masterpieces of a mediocrity, or as Charles Caleb Colton so cheerfully put it, "Love is a spaniel that prefers even punishment from one hand to caresses from another." Which is not to say Schubert's Masses are in any way second-rate: the works contain a wealth of lovely melody and sincere religious feeling, and if they lack the sustained dramatic impact of Haydn's or Beethoven's sacred music, they are nonetheless fresh and engaging and deserve to be far better known.

In these two medium-priced collections, Wolfgang Sawallisch and his brilliant forces make exceptionally strong cases for three of the composer's finest settings, especially the richly moving Mass in A-flat from 1828. Both the chorus and orchestra are warm and responsive, and the fact that some of the soloists—Helen Donath, Brigitte Fassbaender, Dietrich Fischer-Dieskau, and the late Lucia Popp—were and are major Schubert lieder specialists is evident in every phrase.

Octet in F for Strings and Winds

**Academy of St. Martin-in-the-Fields Chamber Ensemble.
Chandos CHAN-8585 [CD], ABTB-1276 [T].**

This sublimely entertaining chamber work, which in some performances can last very nearly as long as Beethoven's Ninth Symphony, is as much fun as eight musicians can have with all their clothes on. (Rumors of an Octet au naturel given at a well-known music festival in Southern California continue to prove groundless. The festival's director told me in confidence that though they were certainly open to the idea, it was not only impossible to find a clarinetist who was willing to appear in that condition, but also one whom relatively normal people would be willing to look at.)

As in their Philips recording made in the late 1970s, the Academy of St. Martin-in-the-Fields Chamber Ensemble gives a performance for Chandos in which both the simplicity and sophistication of Schubert's great score are given full rein. Mechanically, the playing is all but flawless; yet it is the sheer *enjoyment* we hear in the playing that makes the recording stand out. For years, Angel's recording with the Melos Ensemble, now available in England on an EMI compact disc, set a standard I thought would never be approached. This one joins it at the very top of any list.

Piano Sonatas: in C minor, D. 958; in A, D. 959; in B-flat, D. 960

Pollini, piano. Deutsche Grammophon 419229-2 [CD].

Though Schubert produced some twenty piano sonatas over the course of his career, he was never really comfortable with the form. It was only with these last three, written during the final year of his life, that Schubert, the incomparable miniaturist of the Impromptus and *Moments musicaux*, produced a trio of large-scale piano works whose depth and quality rival any that his revered Beethoven ever wrote. Not since Arthur Schnabel (who once said, "I play Beethoven to make my living; Schubert I play for love") have these works had a more probing or poetic interpreter than Maurizio Pollini. If other performances of the C minor Sonata have unleashed a more torrential strength, Pollini stands virtually alone in evoking the bitter tragedy of the A Major, and the heroic grandeur of the Sonata in B-flat. While all the interpretations are full of the special insights (his detractors would call them "mannerisms") that have made Pollini the most deeply personal keyboard artist of his generation, the occasional eccentricities are far outweighed by the extraordinary depth and beauty of this set.

For those wanting to explore the entire cycle, Wilhelm Kempff's magisterial recordings from the mid- to late-1960s have been reissued on a set of seven medium-priced Deutsche Grammophon CDs (423496-2). As in the pianist's two separate versions of the Beethoven sonatas, the level of inspiration is extraordinarily high, with a freshness of insight and sense of discovery that prevent the slightest hint of the perfunctory or the routine. A classic recording and an outstanding bargain.

Quintet in A for Piano and Strings, *Trout*

Curzon, piano; Vienna Octet. London 417459-2 [CD].

Like his near-contemporary Solomon, Sir Clifford Curzon was one of the most physically unprepossessing of the great modern pianists, looking like a cross between a Talmudic scholar and an Oxford don. But Curzon possessed a blazing technique and a temperament to match. His penchant for canceling appearances eventually became legendary, and in my own personal experience only the high-strung Byron Janis backed out on more concerts for which I had tickets in hand. (A musical wit once suggested that the pianist's management should announce, "Mr. Curzon is available for only a limited number of cancellations this season.")

Nonetheless, when Curzon came to play—as he did in this celebrated 1958 recording of the *Trout* Quintet—all grumbles about his personal quirks were silenced. The playing is both completely relaxed and supremely magisterial, with a bracingly vigorous account of the Scherzo to keep the listeners on their toes. Combined with a loving account of the *Death and the Maiden* Quartet, this is a bargain that few can afford to pass up.

Quintet in C for Strings, D. 956

Ma, cello; Cleveland String Quartet. CBS MK-39134 [CD], IMT-39134 [T].

From works like the sublime and serene C Major Quintet, it would be impossible to deduce that the last eighteen months of Franz Schubert's life were an inexpressible nightmare. Dying of syphilis, the composer was nonetheless able to churn out a body of work of such unearthly beauty and purity that the only creative period like it was that equally astonishing *annus mirabilis* of the English poet John Keats.

While the great Cello Quintet has had many distinguished recordings over the years, beginning with an unforgettable account by the old Hollywood Quartet dating from the mid-1950s, now available on Testament CD (SBT 1031) coupled with their equally memorable version of Schoenberg's *Verklärte Nacht*—no recorded performance has been more sensitive or moving than this CBS release by cellist Yo-Yo Ma and the brilliant Cleveland String Quartet. One of the most impassioned and committed of all the Quintet's recent recordings of the work, this is also one of the most polished and meticulous. The attentive and generous contribution made by the "fifth wheel" offers further evidence that Yo-Yo Ma is the most breathtakingly complete cellist of his generation, and with good playback equipment, the amazingly lifelike recorded sound will almost persuade you that the players are in your living room.

*R*osamunde (incidental music)

Von Otter, soprano; Chamber Orchestra of Europe,
Abbado. Deutsche Grammophon 431655-2 [CD].

Once on the air, in introducing a work by Anton Rubinstein, I addressed the old Romantic legend that that fiery Russian composer and pianist, because of his astonishing physical resemblance to Beethoven, was in fact the great man's illegitimate son. I pointed out that as Beethoven had died in 1827 and Rubinstein was born in 1829 this would have been extremely difficult, given the fact that in the 1820s there were no sperm banks in the city of Vienna, other than Helemina von Chézy. Not only would this giftless clown supply the transcendentally stupid libretto that would completely scuttle *Euryanthe*, the grandest of Carl Maria von Weber's operas, but she would also give Franz Schubert the material for one of his worst theatrical disasters, a play called *Rosamunde*, which closed after only two performances.

Claudio Abbado's masterful recording of the *Rosamunde* incidental music is a sheer delight from beginning to end. The Chamber Orchestra of Europe plays this enchanting music with just the right combination of youthful zest and mature gentility, and the soprano and chorus are utterly delectable. Given wonderfully life-like sound by the Deutsche Grammophon engineers, this is easily one of the best Schubert recordings of the decade.

*D*ie schöne Müllerin

Fischer-Dieskau, baritone; Moore, piano. Deutsche
Grammophon 415186-2 [CD].

Unlike his half dozen operatic projects, which came to nothing or ended in total disaster, Schubert's setting of twenty interrelated lyrics by the irredeemably minor poet Wilhelm Müller is one of the most successful music dramas ever written. In this simple, loosely structured tale of a wandering young miller who falls in love, is spurned by the title character (The Fair Maid of the Mill), and finally commits a Romantic suicide by drowning himself in a brook, Schubert fashioned history's first great song cycle and one of the two supreme masterpieces in the form.

Although there have been some memorable recordings of *Die schöne Müllerin* over the years—in many ways, the famous 1941 recording by the Danish tenor Aksel Schiøtz has never been surpassed, and that other celebrated wartime recording by Julius Patzak is now available on a Preiser CD (93128)—Dietrich Fischer-Dieskau's several recordings are all impressive, most notably the now-withdrawn 1962 version for EMI, followed closely by this 1972 remake for Deutsche Grammophon.

Unlike some of the baritone's later recordings, which are ruined by archness and a host of exasperating mannerisms, his third version of the cycle still finds the voice at its freshest and fullest (thereby eliminating the need to posture, primp, and snort) and captures one of the greatest musical storytellers since John McCormack was in his prime. The unerringly perceptive, quietly inventive accompaniments of the great Gerald Moore are the stuff of which legends are made.

Songs

Although it is still difficult to offer any coherent recommendation of Schubert song recordings, the task is certainly easier than it was a couple of years ago. Even though the major companies now seem intent on reissuing *everything* on CD, this pleasantly profligate policy does not seem to extend to lieder, which continue to appeal to a relatively small but rabid crowd. Unbelievably, not *one* of Hermann Prey's Schubert recordings (other than some late recordings of the cycles and two versions of *Winterreise*) is to be had anywhere at any price. Apparently, no one at the several recording companies that have dealt with the baritone over the years has heard that he is—no kidding, guys—one of the greatest Schubert singers in history and, in the opinion of many of us, the foremost lieder specialist to have emerged since the end of the war.

If the Prey situation is surprising, that of Hans Hotter is a scandal. It is as if that noblest German bass of his generation, whose recordings of Schubert came closest to sounding the ultimate depths and most profound stillnesses of the composer's heart, simply never existed. The wonderful Austrian company Preiser, which specializes in historic vocal reissues, has released one CD (93145), but again, for an artist of Hotter's stature, this is inexcusable. By that same token, the wonderful and still vigorously active Dutch soprano Elly Ameling remains woefully underrepresented: only two of her Philips recordings have made the jump to CD (416294-2 and 420870-2), although there is an attractive, if somewhat redundant recital of sixteen songs available from Etcetera (KTC-1009 [CD], XTC-1009 [CD]).

On the brighter side, things on the Fischer-Dieskau front are definitely looking up. In addition to that ageless *Schöne Müllerin*, two other Angel recordings from the 1950s and '60s have also resurfaced on compact disc: a dandy *Schwanengesang* with Gerald Moore (CDMC-63559), and two lovely recitals of some of the best-known songs (CDM-69503 and CDMB-63566), in which the singing is so effortless and unaffected that those who only know the barking, hammy "Fish" of recent years will hardly believe it's the same singer. And finally, Orfeo provides perhaps the most telling recording of all: a group of sixteen songs from an exhilarating recital the baritone gave with Moore at the 1957 Salzburg Festival (C-140101 [CD]). As singing, as drama, as human communication, it captures a unique musical force at its most compelling.

Among recent historic reissues, recitals from Pearl (PEA-9479 [CD]) and Preiser (89017 [CD]) document the phenomenal artistry of the German baritone Gerhard Hüsch, whose insight, musicianship, and sheer manliness have rarely been equalled before or since. Elisabeth Schwarzkopf is finally represented on two CDs from EMI: her classic recordings made in 1952 with the great Swiss pianist Edwin Fischer (CDH-64026) and the more recent ones with Gerald Moore and Geoffrey Parsons (CDM-63656). In both, incomparable musicianship, perception, and sex are combined in an irresistibly heady brew. Though he died before his gifts as a lieder singer had fully matured, the uniquely beautiful voice of tenor Fritz Wunderlich is preserved on a pair of CDs from Deutsche Grammophon (429933-2) and Acanta (CD-43529), along with exquisitely lovely versions of songs by Beethoven and Schumann.

Of the newer collections, Brigitte Fassbaender's extraordinary reading of *Schwanengesang* for Deutsche Grammophon (429766 [CD]) is one of the most exciting lieder recordings in a decade, combining fire and poetry in a manner reminiscent of Lotte Lehmann at her best. Margaret Price's Orfeo release (C-001811-A [CD]) features some captivating singing and perhaps the finest available version of *Der Hirt auf dem Felsen* (The Shepherd on the Rock), and the late Arleen Augér's Virgin recital with fortepiano (59630 [CD]) is as beautifully sung as it is intelligently conceived.

Finally, Hyperion's quixotic and largely successful series that will attempt to record *all* the songs has already yielded several clear winners. Volume 1 (CDJ-33001 [CD], KJ-33001 [T]) finds Dame Janet Baker at the height of her mature interpretive powers and the voice showing only the slightest signs of wear and tear; Volume 3 (CDJ-33003 [CD], KJ-33003[T]) offers the lovely mezzo-soprano Ann Murray in beautiful voice, and on Volume 4 (CDJ-33004 [CD], KJ-33004 [T]) Philip Langridge continues to demonstrate that he is one of the most intelligent and musical Schubert singers in the world today.

All in all, things could be worse.

String Quartets (15)

Melos Quartet. Deutsche Grammophon 419879-2 [CD].

In addition to providing beautifully thought out and handsomely executed versions of the more familiar later quartets, the principal value of this attractive six-CD set is the warmly graceful performances the Melos give of the early ones. While obviously not in the same league as the masterworks Schubert would compose toward the end of his life, they are astonishingly confident and tuneful pieces that deserve to be far better known. These gifted German musicians miss no opportunity to underscore the charm and innocence of the music, and if the remastered recorded sound tends to be a trifle distant and harsh, that is the only minor reservation about an otherwise splendid release.

String Quartets: No. 13 in A minor; No. 14 in D minor, *Death and the Maiden*

Alban Berg Quartet. Angel CDC-47333 [CD].

As in their recordings of the Beethoven Quartets, Vienna's Alban Berg Quartet are all but impossible to better in these performances of the great last quartets of Schubert. The ensemble's almost obscenely beautiful physical sound has never been captured to more thrilling effect (the hushed yet paradoxically full-bodied *pianissimos* of which they are capable continually remind me of the high notes that only Leontyne Price in her prime could pop out with such bewitching ease), but as always in their recordings, the Bergs offer us considerably more than a collection of pretty sounds. The *Death and the Maiden* Quartet (so called because one of its movements is a set of variations on Schubert's song of that name) has rarely sounded this dark and disturbing (there are, of course, ample doses of light and life as well), and the great A minor Quartet explodes with a dramatic intensity that no other recording can match. The sound that Angel's engineers have supplied is as opulent as the performances. For Schubert lovers, or simply anyone interested in three of the greatest string quartets written after those of Beethoven, these are absolute musts.

Symphonies: No. 3 in D; No. 5 in B-flat; No. 6 in C, *Little C Major*

Royal Philharmonic, Beecham. EMI CDM-69750 [CD].

Like her one-time Prague neighbor, Franz Kafka, my grandmother held a fairly dark view of the human condition. For instance, she was persuaded that virtually all useful wisdom was contained in the old Czech beatitude, "Blessed are they who expect nothing, for they shall not be disappointed." She was also a devout believer in the Czech time payment plan (100 percent cash down, and *no* easy monthly installments) and was firmly convinced that there was no such thing as a "bargain." She lived to be ninety-four.

Had she lived to be 109—as well she might have, had it not been for that final pileup on her fully paid-for though, as she often complained, ridiculously overpriced Harley-Davidson—she might have admitted that bargains *do* exist. For here are three of Schubert's most endearing early symphonies in the finest recorded performances they are ever likely to receive on one "medium-priced" compact disc.

As far as Sir Thomas Beecham was concerned, early Schubert was merely an extension of Mozart and Haydn (which, to a large extent, it was), and he treats the music with the same easy wit and amiability. Which is not to say that he sees them as warmed-over versions of the *Surprise* and *Haffner* Symphonies. Never forgetting for a moment that even as a boy Schubert was one of the great masters of melody, Beecham caresses the glorious tunes with an affection and knowledge of breath that suggest a great lieder specialist. As always, the Royal Philharmonic give the impression they would do anything for their unpredictable founder, and the recorded sound from the late 1950s is fine. Alas, the recording is becoming difficult to find domestically. If necessary, it is definitely worth the time and expense to import it directly from any of the large English mail order houses. (Addresses can be found in any copy of *Gramophone* magazine.)

Anyone hunting for comparable versions of the other early symphonies will find that the Deutsche Grammophon recordings by Claudio Abbado and the Chamber Orchestra of Europe come closest to approximating the Beecham spell. The relaxed, yet buoyant romps through Nos. 1 and 2 are especially enjoyable (423652-2), while the performance of the *Tragic* (No. 4) is both weightier and more supple than those we usually hear. Although this disc (423653-3) comes with the best modern recording of the Third Symphony, the Beecham remains in a universe by itself.

Symphony No 8 in B minor *Unfinished*

Vienna Philharmonic, Solti. London 414371-2 [CD].

With Bruno Walter's timeless recording available only on an Odyssey tape (YT-30314), Sir Georg Solti's version of Schubert's best-loved symphony will fill the bill nicely until Walter's inevitable return on compact disc. As always, the conductor gets the very best out of this frequently crotchety orchestra: the strings glow with a burnished intensity; the winds play with point, self-assurance, and enormous individuality. The interpretation itself is virile and straightforward, with the characteristic Solti drama and color. In fact, for many this will be more than a stopgap, especially those who prefer the *Unfinished* on the more heroic, driven side.

Symphony No. 9 in C, *The Great C Major*

Berlin Philharmonic, Furtwängler. Arkadia 525 [CD].
Vienna Philharmonic, Solti. London 400082-2 [CD].

Schubert's final completed symphony can be a very problematic work. Since the *Great* of the sobriquet refers as much to its massive length as to the divinity of its melodic inspiration, the Ninth Symphony can degenerate (and often has) into nothing more than a collection of Sunday school tunes. Like his famous Deutsche Grammophon studio recording from the same period, Wilhelm Furtwängler's live performance from 1953 is the one version of the piece that makes it seem as structurally sound, and dramatically inevitable, as the Beethoven Ninth. The performance is a triumph of Furtwänglerian brinkmanship at its most magical. The unwritten, yet electrifying, accelerando that leads out of the Introduction to the first movement's principal theme, the spring in the Scherzo's rhythm, and the headlong forward thrust of the finale make this one of the most exciting orchestral recordings ever made.

The same qualities that made his version of the *Unfinished* so successful can be heard in Sir Georg Solti's recording of the *Great C Major*, an unforced yet vivid interpretation that is both beautifully played and recorded.

Trios for Piano, Violin, and Cello: No. 1 in B-flat, D. 898; No. 2 in E-flat, D. 929; Nocturne in E-flat, D. 897; Sonata Movement in B-flat, D. 28

Golub, piano; Kaplan, violin; Carr, cello. Arabesque Z-6580-2 [CD].

This divine music has had more than its fair share of outstanding recordings, beginning with a still electrifying (if technically and interpretively wayward) performance of the Trio No. 1 by the *always* electrifying and wayward Corot-Thibaud-Casals Trio from 1926. A decade later, an even more fabulous version of the Trio No. 2 appeared, featuring violinist Adolf Busch, his cello-playing brother Hermann, and son-in-law to be, Rudolf Serkin. Since then, all of the leading groups — Beaux Arts, Suk, Borodin — have come to terms with these cornerstones of the trio literature, as have some superb ad hoc ensembles such as Rubinstein-Heifetz-Feuermann and Rubinstein-Szeryng-Fournier.

That these recent recordings by Golub-Kaplan-Carr are so superb will come as no surprise to anyone familiar with their versions of the Brahms trios (see page 112); what *might* be surprising is how easily these three young musicians place all previous recordings in the shade. Mechanically, the playing is impeccable, as is the individual and collective musicianship. Yet it is the unusual combination of wisdom and freshness—qualities so central to the music itself—that make the interpretations such revelations.

In addition to the two rarely heard miniatures, the performance of the Trio No. 2 concludes with two fourth movements: the finale as it was published and is usually performed, together with the original version, which contains one hundred bars of very worthy music that Schubert persuaded himself to cut.

Wanderer Fantasie

Rubinstein, piano. RCA 6257-2-RC [CD].

Even when Sviatoslav Richter's overwhelming Angel recording from the early 1960s is released domestically (it can be found in Europe on an EMI compact disc), Artur Rubinstein's startling performance from the same period won't have to yield an inch. While not known as a Schubert specialist, Rubinstein was uniquely equipped to probe one of the most influential and forward-looking of the composer's works. For in his rhapsodic, possibly *overly* Romantic performance, Rubinstein draws the obvious parallel to the music that can trace its roots back to this path-breaking composition: the piano music of Schumann, Liszt, and his beloved Chopin.

The performances of the B-flat Major Sonata and the last two Op. 90 Impromptus are also superb, but it's this *Wanderer*— possibly the *Wanderer* of a lifetime—that counts.

Winterreise

Prey, baritone; Bianconi, piano. Denon C37-7240 [CD].

Hotter, bass; Moore, piano. Angel CDH-61002 [CD].

There aren't too many vocal works that can make Mahler's *Kindertotenlieder* or the Shostakovich Fourteenth Symphony seem cheerful in comparison, but that greatest of all song cycles, Schubert's *Winterreise*, is one of them. In the entire lieder repertoire, nothing can match the heartbreaking despair of this "Winter Journey" based on twenty-four poems by Wilhelm Müller; even the relatively bright moments, like "Der Lindenbaum," which has almost acquired folk-song status, are shot through with desolation and foreboding. And yet, like *King Lear*, *Winterreise* is neither self-pitying nor self-deluding. It is an unflinchingly courageous look at a horrible truth, and as such, a central musical catharsis of the Western imagination.

Hermann Prey's interpretation of *Winterreise* has been a classic of the recital platform for more than a quarter of a century. On stage, he typically performs it by itself, without preamble or encores and often, it is said, without taking any bows. It is a mature and completely selfless conception, dark without being dour, tragic with no hint of lugubriousness, effortless yet never glib. While none of his several recordings manages to fully capture the kind of devastating experience this *Winterreise* can be in the concert hall, the most recent version comes perilously close.

Hans Hotter's classic recording is also indispensable, but only for those who are willing to look directly into the black heart of absolute despair. More than any other singer, Hotter elevates this music to the shattering heights of Greek tragedy, in one of the most chilling vocal recordings ever made and one of the most courageous.

Schuman, William

(1910–1992)

New England Triptych; *Judith* (choreographic poem);
Variations on "America" (orchestration of organ work
by Charles Ives); Symphony No. 5

Seattle Symphony, Schwarz. Delos DE-3115 [CD].

The music William Schuman produced over a period of more
than fifty years represented the fusion of an essentially late-
Romantic temperament, a commanding modern intellect, and perhaps the most highly evolved sense of craftsmanship of any
American composer of his time. One of his greatest advocates,
Leonard Bernstein, provided a succinct summary of Schuman's art:
"vitality, optimism, enthusiasm, long lyrical line, rhythmic impetuosity, bristling counterpoint, brilliant textures, dynamic tension."
All of these qualities can be heard in the four works contained on
what may very well be the most completely successful Schuman
recording yet released.

In the capable hands of Gerard Schwarz and his finely honed
Seattle Symphony, the *New England Triptych* and the orchestration of Ives's *"America" Variations* emerge with a point and presence they have rarely enjoyed in the recording studio; the rarely
heard choreographic poem *Judith* and the magnificent Fifth Symphony are revealed as modern American masterworks.

For anyone interested in American music, this is a cause for
serious rejoicing.

Schumann, Robert

(1810–1856)

Carnaval; *Fantasiestücke*; *Waldscenen*

Rubinstein, piano. RCA 5667-2-RC [CD].

Nowhere is the genius of this purest and most tormented of the German Romantics heard to better advantage than in his works for solo piano. Beginning with *Carnaval*, which in 1834 announced the arrival of a major new composer, Robert Schumann began to evolve an entirely novel form of piano music: a large structure made up of many smaller parts that were tied together by a single, unifying poetic idea. Within this loose-knit "literary" framework, which allowed for the widest possible range of musical expression, Schumann produced the most fanciful, wildly imaginative piano works written up to that time. Compared to Schumann, Liszt (aside from the great B minor Sonata) was a purveyor of empty bombast, and Chopin was a broken record stuck in the same gloomy groove, a mood that H. L. Mencken aptly described as "two embalmers doing a post-mortem on a minor poet; the scent of tuberoses; autumn rain."

Until that most phantasmagorical of all *Carnaval* recordings returns to circulation—a version from the early '50s by the English pianist Solomon—Artur Rubinstein's RCA recording from the mid-1960s will probably remain unchallenged. The playing has ample color and sentiment, and just the right amount of rhythmic flippancy to make the individual pieces leap into life. The "Chopin" section is particularly lovely in its quiet restraint, and the final March of the Davidsbündler (Schumann's society of young, iconoclastic champions of the highest ideals in life and art) against the Philistines (represented by a mean-spirited little waltz) is unusually exciting.

Another Rubinstein recording (RCA 6258-2-RC [CD]), which features the pianist's unforgettable interpretations of *Kreisleriana* and the *Fantasia* in C is, if anything, even more successful, while CBS recordings by Murray Perahia offer subtle, spontaneous, and richly expressive versions of *Davidsbündlertänze* and the Op.

12 *Fantasiestücke* (MK-32299 [CD]), as well as performances of *Papillons* and the *Symphonic Etudes* (MK-34539 [CD]) in which poetry drips from every bar.

Concerto in A minor for Cello and Orchestra

Du Pré, cello; New Philharmonia Orchestra, Barenboim. EMI CDM-64626 [CD].

Until Sir Edward Elgar unveiled his masterpiece in the form in 1919, this soaring work by Schumann had the field to itself as the World's Second-Best Cello Concerto. Even now, the choice of which of these very different works should be ranked just behind the B minor Concerto of Antonín Dvořák is largely a matter of personal taste: whether one prefers the passionate lyricism of the Schumann or the Elgar's depth and starkly beautiful despair.

For years, the glowing early recording by the young Jacqueline du Pré stood alone among all versions of the Schumann Concerto, and its return to the catalog cannot be welcomed too warmly. Like her performance of the Elgar Concerto, this winsome, ebullient interpretation will remain one of her most enduring monuments, a fitting memorial to a great and tragically shortlived talent.

Concerto in A minor for Piano and Orchestra

Bishop-Kovecevich, piano; BBC Symphony, Davis. Philips 412923-2 [CD].

Like Edvard Grieg's A minor Concerto, a work with which it is almost invariably paired on recordings, the Schumann Piano Concerto represents something close to the finest work the Romantic era produced in the form. Moody, sensual, and heroic, it was also one of Schumann's greatest achievements with music cast on a larger scale. Like his admired Chopin, Schumann is still accused of being a miniaturist, incapable of sustaining extended forms; works like the Piano Concerto and the four symphonies triumphantly lay *that* nonsense to rest.

Neither the inspired, albeit slightly insane, version by Sviatoslav Richter and Lovro von Matačič nor the poetic and impulsive mid-'50s recording by Solomon available domestically, but Stephen

Bishop-Kovecevich and Colin Davis prove to be as persuasive in this warhorse as they are in the performance of the Grieg Concerto that accompanies it. Although the playing has an exhilarating Romantic waywardness about it, the Concerto's structure—to say nothing of its countless little details—is kept under admirable control. The immaculately balanced early '70s recorded sound barely shows its age.

Dichterliebe; Liederkreis, Op. 39

Fischer-Dieskau, baritone; Brendel, piano. Philips 416352-2 [CD].

When in 1840 a cigar-chomping, beer-guzzling, foul-mouthed womanizer named Robert Schumann settled down to the joys of what his near-contemporary Friedrich Engels called "that leaden boredom known as domestic bliss," not only the composer's life but also the history of art song would be altered forever. After a protracted legal struggle with his bride's domineering father, Schumann found that his marriage to Clara Wieck unleashed an astonishing outburst of creativity, that "Year of Song" in which he wrote most of the works that established him as Schubert's first great successor as a master of German lieder.

Schumann's sensitivity to the infinite shades of meaning in any text was extraordinary, helped no doubt by the fact that the composer, in his youth, had intended to become a poet. At Schumann's best, only Schubert and Hugo Wolf are his legitimate peers; even Brahms, Mahler, and Strauss, as important as their songs most certainly are, cannot really begin to approach the scope or quality of Schumann's achievement.

This Philips recording by Dietrich Fischer-Dieskau, like his now-deleted Deutsche Grammophon version with Christoph Eschenbach, is one of the best introductions to this tender, turbulent universe, offering superlative recordings of Schumann's most important cycles, the frequently bitter and desperate Dichterliebe (A Poet's Love) and the marvelous Op. 39 Liederkreis (literally, Song Cycle) on poems of Joseph von Eichendorff.

While Schumann is also being seriously affected by the protracted and frustrating lieder drought we're passing through, a spate of fine recent recordings suggests that relief may finally be in sight. A recording from the small British label Saga (SCD-9001 [CD]) offers Dame Janet Baker's incomparable version of Schumann's great female cycle, *Frauenliebe und-leben* (Woman's Love and Life). Though feminists have taken some undoubtedly warranted exception to this anthropologically accurate by-product of mid-nineteenth-century male chauvinism (the text says, in essence, that a woman's purpose is to love and serve her husband), the sweetly sentimental songs are so entrancing, you wind up not caring what the wretched words say.

Hermann Prey's Denon recording (CO 1518 [CD]) finds the great German baritone at his most musical and probing, with an approach that is both more direct and far less fussy than Fischer-Dieskau's. Elly Ameling's equally persuasive way with Schumann is captured on a single Edito Classica CD (77085-2), and two of the rising lieder stars of the current generation, Olaf Bär and Thomas Hampson, are featured on a pair of carefully chosen, superbly executed collections from Angel (CDC-54027 [CD]) and Teldec (2292-44935-2 [CD]).

Kinderscenen

Moravec, piano. Supraphon 11-0359-2 [CD]; Nonesuch 79063-4 [T].

Ivan Moravec's performance of Schumann's greatly beloved suite of childhood recollections as captured by Nonesuch is probably the most beautiful ever recorded. Its wide-eyed innocence is matched only by its technical perfection, and it is one of several recordings which make the convincing case that as a tonal colorist, Moravec is the late-twentieth-century equivalent of the legendary Walter Gieseking. Listen, especially, to the utterly unaffected, yet gently devastating performance of the famous "Träumerei," or the ambling miracle he makes of the celebrated opening bars of the piece, which have been pressed into service in recent films such as *My Brilliant Career* and *Sophie's Choice*.

The more recent Supraphon recording is every bit as distinguished; it comes with somewhat less appropriate—though magnificently turned out—partners, Bach's *Chromatic Fantasy* and the B-flat Major Sonata of Mozart.

Quartet in E-flat for Piano and Strings; Quintet in E-flat for Piano and Strings

> Beaux Arts Trio; Rhodes, viola; Bettleheim, violin. Philips 420791-2 [CD].

In addition to the three string quartets that popped out within a few weeks' time, both these vibrant works date from 1842, which musicologists have called "The Year of Chamber Music," possibly because Schumann produced more important chamber music in 1842 than at any other time of his life. (At college, my astronomy professor, the distinguished Hazel Losh, once amazed us all by pointing out the big red spot that can be seen in Jupiter's southern hemisphere and saying, with a perfectly straight face, "Now this is what we professional astronomers call 'The Big Red Spot of Jupiter.' ")

While the Quartet is a spectacularly fine piece, the Quintet is Schumann's greatest chamber work. Not only is it one of the most fruitful and compelling of all his compositions—I've never met anyone yet who could keep his feet from tapping in the dynamic final movement, or his jaw from going slack during its incredible double fugue—but also one of the most surprisingly original. For oddly enough, prior to 1842, no one had ever written a significant work for piano and string quartet.

The Beaux Arts Trio and company are at once meticulous and enthusiastic in both works, and the recordings are vivid and warm. It could be argued that the playing doesn't have the abundance of "character" that Glenn Gould brought to his wildly peculiar collaboration with the Juilliard String Quartet, available on a Sony CD (SMK-52684). On the other hand, the "Beaux-os' " performances are recognizably those by musicians from planet Earth.

Romances for Oboe and Piano; *Fantasiestücke*, Op. 73 (arrangement for oboe and piano); Violin Sonata in A minor (arrangement for oboe and piano); *Stücke im Volkston* (arrangement for oboe and piano)

> Kiss, oboe; Jandó, piano. Naxos 8.550599 [CD].

German Romanticism has little to offer in the way of significant solo music for the oboe; these delightful Schumann miniatures are just about it. The Hungarian oboist Josef Kiss proves as good as his name in these gently caressing performances, and the indefatigable Jenö Jandó is as musical and supportive as always.

What a charmer!

Scenes from Goethe's Faust

> Fischer-Dieskau, Pears, Harwood, Shirley-Quirk, Vyvyan, Aldeburgh Festival Chorus, English Chamber Orchestra, Britten. London 425705-2 [CD].

During a climactic moment in *Song of Love*, MGM's lavish, high-cholesterol screen biography of Schumann Paul Henried, as the composer, is happily conducting a big choral work when he begins hearing a disturbing, high-pitched noise. Since the producers could hardly tell audiences in 1947 that this was the initial symptom of the hideous venereal disease that would eventually drive Schumann mad, they tried to sidestep the issue in another, unintentionally uproarious scene. The brave Clara (Katharine Hepburn) emerges from her husband's study with a worried-looking medico who has just examined him. To the equally worried-looking Brahms (Robert Walker), she delivers the classic line: "Johannes, the doctor thinks that Robert may be suffering from *melancholia*."

The stirring music Henried was conducting was the *Scenes from Goethe's Faust*, one of the least-known of the composer's major works and, in its best pages, one of the most inspired. The reissue of Benjamin Britten's enthusiastic and deeply committed 1973 recording makes one wonder, all over again, why this generally magnificent score isn't heard more often. Anyone with an interest in Schumann and/or Romantic choral music should investigate this one immediately.

Sonatas (2) for Violin and Piano

> Kremer, violin; Argerich, piano. Deutsche Grammophon 419235-2 [CD].

Adolf Busch, the greatest German violinist of his generation, would occasionally program Schumann's A minor Violin Sonata, but for the most part musicians have tended to ignore it and its D minor companion piece for reasons that are difficult to explain. Although the Sonatas were written in 1851 at a time when he was becoming increasingly nervous and irritable as well as gradually losing his powers of concentration, both are unusually fresh and powerful works, showing no sign of the mental disorders that would soon completely envelop him.

Like Adolf Busch, Gidon Kremer is a serious musician with little time for idle virtuosity, and he proves to be an ideal exponent of these richly Romantic works. With able support from Martha Argerich, he places these brilliant, brooding works where they properly belong: among the masterpieces of the instrument's literature.

Symphonies (4)

Amsterdam Concertgebouw Orchestra, Haitink. Philips 416126-2 [CD].

While there have been performances of the individual symphonies that offer more flair and color—George Szell's CBS recording of the *Spring* and Fourth Symphonies is especially riveting (CBS MYK-38468 [CD], MYT-38468 [T]), and Carlo Maria Giulini's Los Angeles version of the *Rhenish* (Deutsche Grammophon 427818-2 [CD]) is unique in its poetry and adult passion—the most consistently satisfying set of Robert Schumann's four great symphonies is the one led by Bernard Haitink. The interpretations are utterly free of exaggeration: tempos are judicious; textures are beautifully controlled and balanced, and throughout all these carefully judged, meticulously executed performances is a sense of inevitability and rightness few modern recordings can equal. Compared to some of the more strong-willed recordings on the market (those by Levine, Bernstein, and Furtwängler, as well as those listed above), Haitink, at first, might seem a trifle colorless and bland. With repeated exposure, however, his maturity and enormous dignity, together with the fabulous playing of the orchestra, more than carry the day.

Scriabin, Alexander

(1872–1915)

Symphonies (5)

Philadelphia Orchestra, Muti. Angel CDC-54251 [CD].

Even by the transcendentally self-indulgent standards of late-Imperial Russia, Alexander Scriabin was an extravagant figure: a musician, poet, philosopher, and mystic who sought to unite music, poetry, drama, and dance into a new visionary art form he called the "Mystery." Less an aesthetic principal than a theological one, "Mystery" was intended to be an all-embracing new gospel into which the whole of human experience would be subsumed, a kind of artistic equivalent of Einstein's elusive unified field theory.

Needless to say, no one—including Scriabin himself—was precisely certain what any of this mumbling mumbo-jumbo meant, yet it led to some of the most interesting, and understandably decadent, music to have emerged from the final years of the Romanov dynasty. Scriabin is at his intensely overwrought best in the final three symphonies, which were naturally given the excessively dramatic subtitles of *Divine Poem*, *Poem of Ecstasy*, and *Prometheus, the Poem of Fire.*

While they are not the most completely persuasive recordings these problematical works have ever received—another conductor of the Philadelphia Orchestra, Leopold Stokowski, left some hair-raising interpretations during the 78 era—Riccardo Muti's performances are alert, sensuous, and wholly sympathetic. The two early symphonies come off equally well (no finer recording of either has ever been made), and the playing of the orchestra is a wonder at every turn.

Those who respond to Scriabin's rarefied, deeply personal vision will also want to acquire Vladimir Ashkenazy's brilliant and knowing accounts of the ten Piano Sonatas, now crammed on a pair of medium-priced London CDs (425579-2). If not the ideal performances of all these challenging works—Horowitz virtually owned the final two (CBS MK-42411 [CD])—they still present a balanced, musical, and immensely well-played vision of an exceptionally interesting body of work.

Shchedrin, Rodion

(1932–)

Carmen Ballet (after Bizet), for Strings and Percussion

Bolshoi Theatre Orchestra, Rozhdestvensky. Eurodisc 7933-2-RG [CD].

In the pre-*glasnost* 1960s, some imaginative press people on both sides of what used to be called the Iron Curtain were trying to pass Rodion Shchedrin off as the latest incarnation of the classic Russian enfant terrible, whose predecessors included Sergei Prokofiev and Dmitri Shostakovich. And there probably *were* people in positions of power who were shocked by Shchedrin's music—but they were those who would have been shocked by the music of Lawrence Welk.

The "new Shostakovich" was in reality an irremediably conventional, extremely well-behaved composer: if not a Party hack like Marian Koval, Mikhai Chulaki or Tikhon Khrennikov, then still a man whose music was unlikely to offend the most reactionary *appartchik*'s grandmother. (How subversive could someone be who in 1969 produced a cantata called—and surely you can whistle its principal themes, can't you?—*Lenin in the People's Heart?*)

The *Carmen Ballet*, Shchedrin's most "original" work to date, is a cutesy though frequently inspired arrangement for strings and a ridiculously overstocked percussion section of familiar themes from the Bizet opera. After a half dozen exposures its charm begins to wear a little thin, but it's fun to hear every couple of years or so. In spite of the fairly harsh recorded sound, Gennadi Rozhdestvensky's barn-burner of a performance is the preferred one.

Shostakovich, Dmitri

(1906–1975)

Concerto No. 1 in C minor for Piano, Trumpet, and Orchestra; *Chamber Symphony*; Preludes

Kissin, piano; Moscow Virtuosi, Spivakov. RCA 7947-2-RC [CD].

Yevgeny Kissin is one of the latest in that seemingly inexhaustible line of gifted young pianists with which the Soviet Union had peacefully bombarded the world since a diminutive firebrand named Vladimir Ashkenazy burst on the scene in the mid-1950s. Kissin, who like his predecessors seems to have unlimited reserves of technique and temperament, is extremely well suited to both the wiseacre exuberance and unexpected tenderness of Shostakovich's most familiar concerto. Vladimir Spivakov and the more or less aptly named Moscow Virtuosi give the kid admirably pointed support and are equally efficient in the *Chamber Symphony*, arranged by Rudolf Barshai from Shostakovich's dramatic String Quartet No. 8.

In the Violin Concertos written for David Oistrakh, whose live Royal Albert Hall performances are available on an Intaglio CD (INCD-7241), the Virgin recording by Dmitri Sitkovetsky and the BBC Symphony under Andrew Davis is a revelation, with playing of such fiery commitment, it seems to place both concertos (even the problematical Second) among the instrument's most important modern works.

For those who believe in the Shostakovich cello concertos—I have little faith in them myself—Heinrich Schiff and the Bavarian Radio Orchestra led by the composer's son Maxim offer a polished, authoritative version of the First Concerto and the only available recording of the somewhat aimless Second (Philips 412526-2 [CD]).

Lady Macbeth of Mtsensk

> Vishnevskaya, Finnilä, Gedda, Petkov, Haugland,
> Ambrosian Opera Chorus, London Philharmonic,
> Rostropovich. Angel CDCB-49955 [CD].

The success of the first Moscow production of *Lady Macbeth of Mtsensk* was such that in January of 1936 the opera-loving Joseph Stalin went to the Bolshoi to find out what all the shouting was about. He didn't like what he heard, as *Pravda* explained in the infamous article, "Muddle instead of Music." In the first of many such public denunciations, *Lady Macbeth* was accused of "modernism," "leftism," and "discordance," thus forcing the dazed Shostakovich to cancel the upcoming premiere of the *really* discordant Fourth Symphony and begin planning his great public "apology," the Fifth.

As usual, Joe got it dead wrong. *Lady Macbeth* is not only one of the powerful twentieth-century stage works, but also a Russian opera whose originality and intensity places it in the company of Mussorgsky's *Boris Godunov*. As the murderous heroine, Galina Vishnevskaya gives one of her most thrilling recorded performances in a role where her customary hooting and bellowing actually add to the characterization (a Vishnevskaya Norma or Mimi—perish the thought—would be an entirely different matter). The conducting of her sometime husband Mstislav Rostropovich is also more impressive than it has ever been before, with moments of singular beauty alternating with moments of shattering power. The supporting cast is uniformly excellent, and the recorded sound will stand your hair on end.

*P*reludes and Fugues (24) for Piano

> Nikolaeva, piano. Melodiya SUCD 10-00073/75 [CD].

Shostakovich's most important work for solo piano was inspired by music of Bach that the composer heard Tatiana Nikolaeva play in Leipzig during the Bach bicentennial year of 1950. Though certainly not as even in inspiration as the *Well-Tempered Klavier*, the Preludes and Fugues contain a wide range of emotion and an unusually high level of invention; there may be less successful moments here and there but rarely if ever a dull one. Nikolaeva, who was consulted almost daily during the composition, plays with the same kind of authority Yevgeny Mravinsky brought to his performances of the symphonies. (The pianist actually collapsed during a performance of the Preludes and Fugues in San Francisco and died shortly thereafter.) The interpretation has a depth, a variety of expression, and a galvanizing unity of purpose that will probably never be superseded, making it one of the half dozen definitive Shostakovich recordings.

String Quartets (15)

Borodin Quartet. Angel CDC-49266/70 [CD].

If there was ever the slightest doubt that the fifteen String Quartets of Dmitri Shostakovich rank not only with the major chamber works of the twentieth century, but with the most significant works in the form since Beethoven, this triumphant cycle by the Borodin Quartet should lay it to rest. Begun in 1935, when the composer already had four symphonies to his credit, the Quartets eventually became, as they had for Beethoven before him, the vehicle for expressing the most private of all his thoughts and emotions. (Nevertheless, Shostakovich vigorously discouraged any suggestion that the symphonies were the public statements of the "official" Shostakovich, and that the Quartets were the ruminations of the introverted, painfully shy man within. However, given that some of the early Quartets are genuinely symphonic in their structure and expression, and some of the later symphonies are almost chamberlike in their size and proportions, the oversimplified generalization seems to fit.)

For a time, a superb series of all fifteen Quartets in performances by England's Fitzwilliam Quartet was available domestically on Oiseau-Lyre. As fine as those interpretations certainly were, they have now been superseded by this incredible, and probably historic, version by the Borodin Quartet. Having studied with the composer extensively (they were his favorite chamber ensemble after the celebrated Beethoven Quartet, which gave most of these works their world premieres), the Borodins bring an incomparable authority and understanding to the music that no other ensemble can begin to rival. They also possess one of the most individual physical sounds in the musical world today: a sound at once rich and sparse, pointed and flexible, from a collection of clearly defined individuals who work as a completely unified, indissoluble whole.

With the exception of the autobiographical Eighth Quartet, with its programmatic allusions to the Second World War and quotations from many of the composer's previous works, none of these extraordinary pieces has yet to enter the standard chamber repertoire, nor are they likely to do so any time soon. Still, they represent as individual and uncompromising a body of work as has been produced so far in this century, from the formal complexity of the early quartets, to the wrenching, often lugubrious death throes of the final works in the series. The Quartet No. 15, for instance, is a series of six unrelentingly gloomy Adagios, all cast in the key of E-flat minor. In short, while this is certainly not a series of recordings that will appeal to admirers of the *1812 Overture* and *Victory at Sea*, it represents one of the most daring and significant recording projects of the last decade. At present, there would seem to be no plans to release these amazing performances on cassette. Which means we will have to content ourselves with one of the first authentic milestones in the brief history of the compact disc.

Symphony No. 1 in E

London Philharmonic, Haitink. London 414667-2 [CD].

There is a case to be made that Dmitri Shostakovich never wrote a more audaciously original work than this youthful masterpiece, submitted as a graduation exercise to Leningrad Conservatory when he was only eighteen. In it, many of the Shostakovich hallmarks—the sardonic humor, the grand gestures, the often brilliantly eccentric orchestration—are clearly in evidence, together with a freshness and almost palpable joy in the act of composition that none of his fourteen subsequent symphonies would ever really recapture. (Within several years of its premiere, the First Symphony had made Shostakovich a world-famous figure, and hence, from the mid-1920s onward, a man Soviet officialdom would try to keep on an increasingly tight leash.)

Bernard Haitink's excellent London recording is easily the first choice among all versions on compact disc. Less immediate and personal than the Bernstein recording on Deutsche Grammophon, it is nevertheless a powerful, deeply committed reading, and one that is exceptionally well played and recorded.

Symphony No. 5 in D minor

New York Philharmonic, Bernstein. CBS MYK-37218 [CD], MYT-37218 [T].

Not to be confused with their second recording of perhaps the most famous twentieth-century Russian symphony (a performance taped on tour in Tokyo in 1979), this is the celebrated recording Bernstein and the Philharmonic made two decades earlier, after returning from a highly publicized tour of the Soviet Union. The reasons this remains the most satisfying of all recordings of the Shostakovich Fifth—a work that Bernstein's mentor, Serge Koussevitzky, found as indestructible and universal as the Fifth Symphony of Beethoven—are as clear today as they were when the recording was first released.

Bernstein's interpretation succeeds because he views the Symphony not as an ironic or paradoxical work, but rather as one that marks the culmination of the nineteenth-century Russian symphonic tradition. Which is not to say, exactly, that he treats the work as though it might have been written by a harmonically advanced Tchaikovsky, but that *does* seem to be the overall impression he wants the Symphony to make. From the crushing opening statement of the principal theme, through the unusually expansive (and expressive) Adagio, to the giddy, helter-skelter finale, this is a Shostakovich Fifth that is as direct, vibrant, and openhearted as any large-scale orchestral work any Russian ever composed.

And if, in light of some of the more recent performances of the work, Bernstein's view might seem a bit *too* Romantic and literal, it should be remembered that the composer often said Bernstein was his favorite American interpreter. The New York Philharmonic plays as well as they ever have in their history, and the recorded sound—especially in the compact disc version—barely shows its age.

Symphonies: No. 6 in B minor; No. 9 in E-flat

Oslo Philharmonic, Jansons. Angel CDC-54339 [CD].

Even though the Sixth Symphony has no subtitle, this profoundly pessimistic work could easily be called "Music to Go Out and Shoot Yourself By." The Largo, regarded by some as the greatest slow movement in Shostakovich, is so full of angst and unrelieved anguish that the two slight and apparently lighthearted movements that follow it come off as a sinister, horribly unfunny joke. On the other hand, Stalin and his musical flunkies considered the Ninth Symphony another kind of very bad joke. Following the conclusion of the Great Patriotic War, he expected some grandiose paean of thanksgiving (with Stalin the principal honoree), not one of the lightest and most amusing of all Shostakovich's works.

The Riga-born, Leningrad-trained Mariss Jansons leads compellingly idiomatic performances of both symphonies, each cut from the same cloth as, but by no means slavishly imitative of, those of his teacher, Yevgeny Mravinsky. The playing of the Oslo Philharmonic is refined and sophisticated, as is the recorded sound.

Symphony No. 7 in C, *Leningrad*

Chicago Symphony, Bernstein. Deutsche Grammophon 427632-2 [CD].

Thanks to conductors like Bernard Haitink, Paavo Berglund, Mariss Jansons, Gennadi Rozhdestvensky, and Neeme Järvi, all of whom have made dignified, searching, musical, or illuminating recordings of the composer's most controversial symphony, the once wildly lionized, once savagely pilloried *Leningrad* seems well on the way to a general rehabilitation, to use an expression from the bad old post-Stalinist days. Though it can never recapture the phenomenal popularity it enjoyed as a symbol of Soviet resistance during the Second World War, the *Leningrad* is being widely accepted now as a serious, substantial, worthwhile work.

Don't believe it for a moment.

Béla Bartók, who parodied the famous first-movement march theme so mercilessly in his *Concerto for Orchestra*, was absolutely right: The *Leningrad* is seventy minutes of understandably shallow, grossly manufactured, spur-of-the-moment junk that no amount of interpretive devotion can redeem.

Leonard Bernstein, in this live recording with the Chicago Symphony, refuses to take the revisionist view of the *Leningrad* Symphony, with predictably pleasurable results. The only *enjoyment* to be had in this bellicose nonsense lies in accepting it for the trash it is and having a good, messy wallow. In a performance even more agreeably vulgar and theatrical than his old New York Philharmonic recording, this is precisely what Bernstein allows us to do.

Symphony No. 8 in C minor

Leningrad Philharmonic, Mravinsky. Philips 422442-2 [CD].

Completed only two years after the windy and prolix *Leningrad* Symphony, the Shostakovich Eighth is (with the single possible exception of the Tenth) the masterpiece among the composer's mature orchestral works. Beginning with one of the greatest symphonic Adagios written after Mahler, the Eighth is a dark, sprawling, grotesque, and enervating work, a combination of a stark outcry against the terrors of the Second World War and the soundtrack for some unimaginable Hollywood horror movie which, fortunately for everyone, was never made. The reactions this great and controversial work continue to provoke are perhaps more extreme than those caused by all of Shostakovich's other works put together: Koussevitzky considered it the greatest orchestral piece of this century; Stalin, as well as other infinitely more civilized listeners, considered it unpleasant, irredeemable trash.

The live 1982 recording of a performance led by Yevgeny Mravinsky, the Symphony's dedicatee, is certainly worth owning, not only as a souvenir of a great musician but as an incomparable interpretation. Although as always, Mravinsky's tempos tend to be on the brisk side, these in no way lessen the cumulative impact of the performance: at its conclusion, you feel very much as though you'd been squashed by a tank, which was precisely the effect the composer intended. It is a great interpretation and one that suggests why the composer entrusted this man with the premieres of so many of his works.

Symphony No. 10 in E minor

Leningrad Philharmonic, Mravinsky. Erato 2292-45753-2 [CD].

If we are to believe Shostakovich in his posthumously published *Testimony*, the Tenth Symphony was his rueful, bitter, sardonic reflection on the Stalin years. In fact, the composer even goes so far as to tell us that the diabolical Scherzo of the work was a portrait of that murderous psychopath himself. Whatever the immediate source of the Tenth's inspiration, it is one of the greatest symphonies of the twentieth century and one of the most compelling works a Russian composer has so far produced.

In the late 1960s, Herbert von Karajan, in one of his last palatable recordings (Deutsche Grammophon 429716-2 [CD]), left a staggeringly brilliant account of the Tenth, since superseded by one of his typical smooth-shod monstrosities, which is to be avoided at all costs. On the other hand, Bernard Haitink's sober, sobering, yet ultimately triumphant and inexplicably withdrawn London recording showed what an ego of human proportions coupled with an immense talent can do. The performance had a sense of dogged decency about it, as if the conductor felt the need to keep the work as far removed from the obscenity that inspired it. It also had moments of snarling rage and dizzy excitement, and was exceedingly well played. One can only hope that it, as well as Haitink's other fine Shostakovich recordings which have fallen under the deletions ax, will reappear on one of London's budget labels soon.

On a medium-priced Erato recording, Mravinsky leads a typically fierce and withering interpretation in very acceptable modern sound. To be sure, it is not a note-perfect performance (toward the end, a few technical chinks finally begin to appear in the old knight's armor), but in the main it is an exhausting and exhilarating experience and one not to be missed.

Symphony No. 15 in A; *From Jewish Folk Poetry* for Soprano, Contralto, Tenor, and Piano (orchestrated 1964)

> Söderström, soprano; Wenkel, contralto; Karczykowski, tenor; Concertgebouw Orchestra of Amsterdam, Haitink. London 417581-2 [CD].

Even for those of us who consider Shostakovich the most important symphonist of the twentieth century, the Thirteenth and

Fourteenth Symphonies are difficult pills to swallow. As great as they clearly are, they are also unspeakably depressing. *Babi Yar*, a setting of Yevtushenko's powerful poem on the subject of an infamous Nazi atrocity, and its haunted successor, which is less a symphony than a cycle of orchestral songs on the subject of death, are too painful to be heard more than once or twice in a lifetime.

For those who are inclined to approach them more frequently, Bernard Haitink's Philips recordings are unlikely to be superseded. The performance of *Babi Yar* bristles with anger and savage indignation (417261-2 [CD]), and the exhausting interpretation of the Fourteenth (417514-2 [CD]) is marked by the unusual but highly effective novelty of presenting each of the poems by García Lorca, Apollonaire, Rilke, and the rest in their original languages instead of the run-of-the-mill Russian translations that were sung in earlier recordings. If the purpose was to make this death-obsessed work even more universal, it succeeded admirably.

If with its peculiar quotations of the *William Tell* Overture and a motif from Wagner's *Götterdämmerung* the Fifteenth Symphony would seem to be a far less serious work, it was Haitink's recording that finally demonstrated that the quirks and clowning were only skin-deep. Although some of the material still sounds rather thin for a valedictory, Haitink was the first, and to date the *only*, conductor to prove conclusively that Shostakovich's cryptic final symphony was not some sort of elaborate practical joke. The orchestral version of *From Jewish Folk Poetry*, one of the most engaging song cycles by a Russian composer since the death of Mussorgsky, rounds out this generous and important release.

Trio No. 2 in E minor for Piano, Violin, and Cello

Palsson-Tellefsen-Helmerson. Bis CD-26 [CD].

The E minor Piano Trio might just be Shostakovich's chamber masterpiece; at very least, it is one of his most powerful and deeply personal works. Written in memory of the composer's closest friend, the brilliant musicologist Ivan Sollertinsky, who somehow survived both the Stalinist purges of the 1930s and the Nazis only to drink himself to death in 1944, the Trio is an exercise in hilarious anguish, or anguished hilarity, depending on which paradoxical designation you prefer. Its most excruciating moment is the finale, a jovial *danse macabre* that breaks the bonds of conventional gallows humor to enter a previously unexplored realm of darkness.

After more than twenty years, this remains one of the greatest of all Shostakovich recordings. The three young Swedish musicians exposed the bitter heart of the Trio more fearlessly than any ensemble ever has. They bring a special insight and finish to each of these problematical movements, but it is their performance of the grotesque final dance that will chill you to the bone. In spite of its age, the recorded sound is still a model of warmth and intimacy.

Viola Sonata

Bashmet, viola; Muntian, piano. RCA 09026-61273-2 [CD].

In addition to being Shostakovich's swan song, the Viola Sonata is among the most pitiless and terrifying works of twentieth-century music: the composer's cold, steady look at his own rapidly approaching death, which he awaits with neither hope, nor bitterness, nor even very much emotion. Yuri Bashmet gives a suitably devastating performance of the piece, with playing in the final bars so purposefully drained of life that you begin to wonder how he could have survived it. Although it makes for a thoroughly chilling experience, the work is strangely heroic, too: a great atheist's stubborn refusal to even consider the possibility of a deathbed conversion.

Sibelius, Jean (1865–1957)

The Bard; *En Saga*; *In Memoriam* (Funeral March for Orchestra); *Lemminkäinen's Return*; Symphony No. 4; *Valse triste*

> London Philharmonic, Beecham. Koch Legacy 3-7061-2 [CD].

These famous interpretations from the late 1930s are among the greatest Sibelius recordings ever made; in fact, the only Sibelius symphony recording that can be mentioned in the same breath with Sir Thomas Beecham's ripely eloquent Fourth is that conductor's 1947 version of the Sixth, said to have been Sibelius's favorite recording of any of his works. Although the sound in Koch's transfer is not ideal (it is rather opaque and tubby compared to the now withdrawn EMI reissue), nothing can dull the sheen of these magical performances, which set an unapproachable standard for all these works.

Concerto in D minor for Violin and Orchestra

> Perlman, violin; Pittsburgh Symphony, Previn. Angel CDC-47167 [CD].

In many respects, Jean Sibelius remains the most mysterious composer of modern times. A national hero in his native Finland while still quite a young man, and a composer who, during his lifetime, enjoyed as much critical and popular adulation as any composer ever has, Sibelius simply closed up his musical shop in the mid-1920s, writing nothing of significance for the next thirty years. (Rumors of a completed Eighth Symphony circulated for more than three decades, although no such work was found in his papers at the time of his death.)

The popular Violin Concerto dates from 1903, the period of some of his finest theatrical music (*Pélleas et Mélisande*), the tone poem *Pohjola's Daughter*, and the Second Symphony. Beginning with a famous early electrical recording by Jascha Heifetz and Sir

Thomas Beecham, the Concerto has always been brilliantly represented on records, from an unforgettable performance in the late
1940s by the French violinist Ginette Neveu to the more recent—
and finer—of Itzhak Perlman's two versions. Compared to his earlier outing with Erich Leinsdorf and the Boston Symphony, the new
recording with André Previn and the Pittsburgh Symphony is at
once more dramatic and more relaxed. While tempos, especially in
the first two movements, tend to be on the leisurely side, there is
nothing in the performance that could be considered even remotely
lethargic or slack. The interpretation has a wonderful feeling of
expansiveness to it, a performance cast and executed on the grandest possible scale. The support Perlman receives from Previn and his
forces is, as usual, exemplary, and the recorded sound is absolutely
first-rate.

Finlandia; *En Saga*; *The Swan of Tuonela*; *Night Ride and Sunrise*; *Pohjola's Daughter*

> L'Orchestre de la Suisse Romande, Stein. London 417697-2 [CD].

Except for the *Karelia Suite* and *Tapiola*, which are now being
brilliantly served on another London recording by the Philharmonia Orchestra led by Vladimir Ashkenazy (417762-2 [CD]),
this reissue of material originally recorded in the early 1970s represents the most complete and generous selection of Sibelius's shorter
works now being offered on compact disc.

On the basis of this and a handful of other recordings made
two decades ago, many (myself included) predicted that Horst
Stein, a German conductor known primarily for his work in the
opera house, was on the brink of a major international career. (God
knows, with plum posts like the Concertgebouw Orchestra of Amsterdam and now the New York Philharmonic going to either rank
incompetents or plodding kapellmeisters, the conductor shortage
has become dangerously acute.)

Be that as it may, these versions of some of the composer's
most popular tone poems are among the best on the market, with
Night Ride and Sunrise and *Pohjola's Daughter* being especially
well-played and thrilling. Those who grew up on L'Orchestre de la
Suisse Romande during the long and memorable Ansermet era will

hardly recognize the ensemble. The solo woodwinds manage to lose that pinched quality, which suggested the players weren't being adequately fed, and the brass bring off feats that recall the exploits of their colleagues in Vienna and Berlin.

*F*our Legends from the Kalevalá (*Lemminkäinen and the Maidens of Saari*; *The Swan of Tuonela*; *Lemminkäinen in Tuonela*; *Lemminkäinen's Return*)

Gothenberg Symphony, Järvi. Bis CD-294 [CD].

Unfortunately, the second of this group of four tone poems based on the Finnish national epic was once so popular that many people were unaware it was only part (and in some ways, the least interesting part) of a larger, superbly dramatic, hugely entertaining score. It has taken some time, but the *Four Legends* have finally begun to come together again into an indissoluble whole, thanks largely to the recording industry.

One of the most brilliant installments in his distinguished Sibelius series for Bis, Järvi's is easily the most impressive version in a still uncrowded field. The richly atmospheric recorded sound is a perfect complement to these darkly brooding performances; the Gothenberg Orchestra again play their hearts out for the conductor, while Järvi misses few opportunities to paint the scenes in the most vivid possible hues.

Another fine Bis collection (CD-359 [CD]) features the lushly erotic *Belshazzar's Feast*, the charming *Swanwhite* incidental music, together with the Dance Intermezzo, *The Dryad*, and *Pan and Echo* in similarly idiomatic, beautifully recorded performances. An anthology of generally lighter pieces (except for *The Bard*, given a powerfully introspective performance) is also delightful (CD-384 [CD]).

*S*ongs for Male Choir (complete)

Helsinki University Chorus. Finlandia FACD-205-S [CD].

Since almost all of Sibelius's vocal music remains terra incognita (how many people know he actually wrote an opera called *The Maid in the Tower*, a pair of cantatas with the irresistible titles

Oma maa and *Maan virsi*, and more than a hundred songs?), here is an unusually alluring invitation to wander down this completely unbeaten path. In addition to a stunning vocal setting of the hymn from *Finlandia* that will snap the goose pimples to attention, the Helsinki University Chorus offers elegant, virile performances of twenty-four other a capella works whose quality ranges from the merely splendid to the nearly sublime.

Symphonies (7)

Boston Symphony, C. Davis. Philips 416600-2 [CD].

There was a time, not so terribly long ago, when some of these seven extraordinary works were heard with the same frequency as the nine symphonies of Beethoven. In fact, during the 1930s and '40s they were probably the most frequently performed orchestral works written during the preceding hundred years. Much of the credit for Sibelius's popularity, aside from the power and originality of the music itself, was due to a group of gifted and tireless champions, including Sir Thomas Beecham, Leopold Stokowski, and Serge Koussevitzky, men whose compelling, highly individual interpretations made the Finnish symphonist's name a household word throughout the musical world.

From Koussevitzky's time to the present, the Boston Symphony has remained one of the world's great Sibelius orchestras. And while several individual interpretations might be marginally preferable—the thrilling new EMI recordings by Mariss Jansons and the Oslo Philharmonic of the First (CDC-54273 [CD]) and Second (CDC-54804 [CD]), and Sir Simon Rattle's dazzling Angel recording of the Fifth (CDM-64122 [CD]) deserve all the lavish critical praise they have received—the BSO's complete set of the symphonies under Sir Colin Davis is one of the best imaginable introductions to the music, either for the novice or the most jaded of collectors. As a Sibelius conductor, Davis represents a golden mean between the audacity of his predecessors and the somewhat cooler approach of the modern school. All the strength and cragginess of the music remains intact, though Sir Colin is also meticulous with textures and details. In short, these are performances which, while they remove some of the bark, leave the trees healthy and intact.

The Boston Symphony plays this music like no other orchestra in the world, and Philips's recorded sound, after nearly two decades, remains a model of clarity and warmth. As a bonus, the generously packed discs include superlative performances of the ever-popular *Finlandia*, *Swan of Tuonela*, and *Tapiola*. All in all, one of the few authentic bargains on the market today.

Smetana, Bedřich (1824–1884)

The Bartered Bride

Běnáčková-Capová, Dvořsky, Novák, Czech Philharmonic Orchestra and Chorus, Kosler. Supraphon 10-3511 [CD].

Three Dances from *The Bartered Bride*

Cleveland Orchestra, Szell. CBS MYK-36716 [CD], MYT-36716.

As immensely and eternally entertaining as *The Bartered Bride* certainly is, its historical importance in the development of Czech music is all but impossible to calculate. Prior to *Prodaná Nevěsta*, Bohemia had been widely known as the conservatory of Europe, a tiny province of the sprawling Austro-Hungarian empire that had always supplied the courts of Europe with some of their finest musicians. Yet Czech composers, before Smetana, were indistinguishable from their German and Austrian counterparts; many, in fact, in order to secure important positions, Germanized their names.

The Bartered Bride was Bohemia's musical Declaration of Independence. A work that not only was based on decidedly Czech themes but also captured the essential spirit of Czech folk music and dance, *Prodaná Nevěsta* made its difficult, irascible composer a national hero. (The only Czech opera that has entered the standard repertoire of every major opera house, it is revered as a national monument in Czechoslovakia.) Without it, the master-works of Smetana's maturity are virtually unthinkable, and had it never been written, composers like Dvořák and Janáček might never have evolved as they did.

A number of fine recorded performances of the opera have been available through the years, but none can begin to approach the brilliant Supraphon release, which will undoubtedly set the standard for *Bartered Brides* for decades to come. In the title role, Gabriela Běnáčkova-Capová—the reigning queen of Prague's National Theater and one of the finest dramatic sopranos in the world today—will probably not be bettered for the remainder of this century. She sings with an ease, warmth, femininity, and freshness that only Elisabeth Schwarzkopf, in a few tantalizing German-language excerpts from the late 1950s, could begin to match. Peter Dvořsky is equally outstanding as the wily hero Jenik, and the rest of the cast—especially the marriage broker of Richard Novák—could not have been bettered either on records or off.

Although Zdeněk Košler's interpretation is as zestful and refreshing as any the opera has ever received, the principal selling point in a recording loaded with selling points is the playing of the great Czech Philharmonic. They perform this music as no other orchestra possibly could, and the lusty, brilliantly trained chorus is as rowdy, rousing, and tender as anyone could wish.

For those poor misguided souls who think they can do without a complete recording of *The Bartered Bride* (then, too, there are probably people who can live without sunshine, root beer popsicles, and sex), George Szell's classic recording of the three popular dances (the Polka, Furiant, and Dance of the Comedians) is the greatest single performance ever given of the opera's most frequently heard orchestral excerpts. Actually, this is one of the most valuable recordings of Czech music ever made, including, as it does, what may easily be the definitive versions of Smetana's popular *Moldau*, and the *Carnival Overture* of Dvořák.

Hakon Jarl; *Prague Carnival*; *Richard III*; *Wallenstein's Camp*

Bavarian Radio Symphony, Kubelik. Deutsche Grammophon 437254-2 [CD].

Apart from the well-intentioned but ultimately disastrous *Festive Symphony*—which in attempting to placate Emperor Franz Josef used Haydn's "Emperor's Hymn" as its principal theme thus effectively consigning itself to oblivion among the freedom-loving Czechs (an adequate if hardly inspired performance of the work is available on Marco Polo 8.223120)—this appealing collection offers virtually all of Smetana's significant orchestral music written before and after *Má Vlast*. The earlier tone poems (*Hakon Jarl, Richard III, Wallenstein's Camp*) are full of Romantic enthusiasm and good ideas, and the *Prague Carnival* is top-drawer Smetana, effectively argued and brilliantly scored.

Packaged with his superlative version of Janáček's *Sinfonietta*, Kubelik's 1971 recordings are wholly idiomatic and persuasive, with a fine eye for detail and a benign tolerance of the composer's early tendency toward melodramatic overstatement (the wonderfully corny offstage bugle calls in *Wallenstein's Camp* are especially effective). The Bavarian Radio Symphony is at the top of its form throughout, as are DG's engineers.

Má Vlast (*My Fatherland*)

Czech Philharmonic, Kubelik. Supraphon 111208 [CD].

Smetana began work on what would prove to be his only major contribution to symphonic thought in the same week of 1874 that he resigned his post as principal conductor of Prague's Provisional Theatre. At the age of fifty, the composer of *The Bartered Bride* was totally deaf. What had at first been diagnosed as a minor ear infection proved to be the first symptom of the neurosyphilis that would also claim his sanity and, ultimately, his life.

Má Vlast, his magnificent, uneven, terribly moving collection of six symphonic poems, is perhaps the greatest musical love letter a composer ever wrote to his native country. *The Moldau* has become justly famous, and the entire cycle contains much of the best that the father of Czech music had to give to nineteenth-century music. It is one of the cornerstones of Romantic art, and one of the purest expressions of the nationalistic spirit ever heard in Western music.

As a performance of the cycle, no modern recording has ever managed to efface the memory of those two versions the great Václav Talich made in 1929 and 1954. (A third version, from 1941, is one of the rarest recordings any major conductor has ever made.) Both versions are finally available, the earlier from Koch (3-7032-2 [CD], 3-7032-4 [T]), the later from Supraphon (SUP-111896 [CD]), each in excellent transfers that merely serve to confirm all the legends.

Among modern recordings of *Má Vlast*, none is more highly charged emotionally than the live performance from the 1990 Prague Spring Festival, which marked Rafael Kubelik's return to his native city after an exile of more than forty years. As in the conductor's three earlier recordings of the cycle, all of which are currently available, this is a large, full-throated, yet deeply poetic reading, made all the more electric by the special circumstances of the occasion. The orchestra plays brilliantly for its old music director, and the recorded sound is first-rate.

String Quartet No. 1 in E minor, *From My Life*

Panocha Quartet. Supraphon 11-1514-2 [CD].

London Symphony, Simon. Chandos CHAN-8412 [CD], ABTD-1149 [T] (orchestration by George Szell).

There is no more poignant chamber work in music than this autobiographical string quartet Smetana completed shortly after he was engulfed by the deafness that would remain with him throughout the remaining ten years of his life. While the final movement, which contains the famous high-pitched E in the first violin (representative of the initial symptom of his hearing loss), is one of the most shattering moments in nineteenth-century music, the Quartet is in fact a predominantly buoyant and cheerful work. It looks backward to the composer's youth with a charming and gentle nostalgia, and even manages to look forward to the troubled future with great dignity and courage.

The Panocha Quartet gives a wonderfully alert and compassionate performance of this great work, with a slow movement aching with tenderness and a finale that bristles with excitement. And instead of the inevitable coupling of Dvořák's *American* Quartet, they offer Smetana's rarely heard Second Quartet, which is certainly not as memorable as the E minor but has its undeniable charms.

George Szell's orchestration is one of the few such arrangements of a chamber piece—Schoenberg's inspired transcription of Brahms's G minor Piano Quartet is another—that actually expands and clarifies the composer's intentions rather than obscuring them. Geoffrey Simon leads a performance full of fire and conviction, which is also as thrillingly played as the old Szell version that was once available on a 10-inch LP.

The Overture and Dances from *The Bartered Bride* are also brilliantly done.

Smyth, Dame Ethel

(1858–1944)

Mass in D; *The March of the Women*; *The Boatswain's Mate*: Mrs. Water's Aria

> Soloists, Plymouth Music Series Orchestra and Chorus, Brunelle. Virgin CDC-59022 [CD].

Though not in all probability a major composer, Dame Ethel Smyth was a classic English character in the manner of Edith Sitwell and Lord Berners. After study in Germany, she returned to England where she devoted herself primarily to opera; Sir Thomas Beecham was an enthusiastic advocate of *The Wreckers*, which he introduced to London in 1909 (the world premiere had been led three years earlier by no less a figure than Arthur Nikisch). Smyth was also a gifted writer and polemicist, as well as a passionate leader of the women's suffrage movement; her *March of the Women* became its unofficial anthem. For her services to the cause she was made a Dame Commander of the British Empire in 1922.

It was Smyth's Mass in D from 1893 that established her initial reputation. A large, ambitious work, it bites off a little more than it can chew but is nonetheless full of good ideas. Philip

Brunelle leads a powerfully committed performance that minimizes the work's obvious debts to Beethoven, Brahms, and Schumann, while finding as much of its original voice as there is. The aria from the comic opera *The Boatswain's Mate* is impressively done, although the *March of the Women* comes off rather tame.

Sousa, John Philip (1854–1932)

Marches

> Philip Jones Brass Ensemble, Howarth. London 410290-2 [CD], 410290-4 [T].
>
> Eastman Wind Ensemble, Fennell. Mercury 416147-2 [CD] ("Stars and Stripes Forever"); Mercury 434300-2 [CD] ("Sound Off!" and "Sousa on Review").
>
> John Philip Sousa and His Band. Delos DE-3102 [CD], CS-3102 [T].

What, I hear you ask, is an entry on John Philip Sousa doing in a book dealing with Official Classical Music? Has the author no standards? Is nothing sacred? The answer to both of the above questions is "No."

If, like me, you find the music of the March King irresistible, by all means snatch up four of the seven finest Sousa March collections ever released. (The others were a collection led by the late Henry Mancini, an ace piccolo player and a top-notch bandsman in his day, and an old Capitol album called "The Military Band," presided over by the hugely gifted Felix Slatkin.) The playing on the London recording is as clean as the most demanding drum major could wish. Rhythms are crisp, the ensemble is razor-sharp, for a British ensemble, and this British group can certainly teach us a thing or two.

The first CD reissues of Frederick Fennell's storied Mercury recordings from the early 1960s are unusually welcome, not only because of the impeccable performances but also for the unusual repertoire. The half dozen "greatest hits" are here, and so are *Bullets and Bayonets, National Game, Riders for the Flag, The Pride of the Wolverines,* and other worthy rarities.

Needless to say, Sousa's own recordings (and he made quite a few) have a special snap and authority in spite of the vintage 1917–1923 acoustical recorded sound. Packaged with a 1929 radio speech made by Sousa and seven marches the composer conducts, are splendid modern recordings of thirteen marches performed by Keith Brion and His New Sousa Band.

Finally, Arthur Fiedler never made a finer recording than the version of Hershey Kay's irresistible Sousa ballet *Stars and Stripes,* which is finally available on a generously crammed RCA release (09026-61501-2 [CD], 09026-61501-4 [T]), which also includes Kay's Gottschalk-inspired *Cakewalk* ballet as well as selections from Bernstein's *Fancy Free* and Morton Gould's *Interplay.*

In short, fellow Sousa cuckoos, rejoice.

Still, William Grant

(1895–1978)

*A*fro-American Symphony

Detroit Symphony, Järvi. Chandos CHAN-9154 [CD].

Revered for decades as the dean of Afro-American composers, William Grant Still was one of the first musicians to incorporate elements of his African heritage into the symphonic mainstream of European music. His extraordinary and shamefully neglected *Afro-American Symphony* of 1930 was a milestone in the history of American music, and not simply because it was the first modern symphony by an American composer of African descent. In its best pages, it ranks with the finest symphonic works written by *any* American and has finally gotten the first-rate modern recording it has long deserved. Neeme Järvi's performance is both skillful and committed, with a seemingly instinctive feel for Still's jazz-inflected idiom and a firm grasp of the Symphony's sometimes elusive architecture. The Detroit Symphony plays the piece as though they own it, and are equally persuasive in the suite from Duke Ellington's vivid ballet *The River*.

Still never had a more tireless or eloquent champion than the wonderful American violinist, the late Louis Kaufman, whose pioneering recordings are now finding their way onto compact disc (Music and Arts CD-638). While the recorded sound of these performances, many of them taken from radio airchecks, is understandably variable, the interpretations themselves are marvels of fire, color, and finesse, especially those involving Kaufman's gifted wife, Annette. Either as music by an important American composer or souvenirs of a great American violinist, the recording is indispensable.

Strauss, Johann II (1825–1899)

*D*ie Fledermaus

> Gueden, Köth, Resnik, Zampieri, Wächter, Kmentt, Berry, Kunz, Vienna State Opera Chorus, Vienna Philharmonic, Karajan. London 421046-2 [CD].

> Varady, Popp, Kollo, Prey, Rebroff, Bavarian State Opera Chorus and Orchestra, C. Kleiber. Deutsche Grammophon 415646-2 [CD].

More than 125 years since the first production of *Die Fledermaus*, it is difficult to imagine how Vienna could have been so cool to the greatest operetta ever written—that is, of course, unless you know the Viennese. Their overwhelming indifference to the original production in 1874 places *Die Fledermaus* in some very good company. The city was also unqualified in its scorn of Mozart's *Don Giovanni*, Beethoven's *Fidelio*, and countless other new works, proving that although it was at one time the musical capital of the world, Vienna in the 1870s was as reactionary as its brutally despotic emperor, Franz Josef.

Die Fledermaus has never had a more effervescent recording than London's "Gala" production of the late 1950s. In addition to memorable star turns from many of the finest singers of the day in the Act II party scene (Leontyne Price's version of Gershwin's "Summertime" is especially haunting), the rest of the production is an unqualified triumph. As in her earlier London recording from the late 1940s, the scrumptious Hilde Gueden was and remains the ideal Rosalinde—wise, wily, sexy—and captured here in wonderful voice. The supporting cast, led by Regina Resnik as the marvelously dissolute Prince Orlovsky and the ageless Erich Kunz as the drunken, irrepressible Frosch, is one of the best ever mustered in a recording studio. The Vienna Philharmonic plays *Fledermaus* as only they can play *Fledermaus*, and Herbert von Karajan, in one of his last successful recordings, conducts with tremendous joy, delicacy, and verve.

As a more modern alternative, the performance led by Carlos Kleiber is only slightly less engaging than London's classic release. The choice of the Russian bass Ivan Rebroff as Prince Orlovsky, generally a mezzo-soprano role, had a particularly daffy inspiration to it, and Kleiber, as always, finds many new and interesting things to say.

Waltzes, Polkas, etc.

Vienna Philharmonic, Boskovsky. London 417885-2 [CD], 417885-4 [T].

Vienna Johann Strauss Orchestra, Boskovsky. Angel CDC-47052 [CD]; EMI CDE-67788 [CD].

Chicago Symphony, Reiner. RCA 60177-2-RG [CD].

The next time you hear a serious-music snob say something demeaning about the waltzes and polkas of Johann Strauss, tell him or her that he or she is full of it. Or even better, haul off and kick the person in the shin. Johann Strauss II was admired by Brahms, Wagner, and almost every other important musician of his time. His waltzes are every bit as important as, and even more memorable and entertaining than, those of Chopin, and to dismiss them as "light music" or mere pops-concert fare is to miss the point entirely. Almost all of them are brilliantly made, ingeniously crafted little tone poems that will undoubtedly survive long after most of the serious music of that era is forgotten.

The recordings listed above have much to offer both the beginning and experienced collector. All of the many recordings made by the longtime concertmaster of the Vienna Philharmonic, Willi Boskovsky, are graceful, stunningly played, and close to the last word in idiomatic grace. The generous RCA compact disc of recordings made by Fritz Reiner and the Chicago Symphony in the late 1950s is a bargain no Strauss lover can afford to resist. The interpretations are full of Viennese lilt and schmaltz, and the performances are more zestful and precise than any others I know.

Strauss, Richard (1864–1949)

Eine Alpensinfonie

Concertgebouw Orchestra of Amsterdam, Haitink. Philips 416156-2 [CD].

Probably the best thing that can be said about *An Alpine Symphony* is that it is not quite as embarrassing as the *Sinfonia domestica*, written eleven years before. Unlike the epically vulgar and, in its bedroom sequence, blatantly pornographic *Domestic Symphony*, this loud and aimless hike through the Alps is merely overblown, overwritten, and dumb. For all practical purposes, there is only one viable theme, a rising, slightly menacing fanfare, which the composer beats to death.

Pervert that I am, I have collected almost every recording of this magnificent trash ever made, beginning with an amazing performance led by the half-mad Oskar Fried that was crammed onto a set of acoustical 78s. Among versions in which you can hear something more than the trumpet and an occasional violin, Bernard Haitink's spectacular Philips recording offers an interpretation of genuine stature as well as state-of-the-art orchestral execution and recorded sound. The misty, dizzying introduction is evocative enough to give you a serious dose of acrophobia, and the first brassy climax will lift you right out of your seat. In addition to being one of the most exciting recent recordings of *An Alpine Symphony*, this is one of the most thoroughly adult: a performance that not only strives to give the music a meaning and dignity it probably doesn't possess but succeeds to an amazing degree.

Also sprach Zarathustra

> Chicago Symphony, Reiner. RCA 09026-61494-2 [CD], 09026-61494-4 [T].

Since Stanley Kubrick's *2001* made it a popular hit, Strauss's tone poem after Nietzsche, *Also sprach Zarathustra*, has had dozens of recordings, most of them with some outer space scene cleverly placed on the record jacket. (Say what you will about them, but recording companies are no dolts when it comes to marketing.)

In spite of the flood of new *Zarathustras*, the one that continues to speak most eloquently is Fritz Reiner's phenomenal 1954 recording with the Chicago Symphony. It was one of RCA's very first stereo efforts, and one of the first recordings Reiner made with his new orchestra; no one could have expected quite so great a result. The playing remains a wonder of alertness, fire, and whiplash attacks, while the recording, old though it may be, is as warm, detailed, and sensual as many recordings made in the 1970s. Incidentally, Reiner was one of Strauss's favorite conductors. This classic recording will show you why.

The CD comes with what remains that most sparkling of all recordings of the *Bourgeois gentilhomme* Suite and Reiner's own arrangement of the *Rosenkavalier* Waltzes. The tape offers the conductor's 1962 remake of *Zarathustra*, which was not quite as superhuman as the 1954 effort, nor, strangely, as brilliantly recorded. This *Zarathustra* (also available on CD as 6722-2 RG) is accompanied by Leontyne Price's languorous version of the *Four Last Songs* and a stunning account of the Empress's Awakening Scene from *Die Frau ohne Schatten*.

Arabella

> Donath, Varady, Fischer-Dieskau, Schmidt, Berry, Bavarian State Opera Chorus and Orchestra, Sawallisch. Orfeo 169882 [CD].

For the last of his operas on a text by his greatest collaborator, Hugo von Hoffmannsthal, Strauss returned to the scene of his greatest triumph, the Vienna of *Der Rosenkavalier*. If *Arabella* does not begin to match the earlier opera's sustained inspiration, it has much of the same scintillating atmosphere, to say nothing of a superb libretto and many inspired touches. A fine performance can persuade you that it is the finest of the composer's later operas; a performance as good as this one might almost have you believing it's something more.

Julia Varady has much of the shrewd intelligence and innate musicality that characterized the work of Vienna's first Arabella, the great Lotte Lehmann. Varardy's singing is rich, warm, and irresistibly feminine, and she is offered able support by her real-life husband, Dietrich Fischer-Dieskau, as Mandryka. The conducting of Wolfgang Sawallisch represents his finest work in the recording studio, and the recorded sound is superb. In short, this is the one *Arabella* that seems like anything but a cut-rate *Rosenkavalier*.

*A*riadne auf Naxos

Schwarzkopf, Seefried, Schock, Streich, Donch, Cuénod,
   Philharmonia Orchestra, Karajan. Angel CDMB-69296
   [CD].

No less a Strauss authority than Sir Thomas Beecham insisted in his book *A Mingled Chime* (1944) that in the original version of *Ariadne auf Naxos*, "the musical accomplishment of Strauss attained its highest reach, yielding a greater spontaneity and variety of invention, together with a subtler and riper style, than anything that his pen has yet given to the stage . . ."

While *Ariadne* has always skirted the edges of the standard repertoire, it has enjoyed a charmed life in the recording studio, beginning with this miraculous version taped in London in 1954. Even those who fail to respond to either the chamber dimensions (the orchestra is limited to thirty-nine players) or the studied artificiality of the play within the play cannot help but be bowled over by the singing of Rita Streich, Elisabeth Schwarzkopf, and the amazing Irmgard Seefried at the height of their powers, or the deft, imaginative conducting of Herbert von Karajan, who very nearly equals the achievement of his historic *Rosenkavalier* (see page 522).

Le Bourgeois gentilhomme Suite; Divertimento (after keyboard pieces by François Couperin)

Orpheus Chamber Orchestra. Deutsche Grammophon 435871-2 [CD].

Strauss's *Le Bourgeois gentilhomme* and the Divertimento after Couperin contain some of the most refined and elegant of his musical inspirations, especially the incidental music for Molière's play, which includes a dinner sequence full of musical quotations that suggest what the guests are eating (the mutton course is hinted at by a reference to the "sheep" variation from *Don Quixote*) and a fizzing final movement that contains some of the most mercurial music Strauss ever wrote.

The always meticulous, always enthusiastic Orpheus Chamber Orchestra does handsomely by both these marvelous scores, as do DG's engineers. For the most passionate of *Le Bourgeois gentilhomme*'s admirers, Gerard Schwarz's recording with the New York Chamber Symphony and Chorus of the complete incidental music for Pro Arte (CDD-448 [CD]) is certainly worth investigating. The performance is bright and committed, though it might prove in the end to be a little too much of an admittedly very good thing.

Capriccio

Schwarzkopf, Moffo, Ludwig, Gedda, Fischer-Dieskau, Wächter, Hotter, Philharmonia Orchestra, Sawallisch. Angel CDCB-49014 [CD].

Although Strauss's final opera has had its detractors (an opera *about* opera and the relative importance of music versus poetry is nothing if not a trifle ingrown, and at two and a half hours this "conversation piece for music," as its authors called it, can seem more than a little verbose), no modern opera has had a more persuasive recording than this one. If anything, Elisabeth Schwarzkopf's Countess is even more compelling than her Marschallin, a characterization bursting with life as well as infinite shades of nuance and meaning. The rest of the cast is no less ideal, as is Wolfgang Sawallisch's conducting. The remastered monophonic sound, which somehow seems more boomy and opaque than the original LPs, is the only minor disappointment—a very minor disappointment in one of the greatest opera recordings yet made.

Concertos (2) for Horn and Orchestra

Brain, horn; Philharmonia Orchestra, Sawallisch. Angel CDC-47834 [CD].

When Dennis Brain died in a car crash September 1, 1957, while rushing back to London from the Edinburgh Festival, the world lost not only the preeminent French horn player of the century but one of its greatest musicians. In the years since his death, players of comparable technical prowess have arisen, but none has managed to combine a flawless technique with such an audacious yet aristocratic musical personality. He was, to use a hackneyed phrase, a one-of-a-kind phenomenon, and it would seem extremely unlikely that we will see his equal again.

With his famous recordings of the Mozart concertos, these versions of the two concertos of Richard Strauss constitute Dennis Brain's most lasting memorial. The actual playing, of course, is breathtaking, but so is the unerring rightness of the interpretations, from the youthful ardor he projects in the early concerto to the mellow wisdom he finds in its successor.

The highest praise that can be heaped upon Wolfgang Sawallisch's accompaniments is to say that they are completely worthy of the soloist. The definitive recording of the Horn Concerto Paul Hindemith wrote for Brain, with the Philharmonia conducted by the composer, fills out the disc.

The composer's overly ripe, phenomenally difficult Oboe Concerto has finally been recorded by the man whose chance remark inspired it. As a GI serving in Germany after the war, John de Lancie, later the principal oboist of the Philadelphia Orchestra, happened to ask the aging composer why he had never written a concerto for the instrument. The Concerto for Oboe and Small Orchestra was the result. Though one could only wish that de Lancie had recorded the work in his prime, his 1987 recording (RCA 7989-2-RG [CD]) is a brilliant one and a significant historical document.

Strauss's impossibly difficult *de facto* piano concerto, *Burleske*, is currently best served on another RCA recording featuring the phenomenal, albeit tightly wound, Byron Janis with the Chicago Symphony led by Fritz Reiner (5734-2-RC [CD]).

Although no one has ever pretended that the composer's youthful Violin Concerto is a particularly original or significant work, someone forgot to tell the brilliant Chinese violinist Xue Wei, who, accompanied by an equally committed Jane Glover and the London Symphony, gives it the most electrifying recorded performance ever (ASV CD-DCA-780 [CD]).

Daphne

Gueden, Little, King, Wunderlich, Schoeffler, Vienna State Opera Chorus, Vienna Symphony, Böhm. Deutsche Grammophon 423579-2 [CD].

In many respects, *Daphne* is a perfect living room opera: not much happens in this stately pastoral romp, and its central event— the transformation of the heroine from a flesh-and-blood fisherman's daughter into a warbling tree—is best left to the listener's imagination. Yet of all the late Strauss operas, *Daphne* is also, paradoxically, the least artificial and possibly the most charming. The level of musical invention, while certainly not that of *Der Rosenkavalier*, rises well above decadent, stillborn efforts like *Die Liebe der Danaë* and *Friedenstag*, and the central character—in the proper hands—can be one of the most enchanting of Strauss's creations.

The incomparable Hilde Gueden gives a gleaming performance in this live 1964 recording led by the man to whom the opera was dedicated. The rest of the cast is an unusually strong one and Karl Böhm's suave, incisive conducting makes even the least inspired pages come alive.

Perhaps as a memorial to Lucia Popp, who never made a more affecting or physically beautiful performance on records, EMI will reissue the brilliant studio recording she made in Munich with Bernard Haitink, but don't hold your breath.

Death and Transfiguration; Don Juan; Till Eulenspiegel's Merry Pranks

Cleveland Orchestra, Szell. CBS MKY-36721 [CD], MYT-36721 [T].

The young Richard Strauss initially made his reputation with this trio of early tone poems, which remain the most popular and frequently performed of his orchestral works. Although there may have been finer individual recordings of each (a live Salzburg Festival recording of *Death and Transfiguration*, led by Victor de Sabata, is so white-hot in its intensity that it might melt the plastic elements in your speaker system), no collection of all three has ever been more successful than this one.

The Cleveland Orchestra is honed to a fine state of perfection by George Szell, who leads them through a *Till Eulenspiegel* of enormous wit and character, a *Death and Transfiguration* of great power and grandeur, and a *Don Juan* that is a model of swagger and romance. Given the 1960s vintage, the sound is surprisingly good, although the compact disc remastering, like most of CBS's efforts with recordings from this period, tends to be on the hissy side. This is a minor drawback, though, to one of the great Strauss recordings of modern times.

Don Quixote

Tortelier, cello; Dresden State Orchestra, Kempe. EMI CDZC-64350 [CD].

Not counting the shamelessly self-indulgent *Ein Heldenleben* (A Hero's Life), *Don Quixote* is easily the greatest of the mature Strauss tone poems. The structure—a set of variations "on a theme of knightly character"—is beautifully worked out, the orchestration a wonder of subtle ingenuity, and the dramatic content (who can forget the final, sliding note in the cello as old Don dies?) among the most powerful and moving of all Strauss's works.

While I continue to have great affection for Fritz Reiner's Chicago Symphony recording, now available on an RCA compact disc (5734-2-RC), Rudolf Kempe's 1973 EMI version, part of his complete cycle of the composer's orchestral music, remains in a special category. Although Paul Tortelier's projection of the Knight of the Woeful Countenance is both poignant and heroic, it is the incomparable burnished copper glow of the Dresden Staatskapelle, Richard Strauss's favorite orchestra, that makes the recording unique. Kempe weaves an orchestral fabric of uncommon richness and sophistication, and the analog recorded sound remains ideal in its warmth and clarity. The only minor drawback is that it is only available as Volume 3 of Kempe's Strauss edition, a three-CD set that nonetheless contains equally splendid accounts of *An Alpine*

Symphony, the Couperin Divertimento, the autumnal *Metamorphosen*, and, in the finest of all their modern recordings, the youthful *Aus Italien* and *Macbeth*.

Elektra

Nilsson, Collier, Resnik, Stolze, Krause, Vienna
Philharmonic, Solti. London 417345-2 [CD].

In many ways, *Elektra* is the most successful and satisfying of all the Strauss operas. For one thing, it is loaded with all those ingredients that make an opera great (cruelty, horror, bloodshed, and revenge), and for another, it is *not* twenty minutes too long (a charge that has been leveled at every other Strauss opera, with the exception of the equally compressed and gory *Salome*).

There is only one completely acceptable recording of the opera currently available, and a very great one it is. In the title role, Birgit Nilsson gives one of her most absorbed and shattering recorded performances, from the savage confrontations with her mother, Klytemnestra, sung to chilling effect by Regina Resnik, to one of the most beautiful and moving versions of the thrilling Recognition Scene. The rest of the cast is splendid. Sir Georg Solti's conducting is vividly dramatic and intense, and the recorded sound in the compact disc format—the only one currently available—will rattle the rafters of the best built house.

RCA has recently issued on another compact disc some generous selections from the opera, together with excerpts from *Salome*, in the classic recordings made by Inge Borkh and the Chicago Symphony conducted by Fritz Reiner (09026-60874-2 [CD], 09026-60874-4 [T]). As much as I tend to dislike operas chopped up into what George Bernard Shaw called "bleeding chunks of meat," this recording is a very special one and shouldn't be passed up.

Four Last Songs

Schwarzkopf, soprano; Berlin Radio Symphony, Szell.
Angel CDC-47276 [CD].

Written when Strauss was in his early eighties, the ravishing *Four Last Songs* is the work of a man who, if he was not anxious to die, was certainly more than ready for death. There is a case to be made that Strauss was artistically dead long before his actual demise in 1949. He was a nineteenth-century revolutionary who lived to see himself become a twentieth-century reactionary; his music from the 1920s onward became increasingly repetitive and uninspired until he was finally reduced to such drivel as *The Happy Workshop* and the pleasant but featherweight Oboe Concerto. With the *Four Last Songs* Strauss dug deeply into himself and the past and became, for the final time, the great composer he had once been: the Strauss of *Der Rosenkavalier* and *Death and Transfiguration*, one of whose themes is quoted so movingly in the last of the songs.

Among all the superb interpretations of Strauss's final masterpiece, by Lucia Popp, Arleen Augér, Jessye Norman, and Leontyne Price (to say nothing of the recording of the world premiere with Kirsten Flagstad and Wilhelm Furtwängler that has been slipping in and out of print for forty years), no performance has ever captured more of the serenity or melancholy intensity of the music than this one Elisabeth Schwarzkopf taped in the mid-1960s with the Berlin Radio Symphony and George Szell. Both these superlative musicians respond to every musical nuance in the score, and the soprano brings a depth of understanding to the words that demonstrates why she was the greatest German singer since Lotte Lehmann.

A generous selection of the composer's orchestral songs rounds out what may be the finest Strauss recording available today.

Die Frau ohne Schatten

> Varady, Behrens, Domingo, van Dam, Vienna State Opera Chorus, Vienna Philharmonic, Solti. London 436243-2 [CD].

> Nilsson, Rysanek, Hesse, King, Berry, Vienna State Opera Orchestra and Chorus, Böhm. Deutsche Grammophon 415472-2 [CD].

Many consider this heavily symbolic Wagnerian fairy tale the high point of Richard Strauss's collaboration with the doomed, brilliantly accomplished Viennese poet and playwright Hugo von Hofmannsthal, which is to say it is an even greater work than

Elektra, Ariadne auf Naxos, or *Der Rosenkavalier*. There are also those who believe that the composer always got the better end of the bargain, including Hofmannsthal himself, who is alleged to have confessed to a friend, "How nice it would be if (Franz) Lehár had composed the music for *Rosenkavalier* instead of Strauss." (Apropos of absolutely nothing, the opera served as the basis for one of the most arcane musical bumper stickers I have ever seen. Unlike the amusing though rather obvious "*Carmen* made Mérimée Prosper," "O Milhaud My," and "The Sugar Plum Fairy made the Nutcracker Suite," this one read "Die Frau ohne Schatten once a day." Think about it.)

Although history has not been especially kind to this most demanding and far-reaching of Strauss's creations, *The Woman without a Shadow* has had a small but fanatically loyal following from the very beginning; it can be an extremely difficult nut to crack, but it will more than repay any amount of time the listener is willing to invest.

Sir Georg Solti's recording is among the most impressive of his career, a near-perfect fusion of superlative singing, staggering orchestral execution, and ear-popping recorded sound. Chief among its many glories is Solti's conducting, which among his many disappointing recent recordings is the one that fully recaptures the vigorously imaginative Solti of old. The interpretation is a triumph of dramatic power and psychological insight in which an almost fanatical attention to detail is wedded to a glorious human warmth and projection of the big Straussian line.

The live 1977 performance led by the composer's old crony Karl Böhm also makes a very persuasive case for the opera. The cast is an extremely strong one, headed by the ageless Leonie Rysanek as the Empress and Birgit Nilsson as the Dyer's Wife. Still, for all the fine, frequently superlative singing, it is Böhm's warm, effortlessly dramatic, infinitely resourceful conducting that best convinces us that *Die Frau*'s admirers could be right. For a live performance, the recording is exceptionally clear and detailed, with both the foot-shuffling onstage and noises from the usually rude Viennese audience kept to a bare minimum.

Ein Heldenleben

> Chicago Symphony, Reiner. RCA 09026-61494-2 [CD], 09026-61494-4 [T].

Richard Strauss was not, by any stretch of the imagination, a lovable, or even particularly likable, man. He collaborated openly with the Nazis from the late 1930s onward, was shamelessly mercenary throughout his life, and was probably the only composer in history whose ego could be compared with Richard Wagner's. The great German conductor Hans Knappertsbusch may have summed it up best when he said, "I knew him very well. We played cards every week for forty years and he was a pig."

In spite of the fact that it is one of the most self-indulgent pieces in the history of art, *Ein Heldenleben* is a very great work. The "Hero's Life" that the tone poem celebrates is, of course, Strauss's own. And though we blush for the sheer audacity of the man, he does blow his own horn (in fact, all eight of them) magnificently.

In a heroically crowded field of superb recordings, the one by Fritz Reiner should now be regarded as the very best. Perhaps more than any of his other Strauss recordings, the Reiner *Heldenleben* is a study in disciplined lunacy: the battle music erupts with a horrible, yet carefully studied violence, and the love music is infused with an overt yet almost gentlemanly eroticism. Like all of RCA's Reiner recordings, this one wears its age with exceptional grace.

Music for Winds (complete)

London Winds, Collins. Hyperion CDA-66731/2 [CD].

This ingratiating Hyperion collection brings together all the music Strauss wrote for wind ensemble, from the youthful Suite in B-flat of 1884 to the genially overripe wind symphony *The Happy Workshop* of 1944. Although none of the pieces can be considered great music or even top-drawer Strauss, there is much here that will delight admirers of his music, especially in these consistently captivating performances by the London Winds. Predictably, Hyperion's recorded sound is a model of naturalness and warmth.

Der Rosenkavalier

**Schwarzkopf, Ludwig, Stich-Randall, Edelmann,
Philharmonia Orchestra and Chorus, Karajan. Angel
CDCC-49354 [CD], 3CDX-3970 [T].**

Shortly after his last and dreadful Deutsche Grammophon recording of the loveliest of the Strauss operas was released, Herbert von Karajan, tactful gentleman that he always was, said something to the effect that he was *so* happy to have finally made a recording of *Der Rosenkavalier* with "an adequate cast." Taking nothing away from Anna Tomowa-Sintow, just what did the maestro think he had in Elisabeth Schwarzkopf thirty years ago? Chopped liver?

The first Karajan *Rosenkavalier* has all the tenderness, charm, impetuosity and dramatic tension that his newer recording lacks. And with Madame Schwarzkopf, he clearly has the finest Marschallin since Lotte Lehmann was singing the role in the 1930s. From either the compact disc or the tapes, the recording emerges as what it has clearly been since it was first released: one of the great opera recordings of the century.

Salome

Nilsson, Hoffman, Stolze, Kmentt, Wächter, Vienna Philharmonic, Solti. London 414414-2 [T].

Salome, that tasteful, wholesome entertainment whose first Berlin performance Kaiser Wilhelm II personally banned, has served as the vehicle for some of the most startling operatic creations of recent years. Monserrat Caballé, whom one would not immediately think of as the nubile heroine, made a dazzling recording for RCA a number of years ago that has finally resurfaced on compact disc (6644-2-RG). Vocally and visually, Maria Ewing's recent performances with the Los Angeles Opera proved a revelation. In addition to a Dance of the Seven Veils in which this disturbingly beautiful soprano did not stop, as is the custom, with veil number six (in the original production she wore a G-string under protest; in the revival, she eschewed it, arguing that Salome herself would never have given in to something so ridiculously modest), the final scene was a musical and dramatic tour de force. If someone doesn't record it soon, it will only prove what I have long assumed—to wit, that the recording industry is nuts.

As Strauss's terrifying, oversexed adolescent, Birgit Nilsson gives one of the most powerful performances of her long and brilliant career. The closing twenty minutes, when she has that grisly "duet" with the head of John the Baptist, are among the most terrifying ever captured in a recording studio. Sir Georg Solti, here as elsewhere, lends the kind of sympathetic, though never sycophantic, support of which most singers only dream. The rest of the cast, especially Gerhard Stolze as King Herod, is overwhelming, and the remastered sound will take your breath away.

Songs

Fischer-Dieskau, baritone; Moore, piano. Angel CDMF-63995 [CD].

Hotter, bass; Klein, piano. Preiser 93367 [CD].

Reining, soprano; Piltti, soprano; Dermota, tenor; Strauss, piano. Preiser 93262 [CD].

Te Kanawa, soprano; Solti, piano. London 430511-2 [CD].

Norman, soprano; Parsons, piano. Philips 416298-2 [CD].

It was with song that Richard Strauss began and concluded his career, from a little Christmas ditty written when he was six to the serenely majestic *Four Last Songs* of 1948, composed when he was eighty-four. Although his achievement was not as consistent as that of Schubert, Schumann, Brahms, or Wolf—his choice of texts was not always ideal nor was his musical invention always inspired—the best Strauss lieder rank with the most moving and sinuously beautiful ever written.

Dietrich Fischer-Dieskau's epic six-CD collection of 134 songs is the ideal place to begin investigating this generally marvelous repertoire. Recorded between 1967 and 1970, a golden era in this singer's career when the voice was at its freshest and the singing at its least mannered, the baritone's understanding and enthusiasm prove irresistible, especially in the gorgeous early songs of Opp. 10, 15, and 17.

Although the Hotter recordings were made toward the end of his singing career (in 1967, two years after his incomparable, albeit vocally woolly *Die Walküre* for London), the depth of feeling and nobility of utterance in songs like "Die Nacht" is incomparable. Incomparable, too, are the recordings Strauss himself made with three of his favorite singers in 1942, especially those with the lovely Maria Reining, one of the composer's favorite Marshallins. Strauss proves a sympathetic (and understandably authoritative) accompanist, and the wartime recorded sound is perfectly acceptable.

Among the more recent recitals, those by Jessye Norman and Kiri Te Kanawa capture two of the most impressive voices of our time in peak condition, with Norman at her most dramatically expressive and Dame Kiri at her most seductively feminine.

Symphonia domestica

Chicago Symphony, Reiner. RCA 60388-2-RG [CD].

Say what you will about the *Domestic Symphony*, it is one of the most shamelessly vulgar musical works ever written by the man who once claimed he could set anything to music. It traces, in gruesome detail, the singularly banal events transpiring in the Strauss household during an average day, including the composer's young son being given his bath and the composer and his wife fulfilling their conjugal obligations. Many of Strauss's closest musical friends pleaded with him not to publish the Symphony's program; he did, and ever since, the *Sinfonia domestica* has remained his most justly maligned work.

Fritz Reiner's classic recording from 1956 is so completely spellbinding that you can almost overlook the yawning vapidity of the work itself and simply revel in the phenomenal execution. Even the closing pages, which can seem so overwritten and overblown, have a magnificent inevitability about them, together with a brassy grandeur that will silence all criticism. The recorded sound, like the Chicago Symphony's playing, remains a marvel.

Stravinsky, Igor (1882–1971)

Apollo

City of Birmingham Symphony, Rattle. Angel CDC-49636 [CD].

From early 1920s, when the Russian "primitive" was busy transforming himself into a Parisian gentleman, to the mid-1950s, when his discovery of the music of Anton Webern lured him, belatedly, into the serialism and twelve-tone procedures of the Schoenberg camp (many of his closest musical friends never forgave him for the "defection"), the longest and most productive creative phase of Igor Stravinsky's career—the so-called neoclassical phase —yielded many of the finest works that great chameleon of twentieth-century music would produce.

The 1928 ballet *Apollon Musagète* (Apollo, Leader of the Muses) is one of the purest expressions of Stravinsky's fascination with the musical procedures and disciplines of the past. The music not only projects a cool, detached tranquility that is perfectly attuned to its subject matter, it manifests a sweet and unmistakable sentimentality of which this tough-minded realist was very rarely accused.

Sir Simon Rattle's interpretation is amiable and unfussy, with some typically affectionate playing from the Birmingham strings. Until John Lubbock's incandescent ASV recording with the Orchestra of St. John's of Smith Square finds an American distributor, Rattle's will more than do.

Concerto in E-flat, *Dumbarton Oaks*; Eight Instrumental Miniatures for Fifteen Players; *Pulcinella* Suite

Orpheus Chamber Orchestra. Deutsche Grammophon 419628-2 [CD].

Stravinsky once said with disarming honesty, "I love Mozart so much, I steal his music." And so, with *The Rake's Progress*, the twentieth century's great recycler produced a complete eighteenth-century number opera modeled on *Don Giovanni*. Rossini,

Tchaikovsky, American jazz, Russian folk song, Webern, and the fourteenth-century Frenchman Guillaume de Machaut were all grist for Stravinsky's incredible refracting mill, as were his two favorite Baroque composers, Bach and Giovanni Battista Pergolesi. It was music attributed to the startlingly ugly, sadly short-lived Pergolesi that he arranged into *Pulcinella*, the first of his great neoclassical ballets, and the spirit, to say nothing of the actual letter, of Bach's *Brandenburg* Concertos that he lifted for the *Dumbarton Oaks* Concerto of 1938.

The Orpheus Chamber Orchestra give predictably polished and enthusiastic performances of the Concerto and the *Pulcinella* Suite, as well as the equally marvelous Eight Instrumental Miniatures for Fifteen Players. This is prime middle-period Stravinsky, affectionately played and handsomely recorded.

For anyone interested in the complete *Pulcinella* (and it's such a hospitable, thoroughly outgoing work, everyone *should* be interested in it), Richard Hickox's enchanting performance on Virgin's dirt-cheap Virgo label (CDZ-61107 [CD]) is a phenomenal bargain no one can afford to pass up. If anything, the playing and singing has even more comic bite and character than on Claudio Abbado's recently withdrawn Deutsche Grammophon recording, and it comes with a superb performance of the preposterously neglected *Danses concertantes* of 1942. In short, a steal.

*T*he Fairy's Kiss

Scottish National Orchestra, Järvi. Chandos CHAN-8360 [CD].

With the possible exception of *Perséphone* (the 1934 ballet with recitation and chorus, which eventually led to a bitter mud-slinging match between the composer and his collaborator, André Gide), *The Fairy's Kiss* is probably the most physically beautiful score Stravinsky ever wrote. Taking Tchaikovsky's music as its point of departure—Stravinsky always claimed that about half the melodies in the ballet were by his great predecessor, half were his own—*Le Baiser de la fée* is a fetching amalgam of instantly lovable tunes (the final apotheosis on "None But The Lonely Heart" makes every audience melt), inspired instrumentation (a graduate seminar in orchestration could be devoted solely to the composer's use of the horns), and that quirky, increasingly sophisticated rhythmic thinking that characterized Stravinsky's work throughout the 1920s.

Neeme Järvi's recording of the complete ballet, which features more than twice the music of the far more familiar Divertimento, is a delightful one. If it's not *quite* as good as the composer's own version (and I must admit my fondness for that recording may have something to do with the fact that it revives fond memories of a performance I once heard with Stravinsky himself and the Chicago Symphony), it's close enough. As they habitually do for Chandos, the Scottish National Orchestra sounds like a world-class ensemble in both the ballet and the fascinating "freeze-dried" arrangement Stravinsky made of the Bluebird pas de deux from Tchaikovsky's *Sleeping Beauty*.

The Firebird (complete ballet)

Concertgebouw Orchestra of Amsterdam, Davis. Philips 400074-2 [CD].

At a fashionable party, Igor Stravinsky was once thanked by an effusive grande dame for writing her favorite work, *Scheherazade*. "But Madame, I did not write *Scheherazade*," he tried to explain. To which she allegedly replied, "Oh, all of you composers are so modest."

In Stravinsky's first great popular success, *The Firebird*, it's easy to hear why the poor woman was so confused. In its opulence, drama, and brilliant orchestration, *The Firebird* is a direct descendant of Stravinsky's teacher's masterwork. Only in the closing bars, with its majestic apotheosis in 7/4 time, does this early ballet give any clue to the rhythmic experimentation that eventually would change the course of twentieth-century music.

Although many great *Firebird* recordings have come and gone over the years, this stunning version by Sir Colin Davis and the Concertgebouw Orchestra is as fine as any. Davis's approach is extremely colorful and dramatic. The Scherzo barely rises above a whisper, and some of the more aggressive moments suggest that this was, indeed, a work by the future composer of *The Rite of Spring*. The orchestra is virtually unbelievable in its ease and power of execution, and the recorded sound is top-drawer.

L'Histoire du soldat (complete)

Lee, speaker; Scottish Chamber Orchestra, Friend. Nimbus NIM-5063 [CD].

The composer's old friend Lukas Foss has always insisted that *L'Histoire du soldat* was Stravinsky's most utterly original work. And as was so often the case in Stravinsky's career, the mother of originality was necessity.

Sitting out the First World War in Switzerland, cut off not only from his native roots but also from the immense orchestra of Sergei Diaghilev's Ballets Russes, the composer gradually abandoned both the Russian themes and opulent scoring of his early ballets. Convinced that the impoverishment of the postwar world would require a new economy in musical settings, he produced *The Soldier's Tale*, music for an ensemble of only seven musicians to accompany a sparse, sinister morality play by the Swiss novelist C. F. Ramuz.

For the producers of this recording to choose Count Dracula to perform all the speaking parts was both surprising and exceptionally canny. Christopher Lee's close association with things that go bump in the night lends an added dimension of eeriness to the supernatural tale; he is also a gifted and versatile actor who turns in a major theatrical tour de force. Lionel Friend and the members of the Scottish Chamber Orchestra prove to be worthy minions for the Count, and the recorded sound is excellent.

The best available recording of the popular Suite is the composer's own, made in the early 1960s, which comes with his rather spartan but intriguing version of *The Firebird* (CBS MK-42432 [CD]).

"The Igor Stravinsky Edition"

Various soloists, choruses, orchestras, ensembles, Stravinsky. Sony SX22K-46290 [CD].

Here, on twenty-two tightly packed compact discs, is one of the unique achievements in the history of the gramophone: the bulk of the music of one of the two major composers of the twentieth century in performances led by the composer himself.

Sony's "Igor Stravinsky Edition" is essentially a CD re-mastering of the thirty-one-LP set originally issued in 1982. Predictably, the sound has been substantially improved, and the performances retain the special energy and insight the ageless composer brought to his music toward the end of his life.

Aside from the obvious convenience and the handsome packaging, the principal reason to invest in this lavish collection is to acquire the recordings that are not yet available separately. For instance, more refreshing, idiomatic versions of *The Fairy's Kiss* and *Les Noces* (whose pianists were the composers Aaron Copland, Samuel Barber, Lukas Foss, and Roger Sessions), are not likely to be made. Moreover, worthy oddities such as the television ballet *The Flood* and Stravinsky's last major score, the *Requiem Canticles*, simply can't be found in any other form.

Needless to say, the investment is substantial. But so too is the amount of history and enjoyment this invaluable document contains.

*L*es Noces; *Mass*

Soloists, English Bach Festival Orchestra and Chorus, Bernstein. Deutsche Grammophon 423251-2 [CD].

Written as long ago as 1917, *Les Noces*, the "Four Choreographic Scenes" for vocal soloists, mixed chorus, four pianists, and a percussion ensemble of seventeen instruments, has remained one of the most paradoxical and underappreciated of all Stravinsky's works. An apparently guileless celebration of a Russian peasant wedding, the ballet is in fact one of the century's most audacious rhythmic experiments. It is also an unprecedented study in monochromatic orchestral color. (In addition to the "orchestra" of pianos, bells, mallet instruments, and drums, the voices, with all their barking and chanting, are treated almost as components of an extended percussion section.)

Similarly, the *Mass* is a major sacred work that manages to complement without repeating the achievement of *Symphony of Psalms*, written eighteen years before. (It was this austere yet moving *Mass* that marked the beginning of the end of Stravinsky's association with his old friend, the conductor Ernest Ansermet. Ansermet, who led the world premiere in 1948, was tactless enough to wonder aloud how someone who pretended to be a lifelong nonbeliever—as the composer was doing at the time—could write such deeply spiritual music.)

Leonard Bernstein leads the most expressive and dramatic recorded performances either work has ever received. *Les Noces* has a driven intensity that serves the choppy, primitive rhythms extremely well, while the passionate simplicity he reserves for the *Mass* makes it seem like one of the key sacred works of modern times.

Oedipus Rex

> Otter, Cole, Gedda, Estes, Sotin, Chéreau, Eric Ericson
> Chamber Chorus, Swedish Radio Symphony and
> Chorus, Salonen. Sony SK-48057 [CD].

In addition to *The Rite of Spring* and *L'Histoire du soldat*, the opera-oratorio (its closest approximate formal designation) *Oedipus Rex* is one of the most staggeringly original of Stravinsky's works. Even more than *Pulcinella*, *Oedipus Rex*, with the "statuesque plasticity" of its Latin text, fully engaged the composer's interest in the classical past and launched the neoclassical phase of his career. Yet for all its stylized aloofness, *Oedipus* also possesses a ferocious power that many later works of the period would not. In spite of the remoteness of the subject matter and the use of a dead language, the emotional drama is intense and immediate; the musical expression is among the most impassioned in Stravinsky's output.

No recording of *Oedipus Rex*, including the composer's own, has ever been more successful in capturing the paradoxical nature of the piece than the incandescent version led by Esa-Pekka Salonen. A performance of withering power and disarming tenderness, it is also flawlessly played and brilliantly sung. Each of the soloists easily eclipses all competitors, as do Sony's engineers. At the end, it leaves the listener exhausted and uplifted, precisely as it should.

Perséphone

> Fournet, Rolfe-Johnson, Tiffen Boys' Choir, London
> Philharmonic Orchestra and Chorus, Nagano. Virgin
> 59077 [CD].

It's almost impossible to believe that this unutterably beautiful "melodrama in three scenes" sparked one of the bitterest public debates of Igor Stravinsky's career. The composer and his librettist, the Nobel Prize–winning novelist André Gide, traded vicious insults over the supposed inadequacies of both the music and the text. What they were arguing about is anybody's guess: Gide had in fact supplied Stravinsky with one of the loveliest, albeit purposefully old-fashioned, texts he would ever receive, and Stravinsky responded with some of his most charming, unaffected, thoroughly heartwarming music.

Compared to the composer's own recording from the 1960s, this new version is a revelation. Kent Nagano transforms Perséphone into a far more French and sensual work, with obvious musical ties to the later scores of Ravel and Debussy. Anne Fournet reads the spoken narration with far greater sensitivity than Vera Zorina did for Stravinsky, and the orchestra plays with more point and sophistication. Those who have postponed investigating this authentic Stravinsky masterpiece no longer have any excuse, especially since the recording comes with a very fine version of *The Rite of Spring* on a separate CD in what amounts to a two-for-one offer.

*P*etrouchka (complete ballet)

London Symphony, Abbado. Deutsche Grammophon 423901-2 [CD].

Given its first performance the year after *The Firebird* made Stravinsky an international sensation, *Petrouchka* not only confirmed the young Igor Stravinsky's remarkable gift but also proved he was neither a flash in the pan nor a composer who was willing to simply go on repeating himself for the rest of his life. Harmonically, structurally, and most importantly, rhythmically, *Petrouchka* marked a significant leap ahead of *The Firebird*, and was one of his earliest works that the elderly Stravinsky professed to like. (He often said that aside from some of the orchestration, he found *The Firebird* utterly uninteresting.)

At least a dozen superlative recordings of the ballet are available today; the most thoroughly satisfying of them is Claudio Abbado's London Symphony version on Deutsche Grammophon. No nuance of texture, no quirky rhythm, no elegant phrase or ingratiating tune escapes Abbado's attention. And unlike the composer's own celebrated recording (CBS MK-42433), a "revisionist" inter-pretation that tried to prove the ballet was a little drier, more acerbic, and more "modern" than it actually was, Abbado refuses to deny *Petrouchka*'s Romantic roots, and in so doing does a great service to both the listener and the work itself.

The Rake's Progress

Raskin, Young, Reardon, Sarfaty, Miller, Manning, Sadler's Wells Opera Chorus, Royal Philharmonic, Stravinsky. Sony SM2K-46299 [CD].

The culminating work of Stravinsky's richly productive neo-classical period, *The Rake's Progress* is also the composer's most ambitious and controversial work. Inspired by the famous series of etchings by William Hogarth and consciously modeled on Mozart's *Don Giovanni*, the piece is a full-fledged eighteenth-century num-ber opera with arias, ensembles, and harpsichord-accompanied rec-itatives, a fact which naturally led to charges that the score is little more than decadent pastiche with no real style, expression, or feelings of its own. Balderdash. With a brilliantly witty text by W. H. Auden and Chester Kallman, not only is *The Rake's Progress* among the most tuneful, exuberant, and emotionally involving of twentieth-century operas, it is one of the most consistently entertaining.

The composer's own recording of the opera is one of the finest he would ever make, with engaging performances from all the principals—especially Regina Sarfaty as the bearded Baba the Turk —together with lusty singing from the Sadler's Wells Opera Chorus and spirited playing from the Royal Philharmonic. The recording's principal glory, though, is Stravinsky's conducting, which releases both the lyric tenderness of the score—Anne Truelove's closing lullaby is especially touching—as well as its sparkling gaiety. The 1964 recorded sound remains lively and faithful.

The Rite of Spring

Columbia Symphony, Stravinsky. CBS MK-42433 [CD], MGT-39015 [T].

Philadelphia Orchestra, Muti. EMI CDM-64516 [CD].

Le Sacre du printemps and Schoenberg's *Pierrot Lunaire* (premiered only a few weeks apart) are the two seminal works that began modern music. While *Pierrot* remains under a cloud of polite neglect, *The Rite of Spring* has nearly become a pops-concert staple. (As early as 1940, a mauled and emasculated edition of the ballet was used as part of the soundtrack of that tedious Disney classic *Fantasia*.)

For one of the clearest and most provocatively objective of all the ballet's many recordings, the composer's own is irreplaceable. As in so many recordings of his own music, Stravinsky the conductor sought to tone down the overtly barbarous moments in the music in favor of greater clarity and restraint (though by this time, much of the nuts-and-bolts rehearsal work was being done by his protégé and amanuensis, Robert Craft). In short, Stravinsky seemed intent on proving, late in life, that stylistically there wasn't all that much separating his music from that of Rossini, Mozart, or Bach.

The approach, needless to say, casts some fascinating light on this great twentieth-century watershed. But for those who want a vicious, untamed, and yet to be housebroken version of the ballet, Riccardo Muti's EMI recording is a bracing tonic to the composer's own. The Philadelphia Orchestra play as though they were possessed, and the recorded sound will rid you of any loose putty on the living room windows, and possibly even the family cat.

Symphony of Psalms; Symphony in Three Movements; Symphony in C

CBC Symphony, Toronto Festival Singers, Stravinsky. CBS MK-42434 [CD].

If *The Rite of Spring* was not Stravinsky's masterpiece, then the proud, aloof, deeply stirring *Symphony of Psalms* probably was. Written "To the Glory of God and Dedicated to the Boston Symphony Orchestra" (Serge Koussevitzky never forgave Stravinsky for giving his orchestra second billing), the *Symphony* is one of the half dozen great sacred works of modern music. In fact, with a small handful of companion pieces—Poulenc's *Gloria*, Schoenberg's *Moses und Aron*, Vaughan Williams's *Hodie*—it is one of the few works of this century that has kept the divine spirit in music alive and well.

Stravinsky's own performance from the 1960s has been issued on a generous CBS compact disc that also features his somewhat spartan but always revealing performances of the *Symphony in Three Movements* and *Symphony in C*. Here, for once, the composer's predilection for a drier sound in his music than most conductors favored serves this particular masterpiece extremely well. The *Symphony of Psalms* emerges with all of its pride, devotion, and admiration (as opposed to adoration) of the Supreme Being blissfully intact.

Suk, Josef (1874–1935)

Serenade for Strings in E-flat

London Chamber Orchestra, Warren-Green. Virgin Classics VC-91165-2 [CD].

Josef Suk composed his most celebrated work while still a student at the Prague Conservatory. Impressed by the young man's talent but concerned that both his musical and personal outlook were far too serious, Suk's teacher, Antonín Dvořák, suggested that his grim young pupil lighten up with something a bit less earnest than the sternly academic music he was writing at the time. The result was the luscious Serenade for Strings.

Although written when its composer was only eighteen and modeled quite consciously on Dvořák's famous E Major String Serenade, Suk's piece, rather incredibly, is the superior work. Although it owes much to Dvořák—the lilting Waltz, particularly, has an unmistakably Dvořákian flavor—the Serenade is also the work of a precocious master, who is melodically and rhythmically far more subtle than his teacher was when his own Serenade was written, and who projects a melancholy tenderness that is already very much his own.

If no recording will ever surpass the magical ones made by the composer's friend Václav Talich, whose 1938 version is now available on a Koch CD (3-7060-2), and the 1951 remake is available from Supraphon (SUP-111899 [CD]), then the recent version by Christopher Warren-Green's brilliant London Chamber Orchestra is the best modern alternative. Not only is the Suk given a graceful, if somewhat overly animated performance, it comes with delectable versions of the Dvořák and Tchaikovsky serenades, therefore making it an irresistible bargain.

For the adventurous, a far more important release is the newest version of Suk's masterpiece, the *Asrael Symphony*. Begun shortly after Dvořák's death in 1904, the Symphony was already well underway when Suk's wife, Dvořák's favorite daughter Otilie, died in the following year. The result is a powerful, crippling eruption of grief equal to the greatest Requiems in music. Either Talich's pioneering recording (Supraphon SUP-111902 [CD]) or the stunning new version by Libor Pesek and the Royal Liverpool Philharmonic (Virgin CDC-59838 [CD]) will serve to introduce many to a neglected but authentic late-Romantic masterwork.

Nearly as important as the *Asrael Symphony* is the vast symphonic poem *The Ripening*, a bewitching essay in hedonistic (albeit elegantly crafted) pantheism that is probably Suk's most physically beautiful score. On another invaluable Virgin CD (CDC-59318 [CD]), Pesek and the Royal Liverpool Philharmonic perform the works with commanding skill and utter devotion, as they also do in *Praga*, the colorful celebration of the Czech capital that comes as the generous filler.

Sullivan, Sir Arthur

(1842–1900)

(Also see Gilbert and Sullivan)

*P*ineapple Poll

Royal Philharmonic, Mackerras. Arabesque Z-8016 [CD].

The life of that Eminent Victorian Arthur Seymour Sullivan is a mournful study in the seemingly endless human capacity for self-delusion. To the end, Sullivan remained unshakably convinced that he was an important composer who only wrote those flippant entertainments with W. S. Gilbert to maintain himself in a style to which few composers of *any* sort ever become accustomed. Even a passing acquaintance with Sullivan's "serious" music—the turgidly pious oratorio *The Light of the World* and his positively lethal opera after Sir Walter Scott's *Ivanhoe* (the mere titles of cantatas like *The Martyr of Antioch* speak for themselves)—proves conclusively that had Sullivan never met Gilbert, he would be best remembered today for his bellicose, imperialistic, loot-the-world-for-Queen-and-Christ hymn, "Onward, Christian Soldiers," and that wilted hothouse flower, "The Lost Chord."

For those who, for inexplicable (I am almost tempted to say *demented*) reasons of their own, can't seem to abide Sullivan *with* Gilbert, Sir Charles Mackerras's frothy pastiche ballet *Pineapple Poll* is one of the best ways of absorbing these immortal melodies without their equally immortal lyrics. Sir Charles's EMI recording from the early 1960s, available now on Arabesque, is marginally preferable to the more recent version from London: the playing of the Royal Philharmonic is as precise and polished as it is wantonly giddy, and the interpretation—needless to say—is definitive.

Three of Sullivan's most important and engaging serious works, the delightful *Irish* Symphony and *Overture di Ballo* together with the unpretentious 1866 Cello Concerto in Mackerras's loving reconstruction (the original score was lost in a 1964 fire) can now be sampled on an appealing EMI CD (CDM7-64726), which features the spanking performances led by the late Sir Charles Groves.

Another fine album of Sullivan going solo is Alexander Faris's recording with the Scottish Chamber Orchestra of the overtures (Nimbus NIM-5066).

Suppé, Franz von (1819–1895)

Overtures

Montreal Symphony, Dutoit. London 414408-2 [CD].

In some quarters, an enthusiasm for Suppé overtures (the operas and operettas they served to introduce have long since disappeared) is looked on very quizzically. It is as though the person who professes the enthusiasm also admits a fondness for cheap detective movies of the 1940s, spy novels, and long summer afternoons in front of the television, watching baseball and drinking beer.

I admit that, like millions of others, I am thoroughly addicted to these cornball classics. And listening to these crisp, no-nonsense, and most importantly, uncondescending performances by Charles Dutoit and the Montreal Symphony may even make a believer out of you. Dutoit and his forces play these familiar classics as though they were crammed to the gunnels with zest, unforgettable melody, and brilliant craftsmanship. In short, they only show us why these imperishable warhorses deserve to be just that.

Suppé-lovers, rejoice. Suppé-haters, in your ear.

Szymanowski, Karol

(1882–1937)

During the last years of his unhappy life, Karol Szymanowski lamented the fact that he ever became a composer. One can hardly blame him. Even now, more than a half century after his death, his music remains an unknown commodity to most people, in spite of the fact that he was the only incontestably great Polish composer after Chopin and one of the giants of twentieth-century music.

To some extent, the recording industry must bear the brunt of the responsibility for the shabby treatment Szymanowski has received. Compared to his compatriots Witold Lutoslawski, whose inspiration has grown increasingly threadbare with the passage of time, and Krzysztof Penderecki, one of the founding fathers of the grunt-and-groan school of modern music, Szymanowski has been recorded far less frequently over the years, even though he could outcompose both of them standing on his head with one hand tied behind his back while lighting a cigarette.

King Roger, one of the most beautiful of all modern operas, is finally back in circulation on a set of Koch compact discs (CD-314014-K2). The performance by the Warsaw Opera is polished and idiomatic and the recorded sound, while less than ideal, is perfectly acceptable.

The adventurous Marco Polo company has so far issued two invaluable Szymanowski CDs. The first (8.223292) contains the wonderful ballets *Mandragora* and *Harnasie*—the latter sounding like an impossibly profound and civilized *Carmina Burana*—and the second (8.223293) is devoted to the choral music, including a setting of the *Stabat Mater* that ranks with the great sacred works of Western music.

On a recent London compact disc (436837-2), Chantal Juliet, the Montreal Symphony and Charles Dutoit give the most shimmering performances of the two ravishing Violin Concertos ever recorded, surpassing even the classic version of the First Concerto made in 1959 by David Oistrakh; the Carmina Quartet's Denon recording of the two quartets (CO-79462 [CD]) places them firmly among the major chamber works of the twentieth-century.

The breathtaking *Myths* for violin and piano is the centerpiece of a beautiful Szymanowski recital on Chandos (CHAN-8747

[CD], ABTD-1386 [T]) featuring the bewitching violinist Lydia Mordkovitch. Carol Rosenberger's lovely Delos recording of some of the piano music (DE-1002 [CD]) only serves to underscore his position as Chopin's heir, and the RCA recording of the *Symphonie concertante* with Artur Rubinstein (60046-2 [CD]), while not the greatest performance of one of the composer's weaker pieces, is more than worth the investment.

Finally, although Antal Dorati's matchless recordings of the Symphony No. 2 in B-flat and the Symphony No. 3, called *Song of the Night*, has been recently withdrawn, a pair of equally fine performances by the Polish Radio Symphony led by Jacek Kaspryzk (try saying that three times with a load of marbles in your mouth) and Jerzy Semkow have resurfaced on a medium-priced Matrix CD (CDM-5-65082) from EMI. While the earlier work is an intriguing, if somewhat derivative, piece that clearly shows an interesting, ambitious young composer on the verge of becoming a major one, the *Song of the Night* is one of the undoubted masterworks of twentieth-century orchestral music: strange, exotic, wholly original, and, once heard, never to be forgotten.

Tallis, Thomas (c. 1505–1585)

Church Music

The Tallis Scholars, Philips. Gimell GDGIM-006 [CD].

After rudely dismissing the music of his contemporary Ralph Vaughan Williams as was his wont—following a BBC broadcast of the *Pastoral* Symphony, the conductor could be heard to say quite audibly, "A city life for me!"—Sir Thomas Beecham was reprimanded by a friend, who said: "But surely you wouldn't write off that wonderful *Fantasia on a Theme by Thomas Tallis*?" "No," Beecham said, "But Vaughan Williams made the cardinal error of not including in all his compositions a theme by Tallis."

If the modern revival of interest in this colossus of Tudor music then began with Vaughan William's haunting masterpiece of 1910, its continuation has depended on the extraordinary quality of Tallis's music itself, including one of the most complex of all polyphonic studies, the celebrated *Spem in alium non habui*, a "Song of Forty Parts" for eight five-part choirs. In addition to the famous motet, the Tallis Scholars under Peter Phillips offer some ethereally beautiful performances of their eponym's other sacred hits, including a perfectly bewitching setting of *Sancte Deus* that may be even more eloquent.

As Tallis was one of the first composers to write sacred music on English texts for Henry VIII's newly founded Church of England, his English anthems are of special historic interest and can be heard on a superlative companion album (Gimell CDGIM-007 [CD], 1585T-07 [T]) in which the singing of the Tallis Scholars is equally inspired.

Taylor, Deems (1885–1966)

Through the Looking-Glass

Seattle Symphony, Schwarz. Delos DE-3099 [CD].

Although best known as a commentator and critic—for seven years he hosted the intermission broadcasts of the New York Philharmonic, and who could forget his introduction to Disney's *Fantasia* or his fascinating explanation of how the canons and bells were recorded in Antal Dorati's early stereo version of the *1812 Overture*?—Deems Taylor was also a composer of considerable accomplishment. His operas *The King's Henchman* (on a text by Edna St. Vincent Millay) and *Peter Ibbetson* were both mounted by the Metropolitan Opera, and his five pictures from Lewis Carroll, *Through the Looking-Glass*, is among the most endearing orchestral scores ever written by an American. From the tender Introduction with its heart-dissolving principal theme, through the witty

"Jabberwocky," to the soaring romance of "The White Knight," *Through the Looking-Glass* is one of those magical, instantly memorable works that most listeners find impossible to forget.

Gerard Schwarz and his fine orchestra miss none of the work's color, vitality, or charm, making this a worthy successor to Howard Hanson's celebrated 1953 recording. The playing has a wonderful (albeit paradoxical) sense of relaxed intensity, with first-rate solo contributions from the orchestra's principals, and the conductor has never led a more sensitive, completely understanding performance. With equally evocative versions of four marvelous works by the hugely underrated Charles Tomlinson Griffes, including his masterpieces, *The Pleasure-Dome of Kubla Khan* and *The White Peacock*, this cannot possibly be missed.

Tchaikovsky, Piotr Ilyich (1840–1893)

Capriccio italien; *Marche slave*; *Nutcracker* Suite; *1812 Overture*

Montreal Symphony, Dutoit. London 417300-2 [CD].

Although an enormous percentage of music lovers first made their way into Serious Music via the works of Tchaikovsky, many seem strangely loath to admit it. As our tastes mature and we become ever more knowledgeable and sophisticated, we tend to abandon—or perhaps even be ashamed of—our youthful enthusiasms. (Who was it who said, "Don't let the young confide to you their dreams, for when they drop them, they'll drop you"?)

Although he can be extremely obvious, bellicose, cheap, and vulgar, Tchaikovsky more than earns his position as one of the three or four most popular composers. He never cheats his listeners, giving them huge doses of overwhelming (and often surprisingly complex) emotions, a keen sense of orchestral color, and one of the greatest melodic gifts any composer possessed. In short, if you love Tchaikovsky, don't be ashamed. And don't think you're alone. Uncounted millions of us can't *all* be wrong.

This superb and unusually generous London collection brings together four of the composer's most popular works in performances as civilized as they are exciting, as brash and brazen as they are thoughtful and refined. Although the *1812 Overture* could be a bit noisier for my taste (remember the great old Mercury recording with Antal Dorati and the Minneapolis Symphony, and Deems Taylor explaining how they got the bells and cannon blasts?), these are the performances I turn to whenever the mood strikes.

Concerto for Piano and Orchestra No. 1 in B-flat minor

Cliburn, piano; RCA Symphony, Kondrashin. RCA 07863-55912-2 [CD], 07863-55912-4 [T].

It's no accident that this is one of the best-selling classical recordings of all time. Naturally, much of it had to do with the ballyhoo that attended Van Cliburn's winning of the Tchaikovsky competition in Moscow during one of the chilliest moments of the Cold War. (Yes, the Russians had a definite jump in the space race —remember all those films of our rockets blowing up on the pad?— but we had this long, lanky Texan who beat them, and beat them decisively, at their own game.)

Three decades later, in the midst of the *glasnost* thaw, it's time we started judging this recording on its own merits, and not its historical context. I have, and simply stated, in *any* context, this is one hell of an exciting performance. Cliburn's mixture of elfin delicacy and animal ferocity has remained intact since the recording was first released. It is a poetic, explosive, lyrical, and deeply humane interpretation that no recording of the last thirty years begins to match.

Concertos for Piano and Orchestra: No. 2 in G; No. 3 in E-flat

Douglas, piano; Philharmonia Orchestra, Slatkin. RCA 09026-61633-2 [CD]

The long overdue rehabilitation of Tchaikovsky's "other" piano concertos would not be long delayed if performances of them were as committed and electrifying as these. Using the composer's uncut original version, Barry Douglas is perhaps even more impressive in the Second Concerto than he was in his version of the First. Like Peter Donohoe in his superb but now deleted Angel recording, Douglas transforms the Second into something engrossing and exciting: with substantial contributions from the concertmaster and principal cellist, the slow movement emerges as one of Tchaikovsky's most original inspirations, and the finale erupts in a blaze of Vesuvian fireworks that outshines even the startling version Gary Graffman recorded a generation ago. Though it is a much lesser piece, the Third Concerto also responds brilliantly to Douglas's poetry and panache, and Leonard Slatkin is as quick and canny a partner as always.

Concerto in D for Violin and Orchestra

Heifetz, violin; Chicago Symphony, Reiner. RCA
09026-61495-2 [CD], 09026-61495-4 [T].

Oistrakh, violin; Philadelphia Orchestra, Ormandy. Sony
SBK-46339, SBT-46339 [T].

From a purely technical point of view, there has never been a recording to match Jascha Heifetz's famous version with Fritz Reiner and the Chicago Symphony. Although the violinist was placed uncomfortably close to the microphone, which accounts for the unaccustomed rasp in his famous tone, the playing is genuinely spellbinding. Listen especially to the first movement cadenza, in which the soloist uses one of his own devising that makes Tchaikovsky's original seem like child's play.

On the other hand, if you're after the warmth, color, and abiding romance of the Tchaikovsky Concerto, then David Oistrakh's meltingly lovely recording with Eugene Ormandy and the Philadelphia Orchestra is clearly the one to own.

Eugene Onegin

Focile, Hvorostovsky, Shicoff, Walker, Arkhipova, St.
Petersburg Chamber Choir, Orchestre de Paris, Bychkov.
Philips 438235-2 [CD].

Of the ten Tchaikovsky operas that survive, only *Eugene Onegin* and *The Queen of Spades*, both based on works by Pushkin, have made any inroads into the standard repertoire. (For any Slavic opera to do so has been next to impossible, given the language barrier. To this day, Smetana's masterpiece is usually heard as *Die Verkaufte Braut* or *The Bartered Bride*, as opposed to *Prodaná Nevěsta*, and even *Boris Godunov* didn't begin making the international rounds until the title role was taken over by a lunatic named Chaliapin.) Although *Onegin* can often seem to lack sustainable dramatic interest or clearly delineated characters (part of the problem lay in the fact that the composer adored Pushkin's heroine and regarded his hero as "a cold, heartless coxcomb"), it is full of unforgettable set pieces like Tatiana's Letter Scene, the Waltz and Polonaise, and the exquisite aria in which the doomed Lensky recalls his youth. (Like his tenor, Pushkin himself was killed in a duel only six years after completing *Onegin*, defending the "honor" of his not entirely honorable wife.)

The impassioned Philips recording with Dmitri Hvorostovsky in the title role easily supplants all previous and currently available versions of *Onegin*, including the recently deleted London version conducted by Sir Georg Solti. Vocally and dramatically, Nuccia Focile who possesses an astounding command of Russian diction and Tchaikovsky's soaring line, is a far more impressive Tatiana than Teresa Kubiak in Solti's version. Semyon Bychkov's conducting is as passionately committed as Solti's, but it is also far more flexible and idiomatic, capturing the music's Russian inflections to perfection. Hvorostovsky demonstrates why he is the most exciting Russian singer of his generation, combining an abundance of old-fashioned temperament and high intelligence with a startlingly large and beautiful voice. All in all, an *Onegin* to set the standard well past the turn of the century.

Hamlet; *Francesca da Rimini*

Stadium Symphony of New York, Stokowski. Dell'Arte CDDA-9006 [CD].

This is a thoroughly impossible recording. Those with any taste know that Tchaikovsky's *Hamlet* is trash, pure and simple, and that *Francesca da Rimini*, on the dreck-o-meter, isn't far behind. Moreover, those who have heard the Stadium Symphony of New York—a name the New York Philharmonic minus its first-deck musicians adopted to protect the identity of its players—must suspect, as I do, that their summer evening concerts may have provided the inspiration for George A. Romero's film, *Night of the Living Dead.*

So here are two second-rate works performed by a third-rate orchestra under the direction of a man whose podium antics, tabloid romances, Bach arrangements, and other glitzy hokum made the word *charlatan* lose all its respectability. After more than thirty years, the results are *still* not to be believed. *Francesca da Rimini,* in an interpretation whose sheer ferocity is matched only by its tenderness and subtlety, transforms into what sounds like the most electrifying tone poem ever written; *Hamlet* becomes what it cannot possibly be: not only something worthy of the name, but also one of the most pointed and perceptive Shakespeare commentaries in all of music.

Add this to Stokowski's 1927 Philadelphia Scheherazade, and you have two of the ten greatest recordings of Russian music ever made.

Impossible, but true.

*T*he Nutcracker

L'Orchestre de la Suisse Romande, Ansermet. London 417055-4 [T].

Berlin Philharmonic, Bychkov. Philips 420237-2 [CD].

If ever a recording deserved the designation "Imperishable," it is Ernest Ansermet's triumphant early stereo version of *The Nutcracker*, which has more sheer interpretive magic than you can shake a sugarplum at. Although the sound has definitely begun to show its age, the performance never will. Ansermet's conception brings out every ounce of charm and color that this often hackneyed work offers, and does it with a touch so light and sure, we're reminded once again of what we all owe this great pioneer of the early stereo age.

While the Philips compact disc recording by Semyon Bychkov and the Berlin Philharmonic can't quite match the winsomeness and delicacy of the Ansermet, it still has much to recommend it. In addition to some razor-sharp playing from one of the world's great orchestras, this compact disc will introduce many to a stupendously gifted young conductor.

Romeo and Juliet (fantasy overture)

Royal Philharmonic, Ashkenazy. London 421715-2 [CD].

London Symphony, Simon. Chandos CHAN-8310/11 [CD], DBR-2003 [T].

Vladimir Ashkenazy's Royal Philharmonic recording offers an excellent, old-fashioned *Romeo*. While it lacks the dash and drama of Leonard Bernstein's inexplicably withdrawn Deutsche Grammophon recording with the Israel Philharmonic, it does feature superior playing and recorded sound. With stellar performances of *Francesca da Rimini*, *Capriccio italien*, and the *Elegy for Strings* tossed in as a bonus, it makes for an easy first recommendation.

Geoffrey Simon's Chandos recording is an entirely different matter. In this fascinating and, for Tchaikovsky aficionados, can't-live-another-day-without-it release, Simon unearths the original 1869 version of the work that put the composer on the musical map of Europe in the early 1880s. This is not simply an early version of *Romeo and Juliet*, but a virtually unrecognizable piece: less finished and professional than the *Romeo* we're used to, yet one whose unvarnished enthusiasm and power are hard to resist. In addition to this proto-*Romeo*, the Simon collection offers a version of *Hamlet* that features both the overture and the incidental music, including a mad scene for Ophelia and a lively (if that's really the right word) "Gravedigger's Song," together with some bona fide off-the-wall discoveries such as the *Festival Overture on the Danish National Anthem* and, as I have now come to think of it, the absolutely indispensable *Serenade for Nikolai Rubinstein's Saint's Day*.

Serenade in C for String Orchestra

Australian Chamber Orchestra, Pini. Omega OCD-1010 [CD].

Academy of St. Martin-in-the-Fields, Marriner. London
417736-2 [CD].

With so many first-rate recordings of the popular Serenade
for Strings floating around, the final choice for many people might
depend on how the piece is packaged. For those who want the
traditional pairing with the Dvořák Serenade, Sir Neville Marriner's London recording isn't going to be bettered, at least until
Angel bestirs itself and issues those spellbinding Barenboim–
English Chamber Orchestra performances on a medium-priced CD.

For a less predictable yet far more logical coupling, the brilliant Australian Chamber Orchestra and Carl Pini offer one of
the most alert and amiable performances on the market, together
with an arresting version of the composer's own favorite piece, the
Souvenir of Florence.

String Quartets (3)

Borodin Quartet. EMI ZDCB-49775 [CD].

The Tchaikovsky string quartets along with those of Alexander Borodin, are among the pivotal Russian chamber works of
the nineteenth century: the first important Russian string quartets
and virtually the only ones until the advent of Dmitri Shostakovich's. Beginning with the early D Major Quartet of 1871, with its
unforgettable slow movement, the famous *Andante cantabile*, the
level of inspiration and invention remained extremely high, as these
vivid, mercurial performances by the Borodin Quartet demonstrate.
With the finest available recording of the sextet version of the
Souvenir of Florence thrown in as a bonus, it is extremely unlikely
this collection will ever be bettered.

Suites for Orchestra: No. 3 in G; No. 4 in G, *Mozartiana*

USSR Academic Symphony, Svetlanov. Melodiya SUCD
10-00104 [CD].

Their small but devoted circle of admirers has always realized
how much wonderful music is to be found in Tchaikovsky's four
orchestral suites; now, thanks to what have to be counted as the

most inspired of Yevgeny Svetlanov's recordings thus far, everyone else will, too. In these miraculous performances of the Third and Fourth Suites, a new insight, a fresh inspiration, an astonishing gee-why-didn't-anyone-ever-think-of-doing-it-that-way-before? solution seems to leap out at every turn. Under Svetlanov's firm but infinitely flexible guidance, the USSR Academic Symphony performs the music with such effortless grace and joy that you're very nearly persuaded they must be making it up as they go along. One can only hope the equally persuasive versions of the First and Second Suites are slated for reissue soon.

Swan Lake (complete ballet)

Philharmonia Orchestra, Lanchbery. Angel CDCB-49171 [CD].

To his everlasting credit, Tchaikovsky never gave up on the two forms he most wanted to master but whose perplexing secrets always just eluded him. And it is his masterpiece, *Swan Lake*, that best explains why he never became the great opera composer and symphonist he so earnestly wanted to be. For the glory of Tchaikovsky's art was neither its intellectual depth nor grasp of structure, but its ability to make melody and emotion indistinguishable from one another. In no other composer's work is melody the *meaning* of the music to the extent that it is in Tchaikovsky, and nowhere else is his melodic genius more finely tuned than it is in *Swan Lake*. In none of his major works, except perhaps for *The Sleeping Beauty*, do we have the sense of such concentration and economy, even in spite of its formidable length; the sense that every tune is not only memorable but absolutely necessary, and that not a note or gesture is wasted. It is a unique achievement which by itself would refute the nonsensical suggestion that Tchaikovsky was not a great composer.

If it doesn't have all the character of other fine recordings of the recent past—Gennadi Rozhdestvensky's Moscow Radio, as opposed to his BBC, performance—John Lanchbery's is an enthusiastic and completely professional job and is easily the best *Swan Lake* left on the map. The playing of the Philharmonia Orchestra is fairly stupendous, though it might not be *quite* as impressive as that of the London Symphony in their classic recording with André

Previn, recently restored by EMI (CDQB-54814 [CD], 4D2Q-54814 [T]). For those who might not need the entire ballet(s), Riccardo Muti and the Philadelphia Orchestra offer colorful, spectacularly well-played versions of excerpts from *Swan Lake* and *Sleeping Beauty* (Angel CDC-47075 [CD], 4DS-38117 [T]).

Symphonies: Nos. 1–6; *Manfred* Symphony

Oslo Philharmonic, Jansons. Chandos CHAN-8672/78 [CD], DBTD-7001 [T].

My own introduction to the Tchaikovsky symphonies came via an RCA Victor Camden recording of the Fifth with the Oslo Philharmonic led by its longtime (1931–1961) conductor, Odd Grünner-Hegge. I remember that exciting interpretation virtually note for note, not only because it was so exceptionally good but also because, forever after, no other performance of the piece has ever sounded quite right. Grünner-Hegge, who studied conducting with Felix Weingartner, observed the whopping cuts his old teacher made in the score, including the whole of the last movement's development section. This still heads my list of must have Tchaikovsky Fifth recordings, followed closely by the zany Paul van Kempen version made with the Concertgebouw Orchestra of Amsterdam at about the same time (Philips 438-310-2 [CD]), which includes, among *its* enthralling perversities, a pair of cymbal crashes just before the final stretto and an additional horn note that creates an unresolved seventh chord at that great pause before the march—undoubtedly a hold-over of one of the many tricks conductors have tried in an attempt to head off the applause that customarily breaks out at that inopportune moment. (Stokowski tried to cure this premature congratulation by simply having the timpani keep rolling through the break, but the only time I heard him do it, with the Chicago Symphony, the unwashed and unsanctified fell in where they always do, earning a withering Stokie glare.)

But I digress.

The current conductor of the Oslo Philharmonic, Mariss Jansons, has built a considerable reputation as a Tchaikovsky conductor thanks to his Chandos recordings, and all of them—even his game go-round with the hopeless *Manfred* Symphony—are among the finest currently available and will probably remain the standard versions for years. The interpretations are both disciplined and spontaneous, with wonderful playing from an orchestra which sounds, for much of the time, like a junior edition of the Berlin Philharmonic. Nearly as fine are the fresh and exhilarating readings of the first two symphonies by Gerard Schwarz and the Seattle Symphony for Delos (DE 3087 [CD]), while two classic recordings should also be returned to print: Carlo Maria Giulini's whirlwind version of the *Little Russian* for EMI, and the *Winter Dreams* with the Boston Symphony conducted by Michael Tilson Thomas on Deutsche Grammophon, one of the most electric Tchaikovsky symphony recordings ever made.

For those who prefer to acquire the later symphonies singly, a few reasonable alternatives exist. Leonard Bernstein's early CBS recording of the Fourth (MYK-37766 [CD], MYT-37766 [T]) still packs plenty of wallop and highly individual pizzazz. Claudio Abbado's brooding yet exhilarating performance of the Fifth ranks with the finest recordings to date (CBS MK-42094 [CD]). And an Erato recording of a live performance of the *Pathétique* led by Jansons's old mentor Yevgeny Mravinsky (2292-45756-2 [CD]) takes at least some of the sting out of Deutsche Grammophon's criminally insensitive decision to withdraw his classic studio recordings of the last three symphonies from circulation.

Variations on a Rococo Theme for Cello and Orchestra

Rostropovich, cello; Berlin Philharmonic, Karajan. Deutsche Grammophon 413819-2 [CD].

By common consent, Mstislav Rostropovich has all but owned Tchaikovsky's de facto cello concerto for a generation, and this most eloquently argued of his several recordings demonstrates why. The cellist refuses to treat the piece as merely an engaging ball of cuddly virtuoso fluff, but approaches it as a major work that requires major concentration. Which is not to say he misses any of the charm or fun of the piece. Quite the contrary. His impish enthusiasm even infects his usually grim-lipped conductor, who here delivers one of the most uncharacteristically witty and humane of his later performances.

A good though by no means exceptional performance of the Dvořák Concerto rounds out the CD, and on cassette Rostropovich's earlier Deutsche Grammophon recording with Gennadi Rozhdestvensky and the Leningrad Philharmonic is an equally obvious first choice (413161-4).

Telemann, Georg Philipp

(1681–1767)

During his lifetime, Georg Philipp Telemann completely over-shadowed his near-contemporary, an obscure German organist and composer named Johann Sebastian Bach. Later centuries slowly realized that what had made Telemann so fashionable during his lifetime—the clear, uncomplicated structures, the easy-to-follow contents of a music that had nothing profound to say—ultimately gave him next to no staying power, especially in comparison with the *real* Baroque giants, Handel and Bach.

While I can make no specific recommendations for recordings of the man's music (it all sounds more or less the same to me), I will offer a few general hints for the Telemann shopper: (1) Avoid any recording with a reproduction of an eighteenth-century landscape painting on the front cover. (2) Avoid any concerto for more than one instrument (anything more complicated seems only to have confused him). (3) Avoid any recording featuring Nikolaus Har-noncourt, his wife Alice, or their friend Gustav Leonhardt. If you see them in the cut-out or used-record bins, and I mean *anything* produced by the Telemann Society, shun them as though your life depended on it. (Several people have laughed themselves to death listening to their well-intentioned but hopelessly feeble efforts.) (4) If the temptation to buy a Telemann recording proves irresist-ible, make certain your cupboard is well stocked with strong, and I do mean *strong*, coffee.

Thomas, Ambroise

(1811–1896)

Hamlet

Anderson, Hampson, Graves, Kunde, Ramey, Ambrosian
Singers, London Philharmonic, de Almeida, EMI CDCC-
54820 [CD].

If the Germans have never been able to tolerate the celebrated
Faust travesty of Charles Gounod, calling it *Marguerite* whenever
it is staged there, then the English have never been particularly
sanguine on the setting of *Hamlet* by Gounod's near-contemporary,
Ambroise Thomas. Yet it spite of its more obvious outrages, such
as a mad scene in lilting ¾ time and an exuberant drinking song put
in the mouth of the melancholy Dane, *Hamlet* can be an effective
piece of theater, given the proper singers. The title role was a major
star vehicle for the "Caruso of Baritones," the legendary Titta
Ruffo, and Ophelia has been a favorite of coloraturas from the age
of Adelina Patti to that of Joan Sutherland.

The foremost living heirs to that great tradition, Thomas
Hampson and June Anderson, make the strongest possible case for
the opera in this superb EMI recording, with Hampson virile yet
sensitive in the title role and Anderson suitably agile and pliant in
hers. Anderson's mad scene does not completely efface the memory
of Luisa Tetrazzini's or Sutherland's, but it is a staggering piece of
singing: accurate, fearless, and perfectly on pitch. Hampson's brindisi, on the other hand, is every bit the equal of Ruffo's, with
possibly even more fire and rhythmic dash. Antonio de Almeida
does his best to keep the rest of the action from flagging, and the
supporting cast is first-rate.

Those with a *Faust* sweet tooth should waste no time giving
this delightful confection a try.

Thompson, Randall

(1899–1984)

Symphonies: No. 2; No. 3

**New Zealand Symphony, Schenck. Koch International
Classics 3-7074-2 [CD].**

One of the most urbane and gentlemanly of American composers, Randall Thompson was primarily known for vocal works like the elegant *Alleluia* of 1940 and the stirring *Testament of Freedom* on a text by Jefferson, currently available on a very fine Reference CD (RR-49). He was also the composer of two of the finest of all American symphonies, both of which are memorably served on this recent Koch recording.

Although the Third Symphony of 1949 is a spirited, beautifully made work that never wears out its welcome or wastes a single gesture, the Second Symphony of 1931 is a masterpiece: virile, tuneful, seamlessly argued, and completely satisfying.

The New Zealand Symphony under the late Andrew Schenck makes a virtually airtight case for both works. The young orchestra plays with polish and enthusiasm; only the occasional thinness in the upper strings reveals that it is not quite a world-class ensemble. The recording, if slightly distant, is excellent.

Thomson, Virgil

(1896–1989)

The Plow That Broke the Plains (orchestral suite); *The River* (orchestral suite); *Autumn* (Concertino for Harp, Strings, and Percussion)

Los Angeles Chamber Orchestra, Marriner. Angel
CDC-47715 [CD].

Even if it's still too soon to get a clear picture of Virgil Thomson's stature as a composer, his position as one of America's most perceptive, courageous, and bitchy music critics is assured. During his enlightened reign of terror (1940–1954) as the critic at the New York *Herald Tribune*, Thomson enraged and delighted readers with countless inflammatory observations, including the then-heretical suggestions that Arturo Toscanini was *not* the risen Christ, and that the Second Symphony of Jean Sibelius, at the height of his popularity at the time, was "vulgar, self-indulgent, and provincial beyond all description."

After *Four Saints in Three Acts*, the transcendentally daffy opera he wrote with Gertrude Stein—which can be heard on a superbly successful Nonesuch CD (79035-2)—Thomson the composer is probably best represented on record these days by the music he wrote for Pare Lorentz's WPA documentary films, *The Plow That Broke the Plains* and *The River*. Like his *Symphony on a Hymn Tune*, an ingenuous portrait of the nineteenth-century American Midwest painted by a citified Parisian in the 1920s, now available in Howard Hanson's classic Mercury recording (434310-2 [CD]), these are folksy, openhearted, sophisticated works that immediately enfold the listener in a bear-hug embrace. The performances by Sir Neville Marriner and the Los Angeles Chamber Orchestra are even more affectionate and evocative than Leopold Stokowski's famous Symphony of the Air recordings, and the twenty-year-old recorded sound remains fertile and uneroded.

Tippett, Sir Michael (1905–)

A Child of Our Time

Armstrong, Palmer, Langridge, Shirley-Quirk, Brighton
Festival Chorus, Royal Philharmonic, Previn. RPO
Records RPO-7012 [CD].

Sir Michael Tippett, England's greatest living composer, has spent most of his career in the tremendous shadow cast by his far more famous contemporary, Benjamin Britten. In many ways, Tippett is the more interesting composer (and this from someone who has always adored Britten's music). Unlike Britten, Tippett has ventured down several important modern roads in his later years. His idiom has become increasingly harsh and dissonant, while his expression has become ever more concentrated and precise. Late Tippett (from, say, the early 1970s onward) can be a very thorny, though immensely rewarding, row to hoe.

A Child of Our Time, completed in 1941, is not only one of Tippett's most accessible pieces, it is one of the most shattering, yet heartbreakingly lovely choral works of the last hundred years. Patterned consciously after the Passions of Bach, Tippett's oratorio presents black spirituals in place of the familiar chorales at key moments in the drama. Their effect, especially in a recording like this one, is overwhelmingly moving and beautiful.

The oratorio has been recorded twice before, in handsome performances led by John Pritchard and Sir Colin Davis, but this new version by André Previn is one of the conductor's finest recordings to date, and the greatest recorded performance *A Child of Our Time* is ever likely to receive. The complex textures of the work are untangled with a pristine clarity, and the soloists are inspired to do some of the finest work of their careers. And the way Previn has the often gigantic forces swing their way through the spirituals is enough to raise the hair on the back of your neck, particularly in "Steal Away." In short, this is an indispensable performance of a great modern classic that belongs in every recording library.

For Tippett admirers (and the man certainly deserves millions more than he has so far attracted), two other important recordings can also be recommended without reservation. The first is an invaluable two-CD set from EMI (ZDMB-63522), which offers irreproachable versions of the Concerto for Double String Orchestra, the *Fantasia Concertante on a Theme of Corelli* (conducted by the composer), the First String Quartet, and the First and Second Piano Sonatas played by John Ogdon. The second, from London (425646-2 [CD]), features all four of the symphonies Sir Michael has written to date, packaged with the slender but enchanting *Suite for the Birthday of Prince Charles*, in the virtually definitive performances led by Sir Colin Davis (1–3) and Sir George Solti (4, *Suite*).

Philips and London have temporarily withdrawn all the re cordings of the Tippett operas. In the case of the extremely knotty *Knot Garden*, such bad manners can be overlooked, if not excused. But for Philips to deep-six the mysterious, exuberant *Midsummer Marriage*—which has a fair claim to being (with all due apologies to Benjamin Britten) the greatest modern English opera—is an act of wanton barbarism that can be expiated *only* by its immediate reissue on compact disc. The wonderful *Ritual Dances* can be found on a fine Nimbus recording (NI-5217 [CD]) in company with other composer-led versions of the *Praeludium* for Brass, Bells, and Percussion and the *Suite for the Birthday of Prince Charles*.

Tubin, Eduard (1905–1982)

Symphonies: No. 4, *Sinfonia lirica*; No. 9, *Sinfonia semplice*

Bergen Symphony, Gothenberg Symphony, Järvi. Bis CD-227 [CD].

Unlike sex, politics, and television, music is always full of surprises. Until quite recently, the surprising music of Eduard Tubin was a carefully guarded secret outside of his native Estonia and adopted Sweden; now, thanks largely to the Estonian conductor Neeme Järvi and the enterprising Swedish label Bis, Tubin has at last begun to take his rightful place among the most substantial and original of mid-twentieth-century symphonists.

Each of the ten completed symphonies that Tubin composed over a fifty-year period (an eleventh was left unfinished at the time of his death) manages to say something fresh and individual. Although the spirits of near-contemporaries Sibelius, Prokofiev, and Shostakovich might flit in and out of the music from time to time, Tubin is very much his own man: a rational yet emotionally intricate personality whose superbly crafted, immediately engaging music says what it has to say—which is often an earful—without wasting a moment of our time, or its.

The pairing of the Fourth Symphony of 1943 and the Ninth of 1969 is an ideal introduction to Tubin's bracing, lucid, mysterious universe, and Järvi's interpretations reveal a deep and obvious affection for his countryman's music. The only serious drawback is that the recording may prove addictive, forcing you to snap up the other symphonies as quickly as possible.

Varèse, Edgar (1883–1965)

Amériques; *Arcana*; *Density 21.5*; *Intégrales*; *Ionisation*; *Octandre*; *Offrandes*

Ensemble InterContemporain, New York Philharmonic, Boulez. Sony SK-45844 [CD].

Following a brief bout of unlikely popularity in the 1960s —due in part to the *Poème électronique*, which, when performed over four hundred speakers at the Philips Pavilion, became an unexpected hit at the 1958 Brussels World's Fair, and thanks, too, to the spirited advocacy of the late Frank Zappa, another unruly genius who immediately knew a kindred spirit when he heard one —Edgar (née Edgard) Varèse slipped back into the not-so-benign neglect in which he languished for most of his career.

In his entry on Varèse in *Baker's Biographical Dictionary of Musicians*, Nicolas Slonimsky drops the usual one- or two-word preparatory appraisal ("Distinguished conductor"; "Famous Bulgarian heckelphone virtuoso") in favor of this: "One of the most remarkable composers of his century, who introduced a totally original principle of organizing the materials and forms of sound, profoundly influencing the direction of new music." That just about says it.

Pierre Boulez's recordings are by far the most valuable yet made of this composer's music, and with seven major works crammed onto a single medium-priced CD, this is a bargain that no one interested in twentieth-century music should be able to resist. Predictably, the French conductor is most impressive whenever Varèse is at his thorniest: the dense, barbaric fabric of *Arcana*, for instance, is untangled to an astonishing degree, and *Offrandes* emerges with a Mozart-like clarity coupled with a sensuousness that will remind many listeners of Debussy.

All in all, the major step to date in the rehabilitation of a modern giant.

Vaughan Williams, Ralph (1872–1958)

Fantasia on a Theme by Thomas Tallis; Symphony No. 2, *A London Symphony*

London Philharmonic, Boult. Angel CDM-64017 [CD].

For those who have yet to acquire the gentle addiction of Ralph Vaughan Williams's music, this superb Angel recording should do the trick. On it are two of his finest and most characteristic pieces, the ravishing *Fantasia on a Theme by Thomas Tallis* and that greatest of modern English musical travelogues, *A London Symphony*.

Although both works have had marginally finer, but currently unavailable, performances (Sir John Barbirolli's version of the Symphony ranks with the great Vaughan Williams recordings yet made), these performances by Sir Adrian Boult are excellent in every way. A close friend of the composer, Boult has unimpeachable credentials as a Vaughan Williams conductor, which shine through every bar of these works. The *Fantasia* has enormous dignity, as well as sensual beauty; the performance of the Symphony, if not quite as colorful a tour as Barbirolli's, is unforgettable. The London Philharmonic is at the top of its form in both performances, and the remastered sound of the compact disc is extremely impressive.

Five Mystical Songs; Dona nobis pacem

> Wiens, soprano; Rayner-Cook, baritone; London
> Philharmonic Orchestra and Choir, Thompson. Chandos
> CHAN-8590 [CD], ABTD-1297 [T].

As his Chandos cycle of the Vaughan Williams symphonies clearly proves, in the decade prior to his untimely death the gifted Bryden Thomson was just beginning to come into his own as a conductor. With a few exceptions (such as his rather too literal version of the highly atmospheric *Sinfonia Antartica*, a considerable disappointment), the Thomson recordings are in most respects competitive with the far more celebrated ones of Sir Adrian Boult and André Previn.

The early *Five Mystical Songs* and *Dona nobis pacem* are two of the most serious and gravely beautiful of all Vaughan William's vocal works, and both are given sumptuous performances under Thomson's direction. The soloists acquit themselves admirably, as does the chorus, the orchestra, and Chandos's highly skilled engineers.

Five Tudor Portraits

> Soloists, London Symphony Orchestra and Chorus,
> Willcocks. EMI CDM-64722 [CD].

Based on the crackbrained, near-doggerel verse of the Tudor poet and eccentric John Skelton, *Five Tudor Portraits* is one of the most exhilarating and enjoyable of all Vaughan Williams's large-scale works. The choral suite is an affable and consistently surprising tour of Skelton's surreal and bawdy world, which culminates in the roaring "Jolly Rutterkin." Sir David Willcocks leads a performance that admirably captures both the warmth and vitality of the piece, with lusty, full-throated singing from the chorus and sparkling playing by the London Symphony. Packaged with a lovely version of the radiant and rarely heard *Benedictine* for Soprano, Chorus, and Orchestra and a very fine account of the *Five Variants of Dives and Lazarus*, this is a release than no Vaughan Williams lover can afford to pass up.

Job (A Masque for Dancing)

London Philharmonic, Handley. Angel CDC 54421 [CD].

Here, as in his admirable Elgar, Delius, and Walton recordings, Vernon Handley continues to prove that he is one of the most gifted and comprehensive conductors of English music now before the public. His enthusiasm for Vaughan Williams is more than understandable: he studied these scores with the composer's old friend Sir Adrian Boult.

In the oddly neglected ballet *Job*, one of Vaughan Williams's supreme creations, Handley's only competition comes from his old teacher on another Angel recording; Boult no doubt would have been proud (if not necessarily pleased) to have been bested so handily by his former pupil. From its subtlest shadings to its most booming climaxes, this is the first and only recording to date that seems to release the full scope and drama of this spectacular score. Even with the generous bonus of the Partita for Double String Orchestra, the Boult version simply cannot compete.

The Pilgrim's Progress

Noble, et. al., London Philharmonic Choir and Orchestra, Boult. EMI CDMB-64212 [CD].

Completed in 1952 when the composer was seventy-nine, *The Pilgrim's Progress* has strong claims to being Vaughan Williams's masterpiece. The composer called it neither an opera nor an oratorio, but a Morality, whose purpose was to examine the mystical implications of John Bunyan's classic tale rather than its limited dramatic content. Using material that also appeared in the beautiful Fifth Symphony, Vaughan Williams fashioned a score of extraordinary beauty and spiritual depth that ranks with Elgar's *Dream of Gerontius* as one of the central works of modern English choral music.

Sir Adrian Boult's lifetime of devotion to his friend's music is obvious at all points in this magnificent performance, one of the crowning glories of that venerable conductor's career. In addition to plumbing the work to its depths, Boult also reveals its enormous variety, from the pastoral Shepherds of the Delectable Mountains episode to the seductive evils of Vanity Fair. John Noble gives a searching and resourceful performance as the Pilgrim, and the other members of the cast are no less fine. Now if only EMI could be persuaded to reissue their superlative recording of the composer's Falstaff opera, *Sir John in Love*, the full range of Vaughan Williams's achievement could be even better understood.

Serenade to Music

London Philharmonic, Boult. Angel CDM-64022 [CD].

Written to a text from Shakespeare's *Merchant of Venice*, the *Serenade to Music* may be the most bewitchingly beautiful work Vaughan Williams ever wrote. And to say that of the man who wrote *The Lark Ascending*, the *Fantasia on a Theme by Thomas Tallis*, *Flos Campi*, and the folk opera *Sir John in Love*, is to say a very great deal indeed.

Although it is usually performed with a full chorus, Sir Adrian Boult gives a gleaming performance of the work as it was originally written. Composed for Sir Henry Wood's Golden Jubilee, the *Serenade* included solo parts for sixteen singers with whom Sir Henry had been especially close. That historic interpretation, recorded by Sir Henry and company in 1938 only a week after the *Serenade*'s premiere, is now out on a Pearl compact disc (GEMM CD-9342). While obviously for specialists, it is a lovely performance and a recording of considerable historic importance.

For those who can do without history—especially the late '30s recorded sound (which isn't all that bad, by the way)—the Boult interpretation remains a modern classic. Packaged with equally charming and authoritative versions of *In the Fen Country*, *The Lark Ascending*, the *English Folksong Suite*, the *Norfolk Rhapsody*, and the *Fantasia on "Greensleeves"*, this is probably the most desirable Vaughan Williams recording now available.

Symphonies: No. 4 in F minor; No. 6 in E minor

New Philharmonia Orchestra, Boult. Angel CDM-64019 [CD].

A number of years ago at the first San Francisco Symphony performance of Vaughan Williams's Sixth Symphony, the conductor—a very fine conductor, who will remain nameless—decided that since the piece was bound to be unfamiliar to most of the audience, he should probably say a few words about it. He began his impromptu talk with the unfortunate sentence, "The Vaughan Williams Sixth is basically a very depressing piece . . ." Before uttering another syllable, he was abruptly cut off by a shy, retiring friend of mine (a full professor of Vaughan Williams), who pointed an accusing finger at the luckless musician and said, "But that *simply* isn't true!" Stunned and speechless, the conductor broke off his comments and began the piece without further ado.

The most bleakly pessimistic of the composer's symphonies it most certainly is; yet it is no more "depressing" than Robert Lowell's poetry, Max Beckmann's paintings, or some of Ingmar Bergman's films. Begun in the midst of the Second World War and completed two years after the war ended, the Sixth is an appropriately dark vision of life from the middle of the darkest century in recorded history.

Sir Adrian Boult's powerful recording is one of the best from his historic Vaughan Williams cycle. The performance is honest and unblinkingly courageous, with a final movement that rises to tragic heights reminiscent of the greatest Mahler Adagios. Coupled with the explosive, dissonant Fourth Symphony in an equally unnerving performance, this is *not* a recording for fans of the *"Greensleeves" Fantasia* who are looking for more of the same.

Symphony No. 5 in D

London Symphony, Previn. RCA 60586-2 [CD].

The Fifth is not only the most beautiful of the nine Vaughan Williams symphonies, it is also one of the most completely characteristic. In it, we hear an impeccable craftsman with a complex yet thoroughly humane mind—an utterly modern man who was content with stirring us deeply, and left probing the depths or shaking the heavens to others.

There are many who feel that André Previn is the most persuasive of all living Vaughan Williams conductors, and I agree. This Fifth, part of Previn's cycle of all nine symphonies for RCA, remains one of the best recordings the conductor has made so far. In general, Previn brings more life and freshness to this great work than any conductor ever has. The themes of the first movement unfold with an ease and naturalness that not even Sir Adrian Boult can match. For a very different view of the work, and one packaged with something more substantial than the admittedly delightful Tuba Concerto and *Three Portraits*, Boult's Angel recording comes with perhaps the finest version of the *Pastoral* Symphony (No. 3) (CDM 64018 [CD]).

While space, alas, does not permit a complete discussion of all nine Vaughan Williams symphonies, the other Angel recordings by Boult and those by Previn on RCA can be recommended enthusiastically. The Boult interpretations have the advantage of the conductor's long friendship with the composer and his fifty-year immersion in the music. Previn, on the other hand, brings an engaging spontaneity to the music and a youthful, interpretive insight that make his recordings no less valuable. The wise collector will want them all, especially since all have been reissued on compact disc.

Verdi, Giuseppe (1813–1901)

Aida

Milanov, Barbieri, Björling, Warren, Christoff, Orchestra
and Chorus of the Rome Opera House, Perlea. Victrola
6652-2-RG [CD], ALK3-5380 [T].

Price, Bumbry, Domingo, Milnes, London Symphony,
Leinsdorf. RCA 6198-2 RC [CD], ARK3-2541 [T].

Verdi is unique among the great composers in that his post-
humous fame is of virtually the same magnitude as that which he
acquired during his lifetime. In 1842, the year of *Nabucco*, Verdi
became a national hero in his own country, and in the next few
years he was lionized throughout the opera world. Although there
were occasional setbacks (the famous initial failure of *La Traviata*,
for instance), he experienced more than half a century of increasing
honors, and died, at the age of eighty-seven, steeped in wealth and
adulation.

Aida, which was to have been his final opera, is a good
indication of why Verdi, now as then, is the very heart of Italian opera. Amid all its pomp and spectacle, *Aida* is essentially a
work about human conflict—the conflicting emotions of its central
characters, both with each other and within themselves. Given an
even half-way decent production, *Aida* easily demonstrates why its
power is virtually indestructible, and why it remains one of the
three or four most popular works of the operatic stage.

As a performance, no recording has yet to supersede the
brilliant version made in Rome in the mid-1950s, which featured
what was, and remains, an ideal cast. Beginning with Zinka Milanov, who is as poignant as she is powerful in the title role, all the
parts are covered by superb choices, from the glorious Rhadames
of Jussi Björling to the menacing, ink-black Ramfis of the young
Boris Christoff. The conducting of the vastly underrated Jonel Perlea is full of fire and poetry, and the recorded sound is much better
than you expect from that era.

For the best modern version of the score, Leontyne Price's RCA recording easily sweeps the field. Although not quite so intense and probing as in her London recording with Sir Georg Solti, the singing clearly shows why Price, after Rosa Ponselle, was the greatest Verdi singer America has so far produced.

Arias

Bergonzi, tenor. Philips 432486-2 [CD].

Caballé, soprano. RCA 09026-60941-2 [CD].

Callas, soprano. Angel CDC-47730 [CD]; CDC-47943 [CD].

Caruso, tenor. RCA 09026-61242-2 [CD].

Hvorostovsky, baritone. Philips 426740-2 [CD].

Ponselle, soprano. RCA 7810-2-RG [CD], 7810-4-RG [T].

Price, soprano. RCA RCD1-7016 [CD].

Here, in the work of seven unique singers, are many of the most celebrated Verdi arias in some of the very best recordings now available. Caruso was of course the prototype of the modern Verdi tenor, and this intelligently chosen, superbly remastered RCA collection indicates just how remote the possibility is that we'll ever hear his like again. The performances are thrilling examples of his art, confirming (and then some) all the legends. The Philips anthology by the indefatigable Carlo Bergonzi offers thirty-one arias in performances that are invariably musical, dramatically cogent, and insightful, featuring one of the most consistent and preposterously underrated singers of our time.

In an interview for *Downbeat* magazine, Nat Hentoff once asked Miles Davis to say a few words about the history of jazz. The garrulous trumpet player said, "I only need four: Louis Armstrong, Charlie Parker." By that same token, much of the history of modern Verdi singing can be summed up in four other words: Rosa Ponselle, Leontyne Price. Ponselle's recordings from the mid- to late-20s capture what is still the single most glorious voice America has ever produced. Even through the antique recorded sound, you know you're in the presence of a Niagara Falls–size natural wonder; the famous interpretations mix fire, grandeur, and melting tenderness in a very heady brew. If Ponselle's was the century's most imposing Verdi instrument, then Price's is the most beautiful. The RCA collection captures the voice in its absolute prime, with singing so effortless and ravishing, you suspect its sheer physical beauty will never be surpassed.

The singing on Caballé's "Verdi Rarities" CD is also very beautiful, with many intriguing items given the star treatment they deserve, and Callas's recordings capture the century's foremost singer-actress at the top of her form. Finally, the Philips release from Dmitri Hvorostovsky suggests that there *is* hope for the future of Verdi singing, with performances that are as interpretively commanding as they are beautifully sung.

Un ballo in maschera

> M. Price, Pavarotti, Ludwig, Battle, Bruson, National
> Philharmonic, Solti. London 410210-2 [CD].

At first glance, this didn't look at all promising. (Actually, it did, but I hate to tell you exactly *what* it seemed to promise.) At the time, Luciano Pavarotti was obviously in serious vocal trouble, Margaret Price was merely getting louder and louder, and Sir Georg Solti hadn't made an opera recording with any genuine passion in it for nearly a dozen years.

The surprising result is a milestone in recent operatic history. This *Masked Ball* takes off like a shot, and refuses to let up until the very end. The cast could not have been better (Pavarotti sounds like the Pavarotti of old), and there is no praise too high for Solti's alert, incisive conducting. In short, this is a *Ballo* for you.

Don Carlo

> Caballé, Domingo, Verrett, Milnes, Raimondi, Orchestra
> and Chorus of the Royal Opera House, Covent Garden,
> Giulini. Angel CDCC-47701 [CD].

The universal acceptance of *Don Carlo* as one of the greatest of Verdi's operas is a fairly recent phenomenon that was helped along by two historic productions: the 1950 revival with which Sir Rudolf Bing began his controversial but always lively tenure at the Metropolitan Opera, and Luchino Visconti's Covent Garden production eight years later, which introduced many to a brilliant new Italian conductor named Carlo Maria Giulini.

Taped in London thirteen years later, Giulini's Angel recording of the 1886 five-act Italian version is not only the best *Don Carlo* we are likely to hear this century, but also one of the great Verdi recordings yet made. While the cast is one of the strongest assembled during the 1970s—Placido Domingo as the feckless hero and Ruggero Raimondi as the King are especially engrossing—it is Giulini's subtle intensity that makes the recording click. Even the problematic Auto da fé scene explodes with an uncommon point and veracity; many listeners, no doubt, will be tempted to bring their own weenies and marshmallows. As with most of Angel's CD restorations, the recording sounds as though it had been made last week.

Ernani

> L. Price, Bergonzi, Sereni, Flagello, RCA Italiana Opera
> Chorus and Orchestra, Schippers. RCA 6503-2-RG [CD].

One of *Ernani*'s harshest early critics was Victor Hugo, who considered Verdi's adaptation of his play *Hernani* a complete travesty. A century and a half later, it is this "travesty" alone that keeps the memory of the once popular play alive.

For his fifth opera, Verdi produced a score bursting with vigor, rousing tunes, and good old-fashioned moustache-twirling melodrama. By the standards of the masterworks of the 1850s, much of this can seem fairly naive and obvious stuff; yet in the right hands, the opera can pack a tremendous vocal and emotional wallop, as it does in this powerful recording from 1967.

If Leontyne Price was not at her dramatic peak as Elvira, then it is still her usual vocal tour de force. With suave and powerful support from the always wonderful Carlo Bergonzi and the magnetic conducting of Thomas Schippers, this is the *Ernani* for you.

Falstaff

> Schwarzkopf, Moffo, Merriman, Barbieri, Alva, Gobbi,
> Philharmonia Orchestra and Chorus, Karajan. Angel
> CDCB-49668 [CD].

More than in his two recordings of Strauss's *Rosenkavalier*, the Jekyll-Hyde nature of the old and new Herbert von Karajan is obvious here. This Angel recording from the early 1960s is one of the most nearly perfect opera recordings of the stereo era. Each member of the cast is coaxed into an imperishable performance by a conductor who obviously cares as much for his singers as he does for the score. (In his later Philips catastrophe, it is equally apparent that all Karajan currently cared about was Karajan himself.) In its transfer to compact disc, this early performance sounds even more brilliant and endearing than ever. The opera rushes by, as it should, like quicksilver, and the lyrical moments are given more than their due.

La forza del destino

> L. Price, Cossotto, Domingo, Milnes, Bacquier, John Alldis
> Choir, London Symphony, Levine. RCA RCD3-1864
> [CD].

Of all the great middle-period Verdi operas (from *Rigoletto* of 1851 through *Aida*, 1871), *La forza del destino* is easily the most incredible. And I mean incredible in the literal sense, something that strains belief. The plot of the opera is hopelessly twisted and complicated, the irony so extreme that it would have made Charles Dickens blush. And yet, in spite of the unintentional silliness of its goofy and frequently embarrassing plot, *Forza* is one of the greatest of Verdi's operas. And despite its great length, it is one of the most compressed. In its musical concentration and dramatic power, *Forza* is the one early Verdi work that clearly points the way to *Aida*, and, ultimately, *Otello*.

After Rosa Ponselle, Leontyne Price was probably the finest Leonora of the century. The power of her middle register, the incomparable beauty of her high notes, and the enormous strength and dignity of her characterization turn this performance into the stuff of legend. While it is clearly Price's show, the rest of the cast is splendid. Placido Domingo and Sherrill Milnes are almost as fine as they are in their superb *Otello* (see page 573), and James Levine offers here some of his most assured and sympathetic conducting on records. Without question, this is one of the best opera recordings of the last three decades and, quite clearly, the one *Forza* to own.

I Lombardi

Deutekom, Domingo, Raimondi, Ambrosian Singers, Royal Philharmonic, Gardelli. Philips 422420-2 [CD].

One of the most consistently impressive series of opera recordings was Philips's cycle of Verdi's early "galley slave" operas in performances led by Lamberto Gardelli, most of which have now found their way onto CD. No hidden masterpieces are lurking here, but each offers an abundance of entertaining, if not always inspired or inspiring, music, as well as invaluable insights into the early development of the supreme tragedian of the operatic stage. *I Lombardi*, which followed the extraordinary success of *Nabucco*, has much to recommend it, including the heroine's lovely "Salve Maria" (changed from "Ave Maria" to placate the Church sensors) and a villain who can be seen as an embryonic version of Iago in *Otello*. As the hero Oronte, son of the tyrant of Antioch (well, no one said this was Chekhov), Placido Domingo sings with ringing conviction, while Gardelli shapes a powerfully theatrical performance that breathes fire and pathos from beginning to end.

Those who respond to the rough but often enthralling pleasures of early Verdi should waste no time acquiring the other installments in the Philips series before they're withdrawn: a stirring *Attila* with Ruggero Raimondi giving a formidable performance in the title role (426115 [CD]); a swift and exciting *La Battaglia di Legnano* with José Carreras and Katia Ricciarelli in spectacular form (422435-2 [CD]); Montserrat Caballé and Jessye Norman going at it tooth and claw in the Byronic *Il Corsaro* (426118-2 [CD]); Carreras and Ricciarelli having another high old time in another Byronic melodrama, *I due Foscari* (422426-2 [CD]); Norman, Carreras, and the always wonderful Fiorenza Cossoto proving that the youthful comedy *Un Giorno di regno* is not the unmitigated disaster of legend but in fact a great deal of Rossiniesque fun (422429-2 [CD]); Caballé again sensational as the heroine of *I Masnadieri*, who is stabbed to death by her lover in order to spare her from a fate worse than death—brigandage, not you-know-what, as this *is* early Verdi after all (422423-2 [CD]).

Finally, with its incomparably goofy Prologue trio—a hairbrained Verdian polka interrupted by what sounds like a lost three-part madrigal by Monteverdi in which Joan of Arc, her boyfriend, and the dauphin express their innermost feelings only to swing back into the polka with villainous zeal—the Angel recording of *Giovanna d'Arco* (CDMB-63226 [CD]) is under no circumstances to be missed.

Luisa Miller

Ricciarelli, Obraztsova, Domingo, Bruson, Orchestra and Chorus of the Royal Opera House, Covent Garden, Maazel. Deutsche Grammophon 423144-2 [CD].

Finished just before *Rigoletto* launched the composer's incomparably rich middle period—that canon of works upon which every opera company in the world depends for its very existence—*Luisa Miller* is very nearly a great opera. There are many who insist that it actually is one, including Placido Domingo, who maintains that the tenor's big moment is his favorite single aria. (He facetiously claims it is such because "Quando le sere al placido" contains his name, but it *is* an extravagantly beautiful moment, one of the finest Verdi ever wrote.)

Domingo and almost everyone else perform magnificently in this first-rate Covent Garden production. The only exception is Elena Obraztsova, who again does her best to shatter flower pots with her guttural braying. Lorin Maazel has rarely sounded more confident and relaxed in the recording studio, and the physical sound is superb.

Macbeth

Verrett, Cappuccilli, Ghiaurov, Domingo, Orchestra and Chorus of La Scala, Abbado. Deutsche Grammophon 435414-2 [CD].

In many ways *Macbeth* was Verdi's *Fidelio*, the work that cost him more time and anguish than any other in his career. A comparative failure at its Florence premiere in 1847, it was revised substantially for an 1865 production in Paris, where it proved to be an even bigger flop. In spite of its lack of success, it remained one of Verdi's favorite operas for reasons that aren't difficult to explain. For along with being the finest opera of the 1840s (the decade he called his "years as a galley slave"), *Macbeth* is also the first in which we hear the unmistakable voice of the composer Verdi would eventually become. For here, dramatic values become as important as musical ones, and the revelation of character, which Verdi sought all his life to perfect, had its first great success in the figure of Lady Macbeth, one of the most important female roles he would ever conceive.

If Shirley Verrett's voice isn't really suited to the part, then that has not prevented her from becoming the great Lady Macbeth of our time. In fact, the characterization is so menacing, eerie, and vivid (the Sleepwalking Scene would chill a Sicilian's blood) that it nearly overwhelms the fine performance of Piero Cappuccilli in the title role. Claudio Abbado's sharply dramatic conducting ranks with his best on records, and the rest of the cast is excellent, as is the recorded sound.

*N*abucco

> Suliotis, Prevedi, Gobbi, Cava, Vienna State Opera
> Orchestra and Chorus, Gardelli. London 417407-2
> [CD].

Nabucco, Verdi's first great success, is the only one of his operas—unless one counts that anvil thing in *Trovatore*—that is best known for a chorus: the celebrated lamentation "Va, pensiero," which immediately became the unofficial anthem of the Italian independence movement and, sixty years later, would be sung spontaneously by Milan's heartbroken masses at Verdi's funeral. While certainly not a great opera, *Nabucco* can be an entertaining and intermittently enthralling experience, especially in a performance such as the one London recorded in Vienna in the mid-1960s.

The principal attractions of this fine recording—which, in spite of its age, is to be preferred to Giuseppe Sinopoli's mannered and finicky outing for Deutsche Grammophon—are the Nabucco of Tito Gobbi, who here demonstrates why he was the most accomplished dramatic baritone of his generation, and the spirited, sensitive conducting of Lamberto Gardelli, one of the major Verdi specialists of the last half century.

For those who are interested only in "Va, pensiero," it can be heard to supremely tear-jerking effect (along with other favorite Verdi choruses) on a superb London release by the Chicago Symphony Chorus, drilled to their usual awe-inspiring perfection by

Margaret Hillis, and Chicago Symphony Orchestra led by Sir Georg Solti (430226-2 [CD]).

Otello

Domingo, Scotto, Milnes, National Philharmonic, Levine. RCA RCD2-2951 [CD].

The choice of a recorded *Otello* inevitably becomes a choice between the two great Otellos of modern times, Jon Vickers and Placido Domingo. On balance, I tend to favor the Domingo version, but only by a hairsbreadth. The Domingo *Otello* is a large, powerful, beautifully sung, and ultimately withering experience. While the Vickers is no less enthralling, both his recorded versions have drawbacks: a spotty cast and strangely inert support from Tullio Serafin in the RCA recording, and Herbert von Karajan's heavy hand in the more recent version for Angel.

The Domingo *Otello*, however, is not without its flaws. It features the often shrill Desdemona of Renata Scotto, and conducting from James Levine that is occasionally so enthusiastic some very important singing is lost. (In the opening "Esultate," for instance, Domingo is practically drowned out.) Nevertheless, with the splendid Iago of Sherill Milnes, this *Otello* is an outstanding performance, and we are not likely to hear a finer one any time soon.

Requiem

Schwarzkopf, Ludwig, Gedda, Ghiaurov, Philharmonia Orchestra and Chorus, Giulini. Angel CDCB-47257 [CD].

This is the recording of the Verdi Requiem—that magnificent opera disguised as a sacred work—to make even the most unregenerate sinner *believe*. (If the Day of Judgment isn't as overwhelming as Verdi and Giulini make it sound, I, for one, will be extremely disappointed.) In the quarter of a century since its release, this version of the Requiem has dominated the catalog in a way no other recording has. In its compact disc format, the performance is even more thrilling than ever, and if this one doesn't spur you on to buying a compact disc player, nothing will.

If any recording on tape came within an inch of this one's instep, I'd be the first to recommend it. To date, no such recording exists. Coupled with Giulini's incomparable version of the *Four Sacred Pieces*, this is now a bargain that no Verdi-lover—no music-lover, for that matter—can possibly resist.

Rigoletto

> Callas, di Stefano, Gobbi, Zaccaria, La Scala Orchestra and Chorus, Serafin. Angel CDCB-47469 [CD].

The ultimate test of any performance of *Rigoletto* is your reaction to the final scene. Are tears rolling down your cheeks or are you laughing so hard you're afraid of committing an indiscretion on your seat? *Both* reactions, by the way, are perfectly plausible. Consider the bare bones of the scene itself. A hunchback jester opens a gunnysack, thinking it contains the corpse of the heartless rogue who deflowered his daughter. Much to his surprise, he discovers his daughter herself, who, while bleeding to death, sings one of the most demanding duets in all of opera. (If you think *singing* on your side isn't a tough trick, just try drinking a glass of beer that way.)

Whenever I hear the final duet in this historic version of Verdi's early masterpiece, I am *never* tempted to laugh. One of the most enduring of the many great recorded collaborations of Maria Callas and Tito Gobbi, this *Rigoletto* virtually defines the phrase "grand opera". To Callas and Gobbi, add the slightly edgy but still magnificent Giuseppe di Stefano as the Duke, and the firm yet flexible conducting of Tullio Serafin, and you have something close to a *Rigoletto* for the ages. The mid-1950s recorded sound is more than adequate, and in the compact disc transfer, its bite and clarity are amazing.

Simon Boccanegra

> Cappuccilli, Freni, Carreras, Ghiaurov, van Dam, Fioani, Orchestra and Chorus of La Scala, Abbado. Deutsche Grammophon 415692-2 [CD].

Except for the overly long and generally uninspired *I vespri siciliani* (even the composer himself complained about the excessive length of his made-to-order French grand opera), *Simon Boccane-*

gra is the only one of Verdi's works after *Rigoletto* that has failed to become a staple of the standard repertoire. Part of the reason this masterpiece has been so long in catching on—and a masterpiece it most certainly is—has to do with the casting of the title role.

Whenever a production is blessed with a magnetic star-caliber baritone—Victor Maurel for the premiere of the 1881 revision, Lawrence Tibbett at the Metropolitan in 1932, Sherrill Milnes in more recent years—the opera usually proves to be an overwhelming success. Claudio Abbado's sensational 1977 recording with the bright, musical, though hardly heart-stopping Piero Cappuccilli proves that *Simon* is *not* a one-man show, and that it can stand on its own with any middle-period Verdi opera.

Most of the credit for one of the most exciting and nearly perfect of all modern Verdi recordings must go to Abbado, who has never been more impressive in the recording studio or out; the conducting is noble, poetic, subtle, and intense, with a sense of life and on-the-spot creativity rarely encountered in a commercial recording. The soloists, chorus, and orchestra all catch fire under Abbado's incandescent direction, and DG's engineers come through with their very best recorded sound.

If for you *Simon Boccanegra* is still a question mark, then this is the recording that will turn it into an exclamation point.

La Traviata

> **Sutherland, Pavarotti, Manuguerra, London Opera Chorus,**
> **National Philharmonic, Bonynge. London 430491-2**
> **[CD].**

This fair but generally uninspired run-through of Verdi's popular opera is now the preferred recording of *La Traviata*, although only by default. Everyone, especially Joan Sutherland, sings well enough, yet the performance simply will not grab you by the throat. Sadly, none of the other versions of this usually foolproof opera comes any closer. Until something better comes along, this perfectly serviceable release will have to do.

Il Trovatore

> **Milanov, Björling, Barbieri, Warren, RCA Victor Orchestra**
> **and Chorus, Cellini. RCA 6643-2-RG [CD], CLK2-5377**
> **[T].**

This (to use a phrase without which every sportscaster in America would be unable to do his job) really *is* what it's all about. Add a Leonora made of 50 percent volcano and 50 percent pathos, a gleaming, heroic Manrico (his high C in "Di quella pira" will shake you down to your socks), and a sinister, brooding, old-fashioned Azucena "whose very urine" (to use Philip Wylie's immortal phrase), "would probably etch glass," and you have one of the most electric operatic recordings ever made. The combination of Zinka Milanov, Jussi Björling, Fedora Barbieri, and Leonard Warren, the same team responsible for that greatest of all recorded *Aidas*, is all but unstoppable here. Even the occasionally phlegmatic Renato Cellini catches fire, and turns in what is undoubtedly the performance of his career.

For those who are bothered by the monophonic, mid-1950s recorded sound (and if you're listening to sound instead of music, then you might want to make sure you have the right hobby), another fine RCA release (6194-2-RC) with Price, Cossotto, Domingo, Milnes, and Mehta at the top of *their* forms is the best recent alternative.

I Vespri siciliani

**Studer, Merritt, Zancanaro, Furlanetto, La Scala Opera
Orchestra and Chorus, Muti. Angel CDCC-54043 [CD].**

Tailor-made to the spectacle-loving tastes of the Parisian public, *I Vespri siciliani* (The Sicilian Vespers) scarcely seems the work of the composer of *Rigoletto*, *Il Trovatore*, and *La Traviata*, the operas that immediately preceded it. Part of the problem was that Verdi disliked the libretto—he considered the treacherous behavior of the Sicilian patriots as insulting to all Italians—and he was unable to work comfortably within the unwieldy five-act form of French grand opera. Yet if not one of Verdi's strongest pieces, *I Vespri siciliani* nonetheless contains marvelous music, including one of his finest overtures, one of his finest bass arias ("O tu Palermo" from Act II), one of his most irresistible soprano cabalettas (Elena's Act V bolero, "Mercè, dilette amiche"), and nearly a half hour of top-notch dance music (the Ballet of the Seasons from Act III).

In this live recording from Milan's La Scala, Riccardo Muti leads a performance full of dash and sweep, with Cheryl Studer a fetching and vocally dazzling heroine. The rest of the cast is good to excellent, with recorded sound that captures the excitement of a live performance with few of its pitfalls. On balance, the most persuasive argument yet made for an unjustly (for the most part) neglected score.

Victoria, Tomás Luis de

(c. 1548–1611)

*M*issa *"Ave maris stella"*; *"O quam gloriosum est regnum"* (motet); *Missa "O quam gloriosum"*

> **Westminster Cathedral Choir, Hill. Hyperion CDA-64114 [CD].**

King Philip II was correct in his famous assertion that "the destiny of Spain cannot await upon the fitness of time." Alas, it *did* have to await upon the whims of that arrogant, boneheaded monarch who in a single, ill-advised stroke managed to throw away one of the greatest empires since the fall of Rome. When the Armada went down in the unforgiving waters of the English Channel in 1588, it not only marked the end of the Spanish domination of both the Old and New Worlds, but also the beginning of the end of the golden age of Spanish art, as epitomized by the paintings of El Greco, the fiction of Cervantes, the drama and poetry of Lope de Vega, and the music of composers like Tomás Luis de Victoria.

Nearly four centuries after his death, Victoria's music retains the ardor and spiritual daring that made it one of the purest Renaissance manifestations of Spanish mysticism, an intense, ecstatic, transcendent beauty that is projected to absolute perfection in this lovely Hyperion recording. The committed, emotionally high-powered interpretations that David Hill draws from the Westminster Choir are far removed from the typical dry-as-dust approach to early sacred music, and the warm, enfolding acoustic of Hyperion's recording proves an ideal setting for the spirit of a very great composer and his glittering age.

Vieuxtemps, Henri

(1820–1881)

Concerto No. 5 in A minor for Violin and Orchestra

Mintz, violin; Israel Philharmonic, Mehta. Deutsche Grammophon 427676-2 [CD].

It's frankly shocking that the six Vieuxtemps violin concertos, given their inherent quality and sheer bravura excitement, have fallen on such hard times. Technically, the best of them—the First, Third, Fourth, and Fifth—are every bit the equal of those virtuoso show-stoppers by Paganini and Wieniawski; musically, they frequently have more to say and often say it with greater skill.

The dazzling recording by Shlomo Mintz offers an encouraging sign that virtuosos of the younger generation may be discovering the abundant pleasures of these works. His playing has a thrilling sense of reckless abandon coupled with extraordinary sensitivity, and note for note is even more impressive than Heifetz's on a celebrated recording for RCA. Speaking of whom, the violinist's electrifying 1935 recording of the Fourth Concerto with the London Symphony led by the young John Barbirolli is now available in an attractive anthology of showpieces on Angel CDH 64251-2 [CD].

Villa-Lobos, Heitor

(1887–1959)

Bachianas brasileiras Nos. 1, 5, and 7

Hendricks, soprano; Royal Philharmonic, Bátiz. Angel
CDC-47433.

Almost everyone who discovers the music of South America's foremost composer, the Brazilian Heitor Villa-Lobos, does so through the wordless aria from the hauntingly beautiful *Bachiana brasileira No. 5*. An imaginative transplanting of the spirit of Bach in the soil of Brazil, the *Bachianas* are major contributions to the music of the twentieth century, as is the work of Villa-Lobos in general.

Not since the Brazilian soprano Bidú Sayão made her famous recording with the composer in the 1940s has there been a more heart-stopping version of the work than this gleaming Angel recording by Barbara Hendricks, who certainly has the talent, the drive, and the looks to become one of the dominant singers of the waning years of the twentieth century. This stunning recording is one of her best to date. The singing has a lush yet other-worldly quality that suggests an oversexed seraph, and the accompaniment she receives from Enrique Bátiz is a model of sympathetic support. For something slightly off the beaten track, i.e., as a gift for the collector who seems to have *almost* everything, you can't go wrong with this lovely recording, even if you simply give it as a gift to yourself.

Concerto for Guitar and Orchestra

Williams, guitar; English Chamber Orchestra, Barenboim.
CBS M2K-44791 [CD].

If Villa-Lobos's Guitar Concerto is not one of his most distinguished or characteristic works, it is still one of the instrument's most attractive modern ones and sounds very close to a masterpiece in the ardent, imaginative performance by John Williams. Although

CBS might easily have reissued his masterful performance of the composer's Five Preludes, the Concerto comes as part of a two-CD set that also includes near-definitive readings of Rodrigo's *Concierto de Aranjuez* and *Fantasia para un gentilhombre*, along with the concertos of Castelnuovo-Tedesco, Ponce, Giuliani, and Vivaldi, leaving little doubt that John Williams is the great guitarist of modern times.

Vine, Carl (1954–)

Piano Sonata (1990)

Harvey, piano. Tall Poppies TP013 [CD].

Microsymphony; Symphony No. 2; Symphony No. 3

Sydney Symphony, Challender. ABC Classics 426-995-2 [CD].

There was a time when virtually all anyone knew about Australian music were those immortal chestnuts of Percy Grainger and perhaps John Antill's vivid 1946 ballet *Corroboree*. Times are certainly changing, if the music of Carl Vine is any indication. A formidably equipped musician with a passion for jazz and avant garde experimentation, Vine is clearly one of the most talented young composers working anywhere. His orchestral scores such as the compressed and brilliantly inventive *Microsymphony* define and inhabit a unique musical world; his Piano Sonata of 1990 is one of the most significant works in the form since the great Piano Sonata of Elliott Carter.

Though the performances of the symphonies sound absolutely definitive—what an incredibly fine ensemble the Sydney Symphony has become!—the version of the Sonata is something quite special. The Australian pianist Michael Kieran Harvey, co-winner of the first Ivo Pogorelich International Solo Piano Competition, plays with the same imagination and reckless abandon he displayed in the competition's final round, which featured the Vine Sonata as his closing work. It is a phenomenally creative and compelling performance by the most exciting pianist I've heard in twenty years.

Vivaldi, Antonio (1678–1741)

I'm the first to admit that I have a blind spot when it comes to this composer. Everyone loves Vivaldi, don't they? At very least, he is the perfect yuppie composer, a man whose tuneful, relentlessly good-natured, cleverly made music turns up more frequently at brunch than that of anyone else. And the music *is* inventive, distinctive, and exceedingly well made. Yet apart from the surface details (what instrument is playing, what key the work is in, and so forth), most of his music seems exactly the same to me. Stravinsky certainly had a point when he said that Vivaldi wrote the same concerto several hundred times. This explains why there are only two entries devoted to this composer. Vivaldi lovers, forgive me. Besides, isn't your BMW double-parked?

The Four Seasons

Loveday, violin; Academy of St. Martin-in-the-Fields, Marriner. Argo 414486-2 [CD].

Standage, violin; English Concert, Pinnock. Deutsche Grammophon 400045-2 [CD].

With the possible exception of Pachelbel's *Kanon*, nothing makes me want to start throwing things more than a half dozen bars of *The Seasons*. I hate it with the same irrational intensity I reserve for peanut butter, for reasons that remain as difficult to explain. Like all his other concertos, these four are exceedingly inoffensive and exceptionally graceful. In me, alas, they stimulate nothing but violence, and if allowed to go on too long, reverse peristalsis.

The recording I have found least offensive over the years is the Argo version by Alan Loveday and Sir Neville Marriner. The playing is as exciting as it is tidy, and communicates a deep and abiding sense of enjoyment. Among period-instrument recordings, the interpretation by Simon Standage and Trevor Pinnock's superb English Concert is undoubtedly the best.

Gloria in D

Nelson, Kirkby, Watkinson, Elliott, Thomas, Christ Church Cathedral Choir, Academy of Ancient Music, Preston. Oiseau-Lyre 414678-2 [CD].

This is the sort of recording that almost makes one believe in miracles, for, miraculously, I managed to remain conscious to the very end.

Wagner, Richard (1813–1883)

The Flying Dutchman

Bailey, Martin, Kollo, Talvela, Chicago Symphony Orchestra and Chorus, Solti. London 414551-2 [CD].

It was with this, the first of his operas destined to occupy a place in the standard repertoire, that the musical world encountered the man who, after Beethoven, would become the most influential composer history has so far known. Although much of Der fliegende Holländer places it in the company of traditional nineteenth-century opera (the discreet arias, choruses and other set pieces), there is much to indicate that as early as 1843, Wagner the arch-revolutionary was beginning to evolve. For one thing, The Flying Dutchman, in its original version, was cast in a single, continuous act. (Two and a half hours without a break was an outrageous demand to make on mid-nineteenth century derrières.) Also we can hear the composer flirting with odd harmonies and dissonances, and an embryonic version of the leitmotif technique which would eventually lead to those vast music dramas that changed not only opera but the course of Western music.

Until Angel gives us a compact disc version of the famous, withering performance conducted by Otto Klemperer, Sir Georg Solti's dazzling London recording is clearly the one to have. With a very strong cast led by Norman Bailey, the finest Dutchman of the last twenty years, Solti leads a performance as incisive as it is atmospheric, as brilliantly played as it is wonderfully sung. Unfortunately, the performance is now available only on compact disc, and there is no tape version that warrants a serious recommendation.

Lohengrin

Domingo, Norman, Randová, Nimsgern, Fischer-Dieskau, Vienna State Opera Chorus, Vienna Philharmonic, Solti. London 421053-2 [CD].

Never expect to hear a *Lohengrin* like this at your neighborhood opera house. For one thing, your local opera company couldn't afford to mount one with singers of this caliber. For another, it's not every day that you hear the likes of the great Vienna Philharmonic in the pit. The reasons why this is the finest recording of Wagner's early opera have as much to do with the conducting as with the choice of the tenor for the title role. Given the wonderful idea of casting Placido Domingo as Walther in *Die Meistersinger* a number of years ago, it's a bit surprising that no one ever thought of doing it again until now. No, Domingo is obviously *not* a Wagnerian in the grand tradition: his command of the language is questionable, and his sense of the character is at times rather sketchy. Yet what a pleasure it is to hear a world-class voice *singing* the part, instead of the usual grunting, howling, and groaning that passes for Wagnerian singing today.

For the remainder of the cast, London put together a formidable ensemble, and Sir Georg Solti's conducting is precisely what it needs to be—neither overly measured nor uncomfortably rushed. The Vienna Philharmonic has not sounded this impressive since their epoch-making recording (also with Solti) of Wagner's complete *Ring*, and the recorded sound will send shivers down your spine.

Die Meistersinger von Nürnberg

Bode, Hamari, Kollo, Bailey, Weikl, Moll, Vienna State Opera Chorus, Vienna Philharmonic, Solti. London 417497-2 [CD].

Ligendza, Ludwig, Domingo, Fischer-Dieskau, Orchestra and Chorus of the German Opera, Berlin, Jochum. Deutsche Grammophon 415278-2 [CD].

Frantz, Grümmer, Schock, Frick, Kusche, Unger, Höffgen, Prey, Choruses, Berlin Philharmonic, Kempe. EMI CDMD-64154 [CD].

While *Tristan und Isolde* is probably his masterpiece, and the *Ring*, taken as a whole, his most significant achievement, *Die Meistersinger* finally showed the world the human side of Richard Wagner. Given the nature of the beast that Wagner was, his human side proved to be shockingly warm, generous, and complete. In the only operatic comedy worthy of comparison with Verdi's *Falstaff* and Mozart's *Figaro*, Wagner succeeds in showing us not only what is finest and best in the German people, but also by inference, what is finest and best in ourselves. For this one Wagner opera cast on a completely human scale is about friendship and trust, young love and mature wisdom, tradition and rebellion—in short, the human condition itself.

Among available modern recordings of the opera, the difficult choice is between the versions conducted by Sir Georg Solti and Eugen Jochum. Each has its particular strengths and weaknesses. The Jochum recording suffers from the disappointing Hans Sachs of Dietrich Fisher-Dieskau, which is as badly overacted as it is oversung. On the other hand, Placido Domingo, as Walther, is a vocal revelation. As in the recent recording of *Lohengrin*, it's a pleasure to hear a voice of this stature in the part. The Solti recording, which features the marvelous Hans Sachs of Norman Bailey, has to contend with a very wobbly Walther (René Kollo). The conducting from Solti is only marginally less graceful and stately than what we hear from Jochum.

For my money, neither can begin to match that virtually flawless 1956 Angel recording conducted by Rudolf Kempe (who stepped in at the last moment for Sir Thomas Beecham). Except for the lack of modern recorded sound—which *is* a factor in the riotous Act II finale and the big crowd scenes in Act III—this is a *Meistersinger* for the ages: the best conducted, the best played, and for the most part, the best sung. Although EMI could have easily had the services of the great Hans Hotter as Sachs (a fact for which he has understandably never forgiven them), Ferdinand Frantz gives the performance of his career, as do Gerhard Unger as David and Benno Kusche as a wonderfully snide and snarling Sixtus Beckmesser. Rudolf Schock, best known for his work in operetta, is dashing and ardent as Walther, Gottlob Frick is the finest Pogner ever recorded, and the ladies are absolutely enchanting, with the radiantly girlish Eva of Elisabeth Grümmer surpassing even Elisabeth Schwarzkopf's. As in his EMI *Lohengrin*, Kempe's conducting is warm, dramatic, and utterly natural, with everything vividly alive yet completely unforced, and the Berlin Philharmonic and the superbly trained choruses are models of flexibility and responsiveness.

For the absolute last work in Hans Sachs, though, all of the electrical recordings of the incomparable Friedrich Schorr have been transferred onto a single Pearl CD (PEA-9944). Recorded between 1927 and 1931, these priceless acetates preserve one of the great characterizations in opera history, an interpretation to be mentioned with Chaliapin's Boris Godunov or Lotte Lehmann's Marschallin.

Overtures, Preludes, and Excerpts

For those who accept the old saw that Wagner wrote some of the most inspired minutes and some of the most tedious hours in the history of music—or for people who simply prefer to do without all that singing—the recorded selection of overtures, preludes, and the rest of what George Bernard Shaw called "the bleeding chunks of meat" has always been varied and impressive, all the more so since the introduction of the compact disc.

Fritz Reiner's Chicago Symphony recording for RCA (09026-61792-2 [CD]) of thrillingly played excerpts from *Meistersinger* and *Götterdämmerung* is an absolute necessity, as is George Szell's lean and athletic CBS recording of the best-known orchestral excerpts—including an especially rousing "Ride of the Valkyries" —from *The Ring* (MYK-36715 [CD], MYT-36715 [T]). Solti (London 410137-2 [CD]) and Stokowski (London 411772-4 [T]) also lead highly successful anthologies of *Ring* excerpts that are as individual as they are exciting.

Bruno Walter is handsomely represented on CBS (MPK-45701 [CD]) by that extraordinary version of the overture and Venusburg Music from *Tannhäuser*, together with typically warm and avuncular interpretations of the *Lohengrin*, *Flying Dutchman*, and *Meistersinger* preludes. His *Siegfried Idyll* is also one of the finest ever recorded, combining a disarming tenderness with genuine Romantic ardor. Leonard Bernstein's dramatic, highly charged Wagner recordings have been collected on a pair of Sony CDs (SMK-47643/44), the latter including Eileen Farrell's majestic interpretations of the Immolation Scene from *Götterdämmerung* and the *Wesendonck Lieder*.

Among the newer collections, Mariss Jansons's EMI anthology (CDC-54583-2) offers typically exciting playing from the Oslo Philharmonic and rafter-rattling sound. James Levine's Deutsche Grammophon recording (435874-2) with the resurgent Met Orchestra confirms their status—with the Vienna Philharmonic—as the greatest pit band in the world, while the Philharmonia Orchestra performs with both grandeur and abandon under Yuri Simonov on a pair of stunning Collins Classics CDs (COL-1294, 1207-2). The recorded sound of Lorin Maazel's seventy-minute *Ring* synthesis with the Berlin Philharmonic for Telarc is awe-inspiring in its weight and clarity (CD-80154 [CD], CS-30154 [T]), as is Gerard Schwarz's Seattle Symphony release on Delos (DCD-3053 [CD]), which includes an especially gripping account of the Prelude and "Good Friday Spell" from *Parsifal*.

For something well off the beaten track, Glenn Gould's highly personal piano transcriptions of "Dawn and Siegfried's Rhine Journey" from *Götterdämmerung*, the *Meistersinger* Prelude, and *Siegfried Idyll* have been reissued on Sony (SK-46279 [CD], ST-46279 [T]). The released also includes Gould's conducting debut (and final commercial recording), in which he leads a performance of *Siegfried Idyll* slow enough to stop the clock and moving enough to break the heart.

Finally, if the absence of demonstration-quality recorded sound is not the end of the world for you, four of the most individual of all Wagnerians are still on hand to instruct, amaze, and delight. Hans Knappersbusch's famous Munich recordings

—including the slowest performance of the *Rienzi* Overture ever attempted—are out on a pair of MCA compact discs (MCAD2-9811); two representative collections by perhaps the greatest Wagner conductor of all, Wilhelm Furtwängler, are available from EMI (CDHB-64935 [CD]) and Enterprise (ENTLV-911 [CD]); and the work of the deeply misanthropic, profoundly spiritual Karl Muck may be sampled on an Opal CD (CDS-9843) or an InSync tape (C-4137). In what must be counted among the most exciting Wagner releases in years, Pearl has reissued those legendary Wagner recordings Leopold Stokowski made with the Philadelphia Orchestra in the 1930s and '40s. A marvel in its day, the recorded sound still retains an incredible clarity and presence; the interpretations are inspired and theatrical, with playing that has rarely been approached for its vividness and fearless abandon. Volume I includes extended excerpts from *Tannhäuser* and *Parsifal* (including Stokowski's Act III "Symphonic Synthesis") (PEA-9448 [CD]); Volume II features the *Lohengrin* and *Meistersinger* Preludes and some *very* steamy *Tristan* excerpts (the best is an Act II *Liebesnacht* "Symphonic Synthesis") (PEA-9486 [CD]); and amid the many glories of the two-CD Volume III is perhaps the pick of the entire litter: the version of "Wotan's Farewell" and the "Magic Fire Music" from the final act of *Die Walküre*, with some unspeakably noble and heart-wrenching singing from the great Lawrence Tibbett.

Parsifal

> Dalis, Thomas, London, Hotter, Neidlinger, Bayreuth Festival Orchestra and Chorus, Knappertsbusch. Philips 416390-2 [CD].

There used to be an ancient Metropolitan Opera curse that one still hears from old-timers. "May you be trapped in a performance of *Parsifal* without a sandwich." And truly, nothing can be more thoroughly numbing than an indifferently prepared production of the opera, which does tend to go on and on, just as nothing can be more genuinely stirring when all the parties involved are giving the opera all it demands, which is to say, *everything*.

Recorded live at the 1962 Bayreuth Festival, this performance proves more conclusively than any other that *Parsifal* was in fact a fitting conclusion to Wagner's career, containing as it does many of the most inspired pages the composer ever wrote. With a cast that includes George London, Jess Thomas, and the great Hans Hotter among others, the recording features some of the finest Wagner singing heard on records. *Parsifal* was always a great house specialty of Hans Knappertsbusch, and he leads a performance of unparalleled dignity, depth, and majesty. Although the recording is of an actual performance, the foot-shuffling, coughing, and vocal drop-outs are kept to a bare minimum, and besides, the thrill of hearing those incomparable Bayreuth acoustics more than compensates for the occasional glitch.

Rienzi

> Kollo, Wennberg, Martin, Schreier, Adam, Dresden State Orchestra and Chorus, Hollreiser. Angel CDMB-63980 [CD].

Rienzi, The Last of the Tribunes was Wagner's *Nabucco*. Introduced in October of 1842, only seven months after Verdi's third opera made him an overnight success, Wagner's third effort also proved to be a charm: it soon became the most popular work in the Dresden Opera's repertoire and made the twenty-nine-year-old composer's name known throughout Germany for the first time.

Although long and frequently derivative—the shadow of Giacomo Meyerbeer hangs heavily over the proceedings—*Reinzi* has many wonderful moments, and the ardent Wagnerian will certainly want to give this recording a try. Unfortunately, the performance is one to admire rather than cherish. Heinrich Hollreiser's able conducting and René Kollo's sturdy interpretation of the title role are the best things in the set; the less said about the women, the better. Still, the passion and youthful enthusiasm of the music carry most of the day.

More charming and in many ways more original is Wagner's very first opera, *Die Feen* (The Fairies), written when he was only twenty. Mendelssohn and Beethoven seem to cast a benign shadow over the proceedings, yet the young Wagner's inventiveness is often startlingly fresh and audacious, with many tantalizing suggestions of what was to come. The Orfeo recording (CO-62833 [CD]) is as delightfully engaging as the work itself, with Wolfgang Sawallisch leading an unusually clear-headed yet riveting performance, and

John Alexander and the young Cheryl Studer particularly impressive among the fine cast.

Der Ring des Nibelungen (Das Rheingold, Die Walküre, Siegfried, Götterdämmerung)

> Nilsson, Flagstad, Crespin, Watson, Ludwig, Madeira, Windgassen, Svanholm, King, Stolze, London, Fischer-Dieskau, Hotter, Frick, Neidlinger, Vienna Philharmonic, Solti. London 414100-2 [CD].

It is only fitting that one of the most titanic outbursts of the human imagination inspired one of the genuine cornerstones of recording history: the now legendary English Decca/London version of Wagner's *Ring*. In spite of its obvious flaws, and there are several, this will undoubtedly be our once and future *Ring*—an enterprise so massively ambitious, audacious, and successful that it boggles the mind.

True, this is not the ideal performance of Wagner's sprawling fifteen-hour tetralogy. Then again, much evidence suggests Wagner himself at last concluded that an ideal *Ring* existed only in his mind. The major flaws in the recording include a Siegfried who is barely adequate (although Wolfgang Windgassen was the best the world had to offer at the time) and the rather wobbly Wotan of the once great Hans Hotter.

In spite of these important drawbacks, the great moments far outnumber the uncomfortable ones. Here is Kirsten Flagstad, singing the *Rheingold* Fricka, a role she learned especially for this recording. Here, too, are those extravagant bits of casting, including Christa Ludwig as Waltraute, and Joan Sutherland as the Forest Bird. Through it all, one still feels the spirit of John Culshaw (the most imaginative recording producer of his generation), who here, with Sir Georg Solti in the pit and the finest cast that could then be assembled, puts together not only his greatest achievement but also that of many who were involved.

Tannhäuser

> Dernesch, Ludwig, Kollo, Braun, Sotin, Vienna State Opera Chorus, Vienna Philharmonic, Solti. London 414581-2 [CD].

Sir Georg Solti has now recorded every Wagner opera from *The Flying Dutchman* to *Parsifal*, and none of those recordings is finer than this stupendous version of the Paris edition of *Tannhäuser*. In Helga Dernesch and Christa Ludwig he has a pair of ladies for whom any conductor would give what remains of his hair. And René Kollo, who has had serious vocal problems over the years, here sounds freer and fresher than he ever has on recordings. But it is Solti's conducting, as languorous and limpid as it is ferocious and exultant, that makes this one of the great Wagner recordings of the last twenty years.

As is now so frequently the case, there is no recording of the opera available on cassette.

Tristan und Isolde

> Flagstad, Thebom, Suthaus, Fischer-Dieskau, Greindl, Royal Opera Chorus, Philharmonia Orchestra, Furtwängler. Angel CDC-47321 [CD].
>
> Behrens, Minton, Hofmann, Weikl, Sotin, Bavarian Radio Orchestra and Chorus, Bernstein. Philips 410447-2 [CD].

The famous 1952 recording of *Tristan und Isolde*, most collectors concede, is the greatest single Wagner recording yet made. In spite of a frequently negligible Tristan and an Isolde who was crowding sixty at the time, no other version of this passionate masterwork has captured as much black magic or animal intensity as this one. In her finest studio recording, the legendary Kirsten Flagstad beguiles and terrifies with equal ease, and this Isolde is more convincingly and beautifully sung than any we are ever likely to hear.

Wilhelm Furtwängler's conducting is similarly inspired, and more than confirms his reputation as the greatest Wagner conductor of his time. The dynamic contrasts range from the merest whisper to the most shattering climaxes. Phrases are stretched out to unimaginable lengths, and in general, the performance creates a feeling no Wagner opera ever does—that it is far too short.

The most amazing thing about Leonard Bernstein's amazing Philips recording is how favorably it compares to what has been for years an incomparable recording. Although his Isolde is no match for Flagstad, the Tristan of Peter Hofmann is virile, exciting, and exceptionally musical, and the rest of the cast is extremely strong. Nevertheless, the conducting is so obviously the center of attention that the voices seem to disappear. Rarely has anyone taken so many chances with what is already a very chancy work (some of the tempos are so slow that Furtwängler's seem brisk in comparison), and rarely have such chances paid off as handsomely as here. In another thirty years, posterity will probably view this *Tristan* with the same hushed reverence we now reserve for the Flagstad-Furtwängler recording. Wise collectors will acquire them both.

Die Walküre, Act I

Lehmann, Melchior, List, Vienna Philharmonic, Walter. Angel CHD-61020 [CD].

So much has been said and written about this legendary recording—including the frequently repeated suggestion that it was, is, and will always be (with the possible exception of the Furtwängler *Tristan*) the greatest Wagner recording of all time—that all that really needs to be said is the CD transfer is even better than anyone could have hoped. The voices, especially Lotte Lehmann's, have never sounded more realistic, and the orchestral detail (which was always rather phenomenal for 1935) is clearer and cleaner than ever.

That other desert-island Wagner recording, the 1929 version of the *Tristan* love duet with an even younger Lauritz Melchior, that most warm and feminine of the great Isoldes, Frida Leider, and the astonishing Albert Coates, whose conducting manages to maintain the tension and animal excitement of the scene in spite of the fact that it was recorded in two separate cities (Berlin and London), several months apart, can now be found with other historic versions of excerpts from the opera on a pair of Legato Classics compact discs (LCD-146-2).

Wesendonk Lieder

Flagstad, soprano; Moore, piano. Angel CDH-63030 [CD].

Norman, soprano; London Symphony, Davis. Philips 412655-2 [CD].

Cut from the same cloth as *Tristan und Isolde*, these ravishing songs were settings of the rather feeble poetry of Mathilde Wesendonk, the pretentious wife of one of Wagner's most generous patrons and the composer's real-life model for Isolde. Characteristically, once *Tristan* was finished, Wagner completely lost interest in the woman who inspired it, leaving her to return to her understanding husband.

Although the great Kirsten Flagstad was in her mid-fifties when she recorded the songs with Gerald Moore, the voice was still in magnificent shape. Supple, commanding, and phenomenally voluminous, it allowed Flagstad to explore the full range of expression inherent in these wondrous lieder as no singer has before or since. Moore, as always, is a model of ardor and discretion, and the recorded sound has held up amazingly well.

For those who need modern recorded sound (to say nothing of Wagner's glorious orchestral colors), Jessye Norman's 1976 recording with Sir Colin Davis is splendidly sung, if less than ideal in its projection of meanings and moods.

Walton, Sir William

(1902–1983)

*B*elshazzar's Feast

**Luxon, baritone; Collegium Musicum of London, Previn.
RPO Records RPO-7013 [CD].**

The only disappointing thing about André Previn's newest and finest recording of the most lurid, prurient, suggestive, and rousing of all twentieth-century sacred works is the CD cover photo. While perfectly acceptable, it is certainly no match for the dazzling image that adorned his early Angel recording, which, alas, is no longer in print. In every other respect, however, this exhilarating version of Walton's colorful oratorio is easily the most impressive yet made. The chorus and the huge orchestral forces are managed with the ease of a Haydn symphony, and over the years the interpretation has become both more thoughtful and more rambunctious. The unbridled joy that Previn coaxes out of the final cry of "Alleluia" is as exciting as anything you've heard in years. The filler is the most rousing recording yet made of the suite from Walton's score for Sir Laurence Olivier's screen version of Shakespeare's *Henry V*.

And if there remains any doubt that Previn is now the world's foremost exponent of Walton's music, another recording will more than convince you: an Angel compact disc of the Viola and Violin Concertos with the brilliant Nigel Kennedy (CDC-49628), which contains the most admirable and adult interpretation either work has yet received.

Concerto for Cello and Orchestra; Symphony No. 1

Harrell, cello; City of Birmingham Symphony, Rattle. EMI-CDC 54572 [CD].

This is probably the single most exciting Walton recording ever issued. And it's not that Sir Simon Rattle and company don't face formidable competiton in both of these towering modern masterworks: Gregor Piatigorsky's splendid creator recording of the Cello Concerto is available from RCA (09026-61498-2 [CD], 09026-61498-4 [T]), and the composer himself pronounced André Previn's first version of the Symphony (RCA 7830-2-RG [CD]) the finest he'd ever heard, inside the recording studio or out.

Lynn Harrell plays the Concerto with an unprecedented understanding and panache; his incomparable tone works wonders in the wistful coda, which is here transformed into something unspeakably poignant, and Rattle offers the most alert and sensitive accompaniment ever recorded. The conductor's version of the Symphony is frankly astounding, bringing a withering intensity to the first movement, a snarling bitterness to the Scherzo, a bleak devastation to the slow movement, and a giddy exultation in the finale, which makes this the greatest and most universal recording the piece has ever received. If Rattle would only move on to the Second Symphony, and better still, a complete version of the composer's 1954 opera *Troilus and Cressida*, then life might be worth living again.

Façade

Walton, Baker, speakers; City of London Sinfonia, Hickox.
Chandos-8869 [CD], ABTD-1484 [T].

Listening to the voice of Dame Edith Sitwell, one was
strangely reminded of W. H. Auden's description of his own face
late in life as "a wedding cake left out in the rain." Among the
major modern poets, only Dylan Thomas had a comparably individual instrument. But it was not merely Dame Edith's indescribable voice—to say nothing of her overwhelming authority (she
wrote the poems the piece is based on)—that made her second
version of *Façade* so far and away the greatest recording this daffy
entertainment has ever received. In the faster poems, the superhuman diction of Sir Peter Pears had to be heard to be believed,
and Anthony Collins's conducting was a model of crack-brained
panache.

Since London has criminally withdrawn that classic recording
from circulation (along with most of the other wonderful items in
their medium-priced British Collection series), that leaves the recent
Chandos release featuring the composer's widow to hold the fort
until it reappears. Born in Argentina, Lady Susana Walton's charming accent (and her obvious sympathy with her husband's music)
add immeasurably to her infectiously enthusiastic reading, and
Richard Baker is equally impressive in the virtuoso stuff, offering
Peter Pears his only serious competition. In addition to the witty
contributions of Richard Hickox and company, the recording
comes complete with *Façade 2*: all the poems (some of them very
fine indeed), which for one reason or another failed to make the
final cut.

Film Music

Plummer, speaker; Academy of St. Martin-in-the-Fields
Orchestra and Chorus, Marriner. Chandos CHAN-8892
[CD], ABTD-1503 [T]. (*Henry V—A Shakespeare
Scenario*).

Gielgud, speaker; Academy of St. Martin-in-the-Fields,
Marriner. Chandos CHAN-8841 [CD], ABTD-1460 [T].
(*Macbeth: Banquet and March*; *Major Barbara: A*

Shavian Sequence for Orchestra; *Richard III—A Shakespeare Scenario*).

Bott, soprano; Gielgud, speaker; Academy of St. Martin-in-the-Fields, Marriner. Chandos CHAN-8842 [CD], ABTD-1461 [T]. (*As You Like It*; *Hamlet*).

Academy of St. Martin-in-the-Fields, Marriner. Chandos CHAN-8870 [CD], ABTD-1485 [T]. (*Battle of Britain*; *Escape Me Never*; *The First of the Few: Spitfire Prelude and Fugue*; *Three Sisters*; *Wartime Sketchbook*).

Here, in four indispensable recordings, are most of Sir William Walton's brilliant achievement as a film composer, much of it never recorded before. The *Shakespeare Scenarios*, arranged by the gifted Christopher Palmer, collect the bulk of the composer's two finest scores—those for Sir Laurence Olivier's *Henry V* and *Richard III*—into compelling, virtually self-contained dramas with Christopher Plummer and Sir John Gielgud delivering cleverly chosen excerpts from the plays. (In the case of Gielgud, this is limited to Richard's "Now is the winter of our discontent" monologue, recorded with Walton's witty underscoring, which went largely unheard in the finished film.) If anything, the *Hamlet* and *As You Like It* recordings are even more valuable, since the music is so little known. Gielgud is in even finer form in the "O that this too, too solid flesh" and "To be or not to be" soliloquies, and Walton's invention is never less than memorable, both here and in the 1936 *As You Like It*. Volume 4 is devoted primarily to the wartime music, including the *Wartime Sketchbook* which collects the best moments from three films of the period and the famous *Spitfire Prelude and Fugue* from *The First of the Few*, the screen biography of the heroic R. J. Mitchell whose incomparable fighter plane turned the tide in the Battle of Britain (the stirring March is a close cousin to the noble Henry Tudor theme from *Richard III*).

Sir Neville Marriner and the Academy are in splendid form throughout the series, with vivid interpretations that go to the very heart of this inherently dramatic music and playing that is far more polished and exciting than any which appeared in the original films. With sumptuous, superbly detailed recorded sound and illuminating notes, these are the most valuable issues yet in Chandos's wonderful Walton series and should be snapped up at once by anyone with even a passing interest in this composer or in great film music.

Variations on a Theme by Hindemith

> Cleveland Orchestra, Szell. Sony SBK-53258 [CD], SBT-53258 [CD].

This is infuriating. After issuing what was perhaps the single most valuable Walton recording then available, George Szell's incomparable Cleveland Orchestra recordings of the Second Symphony, Partita for Orchestra and *Hindemith Variations*, Sony withdraws and repackages the latter with Szell's admittedly unparalled version of Hindemith's *Symphonic Metamorphosis on Themes of Carl Maria von Weber* and a mediocre *Mathis der Maler* Symphony with Eugene Ormandy and the Philadelphia Orchestra. Not that the *Hindemith Variations* isn't magnificent: it simply belongs with the other, equally magnificent Waltons, not in this cutesy mix. Apparently the new motto at Sony is "If It Ain't Broke, Break It"—or perhaps simply the tried and true recording company variation on *Caveat emptor*: *Emptor fornicatum est.*

Warlock, Peter (1894–1930)

Capriol Suite

> Ulster Orchestra, Handley. Chandos CHAN-8808 [CD], ABRD-1436 [T].

On the night of December 17, 1930, a brilliant, erratic English composer fulfilled the secret fantasy of every composer who has ever lived by actually murdering a music critic. Tragically, the composer Peter Warlock and his victim, the critic Philip Heseltine, were one and the same person.

At thirty-six, Warlock was already one of the most distinctive English voices of his generation. His charming, gemlike miniatures reflected the two great passions of his life: the gentle impressionism of his friend Frederick Delius and the forms of the great English music of the Renaissance.

His most popular work, the *Capriol Suite*, based on Elizabethan dances that are given an unmistakably modern yet at times
surprisingly sentimental spin, is superbly represented by Vernon
Handley's colorful recording with the Ulster Orchestra. Other
than the undoubted quality of the performance itself, the principal
advantage of the recording is that it presents the composer's rarely
heard version for full orchestra (instead of the more usual
string band), and also offers Warlock's marvelous Serenade for
String Orchestra as a bonus. The Serenade in G and Nocturne—
unqualified winners both—by Warlock's contemporary F. J. Moeran round out this unusually desirable collection.

Warlock's dangerously addictive songs are elegantly served by
Benjamin Luxon, who with pianist David Willison has recorded
thirty-two of them for Chandos (CHAN-8643 [CD]). The incomparable English tenor Ian Partridge, accompanied by his sister Jen-
nifer, can be heard in a dozen of them on Etcetera (KTC-1078); his
version (with the Music Group of London) of Warlock's masterpiece, the song cycle *The Curlew*, is one that ranks with the great
vocal recordings made since the war, and is now available on a
Warlock centenary album from (EMI 65101-2).

Weber, Carl Maria von

(1786–1826)

Concertos for Clarinet and Orchestra: No. 1 in F minor;
No. 2 in E-flat; Concertino in E-Flat for Clarinet and
Orchestra

> Pay, clarinet; Orchestra of the Age of Enlightenment. Virgin
> Classics 59002 [CD].

Midway between the Old Testament (the Concerto, Quintet,
and Trio of Mozart) and the New (the late masterpieces of Brahms)
fall those several appealing works that the third undisputed master

of the instrument, Carl Maria von Weber, composed for the clarinet. Written for his friend, the suave Bavarian clarinetist and lady-killer Heinrich Bärmann, Weber's concertos and chamber works not only represent one of the high-water marks of early Romantic wind writing but also display the composer's talent at its freshest and most inventive.

In his period-instrument recording with the Orchestra of the Age of Enlightenment, the English clarinetist Anthony Pay strikes the perfect balance between swagger and sensitivity in his approach to the music; the playing has both bite and delicacy, as does the finely drilled (but by whom?) contribution of the conductorless orchestra. Again, the Virgin Classics engineers prove that they are among the best in the business with impeccably clear and detailed recorded sound.

Der Freischütz

> Mattila, Lind, Araiza, Moll, Dresden State Orchestra and Chorus, Davis. Philips 426319-2 [CD].

The next time you're trapped in a game of musical trivia and need a question that will stump everyone, ask "What is the second most frequently performed opera in Germany today?" The totally unexpected answer is Albert Lorzing's Zar und Zimmermann. In fact, the work that occupies the number one spot will also come as a surprise to most people, simply because it isn't performed very often outside the German-speaking world. The reasons for the phenomenal popularity of *that* opera, Weber's Freischütz, are as obvious now as they were when it was new. Along with its wonderfully dark atmosphere (Germans love anything set in a forest), Der Freischütz boasts a succession of unforgettable arias, choruses, and other set pieces. Also, with Der Freischütz, Carl Maria von Weber brought Romanticism into the opera house, and thus composers as diverse as Meyerbeer, Berlioz, Wagner, and Strauss owe Weber an incalculable debt.

The splendid Deutsche Grammophon release that marked Carlos Kleiber's recording debut as an opera conductor has been temporarily withdrawn, but what an auspicious debut it had proved to be! Kleiber led the superb cast and the always impeccable

Dresden State Opera forces with tremendous energy, enthusiasm, and imagination. Only in the most darkly brooding moments of the second act did hints of Weber's subtler poetry escape him. Still, it was a bracing introduction to a wonderful opera, and its medium-priced resurrection cannot be awaited more eagerly.

In the interim, Sir Colin Davis's Dresden recording has much to recommend it, not the least of which is an interpretation with considerably more fire and imagination than his generally dull and disappointing German efforts. The cast is excellent and so is the recorded sound, but this should be regarded as little more than a quick fix for *Freischütz* junkies until the Kleiber returns.

Rafael Kubelik's stunning version of Weber's English opera *Oberon is* available on a medium-priced DG reissue (419038-2 [CD]), with Placido Domingo a gleaming hero, Birgit Nilsson overwhelming in "Ocean, thou mighty monster," and Kubelik turning in some of the most refined and pointed conducting of his career. The spoken dialogue and narration, which made the ridiculous plot seem a little less so, has been omitted—a minor reservation in an otherwise invaluable release.

Overtures (6) and *Invitation to the Dance*

Hanover Band, Roy Goodman. Nimbus NI-5154 [CD].

There was a pressing need for a good modern recording of the six Weber overtures and the Berlioz orchestration of *Aufforderung zum Tanze*; alas, Hermann Scherchen's zestful yet scrappy interpretations (now out on an Adès compact disc) have almost outlived their usefulness, while the more recent (and already withdrawn) releases by Herbert von Karajan and Wolfgang Sawallisch were, respectively, perverse and inert.

The Hanover Band under Roy Goodman captures both the sweep and wit of these captivating pieces, and to do so on period instruments is no mean feat. The whirlwind performances of *Peter Schmoll* and *Abu Hassan* are especially marvelous, but so are the others, including an *Invitation to the Dance* that few will be able to refuse. For the last word in that Berlioz-arranged charmer, Fritz Reiner's witty, high-voltage recording is now available on RCA 09026-61250-2 [CD], 09026-61250-4 [T].

Webern, Anton (1883–1945)

Passacaglia for Orchestra; Five Movements for String
Orchestra; Six Pieces for Orchestra; Symphony for
Chamber Orchestra

> Berlin Philharmonic, Karajan. Deutsche Grammophon
> 423254-2 [CD].

Anton Webern was the most tragic member of the so-called
Second Viennese School, whose other members were his teacher,
Arnold Schoenberg, and his fellow pupil, Alban Berg. Webern was
accidentally shot by an American soldier during the postwar occupation of Austria, but his tragedy had in fact begun years earlier.
Both his daughters were married to high-ranking Nazi officials, and
he himself seems to have been extremely sympathetic to the cause,
not because he was evil, but because he was incredibly naive. On
the day the Nazis marched into Vienna, Webern allegedly said,
"Well now at least we will be able to hear Mahler!"

Until quite recently, this pathetic, lonely figure was one of the
most influential composers of the twentieth century. In fact, "Post-
Webern" became a designation that was once used as frequently as
"neoclassicism" or "New Romanticism."

Perhaps it is the inherent aloofness of the music, or perhaps
it was the natural sympathy he felt for a kindred political spirit, but
Herbert von Karajan's performances of these four astounding
works were among the finest of the conductor's later recordings. It
is not only the disturbing precision of the Berlin Philharmonic, but
also the curious sense of nonterrestrial detachment in the conducting that serve the music so effectively.

Those with a more serious interest in Webern's rarefied art
will find the bulk of it collected on three medium-priced Sony CDs
(SM3K-45845), in those meticulous performances from the 1960s
under the general supervision of Pierre Boulez. As always, the
conductor's sense of reverent enthusiasm is matched only by the
depth of his understanding. The orchestral performances are unfailingly refined and beautiful, and the Juilliard String Quartet and
others work comparable wonders with the chamber music. It isn't
often that one can encounter virtually the whole of a major composer's output in such a compact and attractively priced container.

Weill, Kurt (1900–1950)

The Threepenny Opera

Lenya, Litz, Gunter, Mund, Markworth, Murch, Southwest German Radio Orchestra and Chorus, Brückner-Rüggeberg. CBS MK-42637 [CD].

When the gruff, foul-mouthed Marxist playwright was first introduced to the shy young composer after a performance of one of the latter's symphonies, he got right to the point: "My name is Bert Brecht," he announced, "and if you want to work with me you're going to have to stop writing that shit stuff and come up with some *tunes*." And so began the collaboration that would culminate in *The Threepenny Opera* of 1928, the apotheosis of the spirit of Berlin in the '20s, and one of German art's last great creative gasps before the Nazi deluge.

With Kurt Weill's widow, Lotte Lenya, singing Jenny—a role she created and would eventually make world-famous—this *Dreigroschenoper* from the mid-1950s will never be superseded. With the help of an excellent supporting cast and a very canny conductor, Lenya conjures up the darkness, danger, and sense of all-pervasive corruption that hung over the Weimar Republic like a sickeningly sweet poison gas, a decadent miasma that makes a sanitized entertainment like *Cabaret* seem like innocent child's play.

Lenya's sour, world-weary voice can also be heard to beautifully cynical and vulnerable effect in a collection of her husband's German and English songs on another irreplaceable Mastersound recording (DFCD1-110 [CD]), while the best version of the *Threepenny Opera* Suite is Michael Tilson Thomas's mordant and deliciously overripe recording for CBS (MK-44529 [CD]).

The more serious side of Weill's character can be heard in the Philips recording of the two Symphonies (434171-2 [CD]), which are given tough, aggressive, hugely sympathetic performances by the Leipzig Gewandhaus Orchestra conducted by Edo de Waart.

Weinberger, Jaromir
(1896–1967)

Schwanda the Bagpiper

> Prey, Popp, Jerusalem, Killebrew, Malta, Nimsgern,
> Bavarian Radio Chorus, Munich Radio Orchestra,
> Wallberg. CBS M3K-39626 [CD].

One of the most frequently performed of all twentieth-century operas (within five years of its Prague premiere it would be heard in literally thousands of performances in dozens of productions around the world), *Schwanda the Bagpiper* was given an unaccountably cool reception at the Metropolitan Opera in 1931, and two years later, with the advent of Hitler, its fate in Europe was sealed.

As this first commercial recording demonstrated a few years ago, *Schwanda*'s once-phenomenal popularity was obviously no fluke. In fact, it is such a tuneful, vibrant, utterly disarming work that one can only wonder why more companies don't take a chance on it today. It has fantasy, spectacle, romance, and an abundance of unforgettable set pieces: in addition to the well-known Polka and Fugue (the last is in truth a triumphal chorus), the first-act aria "Ich bin der Schwanda" is one of those arias which, once heard, can't be forgotten, no matter how hard you try.

This recording, produced by the late George Korngold, should be mandatory listening for every director of every opera company in the civilized world, especially those who are now planning their seasons and can't face the prospect of yet another *Bohème*. Surefire winners don't come along all that often, and a surefire, iron-clad, gold-plated, hock-your-grandmother-and-bet-the-bundle winner *Schwanda* most certainly is. With Hermann Prey in the title role, the luscious Lucia Popp as his wife, the young Siegfried Jerusalem as the robber Babinsky, a first-rate supporting cast, and superlative conducting from Heinz Wallberg, this is one of the most thoroughly enjoyable opera recordings ever made.

I strongly recommend doing what I did: Buy a half-dozen extra copies to use as *very* special gifts.

Widor, Charles Marie

(1844–1937)

Symphonies for Organ: No. 5 in F minor; No. 10,
Romaine

Chorzempa, organ. Philips 410054-2 [CD].

Like his immensely prolific near-contemporary, Henry
Charles Litolff, Charles Marie Widor is one of history's mercifully
few examples of a Part-of-a-Work Composer. For just as poor
Litolff is remembered only for the mercurial Scherzo from his *Con-
certo Symphonique* No. 4 (most ably represented these days on an
Olympia recording, OCD-325 [CD], in a quicksilver performance
featuring Peter Katin and the London Philharmonic conducted by
Carl Davis), Widor survives almost entirely on the strength of the
Toccata from the Organ Symphony No. 5.

Although it can be found in any number of recorded grab
bags of organ favorites, the best way to hear the remorselessly
buoyant piece is in the context of the Symphony—actually, an
extended suite—in which it originally appeared. The American
organist Daniel Chorzempa gives a crashingly fine performance of
the work on his Philips compact disc, and almost—*almost*—makes
one wonder why the entire Symphony isn't heard more often. The
recorded sound is exceptional, the sort that might melt the fillings
in the unwary listener's teeth.

Wieniawski, Henryk

(1835–1880)

Concertos for Violin and Orchestra: No. 1 in F-sharp minor; No. 2 in D minor

Shaham, violin; London Symphony, Foster. Deutsche Grammophon 431815-2 [CD].

In the century since his death, the Polish composer Henryk Wieniawski has been represented almost exclusively in the concert hall and the recording studio by his D minor Violin Concerto, one of the classic late-Romantic barn-burners and a piece that can still get the blood boiling when a violinist with the right equipment is in charge. As his stunning Deutsche Grammophon versions (437540-2 [CD]) of the Sibelius and Tchaikovsky Concertos demonstrated conclusively, Gil Shaham's equipment is among the most impressive of his generation, and his thundering technique and interpretive élan not only do wonders for the D minor Concerto but are also extremely effective in its lesser-known F-sharp minor companion piece. Lawrence Foster and the London Symphony offer pointed and ingratiating support, and the recorded sound could hardly be improved.

Wilder, Alec (1907–1980)

Concerto for Oboe, Strings, and Percussion

Lucarelli, oboe; Brooklyn Philharmonic, Barrett. Koch 3-7187-2 [CD].

Alec Wilder, one of the most diverse and difficult to classify of all American composers, was best known for his *sui generis* octets that fused elements of classical chamber music with jazz rhythms and melodies suggestive of popular songs. Largely self-taught, he produced an enormous number of works in a bewildering variety of forms from ballets and operas to tunes for his friend Frank Sinatra, all of them urbane, ingratiating, and enormously appealing.

Bert Lucarelli gives a superb account of the Oboe Concerto Wilder wrote for Mitch Miller, together with limpidly beautiful performances of miniatures by John Corigliano and Robert Bloom. The recital opens with Wayne Barlow's ineffably haunting *The Winter's Past*, which in itself is more than worth the price of the compact disc.

Wirén, Dag (1905–1986)

Serenade for Strings

Guildhall String Ensemble. RCA 60439-2-RC [CD].

Dag Wirén was a Swedish composer of enormously agreeable music who remains best known outside his native country for a single work, the enchanting Serenade for Strings of 1937. It is an infectiously tuneful, immediately appealing piece that bears more than favorable comparison with Grieg's *Holberg Suite* or Nielsen's *Little Suite for Strings*, the other major pieces on this irresistible anthology of Scandinavian music. The Guildhall String Ensemble play with equal amounts of enthusiasm and finesse, and the recorded sound is as fresh and bracing as a northern breeze.

By the way, this is a perfect recording with which to catch a reluctant object of your affections off guard. (It's worked for me; it will work for you.)

Wolf, Hugo (1860–1903)

Songs

After Schubert, there were only three incontestably great composers of German lieder: Schumann, Brahms, and Hugo Wolf. And if Schubert practically invented the form, then it was Wolf who presided over its final, bittersweet flowering. In the work of no other composer are words and music so intimately connected, and in no other German songs do we encounter so much effortless perfection.

Among the available recordings of Wolf songs, and there are shamefully few, the Globe recording (GLO2-5008) of the *Italian Song Book* is exceptionally appealing. Elly Ameling sings flawlessly, and Tom Krause gives one of his best performances in years. Nor would any Wolf fan want to miss the classic version from the mid-1950s with Irmgaard Seefried and Dietrich Fischer-Dieskau accompanied by Erik Werba and Jörg Demus, reissued on a medium-priced Deutsche Grammophon CD (435752-2).

Thomas Allen's Virgin recital (CDC-59221 [CD]) features performances that are both interpretively probing and handsomely sung, and Brigitte Fassbaender's London recording of the fifty-four lieder on texts by Eduard Mörike (440208-2 [CD]) confirms her growing reputation as the foremost female recitalist of her generation: among its many glories is the most dramatic, spine-tingling version of "Der Feuerreiter" since Hermann Prey's long-deleted London recording of a generation ago. Arleen Augér's Hyperion recording is a treasurable reminder of a lovely artist (CDA-66590 [CD]), and although Elisabeth Schwarzkopf's legendary 1953 Salzburg recital with Wilhelm Furtwängler and enchanting *Spanish Song Book* with Fischer-Dieskau are temporarily out of circulation, some of her other incomparable Wolf interpretations are available on a pair of CDs from EMI (CDM-63653, CDM-64905).

Among available recordings of the magical *Italian Serenade*, the Orpheus Chamber Orchestra offer a gossamer-light chamber orchestra version on Deutsche Grammophon (431680-2 [CD]), and on another DG recording (427669-2 [CD]), the gifted young Hagen String Quartet play with youthful ardor and phenomenal precision.

Zelenka, Jan Dismas

(1679–1745)

Orchestral Works

Camerata Bern. Deutsche Grammophon 423703-2 [CD].

Among the odd fish washed up on the wave of the great Baroque Revival of the 1960s, none was odder or more interesting than that Bohemian recluse Jan Dismas Zelenka. Little is known about the man's life other than the fact that Bach was one of his most passionate admirers. He may or may not have been a mystic, a visionary, or simply a short-tempered hypochondriac (two of his works are called *The Angry Man* and *Hipocondria*); the lack of an authenticated portrait has fueled the legend that he was either severely deformed or hideously disfigured.

Whatever it was that combined to create this strange and mysterious figure, he was one of the most startlingly original composers of his period, a kind of nonvocal Central European equivalent of the batty Carlo Gesualdo, whose experiments in form, harmony, and expression were as radically daring a century before.

The recordings by Camerata Bern, highlighted by some truly phenomenal contributions by oboist Heinz Holliger and horn player Barry Tuckwell, are the perfect introduction to Zelenka's peculiar and beautiful world. While some of the music is so advanced that Zelenka might sometimes seem a contemporary of Chopin and Schumann rather than of Handel and Bach, he remains, for all his apparent flirtations with Romanticism, a figure of the Baroque era, and possibly a major one at that.

Zwilich, Ellen Taaffe

(1939–   )

Concerto Grosso 1985 (after Handel); Concerto for
Trumpet and Five Players; Double Quartet for Strings;
Symbolon

Smith, trumpet; New York Philharmonic, Mehta, Zwilich.
New World NW-372-2 [CD].

Born in Miami in 1939, Ellen Taaffe Zwilich is a member of
that talented generation of musicians who have finally been able to
shake off the designation "female composer." There was always
something condescending and faintly preposterous in that usage;
how often, for instance, does one hear the phrase, "the celebrated
male composer, Beethoven"?

As these recordings of four of her works from 1984 to 1988
clearly show, Zwilich is an intelligent, important composer whose
music more than deserves the celebrity it has begun to receive.
While the *Concerto Grosso 1985*, written for the tercentenary of
Handel's birth, is the most immediately accessible piece in the
collection, the others are also challenging and enjoyable, proving,
if nothing else, that music is neither a "male" nor a "female," but
a wholly human art.

Index